SPARKNOTES®

5 practice tests for the ACT®

SPARKNOTES PUBLISHING

SparkNotes Publishing
A Division of Barnes & Noble
76 Ninth Avenue
New York, NY 10011
www.sparknotes.com

Please submit all comments and questions or report errors to www.sparknotes.com/errors.

Library of Congress Cataloging-in-Publication Data

5 Practice Tests for the ACT.
        p. cm.
    "SparkNotes."
    ISBN 978-1-4114-1775-5 (alk. paper)
    1. ACT Assessment—Study guides. I. Spark Publishing. II. Title: Five practice tests for the ACT.
    LB2353.48.A15 2009
    378.1'662—dc22

                                            2008055391

Printed and bound in Canada

10 9 8 7 6 5 4 3 2 1

Contents

Introducing the ACT

WELCOME TO *SPARKNOTES 5 PRACTICE TESTS FOR THE ACT*. YOU'VE bought this book because you want to take the ACT and do well on it. That requires a little extra practice on your part. That's where we come in. We created this book to help you get the practice you need so you can identify your weaknesses in knowledge and test-taking methods.

First, you'll learn a bit about the test itself—what types of questions you can expect and how best to tackle them. Then we'll give you some strategies that you can use in your preparation and on the day of the test.

Now, let's meet the ACT.

The Content and Structure of the ACT

The ACT consists of four multiple-choice "Subject Tests" covering English, Mathematics, Reading, and Science. There is also an "optional" writing section at the very end of the test (more on this "optional" business later). These Subject Tests will always appear on the ACT in the order in which we just named them. We'll give you brief introductions to the subject tests and the material they cover in a minute. First, though, we'll briefly discuss the unvarying content of the test.

The writers of the ACT pride themselves on the regularity and predictability of their tests. They claim that every test has the same breakdown of question types. For example, every English Subject Test will contain ten punctuation questions, and every Mathematics Subject Test will contain four trigonometry questions. The ACT writers believe that it is very important to maintain these numbers exactly. They will not vary.

The essentially unchanging content of the ACT means you can be thoroughly prepared for the test. The ACT doesn't want to trick you. They want to tell you exactly what will be on the test and give you every chance in the world to prepare for the test. The ACT wants to test your knowledge, and it makes sense that the best way to do that is to let you know precisely what you need to know and then see how well you can learn it. You won't be caught off guard by unfamiliar material on test day.

You can also take advantage of the regularity of the ACT to help you pinpoint your weaknesses on the test by using practice tests. We explain how to use practice tests as a powerful study tool in the section called "Practicing with Practice Tests," located just before the practice tests (page 15).

The English Subject Test (75 Questions, 45 Minutes)

The English Subject Test contains five reading passages laced with grammatical and stylistic errors. Each passage is accompanied by fifteen questions. You are given 45 minutes to answer these 75 questions. The questions ask you to make corrections to the text through multiple-choice options.

The English Test assesses your understanding of the basic grammar of the English language, as well as your grasp of the tools and strategies a writer can use to put sentences together to form paragraphs and arguments. The ACT calls grammar "Usage/Mechanics" and essay writing skills "Rhetorical Skills." The English Subject Test includes 40 questions on Usage/Mechanics and 35 on Rhetorical Skills. These two types of question can be further broken down into the following categories:

Subject	Number of Questions
Usage/Mechanics	**40**
Punctuation	10
Grammar and Usage	12
Sentence Structure	18
Rhetorical Skills	**35**
Strategy	12
Organization	11
Style	12
Total	**75**

Perhaps the only category that isn't self-explanatory is Strategy, which tests your understanding of a writer's strategic decisions in putting together a passage. The rest of the categories should be fairly obvious.

What the English Test Really Tests

The English Test assesses your sense of correct English writing. You do not have to memorize esoteric grammatical terminology to do well on this Subject Test. You do not need to know, for example, an appositive from a prepositional phrase. However, though you don't need to know precise grammatical terms and definitions, a good intuitive grounding in grammar is important for doing well on this Subject Test.

The Mathematics Test (60 Questions, 60 Minutes)

The Mathematics Subject Test covers six areas of high school math: pre-algebra, elementary algebra, intermediate algebra, coordinate geometry, plane geometry, and trigonometry. The test will cover those topics according to the following breakdown:

Subject	Number of Questions
Pre-Algebra	14
Elementary Algebra	10
Intermediate Algebra	9
Coordinate Geometry	9
Plane Geometry	14
Trigonometry	4
Total	**60**

As you can see, the majority of questions deal with pre-algebra, elementary algebra, and plane geometry, which are topics usually covered at the beginning of high school.

The other three topics—intermediate algebra, coordinate geometry, and trigonometry—constitute only 22 of the 60 questions on the test. You should learn these more difficult topics by the end of junior year in high school. If you have not learned trigonometry by that time, don't sweat it: There are only four trig questions on the test, and four questions won't ruin your score.

The Mathematics Test differs from the other Subject Tests in two significant ways:

1. Calculator use is allowed.

2. There are five answer choices for each question, rather than four.

The Reading Test (40 Questions, 35 Minutes)

The Reading Test consists of four passages, each approximately 750 words long. The passages cover Prose Fiction, Social Science, Humanities, and Natural Science. These passages always appear in the above order, and they are given equal weight in scoring. Each passage is accompanied by ten questions of varying levels of difficulty. You are given 35 minutes to read the four passages and answer the 40 questions.

Unlike the English and Mathematics Tests, the Reading Test evaluates a set of skills you've acquired rather than subjects you've learned. As the name of this Subject Test implies, these skills are your ability to read and to comprehend different types of passages. The Reading Test assesses these skills through a variety of questions that ask you to do the following:

1. Identify details and facts.

2. Draw inferences from given evidence.

3. Make character generalizations.

4. Identify the main idea of a section or the whole passage.

5. Identify the author's point of view.

6. Identify cause-effect relationships.

7. Determine the meaning of words through context.

8. Make comparisons and analogies.

The Science Test (40 Questions, 35 Minutes)

Despite its name, the Science Test doesn't test your understanding of any scientific field. Instead, this test assesses your ability to reason like a scientist—it tests your ability to understand and think about data. All of the information you need to know for the Science Test will be presented in the questions. You just have to dig it out.

The Science Test consists of seven passages that contain a mixture of graphs, charts, and explanatory text. Each passage is followed by five to seven questions. You will encounter three different types of passages on the test:

- **Data Representation Passages.** The three Data Representation passages are each accompanied by five corresponding questions. These passages ask you to understand and use information presented in graphs or tables.

- **Research Summaries Passages.** The three Research Summaries passages each come with six questions. These passages put scientific data in the context of an experiment; the questions are similar to those in Data Representation, but they demand a greater degree of analysis from you. They require you to evaluate an experimental design.

- **Conflicting Viewpoints Passage.** The one Conflicting Viewpoints passage is accompanied by seven questions. This type of passage presents you with two or three alternative theories on a natural phenomenon. The questions test your understanding of the differences between the viewpoints and ask you to evaluate the soundness of the arguments.

You are given 35 minutes to read the seven passages and answer the 40 questions.

Science "Content"

The ACT says that the Science passages cover biology, earth/space sciences, chemistry, and physics. This is true, but the subject matter of the passages is largely irrelevant to what you're trying to accomplish on the test itself. In other words, all the answers are in the readings. You just need to know how to find them.

The Optional Writing Test (1 Essay Question, 30 Minutes)

In a nutshell, you are given 30 minutes to construct an essay based on a given issue. The issue will be relevant to your life as a high school student. You can either choose to support the perspective given on the issue or relate one of your own. Two "raters" will score your essay on a scale of 1–6. These raters have been trained and certified to evaluate your writing specifically for this test. The two scores from the raters are then added together to make up your subscore, ranging from 2–12. If the two raters come to a substantially different score, a third rater will be brought in.

Your score on the Writing section will be incorporated into your Combined English/Writing score. You will also see a Writing subscore separate from the English score on your test results. Your essay will be scanned and made available online so schools can look up and see exactly what you wrote (and how bad your handwriting is).

Though you can't score the Writing Test the same as you might score other portions of a practice test, we've included this section in each test in this book. By including this portion of the ACT in your preparation, you'll become familiar with the essay prompts and you'll be more comfortable when it comes to taking the real thing.

Optional, you say?

Yes, the Writing Test is optional, but read the fine print closely: The test is optional in the sense that institutions have the "option" of requiring it. You might not necessarily have the "option" of not taking it. The only way for you to get out of taking the Writing section is to know well in advance that you won't be applying to a school that requires it for admission. If there's even a chance that you'll want to apply to a school that requires the Writing Test, then you should spend the extra 30 minutes taking it.

SPECIAL NOTE: If you take the Writing Test, all scores, including the Combined English/Writing score and Writing subscore, will be sent to all the institutions you requested to receive your scores during the registration process. *This is regardless of whether or not those schools require the writing test.* A school must specifically request not to receive the results of the Writing Test or they will be sent to them automatically.

ACT Scoring and the Score Report

The way the ACT is scored might be the most confusing aspect of the test. The number of different scores a single ACT test produces is mind-boggling.

1. First, you receive four **raw scores**, one for each Subject Test, in addition to **raw subscores** for subsections of the Subject Test (for example, Usage/Mechanics and Rhetorical Skills are the two subsections of the English Test).

2. Those raw scores are converted into **four scaled scores** for the Subject Tests and **scaled subscores** for the subsections.

3. The four scaled scores are averaged, producing the **Composite Score**.

4. Finally, every single score is assigned a corresponding **percentile ranking**, indicating how you fared in comparison to other test takers.

The two scores that will matter most to you and the colleges you apply to are the Composite Score and the overall percentile ranking. You will receive these two numbers, plus your scaled scores and subscores, in a score report about four to seven weeks after you take the test.

Raw Scores

Although you will never see a raw score on your score report, you should know how the raw score is computed. All raw scores are based on the number of questions you answered correctly. To compute the raw score of a Subject Test, simply count up the number of questions you answered correctly in that Subject Test. For each correct answer, you receive one point. Your raw score is the total number of points you receive. There are no point deductions for wrong answers.

Raw Subscores

Each Subject Test contains component subsections, each of which is assigned a raw subscore. For example, the English Subject Test breaks down into Usage/Mechanics and Rhetorical Skills. Let's say you correctly answered 32 Usage/Mechanics questions and 21 Rhetorical Skills questions. Your raw scores for those two subsections would be 32 and 21, respectively.

Scaled Scores

Scaled scores account for disparities among different versions of the ACT. Without scaled scores, you wouldn't be able to compare your score on a particular test with the score that someone else received on a different test taken on a different date. One version of the test might be more difficult than another, affecting the overall raw scores received.

The makers of the ACT don't reveal the formula used to convert raw scores into scaled scores, but we provide you with conversion charts that mimic the ACT conversion formula, so you can get an idea of your scaled performance. These conversion charts are located with the practice tests at the back of this book.

Scaled Subscores

To add to the confusion, the subscores of a Subject Test are not scaled according to the same curve as the entire Subject Test of which they are a part: Adding together scaled subscores will not necessarily produce a Subject Test's scaled score. For example, if you receive scaled subscores of 14 on Usage/Mechanics and 15 on Rhetorical Skills, your English scaled score will not necessarily be 29. More likely, it will be either 27 or 28.

The fact that the ACT uses these different scale conversions throws a real kink into any plans to take and score the test at home. The makers of the ACT use computers and programs—to which you don't have access—to compute their scaled scores. For this reason, when we provide you with a conversion key to compute your scaled scores on practice tests, we skip the step of scaling the subsections separately. This means that the scores you receive on our practice tests will be very close to the scores you would get on an ACT, but they will not always be exact. Any test-preparation book that implies the scores you receive on its practice test are exactly right isn't telling you the truth.

Use of Scaled Scores

When you receive your score report, you will see both your scaled scores and scaled subscores. Colleges will care primarily about your scaled scores for Subject Tests. Your scaled subscores will come in handy if you plan to take the test again. They can help you identify your weak and strong areas so you can better focus your studying.

Percentile Rankings

Percentile rankings indicate how you performed compared to the other students in the nation who took the same test you did. A percentile ranking of 75 means that 74 percent of test takers scored worse than you and 25 percent scored the same or better.

The percentile rankings that matter most are the ones for each Subject Test and the one accompanying the Composite Score (the chart below gives a sampling of percentile rankings and their corresponding Composite Scores). You will receive these percentiles on your score report.

The Composite Score

The Composite Score is the big one. It is the score your parents will tell their friends and the one your curious peers will want to know. More precisely, it is the average of your scaled scores for the four Subject Tests. So, if you got a 28 on the English Test, a 26 on the Mathematics Test, a 32 on the Reading Test, and a 30 on the Science Reasoning Test, your composite score will be:

$$\left(\frac{28 + 26 + 32 + 30}{4}\right) = \frac{116}{4} = 29$$

Look for the Composite Score at the bottom of your score report.

Correspondence of Composite Score, Percentile Rank, and Correct Answers

The chart below shows a sample of Composite Scores and how they correspond to percentile rankings and percentages of questions answered correctly. This chart should give you some context for understanding the relative levels of achievement indicated by these Composite Scores:

Composite Score	ACT Approximate Percentile Rank	Percentage of Correct Answers
31	98%	89%
26	86%	76%
23	70%	66%
20	49%	55%
17	26%	44%

Who Receives the Scores? Not You.

That heading is a little misleading, but we thought we'd draw your attention to a bizarre aspect of the test. If you follow the ACT's registration instructions, you probably won't receive your score directly—your high school guidance counselor and any colleges you list (see "Sending Scores to Colleges," below) will get it first, and then you must retrieve your score from your guidance counselor. But there are ways around this bureaucracy.

If you want to receive the report directly at home rather than through a third party at your high school, you can do one of two things:

1. Have your high school give ACT permission to send your score to your home.

2. Leave the High School Code blank when you sign up for the test.

Option 2 is less complicated than Option 1, and there are no repercussions from leaving the Code blank. Although ACT won't explicitly tell you about Option 2, it will work.

Sending Scores to Colleges

In the moments before you take the ACT, test administrators will give you a form allowing you to submit a list of up to six colleges that will receive your score directly from the company that makes the test. Don't submit a list unless you feel extremely confident that you will achieve your target score on the exam. After all, once you receive your score report and know you got the score you wanted, you can always order score reports to be sent to colleges. True, this service of forwarding your scores costs a small fee after the first three reports, but the security it provides is worth it.

There is only one reason that you should opt to have your score sent directly to colleges. If you take the test near college application deadlines, you will probably have to choose this service to ensure that your scores arrive at the colleges on time.

Canceling the Score Report

If you choose to send your score report directly to colleges, but then have a really horrible day at the test center, don't panic. You have several days to cancel your score report. To do this, call ACT at (319) 337-1270. You have until noon, Central Standard Time, on the Thursday immediately following your test date to cancel your score.

Taking the ACT Twice (or Three Times)

If you do have one of those really horrible days at the test center but you didn't choose to send your score report directly to colleges, don't cancel the report. No matter how many times you take the ACT, the colleges you apply to will see only one of your scores—the one you pick. If you don't score as well as you want to the first time, you can take the test again (and again and again) with impunity until you receive a score that you are happy with.

You have a good opportunity to improve your ACT score on the second try. More than half of second-time test takers increase their scores. Taking the test a third or a fourth time probably won't make much difference in your score unless something went seriously awry on your previous tries.

What an ACT Score Means

So, you've taken the test and received your score; now what happens? If you're in your junior year of high school, your ACT score can help you determine which colleges to apply to. Numerous publications each year issue reports on college profiles. Both these reports and your high school guidance counselor should help you determine your safety, 50/50, and reach schools, based on your ACT score, high school GPA, and other factors such as recommendations and extracurricular activities. While an applicant's total package is what counts, a good ACT score will never hurt your chances of getting into the schools you want. If you scored better than you expected, your score may help your applications at schools that you previously considered reaches.

How Your ACT Score Fits into Your Application Package

You may be wondering why a standardized test score matters at all in your college application. Let's compare two students, Megan and Chloe. Megan and Chloe are both straight-A students at their respective high schools. These grades reflect the girls' relative standings at their schools (unless everyone at these two schools gets A's), but how can college administrator Tim use these grades to compare Megan and Chloe? It seems like we're leading you to answer, "ACT scores!" Well, that's not entirely true. The truth is that Tim will look at a number of things to differentiate between the two girls. He'll carefully consider extracurricular activities, the girls' essays, and their recommendations. He'll also look at course descriptions to see whether Megan has long been acing Advanced Number Theory and Sanskrit while Chloe has been queen of her Shop class.

So where does the ACT fit into this? Well, it's just another way of confirming relative standing among applicants. Tim may have access to course descriptions, but that curious college administrator is always on the lookout for other means of comparison. The ACT provides that means: It is a national standard by which colleges can evaluate applicants. The ACT is merely one factor in your total application package, but it is an important factor that should not be overlooked or slighted. Although many schools hesitate to admit it, the fact is that your ACT score is one of the first things that stands out to someone reading your application. That person will eventually get around to reading teacher recommendations and your personal essay, but your ACT score is an easily digestible piece of information that will allow an admissions staff to form an early impression of your academic achievement. We're telling you this not to scare you, but to give you an honest assessment of what the ACT means to your college application.

That said, you should think of the ACT not as an adversary but as a tool that will help you get into college. For example, if Chloe is really a class-A student, but her high school doesn't give her the opportunity to extend her talents beyond Shop class, the ACT provides an opportunity for her to show Tim she isn't a flake. If you approach the ACT pragmatically and don't hope for a knockout score you can't achieve, and if you study with some vigor, you can control your ACT destiny and get the score you need to get into the colleges of your choice.

The ACT Versus the SAT

The SAT dominates the national discussion of standardized testing; the ACT seldom gets mentioned. However, each year, nearly the same number of students take each test. Traditionally, American colleges used the SAT, rather than the ACT, as the standard-bearer in college admissions. But recently an increasing number of colleges around the country have begun to accept ACT scores from applicants, either in addition to SAT scores or in lieu of them. For you, the important question is which of the two tests should you take?

You should do the following two things when deciding whether to take the ACT or the SAT:

1. Find out whether the colleges to which you are applying require one test rather than the other.

2. If it doesn't matter which test you take, decide which test is better suited to your skills (i.e., the test on which you'll score better).

College Requirements

The majority of colleges in the United States, particularly those on the East and West Coasts, still require an SAT score as part of the application. But depending on the schools to which you are applying, you may have a choice between the ACT and the SAT, so be aware of your options. Given the varying preferences at U.S. colleges, you should carefully examine your application requirements before registering for either test. Beware of tricky wording as well: When the writers of the ACT tell you that most U.S. colleges and universities "accept" ACT results, don't be fooled into thinking that those schools will take the ACT in place of the SAT—many are merely willing to look at your ACT score in addition to your SAT score. To avoid confusion (and possibly despair) near application deadline time, make sure you know which scores schools want.

Also remember that the Writing Section is an optional requirement. Some schools will require it and others won't, so make sure you know each institution's requirements. Note that if you do choose to take the Writing Test, your writing scores will be sent to all schools regardless of whether they require the writing test. Schools must specifically request not to be sent the writing scores, which is fairly unlikely.

Choosing the Right Test for You

The ACT and the SAT are both meant to test your knowledge of the fundamentals of a high school education in the United States. Yet the writers of the two tests are guided by very different philosophies, and the two exams have different formats and test different subject matter. These differences are significant enough that you might feel much more comfortable taking one test over the other. We will describe these differences on the next page.

Differences in Testing Philosophy

ACT	SAT
The ACT strives to assess the knowledge you've acquired, meaning that the test focuses on subjects and skills taught in high school.	The SAT tries to assess "innate ability." It does so using tricky and confusing phrasing to determine your test-taking skills (i.e., your performance under pressure and your ability to identify what's being asked).

You should consider your strengths in comparison with the subjects tested by both tests. The ACT may appear more difficult than the SAT because it tests a broader range of subjects, but keep in mind that a weakness in one subject may not be as damaging on the ACT as on the SAT. You should also keep in mind that although the SAT may deal with simpler topics than the ACT, the SAT questions are often deliberately worded to confuse the test taker. In addition, you can study actual subject matter to improve your ACT score, while improving your SAT score requires you to understand test-taking tricks.

The differences in format, shown in the table below, are not terribly significant.

Differences in Format

	The ACT	The SAT
Total Time	175 minutes (plus 30 minute optional Writing Test)	225 minutes (plus 25 minute experimental section)
Total Number of Sections	4 (plus the optional Writing Test)	3 (plus 1 experimental section)

Taking Both Tests

If time and money allow, you may want to consider taking both the ACT and the SAT. That way, you can have your choice of the two scores when applying to colleges. If you're applying to a mix of schools, some of which accept the SAT and some the ACT, you're covered on all sides. While we emphasized the differences between the two tests, studying for both tests actually would overlap a great deal. Both the ACT and the SAT ultimately test your ability to think, and both cover the basics of a high school education.

When to Take the Test

Most people take the ACT at the end of junior year or the beginning of senior year. We recommend taking it at the end of junior year for a number of reasons:

1. Taking the test junior year will give you time to retake it if necessary.

2. You will have covered most of the material on the ACT by the end of junior year, and it will be fresh in your mind.

3. You are likely to forget some material during the summer before your senior year.

Ultimately, when you choose to take the test depends on only one thing: you. If you don't feel comfortable taking it junior year, spend some time during the summer reviewing and take the test during the fall of your senior year. If you are applying for regular admission to colleges, you will probably have a couple of test dates with which to work during your senior year, but take the earliest possible test if you are applying for early admission.

Registering for the ACT

To register for the ACT, you must first obtain an ACT registration packet. Your high school guidance counselor will probably have these packets available for you. If you can't get the packet through your high school, you can request a packet online at actstudent.org/forms/stud_req.html, or write to or call ACT at:

ACT Registration
301 ACT Drive
P.O. Box 414
Iowa City, IA 52243-0414
(319) 337-1270

You can also register for the test by visiting ACT's website (actstudent.org) or, if your high school has it, by using ACT's software program College Connector. If you have taken the ACT within the last two years, you may reregister over the phone for an additional fee. You must make a credit card payment if you register on the Web, through College Connector, or by phone.

Regular, Late, and Standby Registration

There are three types of registration: regular, late, and standby.

- **Regular registration** deadlines are approximately five weeks before the test date. The basic fee is $31 in most of the United States and $56 for students testing internationally. In addition to the basic fee, the optional Writing Test is $15 for all students. (An additional fee of $12 is applied for phone registration.)

- **Late registration**, which costs you an additional $20, ends three weeks before the test date.

The ACT registration packet will contain the exact dates for regular and late registration deadlines.

- **Standby registration** is for those students who missed the late registration deadline and need to take the test by a certain date. Standby registration occurs on the day of the test. It costs an additional $40, and it does not guarantee you a seat or a test booklet. Standby registration is a last resort. If you must use standby registration, make sure to bring a completed registration folder, fee payment, and appropriate personal identification to the test center.

The ACT Admission Ticket

If you register for the ACT using regular or late registration, you will receive an admission ticket in the mail. This ticket will tell you when and where the test will be administered. It will also list the information you submitted to ACT, such as any colleges that will receive your score directly. You should read the admission ticket carefully to make sure there are no mistakes. If you find a mistake, follow the instructions on the back of the ticket for correcting information. You'll also need to bring this ticket with you the day of the test.

Test Dates

ACT test dates usually fall in October, December, February, April, and June. Certain states also have a September test date. Double-check your test dates by going to ACT's student website at actstudent.org.

SparkNotes Online Test Prep

Additional resources are available through the SparkNotes Online Test Prep for the ACT. SparkNotes ACT website provides the following features:

- Additional practice tests, backed by diagnostic software that immediately analyzes your results and directs your study for efficiency and effectiveness.

- Additional, fully searchable review material for the ACT's Subject Tests, with all the latest updates to keep you up to speed.

In addition to the ACT, SparkNotes Online Test Prep also covers the SAT and the most popular SAT Subject Tests.

Practicing with Practice Tests

As WE MENTIONED BEFORE, THE ACT IS ALL ABOUT UNIFORMITY: every test presents the same number of questions on the same basic material. This constancy from test to test can be of great benefit to you as you study for the ACT. By taking and reviewing practice tests, you can identify and target your weaknesses and conquer them before you take another test. If you take the time to study up on your weak spots, you'll see improvement from one practice test to the next. You'll also gain confidence for test day.

Because practice tests can be such a powerful ACT prep tool, we've given you access to additional resources online at testprep.sparknotes.com. Below, we explain step-by-step exactly how to do it yourself.

Controlling Your Environment

Although no one but you needs to see your practice test scores, you should do everything in your power to make the practice test feel like the real ACT. The closer your practice resembles the real thing, the more helpful it will be. When taking a practice test, follow these rules:

Take the tests timed. Don't give yourself any extra time. Be stricter with yourself than the meanest proctor you can think of. Also, don't give yourself time off for bathroom breaks. If you have to go to the bathroom, let the clock keep running; that's what'll happen on the real ACT.

Take the test in a single sitting. Training yourself to endure the full duration of the test should be part of your preparation.

Find a place to take the test that offers no distractions. Don't take the practice test in a room with lots of people walking through it. Go to a library, your bedroom, a well-lit closet, anywhere quiet. And, if possible, find a place that you can use for each practice test you take.

Take each practice test as if it were the real ACT. Don't be more daring than you would be on the actual test, guessing blindly even when you could first eliminate an answer. Don't carelessly speed through the test. Follow the rules for guessing and for skipping questions that we outline in "General Test-Taking Strategies" (page 19). Don't sneak a peak through this book while taking the practice exam. The more closely your attitude and strategies during the practice test reflect those you'll employ during the actual test, the more predictive the practice test will be of your strengths and weaknesses and the more fruitful your studying.

Scoring Your Practice Test

After you take your practice test, you'll no doubt want to score it and see how you did. When you score your test, don't just write down how many questions you answered correctly and tally up your score. Instead, keep a list of every question you got wrong and every question you skipped. This list will be your guide when you study your test.

Studying Your Practice Test

Studying your test involves examining each question you skipped or answered incorrectly. When you look at each question, you shouldn't just look to see what the correct answer is but also why you got the question wrong and how you could have gotten the question right. Train yourself in the process of getting the question right.

Why Did You Get the Question Wrong?

There are three reasons why you might have gotten an individual question wrong:

1. You thought you knew the answer, but actually you didn't.

2. You managed to eliminate some answer choices and then guessed among the remaining answers; sadly, you guessed wrong.

3. You knew the answer but made a careless mistake.

You should know which of these reasons applies to every question you got wrong.

What Could You Have Done to Get the Question Right?

The reasons you got a question wrong affect how you should think about studying your practice test.

Reason 1: Lack of Knowledge

A question answered incorrectly for Reason 1 identifies a weakness in your knowledge of the material tested on the ACT. Discovering this wrong answer gives you an opportunity to target your weakness. When addressing that weakness, make sure that you don't just look at the facts.

For example, if the question you got wrong covers the formula for the area of a circle, don't just look at that formula and memorize it. Take a quick look at circles in general, since if you were confused about this one topic, you might also be unsure about others related to it. Remember, on the real ACT you will not see a question exactly the same as the question you got wrong. But you probably will see a question that covers the same topic as the practice question. For that reason, when you get a question wrong, don't just figure out the right answer to the question. Learn the broader topic of which the question tests only a piece.

Reason 2: Guessing Wrong

If you guessed wrong, review your guessing strategy. Did you guess intelligently? Could you have eliminated more answers? If yes, why didn't you? By thinking in this critical way about the decisions you made while taking the practice test, you can train yourself to make quicker, more decisive, and better decisions. If you took a guess and chose the incorrect answer, don't let that sour you on guessing.

Even as you go over the question and figure out if there was any way for you to have answered it without having to guess, remind yourself that you should always guess. It pays to engage in educated guessing where you eliminate as many wrong answers as you can—even if educated guessing doesn't always result in you getting the right answer. (See "General Test-Taking Strategies" for more on guessing.)

Reason 3: Carelessness

If you discover you got a question wrong because you were careless, it might be tempting to say to yourself, "Oh, I made a careless error," and assure yourself you won't do that again. That is not enough. You made that careless mistake for a reason, and you should try to figure out why. While getting a question wrong because you didn't know the answer constitutes a weakness in your knowledge about the test, making a careless mistake represents a weakness in your method of taking the test. To overcome this weakness, you need to approach careless errors in the same critical way you would approach a lack of knowledge. Study your mistake. Reenact your thought process and see where and how your carelessness came about. Were you rushing? Did you jump at the first answer that seemed right instead of reading all the answers? If you learn precisely what your mistake was, you are much less likely to make that mistake again.

One last comment: Don't leave a blank!

Since there is no penalty for wrong answers on the ACT, you should never leave a question blank. If you're not sure of the right answer, make your best guess.

The Secret Weapon: Talking to Yourself

Yeah, it's embarrassing. Yeah, you might look silly. But talking to yourself is perhaps the best way to pound something into your brain. As you go through the steps of studying a question, you should talk them out. Verbalizing something makes it much harder to delude yourself into thinking that you're working if you're really not.

General Test-Taking Strategies

IMAGINE TWO CHILDREN PLAYING TAG IN THE FOREST. WHO WILL win—the girl who never stumbles because she knows the placement of every tree and all the twists and turns and hiding spots, or the kid who keeps falling down and tripping over roots because he doesn't pay any attention to the landscape? The answer is obvious. Even if the other kid is faster and more athletic, the girl will win because she knows how to navigate the territory and use it to her advantage.

This example of tag in the forest is extreme, but it illustrates a point. The structure of the ACT is the forest; taking the test is the game of tag.

In this section, you'll learn how to take advantage of the ACT's structure to achieve the score you want. You'll learn basic rules for taking the ACT, as well as pacing and preparation strategies. These are the general test-taking strategies that you should use in all sections of the test. You can also go to our website for specific strategies for each Subject Test.

Seven Basic Rules for Taking the ACT

These seven rules apply to every section of the ACT. They really are just commonsense guidelines, but it's amazing how the pressure and time constraints of the ACT can warp and mangle common sense. We list them here because you should always have these rules of test taking resting gently in your mind as you take the test. You don't need to focus on them obsessively, but you should be sure not to forget them. They will help you save time and cut down on careless errors.

1. **Know the Instructions for Each Subject Test**

   Since you'll need all the time you can get, don't waste time reading the Subject Test instructions during the actual test. Learn the instructions beforehand by taking practice tests.

2. **Use Your Test Booklet as Scratch Paper**

   Some students seem to think their test booklet has to look "pretty" at the end of the test. Don't be one of those students. A pristine test booklet is a sad test booklet. In the Mathematics Test, the ACT writers even give you "figuring" space for drawing diagrams and writing out solutions. The Mathematics Test isn't the only place where you can benefit from marginal scribbling, though. Making margin notes alongside the Reading and Science passages can help you stay on track when answering the subsequent questions. In addition, if you want to skip a question and come back to it later, you should make a distinctive mark next to it, so you won't miss it on your second pass through the questions.

3. **Answer Easy Questions Before Hard Questions**

   This is a crucial strategy for the ACT. Since all questions within a Subject Test are worth the same number of points, there's no point slaving away over a difficult question if doing so requires several minutes. In the same amount of time, you probably could have racked up points by answering a bunch of easy, less time-consuming questions. In summary, answer the easy and moderate questions first. That way you'll make sure that you get to see all the questions on the test that you have a good shot of getting right, while saving the leftover time for the difficult questions.

4. **Don't Get Bogged Down by a Hard Question**

   This rule may seem obvious, but many people have a hard time letting go of a question. If you've spent a significant amount of time on a problem (in ACT world, a minute and a half is a lot of time) and haven't gotten close to answering it, just let it go. Leaving a question unfinished may seem like giving up or wasting time you've already spent, but you can come back to the problem after you've answered the easy ones. The time you spent on the problem earlier won't be wasted. When you come back to the problem, you'll already have done part of the work needed to solve it.

   This strategy goes hand in hand with Rule 3. After all, the tough question that's chewing up your time isn't worth more to the computer grading your answer sheet than the easy questions nearby.

5. **Avoid Carelessness**

   There are two kinds of carelessness that threaten you as an ACT test taker. The first kind is obvious: making mistakes because you are moving too quickly through the questions. Speeding through the test can result in misinterpreting a question or missing a crucial piece of information. You should always be aware of this kind of error because the ACT writers have written the test with speedy test takers in mind: They often include tempting "partial answers" among the answer choices. A partial answer is the result of some, but not all, of the steps needed to solve a problem. If you rush through a question, you may mistake a partial answer for the real answer. Students often fall into the speeding trap when they become confused, since confusion brings nervousness and fear of falling behind. But those moments of confusion are precisely the moments when you should take a second to slow down. Take a deep breath, look at the question, and make a sober decision about whether you can answer it. If you can, dive back in. If you can't, skip the question and go on to the next one.

The second kind of carelessness arises from frustration or lack of confidence. Don't allow yourself to assume a defeatist attitude toward questions that appear to be complex. While some of these questions may actually be complex, many will be fairly simple questions disguised in complex-sounding terms. You should at least skim every question to see whether you have a feasible chance of answering it. Assuming you can't answer a question is like returning a present you've never even opened.

6. Be Careful Bubbling in Your Answers

Imagine this: You get all the right answers to the ACT questions, but you fill in all the wrong bubbles. The scoring computer doesn't care that you did the right work; all it cares about are the blackened bubbles on the answer sheet and the wrong answers that they indicate.

Protect yourself against this terrifying possibility with careful bubbling. An easy way to prevent slips on the ACT answer sheet is to pay attention to the letters being bubbled. Odd-numbered answers are lettered **A, B, C, D** (except on the Mathematics Test, where they are **A, B, C, D, E**), and even-numbered answers are lettered **F, G, H, J** (except on the Mathematics Test, where they are **F, G, H, J, K**).

You may also want to try bubbling in groups (five at a time or a page at a time) rather than answering one by one. Circle the answers in the test booklet as you go through the page, and then transfer the answers over to the answer sheet as a group. This method should increase your speed and accuracy in filling out the answer sheet. To further increase your accuracy, say the question number and the answer in your head as you fill out the grid: "Number 24, **F**. Number 25, **C**. Number 26, **J**."

7. Always Guess When You Don't Know the Answer

We will discuss guessing in "The Meaning of Multiple Choice," but the basic rule is this: Always guess! There is no penalty for wrong answers. You're much better off guessing than leaving an answer blank.

The Meaning of Multiple Choice

The multiple-choice format of the ACT should affect the way you approach the questions. In this section, we'll discuss exactly how.

Only the Answer Matters

A machine, not a person, will score your test. This scoring machine does not care how you came to your answers; it cares only whether your answers are correct and readable in little oval form. The test booklet in which you worked out your answers gets thrown in the garbage or, if your proctor is conscientious, into a recycling bin.

On the ACT, no one looks at your work. If you get a question right, it doesn't matter whether you did impeccable work. In fact, it doesn't even matter whether you knew the answer or guessed. The multiple-choice structure of the test is a message to you from the ACT: "We only care about your answers." Remember, the ACT is your tool to get into college, so treat it as a tool. It wants right answers? Give it right answers, as many as possible, using whatever strategies you can.

Multiple Choice: You've Already Got the Answers

When you look at any ACT multiple-choice question, the answer is already right there in front of you. Of course, the ACT writers don't just give you the correct answer; they hide it among a bunch of incorrect answer choices. Your job on each question is to find the right answer. Because the answer is right there, begging to be found, you have two methods you can use to try to get the correct answer:

1. Look through the answer choices and pick out the one that is correct.

2. Look at the answer choices and eliminate wrong answers until there's only one answer left.

Both methods have their advantages: You are better off using one in some situations and the other in others. In a perfect scenario in which you are sure how to answer a question, finding the right answer immediately is clearly better than chipping away at the wrong answers. Coming to a conclusion about a problem and then picking the single correct choice is a much simpler and quicker process than going through every answer choice and discarding the four that are wrong.

However, when you are unsure how to solve the problem, eliminating wrong answers becomes more attractive and appropriate. By focusing on the answers to problems that are giving you trouble, you might be able to use the answer choices to lead you in the right direction, or to solve the problem through trial and error. In some cases, you might be able to eliminate all the wrong answers. In others, you might only be able to eliminate one, which will still improve your odds when you attempt to guess.

Part of your preparation for the ACT should be to get some sense of when to use each strategy. Using the right strategy can increase your speed without affecting your accuracy, giving you more time to work on and answer as many questions as possible.

Guessing and the ACT

We've said it once, but it's important enough to bear repetition: *Whenever you can't answer a question on the ACT, you must guess.* You are not penalized for getting a question wrong, so guessing can only help your score.

Random Guessing and Educated Guessing

There are actually two kinds of guesses: random and educated. Random guesser Charlie Franklin will always guess C or F because he really, really likes those letters. Using this method, Charlie has a pretty good chance of getting about 25 percent of the questions right, yielding a Composite Score of about 11. That's not too shabby, considering Charlie expended practically no intellectual energy beyond identifying C and F as the first letters of his first and last names.

But what about educated guesser Celia? Instead of immediately guessing on each question, she works to eliminate answers, always getting rid of two choices for each question. She then guesses between the remaining choices and has a 50 percent chance of getting the correct answer. Celia will therefore get about half of the questions on the test correct. Her Composite Score will be about a 19, which is an average score on the ACT.

The example of these two guessers should show you that while blind guessing can help you, educated guessing can *really* help you. For example, let's say you know the correct answer for half of the questions and you guess randomly on the remaining half. Your score will probably be a 22—three points higher than the score you'd get leaving half of the answers blank. Now let's say you know the correct answer for half of the questions and you make educated guesses on the remaining half, narrowing the choices to two. You can probably score a 26 with this method, landing you in the 90th percentile of test takers. This is a good score, and to get it you only need to be certain of half the answers.

"Always guess" really means "always eliminate as many answer choices as possible and then guess."

A Note to the Timid Guesser

Some students feel that guessing is like cheating. They believe that by guessing, they are getting points they don't really deserve. Such a belief might be noble, but it is also mistaken, for two reasons.

First, educated guessing is actually a form of partial credit on the ACT. Let's say you're taking the ACT and come upon a question you can't quite figure out. Yet while you aren't sure of the definite answer, you are sure that two of the answer choices can't be right. In other words, you can eliminate two of the four answer choices, leaving you with a one-in-two chance of guessing correctly between the remaining two answer choices. Now let's say someone else is taking the same test and gets to the same question. But this person is completely flummoxed. He can't eliminate any answer choices. When this person guesses, he has only a one-in-four chance of guessing correctly. Your extra knowledge, which allowed you to eliminate some answer choices, gives you better odds of getting this question right, exactly as extra knowledge should.

Second, the people who made the ACT thought very hard about how the scoring of the test should work. When they decided that they wouldn't include a penalty for wrong answers, they knew that the lack of a penalty would allow people to guess. In other words, they built the test with the specific understanding that people would guess on every question they couldn't answer. The test wants you to guess. So go ahead and do it.

Pacing

The ACT presents you with a ton of questions and, despite its three-hour length, not that much time to answer them. As you take the test, you will probably feel some pressure to answer quickly. As we've already discussed, getting bogged down on a single question is not a good thing. But rushing isn't any good either. In the end, there's no real difference between answering very few questions and answering lots of questions incorrectly: Both will lead to low scores. What you have to do is find a happy medium, a groove, a speed at which you can be both accurate and efficient, and get the score you want. Finding this pace is a tricky task, but it will come through practice and strategy.

Setting a Target Score

The ACT is your tool to get into college. Therefore, a perfect score on the ACT is not a 36; it's the score that gets you into the colleges of your choice. Once you set a target score, your efforts should be directed toward achieving that score and not necessarily a 36. In setting a target score, the first rule is to be honest and realistic. Base your target score on the schools you want to attend, and use the results from your practice tests to decide what's realistic. If you score a 20 on your first practice test, your target score probably should not be a 30. Instead, aim for a 23 or 24. Your scores will likely increase on your second test simply because you'll be more experienced than you were the first time, and then you can work on getting several extra problems right on each Subject Test.

Your Target Score Determines Your Strategy and Pace

Your target score should affect your overall approach to the test. Cathy, whose target score is 31, is going to use a different strategy and pace from Elvie, whose target score is 20. Cathy must work quickly without becoming careless to get 90 percent of her questions right. Elvie, on the other hand, can afford to work more slowly; to get a 20, she needs to answer approximately half of the questions correctly. Elvie can focus her energy on carefully answering about 60 percent of the questions, allowing for some wrong answers; then she can guess on the remaining questions. Cathy needs to focus on every question to get her 90 percent. Also allowing for some wrong answers, she should aim to answer all the questions correctly.

Of course, this is all a bit like the chicken and the egg conundrum. Cathy's target score is probably higher than Elvie's because she is a faster and better test taker than Elvie. Elvie needs the extra time to spend on each problem because she is a slower worker than Cathy. It's not as though Elvie generates a lot of extra time in which she can doodle or draw elaborate diagrams by concentrating on a smaller number of questions. All of that extra time per question is being put to use by Elvie because she needs it to get the right answer.

The point of this anecdote: Adjust your pacing to the score you want, but also be honest with yourself about what pace you can maintain. The following charts will give you an idea of the number of questions you need to get right to receive certain scaled scores on the ACT. Use these charts to determine the number of correct answers you need to achieve your target score.

English		Mathematics	
Target Score	# Right	Target Score	# Right
36	75	36	60
30	69–70	30	53–54
26	60–62	26	44–45
23	52–54	23	38–39
20	44–46	20	32–33
17	36–38	17	23–25
11	19–21	11	7–8

Reading		Science	
Target Score	# Right	Target Score	# Right
36	40	36	40
30	35	30	37
26	30–31	26	32–33
23	26–27	23	27–28
20	22	20	22–23
17	18	17	16–17
11	9–10	11	7

The first target score you set doesn't have to be your last. If you reach your initial target score, set a new, higher score and try increasing the pace at which you work. In setting preparatory target scores, focus on improving a couple points at a time. In the end, incremental change will work better than a giant leap.

The White Rabbit Syndrome: Watching the Clock

Because the ACT is a timed test, you should always be aware of the time. The proctor at the test center will strictly enforce the time limits for each Subject Test. Even if you have only one question left to answer, you won't be allowed to fill in that bubble. As you take the test, watch the clock. You shouldn't be checking it every two minutes, since you will only waste time and give yourself a headache. But you should check occasionally to make sure you are on pace to achieve your target score. If you're Cathy, aiming to answer 90 percent of the questions correctly, you'll be in trouble if you've answered only 40 of the 75 English questions in 30 minutes (the English Test is 45 minutes long). If you're Elvie, aiming for 60 percent of the questions, answering 40 English questions in 30 minutes is a pretty good pace.

Preparing for the ACT

Preparation is the key to success on the ACT. When the ACT is lurking sometime far in the future, it can be difficult to motivate yourself to study. Establishing an organized study routine can help keep you on track as you approach the test date.

Setting Up a Study Schedule

Rather than simply telling yourself to study each week, you might want to write down an actual schedule, just as you have a schedule of classes at school. Keep this schedule where you'll see it every day, and consider showing it to a parent who will nag you incessantly when you don't follow it. (You might as well use your parents' nagging capabilities to your own advantage for once.)

You should allot at least a few hours a week to studying, depending on how much time you have before the test date. If you start preparing five weeks in advance, you might consider studying one subject per week, with the last week left over for light review.

To complement your studying, take one test, or at least part of one test, each week. We've given you five practice tests in this book. You don't necessarily have to take a full practice test each week—if you want to focus on English one week, take the practice English Test to help narrow your studying.

The Day of the Test

You must bring the following items to the test center on the day of the test:

1. Your admission ticket.

2. Photo ID or a letter of identification.

Unless a test proctor recognizes you, you will not be allowed in the test room without appropriate identification. We also suggest that you bring the following:

3. Some No. 2 pencils and a sharpener.

4. A calculator. You should bring the calculator you normally use (preferably with an extra battery). You don't want to get stuck searching frantically for the right buttons on an unfamiliar calculator.

5. A watch. Your test room may not have a clock, or the clock may not be visible from where you're sitting. Since the test proctors only call out the time five minutes before the end of each section, you have to rely on yourself to know how much time remains.

6. A snack, to keep up that energy.

7. Lucky clothes. Why not?

ACT Practice
Test 1

DIRECTIONS: The ACT consists of tests in four separate subject areas: English, Mathematics, Reading, and Science. These four tests measure skills learned through high school course-work that are relevant to success in college. *YOU MAY USE CALCULATORS ON THE MATHEMATICS TEST ONLY.*

Each test contains a set of numbered questions. The answer choices for each question are lettered. On your answer sheet, you will find rows of ovals that are numbered to match the questions. Each oval contains a letter to correspond to a particular answer choice.

Choose the best answer for each question. Then, on your answer sheet, find the row of ovals that is numbered the same as the question. Find the oval containing the letter of your chosen answer, and fill in this oval completely. You must use a soft lead pencil for this purpose, and your marks must be heavy and black. *BALLPOINT PENS SHOULD NOT BE USED TO FILL IN THE ANSWER SHEET.*

Fill in only one answer choice oval for each question. If you wish to change an answer, make sure that your original answer is thoroughly erased before marking the new one. After filling in your answer, double-check to be sure that you have marked the row of ovals that corresponds to the question number being answered.

Responses will be scored only if they are marked on your answer document. Your score for each test is determined by the number of questions answered correctly during the testing period. Your score will NOT be reduced if you choose an incorrect answer. *FOR THIS REASON, IT IS ADVANTAGEOUS FOR YOU TO ANSWER EVERY QUESTION, EVEN IF YOU GUESS ON SOME QUESTIONS.*

You may work on a test ONLY when the test supervisor gives you permission to do so. If you finish a test before the end of the time allowed, use any remaining time to review questions that you are unsure about. You are permitted to review ONLY your answers for the test on which you are currently working. You may NOT look back to a test you have already completed, and you may NOT continue on to another test. If you do so, you will be disqualified from the examination.

When the end of each test is announced, put your pencil down immediately. You are NOT permitted to fill in or change ovals for a test after the end of that test has been called. If you do so, for any reason, you will be disqualified from the examination.

You may not fold or tear the pages of your test.

DO NOT TURN TO THE FIRST TEST
UNTIL YOU ARE TOLD TO DO SO.

ACT Practice Test 1: Answer Sheet

TEST 1

1 Ⓐ Ⓑ Ⓒ Ⓓ	16 Ⓕ Ⓖ Ⓗ Ⓙ	31 Ⓐ Ⓑ Ⓒ Ⓓ	46 Ⓕ Ⓖ Ⓗ Ⓙ	61 Ⓐ Ⓑ Ⓒ Ⓓ
2 Ⓕ Ⓖ Ⓗ Ⓙ	17 Ⓐ Ⓑ Ⓒ Ⓓ	32 Ⓕ Ⓖ Ⓗ Ⓙ	47 Ⓐ Ⓑ Ⓒ Ⓓ	62 Ⓕ Ⓖ Ⓗ Ⓙ
3 Ⓐ Ⓑ Ⓒ Ⓓ	18 Ⓕ Ⓖ Ⓗ Ⓙ	33 Ⓐ Ⓑ Ⓒ Ⓓ	48 Ⓕ Ⓖ Ⓗ Ⓙ	63 Ⓐ Ⓑ Ⓒ Ⓓ
4 Ⓕ Ⓖ Ⓗ Ⓙ	19 Ⓐ Ⓑ Ⓒ Ⓓ	34 Ⓕ Ⓖ Ⓗ Ⓙ	49 Ⓐ Ⓑ Ⓒ Ⓓ	64 Ⓕ Ⓖ Ⓗ Ⓙ
5 Ⓐ Ⓑ Ⓒ Ⓓ	20 Ⓕ Ⓖ Ⓗ Ⓙ	35 Ⓐ Ⓑ Ⓒ Ⓓ	50 Ⓕ Ⓖ Ⓗ Ⓙ	65 Ⓐ Ⓑ Ⓒ Ⓓ
6 Ⓕ Ⓖ Ⓗ Ⓙ	21 Ⓐ Ⓑ Ⓒ Ⓓ	36 Ⓕ Ⓖ Ⓗ Ⓙ	51 Ⓐ Ⓑ Ⓒ Ⓓ	66 Ⓕ Ⓖ Ⓗ Ⓙ
7 Ⓐ Ⓑ Ⓒ Ⓓ	22 Ⓕ Ⓖ Ⓗ Ⓙ	37 Ⓐ Ⓑ Ⓒ Ⓓ	52 Ⓕ Ⓖ Ⓗ Ⓙ	67 Ⓐ Ⓑ Ⓒ Ⓓ
8 Ⓕ Ⓖ Ⓗ Ⓙ	23 Ⓐ Ⓑ Ⓒ Ⓓ	38 Ⓕ Ⓖ Ⓗ Ⓙ	53 Ⓐ Ⓑ Ⓒ Ⓓ	68 Ⓕ Ⓖ Ⓗ Ⓙ
9 Ⓐ Ⓑ Ⓒ Ⓓ	24 Ⓕ Ⓖ Ⓗ Ⓙ	39 Ⓐ Ⓑ Ⓒ Ⓓ	54 Ⓕ Ⓖ Ⓗ Ⓙ	69 Ⓐ Ⓑ Ⓒ Ⓓ
10 Ⓕ Ⓖ Ⓗ Ⓙ	25 Ⓐ Ⓑ Ⓒ Ⓓ	40 Ⓕ Ⓖ Ⓗ Ⓙ	55 Ⓐ Ⓑ Ⓒ Ⓓ	70 Ⓕ Ⓖ Ⓗ Ⓙ
11 Ⓐ Ⓑ Ⓒ Ⓓ	26 Ⓕ Ⓖ Ⓗ Ⓙ	41 Ⓐ Ⓑ Ⓒ Ⓓ	56 Ⓕ Ⓖ Ⓗ Ⓙ	71 Ⓐ Ⓑ Ⓒ Ⓓ
12 Ⓕ Ⓖ Ⓗ Ⓙ	27 Ⓐ Ⓑ Ⓒ Ⓓ	42 Ⓕ Ⓖ Ⓗ Ⓙ	57 Ⓐ Ⓑ Ⓒ Ⓓ	72 Ⓕ Ⓖ Ⓗ Ⓙ
13 Ⓐ Ⓑ Ⓒ Ⓓ	28 Ⓕ Ⓖ Ⓗ Ⓙ	43 Ⓐ Ⓑ Ⓒ Ⓓ	58 Ⓕ Ⓖ Ⓗ Ⓙ	73 Ⓐ Ⓑ Ⓒ Ⓓ
14 Ⓕ Ⓖ Ⓗ Ⓙ	29 Ⓐ Ⓑ Ⓒ Ⓓ	44 Ⓕ Ⓖ Ⓗ Ⓙ	59 Ⓐ Ⓑ Ⓒ Ⓓ	74 Ⓕ Ⓖ Ⓗ Ⓙ
15 Ⓐ Ⓑ Ⓒ Ⓓ	30 Ⓕ Ⓖ Ⓗ Ⓙ	45 Ⓐ Ⓑ Ⓒ Ⓓ	60 Ⓕ Ⓖ Ⓗ Ⓙ	75 Ⓐ Ⓑ Ⓒ Ⓓ

TEST 2

1 Ⓐ Ⓑ Ⓒ Ⓓ Ⓔ	13 Ⓐ Ⓑ Ⓒ Ⓓ Ⓔ	25 Ⓐ Ⓑ Ⓒ Ⓓ Ⓔ	37 Ⓐ Ⓑ Ⓒ Ⓓ Ⓔ	49 Ⓐ Ⓑ Ⓒ Ⓓ Ⓔ
2 Ⓕ Ⓖ Ⓗ Ⓙ Ⓚ	14 Ⓕ Ⓖ Ⓗ Ⓙ Ⓚ	26 Ⓕ Ⓖ Ⓗ Ⓙ Ⓚ	38 Ⓕ Ⓖ Ⓗ Ⓙ Ⓚ	50 Ⓕ Ⓖ Ⓗ Ⓙ Ⓚ
3 Ⓐ Ⓑ Ⓒ Ⓓ Ⓔ	15 Ⓐ Ⓑ Ⓒ Ⓓ Ⓔ	27 Ⓐ Ⓑ Ⓒ Ⓓ Ⓔ	39 Ⓐ Ⓑ Ⓒ Ⓓ Ⓔ	51 Ⓐ Ⓑ Ⓒ Ⓓ Ⓔ
4 Ⓕ Ⓖ Ⓗ Ⓙ Ⓚ	16 Ⓕ Ⓖ Ⓗ Ⓙ Ⓚ	28 Ⓕ Ⓖ Ⓗ Ⓙ Ⓚ	40 Ⓕ Ⓖ Ⓗ Ⓙ Ⓚ	52 Ⓕ Ⓖ Ⓗ Ⓙ Ⓚ
5 Ⓐ Ⓑ Ⓒ Ⓓ Ⓔ	17 Ⓐ Ⓑ Ⓒ Ⓓ Ⓔ	29 Ⓐ Ⓑ Ⓒ Ⓓ Ⓔ	41 Ⓐ Ⓑ Ⓒ Ⓓ Ⓔ	53 Ⓐ Ⓑ Ⓒ Ⓓ Ⓔ
6 Ⓕ Ⓖ Ⓗ Ⓙ Ⓚ	18 Ⓕ Ⓖ Ⓗ Ⓙ Ⓚ	30 Ⓕ Ⓖ Ⓗ Ⓙ Ⓚ	42 Ⓕ Ⓖ Ⓗ Ⓙ Ⓚ	54 Ⓕ Ⓖ Ⓗ Ⓙ Ⓚ
7 Ⓐ Ⓑ Ⓒ Ⓓ Ⓔ	19 Ⓐ Ⓑ Ⓒ Ⓓ Ⓔ	31 Ⓐ Ⓑ Ⓒ Ⓓ Ⓔ	43 Ⓐ Ⓑ Ⓒ Ⓓ Ⓔ	55 Ⓐ Ⓑ Ⓒ Ⓓ Ⓔ
8 Ⓕ Ⓖ Ⓗ Ⓙ Ⓚ	20 Ⓕ Ⓖ Ⓗ Ⓙ Ⓚ	32 Ⓕ Ⓖ Ⓗ Ⓙ Ⓚ	44 Ⓕ Ⓖ Ⓗ Ⓙ Ⓚ	56 Ⓕ Ⓖ Ⓗ Ⓙ Ⓚ
9 Ⓐ Ⓑ Ⓒ Ⓓ Ⓔ	21 Ⓐ Ⓑ Ⓒ Ⓓ Ⓔ	33 Ⓐ Ⓑ Ⓒ Ⓓ Ⓔ	45 Ⓐ Ⓑ Ⓒ Ⓓ Ⓔ	57 Ⓐ Ⓑ Ⓒ Ⓓ Ⓔ
10 Ⓕ Ⓖ Ⓗ Ⓙ Ⓚ	22 Ⓕ Ⓖ Ⓗ Ⓙ Ⓚ	34 Ⓕ Ⓖ Ⓗ Ⓙ Ⓚ	46 Ⓕ Ⓖ Ⓗ Ⓙ Ⓚ	58 Ⓕ Ⓖ Ⓗ Ⓙ Ⓚ
11 Ⓐ Ⓑ Ⓒ Ⓓ Ⓔ	23 Ⓐ Ⓑ Ⓒ Ⓓ Ⓔ	35 Ⓐ Ⓑ Ⓒ Ⓓ Ⓔ	47 Ⓐ Ⓑ Ⓒ Ⓓ Ⓔ	59 Ⓐ Ⓑ Ⓒ Ⓓ Ⓔ
12 Ⓕ Ⓖ Ⓗ Ⓙ Ⓚ	24 Ⓕ Ⓖ Ⓗ Ⓙ Ⓚ	36 Ⓕ Ⓖ Ⓗ Ⓙ Ⓚ	48 Ⓕ Ⓖ Ⓗ Ⓙ Ⓚ	60 Ⓕ Ⓖ Ⓗ Ⓙ Ⓚ

TEST 3

1 Ⓐ Ⓑ Ⓒ Ⓓ	9 Ⓐ Ⓑ Ⓒ Ⓓ	17 Ⓐ Ⓑ Ⓒ Ⓓ	25 Ⓐ Ⓑ Ⓒ Ⓓ	33 Ⓐ Ⓑ Ⓒ Ⓓ
2 Ⓕ Ⓖ Ⓗ Ⓙ	10 Ⓕ Ⓖ Ⓗ Ⓙ	18 Ⓕ Ⓖ Ⓗ Ⓙ	26 Ⓕ Ⓖ Ⓗ Ⓙ	34 Ⓕ Ⓖ Ⓗ Ⓙ
3 Ⓐ Ⓑ Ⓒ Ⓓ	11 Ⓐ Ⓑ Ⓒ Ⓓ	19 Ⓐ Ⓑ Ⓒ Ⓓ	27 Ⓐ Ⓑ Ⓒ Ⓓ	35 Ⓐ Ⓑ Ⓒ Ⓓ
4 Ⓕ Ⓖ Ⓗ Ⓙ	12 Ⓕ Ⓖ Ⓗ Ⓙ	20 Ⓕ Ⓖ Ⓗ Ⓙ	28 Ⓕ Ⓖ Ⓗ Ⓙ	36 Ⓕ Ⓖ Ⓗ Ⓙ
5 Ⓐ Ⓑ Ⓒ Ⓓ	13 Ⓐ Ⓑ Ⓒ Ⓓ	21 Ⓐ Ⓑ Ⓒ Ⓓ	29 Ⓐ Ⓑ Ⓒ Ⓓ	37 Ⓐ Ⓑ Ⓒ Ⓓ
6 Ⓕ Ⓖ Ⓗ Ⓙ	14 Ⓕ Ⓖ Ⓗ Ⓙ	22 Ⓕ Ⓖ Ⓗ Ⓙ	30 Ⓕ Ⓖ Ⓗ Ⓙ	38 Ⓕ Ⓖ Ⓗ Ⓙ
7 Ⓐ Ⓑ Ⓒ Ⓓ	15 Ⓐ Ⓑ Ⓒ Ⓓ	23 Ⓐ Ⓑ Ⓒ Ⓓ	31 Ⓐ Ⓑ Ⓒ Ⓓ	39 Ⓐ Ⓑ Ⓒ Ⓓ
8 Ⓕ Ⓖ Ⓗ Ⓙ	16 Ⓕ Ⓖ Ⓗ Ⓙ	24 Ⓕ Ⓖ Ⓗ Ⓙ	32 Ⓕ Ⓖ Ⓗ Ⓙ	40 Ⓕ Ⓖ Ⓗ Ⓙ

TEST 4

1 Ⓐ Ⓑ Ⓒ Ⓓ	9 Ⓐ Ⓑ Ⓒ Ⓓ	17 Ⓐ Ⓑ Ⓒ Ⓓ	25 Ⓐ Ⓑ Ⓒ Ⓓ	33 Ⓐ Ⓑ Ⓒ Ⓓ
2 Ⓕ Ⓖ Ⓗ Ⓙ	10 Ⓕ Ⓖ Ⓗ Ⓙ	18 Ⓕ Ⓖ Ⓗ Ⓙ	26 Ⓕ Ⓖ Ⓗ Ⓙ	34 Ⓕ Ⓖ Ⓗ Ⓙ
3 Ⓐ Ⓑ Ⓒ Ⓓ	11 Ⓐ Ⓑ Ⓒ Ⓓ	19 Ⓐ Ⓑ Ⓒ Ⓓ	27 Ⓐ Ⓑ Ⓒ Ⓓ	35 Ⓐ Ⓑ Ⓒ Ⓓ
4 Ⓕ Ⓖ Ⓗ Ⓙ	12 Ⓕ Ⓖ Ⓗ Ⓙ	20 Ⓕ Ⓖ Ⓗ Ⓙ	28 Ⓕ Ⓖ Ⓗ Ⓙ	36 Ⓕ Ⓖ Ⓗ Ⓙ
5 Ⓐ Ⓑ Ⓒ Ⓓ	13 Ⓐ Ⓑ Ⓒ Ⓓ	21 Ⓐ Ⓑ Ⓒ Ⓓ	29 Ⓐ Ⓑ Ⓒ Ⓓ	37 Ⓐ Ⓑ Ⓒ Ⓓ
6 Ⓕ Ⓖ Ⓗ Ⓙ	14 Ⓕ Ⓖ Ⓗ Ⓙ	22 Ⓕ Ⓖ Ⓗ Ⓙ	30 Ⓕ Ⓖ Ⓗ Ⓙ	38 Ⓕ Ⓖ Ⓗ Ⓙ
7 Ⓐ Ⓑ Ⓒ Ⓓ	15 Ⓐ Ⓑ Ⓒ Ⓓ	23 Ⓐ Ⓑ Ⓒ Ⓓ	31 Ⓐ Ⓑ Ⓒ Ⓓ	39 Ⓐ Ⓑ Ⓒ Ⓓ
8 Ⓕ Ⓖ Ⓗ Ⓙ	16 Ⓕ Ⓖ Ⓗ Ⓙ	24 Ⓕ Ⓖ Ⓗ Ⓙ	32 Ⓕ Ⓖ Ⓗ Ⓙ	40 Ⓕ Ⓖ Ⓗ Ⓙ

ENGLISH TEST

45 Minutes—75 Questions

DIRECTIONS: There are five passages on this test. You should read each passage once before answering the questions on it. In order to answer correctly, you may need to read several sentences beyond the question.

There are two question formats within the passages. In one format, you will find words and phrases that have been underlined and assigned numbers. These numbers will correspond with sets of alternative words/phrases given in the right-hand column of the test booklet. From the sets of alternatives, choose the answer choice that works best in context, keeping in mind whether it employs standard written English, whether it gets across the idea of the section,

and whether it suits the tone and style of the passage. You will usually be offered the option "NO CHANGE," which you should choose if you think the version found in the passage is best.

In the second format, you will see boxed numbers referring to sections of the passage or to the passage as a whole. In the right-hand column, you will be asked questions about or given alternatives for the sections marked by the boxes. Choose the answer choice that best answers the question or completes the section. After choosing your answer choice, fill in the corresponding bubble on the answer sheet.

Passage I

A Volunteer Effort

[1]

Starting a volunteer movement is a time-consuming but rewarding experience, as I learned, when I established an
<u>1</u>

organization to help the residents in a nearby local nursing
<u>2</u>
home.
<u>2</u>

1. **A.** NO CHANGE
   B. learned; when
   C. learned when
   D. learned. When

2. **F.** NO CHANGE
   G. a local nursing home
   H. a nearby and local nursing home
   J. a nursing home located nearby

[2]

When I was a teenager, my grandmother lived in a nursing home, and my sister and I enjoy spending time with
<u>3</u>
her talking and playing Scrabble. Fortunately, the nursing
<u>4</u>
home was not too far from our house, so we visited her every weekend and sometimes during the week.

3. **A.** NO CHANGE
   B. are enjoying spending
   C. do enjoy spending
   D. enjoyed spending

4. **F.** NO CHANGE
   G. Consequently,
   H. Finally,
   J. However,

GO ON TO THE NEXT PAGE.

[3]

5 One afternoon my sister encouraged me to help her start a conversation with an elderly lady who was sitting

alone in the television room. <u>The woman proceeded to tell us,</u> <u>delighted to talk with someone, about her 19 grandchildren.</u>

She also shared romantic stories about meeting her husband and <u>exchanged</u> letters with him during his World War II military tour. Our simple gesture toward one woman helped us realize that many older people <u>earn</u> great joy from the simple act of conversation.

[4]

As a result of our experience, my sister and I organized a group of teenage volunteers <u>regularly to visit the nursing</u> <u>home residents.</u> Group members play games with the

men and <u>women they</u> sometimes help the residents write letters to loved ones. One of the volunteers is working on a scrapbook with <u>their</u> buddy, Elsie, who has been at the nursing facility for two years. The teenagers

5. Given that all the answers are true, which of the following sentences, if added here, would most effectively introduce the new subject of paragraph 3?
A. Our grandmother had developed many friendships with the other residents during her three years in the home.
B. If our mother could not drive us to the nursing home, my sister and I took the bus or rode our bicycles.
C. We were saddened by the fact that some residents never had visitors, and they were obviously very lonely.
D. When we visited the nursing home, our grandmother proudly introduced us to the nurses, doctors, and residents.

6. F. NO CHANGE
G. The woman told us she had 19 grandchildren delighted to talk with someone.
H. As she proceeded to talk with my sister and me, the woman's 19 grandchildren delighted her.
J. Delighted to talk with someone, the woman proceeded to tell us about her 19 grandchildren.

7. A. NO CHANGE
B. having exchanged
C. was exchanging
D. exchanging

8. F. NO CHANGE
G. generate
H. assess
J. derive

9. A. NO CHANGE
B. to visit the nursing home residents on a regular basis.
C. to on a regular basis visit the nursing home residents.
D. to regularly visit the nursing home residents.

10. F. NO CHANGE
G. women, they
H. women, and they
J. women; and they

11. A. NO CHANGE
B. her
C. our
D. your

enjoy listening to the amazing stories of the home's elderly citizens. 12

[5]

We have received enthusiastic support from the nursing homes' administrators and staff, who are pleased that

13

we care enough to make a difference. The staff expected

14

the program to be a huge hit, and they were correct. The residents and the volunteers look forward to their time together, and both parties are rewarded by the experience. 15

12. Upon reviewing this paragraph, the author is thinking of deleting the preceding sentence. If the author were to delete the sentence, the paragraph would primarily lose:
F. a defense in favor of the teenager's volunteer efforts.
G. a summation of the main idea of paragraph 4.
H. an illustration of the benefits received by the nursing home residents.
J. a comment on what the teenagers gain from their visits to the home.

13. A. NO CHANGE
B. home's administrators
C. homes' administrator's
D. homes administrators

14. F. NO CHANGE
G. expects
H. have expected
J. are expecting

15. For the sake of logic and coherence, paragraph 1 should be placed:
A. where it is now.
B. after paragraph 2.
C. after paragraph 4.
D. after paragraph 5.

GO ON TO THE NEXT PAGE.

Passage II

Major Winters and Easy Company

[1]

Richard "Dick" Winters gained fame through his portrayal by actor Damien Lewis in the Steven Spielberg series *Band of Brothers*. The miniseries chronicling the
16
journey of Easy Company, a World War II paratrooper airborne division that fought in two significant campaigns: the Battle of Normandy and the Battle of the Bulge. Company "E," which was heavily utilized during World War II, was authorized by Major Winters.
17

[2]

Born in Lancaster, Pennsylvania in 1918 Winters was
18
raised as a Mennonite and upheld a very strict moral code that was apparent during his years in the military. Winters
19
will enlist in the Army in 1941, after graduating from
19   20
basic training, he was chosen for officer's training school.

The Army gained an officer who displayed leadership, had camaraderie, and is understanding with his charges
21
both on and off the battlefield. The upright Winters developed a remarkable friendship with Lewis Nixon, a fellow lieutenant whose struggle with personal issues led to a demotion during the war. 22

16. **F.** NO CHANGE
    G. chronicles
    H. will chronicle
    J. has been chronicling

17. **A.** NO CHANGE
    B. organized
    C. governed
    D. commanded

18. **F.** NO CHANGE
    G. Lancaster, Pennsylvania in 1918,
    H. Lancaster Pennsylvania, in 1918
    J. Lancaster, Pennsylvania in, 1918,

19. **A.** NO CHANGE
    B. does enlist
    C. enlisted
    D. is enlisting

20. **F.** NO CHANGE
    G. 1941
    H. 1941 and
    J. 1941, and

21. **A.** NO CHANGE
    B. had camaraderie, and understanding
    C. camaraderie, and was understanding
    D. camaraderie, and understanding

22. If the author were to delete the preceding sentence, the paragraph would primarily lose:
    F. an irrelevant but interesting fact about Lewis.
    G. information that explains Winters' morality.
    H. an example of Winters's compassion for others.
    J. information that contrasts Winters with most soldiers.

[3]

Winters co-wrote a book about his experiences with
                                                  23
Easy Company during World War II. One of his most
                                    23
distinguished accomplishments took place during a battle

in Germany when Winters and 13 men only destroyed an
                                            24
entire artillery battery. However, Winters managed to
                          25
ascertain a map of all the German defenses in Utah Beach.

Winters later trained Army Rangers for the Korean War,
                                                        26
and his groundbreaking attack style is still taught at
26
West Point today.

[4]

As shown in *Band of Brothers*, on the battlefield Winters
                                 27
demonstrated great strength and determination. Winters
                                                   28
never saw himself as a hero or as a brave individual, and
                                                    28
he never failed to tell others about the accomplishments and

bravery of his men. As the retired Major Winters said when

23. Given that all of the following sentences are true, which one would be the most effective first sentence of paragraph 3?
A. NO CHANGE
B. Winters and his wife have retired to a small farm in Hershey, Pennsylvania, where they enjoy the peace and quiet.
C. Winters's best strengths were his bravery in the face of fighting and his ability to lead no matter the circumstances.
D. A letter-writing campaign is underway to encourage the U.S. House to retroactively award Winters with the Medal of Honor.

24. F. NO CHANGE
G. 13 men destroyed only
H. 13 of his only men destroyed
J. only 13 men destroyed

25. A. NO CHANGE
B. In addition,
C. Nonetheless,
D. For example,

26. Which of the following alternatives to the underlined portion would NOT be acceptable?
F. War. Moreover, his
G. War; and his
H. War. His
J. War; his

27. The best placement for the underlined portion would be:
A. where it is now.
B. at the beginning of the sentence (revising the capitalization accordingly).
C. after the word *strength*.
D. after the word *determination* (ending the sentence with a period).

28. F. NO CHANGE
G. Winters never thought of himself as heroic or courageous,
H. Winters never saw himself as a hero,
J. Winters, who never thought of himself as a hero,

asked by his grandson whether he was a hero in World War

II, "No, but I served in a company of heroes." 29 30

29. What function does the quotation in paragraph 4 serve in relation to the rest of the essay?
   A. It illustrates the paragraph's main point that Winters is a humble leader.
   B. It refers back to the opening sentence of the essay and the title of the miniseries.
   C. It suggests that Winters dislikes remembering the difficulties of World War II.
   D. It indicates that Winters's grandson is unfamiliar with the heroics of his grandfather.

30. Suppose the writer had intended to write a brief essay that describes the importance of paratroopers during World War II. Would this essay successfully fulfill the writer's goal?
   F. Yes, because it offers such details as how paratroopers were able to get behind enemy lines to gather important information.
   G. Yes, because it explains in detail how paratroopers were trained in preparation for military operations.
   H. No, because it focuses primarily on the character and life of a single paratrooper.
   J. No, because it is primarily a historical essay about how military tactics have changed.

Passage III

Amish Quilts

"Plain and simple" is a phrase often associated with the

<u>Amish. An</u> Anabaptist Christian denomination
   31

formed in 1693 with communities scattered across

Pennsylvania, Indiana, and Ohio. Horse-drawn buggies,

black clothing, and wide-brimmed hats are the typical

images of the Amish lifestyle. With little use for items in

their homes that serve no practical purpose, the Amish

typically shun <u>art for art's</u> sake. However, form and
                   32

function <u>come</u> together in creative and artistic ways
          33

when Amish women took up quilting in the 1870s.

[1] <u>Quilting was brought to America, which had become a</u>
                                                        34

<u>popular pastime in neighboring communities, by British</u>
                                                        34

<u>Quakers.</u> [2] At the time, Amish families used plain
   34

bed coverings in their homes. [3] Amish women saw no need

to create elaborate quilts merely for the purpose of staying

warm. [4] Over time, the quilting fad passed, which is when

Amish women began piecing fabric together. ⑤

31. A. NO CHANGE
B. Amish, an
C. Amish; an
D. Amish.

32. F. NO CHANGE
G. art for arts'
H. art, for arts
J. art, for art's

33. A. NO CHANGE
B. will be coming
C. have come
D. came

34. F. NO CHANGE
G. Quilting had become a popular pastime in neighboring communities after the skill was brought to America by British Quakers.
H. British Quakers brought to America quilting, which had become a popular pastime in neighboring communities.
J. A popular pastime in neighboring communities after the skill was brought to America; quilting was brought by British Quakers.

35. The writer is considering adding the following true statement to this paragraph:

During Colonial times in America, many women occupied their time by weaving.

Should the sentence be added to this paragraph, and if so, where should it be placed?
A. Yes, after sentence 1.
B. Yes, after sentence 2.
C. Yes, after sentence 3.
D. The sentence should NOT be added.

GO ON TO THE NEXT PAGE.

In keeping with their <u>feelings,</u> Amish women created
[36]
unadorned quilts from solid fabrics instead of trendy <u>prints</u>
[37]

<u>and early</u> Amish quilts were typically made in one
[37]

dark color, such as rust, blue, or black. The simple color

selections contrasted with <u>intricately quilting styles.</u>
[38]

Swirling feathers and curves brought the plain fabric to

life. Although Amish quilters often used a sewing machine

for piecing fabric together, they always quilted the layered

fabric and batting together by hand.

<u>Amish quilts are frequently featured in national quilt</u>
[39]
<u>shows sponsored by museums and quilting organizations.</u>
[39]
For example, a traditional Amish quilt may consist

of a large diamond-shaped piece of fabric <u>centering in</u>
[40]

<u>the middle, surrounded by</u> a contrasting fabric.
[40]

36. **F.** NO CHANGE
   G. values,
   H. routines,
   J. strategies

37. **A.** NO CHANGE
   B. prints, early
   C. prints. Early
   D. prints but early

38. **F.** NO CHANGE
   G. styles of intricately quilts.
   H. quilting by intricate styles.
   J. intricate quilting styles.

39. Which choice most effectively guides the reader from
   the preceding paragraph into this new paragraph?
   A. NO CHANGE
   B. In honor of their customs, many Amish quilters continue to use non-electric sewing machines, despite
   the convenience of electric machines.
   C. Many Amish communities hold large quilt auctions
   and craft shows each spring and summer to sell
   their homemade goods.
   D. Over time, Amish quilts began to include additional
   colors, but designs remained simple.

40. **F.** NO CHANGE
   G. centered in the middle, to surround
   H. centered in the middle, surrounded by
   J. centering in the middle surrounding by

While additional designs have been added to the Amish
41

quilting style throughout the years, solid colors remain the
41

standard. Brighter hues, such as violet, and red, now
41   42

enhance the modern quilting palette. The contrast

of black fabric with a vibrant solid color in an uncluttered

pattern creates an almost contemporary looking quilt,
43

who are beautiful in its simplicity. 45
44

41. **A.** NO CHANGE
  B. Throughout the years, while additional designs are added to the Amish quilting style, solid colors have remained the standard.
  C. To the Amish quilting style, for which solid colors remain the standard, additional designs are being added throughout the years.
  D. Solid colors remain the standard of the Amish quilting style throughout the years, to which additional designs have been added.

42. **F.** NO CHANGE
  G. violet and red, now,
  H. violet, and red now
  J. violet and red, now

43. **A.** NO CHANGE
  B. contemporary and modern
  C. modern-day, up-to-date
  D. progressive, new, and fresh looking

44. **F.** NO CHANGE
  G. which is
  H. that are
  J. who is

45. Suppose the author had chosen to write a brief essay about the history of Amish quilting. Would this essay successfully fulfill the author's goal?
  A. Yes, because the essay describes when Amish women began quilting and how their quilting styles have changed.
  B. Yes, because the essay compares the quilting traditions of the Amish with those of the British Quakers who came to the United States.
  C. No, because the essay presents theories regarding why the Amish did not quilt when the fad first arrived in the United States.
  D. No, because the essay explains why Amish quilts are highly sought by quilt collectors and museums.

Passage IV

Where Is the Ivory-billed Woodpecker?

With a wing span of 30 inches and a height of 20 inches, it would seem that an Ivory-billed Woodpecker would be simple enough to identify. Moreover, a flurry

46.
F. NO CHANGE
G. Furthermore,
H. Finally,
J. However,

of questions surround the reported 2004 Arkansas sighting of the largest member of the woodpecker family.

47.
A. NO CHANGE
B. surrounds
C. are surrounding
D. do surround

The Ivory-billed Woodpecker was categorized as an endangered and rare species in 1967, similarly the large

48.
F. NO CHANGE
G. extraordinarily rare and endangered species
H. uncommon and rarely seen species
J. endangered species

49.
A. NO CHANGE
B. therefore
C. although
D. as a result

bird was presumed extinct because it had not been spotted since the 1940s. Over the years unconfirmed sightings surfaced among bird enthusiasts. However, reports from the swamps of Arkansas in 2004 generated immense excitement among both ornithologists and the media.

50.
F. NO CHANGE
G. Over the years, unconfirmed sightings
H. Over the years unconfirmed sightings,
J. Over the years, unconfirmed sightings,

The Arkansas spotting came from a member of an ornithologist group who was kayaking in the river through

51.
A. NO CHANGE
B. in the federally protected river
C. in the heavily wooded river
D. OMIT the underlined portion.

the Cache River National Wildlife Refuge. According with

52.
F. NO CHANGE
G. According by
H. According to
J. According from

the bird <u>watchers report</u>, a very large woodpecker <u>with a</u>
            53   54

<u>red crest and markings</u> similar to those of an Ivory-billed
  54

Woodpecker was observed. <u>The alleged sighting spurred</u>
                                   55

<u>further intense searches of the area over the next year.</u>
                               55

    Fearing an onslaught of overeager bird enthusiasts,

experts kept the outings secretive while trying to gather

more information. [56] <u>At least seven other eyewitness</u>

<u>sightings were noted within the area, following the first</u>
                             57

<u>report, during that time period.</u> One bird was captured on a
         57

53. A. NO CHANGE
    B. watcher's report
    C. watchers' report
    D. watcher whose report

54. F. NO CHANGE
    G. with a red crest and having markings
    H. displaying a red crest and with markings
    J. topped with a red crest and showing markings

55. Which choice best leads the reader into the subject
    matter of the next paragraph?
    A. NO CHANGE
    B. The Ivory-billed Woodpecker is blue and black with
       white markings on its neck, back, and wings.
    C. Hunting of the Ivory-billed Woodpecker, combined
       with heavy logging, led to the bird's reduction in
       number.
    D. Ornithologists used robotic video cameras to record
       birds discovered in the woods of Arkansas.

56. The writer is considering deleting the following phrase
    from the preceding sentence:

    Fearing an onslaught of overeager bird enthusiasts

    If the writer were to make this deletion, the sentence
    would primarily lose:
    F. an explanation for the experts' secrecy about the
       woodpecker sightings.
    G. an element of humor.
    H. a detail providing the author's opinion about the
       purported woodpecker sightings.
    J. historical information about the Ivory-billed Wood-
       pecker.

57. A. NO CHANGE
    B. During that time period, within the area not far
       from the area of the first report, at least seven other
       eyewitness sightings were noted.
    C. Within the area not far from the first report during
       that time period, at least seven other eyewitness
       sightings were noted.
    D. During that time period, at least seven other eye-
       witness sightings were noted within the area of the
       first report.

blurry videotape. Despite the poor quality of the video, the

bird caught on film shared many similarities to the elusive

Ivory-billed Woodpecker. The bird's size, wing markings,

and plumage seemed to match. 58

58. At this point, the writer wants to add a sentence that would provide further evidence that the bird spotted in Arkansas shared characteristics with the Ivory-billed Woodpecker. Which of the following sentences would best accomplish this goal?

F. Experts on the scene noticed a nest in the area similar to ones built by Imperial Woodpeckers, which are related to Ivory-billed Woodpeckers.

G. Reports also indicated that a drumming sound consistent with that of the Ivory-billed Woodpecker was heard in the same area.

H. The Ivory-billed Woodpecker uses its large white bill to hammer away at the bark of dead trees in the hope of finding insects.

J. Additional information suggests that Ivory-billed Woodpeckers travel in pairs, and the mating season occurs between January and May.

Skeptics of the Arkansas findings assert that the

purported Ivory-billed Woodpecker was actually a Pileated

Woodpecker, the largest woodpecker in North America. 59

59. At this point, the writer is considering adding the following sentence:

The markings of a Pileated Woodpecker and an Ivory-billed Woodpecker are very similar.

Should the writer make this addition?

A. Yes, because the information explains why Pileated Woodpeckers are still seen today and why Ivory-billed Woodpeckers are not.

B. Yes, because the additional detail provides support for the theory that the bird seen in Arkansas was a Pileated Woodpecker.

C. No, because the additional detail distracts the reader from the focus of the essay, which is the sighting of an Ivory-billed Woodpecker.

D. No, because the information is inconsistent with the theory presented in the essay about the Ivory-billed Woodpecker.

No conclusive evidence exists to support either theory, so

the debate, the arguments, and the search continue.
60

60. F. NO CHANGE

G. the debate and the search continue.

H. the search continues, as well as the arguments.

J. the debate continues along with the search.

Passage V

The Great Storm

In the history of the United States, Hurricane Katrina is considered one of the most destructive and costly hurricanes, having claimed the lives of approximately 1,800 victims in 2005. <u>Otherwise,</u> a Category 4 storm
61

with winds estimated at 135 mph struck the island city of Galveston, Texas, on September 8, 1900, and ended the lives of nearly 8,000 of the city's 38,000 citizens. Considered the deadliest natural disaster faced by the United States, the hurricane occurred before code names were assigned to tropical storms. <u>People interested in history and the</u>
62
<u>residents of Galveston</u> refer to the disaster by a number
62

of different <u>names.</u> "The Great Storm," "The Great
63

Galveston Hurricane," and "The Galveston Hurricane of

1900."

At the end of the nineteenth century, the only tools

<u>questionable</u> for weather predictions were ship reports,
64

61. A. NO CHANGE
 B. Then,
 C. Besides,
 D. However,

62. F. NO CHANGE
 G. History experts and those who are longtime residents of Galveston
 H. People who have an interest in history and residents of Galveston
 J. Historians and Galveston residents

63. A. NO CHANGE
 B. names:
 C. names.
 D. names

64. Three of the choices below indicate that weather prediction devices were limited at the time of the Galveston storm. Which choice does NOT do so?
 F. questionable
 G. accessible
 H. available
 J. obtainable

but information about storms <u>were delayed</u> until ships
65

could reach port. Reports received on September 6 and

7 indicated that a storm was moving through the Gulf

of Mexico. A hurricane warning was put into effect on

September 7, <u>though</u> few people evacuated the island
66

that lies southeast of Houston. <u>Accustomed to regular and</u>
67
<u>frequent coastal storms</u> and water rushing onto the
67

beachfront, the majority of Galvestonians went about <u>there</u>
68

daily business instead of <u>to evacuate or heading</u> to the
69

shelter of downtown buildings.

In 1900, the highest point on the island was 8.7 feet

above sea <u>level, however,</u> the Galveston Hurricane
70

brought storm surges of 15 feet. <u>Meanwhile, the</u> houses
71

65. **A.** NO CHANGE
    B. are delayed
    C. have been delayed
    D. was delayed

66. Which of the following alternatives to the underlined
portion would be LEAST acceptable?
    F. except
    G. therefore
    H. yet
    J. although

67. **A.** NO CHANGE
    B. Accustomed to coastal storms at a high rate of frequency
    C. Accustomed to and comfortable with coastal storms
    D. Accustomed to coastal storms

68. **F.** NO CHANGE
    G. their
    H. they're
    J. its

69. **A.** NO CHANGE
    B. evacuating or to head
    C. evacuating or heading
    D. to evacuate or by heading

70. **F.** NO CHANGE
    G. level however,
    H. level, however;
    J. level; however,

71. **A.** NO CHANGE
    B. Finally, the
    C. In contrast, the
    D. The

along the coastline were the first to fall once the hurricane

struck. <u>Like dominos, one house pushed down the next until</u>
₇₂

<u>over 3,600 homes were damaged by wind gusts of 100 to 120</u>
₇₂

<u>mph.</u> Buildings were pushed from foundations, bridges
₇₂

were washed out, and <u>repairs were time-consuming.</u> In
₇₃

the aftermath, the citizens of Galveston pulled together to

rebuild their once bustling metropolis, but the Great Storm

remains an integral part of the island's history. 74 75

72. F. NO CHANGE
   G. With wind gusts of 100 to 120 mph like dominos, one house pushed down the next until over 3,600 homes were damaged.
   H. One house pushed down the next until over 3,600 homes like dominos were damaged by wind gusts of 100 to 120 mph.
   J. Damaging wind gusts of 100 to 120 mph, like dominos pushed down over 3,600 homes one house after another.

73. Given that all of the choices are true, which option provides information most relevant to the main focus of this paragraph?
   A. NO CHANGE
   B. telegraph lines were destroyed.
   C. people on the mainland were worried.
   D. many residents were frustrated.

74. The writer is considering revising the preceding sentence by deleting "but the Great Storm remains an integral part of the island's history" (placing a period after the word *metropolis*). If the writer did this, the paragraph would primarily lose:
   F. specific descriptive material about Galveston.
   G. a reference to the hurricane's destruction.
   H. a comment about the hurricane's effect on Galveston.
   J. an illustration of community development.

75. Suppose the writer had intended to write a brief essay that describes the history of hurricanes in the United States since 1900. Would this essay successfully fulfill the writer's goal?
   A. Yes, because it describes the impact of the Galveston Hurricane and other recent hurricanes.
   B. Yes, because it explains in detail why the Galveston Hurricane was more destructive than recent hurricanes.
   C. No, because it focuses primarily on one hurricane rather than on the history of hurricanes.
   D. No, because it is primarily a history of Galveston Island and its recovery after a major hurricane.

END OF TEST 1
STOP! DO NOT TURN THE PAGE UNTIL TOLD TO DO SO.

MATHEMATICS TEST

60 Minutes—60 Questions

DIRECTIONS: After solving each problem, pick the correct answer from the five given and fill in the corresponding oval on your answer sheet. Solve as many problems as you can in the time allowed. Do not worry over problems that take too much time; skip them if necessary and return to them if you have time.

Calculator use is permitted on the test. Calculators can be used for any problem on the test, though calculators may be more harm than help for some questions.

Note: Unless otherwise stated on the test, you should assume that:

1. Figures accompanying questions are not drawn to scale.
2. Geometric figures exist in a plane.
3. When given in a question, "line" refers to a straight line.
4. When given in a question, "average" refers to the arithmetic mean.

---

1. What is the value of the expression $(x + y)^2$ when $x = -2$ and $y = 6$?

   A. 16
   B. 36
   C. 64
   D. 68
   E. 100

2. Given that ΔDEF is a right triangle, how many inches long is $\overline{DF}$?

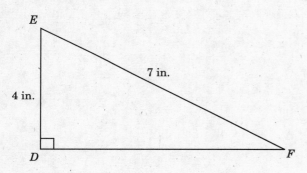

   F. $\sqrt{24}$
   G. 5
   H. $\sqrt{33}$
   J. 6
   K. 33

DO YOUR FIGURING HERE.

3. In △ABC, pictured below, $\overline{AB} \cong \overline{AC}$ and the measure of ∠B is 62°. What is the measure of ∠A?

DO YOUR FIGURING HERE.

A. 42°
B. 48°
C. 56°
D. 62°
E. 88°

4. Which of the following expressions is equivalent to $(5a^4)^2$?

F. $5a^6$
G. $5a^8$
H. $10a^8$
J. $25a^6$
K. $25a^8$

5. A taxi company charges a flat fee of $20, with an additional charge of $0.15 for every mile driven. Which of the following expressions represents the cost, in dollars, of taking a taxi to the airport and traveling m miles?

A. $0.15m + 20$
B. $20m + 15$
C. $15m + 20$
D. $20.15m$
E. $35m$

6. The figure below shows quadrilateral ABCD. What is the measure of ∠C?

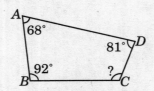

F. 119°
G. 114°
H. 109°
J. 100°
K. 94°

GO ON TO THE NEXT PAGE.

7. If $3(a - 7) = -14$, then $a = ?$

A. $11\frac{2}{3}$

B. $2\frac{1}{3}$

C. $1\frac{2}{3}$

D. $-2\frac{1}{3}$

E. $-11\frac{2}{3}$

8. Jack is a guitar instructor who earns \$44,000 per year. He is paid on a per-session basis and teaches 80 sessions per year. When Jack takes a day off without pay and one of his assistants teaches the session, the assistant is paid \$375. How much less than Jack does the assistant earn per session?

F. \$117

G. \$175

H. \$280

J. \$375

K. \$550

9. $| \, 5 - 9 \, | - | \, 10 - 2 \, | = ?$

A. -8

B. -4

C. 4

D. 6

E. 8

10. To determine an individual bowler's overall score for the season, a bowling league throws out the lowest score and takes the average of the remaining scores. Elise earned the following bowling scores this season: 165, 190, 210, 228, and 242. What is Elise's overall score for this season?

F. 200

G. 207

H. 210

J. 217.5

K. 240.5

DO YOUR FIGURING HERE.

11. In the figure below, $\angle ADC$ measures $6n$ degrees and $\angle CDB$ measures $2n - 20$ degrees. What is the degree measure of the smaller of the two angles?

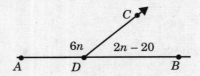

A. 25
B. 30
C. 65
D. 80
E. 150

DO YOUR FIGURING HERE.

12. Travis wants to cover his entire living-room floor in carpet. The floor measures 9 feet by 12 feet. How many square feet of carpet does Travis need?

F. 21
G. 42
H. 80
J. 108
K. 144

13. Meghan earns a total of $710 each month at her part-time job at a museum. If 21% of her pay is withheld for taxes and insurance, what is Meghan's monthly take-home pay?

A. $149.10
B. $560.90
C. $670.80
D. $731.00
E. $859.10

14. What two numbers should be placed in the blanks below so that the difference between consecutive numbers is the same amount?

8, ____ , ____ , 26

F. 12, 20
G. 12.5, 17
H. 14, 20
J. 14, 17
K. 16, 24

15. For all g, $(6g + 9)^2 = ?$

A. $36g^2 + 108g + 81$
B. $36g^2 + 54g + 81$
C. $12g^2 + 108g + 81$
D. $36g^2 + 81$
E. $12g^2 + 81$

GO ON TO THE NEXT PAGE.

16. Circle O is divided into five sectors, as shown below. Each sector represents a fraction of the circle. What fraction is represented by sector S?

DO YOUR FIGURING HERE.

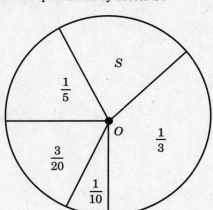

F. $\dfrac{1}{60}$

G. $\dfrac{2}{60}$

H. $\dfrac{13}{60}$

J. $\dfrac{17}{20}$

K. $1\dfrac{47}{60}$

17. If $x^2 = 81$ and $y^2 = 49$, which of the following CANNOT be a value of $x + y$?

A. -16
B. -2
C. 2
D. 16
E. 130

18. If $a \geq 13 + 2a$, which of the following represents the set of all possible values for a?

F. $a \geq 13$
G. $a \geq -13$
H. $a \leq 13$
J. $a \leq -13$
K. $a \leq -26$

19. What value of x will satisfy the equation $\dfrac{1}{x+5} + 4 = 12$?

    A. 46

    B. $\dfrac{41}{8}$

    C. –3

    D. $-\dfrac{17}{8}$

    E. $-\dfrac{39}{8}$

DO YOUR FIGURING HERE.

20. What is the median of the set of numbers contained in set T below?

$$T: \{2, 19, 81, 27, 60, 19, 33, 46\}$$

    F. 19
    G. 30
    H. 35.875
    J. 46
    K. 79

21. Rectangle $ABCD$ measures 60 feet by 144 feet. $\overline{AC}$ represents one diagonal of the rectangle. What is the length, in feet, of $\overline{AC}$?

    A. 130
    B. 156
    C. 243
    D. 508
    E. 769

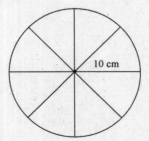

22. The toy wheel, shown in the figure below, has a radius of 10 centimeters. What is the maximum number of complete revolutions the wheel will make if it rolls along a smooth surface for a distance of exactly 200 centimeters?

10 cm

    F. 1
    G. 2
    H. 3
    J. 4
    K. Cannot be determined from the given information

GO ON TO THE NEXT PAGE.

23. A triangle with a perimeter of 78 inches has one side that is 15 inches long. The lengths of the other two sides have a ratio of 3:4. What is the length, in inches, of the *longest* side of the triangle?

   A. 15
   B. 21
   C. 27
   D. 36
   E. 42

DO YOUR FIGURING HERE.

24. Mr. Oliveri is a social studies teacher. He grades his students' papers each night. At the beginning of each grading session, he spends 7 minutes putting the papers in alphabetical order by student name. The equation $g = 12s + 7$ shows the time, g minutes, that Mr. Oliveri budgets for a grading session with s student papers. Which of the following statements is definitely true, according to Mr. Oliveri's model?

   F. Mr. Oliveri spends 12 minutes grading each paper.
   G. Mr. Oliveri spends 19 minutes grading each paper.
   H. Mr. Oliveri spends 7 minutes grading each paper.
   J. Mr. Oliveri spends 5 minutes grading each paper.
   K. Mr. Oliveri takes a 7-minute break between papers.

25. Which of the following is a factored form of the expression $4x^2 + 2x - 30$?

   A. $(2x + 5)(2x - 6)$
   B. $(2x - 6)(2x - 5)$
   C. $(x + 2)(4x - 15)$
   D. $(2x - 5)(2x + 6)$
   E. $(x - 2)(4x + 15)$

26. A square is circumscribed about a circle of 11-foot radius. What is the area of the square, in square feet?

   F. 44
   G. 121
   H. 121π
   J. 484
   K. 512

27. The graph below shows the number of CDs available at 5 different music fairs across the nation, to the nearest 2,000 CDs. According to the graph, what fraction of the CDs available at all 5 fairs were available at the Chicago Music Fair?

DO YOUR FIGURING HERE.

Key

♫ = 4,000

City	CDs available
Atlanta	♫ ♫ ♫ ♫ ♫
Chicago	♫ ♫ ♫ ♪
Dallas	♫ ♫ ♫
New York	♫ ♫ ♪
Washington, D.C.	♫ ♫

A. $\frac{3}{16}$

B. $\frac{1}{4}$

C. $\frac{7}{32}$

D. $\frac{5}{16}$

E. $\frac{9}{16}$

28. For all pairs of real numbers j and r, where $j = 24 - 2r$, $r = ?$

F. $24 - j$

G. $24 + \frac{j}{2}$

H. $12 + j$

J. $12 - \frac{j}{2}$

K. $\frac{12 - j}{2}$

Practice Test 1

DO YOUR FIGURING HERE.

A solid rectangular wooden block has dimensions 12 inches × 6 inches × 7 inches. A diagram of the block is shown below.

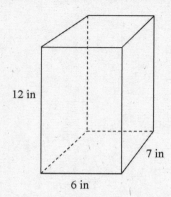

12 in

7 in

6 in

29. What is the surface area, in square inches, of the wooden block?

   A. 56
   B. 198
   C. 224
   D. 396
   E. 504

30. A smaller rectangular solid is cut out of the upper left corner of the wooden block, as shown in the figure below. The volume of the cut-out portion represents approximately what percentage of the original volume of the entire block?

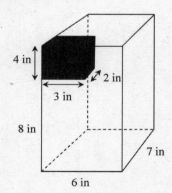

4 in

2 in

3 in

8 in

7 in

6 in

   F. 2.1
   G. 4.76
   H. 6
   J. 13.13
   K. 24.9

31. $\dfrac{1}{4} \times \dfrac{2}{5} \times \dfrac{5}{7} \times \dfrac{8}{9} \times \dfrac{2}{3} \times \dfrac{1}{6} \times \dfrac{4}{8} \times \dfrac{3}{10} = ?$

A. $\dfrac{1}{2}$

B. $\dfrac{2}{15}$

C. $\dfrac{1}{30}$

D. $\dfrac{1}{620}$

E. $\dfrac{1}{945}$

DO YOUR FIGURING HERE.

32. If a line has a slope of $m = -\dfrac{1}{2}$, what two points listed below are possible points on that line?

F. $(3, -1)$ and $(2, 4)$
G. $(6, 3)$ and $(4, -1)$
H. $(8, -4)$ and $(2, 2)$
J. $(4, -5)$ and $(0, -3)$
K. $(-5, 4)$ and $(2, -3)$

33. Parallelogram *WXYZ* is shown below. What is the area of the parallelogram, in square centimeters?

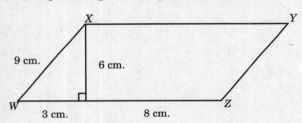

A. 42
B. 50
C. 58
D. 66
E. 99

34. Desmond is on vacation in Scotland. He wants to visit a castle located 320 kilometers from his hotel. He plans on driving an average of 40 kilometers per hour. How many kilometers per hour faster must he average in order to reduce his total driving time by 3 hours?

F. 5
G. 8
H. 24
J. 32
K. 64

GO ON TO THE NEXT PAGE.

35. The inequality $6(y - 1) < 2(2y + 2)$ is equivalent to which of the following inequalities?

    A. $y < -1$
    B. $y < 5$
    C. $y < 7$
    D. $y < 10$
    E. $y < 12$

36. A circular birthday cake with a diameter of 22 inches is cut into 10 equal slices. What is the degree measure of the central angle of each slice of cake?

    F. 36
    G. 42
    H. 48
    J. 72
    K. 108

37. A drawer contains 10 red pens, 6 black pens, and 2 blue pens. What is the minimum number of additional black pens that must be added to the pens already in the drawer so that the probability of picking a black pen is $\frac{4}{7}$?

    A. 8
    B. 10
    C. 14
    D. 18
    E. 20

38. In the figure shown below, lines X and Y are parallel lines crossed by transversals T and Z. Which of the following angles must be congruent to $\angle c$?

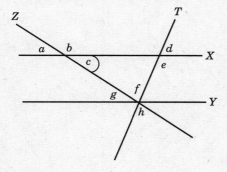

    F. $\angle d$
    G. $\angle d, \angle e$
    H. $\angle a, \angle g$
    J. $\angle a, \angle b, \angle g$
    K. $\angle d, \angle e, \angle f, \angle h$

DO YOUR FIGURING HERE.

Practice Test 1

39. For a chemistry experiment, water needs to have a certain salinity level. The maximum amount of sodium chloride in the water is 1.3×10^{-4} milligrams per gallon. A chemist just tested the water and found that the amount of sodium chloride was 1,000 times as great as the acceptable maximum amount. What concentration of sodium chloride, in milligrams per gallon, was in the water the chemist just tested?

  A. $1.3 \times 10^{-1,004}$
  B. 1.3×10^{-2}
  C. 1.3×10^{-1}
  D. 1.3×10^{0}
  E. 1.3×10^{2}

40. If a and b are positive integers such that the greatest common factor of a^3b^2 and a^4b^3 is 72, which of the following could b equal?

  F. 2
  G. 3
  H. 9
  J. 36
  K. 72

41. A sound wave travels at 1,130 feet per second. Approximately how far does a sound wave travel in 3 hours?

  A. 2.26×10^{3}
  B. 3.42×10^{3}
  C. 2.03×10^{5}
  D. 1.22×10^{7}
  E. 2.26×10^{8}

42. In $\triangle FGH$, $\cos F = \dfrac{2}{5}$ and $\overline{FH} = 22$ cm. What is the measure of $\overline{FG}$ in cm?

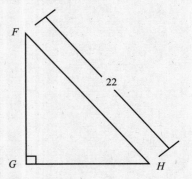

  F. 10

  G. 8

  H. $\dfrac{44}{5}$

  J. $\dfrac{42}{7}$

  K. $\sqrt{5}$

DO YOUR FIGURING HERE.

GO ON TO THE NEXT PAGE.

43. Which of the following lines goes through (6, 9) and is parallel to $y = 10x - 1$?

 A. $y = 9x + 43$
 B. $y = 10x - 51$
 C. $y = 10x + 51$
 D. $y = 8x - 51$
 E. $y = 12x - 18$

DO YOUR FIGURING HERE.

44. If 130% of a number is 520, what is 80% of the number?

 F. 320
 G. 400
 H. 410
 J. 416
 K. 676

45. Line AB, shown below, lies in the standard (x, y) coordinate plane. If $\overline{AB}$ is reflected across the x-axis to form $\overline{A'B'}$, which of the following represents the coordinates for point B'?

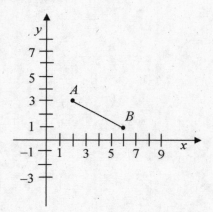

 A. (6, 1)
 B. (6, –1)
 C. (2, 3)
 D. (2, –3)
 E. (–1, 6)

46. Find the matrix product:

$$\begin{bmatrix} -3 \\ 4 \\ 6 \end{bmatrix} \begin{bmatrix} 2 & -3 & -4 \end{bmatrix}$$

DO YOUR FIGURING HERE.

F. $\begin{bmatrix} -6 \\ 9 \\ 12 \end{bmatrix}$

G. $\begin{bmatrix} -6 & 9 & 12 \\ 8 & -12 & -16 \\ 12 & -18 & -24 \end{bmatrix}$

H. $\begin{bmatrix} -6 & 9 & 12 \end{bmatrix}$

J. $\begin{bmatrix} 8 & -12 & -16 \end{bmatrix}$

K. $\begin{bmatrix} -6 & 9 & 12 \\ 8 & 12 & 16 \\ -12 & 18 & 24 \end{bmatrix}$

47. What is the distance in the standard coordinate plane between the points (4, 6) and (5, 12)?

A. $\sqrt{37}$
B. 36
C. 6
D. 7
E. 30

48. In the figure below, $\cos \theta = ?$

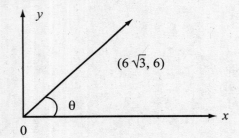

$(6\sqrt{3}, 6)$

F. $\sqrt{3}$

G. $2\sqrt{3}$

H. 1

J. $\dfrac{\sqrt{3}}{2}$

K. $\sqrt{2}$

GO ON TO THE NEXT PAGE.

49. What is the value of t for which the lines $y = tx - 4$ and $y = 3x + 6$ intersect at the point (2, 12) in the standard coordinate plane?

A. 6

B. 7

C. 8

D. $8\frac{1}{2}$

E. 10

DO YOUR FIGURING HERE.

50. A circle is tangent to the x-axis at 10 and tangent to the y-axis at 10 in a standard coordinate plane. Which of the following represents the equation of the circle?

A. $x^2 + y^2 = 10$
B. $(x - 10)^2 + (y - 10)^2 = 100$
C. $(x - 10)^2 + (y - 10)^2 = 10$
D. $x^2 + y^2 = 100$
E. $(x + 10)^2 + (y + 10)^2 = 100$

51. When sec θ is defined, it is equivalent to:

F. $\dfrac{1}{\tan \theta}$

G. $\dfrac{1}{\cos \theta}$

H. $\dfrac{1}{\sin \theta}$

J. $\dfrac{1}{\cos^2 \theta}$

K. $\dfrac{1}{\tan^2 \theta}$

52. Which inequality represents the number line graph shown below?

F. $-6 < x$ and $4 \geq x$
G. $-6 \leq x$ and $4 > x$
H. $-6 < x$ and $4 \leq x$
J. $-6 > x$ or $4 \leq x$
K. $-6 > x$ or $4 \geq x$

53. A function S is defined as follows:

for $x > 2$, $S(x) = \sqrt{x + 3}$

for x $S(x) = x^4 - 6$

What is the value of $S(-5)$?

A. No solution

B. 619

C. $2\sqrt{2}$

D. 631

E. $\sqrt{-2}$

GO ON TO THE NEXT PAGE. •

54. The three parabolas graphed below belong to a family of parabolas. The general equation includes the variables n, x, and y. Which of the following could be the general equation that defines this family of parabolas for all $n \geq 2$?

DO YOUR FIGURING HERE.

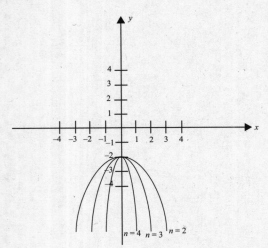

n = 4   n = 3   n = 2

F. $y = -\dfrac{1}{2}nx^2 - 2$

G. $y = -nx^2 - 2$

H. $y = x^2 - n$

J. $y = nx^2 - 2$

K. $y = nx^2 + 2$

55. If $f(a) = 3 - a^2$, then $f(a + r) = ?$

A. $3 - a^2 - r^2$

B. $3 - a^2 + r$

C. $a - 2ar - r^2$

D. $3 - a - 2ar - r^2$

E. $3 + a - 2ar - r^2$

56. Which of the following graphs represents $|x| - 4 < 6$?

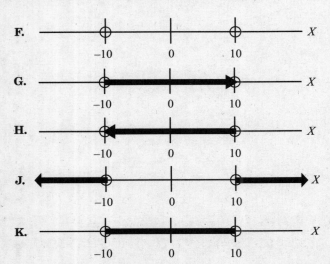

F. −10   0   10   X

G. −10   0   10   X

H. −10   0   10   X

J. −10   0   10   X

K. −10   0   10   X

GO ON TO THE NEXT PAGE.

57. The circle below has a radius of 10 inches and is cut into 4 equal pieces, one of which is arc *DE*. What is the measure of arc *DE* in centimeters?

DO YOUR FIGURING HERE.

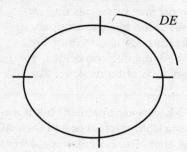

DE

   A. 3π
   B. 2
   C. 2.5π
   D. 4π
   E. 5π

58. If $\cos \theta = -\dfrac{4}{6}$ and $\pi < \theta < 2\pi$, then $\tan \theta = ?$

   F. $\sqrt{3}$

   G. $2\sqrt{3}$

   H. $-\dfrac{\sqrt{5}}{3}$

   J. $\dfrac{\sqrt{5}}{3}$

   K. $\dfrac{\sqrt{5}}{2}$

59. Which of the following quadratic equations has the solutions $y = -2c$ and $y = 8d$?

   A. $y^2 - 16cd = 0$
   B. $y^2 - y(8d - 2c) - 16cd = 0$
   C. $y^2 + y(8d - 2c) + 16cd = 0$
   D. $y^2 - y(8d + 2c) - 16cd = 0$
   E. $y^2 + y(8d - 2c) - 16cd = 0$

60. If $\log_d m = p$ and $\log_d n = q$, then $\log_d (mn)^3 = ?$

   F. $6pq$
   G. $p + q$
   H. $3(p + q)$
   J. $3pq$
   K. pq

END OF TEST 2.
STOP! DO NOT TURN THE PAGE UNTIL TOLD TO DO SO.
DO NOT RETURN TO THE PREVIOUS TEST.

READING TEST

35 Minutes—40 Questions

DIRECTIONS: On this test, you will have 35 minutes to read four passages and answer 40 questions (10 questions on each passage). Each set of ten questions appears directly after the relevant passage. You should select the answer choice that best answers the question. There is no time limit for work on the individual passages, so you can move freely between the passages and refer to each as often as you'd like.

Passage I

PROSE FICTION: This passage is adapted from the short story "Miss Brill" by Katherine Mansfield.

Although the blue sky was brilliant, Miss Brill was glad that she had decided to wear her fur because there was a faint chill in the air. Miss Brill put up her hand and touched her fur. Dear little thing! It was nice to feel it
5 again. She had taken it out of its box that afternoon, given it a good brush, and rubbed the life back into the dim little eyes. "What has been happening to me?" said the sad little eyes. Oh, how sweet it was to see them snap at her again. Little rogue! Yes, she really felt like that about it. Little
10 rogue biting its tail just by her left ear. She could have taken it off and laid it on her lap and stroked it.

There were a number of people out this afternoon, far more than last Sunday. And the band sounded louder and merrier.

15 Only two people shared her "special" seat: a fine old man in a velvet coat, and a big old woman with a roll of knitting on her embroidered apron. They did not speak. This was disappointing for Miss Brill. She had become an expert, she thought, at listening as though she didn't
20 listen, at sitting in other people's lives just for a minute while they talked around her.

The crowd was always interesting to watch. People paraded back and forth in front of the flowerbeds and the band rotunda—stopping to talk and greet. Other people
25 sat on the benches, but they were nearly always the same, Sunday after Sunday, and—Miss Brill had often noticed—there was something funny about nearly all of them. They were odd, silent, nearly all old, and from the way they stared, they looked as though they'd just come from dark
30 little rooms or even—even cupboards!

Two young girls in red came by and two young soldiers in blue met them, and they laughed and went off together. A cold, pale nun hurried by. The old couple on Miss Brill's bench got up and marched away, and a funny old man with
35 long whiskers hobbled by.

Oh, how fascinating it was! How she loved sitting here, watching it all! It was like a play. Who could believe the sky at the back wasn't painted? But it wasn't until a little brown dog slowly trotted on and then off, like a little
40 "theatre" dog, that Miss Brill discovered what made it so exciting. They were all on the stage. They weren't only the audience looking on; they were acting. Even she had a part and came every Sunday. No doubt somebody would have noticed if she hadn't been there; she was part of the
45 performance after all. How strange she'd never thought of it like that before! And yet it explained why she always started from home at just the same time each week—to avoid being late for the performance. It also explained why she felt shy about telling her English students how she
50 spent her Sunday afternoons. No wonder! Miss Brill nearly laughed out loud. She was on the stage.

The band had been having a rest. Now they started again. And what they played made you want to sing. It seemed to Miss Brill that in another moment the whole
55 company would begin singing. Miss Brill's eyes filled with tears, and she looked smiling at all the other members of the company. Yes, we understand, we understand, she thought—though what they understood she didn't know.

Just at that moment a boy and girl came and sat down
60 where the old couple had been. They were beautifully dressed; they were in love. The hero and heroine, of course, had just arrived from his father's yacht. And still soundlessly singing, still with that trembling smile, Miss Brill prepared to listen.

65 "No, not now," said the girl. "Not here, I can't."

"But why? Because of that stupid old thing at the end there?" asked the boy. "Why does she come here at all? Who wants her? Why doesn't she stay at home?"

"It's her fur which is so funny," giggled the girl. "It's
70 exactly like a fried fish."

On her way home she usually bought a slice of honey-cake at the baker's. It was her Sunday treat. But today she passed the baker's, climbed the stairs, went into the little dark room—her room like a cupboard—and sat down. She
75 sat there for a long time. The box that the fur came out of was on the bed. She unclasped the pendant on the fur quickly; quickly, without looking, laid it inside. But when she put the lid on, she thought she heard something crying.

GO ON TO THE NEXT PAGE.

1. The passage makes it clear that Miss Brill:
   A. wears her fur quite frequently.
   B. knows many people at the park.
   C. attends the concert every week.
   D. directs her students in class plays.

2. It can reasonably be inferred from the passage that Miss Brill views her fur as:
   F. a mischievous pet with thoughts and feelings.
   G. an old, worn garment that she dislikes wearing.
   H. a wild animal that makes her feel vibrant and alive.
   J. a soft, warm garment to be worn on special occasions.

3. As she is revealed in the passage, Miss Brill is best described as:
   A. lonely yet eager for human connection.
   B. sociable but quietly emotional and sensitive.
   C. creative and willing to share her feelings.
   D. insightful and outwardly critical of others.

4. Which of the following can most reasonably be inferred from the fourth paragraph (lines 22–30) of the passage?
   F. Miss Brill envies the people sitting on the bench and hopes to befriend them.
   G. Miss Brill knows the people sitting on the bench from previous park concerts.
   H. Miss Brill views the people sitting on the bench as strange and pitiful.
   J. Miss Brill considers the people sitting on the bench similar to her.

5. The passage states that Miss Brill concludes she is involved in a stage play as a result of:
   A. a small dog walking in front of her.
   B. a whiskered old man walking by her.
   C. a class discussion with her students.
   D. a painted backdrop of the blue sky.

6. Which of the following best describes the way the twelfth paragraph (lines 71–78) functions in the passage?
   F. It provides the first indication that Miss Brill regrets eavesdropping on conversations between people in the park.
   G. It represents a change in how Miss Brill sees herself with respect to the other people she encounters.
   H. It reveals that Miss Brill remains unaware of the realities in her life despite the fact that the couple in the park hurt her feelings.
   J. It suggests that Miss Brill will continue attending the park gatherings and that she will try to develop real relationships with others.

7. Which of the following statements does NOT describe one of Miss Brill's actions in the twelfth paragraph (lines 71–78)?
   A. She does not stop for cake at the bakery.
   B. She views her apartment as small and dark.
   C. She strokes the fur while crying to herself.
   D. She takes the fur off and packs it in a box.

8. The main point of the third paragraph (lines 15–21) is to indicate that:
   F. People usually talk with Miss Brill because she is a good listener.
   G. The old couple next to Miss Brill are rude and do not speak to her.
   H. Miss Brill often listens to the conversations of the people around her.
   J. The old couple and Miss Brill always sit next to each other at concerts.

9. It can be reasonably inferred from this passage that if Miss Brill failed to attend a Sunday afternoon performance:
   A. the baker would notice she had not stopped to purchase cake.
   B. the English students would ask her many questions about the band.
   C. the actors would wonder why she was not performing her part.
   D. her presence would go unnoticed by the people in attendance.

10. According to the passage, after Miss Brill determines that she is part of a stage performance she:
    F. cries with joy.
    G. sings out loud.
    H. laughs out loud.
    J. cries with sadness.

Passage II

SOCIAL SCIENCE: This passage is adapted from "Shotgun Houses: A Look at the Past" by Maria Rhodes.

Despite many differences, Elvis Presley and the Neville Brothers have one thing in common—the shotgun house. The King was born in one, while Aaron and his siblings grew up in one of these strangely narrow homes scattered
5 throughout cities in the South. Although the shotgun house originated in New Orleans, the structures became popular in Texas, Mississippi, Alabama, Florida, and California as well. Shotgun houses, or "shotgun shacks" as they are also known, reached the height of popularity
10 between the 1860s and the 1920s because the style fulfilled a need for affordable, urban housing.

The typical shotgun house is single-story, 12 feet wide and 36 feet deep, with no inner hallways. Each room in the home is placed behind another in single file with all
15 the doors on the same side of the house. The style's name may stem from the floor plan of the house: you could potentially shoot a shotgun through the front door and the bullet would come out the back door without touching a wall. However, some historians theorize that the name
20 of the house is a modified version of "to-gun," which is the African word for "place of assembly." The shotgun house trend began in New Orleans in the early 1800s, when more than 1,300 freed Haitians arrived in the city and created a housing boom. Both builders and inhabitants
25 were of African descent, and the to-gun or shotgun houses resemble structures found in Haiti.

Scarcity of land in New Orleans required homes to have a small footprint, which is why shotgun houses were so popular in the area. Characteristically built in
30 lower- and middle-class neighborhoods, shotgun shacks were available in three main variations. A single shotgun house had one door and window in the front, while a double shotgun house had two front doors and two front windows. The double shotgun house was basically two
35 single shotgun homes connected by a central wall, much like a modern duplex. A third style, the camelback shotgun house, included a partial second floor over the back part of the house.

The long, rectangular design of shotgun houses served
40 a number of purposes. In a time before air conditioning, maximizing airflow was of great importance, especially in humid Southern towns. The alignment of doors combined with the length of the house created excellent airflow by encouraging drafts to move from the front door to the
45 back. The number of rooms in a shotgun house varied, but in most cases, the rooms were fairly spacious with high ceilings that encouraged hot air to rise. In addition

to increasing comfort, shotgun houses maximized the limited land available in urban areas. Their narrow
50 width increased the number of houses that could fit along a street, which made shotgun houses excellent rental investments.

After the Civil War, manufacturing centers developed throughout the United States, and more housing became
55 necessary. Before automobile ownership was commonplace, homes needed to be near the workplace or near a railroad station, which explains why so many shotgun houses are found in city centers. Moreover, New Orleans and other cities determined property taxes based on the width of
60 a lot, so shotgun houses were an affordable option for working-class families.

Typically erected near the street with a very small front yard and no porch, shotgun houses were constructed from wood siding, although a few were made of brick.
65 Given that shotgun houses were usually built very close together, they may or may not have had side windows. Chimneys were constructed in the interior of the home, which allowed multiple rooms to be warmed during winter months. Ornamented with decorative moldings and special
70 woodwork, shotgun houses offered a surprising number of features for $100 cash or $12 a month.

Two modern inventions led to the eventual decline of shotgun houses: the automobile and air conditioning. The affordability of automobiles sent workers to the suburbs,
75 while the availability of air conditioning units in the 1950s ended the need for homes with good airflow. With fewer people living in the inner-city, shotgun houses suffered from neglect. Although they had once been a symbol of America's working class, from the 1950s until the 1980s,
80 shotgun houses became viewed as substandard housing in cities throughout the South.

As with many things from the past, the shotgun house is experiencing a revival. Cities such as Santa Monica, Houston, and Charlotte have established shotgun historic
85 districts and are embracing the structures that other cities have bulldozed in the name of urban development. Shotgun houses offer a narrow window to the past and a glimpse at a slower way of life.

11. One of the main points that the author seeks to make in the passage is that shotgun houses:

   A. stand as reminders of a better way of living and should be designated historic landmarks.

   B. provided reasonably priced housing with a surprising number of high-quality features.

   C. enabled working-class families to live conveniently near factories and railroad stations.

   D. served many useful purposes before modern inventions diminished their relevance.

12. According to the passage, shotgun houses became popular in New Orleans because:

   F. city codes prohibited construction of homes with large square footage.

   G. limited property dictated that housing space be maximized.

   H. high summer temperatures demanded houses with high ceilings.

   J. workers built small homes near factories for easy commuting.

13. As it is used in line 83, the word *revival* most nearly means:

   A. descent.

   B. recovery.

   C. duplication.

   D. motivation.

14. The main function of the seventh paragraph (lines 72–81) in relation to the passage as a whole is most likely to:

   F. explain why the popularity of shotgun houses diminished.

   G. provide an argument in favor of rebuilding shotgun homes.

   H. describe the negative impact of cars on urban growth.

   J. contrast living conditions in the South before and after WWII.

15. According to the passage, shotgun houses were beneficial in all of the following ways EXCEPT:

   A. reducing property taxes.

   B. maximizing airflow.

   C. developing neighborhoods.

   D. generating rental income.

16. It can reasonably be inferred from the passage that the author believes that:

   F. shotgun houses are worthy of saving for their unique and valuable histories.

   G. abandoned shotgun houses led to inner-city housing problems throughout the South.

   H. urban development should be better controlled before historic structures are destroyed.

   J. new construction of shotgun houses would invigorate inner-city property values.

17. The passage indicates that single shotgun houses, double shotgun houses, and camelback shotgun houses are alike in that they all have:

   A. rooms on the second floor.

   B. more than one interior fireplace.

   C. windows facing the street.

   D. small front and back porches.

18. According to the passage, what evidence supports the theory that the term "shotgun house" is an adaptation of the term "to-gun"?

   F. A gun's bullet could travel from one end of the house to the other and pass only through open doors.

   G. The construction of shotgun houses coincides with newly freed Haitian slaves moving to Louisiana.

   H. Historians trace the two terms back to the African and Haitian immigrants who settled in New Orleans.

   J. The camelback shotgun house design originated in Haiti and was used as a place to hold religious assemblies.

19. It can be reasonably inferred from the passage that shotgun houses were:

   A. inexpensively constructed by investors hoping to make money from families moving to cities from rural areas.

   B. frequently built by city governments that hoped to lure workers to their area with the promise of affordable housing.

   C. generously decorated with lavish features to justify high prices and give the appearance of quality to first-time home buyers.

   D. usually located in undesirable neighborhoods that had plenty of available property for the construction of multifamily homes.

20. According to the passage, which of the following factors made shotgun houses especially suitable for residents of Southern states?

   F. Post–Civil War poverty

   G. Growing population

   H. Competent workers

   J. Weather conditions

Passage III

HUMANITIES: This passage is adapted from the article "Saving Art" by Elaine Reilly.

Robert Frost wrote that "nothing gold can stay," but those in favor of restoring the works of Old Masters such as Rembrandt, Leonardo da Vinci, and Michelangelo believe that the original nature of a piece of art should be

5 returned to its past glory. At the same time, art restoration raises concerns from many in the art community who fear that disturbing statues and paintings that have existed since the 15th and 16th centuries will damage or diminish the beauty of aging pieces.

10 The goal of art restoration is to return a work of art to a pristine state by repairing damage caused by smoke, neglect, or low-quality materials. Since the artist is usually no longer living by the time a piece is repaired, the individual restoring the art determines the most

15 likely original condition—a subjective opinion. Although some elements of art restoration are reversible, other elements, such as cleaning, are not, which causes alarm that restoration may permanently damage priceless pieces of work.

20 One of the most controversial art restoration projects involved Leonardo da Vinci's mural *The Last Supper*. Painted in the late 15th century on the dining room hall of a church in Milan, Italy, *The Last Supper* has suffered more than many paintings because it cannot be moved.

25 Twenty years after it was completed, the mural began to flake, and by 1556 many of the figures of Jesus' apostles were difficult to recognize. Two attempts were made in the 18th century to repair the painting, but angry citizens insisted that the restoration stop because some of the faces

30 were being repainted. More modern methods of cleaning were attempted in the early 20th century, but by the 1970s the mural was still in poor condition.

In 1978, Pinin Brambilla was given the task of leading a major restoration project of *The Last Supper*. Brambilla's

35 goal was to remove the overpainting that had occurred during previous restoration attempts and to remove the dirt and pollution that had accumulated. For the next twenty years, Brambilla covered every inch of the world's most famous painting with a microscope and a knife in

40 order to return the painting back to da Vinci's original form. Many areas of the mural were so damaged that they were touched up with watercolors. When *The Last Supper* was unveiled to the public, the changes made to face shapes, colors, and tones were both disappointing and

45 shocking. According to Jacques Franck, a da Vinci expert, the restored mural "had lost all its dimension and contrast and there were huge square meters missing including Christ's head. Leonardo would not have approved."

Another restoration controversy arose when

50 Michelangelo's marble figure of David was cleaned in honor of the statue's 500th anniversary. Because the 14-foot statue was displayed outside from 1504 until 1873, it had been damaged by the elements, including a lightning strike in 1512. In addition to withstanding rain, dirt,

55 and freezing temperatures, *David* was injured by 16th-century rioters who broke the statue's left arm, and by an angry Italian artist who struck one of *David*'s toes with a hammer in 1991. A poor attempt was made in 1843 to clean the statue with hydrochloric acid and steel brushes.

60 The strong combination destroyed the protective finish placed on the statue by Michelangelo and left the marble exposed to further degradation.

Although modern-day restorers know better than to use harsh chemicals, the question of how to clean a

65 500-year-old statue remains as debatable as the issue of whether such masterpieces should be restored at all. Discussions on whether to give the statue a dry cleaning or a wet bath drew opinions from art specialists around the world, but it was finally determined that *David* would

70 be cleaned with compresses of distilled water. The decision led to the resignation of a veteran restorer who favored cleaning the marble with dry cloths and soft brushes and felt that cleaning with water would be too harsh.

When the scaffolding around *David* came down,

75 responses were mixed. Art historian James Beck, who had led a movement to fight the cleaning project, said he was relieved that the restoration had been "less intense" than originally planned. Other observers remarked that any changes in *David* were subtle and not as remarkable

80 as anticipated. Beck asserted that the restoration project ignored the statue's main problem—instability due to cracks in *David*'s ankles.

According to Beck, who died in 2007, much of the cleaning and restoring of great art is unnecessary;

85 restoration merely serves as a way for museums to gain publicity and increase tourism. With over one million tourists per year visiting the Italian museum that houses *David*, billions of dollars of revenue from admission tickets, books, and videos are at stake. However, with little

90 consensus regarding the best techniques necessary to clean a piece of art, restoration should be avoided until it is clearly necessary. Restoration cannot turn back the clock, nor is it worth the damage it may cause.

GO ON TO THE NEXT PAGE.

21. One of the main arguments the author is trying to make in the passage is that:

  A. art restoration projects are initiated to celebrate anniversaries.

  B. works of art should be left intact and never be cleaned or restored.

  C. current art restoration practices greatly diminish the risk of damage.

  D. restoration projects often inadvertently ruin art masterpieces.

22. According to the passage, which of the following methods was used during the most recent restoration of *David*?

  F. Cloths soaked in water

  G. Dry cloths and brushes

  H. Hydrochloric acid

  J. Steel reinforcements

23. Which of the following can be inferred from the sixth paragraph (lines 63–73)?

  A. Cleaning marble is time-consuming, and the results are often unnoticeable.

  B. There is not yet an agreed-upon best method for restoring marble statues.

  C. Modern methods of cleaning marble are not permanent, so risks are minimized.

  D. The original color of old marble can be restored most effectively with dry cleanings.

24. It can be reasonably inferred that the author believes:

  F. *The Last Supper* restoration project was essential and well executed.

  G. the *David* restoration project was unnecessary and misguided.

  H. *The Last Supper* restoration project returned the mural to its original beauty.

  J. the *David* restoration project insured the statue's long-term preservation.

25. According to the fourth paragraph (lines 33–48), the intended purpose of the restoration of *The Last Supper* was to:

  A. move the wall on which the mural was attached to a safe location.

  B. modify the original tones of the mural with watercolors.

  C. scrape away paint that had been added during previous restorations.

  D. paint over the flaking portions of the mural with oil paint.

26. According to the passage, *The Last Supper* first showed signs of disrepair in:

  F. the 1400s

  G. the 1500s

  H. the 1700s

  J. the 1900s

27. The main function of the second paragraph (lines 10–19) in relation to the passage as a whole is to:

  A. explain the purpose of art restoration and provide an overview of the controversies involved.

  B. establish the passage's claim that art restoration is damaging and assess various techniques.

  C. emphasize the need for consensus on restoration projects and describe the different theories.

  D. express the necessity for restoring masterpieces and describe how damage initially occurs.

28. As it is used in paragraph 5 (line 62), the word *degradation* most nearly means:

  F. progression.

  G. renovation.

  H. affliction.

  J. deterioration.

29. It can most reasonably be inferred from the fifth paragraph (lines 49–62) that *David* would require less restoration efforts if the statue had:

  A. not been struck with a hammer in the twentieth century.

  B. been coated with a more resilient finish by Michelangelo.

  C. been stored indoors from the time it was completed.

  D. not been cleaned in honor of its 500th anniversary.

30. According to James Beck, large-scale art restoration projects of masterpieces are primarily undertaken to:

  F. improve the resilience of masterpieces by removing harmful grime.

  G. further the interests of the art restoration industry by raising questionable issues.

  H. ease the concerns of art museums regarding the welfare of works by Old Masters.

  J. increase interest in a museum's art collection by providing reasons for media publicity.

Passage IV

NATURAL SCIENCE: This passage is adapted from the article "The Inner-Workings of Geysers" by Nicholas Apostol.

A visit to Yellowstone National Park would be incomplete without stopping to see Old Faithful, the world's most renowned geyser. Twenty times every day the geyser releases an average of 6,000 gallons of steam to the
5 astonishment of park visitors. Although Old Faithful erupts on a fairly predictable schedule, as indicated by its name, the duration of each eruption varies from one to five minutes.

Since Yellowstone is home to more than half of the earth's estimated 1,000 geysers, the park offers the
10 greatest opportunity to view the geologic phenomena. Defined as hot springs that periodically discharge boiling water and steam hundreds of feet into the air, geysers exist on every continent except Antarctica.

The geologic conditions in Yellowstone National Park
15 make it an especially ideal location for the formation of geysers. Geyser activity requires that a plentiful supply of surface water seeps down through the ground until it reaches hot volcanic rock. The water ejected by a geyser originates as snow and rain that soaks into the ground
20 and finds its way through cracks until it reaches rock heated by magma. Experts estimate that it takes surface water 500 years to travel 7,000 feet below the surface.

Once surface water reaches the hot rock below, it begins rising to the top through volcanic rhyolite rock. Rhyolite
25 rocks dissolve in hot water and produce geyserite, which is then deposited along the inside of the geyser's plumbing system and also near the geyser's surface. The geyserite creates a pressure-tight channel by cementing rocks and loose soil together, thus eliminating any water leaks.

30 While all natural springs have channels underneath them that enable water to flow towards the surface, only geysers have constrictions near the top. After the hot water passes through the tightly sealed plumbing system, it reaches a narrow spot just underneath the surface.
35 Naturally, the hot water and steam want to continue rising, but the narrow space prevents an immediate release. Only when enough pressure builds in the constricted area does the geyser erupt. The eruption will not cease until either all the water has been expelled or the water temperature
40 falls below boiling. In some cases, a geyser's expulsion of water is followed by a period of steam release. For example, Steamboat Geyser in Yellowstone throws water over 300 feet into the sky and then shoots steam out for hours afterward. Once a geyser has erupted, the cycle of filling,
45 heating, and releasing begins all over again.

Although geysers such as Old Faithful appear to be never-ending, the unique circumstances required for a geyser to exist cannot last forever. While Yellowstone's Castle Geyser has been going strong for at least 5,000
50 years, other geysers in the park, such as Porkchop Geyser, illustrate the impact of geothermal changes on geyser activity. Porkchop Geyser changed its status from hot spring to geyser when it erupted for the first time in 1971. Over the years, the geyser sealed itself with geyserite, and
55 in 1985 Porkchop began erupting continuously. The force of the spray was so loud that the sound could be heard over 600 yards away. In 1989, as a result of accumulated pressure, Porkchop Geyser exploded and threw rocks over 200 feet from the vent. Porkchop is now a hot spring, but it
60 appears to be attempting to seal itself once again.

Geysers are affected by underground dynamics as well as more obvious occurrences, such as earthquakes. Correlations have been recorded between earthquakes and geyser activity, most notably in 1959 when an earthquake
65 struck Hebgen Lake, Montana, approximately 30 miles from Yellowstone National Park. Since the earthquake's epicenter was so close to the park, significant changes in geyser activity took place. Immediately following the earthquake, all the park's geysers, even dormant
70 ones, erupted simultaneously, and some eruptions were significantly higher and longer than usual. In addition, the average water temperature of the park's springs and geysers rose 2°C. Most of the park's geysers returned to their normal activity within a month, but the eruption
75 patterns of other geysers were permanently altered. While the Hebgen Lake earthquake had an expected impact on the geysers in Yellowstone due to its proximity, the eruption pattern of Old Faithful was also surprisingly affected in 2003 by an 8.5 magnitude earthquake in
80 Alaska, which is over 1,800 miles away.

Geysers provide geologists with windows to the center of the earth and offer tourists amazing sights to see. These rare natural fountains that are scattered around the globe exist only when essential conditions are met,
85 and their delicate nature makes them susceptible to the earth's rumblings. A geyser's lifespan depends on so many uncontrollable conditions that its longevity cannot be predicted.

31. According to the passage, steam that erupts from a geyser today began as water runoff:

A. in the last 10 years.
B. between 100 and 200 years ago.
C. over 500 years ago.
D. over 2,000 years ago.

32. It is reasonable to infer from the passage that a connection between earthquakes and geysers relates to:

F. decreases in water supply.
G. changes in nearby hot springs.
H. disruptions in seismic activity.
J. increases in underground temperatures.

33. The passage indicates that Porkchop may change from a hot spring back to a geyser because:

A. geyserite has been stopping leaks in the plumbing.
B. rhyolite deposits have been discovered nearby.
C. geyserite has been eroding near the surface.
D. rhyolite rocks surround the surface of the vent.

34. According to the passage, of all the geysers in Yellowstone, Old Faithful is characterized as:

F. being the tallest geyser in the park.
G. having the longest lasting eruption.
H. being the oldest known geyser in the park.
J. having the most predictable eruption schedule.

35. The passage indicates that geysers and hot springs are similar in that they both have:

A. narrow openings near ground level.
B. patterns of releasing steam and water.
C. rhyolite rocks within their plumbing systems.
D. underground paths enabling water to rise to the surface.

36. According to the passage, which of the following occurs immediately after a geyser's eruption ends?

F. Rhyolite melts near the surface creating a pressure-inducing seal.
G. Surface water trickles underground toward the geyser's reservoir.
H. Temperatures reach the boiling point near the bottom of the geyser.
J. Volcanic rock heats up the collected water beneath the earth's surface.

37. It may reasonably be inferred from the passage that the rare nature of geysers:

A. can be explained by the instability of the earth.
B. can be used to predict earthquakes and other seismic activity.
C. draws many tourists to see them at Yellowstone National Park.
D. creates concern among geologists who fear humans will damage them.

38. The main function of the sixth paragraph (lines 46–60) in relation to the passage as a whole is to:

F. redirect the passage's focus from the specifics of how geysers work to the effects of underground activities on geyser eruptions.
G. shift the passage from a discussion of geysers in general toward the history of geyser activity in Yellowstone National Park.
H. establish the passage's assertion that the earth's geysers are slowly dying as a result of elevated seismic activity.
J. emphasize the passage's argument that excessive geyser activity indicates a likelihood of stronger and more frequent earthquakes.

39. As it is used in paragraph 7 (line 69), the term *dormant* most nearly means:

A. insignificant.
B. emergent.
C. inactive.
D. shallow.

40. The author indicates that geyserite creates a pressurized situation by:

F. creating a tight seal near the geyser's surface that prevents the boiling water from escaping.
G. narrowing the passageways through the geyser's plumbing and hindering water flow.
H. melting the rhyolite when it reaches the hot volcanic rock, which forces the water upward.
J. increasing the temperature of the water, so that it is boiling by the time it finally erupts.

END OF TEST 3.
STOP! DO NOT TURN THE PAGE UNTIL TOLD TO DO SO.
DO NOT RETURN TO A PREVIOUS TEST.

SCIENCE TEST

35 Minutes—40 Questions

DIRECTIONS: This test contains seven passages, each accompanied by several questions. You should select the answer choice that best answers each question. Within the total allotted time for the Subject Test, you may spend as much time as you wish on each individual passage. Calculator use is not permitted.

Passage I

A J-tube experiment is designed to measure the relationship between the pressure and volume of a gas at a constant temperature. A length of glass tubing is bent into a J-shape. The short end of the J-tube is sealed. The long end of the tube is left open, and is connected to a non-metallic funnel with rubber tubing. The J-tube is then clamped to a ring stand and placed in a plastic tray.

Mercury is poured through the funnel until it fills the curved portion at the bottom of the J-tube. The mercury in the bottom of the tube traps gas (air) in the sealed arm of the tube, as shown in Figure 1 below.

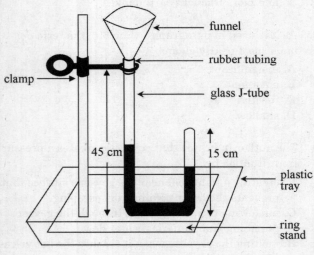

funnel

rubber tubing

clamp

glass J-tube

45 cm   15 cm

plastic tray

ring stand

Figure 1

Two measurements are taken, both in millimeters. One is the difference in mercury (Hg) levels in the two arms of the tube. The second measurement is the height of the column of gas in the sealed, shorter end of the tube. Mercury continues to be poured into the tube, and the two measurements are repeated. Table 1 shows both measurements over a period of six trials.

Trial	Difference in Hg Levels (mm)	Height of Gas Column (mm)
1	26	240.824
2	139	212.643
3	388	164.672
4	542	145.567
5	736	127.315
6	928	115.283

Table 1

Table 2 shows the volume of gas trapped in the sealed end of the J-tube for each trial.

Trial	Volume of Gas (mm³)
1	18,921.92
2	16,707.66
3	12,938.55
4	11,437.39
5	10,003.36
6	9,057.96

Table 2

The air pressure in the sealed end of the J-tube can be measured by adding the atmospheric pressure (760 mm Hg) to the difference in the mercury levels in the two parts of the tube. Table 3 shows the total air pressure for each trial, as well as calculations for the pressure × volume (PV) of air.

Trial	Total Pressure of Gas (mm Hg)	Pressure × Volume (PV)
1	786	14,872,627
2	899	15,020,184
3	1148	14,853,458
4	1302	14,891,482
5	1496	14,965,024
6	1688	15,289,837

Table 3

1. According to Tables 1 and 2, as the difference in mercury levels increased, the volume of the gas in the sealed column:
   A. decreased.
   B. decreased, then increased.
   C. increased.
   D. remained the same.

2. Which of the following correctly lists the pressure × volume (PV) calculations from Table 3 in increasing order by trial?
   F. Trial 1, Trial 4, Trial 3, Trial 2, Trial 5, Trial 6
   G. Trial 3, Trial 1, Trial 4, Trial 5, Trial 2, Trial 6
   H. Trial 6, Trial 2, Trial 4, Trial 5, Trial 1, Trial 3
   J. Trial 3, Trial 4, Trial 1, Trial 2, Trial 5, Trial 6

3. Based on the data in Table 1, at a gas column height of 152 mm, the difference in Hg levels between the two parts of the J-tube would be closest to which of the following?
   A. 106 mm
   B. 227 mm
   C. 434 mm
   D. 1056 mm

4. Which of the following graphs best illustrates the relationship between the total gas pressure shown in Table 3 and the pressure × volume (PV) calculation?

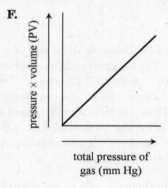

F.

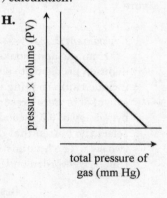

H.

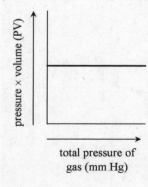

G.

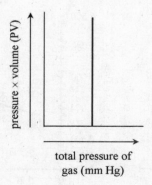

J.

5. Boyle's Law states that for a fixed mass of gas at a constant temperature, as the volume of the gas increases, the pressure of the gas decreases, and vice versa. This means that when the pressure and volume of the gas are multiplied together, the result will be a constant—though not necessarily exact—number. Based on the information in Tables 2 and 3, one can conclude that the results of this experiment:
   A. do not confirm Boyle's Law, because the pressure × volume calculations decrease consistently over all six trials.
   B. do not confirm Boyle's Law, because as the volume of the gas increases, the pressure of the gas increases and then decreases.
   C. confirm Boyle's Law, because the volume and pressure of the gas increase consistently over all six trials.
   D. confirm Boyle's Law, because the pressure × volume (PV) calculations are relatively constant over all six trials.

Passage II

CITATION: Cantlon JF, Brannon EM (2007). Basic math in monkeys and college students. PLoS Biol 5(12): e328.

Current evidence indicates that humans and nonhuman animals share some mathematical abilities. The following experiments show that monkeys can mentally add the numerical values of two sets of objects and choose a visual array that corresponds to the arithmetic sum of these two sets. Researchers tested 2 monkeys (named Boxer and Feinstein) and 14 college-age humans.

Experiment 1

Monkeys were given a set of simple addition problems. The range of addition problems included the numerical values 2, 4, 8, 12, and 16. All possible combinations of addends were tested (e.g., sum of 8 = 1 + 7, 2 + 6, 3 + 5, 4 + 4, 5 + 3, etc.), and all values were equally likely to occur as correct and incorrect choices. The monkeys' performance was affected by the ratio between the addends.

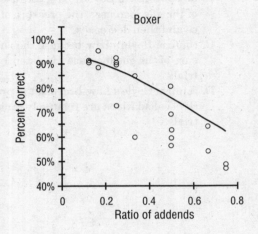
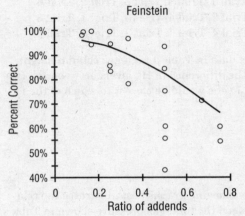

Figure 1

Experiment 2

Humans and monkeys were given identical sets of addition problems to solve. The range of addition problems included sums adding up to 2, 3, 7, 8, 11, 12, and 16. Two sets of dots were presented on a touch screen, separated by a delay of 0.5 seconds. Then, subjects were required to select the button that displayed the numerical sum of the two sets. The humans' and monkeys' accuracy and response time are recorded on the following graphs.

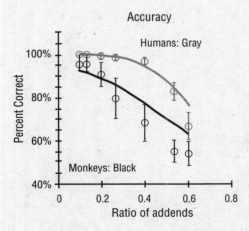
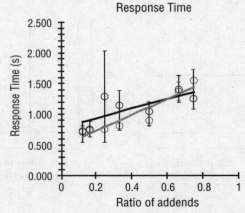

Figure 2

GO ON TO THE NEXT PAGE.

6. In Experiment 1, as the ratio grew closer to 1, the monkeys:

   F. answered more questions correctly.
   G. answered fewer questions overall.
   H. answered fewer questions correctly.
   J. answered more questions overall.

7. In Experiment 2, humans' and monkeys' response times were equal in:

   A. addition problems with a ratio of 0.2.
   B. addition problems with a ratio of 0.4.
   C. addition problems with a ratio of 0.6.
   D. addition problems with a ratio of 0.8.

8. Based on the results of Experiment 2, how did the increasing ratio between numerical values affect both humans' and monkeys' response times?

   F. Humans' response time increased, while monkeys' response time decreased.
   G. Humans' response time decreased, while monkeys' response time increased.
   H. Both humans' and monkeys' response times decreased.
   J. Both humans' and monkeys' response times increased.

9. The results of Experiment 2 support which of the following conclusions?

   A. Humans have a higher accuracy rate than monkeys, but both humans and monkeys answer questions in roughly the same amount of time.
   B. Humans have a lower accuracy rate than monkeys, but humans answer questions more quickly than monkeys.
   C. Monkeys have a lower accuracy rate than humans, but monkeys answer questions more quickly than humans.
   D. Humans and monkeys have both similar accuracy rates and similar response times.

10. Which of the following assumptions was made in the design of Experiment 1?

    F. The two monkeys are capable of solving complex math problems.
    G. The two monkeys are the same age and gender.
    H. The two monkeys' mental capabilities are roughly equivalent.
    J. The two monkeys are able to perform addition as well as humans.

11. If a scientist were to add a third monkey to the study and give that monkey an addition problem with a ratio of 0.4, how quickly could the scientist expect the monkey to solve the problem, and how likely would the monkey be to answer the question correctly?

    A. The monkey could answer the question in 0.500 second with an 85% chance of being correct.
    B. The monkey could answer the question in 1.000 second with an 80% chance of being correct.
    C. The monkey could answer the question in 1.500 seconds with a 70% chance of being correct.
    D. The monkey could answer the question in 2.000 seconds with a 60% chance of being correct.

Passage III

CITATION: Sawatzky R, Liu-Ambrose T, Miller WC, Marra CA (2007). Physical activity as a mediator of the impact of chronic conditions on quality of life in older adults. *Health and Quality of Life Outcomes*, 5: 68.

In older adults, having a *chronic condition* (a medical condition that lasts for six months or more) is associated with a relative decrease in health and a relative increase in mobility limitations, emotional problems, and cognitive limitations. The increased prevalence of chronic conditions in the aging population poses a significant challenge to society and to the health care system.

Studies have demonstrated that physical activity can improve the quality of life in older adults. The objectives of the following study were to: 1) examine to what degree chronic conditions and related health problems could be attributed to a lack of physical activity and 2) examine the effect of physical activity on specific, prevalent chronic conditions such as cardiovascular disorders, diabetes, and strokes. The following table presents information about the participants' health.

12. According to the table, women are most likely to develop which of the following chronic conditions?

F. Respiratory disorders
G. Urinary or bowel disorders
H. Cardiovascular disorders
J. Stroke

13. Which of the following lists the table's chronic-condition groups in increasing order of physical activity?

A. Respiratory disorders, urinary or bowel disorders, cardiovascular disorders, musculoskeletal disorders
B. Musculoskeletal disorders, diabetes, respiratory disorders, stroke
C. Stroke, respiratory disorders, diabetes, musculoskeletal disorders
D. Cardiovascular disorders, respiratory disorders, stroke, diabetes

14. The data in the table support which of the following hypotheses?

F. Diabetes is the most common chronic condition in adults between 75 and 79 years of age.
G. Older adults with no chronic condition are more physically active than older adults with one or more chronic conditions.
H. Older adults with a BMI greater than 25 are less likely to have a chronic condition than older adults with a BMI less than 18.5.
J. Older adults with respiratory disorders are more likely to exercise than older adults with musculoskeletal disorders.

Table 1 - Description of the chronic condition groups

Category	No chronic condition (n = 2,839)	One or more chronic conditions (n = 17,314)	Respiratory disorders (n = 2,722)	Musculoskeletal disorders (n = 11,473)	Cardiovascular disorder (n = 10,741)	Diabetes (n = 2,754)	Urinary or bowel disorders (n = 2,399)	Stroke (n = 894)
Activity								
≥ 1,000 Kcal/week	35.1%	25.8%	20.7%	24.8%	24.7%	24.3%	20.0%	17.2%
Age								
85 – 74 yrs	89.7%	58.3%	58.1%	57.4%	56.3%	61.2%	48.9%	43.1%
75 – 79 yrs	17.1%	21.2%	22.2%	21.3%	22.5%	21.8%	21.9%	26.4%
> 84 yrs	13.2%	20.5%	19.7%	21.3%	21.2%	17.0%	29.2%	30.5%
Sex								
Female	46.2%	50.8%	56.0%	85.0%	50.1%	50.8%	68.3%	50.7%
Smoking								
Yes	16.7%	11.8%	15.8%	11.8%	10.1%	9.0%	11.8%	11.5%
Alcohol use								
Does not use alcohol	28.0%	34.4%	37.8%	34.5%	38.0%	47.1%	37.2%	44.8%
< 2 times/month	19.2%	21.7%	20.3%	22.3%	21.7%	21.7%	24.8%	19.8%
2 to 3 times/month	14.4%	12.9%	11.9%	12.8%	12.8%	10.3%	12.5%	10.8%
> 3 times/month	30.4%	31.0%	30.1%	30.4%	29.5%	21.0%	25.7%	24.7%
Obesity								
BMI < 18.5	55.8%	42.5%	42.3%	40.6%	39.7%	30.9%	41.8%	46.2%
BMI 18.5 – 25	2.8%	3.1%	4.4%	3.1%	2.8%	1.2%	3.3%	4.8%
BMI ≥ 25	41.7%	54.4%	53.4%	58.2%	57.8%	87.9%	55.0%	49.0%

Notes: *N* = 19,953, including those older adults who had no chronic conditions or who had one of the selected chronic conditions and for whom there was no missing data for any of the variables in our analyses.

GO ON TO THE NEXT PAGE.

15. Which of the following graphs best illustrates the relationship between alcohol use and stroke in older adults?

A.

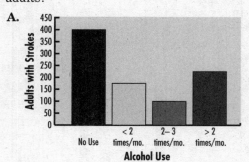

B.

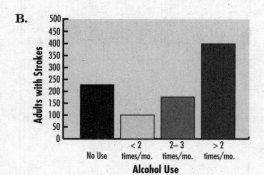

C.

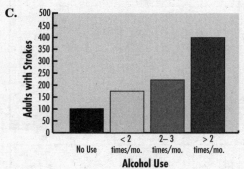

D.

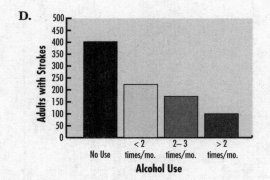

16. Based on the data in the table, one can conclude that older people with a BMI greater than 25 are:

F. less likely to have a cardiovascular disorder than older people with a BMI less than 25.

G. more likely to use alcohol than people with a BMI less than 25.

H. between 75 and 79 years of age.

J. at greater risk for diabetes than older people with a BMI less than 25.

Passage IV

CITATION: Smit GN (2005). Tree thinning as an option to increase herbaceous yield of an encroached semi-arid savanna in South Africa. *BMC Ecology* 5: 7.

Study 1

This investigation was conducted in a South African *savanna* (a grassland scattered with trees). The savanna area was covered by a dense group of trees that caused the suppression of herbaceous plants. The objective of this study was to determine the influence of tree thinning on the yield of herbaceous plants (mostly grasses). Seven 1.17-hectare plots were thinned to differing tree densities. The control plot was left undisturbed (referred to as the 100% plot), and the others were thinned to the approximate equivalents of 75%, 50%, 35%, 20%, 10%, and 0% (total clearing) of that of the 100% plot. Figure 1 shows the results over three seasons.

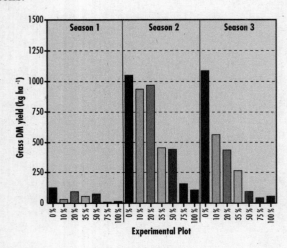

Figure 1

Study 2

In this study, researchers identified three subhabitats: between tree canopies (uncanopied—UCA), under tree canopies (canopied—CA), and where trees have been removed (removed canopies—RCA). Areas covered by each of the three subhabitats were determined for each of the experimental plots. Grass yield within the plots was determined at the end of each growing season, normally in April or May. Figure 2 shows the total seasonal yield within the three defined subhabitats.

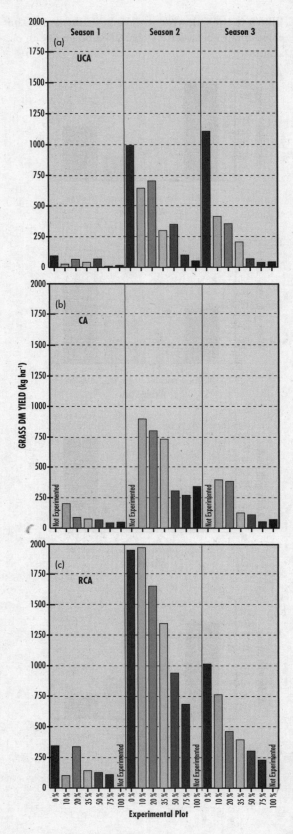

Figure 2

GO ON TO THE NEXT PAGE.

The following bar graph depicts the rainfall across the three seasons.

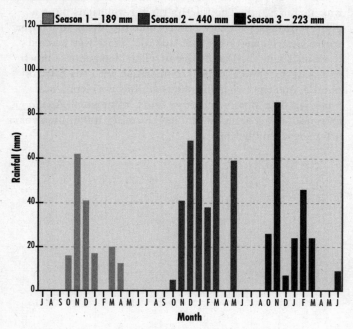

Figure 3

17. In Season 3, researchers harvested nearly 500 kg ha⁻¹ of grass from a particular plot. Based on the results of Study 1, what was the tree density of that plot?

- **A.** 0%
- **B.** 10%
- **C.** 35%
- **D.** 50%

18. According to Study 1, across the three seasons, grass yield on the 20% plot was:

- **F.** always higher than grass yield on the 35% plot.
- **G.** never higher than grass yield on the 35% plot.
- **H.** always the same as grass yield on the 35% plot.
- **J.** sometimes higher and sometimes lower than grass yield on the 35% plot.

19. Based on the information in Figures 1, 2 and 3, what impact did rainfall have on the tree-thinning studies?

- **A.** Rainfall had no impact on the studies.
- **B.** Heavy rainfall in Season 2 led to greater grass yield on nearly all of the experimental plots compared to Season 1.
- **C.** Light rainfall in Season 3 led to greater grass yield on the removed-canopy plots compared to Season 2.
- **D.** Rainfall is usually greater in January than in any other month.

20. Which of the following conclusions is most strongly supported by the information in Study 1?

- **F.** The greatest grass yields are obtained from completely cleared plots.
- **G.** The soil quality of the experimental plots improved in Season 3.
- **H.** On average, plots with thicker tree canopies have a higher grass yield.
- **J.** Grass yields on every plot increased from season to season.

21. According to the information in Study 2, what was the grass yield from the canopied 75% plot in Season 2?

- **A.** 250 kg ha⁻¹
- **B.** 325 kg ha⁻¹
- **C.** 625 kg ha⁻¹
- **D.** 875 kg ha⁻¹

22. Livestock depend upon herbaceous plants for survival. A livestock owner hypothesizes that there is more grass on land where the canopy has been removed than on land where there was never a canopy. Do the results of Study 2 support this hypothesis?

- **F.** No, because the 0% uncanopied plot yielded more grass than the 0% removed-canopy plot in Season 3.
- **G.** Yes, because the RCA bar graphs for Season 2 show that the removed-canopy plots yielded as much grass at 50% as the uncanopied plots yielded at 0%.
- **H.** Yes, because the RCA bar graphs show that the removed-canopy plots yielded up to twice as much grass as the uncanopied plots over three seasons.
- **J.** No, because very little grass grew on the removed-canopy plot in Season 1.

Passage V

There are several conflicting scientific theories about the formation of the Earth's moon. Five serious hypotheses have been presented by astronomers. Today, the two considered the most valid are the Giant Impact theory and the Fission Theory. Both hypotheses are discussed below.

Giant Impact Theory

More than 4.5 billion years ago, a gigantic meteor (or small planet) roughly the size of Mars collided with the young planet Earth. This colliding body, which astronomers have named Theia, was destroyed upon its impact with Earth. Parts of Theia and a large chunk of Earth's mantle hurtled into outer space. Several decades after that initial impact, this large amount of debris coalesced to form the Moon. During the *Apollo* moon landing, astronauts collected rocks with oxygen isotope compositions that are nearly identical to those found in the Earth's mantle.

Fission Theory

At the dawn of our solar system's existence, the Moon was part of Earth. The Earth's rapid revolutions flung a giant rock mass, which would become the Moon, into outer space. (Astronomers say that this rock mass was nestled in what is now the Pacific Ocean.) The Moon shares much of its physical and chemical composition with the Earth's mantle, and the two bodies have similar developmental histories. The Moon's primitive crust, from which *Apollo* astronauts took samples, finished forming 100 million years after the initial fission.

23. Based on the information in both hypotheses, which of the following is a key source of evidence for Moon-formation theories?

    A. Modern telescopic images of the Moon

    B. Surface rock collected by astronauts

    C. Heat readings of Earth's mantle

    D. Depth measurements of the Pacific Ocean

24. The Great Impact Theory does NOT address which of the following?

    F. Space debris

    G. Planetary revolution

    H. The Earth's mantle

    J. Oxygen isotopes

25. The Fission Theory would be most strengthened by:

    A. debris evidence that suggests a massive planetary body collided with Earth.

    B. astronauts' retrieval of moon-rock components that cannot be found on Earth.

    C. the proposal that Earth revolved more slowly billions of years ago.

    D. the discovery of a massive crater at the depths of the Pacific Ocean.

26. The scientists supporting both hypotheses would agree that the Moon:

    F. shares some chemical compositions with Earth.

    G. finished forming millions of years after the formation of Earth.

    H. has its origins in the Earth's core.

    J. formed after the Earth revolved very rapidly.

27. Which of the following questions is raised by the Fission Theory, but NOT answered in the passage?

    A. How did the giant rock mass get into outer space?

    B. Why did it take 100 million years for the Moon to form its primitive crust?

    C. When the Moon was still part of Earth, where was it located?

    D. With which layer of the Earth does the Moon have elements in common?

28. The Giant Impact Theory makes the assumption that:

    F. the Earth rotated quickly enough to expel a giant rock mass.

    G. the Earth is billions of years older than the Moon.

    H. the oxygen isotopes discovered by *Apollo* astronauts are unique to the Moon.

    J. only one huge rock mass collided with Earth to form the Moon.

29. If it was discovered that the Earth lost a significant amount of its mass around 4.5 billion years ago, how would this discovery affect the hypotheses, if at all?

    A. It is consistent with the Fission Theory only.

    B. It is consistent with both hypotheses.

    C. It is consistent with the Giant Impact Theory only.

    D. It would have no effect on either hypothesis.

Passage VI

CITATION: An X, Zhu T, Wang Z, Li C, Wang Y (2007). A modeling analysis of a heavy air pollution episode occurred in Beijing. Atmospheric Chemistry and Physics 7: 3103–3114.

After Beijing, China, succeeded in the competition to host the 2008 Olympic Games, improving the air quality in the region became one of the Chinese government's most important tasks. Researchers used a modeling system to investigate a heavy air-pollution episode in April 2005. The goal was to learn how heavy air pollution forms and how local emissions contribute. Table 1 shows how many tons of certain pollutants go into the air each year.

Region	Volatile Organic Compounds (VOC)	Sulfer Dioxide (SO²)	Nitrous Oxides (NO$_x$)	Carbon Monoxide (CO)	Suspended Particulate Matter (PM$_{10}$)	Thin Particulate Matter (PM$_{2.5}$)	Ammonia (NH$_3$)
Beijing Municipality	285,111 tons	211,306 tons	227,311 tons	1,021,790 tons	106,890 tons	53,367 tons	69,068 tons
Tianjin Municipality	270,000 tons	375,876 tons	178,940 tons	737,041 tons	93,497 tons	37,996 tons	49,981 tons
Hebei Province	855,000 tons	1,353,731 tons	686,000 tons	6,806,000 tons	535,055 tons	264,052 tons	846,462 tons
Shanxi Province	401,000 tons	1,467,420 tons	558,000 tons	3,254,000 tons	173,848 tons	66,899 tons	214,950 tons
Shandong Province	1,088,000 tons	1,575,245 tons	812,000 tons	7,339,000 tons	684,824 tons	379,516 tons	1,093,000 tons

Table 1

To indicate the air pollution level over the Chinese cities, an Air Pollutant Index (API) is issued every day. The API monitors pollutants. An index level under 100 indicates that the air quality of that monitoring station conforms to national air quality criteria. An index value over 100 will worsen symptoms in people with allergies. Figure 1 shows the API values of Beijing and surrounding cities for seven days in April 2005.

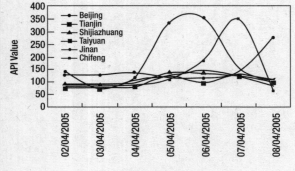

Figure 1

GO ON TO THE NEXT PAGE.

30. According to Table 1, how many tons of ammonia pollute the air in Hebei Province each year?

    F. 69,068 tons/year
    G. 686,000 tons/year
    H. 846,462 tons/year
    J. 1,093,000 tons/year

31. According to Figure 1, the two most polluted cities in China are:

    A. Beijing and Tianjin
    B. Jinan and Taiyuan
    C. Beijing and Chifeng
    D. Jinan and Tianjin

32. Based on the information presented and the data in Figure 1, people with allergies would experience the fewest health problems in:

    F. Jinan
    G. Chifeng
    H. Beijing
    J. Tianjin

33. The following graphs represent projected pollution levels for Beijing during five days of the 2008 Olympics. Which graph represents data that meets national air-quality criteria?

A.
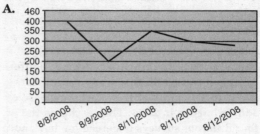

B.
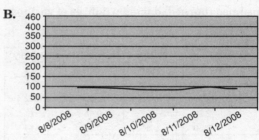

C.
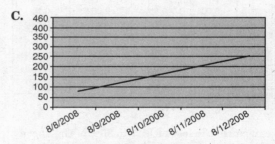

D.
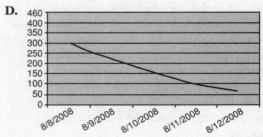

34. Pollutants such as carbon monoxide, nitrogen oxides, and sulfur dioxide are particularly problematic in highly industrialized areas. Based on the information in Table 1, which area is likely to be the most industrialized?

    F. Shandong Province
    G. Beijing Municipality
    H. Tianjin Municipality
    J. Hebei Province

GO ON TO THE NEXT PAGE.

Practice Test 1

Passage VII

CITATION: Zhengxi T, Tieszen LL, Zhu Z, Liu S, Howard SM (2007). An estimate of carbon emissions from 2004 wildfires across Alaskan Yukon River Basin. *Carbon Balance and Management* 2: 12.

Study 1

Wildfires contribute significantly to the carbon (C) cycle and, by extension, to global climate change. Wildfires result in the burning of carbon. In this study, researchers examined the Alaskan Yukon River Basin, where massive, widespread wildfires burned in 2004. They gathered the findings from four different surveys to determine how much carbon was consumed (burned) during wildfires of varying severity levels. The results are in the following table.

Category	Biomass Kg Cm^{-2}	Fraction Consumed (β) Burn Severity		
		High	Moderate	Low
Above-ground Biomass	1.56			
	2.30	0.33	0.23	0.12
	2.30		0.45	
	2.09	0.50	0.34	0.14
Ground Layer (or Organic Soil)	9.00	0.56	0.36	0.18
	6.00		0.36	
	6.89	0.62	0.45	0.27
Mean- above ground	2.06	0.42	0.34	0.13
Mean- Organic soil	7.30	0.59	0.39	0.23

Study 2

Wildfires can cause the loss of 15% to 35% of the above-ground *biomass* (living matter). In this study, researchers measured the association between *fire scars* (the amount of biomass destroyed by a wildfire) and soil drainage quality. The soil drainage classes associated with fire scars were labeled VP (very poorly drained), SP (somewhat poorly drained), W (well drained), and E (excessively drained). Researchers also compared the burned areas in the 2004 fires to all fires in the region from 1950 to 2003. Figure 1 displays the results.

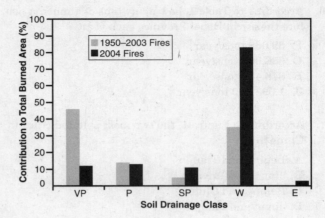

Figure 1

Researchers also measured the contributions of different land-cover types to the total burned area and to total carbon release. The results are in Figure 2.

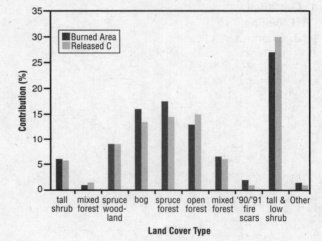

Figure 2

GO ON TO THE NEXT PAGE.

35. According to the table, what was the average fraction of carbon consumed in above-ground biomass during a wildfire of moderate severity?

A. 0.13
B. 0.34
C. 0.39
D. 0.59

36. According to Figure 1, which soil drainage class contributed the most to the total burned area in 2004?

F. Very poorly drained
G. Somewhat poorly drained
H. Well drained
J. Poorly drained

37. Based on Figure 2, the bog and the spruce forest:

A. contributed insignificant amounts of released carbon.
B. contributed equal percentages to the total burned area and the total release of carbon.
C. contributed more to the total release of carbon than to the total burned area.
D. contributed more to the total burned area than to the total release of carbon.

38. According to Figures 1 and 2, in 2004 a near-equal amount of the total burned area was contributed by:

F. bog land cover and well-drained soil.
G. spruce woodland land cover and well-drained soil.
H. tall and low shrub and somewhat poorly drained soil.
J. spruce woodland land cover and somewhat poorly drained soil.

39. The main purpose of Study 1 was to determine:

A. the root causes of the 2004 Alaska wildfires.
B. the amount of carbon consumed in the 2004 Alaska wildfires.
C. the contributions of various types of land cover to the Alaska wildfires.
D. the amount of biomass destroyed in the 2004 Alaska wildfires and in fires from 1950 to 2003.

40. An ecologist wants to prevent the significant loss of biomass in future Alaskan wildfires. Based on the information in Figure 1, which soil drainage class would be the most effective in preventing such a loss?

F. Well drained
G. Excessively drained
H. Very poorly drained
J. Somewhat poorly drained

END OF TEST 4.
STOP! DO NOT RETURN TO ANY OTHER TEST.

WRITING TEST

DIRECTIONS: This test evaluates your writing skills. You will be given thirty (30) minutes to write an original essay. Before you start, read the writing prompt and be sure you understand the task required. Your essay will be scored based on how well you express judgments by taking a clear position on the issue presented; maintain your focus on your argument throughout the entire essay; support your position with logical reasoning and relevant evidence; present your ideas in an organized manner; and demonstrate clear and effective use of language, based on standard written English language conventions.

To plan out your essay, you may use the unlined page provided. You will not be scored on any information written on this unlined page. *Your essay must be written on the lined pages provided.* Your essay will be scored based only on the writing on those lined pages. You may not end up using all of the lined pages provided, but to be sure that you have enough space to complete your essay, do NOT skip any lines. Corrections or additions may be written in neatly between the lines of your essay, but you must NOT include any writing in the margins of the lined pages. *If your essay is illegible, it cannot be scored, so be sure to write or print clearly.*

If you finish your essay early, you may go back and review what you have written. When time is called, stop writing immediately and lay down your pencil.

ACT Assessment Writing Test Prompt

Many high school students consider traveling overseas during the summer after they graduate, prior to starting college. Some people support overseas travel before college because they believe students will benefit from this experience. Others think students will not benefit from the experience, because students will be too busy with the added overseas travel. In your opinion, should high school students travel overseas during the summer before staring college?

Write an essay that develops your position on this question. You may choose to take one of the two viewpoints given, or you may present a different position on this question. Support your position using specific reasons and examples.

Begin WRITING TEST here.

WRITING TEST

Practice Test 1: Answers & Explanations

Question Number	Answer	Right	Wrong	Question Number	Answer	Right	Wrong
	English			38.	J	—	—
1.	C	—	—	39.	D	—	—
2.	G	—	—	40.	H	—	—
3.	D	—	—	41.	A	—	—
4.	F	—	—	42.	J	—	—
5.	C	—	—	43.	A	—	—
6.	J	—	—	44.	G	—	—
7.	D	—	—	45.	A	—	—
8.	J	—	—	46.	J	—	—
9.	B	—	—	47.	B	—	—
10.	H	—	—	48.	J	—	—
11.	B	—	—	49.	C	—	—
12.	J	—	—	50.	G	—	—
13.	B	—	—	51.	D	—	—
14.	F	—	—	52.	H	—	—
15.	A	—	—	53.	B	—	—
16.	G	—	—	54.	F	—	—
17.	D	—	—	55.	A	—	—
18.	G	—	—	56.	F	—	—
19.	C	—	—	57.	D	—	—
20.	J	—	—	58.	G	—	—
21.	D	—	—	59.	B	—	—
22.	H	—	—	60.	G	—	—
23.	C	—	—	61.	D	—	—
24.	J	—	—	62.	J	—	—
25.	B	—	—	63.	B	—	—
26.	G	—	—	64.	F	—	—
27.	D	—	—	65.	D	—	—
28.	H	—	—	66.	G	—	—
29.	A	—	—	67.	D	—	—
30.	H	—	—	68.	G	—	—
31.	B	—	—	69.	C	—	—
32.	F	—	—	70.	J	—	—
33.	D	—	—	71.	D	—	—
34.	G	—	—	72.	F	—	—
35.	D	—	—	73.	B	—	—
36.	G	—	—	74.	H	—	—
37.	C	—	—	75.	C	—	—

Question Number	Answer	Right	Wrong	Question Number	Answer	Right	Wrong
Mathematics				31.	E	—	—
1.	A	—	—	32.	J	—	—
2.	H	—	—	33.	D	—	—
3.	C	—	—	34.	H	—	—
4.	K	—	—	35.	B	—	—
5.	A	—	—	36.	F	—	—
6.	F	—	—	37.	B	—	—
7.	B	—	—	38.	H	—	—
8.	G	—	—	39.	C	—	—
9.	B	—	—	40.	G	—	—
10.	J	—	—	41.	D	—	—
11.	B	—	—	42.	H	—	—
12.	J	—	—	43.	B	—	—
13.	B	—	—	44.	F	—	—
14.	H	—	—	45.	B	—	—
15.	A	—	—	46.	G	—	—
16.	H	—	—	47.	A	—	—
17.	E	—	—	48.	J	—	—
18.	J	—	—	49.	C	—	—
19.	E	—	—	50.	G	—	—
20.	G	—	—	51.	B	—	—
21.	B	—	—	52.	J	—	—
22.	H	—	—	53.	B	—	—
23.	D	—	—	54.	G	—	—
24.	F	—	—	55.	D	—	—
25.	D	—	—	56.	K	—	—
26.	J	—	—	57.	E	—	—
27.	C	—	—	58.	K	—	—
28.	J	—	—	59.	B	—	—
29.	D	—	—	60.	H	—	—
30.	G	—	—				

Question Number	Answer	Right	Wrong	Question Number	Answer	Right	Wrong
Reading				21.	D	—	—
1.	C	—	—	22.	F	—	—
2.	F	—	—	23.	B	—	—
3.	A	—	—	24.	G	—	—
4.	H	—	—	25.	C	—	—
5.	A	—	—	26.	G	—	—
6.	G	—	—	27.	A	—	—
7.	C	—	—	28.	J	—	—
8.	H	—	—	29.	C	—	—
9.	D	—	—	30.	J	—	—
10.	F	—	—	31.	C	—	—
11.	D	—	—	32.	J	—	—
12.	G	—	—	33.	A	—	—
13.	B	—	—	34.	J	—	—
14.	F	—	—	35.	D	—	—
15.	C	—	—	36.	G	—	—
16.	F	—	—	37.	C	—	—
17.	C	—	—	38.	F	—	—
18.	G	—	—	39.	C	—	—
19.	A	—	—	40.	F	—	—
20.	J	—	—				

Question Number	Answer	Right	Wrong	Question Number	Answer	Right	Wrong
Science				21.	A	—	—
1.	A	—	—	22.	H	—	—
2.	G	—	—	23.	B	—	—
3.	C	—	—	24.	G	—	—
4.	G	—	—	25.	D	—	—
5.	E	—	—	26.	F	—	—
6.	H	—	—	27.	B	—	—
7.	C	—	—	28.	J	—	—
8.	J	—	—	29.	B	—	—
9.	A	—	—	30.	H	—	—
10.	H	—	—	31.	C	—	—
11.	B	—	—	32.	J	—	—
12.	G	—	—	33.	B	—	—
13.	C	—	—	34.	F	—	—
14.	G	—	—	35.	B	—	—
15.	A	—	—	36.	H	—	—
16.	J	—	—	37.	D	—	—
17.	B	—	—	38.	J	—	—
18.	F	—	—	39.	B	—	—
19.	B	—	—	40.	G	—	—
20.	F	—	—				

Calculating Your Score

To find your scaled scores for each test, add up the number of questions you answered correctly on each test. That number represents your raw score for the test. Then covert your raw score to a 1–36 score using the table below. To find your Composite Score for the entire exam, add up your scaled scores for all four tests and divide that total by 4. Round off any fractions to the nearest whole number.

Keep in mind that this score is just a rough estimate. The only completely accurate predictors of your current scoring level are the scoring scales provided with official ACT materials, so make sure you practice with them in the week or two before the test to gauge where you stand.

Scaled Score	Raw Scores				Scaled Score
	Test 1	Test 2	Test 3	Test 4	
	English	Mathematics	Reading	Science	
36	75	60	38–40	40	36
35	73–74	58–59	37	—	35
34	71–72	56–57	36	39	34
33	70	55	35	—	33
32	69	54	34	38	32
31	68	52–53	—	—	31
30	67	50–51	33	37	30
29	65–66	48–49	32	36	29
28	64	46–47	30–31	35	28
27	62–63	43–45	29	34	27
26	60–61	41–42	28	32–33	26
25	57–59	39–40	27	30–31	25
24	55–56	37–38	26	29	24
23	53–54	35–36	25	27–28	23
22	50–52	33–34	24	25–26	22
21	47–49	31–32	23	23–24	21
20	44–46	30	22	21–22	20
19	42–43	27–29	21	18–20	19
18	39–41	25–26	20	16–17	18
17	37–38	22–24	19	14–15	17
16	34–36	18–21	17–18	13	16
15	30–33	15–17	16	12	15
14	28–29	12–14	14–15	10–11	14
13	26–27	09–11	12–13	09	13
12	24–25	08	10–11	08	12
11	22–23	06–07	08–09	07	11
10	20–21	05	07	06	10
9	18–19	04	06	05	9
8	15–17	—	05	04	8
7	13–14	03	—	03	7
6	10–12	02	04	—	6
5	08–09	—	03	02	5
4	06–07	—	02	—	4
3	04–05	01	—	01	3
2	02–03	—	01	—	2
1	00–01	00	00	00	1

Practice Test 1: Answers & Explanations

ENGLISH

1. C

Punctuation: Commas   *Easy*

The second half of the sentence consists of the following clause: *when I established an organization to help the residents in a nearby local nursing home.* A comma is unnecessary before the clause because the information in the clause is vital to the sentence. Both a semicolon and a period would be incorrect because the clause cannot stand alone as a complete sentence.

2. G

Style: Redundancy and Wordiness   *Medium*

Choices **F**, **G**, and **J** include both *nearby* and *local*, although each answer choice is worded differently. *Nearby* and *local* have a similar meaning, so including both words in the sentence creates a redundancy. The correct answer offers a clear, concise statement without any repeated information. The elimination of *nearby* in **G** does not alter the meaning, but it does free the sentence of clutter.

3. D

Basic Grammar and Usage: Verb Tenses   *Easy*

The main subject and verb in the first part of the sentence are *grandmother lived*, which is past-tense. Consequently, the second half of the sentence should be past-tense, which would mean *enjoyed spending* is the correct answer. *Enjoy spending*, *do enjoy spending*, and *are enjoying spending* are all present-tense verb phrases.

4. F

Sentence Structure: Connecting and Transitional Words   *Medium*

The author is explaining that she and her sister were able to visit their grandmother regularly because they *fortunately* lived near the nursing home. *Consequently* and *however* would be incorrect because the previous sentence does not indicate a reason that the girls are either able or unable to visit their grandmother. *Finally* might be tempting because the sentence is the last one in the paragraph; however, the author is not making a list of reasons the girls visit the nursing home. The best answer is **F**.

5. C

Organization: Transitions, Topic Sentences & Conclusions *Difficult*

Paragraph 3 describes how the girls met a resident who happily talked with them about her life experiences. **A** and **B** might work well in the previous paragraph, but they do not summarize the main idea of paragraph 3. Although **D** is tempting because it refers to the girls being introduced to residents, the best answer is **C** because the sentence explains why the girls initiated a conversation with the elderly woman.

6. J

Organization: Sentence Reorganization *Difficult*

The current sentence requires reorganization, since it is unclear who is delighted. **G** and **H** suggest that the grandchildren are the ones who are delighted instead of the woman. Moreover, **H** suggests that the grandchildren are presently at the nursing home, but the previous sentence indicates the woman is alone. **J** clearly indicates that the woman is delighted to talk with the girls about her grandchildren.

7. D

Sentence Structure: Parallelism *Difficult*

Sentences are awkward when words and phrases are not phrased similarly. In this case, the two verbs in the prepositional phrase should be expressed in parallel grammatical form. *Exchanged* is past-tense, so **A** is incorrect. Although *having exchanged* and *was exchanging* include *-ing* endings, they are verb phrases, unlike the single word *meeting*. *About meeting her husband and exchanging letters with him* is balanced because the verbs *meeting* and *exchanging* both end in *-ing*.

8. J

Style: Word Choice and Identifying Tone *Difficult*

The original sentence is not accurate because the residents are *receiving* joy from their time with the volunteers, not *earning* joy. *Generate* means to create or produce, and the *older people* are not creating *great joy*—they are receiving *great joy* from spending time with the teenagers. No *assessments* are taking place, so *derive*, which means *gain*, works best.

9. B

Sentence Structure: Misplaced Modifiers *Difficult*

From the original placement of the word *regularly*, it is unclear whether the volunteers will be visiting *regularly* or organizing *regularly*. **C** is wrong because *to* and *on* would not be used together. **D** may be tempting, but the placement of *regularly* between *to visit* results in a split infinitive. **B** clearly expresses the meaning of the sentence.

10. H

Sentence Structure: Run-on Sentences *Medium*

The original sentence is a run-on: Two complete ideas have been joined without the correct punctuation or conjunction. **G** is incorrect because a run-on cannot be repaired with a comma. **J** is incorrect because if a semicolon is used, the conjunction *and* is unnecessary. Run-ons can be corrected with the combination of a comma and a conjunction, therefore **H** is correct.

11. B

Basic Grammar and Usage: Pronoun-Antecedent Agreement   *Medium*

In the original sentence, the pronoun *their* does not match its antecedent *one*. At first glance, it may seem that *their* and *volunteers* match. However, *one* is the subject of the sentence, while *of the volunteers* is a prepositional phrase. Both *our* and *your* fail to match the subject, so the best answer is **B**.

12. J

Writing Strategy: Analysis   *Difficult*

The last sentence of the paragraph details how the program benefits the volunteers, so **J** is the correct answer. **G** is incorrect because the sentence does not summarize the idea of the paragraph. **H** is incorrect because the sentence is not about the residents. Although **F** might be tempting, the author does not indicate that the volunteer program is under attack and needs to be defended.

13. B

Punctuation: Apostrophes   *Easy*

Only one nursing home is discussed in the passage, and in the original sentence *homes'* indicates a plural possession. **C** is incorrect because the plural possessive, *homes'*, is used in addition to *administrators* being made to show ownership when none exists. **D** is incorrect because no indication is made that the home possesses the administrators. **B** correctly shows that a singular *home* possesses *administrators*.

14. F

Basic Grammar and Usage: Verb Tenses   *Easy*

The original sentence is correct because *expected* and *were correct* are both past-tense verbs. Changing the verb tense in the first part of the sentence to present tense would not make sense when the second half of the sentence remains in past-tense, so **G** and **J** are incorrect. **H** includes the helping verb *have*, which creates a present perfect verb phrase that suggests the staff currently expects the *program to be a huge hit*. However, the past-tense verb phrase *were correct* indicates that the staff's expectations occurred in the past and are not ongoing.

15. A

Organization: Passage Reorganization   *Difficult*

The best answer is **A** because paragraph 1 effectively introduces the topic of establishing a volunteer program. **B** might be tempting because paragraph 2 describes how the author became interested in the idea of a nursing home program; however, the passage is not primarily about the author and her grandmother. **C** and **D** are incorrect because toward the end of the passage the author has already explained her volunteer program, so an overview is unnecessary.

16. G

Basic Grammar and Usage: Subject-Verb Agreement   *Easy*

The original version lacks a verb and creates a sentence fragment, although *chronicling* may appear to be the verb at first glance. The best answer is **G** because *chronicles* is a present-tense verb, which is appropriate for the context. The series has already been made, so *will chronicle* and *has been chronicling* do not work.

17. D
Style: Word Choice and Identifying Tone   *Medium*

Winters was the leader of Company "E," and he *commanded* them through *significant campaigns*. Although Winters *organized* the men as part of his leadership duties, *organized* fails to convey the idea that Winters led the men into battle. *Governed* suggests Winters merely directed the soldiers, but Winters also fought beside them in the trenches. While Major Winters had authority over individual soldiers, he did not *authorize* which men would be in Company "E."

18. G
Punctuation: Commas   *Medium*

The original version does not include a comma after *1918*, which would separate the introductory phrase from the main part of the sentence. **G** corrects the problem and is the best answer. **H** includes a comma after *Pennsylvania*, which is acceptable but not always necessary with names of places. But **H** omits the comma separating *Lancaster* (the city) from *Pennsylvania* (the state), and does not include a comma after *1918*. The comma between *in* and *1918* in **J** interrupts a prepositional phrase.

19. C
Basic Grammar and Usage: Verb Tenses   *Easy*

Shifting tenses within a sentence creates confusion for the reader. The past-tense verb phrase *was chosen*, used in the second part of the sentence, indicates that a past-tense verb is needed in the first part of the sentence. The original sentence incorrectly includes the future-tense verb phrase *will enlist*. **B** and **D** are present tense, which leaves **C** as the correct answer.

20. J
Sentence Structure: Comma Splices   *Medium*

The original sentence includes a comma splice (two independent clauses incorrectly joined by only a comma). Correcting the problem requires a comma with a conjunction, so **J** is correct. Although **H** adds the conjunction *and*, a comma is not included. The comma is removed in **G**, which only serves to change the comma splice into a run-on sentence.

21. D
Sentence Structure: Parallelism   *Difficult*

The original sentence is not parallel because the phrases *had camaraderie* and *is understanding* are not the same tense. **B** and **C** are also unbalanced: *had* or *was* is used in front of one word but not the other. Parallel phrases must begin in the same way. The best choice is **D**, which improves the flow of the sentence by eliminating the verbs and making the items in the series all nouns: *leadership*, *camaraderie*, and *understanding*.

22. H
Writing Strategy: Analysis   *Difficult*

As **H** indicates, the sentence in question describes the relationship between Nixon and Winters and relates to the preceding sentence that mentions Winters' *camaraderie* and *understanding*. **F** is incorrect since the information in the sentence is relevant to the discussion of Winters' compassion. The sentence does not offer an explanation to Winters' morality, so **G** is wrong. While Nixon was different from Winters, the purpose of the sentence is not to illustrate that fact but to point out Winters' kindness toward others, so **J** is also wrong.

23. C

Organization: Transitions, Topic Sentences & Conclusions   *Difficult*

The original topic sentence provides a detail unrelated to the rest of the paragraph, and therefore it should be replaced. **B** and **D** both provide details about Winters' life after the military, so they do not relate to the rest of the paragraph. **C** is a general statement that fits the topic of Winters' *distinguished accomplishments*.

24. J

Sentence Structure: Misplaced Modifiers   *Medium*

The modifier *only* is incorrectly placed in front of *destroyed*, implying that the men's great feat sounds like nothing extraordinary. **G** is similarly worded, and also incorrect. **H** is tempting because the modifier describes the men, but *13 of his only men* is a confusing construction. The best option is **J**, which clarifies that Winters and a small number of soldiers, *only 13*, were able to destroy an artillery battery.

25. B

Sentence Structure: Connecting and Transitional Words   *Medium*

The transitional word *however* is inappropriate for the original sentence because no contrast exists with the previous sentence—Winters destroyed a battery and then he attained an important map. *Nonetheless* suggests a contrast, much like *however*, so **C** will not work. The information about the map is not an example, so **D** is incorrect. The best transitional phrase is *in addition* since more details about Winters's bravery are being provided.

26. G

Punctuation: Commas   *Difficult*

The original sentence is a compound sentence, which consists of two independent clauses joined together. Compound sentences can be punctuated with semicolons or separated into two sentences. Compound sentences can also be joined with a comma and a conjunction, as in the underlined version. **F**, **H**, and **J** are all appropriate options. **G** is not acceptable because a semicolon does not need a conjunction; it can stand alone (as in **J**).

27. D

Organization: Sentence Reorganization   *Difficult*

D is the best answer because the prepositional phrase *on the battlefield* describes where *Winters demonstrated strength and determination*. In the original sentence, the location of the prepositional phrase implies that the miniseries was shown on the battlefield. **B** is incorrect for the same reason. In **C**, the flow of the sentence is broken by placing *on the battlefield* between *strength and determination*.

28. H

Style: Redundancy and Wordiness   *Medium*

Heroic, *brave*, and *courageous* are synonyms, so the sentence does not need to include more than one of these words to convey a clear meaning. Repeating words may seem to add emphasis to an important point, but the repetition can distract the reader. The original sentence and **G** both include redundancies. **J** does not include the verb, making the sentence incomplete. **H** is the best answer because *Winters never saw himself as a hero* is a simple yet powerful statement.

29. **A**

Writing Strategy: Analysis   *Difficult*

The main idea of paragraph 4—that Winters was a successful yet modest soldier—is illustrated by the quotation. The quotation does not refer to *Band of Brothers*, so **B** is incorrect. **C** is wrong because Winters does not indicate displeasure at discussing WWII. Although Winters's grandson asks a question, the quotation itself does not relate to his grandson. The best choice is **A**.

30. **H**

Writing Strategy: Big Picture Purpose   *Difficult*

The essay is about the life and character of Major Winters, so the correct answer is **H**. Though the author mentions paratroopers getting behind enemy lines and military training, those details are minor points. **J** is wrong because the essay does not discuss how military tactics have changed.

31. **B**

Sentence Structure: Sentence Fragments   *Medium*

In the original version, the first sentence of the essay is a complete sentence. However, *an Anabaptist Christian denomination formed in 1693 with communities scattered across Pennsylvania, Indiana, and Ohio* is a sentence fragment because it lacks a verb. The addition of a semicolon in **C** is unhelpful because a semicolon should have two independent clauses on either side. Removing *an* in **D** fails to correct the sentence fragment. **B** is the correct answer because the period becomes a comma, and the second half of the sentence becomes a subordinate clause describing *Amish*.

32. **F**

Punctuation: Apostrophes   *Medium*

The original punctuation is correct because *art* is in possession of *sake* and needs an apostrophe to indicate that ownership. Though **J** includes an apostrophe in the correct location, the comma is unnecessary. The plural possessive used in **G** is incorrect because *art* should be singular.

33. **D**

Basic Grammar and Usage: Verb Tense   *Easy*

The past-tense verb *took* is used in the second part of the sentence, so a past-tense verb is required in the first part. **D** is the correct because *came* is a past-tense verb. *Will be coming* is future tense, and *come* is present tense. *Have come* is present perfect, which is a verb tense used to express continued actions. *When Amish women took up quilting in the 1870s* clarifies that the author is only describing events in the past, so **C** is incorrect.

34. **G**

Organization: Sentence Reorganization   *Difficult*

The structure of the original sentence is confusing because *America*, rather than *quilting*, is being described as *a popular pastime*. **H** does not flow well because *to*

America breaks up the phrase *brought quilting*. **J** includes *brought* twice, which makes the sentence too wordy. The best reorganization is **G**, which clearly conveys the intended meaning.

35. D

Writing Strategy: Additional Detail and Evidence   *Difficult*

Indications that colonial women spent their time weaving does not relate to the topic of the essay: when and why Amish women began quilting. The new sentence would not logically follow any of the sentences in the paragraph. Irrelevant information, no matter how interesting, distracts the reader from the focus of the essay.

36. G

Style: Word Choice and Identifying Tone   *Medium*

Values is the best word for the underlined portion. In the previous paragraph, the author illustrates the attitudes of the Amish by explaining that *Amish women saw no need to create elaborate quilts merely for the purpose of staying warm*. The Amish value system dictates their simple quilt designs, and *feelings* play no part. *Routines* and *strategies* do not explain why *Amish women created unadorned quilts from solid fabrics instead of trendy prints*.

37. C

Sentence Structure: Run-on Sentences   *Medium*

The original sentence is a run-on because the conjunction *and* is placed between two complete sentences without a comma. Although **B** includes a comma, a conjunction is also necessary. **D** merely changes *and* to *but*, which still leaves a run-on. The best answer is **C**, which separates the two ideas with a period.

38. J

Basic Grammar and Usage: Adverbs and Adjectives   *Medium*

The author is attempting to show the difference between the *intricate quilting* and the *plain fabric* described in the next sentence of the paragraph. This contrast is very unclear in the original text. The adverb *intricately* cannot be used, since it is not being used to modify an adjective or verb. The preposition *by* makes no sense in **H**. **J** is the best choice because the adjective *intricate* modifies *quilting*, and *quilting* modifies *styles*.

39. D

Organization: Transitions, Topic Sentences & Conclusions   *Difficult*

Paragraph 3 describes the early styles of Amish quilts, and paragraph 4 introduces current Amish quilting trends. Neither the original sentence nor **C** relates to either topic. Though the last sentence of paragraph 3 mentions sewing machines, **B** provides a specific detail that does not relate to paragraph 4. **D** most effectively connects the ideas between the two paragraphs by addressing Amish quilts past and present.

40. H

Sentence Structure: Parallelism   *Difficult*

The verb *may* indicates that other verbs in the sentence should be past-tense to be parallel with each other. *Centering* is not past-tense, so **F** and **J** are both incorrect. **G** is wrong because *surround* is a present-tense verb, and the preposition *to* breaks the flow of the sentence. The parallel way to write the sentence is with **H**, which uses two past-tense verbs, *centered* and *surrounded*, to create balance.

41. A

Organization: Sentence Reorganization   *Difficult*

The original sentence offers the clearest and most logical structure. The verb phrases *are added* and *are being added* make the sentence confusing in relation to the phrase *throughout the years. Throughout the years* modifies *added*, and the two are far apart when they should be close together for clarity.

42. J

Punctuation: Commas   *Medium*

The phrase *such as violet and red* interrupts the main sentence: *brighter hues now enhance the modern quilting palette. Such as violet and red* explains *brighter hues*, and the phrase should be set off with commas before *such* and after *red*. Only two colors are listed, and a comma is not needed to separate them. Therefore, **F** and **H** are wrong. **G** is also incorrect because a comma after *now* breaks up the flow of the sentence.

43. A

Style: Redundancy and Wordiness   *Medium*

The original sentence concisely describes the Amish quilts as *contemporary looking* and requires no change. The other choices include redundancies because *contemporary*, *modern*, *progressive*, *up-to-date*, and *fresh* all share the same basic meaning. Repeating words and phrases does not improve the meaning or style of the sentence. With style questions, the simplest option is often the best answer.

44. G

Basic Grammar and Usage: Pronoun-Antecedent Agreement   *Easy*

The pronoun in the underlined portion should match its antecedent, which is *quilt*. Since a quilt is not a person, and *who* is a pronoun used in reference to people, **F** and **J** are incorrect. A singular quilt is being discussed, so **H** is wrong due to its use of the plural verb *are*. The best answer is **G** because the pronoun *which* is appropriate when referring to things and animals.

45. A

Writing Strategy: Big Picture Purpose   *Difficult*

The correct answer is **A** because the essay briefly describes the development of Amish quilting. Although *British Quakers* are mentioned in the essay as the ones who brought quilting to America, the detail is a minor one. Therefore, **B** is wrong. *Theories regarding why the Amish did not quilt* is not a topic of the passage. The author writes that *Amish women saw no need to create elaborate quilts merely for the purpose of staying warm*, but that eventually they began to see utility of quilting. The author presents no other *theories* regarding why the Amish did not quilt as soon as their neighbors did, so **C** is wrong. The author never mentions Amish quilt collecting, so **D** is incorrect.

46. J

Sentence Structure: Connecting and Transitional Words   *Medium*

The first sentence of the paragraph states that identifying an Ivory-billed Woodpecker should be easy, and the second sentence indicates that a controversy exists over a sighting. *Moreover* and *furthermore* are transitional words used to indicate that additional information has been provided, so both **F** and **G** are incorrect. *Finally* indicates that a period of time has passed, which makes **H** incorrect. *However* illustrates a contrast, so **J** is the correct answer.

47. B

Basic Grammar and Usage: Subject-Verb Agreement   *Medium*

The subject of the sentence is the singular noun *flurry*, so the correct verb is *surrounds*. At first glance, it might seem that *questions* is the subject, but the plural noun, *questions*, is part of the prepositional phrase describing *flurry*. *Surround, are surrounding,* and *do surround* agree with plural nouns, so the correct answer is **B**.

48. J

Style: Redundancy and Wordiness   *Medium*

The original sentence, as well as **G** and **H**, are unnecessarily wordy. The most concise way to describe the woodpecker is with **J**. The most concise answer is often the best answer with style questions where being economical with words is prized above all else.

49. C

Sentence Structure: Connecting and Transitional Words   *Medium*

The author is contrasting the fact that the Ivory-billed Woodpecker was not identified as endangered until twenty years after it was last seen. *Similarly* would be used to compare, not contrast, so the original sentence needs to be corrected. *Therefore* suggests a conclusion, which is not being made in this sentence. *As a result* suggests a connection between the two ideas. The best transitional word is *although*.

50. G

Punctuation: Commas   *Easy*

Over the years is an introductory phrase that needs a comma to set it off from the rest of the sentence. Both the original sentence and **H** lack a comma after *years*. **J** includes an unnecessary comma after *sightings*. **G** includes a comma in the correct place.

51. D

Style: Redundancy and Wordiness   *Medium*

The sentence explains that the bird watcher is kayaking in the Cache River National Wildlife Refuge. Adding that the kayaker is in a river creates a redundancy. Although it may be tempting to include the descriptive phrases *federally protected* and *heavily wooded*, the fact that **B** and **C** repeat *river* makes them incorrect choices. The underlined portion should be omitted because it adds no new information.

52. H

Basic Grammar and Usage: Idioms   *Medium*

An idiom is a way of speaking that follows no specific rules and may vary by culture. For example, someone from England might say, "John went to hospital," while an American would say, "John went to the hospital." *According to* is idiomatic, so **H** is correct. *According with, according by,* and *according from* are not idiomatic and are incorrect.

53. B

Punctuation: Apostrophes *Easy*

According to paragraph 3, *a member of an ornithologist group* reported seeing the bird, so *watcher* should be singular. **B** correctly indicates singular possession of the report. **C** would only be correct if more than one bird watcher made the report. **A** is wrong because no ownership is indicated.

54. F

Sentence Structure: Parallelism *Difficult*

The underlined portion in the original sentence flows well and maintains parallel form, unlike the other answer choices. Both **G** and **H** include *with* and an *-ing* verb, which is unbalanced. **J** ineffectively combines *topped* with *showing*, which breaks the sentence's flow.

55. A

Organization: Transitions, Topic Sentences & Conclusions *Difficult*

Paragraph 4 focuses on search efforts, and the original sentence provides the best transition to it. Although **B** provides a more detailed description of the Ivory-billed Woodpecker, the information does not smoothly move into paragraph 4. **C** does not relate to either paragraph. **D** offers a good detail for paragraph 4, but it does not work as a transition at the end of paragraph 3.

56. F

Writing Strategy: Analysis *Difficult*

The phrase provides neither the author's opinion nor historical information. **G** might be a tempting option because the phrase is somewhat humorous. However, the main purpose of the phrase is to provide a descriptive explanation for why experts maintain secrecy about the outings in search of the Ivory-billed Woodpecker.

57. D

Organization: Sentence Reorganization *Difficult*

In the original sentence, it is unclear what *during that time period* is modifying. **B** is not a good fix because *within the area not far from the area of the first report* is confusing. **C** presents an awkward organization that makes it unclear what *during that time period* is describing. **D** makes it clear that *seven other eyewitness sightings* were noted at the same time as the initial report.

58. G

Writing Strategy: Additional Detail and Evidence *Difficult*

Sentences 4 and 5 of paragraph 4 describe the similarities between the bird captured on video and the Ivory-billed Woodpecker. **G** provides additional information about a drumming sound, which would support the idea that the videotaped bird is the Ivory-billed Woodpecker. **F** undermines the writer's goal by suggesting that an Imperial Woodpecker might be the bird on the videotape. **H** and **J** provide details about the Ivory-billed Woodpecker, but they do not provide evidence of the bird's existence.

59. B

Writing Strategy: Additional Detail and Evidence *Difficult*

The first sentence of paragraph 5 states the theory held by skeptics, and the additional sentence provides evidence for that theory. **B** is the best answer. Although

Pileated Woodpeckers are seen today, as suggested in **A**, the additional sentence does not explain why. **C** and **D** are incorrect because the information about the similarities between the two birds merely supports an alternate theory and does not have a significant impact on the entire essay.

60. G

Style: Redundancy and Wordiness   *Medium*

The original sentence requires revision because *debate* and *arguments* are synonyms and should not be used in the same sentence. Including *as well as* and *along with* in **H** and **J** makes the sentence too wordy. **G** uses the fewest number of words to express the same idea, which is often the best option with style questions.

61. D

Sentence Structure: Connecting and Transitional Words   *Easy*

The opening sentence, which describes the impact of the recent Hurricane Katrina, contrasts with the information in the second sentence about the Galveston storm. *Otherwise* indicates the two storms were very different, while *then* suggests that the Galveston storm occurred after Hurricane Katrina. *Besides* is used to illustrate an additional example. *However* is the best choice because it indicates a contrast between the two events.

62. J

Style: Redundancy and Wordiness   *Medium*

People interested in history and the residents of Galveston is too wordy and requires revision. **G** and **H** are also too wordy. **J** presents the same information in fewer words and without losing any meaning.

63. B

Punctuation: Colons   *Easy*

Colons are appropriate before a list of items introduced by an independent clause. In **B**, the words before the colon make a complete sentence, and the words after the colon compose a list. A period as used in **C** would be incorrect because *"The Great Storm," "The Great Galveston Hurricane,"* and *"The Galveston Hurricane of 1900"* cannot stand alone as a complete sentence. **D** is wrong because the list of storm names needs to be set apart. **A** is incorrect because a comma cannot be used to set off lists.

64. F

Style: Word Choice and Identifying Tone   *Medium*

The question asks for the word that does NOT fit in the sentence. *Ship reports* were the *only tools* that could help with *weather predictions,* which suggests that weather prediction devices had not been developed. *Accessible, available,* and *obtainable* fit with the context of the sentence. Although ship reports might have been *questionable,* that word does not relate to tools being *limited at the time of the Galveston storm.*

65. D

Basic Grammar and Usage: Subject-Verb Agreement   *Medium*

The underlined verb should agree with the singular noun *information,* which is the subject. *Information* and *were delayed* do not agree. *Information are delayed* also lacks agreement. *Have been delayed* would work with a plural noun but not a singular one. The noun and verb in *information was delayed* both agree, making **D** the best answer.

66. G

Sentence Structure: Connecting and Transitional Words   *Medium*

The question is asking for the LEAST acceptable answer, which is **G**. The author is contrasting the fact that a hurricane warning was issued, but no one left the island. All of the transitional words listed illustrate a contrast except *therefore*.

67. D

Style: Redundancy and Wordiness   *Difficult*

Because the word *accustomed* suggests that people on the island were used to storms coming through on a regular basis, it is unnecessary to describe the storms as *frequent* or *regular*. *Accustomed to* and *high rate of frequency* have similar meanings, making **B** repetitive. **C** is also redundant because *comfortable with* repeats *accustomed to*. **D** does not include any repeated information.

68. G

Basic Grammar and Usage: Pronoun Cases   *Easy*

There is an adverb expressing a place, so **F** is incorrect. *They're* is a contraction for *they are*, which means **H** is also incorrect. *Its* is a singular possessive pronoun, and the underlined pronoun is referring to the plural noun *majority*. A possessive pronoun should modify *business*, so *their* is the correct answer.

69. C

Sentence Structure: Parallelism   *Difficult*

The original sentence does not flow well because the underlined portion is not parallel. Parallelism is achieved when words and phrases in a sentence are structured similarly. In this case, *evacuating* and *heading*, both of which end in *-ing*, are structured in parallel form. *To evacuate or heading*, *evacuating or to head*, and *to evacuate or by heading* are not parallel because the two verbs are not similar.

70. J

Punctuation: Semicolons   *Difficult*

A semicolon is required whenever a conjunctive adverb, such as *however*, is used to connect two independent clauses. A comma is placed after *however* to indicate a pause before the next half of the sentence. **J** is the only option that fulfills both of these requirements.

71. D

Sentence Structure: Connecting and Transitional Words   *Medium*

The first sentence of paragraph 3 provides information about the height of *storm surges*, while the second sentence provides information about homes being destroyed. *Meanwhile* is inappropriate because a passage of time is not being indicated. *Finally* would be appropriate if the author were listing off a series of events, but that is not the case. The author is not contrasting any information, so **C** is wrong. The best option is to refrain from using any transitional words and simply begin the sentence with *the*.

72. F

Organization: Sentence Reorganization   *Difficult*

The original sentence does not require reorganization because the author clearly presents the idea that houses were falling on top of each other *like dominos*. **G** is unclear because *like dominos* appears to be describing *wind gusts*. **H** is incorrect because *like dominos* describes *homes* rather than the action of one house pushing *down the next*. **J** is awkwardly structured; *like dominos* describes *damaging wind gusts*.

73. B

Writing Strategy: Analysis   *Difficult*

Paragraph 4 focuses on the destruction caused by the hurricane. The author writes that *buildings were pushed from foundations*, and *bridges were washed out*. Including *telegraph lines were destroyed* in the paragraph is relevant to the discussion of problems caused by the storm. While citizens would have been *frustrated*, their feelings are not as relevant as the damage caused by the storm. The long duration of repairs suggested in the original version does not relate to the sentence. Concerns of *people on the mainland* is also irrelevant.

74. H

Writing Strategy: Analysis   *Difficult*

The second half of the sentence comments on the long-lasting impact the hurricane made on Galveston. The Great Storm is part of Galveston's unique history, so **H** is the best answer. No details or information about the destruction are suggested by the last portion of the sentence, so **F** and **G** are wrong. **J** is incorrect because, although the first part of the sentence relates to *community development*, the second part does not.

75. C

Writing Strategy: Big Picture Purpose   *Difficult*

The essay does not describe the history of hurricanes, only the destruction caused by one specific hurricane. While the introduction compares Hurricane Katrina with the storm that struck Galveston, the author mentions no other storm in the essay. Although the author mentions Galveston's recovery in the last paragraph, the subject is not a primary focus of the essay. The essay *explains in detail why the Galveston Hurricane was more destructive than recent hurricanes,* but the question supposes that the writer intended to write about a more general *history of hurricanes*.

MATHEMATICS

1. A

Algebra: Substitution   *Easy*

Plug in the values given for x and y. Then, simply add -2 to 6, and the result is 4. Next, multiply: 4^2 is 16.

2. H

Plane Geometry: Triangles   *Easy*

This problem presents us with a right triangle. We can find the length of $\overline{DF}$ by using the Pythagorean theorem:

$$a^2 + b^2 = c^2$$

The hypotenuse, $\overline{EF}$, is 7 inches long. The other given side, $\overline{DE}$, is 4 inches long. Plug these numbers in:

$$a^2 + 4^2 = 7^2$$
$$a^2 + 16 = 49$$
$$a^2 + 16 - 16 = 49 - 16$$
$$a^2 = 33$$
$$a = \sqrt{33}$$

3. C

Plane Geometry: Triangles   *Easy*

In an isosceles triangle, the angles opposite the congruent sides are equal. The two congruent sides in $\triangle ABC$ are $\overline{AB}$ and $\overline{AC}$. Therefore, $\angle B$ and $\angle C$ are also equal, both measuring 62°. The sum of the three angles of a triangle always equals 180°, so we find the missing angle by subtracting the known measurements from 180°:

$$180° - 62° - 62° = 56°$$

4. K

Intermediate Algebra: Exponents and Roots   *Easy*

To find the equivalent expression, simplify the one we are given:

$$(5a^4)^2 = (5^2)\left(a^{4\times2}\right)$$
$$= (25)\left(a^{4\times2}\right)$$
$$= (25)\left(a^8\right)$$
$$= 25a^8$$

5. A

Algebra: Writing Expressions and Equations   *Easy*

Every ride to the airport costs the flat fee of $20. On top of this, there is a charge of $0.15 per mile driven. The total cost of a taxi ride to the airport can be expressed by the equation $0.15m + 20$.

6. F

Plane Geometry: Polygons   *Easy*

The sum of all four interior angles in any given quadrilateral is always 360°. Here, the given measures—68°, 92°, and 81°—add up to 241°. The missing angle measure is 360° − 241°, or 119°.

7. B

Algebra: Solving Linear Equations   *Easy*

This question is asking you to solve for a:

$$3(a - 7) = -14$$
$$3a - (3 \times 7) = -14$$
$$3a - 21 = -14$$
$$3a - 21 + 21 = -14 + 21$$
$$3a = 7$$
$$\frac{3a}{3} = \frac{7}{3}$$
$$a = \frac{7}{3}$$
$$= 2\frac{1}{3}$$

8. G

Pre-Algebra: Number Problems   *Easy*

To figure out how much Jack earns per session, divide his yearly salary ($44,000) by the number of sessions he teaches per year (80). His pay per session is $\frac{44,000}{80}$, or $550. When Jack takes an unpaid day off and his assistant teaches the session, the assistant earns $375. After calculating the difference, 550 − 375, we find that the assistant makes $175 less than Jack.

9. B

Pre-Algebra: Absolute Value Simplification and Substitution   *Easy*

The absolute value of | 5 − 9 | is 4. The absolute value of | 10 − 2 | is 8. Find the difference: 4 − 8 = −4.

10. J

Pre-Algebra: Mean, Median & Mode   *Easy*

This question is asking for the average (or mean) of Elise's bowling score for the season. The bowling league throws out an individual player's lowest score, so do not include 165 in the average. We find the average by first adding the four scores together:

$$190 + 210 + 228 + 242 = 870$$

Then, we divide the total by 4:

$$\frac{870}{4} = 217.5$$

Elise's average score is 217.5.

11. B

Plane Geometry: Angles and Lines   *Easy*

In this figure, angles *ADC* and *CDB* lie on a straight line. Therefore, the angles are complementary and their measures (*m*) total 180°. This relationship can be stated in the following equation:

$$m \angle ADC + m \angle CDB = 180°$$

Substitute in the values given for the two angles, and solve for *n*:

$$m\angle ADC + m\angle CDB = 180$$
$$(6n) + (2n - 20) = 180$$
$$8n - 20 = 180$$
$$8n = 200$$
$$n = \frac{200}{8}$$
$$= 25$$

The question asks for the measure of the smallest angle. Angle *ADC* measures 6*n*, or 150°, and ∠*CDB* measures 2*n* − 20, or 30°.

12. J

Plane Geometry: Polygons   *Easy*

Travis needs to know the area of the living room floor to cover it with carpet. Calculate the area by multiplying the floor's length by its width. The result is 9 × 12 = 108.

13. B

Pre-Algebra: Percentages, Fractions & Decimals   *Easy*

Meghan earns $710 per month at her part-time job. Twenty-one percent of that money is withheld for taxes and insurance. First, let's find how much money is withheld from Meghan's take-home pay each month:

$$0.21 \times \$710 = \$149.10$$

To find Meghan's total take-home pay, subtract the amount withheld from the total earnings per month:

$$\$710 - \$149.10 = \$560.90$$

Meghan takes home $560.90 per month.

14. H

Intermediate Algebra: Series   *Easy*

The four numbers presented in this problem form a mathematical series (or sequence). Define the difference between consecutive numbers as *d*. The first term is 8, and the final term is 26. This means that the second number is 8 + *d* and the third number is 8 + *d* + *d*. The final term, 26, is equal to 8 + *d* + *d* + *d*, or 8 + 3*d*. This expression leads to the equation 26 = 8 + 3*d*. Subtract 8 from both sides to get 18 = 3*d*. Dividing both sides by 3, we find that 6 = *d*. The second term is 8 + 6, or 14. The third term is 14 + 6, or 20.

15. A

Algebra: Multiplying Binomials   *Medium*

Follow the steps to multiply binomials:

$$(6g+9)^2 = (6g+9)(6g+9)$$
$$= (6g \times 6g) + (6g \times 9) + (9 \times 6g) + (9 \times 9)$$
$$= 36g^2 + 54g + 54g + 81$$
$$= 36g^2 + 108g + 81$$

16. H

Pre-Algebra: Percentages, Fractions & Decimals   *Medium*

The fractions given in the figure add up to a total of 1 circle. Create an equation and solve for S:

$$\frac{1}{5} + \frac{3}{20} + \frac{1}{10} + \frac{1}{3} + S = 1$$

The lowest common denominator of these four fractions is 60. Convert each fraction to a fraction over 60:

$$\frac{1}{5} \times \frac{12}{12} + \frac{3}{20} \times \frac{3}{3} + \frac{1}{10} \times \frac{6}{6} + \frac{1}{3} \times \frac{20}{20} + S = 1$$

$$\frac{12}{60} + \frac{9}{60} + \frac{6}{60} + \frac{20}{60} + S = 1$$

$$\frac{12+9+6+20}{60} + S = 1$$

$$\frac{47}{60} + S = 1$$

$$S = 1 - \frac{47}{60}$$

$$S = \frac{60}{60} - \frac{47}{60}$$

$$S = \frac{13}{60}$$

17. E

Intermediate Algebra: Exponents and Roots   *Medium*

The only real numbers that satisfy $x^2 = 81$ are −9 and 9. The only real numbers that satisfy $y^2 = 49$ are −7 and 7. Therefore, the possible numerals for $x + y$ are −9 + −7, −9 + 7, 9 + −7, and 9 +7. The answer possibilities are −16, −2, 2, and 16. The one answer choice left is 130.

18. **J**

Algebra: Inequalities   *Medium*

Solve the inequality for a:

$$a \geq 13 + 2a$$
$$a - 2a \geq 13$$
$$-a \geq 13$$
$$\frac{-a}{-1} \geq \frac{13}{-1}$$
$$a \leq -13$$

The inequality sign must always be reversed when multiplying or dividing an inequality by a negative number. **G** is incorrect because that answer represents the result when the inequality sign is not reversed.

19. **E**

Algebra: Solving Linear Equations   *Medium*

Solve the equation for x:

$$\frac{1}{x+5} + 4 = 12$$

Subtract 4 from both sides of the equation:

$$\frac{1}{x+5} = 8$$

Multiply both sides by $x + 5$:

$$(x+5)\frac{1}{x+5} = 8(x+5)$$
$$1 = 8x + 40$$

Subtract 40 from both sides:

$$-39 = 8x$$

Divide both sides by 8:

$$-\frac{39}{8} = x$$

20. **G**

Pre-Algebra: Mean, Median & Mode   *Medium*

For any set of numbers, the median is the number that lies exactly in the middle when the terms are arranged in numerical order. Place the terms from set T in numerical order:

$$T: \{2, 19, 19, 27, 33, 46, 60, 81\}$$

Set T contains 8 terms, so there is no middle number. In such a case, the median is the number that falls exactly between the two middle terms. So, the median equals $\frac{27+33}{2}$, or 30.

F is incorrect, because 19 represents the *mode*, or the term that occurs most frequently in a set of numbers. **H** is incorrect, because 35.875 represents the *average*, or arithmetic mean, of the 8 numbers. **K** is incorrect, because 79 represents the *range*, or the difference between the highest and lowest value in a set of numbers.

21. B

Plane Geometry: Triangles   *Medium*

Diagonal $\overline{AC}$ represents the hypotenuse of a right triangle with legs of 60 feet and 144 feet. Note that this is a special right triangle: a Pythagorean triple with sides in a ratio of 5:12:13. If you divide the lengths of both legs by 12, the legs are in a ratio of 5 feet to 12 feet. Therefore, diagonal $\overline{AC}$ will measure 13 × 12, or 156 feet.

You could also use the Pythagorean theorem to solve this problem. Substitute in the values you know for a, b, and c in the formula:

$$a^2 + b^2 = c^2$$
$$(60)^2 + (144)^2 = c^2$$
$$3,600 + 20,736 = c^2$$
$$24,336 = c^2$$
$$c = \sqrt{24,336}$$
$$c = 156$$

22. H

Plane Geometry: Circles   *Medium*

First, determine the circumference of the wheel. Substitute the value of the radius (10 cm) into the equation for the circumference of a circle:

$$C = 2\pi r$$
$$= 2\pi(10)$$
$$= 20\pi$$
$$\approx 20(3.14)$$
$$\approx 62.8$$

The circumference of the wheel is approximately 62.8 centimeters. Divide the circumference into the total distance traveled: 200 ÷ 62.8 ≈ 3.18. The wheel makes approximately 3.18 revolutions when traveling a distance of 200 centimeters. Thus, it makes a maximum of 3 complete revolutions.

23. D

Plane Geometry: Triangles   *Medium*

This triangle has a perimeter of 78 inches. A triangle's perimeter is calculated by adding the three sides together. We have been given the length of one side. Because that side measures 15 inches, the remaining two sides must be 78 − 15, or 63 inches. The 3:4 ratio tells us there are 3 parts for the first side and 4 parts for the second side, resulting in a total of 7 parts. Divide 63 by 7, and we find that each part is 9 inches long. Therefore, the side with 3 parts is 27 inches long, and the side with 4 parts is 36 inches long. The longest side of the triangle is 36 inches.

24. F

Algebra: Writing Expressions and Equations   *Medium*

In the equation $g = 12s + 7$, the number 12 represents the number of minutes Mr. Oliveri spends grading each paper. **G** is incorrect because it suggests that Mr. Oliveri spends 7 minutes alphabetizing student papers before grading *each* paper.

25. D

Algebra: Multiplying Binomials   *Medium*

Factor the expression using reverse FOIL. Look for the first, outer, inner, and last terms:

$$4x^2 + 2x - 30 = (2x + ?)(2x - ?)$$
$$= (2x + 6)(2x - 5)$$

B is incorrect, because it represents the factored form of $4x^2 - 2x - 30$.

26. J

Plane Geometry: Polygons   *Medium*

To find the area of a square, first find the length of its side. The question states that the square is circumscribed around the circle. The side length of the square is exactly twice as long as the radius of the circle, or $2(11) = 22$ feet. Square the side length to get the area of the square. The area is 484 square feet.

   F is incorrect because it represents the perimeter of the square $(11+11+11+11)$. **H** is incorrect because it represents the area of the circle, πr^2, where r is 11.

27. C

Pre-Algebra: Percentages, Fractions & Decimals   *Medium*

First, translate the pictures to numbers. Each pair of musical notes is equivalent to 4,000 CDs, so each single musical note is equal to 2,000 CDs. Rewrite the chart as follows:

City	CDs available
Atlanta	20,000
Chicago	14,000
Dallas	12,000
New York	10,000
Washington, D.C.	8,000

The fraction of CDs sold at the Chicago Music Fair is $\dfrac{14,000}{64,000} = \dfrac{14}{64} = \dfrac{7}{32}$.

28. J

Algebra: Solving Linear Equations   *Medium*

Solve the equation for r:

$$j = 24 - 2r$$
$$2r = 24 - j$$
$$r = \frac{24 - j}{2}$$
$$r = \frac{24}{2} - \frac{j}{2}$$
$$r = 12 - \frac{j}{2}$$

29. D

Plane Geometry: Three Dimensions   *Medium*

Calculate the surface area using the formula for the surface area of a rectangular solid:

$$\begin{aligned}
SA &= 2(l \times w) + 2(w \times h) + 2(l \times h) \\
&= 2(7 \times 6) + 2(6 \times 12) + 2(7 \times 12) \\
&= 2(42) + 2(72) + 2(84) \\
&= 84 + 144 + 168 \\
&= 396
\end{aligned}$$

The surface area of the solid is 396 in^2.

30. G

Pre-Algebra: Percentages, Fractions & Decimals   *Medium*

First calculate the volume of the entire original solid: $12 \times 6 \times 7 = 504$ in^3. Next, determine the volume of the cut-out portion of the solid: $4 \times 3 \times 2 = 24$ in^3. The question asks what percentage of the original volume (504 in^3) is represented by the cut-out volume (24 in^3). Let p equal the missing percentage. Set up an equation and solve for p:

$$\begin{aligned}
24 &= \frac{p}{100} \times 504 \\
24 \times 100 &= p \times 504 \\
2400 &= 504p \\
p &= \frac{2400}{504} \\
&\approx 4.76
\end{aligned}$$

31. E

Pre-Algebra: Percentages, Fractions & Decimals   *Medium*

To solve this problem, you could perform the multiplication on your calculator and then compare the result with each of the answer choices. You can also break this long multiplication problem down by canceling out and reducing. Starting from left to right, cancel out all of the numbers that are the same in the numerator and denominator. Also reduce any numerators or denominators that you can:

$$\frac{1}{4} \times \frac{2}{5} \times \frac{5}{7} \times \frac{8}{9} \times \frac{2}{3} \times \frac{1}{6} \times \frac{4}{8} \times \frac{3}{10} = \frac{1}{\cancel{42}} \times \frac{\cancel{2}}{\cancel{5}} \times \frac{\cancel{5}}{7} \times \frac{8}{9} \times \frac{\cancel{2}}{3} \times \frac{1}{\cancel{63}} \times \frac{\cancel{42}}{\cancel{84}} \times \frac{3}{10}$$

Rewrite the equation so you can see what numbers you have left. Keep canceling and reducing:

$$\begin{aligned}
&= \frac{8 \times 2 \times 3}{2 \times 7 \times 9 \times 3 \times 3 \times 4 \times 10} \\
&= \frac{2\cancel{8} \times \cancel{2} \times \cancel{3}}{\cancel{2} \times 7 \times 9 \times \cancel{3} \times 3 \times \cancel{4} \times 10} \\
&= \frac{2}{7 \times 9 \times 3 \times 10} \\
&= \frac{1}{7 \times 9 \times 3 \times 5} \\
&= \frac{1}{945}
\end{aligned}$$

32. **J**

Coordinate Geometry: Slope   *Medium*

Use the formula for finding slope and plug in x- and y-values from each pair of points:

$$m = \frac{y_2 - y_1}{x_2 - x_1}$$
$$= \frac{-3 - (-5)}{0 - 4}$$
$$= -\frac{2}{4}$$
$$= -\frac{1}{2}$$

33. **D**

Plane Geometry: Polygons   *Medium*

To find the area of a parallelogram, multiply base times height. The base of parallelogram $WXYZ$, $\overline{WZ}$, is 3 + 8, or 11 centimeters long. Its height is 6 centimeters. Therefore, the area is:

$$A = bh$$
$$= 11 \times 6$$
$$= 66$$

E is incorrect, because it represents the two side lengths multiplied together.

34. **H**

Pre-Algebra: Number Problems   *Medium*

First, find the time that it would take Desmond to drive 320 kilometers at a rate of 40 kilometers per hour:

$$\frac{320}{40} = 8$$

If Desmond reduces his total driving time by 3 hours, he will complete the trip in 5 hours. Find the rate at which Desmond must drive to reach the castle in 5 hours:

$$\frac{320}{5} = 64$$

He must drive 64 kilometers per hour to reach the castle in 5 hours. The question asks how much faster Desmond must drive than his original 40 kilometers per hour:

$$64 - 40 = 24$$

35. **B**

Algebra: Inequalities   *Medium*

Solve the inequality for y:

$$6(y - 1) < 2(2y + 2)$$
$$6y - 6 < 4y + 4$$
$$6y - 4y < 4 + 6$$
$$2y < 10$$
$$y < 5$$

36. F

Plane Geometry: Circles   *Medium*

The entire cake measures 360°. If the cake is cut into 10 equal slices, each slice would measure $\frac{360}{10}$, or 36°.

37. B

Pre-Algebra: Probability   *Medium*

For the probability of picking a black pen to be $\frac{4}{7}$, the total number of pens in the drawer must be divisible by 7. Remember that we are looking for the minimum number of additional black pens needed, so we want to find the lowest multiple of 7 possible. You may find it helpful to set up a proportion, such as $\frac{4}{7} = \frac{x}{28}$. Multiply x by 4 to get 16. There are already 6 black pens in the drawer, so the minimum number of black pens that must be added to the drawer is 10.

38. H

Plane Geometry: Angles and Lines   *Medium*

When two parallel lines are crossed by a transversal, corresponding angles and opposite interior angles are equal. Vertical angles are also always congruent. Thus, the following angles are all congruent to $\angle c$: vertical angle a and opposite interior angle g. **J** is incorrect, because $\angle b$ is supplementary to $\angle c$ but not necessarily equal.

39. C

Intermediate Algebra: Exponents and Roots   *Medium*

The maximum amount of sodium chloride that can be present in the water is 1.3×10^{-4} milligrams per gallon. We can write this as 0.00013 milligrams per gallon. The chemist just measured the water's salinity level and found that it was 1,000 times greater than the acceptable level, or $(0.00013) \times 1,000 = 0.13$. This can also be written as 1.3×10^{-1}.

40. G

Pre-Algebra: Multiples, Factors &Primes   *Medium*

The greatest common factor of a^3b^2 and a^4b^3 is 72. So, we're looking for two numbers, a and b, that when multiplied together as a^3b^2 have a factor of 72. The numbers also have a factor of 72 when multiplied as a^4b^3. And, 72 is the greatest common factor of these two combinations.

The question only gives algebraic expressions, so start by working with these expressions. First, determine the greatest common factor of a^3b^2 and a^4b^3. In algebraic terms, the greatest common factor of a^3b^2 and a^4b^3 is a^3b^2. The question tells us that the greatest common factor of both expressions is 72, so this means that $a^3b^2 = 72$. Look for numbers that can be substituted into this equation. We know that $72 = 8 \times 9$, which can be written as $23 \times 32 = 72$. So, it's possible that b could equal 3. None of the other numbers works for b when placed into the equation $a^3b^2 = 72$.

41. **D**

Pre-Algebra: Number Problems   *Medium*

First, multiply to find the number of seconds in an hour. There are 60 seconds in a minute and 60 minutes in an hour, so there are 3,600 seconds in an hour. The problem asks how far a sound wave travels in 3 hours, so multiply $3,600 \times 3 = 10,800$. Multiply 10,800 by 1,130. The result is 12,204,000, or approximately 1.22×10^7.

    C is incorrect because it represents the calculation performed using minutes per hour rather than seconds per hour.

42. **H**

Trigonometry: Solving Triangles   *Medium*

Find the adjacent side using the cosine formula:

$$\cos F = \frac{\text{adjacent}}{\text{hypotenuse}}$$
$$\frac{2}{5} = \frac{\text{adjacent}}{22}$$
$$5(\text{adjacent}) = 44$$
$$\text{adjacent} = \frac{44}{5}$$

43. **B**

Coordinate Geometry: Parallel and Perpendicular   *Medium*

A parallel line must have the same slope as the given line. The given line is in the form $y = mx + b$, so its slope, m, is 10. This narrows down the possible choices to **B** and **C**.

    Plug the coordinate (6, 9) into the equations to see which one works. Start with **B**:

$$y = 10x - 51$$
$$(9) = 10(6) - 51$$
$$9 = 9$$

This equation holds true, so **B** is correct.

44. **F**

Pre-Algebra: Percentages, Fractions & Decimals   *Medium*

Let x represent the missing number. Set up an equation and solve for x:

$$\frac{130}{100}x = 520$$
$$1.3x = 520$$
$$x = \frac{520}{1.3}$$
$$= 400$$

The missing number, x, is 400. Next, calculate 80% of 400: $.80 \times (400) = 320$.

    J is incorrect, because it represents 80% of 520. **K** is incorrect, because it reflects 520 multiplied by 130%.

45. B

Coordinate Geometry: Transformations   *Medium*

Point B lies at coordinates (6, 1). When $\overline{AB}$ is reflected across the x-axis, the x-coordinate remains the same. Only the y-coordinate changes, as shown in the figure below:

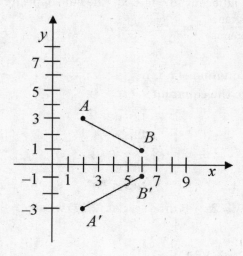

The coordinates for point B' are (6, –1).

    D is incorrect, because these are the coordinates for point A'.

46. G

Intermediate Algebra: Matrices   *Medium*

Multiply:

$$\begin{bmatrix} -3 \\ 4 \\ 6 \end{bmatrix} [2 \ -3 \ -4] = \begin{bmatrix} (-3)(2) & (-3)(-3) & (-3)(-4) \\ (4)(2) & (4)(-3) & (4)(-4) \\ (6)(2) & (6)(-3) & (6)(-4) \end{bmatrix}$$

$$= \begin{bmatrix} -6 & 9 & 12 \\ 8 & -12 & -16 \\ 12 & -18 & -24 \end{bmatrix}$$

47. A

Coordinate Geometry: Distance and Midpoints   *Medium*

Use the distance formula:

$$d = \sqrt{(x_2 - x_1)^2 + (y_2 - y_1)^2}$$

Label the coordinates as x_1, x_2, y_1, and y_2, then substitute their values into the distance formula:

$$= \sqrt{(5-4)^2 + (12-6)^2}$$
$$= \sqrt{(1)^2 + (6)^2}$$
$$= \sqrt{37}$$

48. J

Trigonometry: SOHCAHTOA *Medium*

Draw a vertical line from $(6\sqrt{3}, 6)$ to the x-axis to create a right triangle. Doing so, we can see that the side adjacent to θ is $6\sqrt{3}$, the side opposite θ is 6, and the hypotenuse is 12. $\text{Cos}\theta = \dfrac{\text{adjacent}}{\text{hypotenuse}}$, or $\dfrac{6\sqrt{3}}{12} = \dfrac{\sqrt{3}}{2}$.

49. C

Coordinate Geometry: Equation of a Line *Medium*

Plug the point $(2,12)$ into the equation $y = tx - 4$:

$$12 = t(2) - 4$$
$$12 = 2t - 4$$
$$12 + 4 = 2t$$
$$16 = 2t$$
$$8 = t$$

The lines $y = tx - 4$ and $y = 3x + 6$ intersect at $(2,12)$ when $t = 8$.

50. G

Coordinate Geometry: Conic Sections *Medium*

If the circle is tangent to the x-axis at 10 and tangent to the y-axis at 10, then we know that the radius is 10 and the center is (h, k) is $(10, 10)$. Plug this information into the equation of a circle:

$$(x - h)^2 + (y - k)^2 = r^2$$
$$(x - 10)^2 + (y - 10)^2 = 100$$

51. B

Trigonometry: Trigonometric Identities *Medium*

According to the definition of $\sec\theta$:

$$\text{Sec }\theta = \frac{\text{hypotenuse}}{\text{adjacent}}$$

The definition of $\cos\theta$ states:

$$\text{Cos }\theta = \frac{\text{adjacent}}{\text{hypotenuse}}$$

The functions sec and cos are reciprocals of one another. Thus, $\sec\theta$ also equals $\dfrac{1}{\cos\theta}$.

52. J

Coordinate Geometry: Number Lines and Inequalities *Medium*

The number line shows x is less than -6 or greater than or equal to 4.

53. B

Intermediate Algebra: Functions   *Medium*

The value of $x = -5$ meets the criteria for the second definition, $x < 2$.
Substitute -5 for x in the equation, $S(x) = x^4 - 6$:

$$S(x) = x^4 - 6$$
$$= (-5^4 - 6)$$
$$= 625 - 6$$
$$= 619$$

54. G

Coordinate Geometry: Conic Sections   *Medium*

The parabolas open downward, so **H**, **J**, and **K** can be eliminated. Also note that **K** indicates a shift upward of 2 units. The family of equations is shifted downward 2 units. Also, the stretching of the parabola indicates a multiplication by $-n$, not $-\frac{1}{2}n$. **G** is correct.

55. D

Intermediate Algebra: Functions   *Difficult*

The question tells us that the function $f(a)$ equals $3 - a^2$. The function $f(a + r)$ therefore equals $3 - (a + r)^2$. Using the order of operations, calculate the value of this expression.

$$3 - (a + r)^2 = 3 - (a + r)(a + r)$$
$$= 3 - (a^2 + ar + ar + r^2)$$
$$= 3 - (a^2 + 2ar + r^2)$$
$$= 3 - a - 2ar - r^2$$

56. K

Coordinate Geometry: Number Lines and Inequalities   *Difficult*
Solve the inequality:

$$|x| - 4 < 6$$
$$|x| < 6 + 4$$
$$|x| < 10$$

Look for the graph that shows an absolute distance from 0 of less than 10 units. **K** is the correct answer.

57. E

Plane Geometry: Circles   *Difficult*
Use the arc length formula:

$$\left(\frac{n}{360°}\right)(2\pi r) = \left(\frac{90}{360}\right)(2\pi 10)$$
$$= (0.25)(20\pi)$$
$$= 5\pi$$

58. K

Trigonometry: SOHCAHTOA   *Difficult*

Find sin θ:

$$\sin^2\theta + \cos^2\theta = 1$$

$$\sin^2\theta + \left(-\frac{4}{6}\right)^2 = 1$$

$$\sin^2\theta = 1 - \left(-\frac{4}{6}\right)^2$$

$$\sin^2\theta = \frac{20}{36}$$

$$\sin\theta = \frac{\sqrt{5}}{3}$$

Sin θ = $\frac{\sqrt{5}}{3}$, since sin θ < 0. Next, find tan θ:

$$\tan\theta = \frac{\sin\theta}{\cos\theta}$$

$$= -\frac{\frac{\sqrt{5}}{3}}{\frac{4}{6}}$$

$$= \frac{\sqrt{5}}{2}$$

59. **B**

Intermediate Algebra: Quadratic Equations   *Difficult*

Set both quadratic equations equal to 0:

$$y + 2c = 0 \text{ and } y - 8d = 0$$

Multiply the binomials and set equal to 0:

$$(y + 2c)(y - 8d) = 0$$

$$y^2 - 8dy + 2cy - 16cd = 0$$

$$y^2 - y(8d - 2c) - 16cd = 0$$

60. **H**

Intermediate Algebra: Logarithms   *Difficult*

The properties of logarithms tell us that $\log_d (mn)^3$ can be written as follows:

$$\log_d(mn)^3 = 3\log_d(mn)$$

$$= 3(\log_d m + \log_d n)$$

Substitute in p for $\log_d m$ and q for $\log_d n$:

$$3(\log_d m + \log_d n) = 3(p + q)$$

READING

1. C

Prose Fiction: Specific Detail   *Easy*

In the fourth paragraph, the narrator describes Miss Brill seeing the same people *Sunday after Sunday*, and in paragraph 6, the author writes that Miss Brill *came every Sunday*. **A** is tempting but wrong. When Miss Brill pulls out her fur in the first paragraph, she has not used it in some time, which is why she brushed its fur. **B** and **D** are incorrect because neither idea is suggested in the story.

2. F

Prose Fiction: Inference   *Medium*

Miss Brill wears her fur because the air is chilly, so **J** is incorrect. **G** is wrong because only the young couple at the end of the story is appalled by the fur; Miss Brill is proud of her fur at the beginning of the passage. Some readers may incorrectly choose **H** if they assume Miss Brill's eyes *snap* when she puts on her fur. However, the fur jacket has the animal's head intact, so it is the eyes of the animal that Miss Brill interprets as snapping to life. Miss Brill believes the fur is so glad to be out of the box that it is mischievously biting and snapping; she even refers to it as *Little rogue*.

3. A

Prose Fiction: Character   *Medium*

Throughout the entire passage, Miss Brill never speaks, yet she regularly attends the concert to watch everyone else. **B** is tempting because Miss Brill's emotions change after the comment by the young couple, but Miss Brill is never sociable with other people. **C** and **D** are wrong because Miss Brill does not share feelings or criticisms with anyone else. The best answer is **A**.

4. H

Prose Fiction: Inference   *Medium*

Miss Brill thinks the people on the bench are *funny* and *odd* because they are so different from the other people at the park who walk around and visit with their friends. **J** is tempting because Miss Brill is exactly like the *other people* since she silently sits on the same bench week after week. The author does not indicate that Miss Brill envies the people, so **F** is wrong. **G** is incorrect because Miss Brill never converses with anyone at the concert.

5. A

Prose Fiction: Cause-Effect   *Medium*

Miss Brill watches *a little brown dog* trot by *like a little "theatre" dog*, and she decides that she must be part of a large play. Miss Brill does not talk to her students about her Sunday outings, so **C** is incorrect. Miss Brill notices *a funny old man with long whiskers* and the blue in the sky right before the dog walks in front of her, which means **B** and **D** are incorrect.

6. G

Prose Fiction: Purpose   *Difficult*

The last paragraph is when a change occurs in Miss Brill, so **G** is correct. Until Miss Brill overhears the conversation of the young couple, she does not view herself as old and strange like the other people sitting on benches. In the final paragraph, she no longer acts as she usually does. At that point, Miss Brill begins to compare her own room to a *cupboard*—like the ones that she imagines belong to the *odd, silent, nearly all old* people in the park.

7. C

Prose Fiction: Specific Detail   *Medium*

The last paragraph describes Miss Brill's activities after she hears the young couple's comments about her. Miss Brill passes the bakery, enters her *little dark room*, and puts the fur in the box. **C** is the correct answer because Miss Brill *quickly* places the fur in the box, and only after closing it does she hear a cry. The author suggests that the fur is crying, although readers might misinterpret the text and think Miss Brill is crying.

8. H

Prose Fiction: Main Idea, Argument & Theme   *Easy*

H is correct because the last sentence of paragraph 3 describes how Miss Brill eavesdrops on the conversations of other people *while they talked around her*. **F** is tempting because Miss Brill indicates she *had become an expert, she thought, at listening*, but no one talks with Miss Brill throughout the entire passage. Although Miss Brill is disappointed the old couple does not speak, **G** is incorrect because she merely wanted to eavesdrop. **J** is wrong because the author does not suggest Miss Brill and the old couple know each other, although they are both sitting on Miss Brill's *special* seat.

9. D

Prose Fiction: Inference   *Medium*

In paragraph 6, Miss Brill thinks to herself that *somebody would have noticed if she hadn't been there*, but in reality, no one would notice. Miss Brill is exactly like the people on the benches, as indicated in the tenth paragraph by the young couple who refer to Miss Brill as a *stupid old thing*. The author provides no indication that Miss Brill has a relationship with anyone, so the best answer is **D**.

10. F

Prose Fiction: Specific Detail   *Easy*

Paragraph 6 indicates that Miss Brill *nearly* laughs aloud at her revelation, so **H** is incorrect. The author writes in the eighth paragraph that Miss Brill sings *silently*, so **G** is incorrect. paragraph 7 states that *Miss Brill's eyes filled with tears, and she looked smiling at all the other members of the company*. Miss Brill feels like she belongs to a group, which makes her happy, so the best answer is **F**.

11. D

Social Science: Main Idea, Argument & Theme   *Easy*

B and **C** are true statements, but they are specific details mentioned in the passage rather than main points. **A** is tempting especially after reading the concluding paragraph, but designating shotgun houses as *historic landmarks* is a minor detail rather than a main point of the passage. **D** is the best choice because the *useful purposes* of shotgun homes are a key theme addressed throughout the entire passage.

12. G

Social Science: Cause-Effect

Medium

The first sentence of the third paragraph states that *scarcity of land in New Orleans* led to homes that required minimal property. Although *high ceilings* and *easy commutes* were benefits of many shotgun houses, such features were not limited to one style of home. **F** is incorrect because the author does not indicate that large homes were *prohibited* in New Orleans.

13. B

Social Science: Vocabulary in Context

Medium

Although shotgun houses suffered from a decline in interest, *embracing the structures* suggests that *revival* has a meaning opposite of *descent*. The *motivation* of people interested in shotgun homes is leading the *revival*, so **D** is incorrect. The second sentence of paragraph 8 discusses cities that are creating *shotgun historic districts* in order to save and restore the homes. The house style is not being *duplicated* but being *rescued*, so *recovery* is the best answer.

14. F

Social Science: Purpose

Difficult

Automobiles and air-conditioning are discussed in the seventh paragraph to explain why shotgun houses were no longer popular during the 1950s. Although **J** is tempting because the shotgun house was a prewar style of home, the purpose of the seventh paragraph is not to show the difference between the two periods but to illustrate how the shotgun house was affected by modernization.

15. C

Social Science: Specific Detail

Easy

Remember, the correct answer is the one NOT addressed in the passage. The best answer is **C** because the author does not mention the use of shotgun houses for developing neighborhoods. The passages states the *alignment of doors combined with the length of the house created excellent airflow*, so **B** is incorrect. **D** is wrong because the author writes that shotgun homes made *excellent rental investments*. **A** is incorrect because *New Orleans and other cities determined property taxes based on the width of a lot, so shotgun houses were an affordable option for working-class families.*

16. F

Social Science: Inference

Medium

The best answer is **F** because the unique qualities and historic value of shotgun homes are emphasized throughout the passage. Although paragraph 7 mentions neglected shotgun houses, *inner-city housing problems* are not discussed. **H** and **J** are wrong because the author does not discuss controlling *urban development* or invigorating property values through the *construction of shotgun houses*.

17. C

Social Science: Comparison

Medium

Paragraph 3 states that shotgun houses had front windows but no porches. Although *chimneys were constructed in the interior of the home*, as stated in paragraph 6, only one fireplace warmed multiple rooms. Camelback shotgun houses *included a partial second floor over the back part of the house*, so the correct answer is **C**.

18. G

Social Science: Specific Detail .... *Medium*

According to the second paragraph, historians believe that shotgun houses are based on Haitian *to-guns* since the construction of the houses *coincides* with Haitian slaves arriving in New Orleans and building homes. **F** is mentioned in the second paragraph as well, but it is not evidence supporting the *to-gun* theory. **H** and **J** are tricky because only one term can be traced to Haiti. While *to-gun* translates to *place of assembly*, the author does not state that the term *camelback shotgun house* stems from Haiti.

19. A

Social Science: Inference .... *Difficult*

The author does not discuss *first-time home buyers* or the involvement of *city governments*, so **B** and **C** are incorrect. **D** is wrong because the third paragraph refers to the *scarcity of land* in New Orleans as the reason for the shotgun home's popularity. Paragraphs 4 and 5 discuss shotgun homes as rental investments and the development of manufacturing centers in cities. The inference can be made that people living in rural areas were moving to the city for jobs, so **A** is correct.

20. J

Social Science: Specific Detail .... *Easy*

In the fourth paragraph, the author writes that shotgun houses were popular in *humid Southern towns* because the design maximized *airflow*. Although workers were moving in large numbers to cities across the country after the Civil War, only cities with warm weather climates saw the construction of shotgun houses. The best answer is **J**.

21. D

Humanities: Main Idea and Argument .... *Medium*

Throughout the passage, the author discusses the problems related to restoring works of art and how restoration can damage masterpieces, so **D** is the best answer. **A** and **C** are details from the passage rather than key arguments. **B** is too extreme because the author does not indicate that art should never be cleaned, only *that restoration should be avoided until it is clearly necessary*.

22. F

Humanities: Specific Detail .... *Easy*

H and **J** are wrong because *hydrochloric acid and steel brushes* were used *in 1843*, which is not the most recent cleaning *David* has received. The author writes in the sixth paragraph about the controversy surrounding *a dry cleaning or a wet bath*. The statement *it was finally determined that David would be cleaned with compresses of distilled water* indicates that dry cloths were not used, so the best answer is **F**.

23. B

Humanities: Inference .... *Medium*

The first sentence of the sixth paragraph indicates that restorers no longer use *harsh chemicals* but that cleaning techniques are still *debatable*. Since art restorers cannot agree on the best method, it can be inferred that there is a lack of substantial evidence that one technique is better or worse than another. **A** relates to information found in the seventh paragraph. According to paragraph 2, cleaning methods are permanent, so **C** is incorrect. **D** is the opinion of some restorers, as mentioned in the sixth paragraph, but others argue that wet cleanings are better. The best answer is **B**.

24. G

Humanities: Inference   *Medium*

The information about *The Last Supper* project indicates that the results were *both disappointing and shocking*, so **F** and **H** are incorrect. **J** is wrong because *Beck asserted that the restoration project ignored the statue's main problem—instability due to cracks in David's ankles*. The statement *restoration merely serves as a way for museums to gain publicity and increase tourism* suggests that the author would most likely agree with **G**.

25. C

Humanities: Specific Detail   *Easy*

The author makes no mention of moving the *wall on which the mural was attached*, so **A** is incorrect. The restorer added watercolors, not oil paint, to heavily damaged areas, which changed the tones and colors according to disappointed art specialists, so **B** and **D** are wrong. The restoration involved scraping away *overpainting*, so **C** is correct.

26. G

Humanities: Specific Detail   *Easy*

According to the third paragraph, da Vinci painted *The Last Supper* in the late fifteenth century, or the 1400s. According to the passage, *by 1556 many of the figures of Jesus' apostles were difficult to recognize*, which means **G** is the correct answer. Although attempts were made in the eighteenth and twentieth centuries to restore the mural, signs of disrepair appeared much sooner, so **H** and **J** are wrong.

27. A

Humanities: Purpose   *Medium*

In the second paragraph, the author describes the *goal of art restoration*. The second paragraph also covers the idea that art restoration is *subjective*, which may cause *alarm* and controversy. The author does not express an opinion in the second paragraph about *the need for consensus on restoration projects* or *the necessity for restoring masterpieces*, so **C** and **D** are incorrect. Later in the passage the author suggests that art restoration may be *damaging*, but since this does not occur in the second paragraph, **B** is wrong.

28. J

Humanities: Vocabulary in Context   *Medium*

The last two sentences of the fifth paragraph describe how *David* was harshly cleaned by a *strong combination* of acid and steel brushes that *destroyed the protective finish*. As a result, the statue was *exposed* to additional harm or *deterioration*, so **J** is correct. **F** and **G** are positively charged words, so they are clearly incorrect. Although *affliction* ("misery") has a negative meaning, the word would be used to describe human suffering, not damage done to an inanimate object.

29. C

Humanities: Inference   *Difficult*

The majority of the damage to *David* stems from the fact that it was left outside in the elements for over three hundred years. If *David* had been safely stored indoors, neither rioters nor weather would have damaged the statue, and Michelangelo's protective finish would have remained intact. The anniversary cleaning and the hammer strike had minimal effect on the statue, so **C** is the answer.

30. J

Humanities: Specific Detail   *Medium*

J is the best answer. The author discusses the opinion of James Beck in the eighth paragraph, when he states that *restoration merely serves as a way for museums to gain publicity and increase tourism.* Beck was a critic of unnecessary art restoration, so he would not likely agree with **F**. The author does not address the *interests of the art restoration industry* or the *concerns of art museums*, so **G** and **H** are incorrect.

31. C

Natural Science: Specific Detail   *Easy*

The author states in the third paragraph that *it takes surface water 500 years to travel 7,000 feet below the surface.* Although the passage mentions that some geysers have been erupting for over five thousand years, the question asks about the origination of the water runoff, so **C** is correct.

32. J

Natural Science: Inference   *Medium*

The seventh paragraph details correlations between earthquakes and geysers and notes that *the average water temperature of the park's springs and geysers rose 2°C* as a result of an earthquake. It can be inferred that temperatures in the earth's core rose enough to cause the earthquake and increase geyser eruptions. The other options are distractors that are not mentioned in the text.

33. A

Natural Science: Cause-Effect   *Medium*

The best answer is **A**. The last sentence of the sixth paragraph states that Porkchop *appears to be attempting to seal itself once again.* According to the fourth paragraph, geyserite *creates a pressure-tight channel by cementing rocks and loose soil together, thus eliminating any water leaks.* **B** and **D** are incorrect because rhyolite is found beneath the surface, not near the top.

34. J

Natural Science: Specific Detail   *Easy*

The introductory paragraph explains that Old Faithful earned its name by being *predictable*, so **J** is correct. The oldest geyser is Castle, so **H** is wrong. Steamboat has eruptions that are both long lasting and tall, which eliminates **F** and **G**.

35. D

Natural Science: Comparison   *Medium*

Only geysers have constrictions near the top, so **A** is incorrect. Natural springs do not release steam, which makes **B** wrong. The text does not address rhyolite rocks in relation to hot springs, so **C** is incorrect. The best answer is **D** because *all natural springs have channels underneath them that enable water to flow towards the surface.*

36. G

Natural Science: Specific Detail   *Easy*

The last sentence of the fifth paragraph states that after an eruption, *the cycle of filling, heating, and releasing begins all over again.* The filling stage of the cycle begins with surface water trickling down below, so **G** is correct. **H** and **J** are part of the heating stage. **F** is an untrue statement because *rhyolite rocks dissolve in hot water and produce geyserite, which is then deposited along the inside of the geyser's plumbing system.*

37. C

Natural Science: Inference   *Medium*

No textual evidence suggests that geysers are rare due to the *instability of the earth*, so **A** is wrong. *Correlations have been recorded between earthquakes and geyser activity* but they are not used to predict earthquakes. Earthquakes affect the underground activity of geysers. Although geologists may worry that humans will *damage* geysers, the author does not discuss that concern in the passage, so **D** is wrong. **C** is the best answer because *Yellowstone is home to more than half of the earth's estimated 1,000 geysers*, which makes the park a popular tourist destination.

38. F

Natural Science: Purpose   *Difficult*

The first five paragraphs describe how geysers work, while paragraphs 6–8 describe how earthquakes and geothermal activities affect geyser eruptions. The death of the *earth's geysers* is not addressed by the text, so **H** is wrong. Although correlations have been made between geyser activity and seismic activity, the author does not argue that *excessive geyser activity indicates a likelihood of stronger and more frequent earthquakes.* Several Yellowstone geysers are discussed in the latter part of the passage to illustrate the correlation between earthquakes and geysers. This discussion is not intended as an historical overview, so **G** is wrong.

39. C

Natural Science: Vocabulary in Context   *Medium*

The passage mentions *all the park's geysers, even dormant ones* to suggest that dormant geysers have a different level of activity than other geysers. **C** is the best answer. **D** is wrong because geysers cannot be *shallow* since their water supply is heated by volcanic rock deep inside the earth. Choices **A** and **B** are incorrect because geysers would not be described as *insignificant* or *emergent*.

40. F

Natural Science: Specific Detail   *Medium*

The best answer is **F**. Information in the fourth paragraph explains that *geyserite creates a pressure-tight channel* and that it is deposited *near the geyser's surface*. Geyserite comes from melted rhyolite, so **H** is incorrect. **J** is never suggested in the text. **G** is tempting because the geyserite *creates a pressure-tight channel by cementing rocks and loose soil together*, but this is done to eliminate water leaks, not to hinder water flow.

SCIENCE

1. A

Data Representation: Read the Chart   *Easy*

Table 1 shows that the difference in mercury (Hg) levels increases from Trial 1 to Trial 6. Table 2 shows that from Trial 1 to Trial 6, the volume of gas decreases. **A** is correct.

2. G

Data Representation: Read the Chart   *Easy*

The pressure × volume (PV) calculations can be ranked in the following order: 14,853,458 (Trial 3), 14,872,627 (Trial 1), 14,891,482 (Trial 4), 14,965,024 (Trial 5), 15,020,184 (Trial 2), and 15,289,837 (Trial 6). **G** reflects the correct ordering of the trials.

3. C

Data Representation: Use the Chart   *Medium*

This question requires you to use the information in the table to infer the difference in Hg levels. In Table 1, the gas column heights are presented in descending order. So, a gas column height of 152 mm would fall between the readings for Trial 3 (164.672) and Trial 4 (145.567). The difference in Hg levels for Trial 3 is 388 mm, while the difference in Hg levels for Trial 4 is 542 mm. The correct answer will lie between these two numbers, so **C** is correct.

A and **B** are incorrect because those numbers are too small, and **D** is incorrect because it is too large.

4. G

Data Representation: Handle Graphs   *Medium*

Table 3 shows that as the gas pressure increases, the pressure × volume (PV) calculation stays roughly the same, hovering near the 15,000,000 mark. **G** presents the graph that best reflects this relationship: As gas pressure increases on the *x*-axis, PV remains relatively constant on the *y*-axis. **K** displays the opposite of the correct answer. It indicates that gas pressure remains the same as PV increases, which does not match the values in the table. **F** and **H** are also incorrect, because as gas pressure increases, there is no corresponding large increase or decrease in PV.

5. E

Data Representation: Use the Chart   *Difficult*

Tables 2 and 3 show that for each trial, the gas volume increases and the gas pressure decreases. Table 3 also shows that the pressure × volume (PV) calculations are relatively consistent for all six trials. These calculations lie close to 14,900,000 or 15,000,000. The question states that the PV calculations will not necessarily be exact, so **E** is correct.

A is incorrect, because the pressure × volume calculations do not decrease consistently. **B** and **C** are also incorrect, because they do not match with the data given in Tables 2 and 3.

6. H

Research Summary: Read the Chart   *Easy*

According to the line graphs, the monkeys answered fewer questions correctly as the ratio grew closer to 1, so **H** is the correct choice. **F** is the *opposite* of the correct answer. The information presented makes no mention of the monkeys answering fewer or more questions, so **G** and **J** are incorrect as well.

7. C

Research Summary: Use the Chart   *Easy*

Look at the "Response Time" line graph in Experiment 2. The humans' and monkeys' response times are equal where the two lines intersect, making **C** the correct answer. Humans answered questions with a 0.2 ratio about 0.500 second faster than monkeys, so **A** is not correct. Humans also answered questions with a 0.4 ratio and a 0.8 ratio more quickly than monkeys did, so **B** and **D** are incorrect as well.

8. J

Research Summary: Use the Chart   *Easy*

The correct answer is **J**, because the "Response Time" line graph in Experiment 2 shows that the response times of both humans and monkeys increased as the ratio between numerical values increased. **H** is the *opposite* of the information given in the graph. **F** and **G** are incorrect because both lines have a continuous upward slope.

9. A

Research Summary: Use the Chart   *Medium*

The data presented in Experiment 2 shows that humans have a higher accuracy rate than monkeys (e.g., humans have an 100% accuracy rate answering questions with a 0.2 ratio, while monkeys have an 85% accuracy rate solving the same problems) and that both species answer questions in roughly the same amount of time. **B** is incorrect on both counts. **C** is only half correct (while it's true that monkeys have a lower accuracy rate than humans, they do not answer questions more quickly). **D** is incorrect because humans and monkeys do not have similar accuracy rates.

10. H

Research Summary: Take the Next Step   *Difficult*

This methodology question asks you to think about how researchers designed the experiment. For the data to be useful and valid, the two monkeys would need to possess near-equivalent mental capabilities, so **H** is correct. The addition problems are simple, so **F** is incorrect. **G** is incorrect because the monkeys' age and gender are not relevant to the study. **J** describes a possible outcome of the experiment, not an element of the experiment's design.

11. B

Research Summary: Use the Chart   *Difficult*

This question requires you to synthesize new information based on the data presented in the passage. You need to examine both line graphs in Experiment 2 to answer the question. The "Response Time" line graph shows that monkeys can answer questions with a 0.4 ratio in 1.000 second. The "Accuracy" line graph shows that monkeys get 80% of the questions with a 0.4 ratio correct. **B** is the correct answer. In **A**, the response time is too fast and the chance of being correct is too high. In **C** and **D**, the response times are too fast and the chances of being correct are too low.

12. G

Data Representation: Read the Chart *Easy*

The table shows that 68.3% of women with one or more chronic conditions have a urinary or bowel disorder, so the correct answer is **G**. The percentages of women with respiratory disorders, cardiovascular disorders, or stroke are lower than 68.3%, so choices **F**, **H**, and **J** are all incorrect.

13. C

Data Representation: Read the Chart *Easy*

Only **C** lists physical activity in increasing order: stroke (17.2%), respiratory disorders (20.7%), diabetes (24.3%), and musculoskeletal disorders (24.8%). **B** lists physical activity in *decreasing* order.

14. G

Data Representation: Use the Chart *Medium*

G is the only hypothesis reflected by the data in the table. Among older adults, 35.1% without a chronic condition participate in physical activities, as opposed to 25.8% with a chronic condition. Stroke is the most common chronic condition in adults between 75 and 79, making **F** incorrect. **H** is incorrect because older adults with a BMI greater than 25 are *more* likely to have a chronic condition than adults with a BMI less than 25. **J** gets it backward—older adults with respiratory disorders are *less* likely to exercise than adults with musculoskeletal disorders.

15. A

Data Representation: Handle Graphs *Difficult*

This question asks you to translate information on the table into information on a bar graph. The table shows that 894 of the older adults who participated in the study suffered from stroke ($n=894$). Of those, 44.8% did not use alcohol, 19.8% used alcohol fewer than two times per month, 10.8% used alcohol two or three times per month, and 24.7% used alcohol more than three times per month. These amounts are represented on the bar graph in **A**. **B** gets the numbers backwards. **C** and **D** represent a linear progression that is not supported by the data.

16. J

Data Representation: Use the Chart *Difficult*

The table shows that 67.9% of older adults with diabetes have a BMI greater than 25. **F** has it backwards—older people with a BMI greater than 25 are *more* likely to have a cardiovascular disorder than older people with a BMI less than 25. **G** and **H** are not directly supported by the data.

17. B

Research Summary: Read the Chart *Easy*

Follow the gridline for a Grass DM yield of 500 kg ha^{-1}. In Season 3, the 10% experimental plot yielded nearly that amount. **A** is incorrect because the 0% plot yielded around 1,000 kg ha^{-1}. **C** and **D** are incorrect because the 35% plot and 50% plot yielded around 240 kg ha^{-1} and 75 kg ha^{-1}, respectively.

18. F

Research Summary: Read the Chart   *Easy*

In Seasons 1, 2, and 3, grass yields on the 20% plot were higher than grass yields on the 35% plot, so **F** is the correct answer. **G** is the *opposite* of the correct answer, and **H** and **J** represent a misreading of the data.

19. B

Research Summary: Use the Chart   *Medium*

According to Figure 3, rainfall was heaviest in Season 2 (440 mm). The data in Figures 1 and 2 shows that grass yields were the highest overall in Season 2. Rainfall definitely had an impact on grass yield, so **A** is incorrect. Grass yield in Season 3 was smaller than grass yield in Season 2, making **C** incorrect as well. Finally, while rainfall was greatest in January of Season 2, this was not the case in Season 1 or Season 3.

20. F

Research Summary: Use the Chart   *Medium*

Study 1 shows that, across all three seasons, the highest grass yields came from the 0% plot, so **F** is the correct answer. The information presented does not address soil quality, so **G** is an assumption we cannot make. **H** is incorrect because plots with thicker tree canopies generally have a *lower* grass yield. **J** is incorrect because grass yields did not increase on every plot from season to season (for example, the yield from the 10% and 20% plots decreased in Season 3).

21. A

Research Summary: Read the Chart   *Medium*

The grass yield from the canopied 75% plot in Season 2 was 250 kg ha^{-1}, making **A** the correct answer. The yields in **B**, **C**, and **D** are all too large to be correct.

22. H

Research Summary: Use the Chart   *Difficult*

This question requires you to consider a hypothetical situation related to the information presented. The livestock owners are seeking a high grass yield for their livestock. According to Study 2, grass yield is almost always higher on removed-canopy plots than on plots where there was never a canopy. In fact, in Season 2, the 10% RCA plot yielded more than twice as much grass as the CA plot. **H** is the correct answer. **F** looks at just two data points rather than the overall information. **G** is also too narrow and does not represent the sort of trend on which to build an entire hypothesis. **J** is an incorrect reading of the data—very little grass grew on *any* of the plots in Season 1.

23. B

Conflicting Viewpoints: Comparison   *Easy*

Both hypotheses discuss the moon samples taken by astronauts, so **B** is the correct answer. Neither hypothesis refers to telescopic images of the Moon, so **A** is incorrect. Both hypotheses mention the Earth's mantle—but they don't say anything about heat readings, so **C** is incorrect. **D** is incorrect because the Pacific Ocean is mentioned only in the Fission Theory, and its depth is not addressed.

24. G

Conflicting Viewpoints: Detail   *Easy*

F, **H**, and **J** are all mentioned in the Great Impact Theory. Planetary revolution, however, is not mentioned in this hypothesis. Planetary revolution is only mentioned in the Fission Theory.

25. D

Conflicting Viewpoints: Inference   *Medium*

The Fission Theory hypothesizes that a giant rock mass, which was once part of the Earth, was flung into outer space to form the Moon. Further, astronomers suggest that this rock mass was in what is now the Pacific Ocean. The discovery of a massive crater at the depths of the Pacific Ocean would strengthen the Fission Theory, so the correct answer is **D**. **A** would strengthen the Great Impact Theory, not the Fission Theory. **B** and **C** would weaken the Fission Theory rather than strengthen it.

26. F

Conflicting Viewpoints: Comparison   *Medium*

Supporters of both the Great Impact Theory and the Fission Theory would agree that the Moon shares some chemical compositions with Earth. **G** is incorrect because the Great Impact Theory hypothesizes that the Moon formed not long after the Earth. Neither hypothesis states that the Moon has its origins in the Earth's core, so **H** is incorrect as well. **J** is backed up by the Fission Theory but not the Great Impact Theory.

27. B

Conflicting Viewpoints: Detail   *Medium*

B is correct because the hypothesis never expands upon *why* it took the Moon 100 million years to form its primitive crust. The Fission Theory explains how the rock mass was flung into outer space, so **A** is not correct. The questions posed in **C** and **D** are also answered in the passage.

28. J

Conflicting Viewpoints: Inference   *Difficult*

The Giant Impact Theory assumes that just one huge rock mass (Theia) collided with Earth. **F** is an assumption made by the Fission Theory, not the Great Impact Theory. Neither hypothesis makes the assumptions stated in **G** and **H**.

29. B

Conflicting Viewpoints: Comparison   *Difficult*

Both the Giant Impact Theory and the Fission Theory hypothesize that the Earth lost a significant amount of its mass. Because this new discovery supports both hypotheses, **A**, **C**, and **D** are all incorrect.

30. H

Data Representation: Read the Chart   *Easy*

By reading the chart, we find that Hebei Province is polluted by 846,462 tons of ammonia per year, as expressed in **H**. **F** is the amount of ammonia that pollutes the air in Beijing Municipality. **G** is the amount of carbon monoxide that pollutes Hebei Province. **J** is the amount of ammonia that pollutes Shandong Province.

31. **C**

Data Representation: Read the Chart   *Easy*

The pollution levels in Beijing and Chifeng rise significantly higher than the levels in other cities. Pollution is very high in Beijing but not nearly as high in Tianjin, so **A** is incorrect. Pollution levels are relatively low in Jinan and Taiyuan as well, so **B** and **D** are also incorrect.

32. **J**

Data Representation: Use the Chart   *Medium*

Figure 1 shows that pollution levels are lowest (and mostly under 100 on the API) in Tianjin. People with allergies would feel healthiest in this city. Jinan, Chifeng, and Beijing have pollution levels that would adversely affect people with allergies, so choices **F**, **G**, and **H** are all incorrect.

33. **B**

Data Representation: Handle Graphs   *Medium*

This question asks you to translate information from the passage into chart form. The air must have an index value under 100 to meet national air-quality criteria. The only graph that represents the meeting of this requirement is **B**. The API levels in **A** are consistently over 100, so that choice is incorrect. **C** starts below 100 API but exceeds it by the second day, so that choice is incorrect. **D** is incorrect because its API level starts out at 300.

34. **F**

Data Representation: Use the Chart   *Difficult*

Shandong Province consistently has the greatest amount of pollutants, so the correct answer is **F**. The pollutant levels are not high enough in **G**, **H**, or **J** for those choices to be correct.

35. **B**

Research Summary: Read the Chart   *Easy*

According to the table, the average fraction of carbon consumed in above-ground biomass during a wildfire of moderate severity is 0.34. **A** is the amount of carbon consumed in above-ground biomass during a wildfire of low severity. **C** is the amount of carbon consumed in organic soil during a wildfire of moderate severity. **D** is the amount of carbon consumed in organic soil during a wildfire of high severity.

36. **H**

Research Summary: Read the Chart   *Easy*

The well-drained soil drainage class contributed the most to the total burned area in 2004, so the correct answer is **H**. **F**, **G**, and **J** do not represent enough of the total burned area to be correct.

37. **D**

Research Summary: Use the Chart   *Medium*

The bog and the spruce forest contributed more to the total burned area than to the total release of carbon. **C** is the *opposite* of the correct answer. **B** represents a misreading of the data. The passage never refers to amounts of released carbon as "insignificant," so **A** is incorrect as well.

38. **J**

Research Summary: Use the Chart   *Medium*

Both the spruce woodland land cover and the somewhat poorly drained soil contributed around 10% of the total burned area. The bog land cover and well-drained soil contributed very different percentages, so **F** is incorrect. Additionally, neither **G** nor **H** represent equal percentages.

39. **B**

Research Summary: Use the Chart   *Difficult*

The main purpose of Study 1 was to determine the amount of carbon consumed in the 2004 Alaska wildfires. The study did not address the root causes of the wildfires, so choice **A** is incorrect. **C** and **D** represent goals of Study 2, not Study 1.

40. **G**

Research Summary: Use the Chart   *Difficult*

This question requires you to consider a hypothetical situation. Based on Figure 1, a very small amount of excessively drained soil contributed to the total burned area. This soil drainage class could help prevent the loss of biomass in future wildfires, so the correct answer is **G**. The soil drainage classes listed in **F**, **H**, and **J** contributed too much to the total burned area to be correct.

ACT Practice
Test 2

DIRECTIONS: The ACT consists of tests in four separate subject areas: English, Mathematics, Reading, and Science. These four tests measure skills learned through high school course-work that are relevant to success in college. *YOU MAY USE CALCULATORS ON THE MATHEMATICS TEST ONLY.*

Each test contains a set of numbered questions. The answer choices for each question are lettered. On your answer sheet, you will find rows of ovals that are numbered to match the questions. Each oval contains a letter to correspond to a particular answer choice.

Choose the best answer for each question. Then, on your answer sheet, find the row of ovals that is numbered the same as the question. Find the oval containing the letter of your chosen answer, and fill in this oval completely. You must use a soft lead pencil for this purpose, and your marks must be heavy and black. *BALLPOINT PENS SHOULD NOT BE USED TO FILL IN THE ANSWER SHEET.*

Fill in only one answer choice oval for each question. If you wish to change an answer, make sure that your original answer is thoroughly erased before marking the new one. After filling in your answer, double-check to be sure that you have marked the row of ovals that corresponds to the question number being answered.

Responses will be scored only if they are marked on your answer document. Your score for each test is determined by the number of questions answered correctly during the testing period. Your score will NOT be reduced if you choose an incorrect answer. *FOR THIS REASON, IT IS ADVANTAGEOUS FOR YOU TO ANSWER EVERY QUESTION, EVEN IF YOU GUESS ON SOME QUESTIONS.*

You may work on a test ONLY when the test supervisor gives you permission to do so. If you finish a test before the end of the time allowed, use any remaining time to review questions that you are unsure about. You are permitted to review ONLY your answers for the test on which you are currently working. You may NOT look back to a test you have already completed, and you may NOT continue on to another test. If you do so, you will be disqualified from the examination.

When the end of each test is announced, put your pencil down immediately. You are NOT permitted to fill in or change ovals for a test after the end of that test has been called. If you do so, for any reason, you will be disqualified from the examination.

You may not fold or tear the pages of your test.

DO NOT TURN TO THE FIRST TEST
UNTIL YOU ARE TOLD TO DO SO.

ACT Practice Test 2: Answer Sheet

TEST 1

1 Ⓐ Ⓑ Ⓒ Ⓓ   16 Ⓕ Ⓖ Ⓗ Ⓙ   31 Ⓐ Ⓑ Ⓒ Ⓓ   46 Ⓕ Ⓖ Ⓗ Ⓙ   61 Ⓐ Ⓑ Ⓒ Ⓓ
2 Ⓕ Ⓖ Ⓗ Ⓙ   17 Ⓐ Ⓑ Ⓒ Ⓓ   32 Ⓕ Ⓖ Ⓗ Ⓙ   47 Ⓐ Ⓑ Ⓒ Ⓓ   62 Ⓕ Ⓖ Ⓗ Ⓙ
3 Ⓐ Ⓑ Ⓒ Ⓓ   18 Ⓕ Ⓖ Ⓗ Ⓙ   33 Ⓐ Ⓑ Ⓒ Ⓓ   48 Ⓕ Ⓖ Ⓗ Ⓙ   63 Ⓐ Ⓑ Ⓒ Ⓓ
4 Ⓕ Ⓖ Ⓗ Ⓙ   19 Ⓐ Ⓑ Ⓒ Ⓓ   34 Ⓕ Ⓖ Ⓗ Ⓙ   49 Ⓐ Ⓑ Ⓒ Ⓓ   64 Ⓕ Ⓖ Ⓗ Ⓙ
5 Ⓐ Ⓑ Ⓒ Ⓓ   20 Ⓕ Ⓖ Ⓗ Ⓙ   35 Ⓐ Ⓑ Ⓒ Ⓓ   50 Ⓕ Ⓖ Ⓗ Ⓙ   65 Ⓐ Ⓑ Ⓒ Ⓓ
6 Ⓕ Ⓖ Ⓗ Ⓙ   21 Ⓐ Ⓑ Ⓒ Ⓓ   36 Ⓕ Ⓖ Ⓗ Ⓙ   51 Ⓐ Ⓑ Ⓒ Ⓓ   66 Ⓕ Ⓖ Ⓗ Ⓙ
7 Ⓐ Ⓑ Ⓒ Ⓓ   22 Ⓕ Ⓖ Ⓗ Ⓙ   37 Ⓐ Ⓑ Ⓒ Ⓓ   52 Ⓕ Ⓖ Ⓗ Ⓙ   67 Ⓐ Ⓑ Ⓒ Ⓓ
8 Ⓕ Ⓖ Ⓗ Ⓙ   23 Ⓐ Ⓑ Ⓒ Ⓓ   38 Ⓕ Ⓖ Ⓗ Ⓙ   53 Ⓐ Ⓑ Ⓒ Ⓓ   68 Ⓕ Ⓖ Ⓗ Ⓙ
9 Ⓐ Ⓑ Ⓒ Ⓓ   24 Ⓕ Ⓖ Ⓗ Ⓙ   39 Ⓐ Ⓑ Ⓒ Ⓓ   54 Ⓕ Ⓖ Ⓗ Ⓙ   69 Ⓐ Ⓑ Ⓒ Ⓓ
10 Ⓕ Ⓖ Ⓗ Ⓙ   25 Ⓐ Ⓑ Ⓒ Ⓓ   40 Ⓕ Ⓖ Ⓗ Ⓙ   55 Ⓐ Ⓑ Ⓒ Ⓓ   70 Ⓕ Ⓖ Ⓗ Ⓙ
11 Ⓐ Ⓑ Ⓒ Ⓓ   26 Ⓕ Ⓖ Ⓗ Ⓙ   41 Ⓐ Ⓑ Ⓒ Ⓓ   56 Ⓕ Ⓖ Ⓗ Ⓙ   71 Ⓐ Ⓑ Ⓒ Ⓓ
12 Ⓕ Ⓖ Ⓗ Ⓙ   27 Ⓐ Ⓑ Ⓒ Ⓓ   42 Ⓕ Ⓖ Ⓗ Ⓙ   57 Ⓐ Ⓑ Ⓒ Ⓓ   72 Ⓕ Ⓖ Ⓗ Ⓙ
13 Ⓐ Ⓑ Ⓒ Ⓓ   28 Ⓕ Ⓖ Ⓗ Ⓙ   43 Ⓐ Ⓑ Ⓒ Ⓓ   58 Ⓕ Ⓖ Ⓗ Ⓙ   73 Ⓐ Ⓑ Ⓒ Ⓓ
14 Ⓕ Ⓖ Ⓗ Ⓙ   29 Ⓐ Ⓑ Ⓒ Ⓓ   44 Ⓕ Ⓖ Ⓗ Ⓙ   59 Ⓐ Ⓑ Ⓒ Ⓓ   74 Ⓕ Ⓖ Ⓗ Ⓙ
15 Ⓐ Ⓑ Ⓒ Ⓓ   30 Ⓕ Ⓖ Ⓗ Ⓙ   45 Ⓐ Ⓑ Ⓒ Ⓓ   60 Ⓕ Ⓖ Ⓗ Ⓙ   75 Ⓐ Ⓑ Ⓒ Ⓓ

TEST 2

1 Ⓐ Ⓑ Ⓒ Ⓓ Ⓔ   13 Ⓐ Ⓑ Ⓒ Ⓓ Ⓔ   25 Ⓐ Ⓑ Ⓒ Ⓓ Ⓔ   37 Ⓐ Ⓑ Ⓒ Ⓓ Ⓔ   49 Ⓐ Ⓑ Ⓒ Ⓓ Ⓔ
2 Ⓕ Ⓖ Ⓗ Ⓙ Ⓚ   14 Ⓕ Ⓖ Ⓗ Ⓙ Ⓚ   26 Ⓕ Ⓖ Ⓗ Ⓙ Ⓚ   38 Ⓕ Ⓖ Ⓗ Ⓙ Ⓚ   50 Ⓕ Ⓖ Ⓗ Ⓙ Ⓚ
3 Ⓐ Ⓑ Ⓒ Ⓓ Ⓔ   15 Ⓐ Ⓑ Ⓒ Ⓓ Ⓔ   27 Ⓐ Ⓑ Ⓒ Ⓓ Ⓔ   39 Ⓐ Ⓑ Ⓒ Ⓓ Ⓔ   51 Ⓐ Ⓑ Ⓒ Ⓓ Ⓔ
4 Ⓕ Ⓖ Ⓗ Ⓙ Ⓚ   16 Ⓕ Ⓖ Ⓗ Ⓙ Ⓚ   28 Ⓕ Ⓖ Ⓗ Ⓙ Ⓚ   40 Ⓕ Ⓖ Ⓗ Ⓙ Ⓚ   52 Ⓕ Ⓖ Ⓗ Ⓙ Ⓚ
5 Ⓐ Ⓑ Ⓒ Ⓓ Ⓔ   17 Ⓐ Ⓑ Ⓒ Ⓓ Ⓔ   29 Ⓐ Ⓑ Ⓒ Ⓓ Ⓔ   41 Ⓐ Ⓑ Ⓒ Ⓓ Ⓔ   53 Ⓐ Ⓑ Ⓒ Ⓓ Ⓔ
6 Ⓕ Ⓖ Ⓗ Ⓙ Ⓚ   18 Ⓕ Ⓖ Ⓗ Ⓙ Ⓚ   30 Ⓕ Ⓖ Ⓗ Ⓙ Ⓚ   42 Ⓕ Ⓖ Ⓗ Ⓙ Ⓚ   54 Ⓕ Ⓖ Ⓗ Ⓙ Ⓚ
7 Ⓐ Ⓑ Ⓒ Ⓓ Ⓔ   19 Ⓐ Ⓑ Ⓒ Ⓓ Ⓔ   31 Ⓐ Ⓑ Ⓒ Ⓓ Ⓔ   43 Ⓐ Ⓑ Ⓒ Ⓓ Ⓔ   55 Ⓐ Ⓑ Ⓒ Ⓓ Ⓔ
8 Ⓕ Ⓖ Ⓗ Ⓙ Ⓚ   20 Ⓕ Ⓖ Ⓗ Ⓙ Ⓚ   32 Ⓕ Ⓖ Ⓗ Ⓙ Ⓚ   44 Ⓕ Ⓖ Ⓗ Ⓙ Ⓚ   56 Ⓕ Ⓖ Ⓗ Ⓙ Ⓚ
9 Ⓐ Ⓑ Ⓒ Ⓓ Ⓔ   21 Ⓐ Ⓑ Ⓒ Ⓓ Ⓔ   33 Ⓐ Ⓑ Ⓒ Ⓓ Ⓔ   45 Ⓐ Ⓑ Ⓒ Ⓓ Ⓔ   57 Ⓐ Ⓑ Ⓒ Ⓓ Ⓔ
10 Ⓕ Ⓖ Ⓗ Ⓙ Ⓚ   22 Ⓕ Ⓖ Ⓗ Ⓙ Ⓚ   34 Ⓕ Ⓖ Ⓗ Ⓙ Ⓚ   46 Ⓕ Ⓖ Ⓗ Ⓙ Ⓚ   58 Ⓕ Ⓖ Ⓗ Ⓙ Ⓚ
11 Ⓐ Ⓑ Ⓒ Ⓓ Ⓔ   23 Ⓐ Ⓑ Ⓒ Ⓓ Ⓔ   35 Ⓐ Ⓑ Ⓒ Ⓓ Ⓔ   47 Ⓐ Ⓑ Ⓒ Ⓓ Ⓔ   59 Ⓐ Ⓑ Ⓒ Ⓓ Ⓔ
12 Ⓕ Ⓖ Ⓗ Ⓙ Ⓚ   24 Ⓕ Ⓖ Ⓗ Ⓙ Ⓚ   36 Ⓕ Ⓖ Ⓗ Ⓙ Ⓚ   48 Ⓕ Ⓖ Ⓗ Ⓙ Ⓚ   60 Ⓕ Ⓖ Ⓗ Ⓙ Ⓚ

TEST 3

1 Ⓐ Ⓑ Ⓒ Ⓓ   9 Ⓐ Ⓑ Ⓒ Ⓓ   17 Ⓐ Ⓑ Ⓒ Ⓓ   25 Ⓐ Ⓑ Ⓒ Ⓓ   33 Ⓐ Ⓑ Ⓒ Ⓓ
2 Ⓕ Ⓖ Ⓗ Ⓙ   10 Ⓕ Ⓖ Ⓗ Ⓙ   18 Ⓕ Ⓖ Ⓗ Ⓙ   26 Ⓕ Ⓖ Ⓗ Ⓙ   34 Ⓕ Ⓖ Ⓗ Ⓙ
3 Ⓐ Ⓑ Ⓒ Ⓓ   11 Ⓐ Ⓑ Ⓒ Ⓓ   19 Ⓐ Ⓑ Ⓒ Ⓓ   27 Ⓐ Ⓑ Ⓒ Ⓓ   35 Ⓐ Ⓑ Ⓒ Ⓓ
4 Ⓕ Ⓖ Ⓗ Ⓙ   12 Ⓕ Ⓖ Ⓗ Ⓙ   20 Ⓕ Ⓖ Ⓗ Ⓙ   28 Ⓕ Ⓖ Ⓗ Ⓙ   36 Ⓕ Ⓖ Ⓗ Ⓙ
5 Ⓐ Ⓑ Ⓒ Ⓓ   13 Ⓐ Ⓑ Ⓒ Ⓓ   21 Ⓐ Ⓑ Ⓒ Ⓓ   29 Ⓐ Ⓑ Ⓒ Ⓓ   37 Ⓐ Ⓑ Ⓒ Ⓓ
6 Ⓕ Ⓖ Ⓗ Ⓙ   14 Ⓕ Ⓖ Ⓗ Ⓙ   22 Ⓕ Ⓖ Ⓗ Ⓙ   30 Ⓕ Ⓖ Ⓗ Ⓙ   38 Ⓕ Ⓖ Ⓗ Ⓙ
7 Ⓐ Ⓑ Ⓒ Ⓓ   15 Ⓐ Ⓑ Ⓒ Ⓓ   23 Ⓐ Ⓑ Ⓒ Ⓓ   31 Ⓐ Ⓑ Ⓒ Ⓓ   39 Ⓐ Ⓑ Ⓒ Ⓓ
8 Ⓕ Ⓖ Ⓗ Ⓙ   16 Ⓕ Ⓖ Ⓗ Ⓙ   24 Ⓕ Ⓖ Ⓗ Ⓙ   32 Ⓕ Ⓖ Ⓗ Ⓙ   40 Ⓕ Ⓖ Ⓗ Ⓙ

TEST 4

1 Ⓐ Ⓑ Ⓒ Ⓓ   9 Ⓐ Ⓑ Ⓒ Ⓓ   17 Ⓐ Ⓑ Ⓒ Ⓓ   25 Ⓐ Ⓑ Ⓒ Ⓓ   33 Ⓐ Ⓑ Ⓒ Ⓓ
2 Ⓕ Ⓖ Ⓗ Ⓙ   10 Ⓕ Ⓖ Ⓗ Ⓙ   18 Ⓕ Ⓖ Ⓗ Ⓙ   26 Ⓕ Ⓖ Ⓗ Ⓙ   34 Ⓕ Ⓖ Ⓗ Ⓙ
3 Ⓐ Ⓑ Ⓒ Ⓓ   11 Ⓐ Ⓑ Ⓒ Ⓓ   19 Ⓐ Ⓑ Ⓒ Ⓓ   27 Ⓐ Ⓑ Ⓒ Ⓓ   35 Ⓐ Ⓑ Ⓒ Ⓓ
4 Ⓕ Ⓖ Ⓗ Ⓙ   12 Ⓕ Ⓖ Ⓗ Ⓙ   20 Ⓕ Ⓖ Ⓗ Ⓙ   28 Ⓕ Ⓖ Ⓗ Ⓙ   36 Ⓕ Ⓖ Ⓗ Ⓙ
5 Ⓐ Ⓑ Ⓒ Ⓓ   13 Ⓐ Ⓑ Ⓒ Ⓓ   21 Ⓐ Ⓑ Ⓒ Ⓓ   29 Ⓐ Ⓑ Ⓒ Ⓓ   37 Ⓐ Ⓑ Ⓒ Ⓓ
6 Ⓕ Ⓖ Ⓗ Ⓙ   14 Ⓕ Ⓖ Ⓗ Ⓙ   22 Ⓕ Ⓖ Ⓗ Ⓙ   30 Ⓕ Ⓖ Ⓗ Ⓙ   38 Ⓕ Ⓖ Ⓗ Ⓙ
7 Ⓐ Ⓑ Ⓒ Ⓓ   15 Ⓐ Ⓑ Ⓒ Ⓓ   23 Ⓐ Ⓑ Ⓒ Ⓓ   31 Ⓐ Ⓑ Ⓒ Ⓓ   39 Ⓐ Ⓑ Ⓒ Ⓓ
8 Ⓕ Ⓖ Ⓗ Ⓙ   16 Ⓕ Ⓖ Ⓗ Ⓙ   24 Ⓕ Ⓖ Ⓗ Ⓙ   32 Ⓕ Ⓖ Ⓗ Ⓙ   40 Ⓕ Ⓖ Ⓗ Ⓙ

ENGLISH TEST

45 Minutes—75 Questions

DIRECTIONS: There are five passages on this test. You should read each passage once before answering the questions on it. In order to answer correctly, you may need to read several sentences beyond the question.

There are two question formats within the passages. In one format, you will find words and phrases that have been underlined and assigned numbers. These numbers will correspond with sets of alternative words/phrases given in the right-hand column of the test booklet. From the sets of alternatives, choose the answer choice that works best in context, keeping in mind whether it employs standard written English, whether it gets across the idea of the section,

and whether it suits the tone and style of the passage. You will usually be offered the option "NO CHANGE," which you should choose if you think the version found in the passage is best.

In the second format, you will see boxed numbers referring to sections of the passage or to the passage as a whole. In the right-hand column, you will be asked questions about or given alternatives for the sections marked by the boxes. Choose the answer choice that best answers the question or completes the section. After choosing your answer choice, fill in the corresponding bubble on the answer sheet.

Passage I

The Sherpas of Nepal

[1]

Mount Everest and Sherpas are two terms that often go hand in hand. As an ethnic group that <u>live</u> in the eastern region of the Himalayan Mountains, Sherpas are renowned for their prowess in high altitudes and <u>proving</u> invaluable to foreigners attempting to reach the world's highest peak. Of the more than 10,000 Sherpas who live in Nepal, <u>approximately</u> 3,000 live in the Khumbu Valley, a region <u>of Nepal</u> with elevations ranging from 11,000 feet at the base to 29,035 at the peak of Mount Everest.

[2]

Due to their physical strength and seeming resistance to cold <u>temperatures.</u> Sherpas have become an integral

1. **A.** NO CHANGE
   B. lives
   C. do live
   D. have lived

2. **F.** NO CHANGE
   G. proved
   H. by proving
   J. have proved

3. Three of these choices indicate that the exact number of Sherpas living in the Khumbu Valley is unknown. Which choice does NOT do so?
   A. NO CHANGE
   B. roughly
   C. precisely
   D. nearly

4. **F.** NO CHANGE
   G. which includes Mount Everest
   H. of Nepal near the border of China
   J. OMIT the underlined portion.

5. **A.** NO CHANGE
   B. temperatures,
   C. temperatures;
   D. temperatures

GO ON TO THE NEXT PAGE.

part of mountain-climbing <u>expeditions, few</u> people have
6

reached the peak of Everest without the aid of a Sherpa.

It remains unknown why Sherpas do not feel the typical

effects of high altitude. ⑦

[3]

Not until European mountaineers came to Nepal to

battle Everest did most Sherpas even consider climbing

what the <u>Nepalese refer to as "Goddess Mother,</u> of the
8

Land." <u>Believed to be a home of the gods, the slopes of</u>
9

<u>Mount Everest were once considered too special for humans</u>
9

<u>to cross.</u> Although Mount Everest has now been climbed
9

by many people, Sherpas still honor <u>its</u> holy mountain
10

through special ceremonies before the start of expeditions.

6. Which of the following alternatives to the underlined
portion would NOT be acceptable?
F. expeditions few
G. expeditions. Few
H. expeditions; few
J. expeditions: few

7. At this point, the writer is considering adding the following phrase to the end of the sentence:
such as fatigue and mountain sickness.
Given that this is a true statement, would it be a relevant addition to make here?
A. Yes, because it can give the reader a better understanding of how high altitudes affect the body.
B. Yes, because it helps explain to the reader why high
altitudes do not affect the health of Sherpas.
C. No, because it fails to explain the connection between high altitudes and the health of mountain
climbers.
D. No, because it is unnecessary information that does
not relate to the focus of the essay.

8. F. NO CHANGE
G. Nepalese refer to, as "Goddess Mother
H. Nepalese refer to as "Goddess Mother
J. Nepalese, refer to as "Goddess Mother

9. A. NO CHANGE
B. Believed too special for humans to cross, the Nepalese thought the slopes of Mount Everest were once
considered to be a home of the gods.
C. The slopes of Mount Everest, once considered too
special for humans to cross, were believed by them
to be a home of the gods.
D. Humans were considered too special to cross the
slopes of Mount Everest, which were once believed
to be a home of the gods.

10. F. NO CHANGE
G. it's
H. there
J. their

[4]

The general term "sherpa" <u>often</u> used to describe
₁₁

any porter hired to carry equipment for foreigners climbing

in the Himalayas. However, Nepalese Sherpas try to

distinguish themselves as guides and experts with enough

experience to garner <u>the most highest</u> pay than regular
₁₂

porters. Responsible for <u>carrying heavy loads, having to</u>
₁₃

<u>establish campsites, and setting ropes,</u> Sherpas have
₁₃

enabled the climbing industry to flourish in a once isolated

area of the world. Before Sherpas led expeditions, most of

them worked as traders and farmers. <u>Thus,</u> Nepalese
₁₄

Sherpas embrace the sport for which they seem to have

been born. 15

11. **A.** NO CHANGE
    B. which often is
    C. is often
    D. OMIT the underlined portion.

12. **F.** NO CHANGE
    G. higher
    H. the most high
    J. highest

13. **A.** NO CHANGE
    B. carrying heavy loads, establishing campsites, and setting ropes,
    C. the carrying of heavy loads, establishing campsites, and for setting ropes,
    D. carrying heavy loads, to establish campsites, and to set ropes,

14. **F.** NO CHANGE
    G. Nevertheless,
    H. Now,
    J. In conclusion,

15. Upon reviewing this essay and realizing that some information has been left out, the writer composes the following sentence:

    Experts suspect the physiological abilities of Sherpas stem from a combination of genetics and environmental influences.

    The most logical and effective place to add this sentence would be after the last sentence in Paragraph:
    A. 1
    B. 2
    C. 3
    D. 4

GO ON TO THE NEXT PAGE.

Passage II

Roman Summer

[1]

In Rome, Italy, I had the opportunity to stay with an
aunt who lived when I was 16. At first, I felt homesick
                    16
for my parents, my friends, and even my annoying little

brother, however, my attitude changed once I started to
         17
experience the wonders of Rome.

[2]

18 My aunt taught me important words such as "food,"

"water," and "restroom." By eavesdropping on conversations,

I learned additional Italian phrases, while I still had
           19   20
a hard time making myself understood.

[3]

Visitors to Rome having been rewarded with many
                    21
intriguing sites not likely seen in the United States.

For example, graffiti is everywhere, even on very large
                                                    22
expensive apartment buildings. Moreover, traffic is
    22

16. **F.** NO CHANGE
    G. When I was 16, I had the opportunity to stay with an aunt who lived in Rome, Italy.
    H. I had the opportunity to stay with an aunt in Rome, Italy who lived when I was 16.
    J. An aunt, who I had the opportunity to stay with, lived in Rome, Italy when I was 16.

17. **A.** NO CHANGE
    B. brother, however;
    C. brother—however,
    D. brother; however,

18. Which of the following sentences (assuming all are true), if added here, would best introduce the new subject of paragraph 2?
    F. Rome offers visitors an array of interesting cultural opportunities, which I fully enjoyed.
    G. Upon arrival, I spoke no Italian, so the language barrier proved to be my greatest challenge.
    H. Fortunately, my aunt had been living in Rome for six months and knew how to get around.
    J. My trip to Rome provided me with an excellent opportunity to learn more about my aunt.

19. **A.** NO CHANGE
    B. bonus
    C. optional
    D. intentional

20. **F.** NO CHANGE
    G. so
    H. as
    J. yet

21. **A.** NO CHANGE
    B. were rewarded
    C. are rewarded
    D. OMIT the underlined portion.

22. **F.** NO CHANGE
    G. very large, expensive
    H. very, large, expensive
    J. very large expensive,

a nightmare. Having grown up in Chicago, I thought I knew all about traffic jams, but the ones in Rome were <u>a frightening and disorderly mess.</u> Italian drivers create
23

six lanes from roads intended for three lanes of traffic, which results in a chaotic mass of cars. Due <u>from the</u> the traffic snarls, most people choose to travel around the
24

city on Vespa scooters, but I opted to walk or take public transportation.

[4]

The lifestyle of Roman citizens <u>appeal</u> to me. Although
25

Romans attend school or work like Americans, they end

their busy days by strolling around the city's fountains and <u>a snack</u> on gelato, a delicious, icy treat. The latest
26

fashion trends can be seen on the residents of Rome, which is home to many wealthy individuals who enjoy an upscale lifestyle.

[5]

During my visit, I went to historical sites, such as the Coliseum, and took a day trip with my aunt to Venice, which is considered the <u>worlds'</u> most romantic city. When it was
27

time for me <u>to return home,</u> I was a little forlorn, but my
28

23. A. NO CHANGE
B. a frightening and disorderly mess of cars and scooters.
C. worrisome, disorderly, and frightening.
D. frightening.

24. F. NO CHANGE
G. with
H. to
J. OMIT the underlined portion.

25. A. NO CHANGE
B. are appealing
C. have appealed
D. appeals

26. F. NO CHANGE
G. having a snack
H. snacking
J. to snack

27. A. NO CHANGE
B. world's
C. worlds
D. worlds's

28. F. NO CHANGE
G. to return home on the airplane to Chicago,
H. to finally return home to my family and friends,
J. to leave Italy and return home,

GO ON TO THE NEXT PAGE.

birthday present is a ticket to Rome for summer vacation, which should chase the blues away. 29 30

29. The entire essay is written in the first person (*I, we*). If the essay were revised so that the first-person pronouns were replaced with the pronouns *one* and *one's*, the essay would primarily:
A. gain a polite and formal tone appropriate to the topic of the essay.
B. gain the attention of a wider age range of readers in the audience.
C. lose the sense of sharing a personal experience with the audience.
D. lose the intimacy established by the writer regarding a sensitive subject.

30. Suppose the writer had decided to write an essay discussing the benefits of becoming familiar with a foreign country by spending time exploring its small towns. Would this essay successfully fulfill the writer's goal?
F. Yes, because the essay describes taking daytrips to towns outside of Rome.
G. Yes, because the essay details the simple pleasures the author discovered in Rome.
H. No, because the essay limits itself to the author's difficulties learning Italian.
J. No, because the essay primarily depicts the author's experiences in Rome.

Passage III

Al Jolson: The Jazz Singer

[1]

Before the pyrotechnics, special effects, and <u>intricately dance moves</u> of today's musical performers, there was Al Jolson. Jolson paved the way for the onstage gyrations of Elvis Presley, Michael Jackson, and many more. <u>Jolson engaged audiences dubbed "the world's greatest entertainer" with his musical talents and showmanship from 1911 until his death in 1950.</u>

31. A. NO CHANGE
B. dance moves intricately
C. intricate dance moves
D. intricate as a dance move

32. F. NO CHANGE
G. From 1911 until his death in 1950, Jolson engaged audiences dubbed "the world's greatest entertainer" with his musical talents and showmanship.
H. With his musical talents and showmanship dubbed "the world's greatest entertainer," Jolson engaged audiences from 1911 until his death in 1950.
J. Dubbed "the world's greatest entertainer," Jolson engaged audiences with his musical talents and showmanship from 1911 until his death in 1950.

[2]

Jolson used various theatrical techniques during his

shows, yet he found great pleasure in performing the new
33

jazz music that was becoming popular at the time. Jolson

introduced audiences to such African American musical

styles as jazz, ragtime, and blues—music he greatly
34

admired and respected. Jolson's musical choices have been

credited with opening the door for many African American

musicians, like Cab Calloway, Louis Armstrong, and
35

Duke Ellington.

[3]

Jolson immigrated to the United States with his parents
36

when he was a child, born in Lithuania as Asa Yoelson.
36

He dropped his Jewish name after beginning his career

as a dancer, musician, and comedian, although he never
37

denied his heritage. In addition to showcasing energetic

physical movements, Jolson's unique style included a

comedic combination of opera-style singing and some bird
38

whistles.
38

33. **A.** NO CHANGE
    B. and
    C. since
    D. although

34. **F.** NO CHANGE
    G. blues. Music
    H. blues music,
    J. blues; music,

35. Which of the following alternatives to the underlined portion would NOT be acceptable?
    A. consequently
    B. such as
    C. including
    D. specifically

36. **F.** NO CHANGE
    G. When he was a child, his parents immigrated to the United States with Jolson, who was born in Lithuania as Asa Yoelson.
    H. Born in Lithuania as Asa Yoelson, Jolson immigrated to the United States with his parents when he was a child.
    J. With his parents, Jolson, born in Lithuania as Asa Yoelson, immigrated to the United States when he was a child.

37. **A.** NO CHANGE
    B. as a performer,
    C. as an actor, dancer, and entertainer,
    D. working as an entertainer and performer

38. **F.** NO CHANGE
    G. opera-style songs and bird whistling.
    H. opera-style singing and his bird whistles.
    J. opera-style singing and bird whistling.

GO ON TO THE NEXT PAGE.

[4]

Jolson's onstage performances thrilled audiences, but they often frustrated Broadway producers. Jolson occasionally stopped in the middle of a <u>play turned to the members of the audience, and</u> asked whether <u>it</u> would rather hear
₃₉   ₄₀
him sing or see the rest of the production. After receiving

thunderous encouragement from the audience, Jolson would proceed into a spontaneous one-man show to the <u>alarm</u>
₄₁
of ticket holders.

[5]

<u>Some time later</u>, Jolson starred in *The Jazz Singer*, the
₄₂
first feature-length film with dialogue, music, and sound

effects. 43 Jolson's character opened the film with the remark, "You ain't heard nothin' yet." That line cleverly

39. **A.** NO CHANGE
B. play, turned to the members of the audience, and
C. play turned to the members, of the audience and
D. play turned to the members of the audience and

40. **F.** NO CHANGE
G. they
H. them
J. we

41. **A.** NO CHANGE
B. admiration
C. dismay
D. delight

42. Which of the transitions provides the most effective link from paragraph 4 to paragraph 5?
F. NO CHANGE
G. Although he had never starred in a Hollywood film,
H. In addition to performing in Broadway and vaude-ville productions,
J. After many years of working in the entertainment industry,

43. At this point, the writer wants to add a sentence that would further explain the historical significance of *The Jazz Singer*. Given that all of the following sentences are true, which one would best accomplish this goal?
A. The 1927 debut of *The Jazz Singer* received positive reviews from both the media and audiences.
B. *The Jazz Singer* has been preserved by the Ameri-can National Film Registry because of its cultural and historical relevance.
C. The premier of *The Jazz Singer* in 1927 ended the days of silent films and opened the door to a new type of movie—the "talkie."
D. The storyline of *The Jazz Singer* resembles the life of Jolson, although the film was not written as a biography.

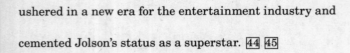

ushered in a new era for the entertainment industry and

cemented Jolson's status as a superstar. 44 45

44. For the sake of logic and coherence, paragraph 3 should be placed:
   F. where it is now.
   G. before paragraph 1.
   H. after paragraph 1.
   J. after paragraph 5.

45. What function does paragraph 5 serve in relation to the rest of the passage?
   A. It summarizes the main point that Jolson's hard work led to his success in the entertainment industry.
   B. It emphasizes that Jolson's film debut was the most fulfilling aspect of his career in the entertainment business.
   C. It refers to the opening paragraph by comparing Jolson to modern-day celebrities.
   D. It explains the connection between modern filmmaking and Jolson's entertainment career.

Passage IV

Downloads and the Digital Age of Music

[1]

In 1998, college student Shawn Fanning became

extremely frustrated and annoyed by the difficulties
46

of downloading music. Fanning put his computer

programming skills to work and will spend months
47

writing the code which would eventually lead to Napster,

a file-sharing platform. 48 Since it was primarily used

46. F. NO CHANGE
   G. frustrated
   H. aggravated and annoyed
   J. very frustrated, aggravated, and discouraged

47. A. NO CHANGE
   B. was spending
   C. spends
   D. spent

48. At this point, the writer wants to add a sentence that would further describe the purpose of Napster. Given that all are true, which of the following sentences would best accomplish this goal?
   F. At first, Napster was driven exclusively by Windows, but in 2000 a Macintosh version became available.
   G. Napster led to the creation of similar file-sharing networks, such as Kazaa and LimeWire.
   H. Napster enabled people to easily share files with one another through a centralized server.
   J. Napster's instant popularity supported Fanning's theory that people desired an easy way to download music.

GO ON TO THE NEXT PAGE.

for sharing <u>music files Napster created</u> a stir within
$\overset{}{\underset{49}{}}$

the recording industry because the free service allowed

users to upload and download copyrighted music without

permission.

[2]

Napster faced lawsuits from recording artists and record

companies for copyright <u>infringement, but</u> alternative
$\overset{}{\underset{50}{}}$

methods of legally downloading music have arisen over the

last decade. For example, iTunes and other online music

stores charge customers a small fee for each downloaded

song. Yet representatives of the recording industry

<u>continues</u> to worry about revenue losses as a result of the
$\overset{}{\underset{51}{}}$

new technology. Recording artists contend that music sales

<u>are lower than expected and money is being lost</u> because
$\overset{}{\underset{52}{}}$

consumers download music instead of buying albums.

[3]

<u>Napster was once so large that every song ever recorded</u>
$\overset{}{\underset{53}{}}$

<u>could be downloaded for free.</u> The recording industry is
$\overset{}{\underset{53}{}}$

49. A. NO CHANGE
B. music files Napster, created
C. music files, Napster created
D. music files Napster created,

50. Which of the following alternatives to the underlined
portion would be LEAST acceptable?
F. infringement; however,
G. infringement, yet
H. infringement, although
J. infringement, since

51. A. NO CHANGE
B. continue
C. does continue
D. has continued

52. F. NO CHANGE
G. are down
H. and profits are taking a downward turn
J. of albums have declined and hurt their profits

53. Which choice is the most effective first sentence of
paragraph 3?
A. NO CHANGE
B. Although its name was creative, Napster sounded
too much like gangster, which suggested illegal
activity to some people.
C. But why should a consumer spend fifteen or twenty
dollars on one album, when downloading a song
costs less than one dollar?
D. Savvy bands began to protect their music by putting distorted versions of their songs on Napster so
people would download flawed music.

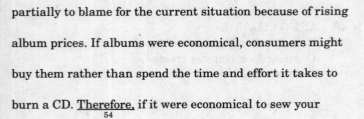

partially to blame for the current situation because of rising

album prices. If albums were economical, consumers might

buy them rather than spend the time and effort it takes to

burn a CD. <u>Therefore,</u> if it were economical to sew your
54

own <u>clothing, or</u> make your own food, the clothing and
55

fast food industries would go out of business. People lack the

incentive to sew or flip burgers because clothing and fast

food can be purchased unlike albums <u>inexpensively</u>.
56

[4]

The recording industry is <u>excited</u> about every new
57

music format. Before MP3 players, cassette recorders were

considered a <u>threat, before</u> that it was reel-to-reel tape
58

recorders. Every new format has provided a better method

54. F. NO CHANGE
G. In contrast,
H. Similarly,
J. However,

55. A. NO CHANGE
B. clothing or
C. clothing; or
D. clothing—or

56. F. NO CHANGE
G. (Place underlined text after *burgers*, followed by a comma)
H. (Place underlined text after *food*, followed by a comma)
J. (Place underlined text after *purchased*, followed by a comma)

57. A. NO CHANGE
B. relaxed
C. eager
D. anxious

58. F. NO CHANGE
G. threat and before
H. threat; before
J. threat before

GO ON TO THE NEXT PAGE.

of music distribution, which ultimately benefits both fans

and musicians. 59 Fighting the digital age is fruitless

because consumers always have the last word. 60

59. The writer is thinking of revising the second part of
the preceding sentence to read:
    which ultimately benefits everyone.
If this revision were made, the sentence would primarily lose:

A. confusing details that distract the reader from the
author's argument.

B. unnecessary information that makes the essay
redundant.

C. important details that emphasize the author's argument.

D. information more clearly established elsewhere in
the essay.

60. Suppose the writer had been assigned to write a short
argumentative essay illustrating why the business
practices of the recording industry should be monitored.
Would this essay successfully fulfill the assignment?

F. Yes, because the essay shows how the recording
industry is losing money through its unwillingness
to adapt to the digital age.

G. Yes, because the essay shows how recording industry executives have initiated lawsuits regarding
illegal downloads.

H. No, because the essay indicates that the free
market will monitor the business practices of the
recording industry.

J. No, because the essay focuses on how music downloads can ultimately benefit the music industry.

Passage V

Animal Shelters

[1]

When I first began volunteering at my local animal shelter, I thought my primary duties would be playing with fluffy little kittens and to train rambunctious but lovable
₆₁ puppies. I was unprepared for the number of adult animals housed in the shelter for various reasons.

[2]

It was disheartening to see rows of cages containing homeless dogs and cats that had been picked up as strays or rescued from unfit homes. 62 However, some of the
₆₃ animals arriving at the shelter as a result of owners
₆₄ who were trying to be responsible. In some cases, pet

---

61. A. NO CHANGE
     B. for training
     C. help train
     D. training

62. The writer is considering revising "to see rows of cages containing homeless dogs and cats" to read "to see dogs and cats." That revision would cause the sentence to lose primarily:
     F. characterizing details about the appearance of the animals.
     G. unnecessary information that has been previously stated.
     H. descriptive details about the situation at the animal shelter.
     J. confusing information that bogs down the description.

63. Which of the alternatives to the underlined portion would NOT be acceptable?
     A. But,
     B. Likewise,
     C. In contrast,
     D. On the other hand,

64. F. NO CHANGE
     G. arrived
     H. will arrive
     J. who have arrived

GO ON TO THE NEXT PAGE.

owners were moving and could not take their pet. In other situations, the owner's lifestyle had altered, and adequately caring for an animal was no longer possible. [65]

[3]

I am a firm believer that fewer animals would end up in shelters if more people were educated <u>about responsible</u>
<u>pet ownership and how to properly care for dogs and</u>
₆₆
<u>cats</u>. My initial advice to new pet owners is to spay or
₆₆
neuter their dogs and cats. While many people <u>are making</u>
₆₇
plans to limit their dog or cat to a single <u>litter pet</u>
₆₈
<u>owners often discover</u> that finding good homes for one
₆₈
litter of puppies and kittens is harder than they anticipated.

<u>Consequently,</u> a new batch of pups or kittens arrives
₆₉
at the door of the local animal shelter a few months later.

65. Given that all of the choices are true, which of the following sentences, if added here, would most effectively lead the reader from paragraph 2 into paragraph 3?
A. Animal shelters across the United States are overcrowded and in need of funding.
B. Many cities offer low-cost spay and neuter services in an attempt to prevent shelter overcrowding.
C. Irresponsible pet owners should be criminally punished for their negligent behavior.
D. Sadly, no matter why a dog or cat enters a shelter, they are deemed homeless once inside.

66. **F.** NO CHANGE
G. about responsibly caring for dogs, cats, and other animals.
H. about responsible pet ownership.
J. OMIT the underlined portion and end the sentence with a period.

67. **A.** NO CHANGE
B. making
C. make
D. made

68. **F.** NO CHANGE
G. litter, pet owners often discover
H. litter pet owners, often discover
J. litter pet owners often discover,

69. **A.** NO CHANGE
B. Similarly,
C. Furthermore,
D. In other words,

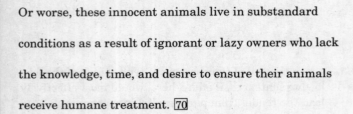

Or worse, these innocent animals live in substandard conditions as a result of ignorant or lazy owners who lack the knowledge, time, and desire to ensure their animals receive humane treatment. [70]

[4]

A pet <u>will provide its owners with many years of</u> <u>happiness</u>. Animals are <u>living, breathing, beings</u> that deserve
        71   72
food, water, shelter, and love every day, regardless of their

<u>owners</u> attitudes or schedules. Pets are <u>time-consuming</u>
     73   74
<u>creatures requiring effort and dedication,</u> and animal
                        74
rescuers around the country only wish more people realized

this fact. [75]

70. The writer is considering revising "Or worse, these innocent animals live in substandard conditions as a result of" to read "Numerous animals live in difficult conditions as a result of". That revision would cause the sentence to lose primarily:
- **F.** the writer's opinion about the effects of irresponsible pet owners.
- **G.** the writer's explanation about the problems with animal shelters.
- **H.** information that is too argumentative for the topic of the essay.
- **J.** unnecessary information that makes the paragraph too emotional.

71. Which choice best leads the reader into the subject matter of the fourth paragraph?
- **A.** NO CHANGE
- **B.** offers children a way to learn about being responsible and caring.
- **C.** can become dangerous as a result of mistreatment or neglect by its owners.
- **D.** should not be considered a toy or a passing interest.

72. **F.** NO CHANGE
- **G.** living breathing, beings
- **H.** living, breathing beings
- **J.** living breathing beings,

73. **A.** NO CHANGE
- **B.** owners'
- **C.** owner's
- **D.** owners's

74. **F.** NO CHANGE
- **G.** a major responsibility requiring great dedication,
- **H.** creatures that require dedication and effort,
- **J.** a big responsibility,

75. Suppose the writer had intended to write a brief essay that describes the process of adopting an animal from a shelter. Would this essay successfully fulfill the writer's goal?
- **A.** Yes, because it describes the experience the author had when adopting an animal from a shelter.
- **B.** Yes, because it offers advice about how to select an animal for adoption and how to be a responsible pet owner.
- **C.** No, because it focuses on the reasons why animals are placed in shelters rather than the process of adopting animals.
- **D.** No, because it is primarily an essay about the duties involved in working at an animal shelter rather than the adoption process.

END OF TEST 1.
STOP! DO NOT TURN THE PAGE UNTIL TOLD TO DO SO.

MATHEMATICS TEST

60 Minutes—60 Questions

DIRECTIONS: After solving each problem, pick the correct answer from the five given and fill in the corresponding oval on your answer sheet. Solve as many problems as you can in the time allowed. Do not worry over problems that take too much time; skip them if necessary and return to them if you have time.

Calculator use is permitted on the test. Calculators can be used for any problem on the test, though calculators may be more harm than help for some questions.

Note: Unless otherwise stated on the test, you should assume that:

1. Figures accompanying questions are not drawn to scale.
2. Geometric figures exist in a plane.
3. When given in a question, "line" refers to a straight line.
4. When given in a question, "average" refers to the arithmetic mean.

1. Naomi decides her babysitting rate b by tripling the number of hours worked w and adding 9. Which of the following equations expresses Naomi's babysitting rate?

A. $b = \frac{1}{3}w - 9$

B. $b = \frac{1}{3}(w + 9)$

C. $b = \frac{1}{3}w + 9$

D. $b = 3(w + 9)$

E. $b = 3w + 9$

DO YOUR FIGURING HERE.

2. Marc needs $2\frac{1}{3}$ cups of sugar for a pecan pie and $3\frac{4}{5}$ cups of sugar for a chocolate cake. What is the total amount of sugar, in cups, that Marc needs to make the pie and the cake?

F. $5\frac{1}{15}$

G. $5\frac{2}{15}$

H. $5\frac{2}{5}$

J. $5\frac{5}{8}$

K. $6\frac{2}{15}$

3. An elementary school playground is shaped like a rectangle. The playground measures 30 meters by 18 meters and is completely surrounded by a chain-link fence. Approximately how long, in meters, is the fence?

A. 48
B. 96
C. 108
D. 540
E. 600

DO YOUR FIGURING HERE.

4. The operator of a commuter train keeps track of how many passengers ride each day. Last Monday through Friday, the daily passenger totals were 301, 280, 212, 313, and 299. What was the average number of passengers who rode the commuter train each day?

F. 101
G. 198
H. 281
J. 299
K. 1,405

5. Which of the following is a simplification of the expression $3(4a - 3) + 5(6a + 4)$?

A. $-18a + 11$
B. $11a + 18$
C. $42a + 11$
D. $42a - 11$
E. $53a$

6. Sam's Sporting Goods sells 20 tennis balls for $13, while Al's Athletics sells the same type of tennis balls 15 for $9. Which store sells tennis balls at the lowest price per ball, and at what price per ball?

F. Sam's Sporting Goods, at $0.60
G. Sam's Sporting Goods, at $0.65
H. Sam's Sporting Goods, at $1.54
J. Al's Athletics, at $0.60
K. Al's Athletics, at $1.67

GO ON TO THE NEXT PAGE.

7. In the figure showing $\triangle XYZ$, line a is parallel to line b. Which of the following angles must be congruent to $\angle m$?

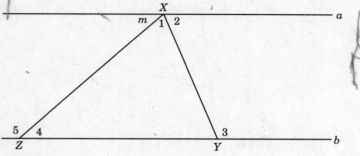

    A. $\angle 1$
    B. $\angle 2$
    C. $\angle 3$
    D. $\angle 4$
    E. $\angle 5$

8. In the 8-sided figure below, adjacent sides meet at right angles and the lengths given are in feet. What is the perimeter of the figure, in feet?

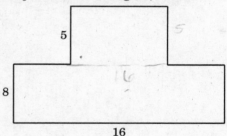

    F. 29
    G. 45
    H. 58
    J. 120
    K. 208

9. When $x + y = 12$, what is the value of

    $$3(x + y) + \frac{x + y}{3} + (x + y)^3 - 3?$$

    A. 181
    B. 187
    C. 1,765
    D. 1,771
    E. 2,224

10. If a is a real number such that $a^2 = 81$, then $a^3 + \sqrt{a} = ?$

    F. 84
    G. 162
    H. 243
    J. 732
    K. 810

11. A DVD originally cost $18, but during a sale its price was reduced by 20%. What is the current price of the DVD?

    A. $3.60
    B. $12.60
    C. $14.40
    D. $15.80
    E. $21.60

12. For all x, $(5x + 9)^2 = ?$

    F. $10x + 18$
    G. $10x^2 + 18$
    H. $5x + 81$
    J. $25x^2 + 45x + 81$
    K. $25x^2 + 90x + 81$

13. When $\frac{1}{5}d + \frac{1}{3}d = 2$, what is the value of d?

    A. $1\frac{1}{4}$

    B. $3\frac{3}{4}$

    C. 6

    D. 15

    E. 30

14. Which of the following lists gives two of the three angle measurements of a triangle in which the third angle measurement is equal to one of the two given measurements?

    F. 20, 40
    G. 20, 60
    H. 35, 110
    J. 45, 100
    K. 80, 100

15. Ilya is a chef. She wants to order 350 pie crusts from a local company. The pie crusts come in cases of 12 boxes with 3 pie crusts in each box. The local company does not allow people to order partial cases. What is the fewest number of cases that Ilya should order?

    A. 9
    B. 10
    C. 15
    D. 16
    E. 29

DO YOUR FIGURING HERE.

GO ON TO THE NEXT PAGE.

16. The ratio of the side lengths of a triangle is 11:13:16. In a second triangle similar to the first, the shortest side is 9 centimeters long. To the nearest tenth of a centimeter, what is the length of the longest side of the second triangle?

    F. 12
    G. 13.1
    H. 13.5
    J. 14
    K. 14.9

DO YOUR FIGURING HERE.

17. What number should be added to the numerator and denominator of $\frac{9}{11}$ to get $\frac{2}{3}$?

    A. −5

    B. $-2\frac{2}{5}$

    C. $\frac{2}{5}$

    D. $2\frac{2}{5}$

    E. 5

18. A clothing store is offering the following special: "Buy four T-shirts, and get the fifth T-shirt free!" This special is equivalent to what discount off the regular price of all 5 T-shirts?

    F. 10%
    G. 20%
    H. 25%
    J. 50%
    K. 80%

19. What is the length, in feet, of diagonal d of the rectangle shown below?

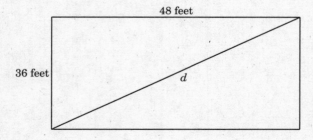

    A. 40
    B. 48
    C. 50
    D. 60
    E. 84

20. We find the area of a trapezoid by using the formula $A = \frac{1}{2}h(b_1 + b_2)$, where h is the height and b_1 and b_2 are the lengths of the parallel bases. What is the area, in square centimeters, of the trapezoid below?

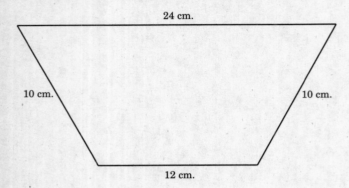

24 cm.

10 cm.   10 cm.

12 cm.

DO YOUR FIGURING HERE.

    F. 96
    G. 144
    H. 180
    J. 210
    K. 1,440

21. A large square box has edges that are 4 times as long as the edges of a small square box. The volume of the large square box is how many times the volume of the small square box?

    A. 4
    B. 8
    C. 16
    D. 64
    E. 256

22. A home-insulation company sells vinyl siding. The width, w millimeters, of each piece of vinyl must satisfy the inequality $|w - 4| \le 2$. What is the maximum width, in millimeters, that such a piece of vinyl can have?

    F. −2
    G. 2
    H. 6
    J. 8
    K. 10

GO ON TO THE NEXT PAGE.

23. The table below shows the numbers of livestock at Richfield Farms. The farm plans to sell its livestock to another farm down the road. If the animals must be sold in pairs of 1 male and 1 female, and exactly twice as many horses are sold as cattle, what is the maximum number of animals that can be sold?

Richfield Farms Animals		
Animal	Male	Female
Goats	12	20
Mules	14	17
Horses	13	18
Cattle	4	9

A. 24
B. 28
C. 38
D. 76
E. 87

DO YOUR FIGURING HERE.

24. As shown in the figure below, a chord 32 inches long is 7 inches from the center of a circle. What is the diameter of the circle, to the nearest tenth of an inch?

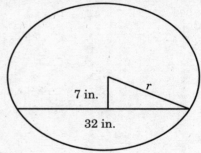

7 in.   r

32 in.

F. 17.5
G. 34.9
H. 42.1
J. 39.0
K. 64.0

25. If a sock is chosen from a drawer that contains exactly 10 red socks, 8 blue socks, and 8 white socks, what is the probability that the sock will NOT be blue?

A. $\frac{1}{13}$

B. $\frac{5}{26}$

C. $\frac{3}{13}$

D. $\frac{9}{13}$

E. $\frac{21}{26}$

26. The temperature F, in degrees Fahrenheit, of a certain liquid is given by the equation $F = \frac{3}{4}H + 5$, where H is the heat units applied. What number of heat units must be applied for the liquid's temperature to be 95 degrees Fahrenheit?

   F. 72.5
   G. 120
   H. 190
   J. 210
   K. 225.5

DO YOUR FIGURING HERE.

27. $QRST$ is a square circumscribed within a circle with center O, as shown below. If the length of $\overline{RT}$ is 264 inches, what is the circumference, in feet, of the circle?

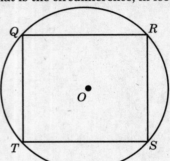

   A. 11π
   B. 22π
   C. 132
   D. 132π
   E. 264π

28. What equation below has a slope of 8?

   F. $16x - 2y + 9 = 0$
   G. $14x - 6y + 8 = 0$
   H. $16x + y - 2 = 0$
   J. $8x + 16y - 4 = 0$
   K. $8x - 2y + 6 = 0$

GO ON TO THE NEXT PAGE.

29. Pete's Pizza Palace charges $7.00 for large pizzas ordered between noon and 5 p.m. on weekdays and all day on Saturday; $8.50 for large pizzas ordered all day on Sunday; and $9.25 for large pizzas ordered after 5 p.m. on weekdays. The table below shows the number of large pizzas ordered in one week by residents of a college dorm, along with the days and times of their orders.

Day	Time	Number of Large Pizzas
Monday	2 p.m.	6
Wednesday	8 p.m.	4
Friday	3 p.m.	3
Saturday	7 p.m.	6
Sunday	4 p.m.	8

DO YOUR FIGURING HERE.

What was the total that Pete's Pizza Palace charged for the pizzas in the table?

A. $124.00
B. $156.75
C. $189.00
D. $201.50
E. $210.00

30. If two numbers a and b are negative, which of the following statements MUST be true?

F. $ab < 1$
G. $a + b < a - b$
H. $a^2 < b^2$
J. $a - b < 1$
K. $ab \neq \dfrac{a}{b}$

31. Which of the following expressions is equivalent to $(3a^2b^4)^3$?

A. $9a^6b^{12}$
B. $9a^5b^7$
C. $9a^5b^9$
D. $12a^6 + b^{12}$
E. $27a^6b^{12}$

32. Which of the following inequalities defines the solution set for the inequality

$$14 - 3x \le 7?$$

F. $x \le \dfrac{7}{3}$

G. $x \le -\dfrac{3}{7}$

H. $x \ge \dfrac{3}{7}$

J. $x \ge \dfrac{4}{3}$

K. $x \ge \dfrac{7}{3}$

DO YOUR FIGURING HERE.

33. Parallelogram $WXYZ$, with its dimensions in centimeters, is depicted below. What is the area of parallelogram $WXYZ$, in square centimeters?

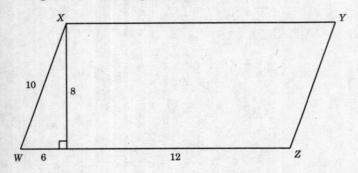

A. 80
B. 120
C. 136
D. 144
E. 180

34. Which of the following equations expresses z in terms of x for all real numbers x, y, and z such that $x^4 = y$ and $y^3 = z$?

F. $z = \dfrac{3}{4}x$

G. $z = x^7$

H. $z = x^{12}$

J. $z = 3x^4$

K. $z = x$

35. There are d doctors in a hospital. Among those doctors, s % perform at least one type of specialized surgery. Which of the following expressions represents the number of doctors who do NOT perform any type of specialized surgery?

DO YOUR FIGURING HERE.

    A. $\dfrac{(100-s)d}{100}$

    B. $.01ds$

    C. ds

    D. $\dfrac{(1-s)d}{.01}$

    E. $100(1-s)d$

36. The larger of two numbers exceeds 3 times the smaller number by 4. The sum of 3 times the larger number and 4 times the smaller number is 82. If b is the smaller number, which of the following equations determines the correct value of b?

    F. $4(3b) + 4b = 82$
    G. $(3b + 4) + 4b = 82$
    H. $(4b + 3) + 3b = 82$
    J. $3(3b + 4) + 4b = 82$
    K. $4(3b + 3) + 4b = 82$

37. A smaller circle is inscribed within a larger circle. Both circles have center O. If the radius of the larger circle is 7 centimeters longer than the radius of the smaller circle, what is the difference, in square centimeters, between the areas of the two circles?

    A. 49π
    B. $14r + 49$
    C. $\pi^2 + 14r + 49$
    D. $\pi(14r + 49)$
    E. $\pi^2 + 2{,}401$

38. Rodrigo works for a car company. His car sales increased by 20% from 2005 to 2006 and by 15% from 2006 to 2007. By what percentage did Rodrigo's car sales increase from 2005 to 2007?

    F. 35%
    G. 38%
    H. 40%
    J. 45%
    K. 47%

39. Isabel is collecting canned goods for a food drive. She collected 40 cans per week for the first 2 weeks, 37 cans during the third week, and 40 cans per week during the fourth and fifth weeks. What is the median number of cans per week that Isabel collected during the food drive?

    A. 3
    B. 37
    C. 39
    D. 40
    E. 42

DO YOUR FIGURING HERE.

40. In the figure below, tan θ = ?

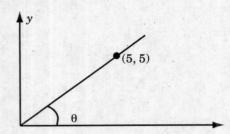

    F. $\sqrt{2}$

    G. 2

    H. 1

    J. $\dfrac{\sqrt{2}}{2}$

    K. 5

41. Which of the following lines goes through (−5, 4) and is parallel to $y = -9x + 3$?

    A. $y = 7x - 14$
    B. $y = -7x + 14$
    C. $y = -9x - 41$
    D. $y = -9x + 41$
    E. $y = 4x + 3$

GO ON TO THE NEXT PAGE.

42. What is the matrix product

$$\begin{bmatrix} 3c \\ 5c \\ -c \end{bmatrix} \begin{bmatrix} 3 & -6 & 4 \end{bmatrix}?$$

F. $\begin{bmatrix} 15c & -30c & 20c \end{bmatrix}$

G. $\begin{bmatrix} -30c \end{bmatrix}$

H. $\begin{bmatrix} 9c & -18c & 12c \\ 15c & -30c & 20c \\ -3c & 6c & 4c \end{bmatrix}$

J. $\begin{bmatrix} 45c & -90c & 60c \end{bmatrix}$

K. $\begin{bmatrix} 9c & 15c & -3c \\ -18c & -30c & 6c \\ 12c & 20c & 4c \end{bmatrix}$

43. Which of the following equations could represent the parabola graphed below?

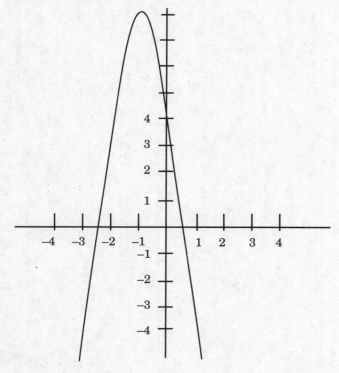

A. $y = 2x^2 - 4 + 8$
B. $y = (-2x + 4)^2 + 8$
C. $y = -(2x + 2)^2 + 8$
D. $y = (2x - 4)^2 - 8$
E. $y = 2(x + 6)$

44. What is the sum of the prime numbers between 20 and 40?

    F. 80

    G. 120

    H. 159

    J. 163

    K. 174

DO YOUR FIGURING HERE.

45. The sides of a right triangle, in centimeters, are shown below, $a > 0$. What is the secant of $\angle E$, in terms of a?

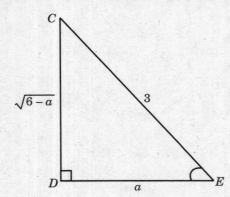

    A. 3

    B. $\dfrac{6}{a}$

    C. $\dfrac{a}{\sqrt{6-a}}$

    D. $\dfrac{\sqrt{6-a}}{a}$

    E. $\sqrt{2}$

46. What is the degree measure of the larger of the two angles formed by the line and ray shown below?

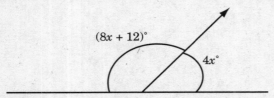

    F. 12

    G. 14°

    H. 56°

    J. 124°

    K. Cannot be determined from the given information

GO ON TO THE NEXT PAGE.

47. What is the distance in the standard coordinate plane between the points $(-5, 8)$ and $(2, 6)$?

A. 51

B. 49

C. $\sqrt{53}$

D. 7

E. $3\sqrt{5}$

48. What is the value of s for which the lines $y = sx + 4$ and $y = -7x - 9$ intersect at the point $(-8, 47)$ in the standard coordinate plane?

F. $-\dfrac{43}{8}$

G. -5

H. 2

J. 3

K. $-\dfrac{39}{2}$

49. In the figure below, $STUV$ is a square and $W, X, Y,$ and Z are the midpoints of its sides. If $ST = 16$ meters, what is the perimeter of $WXYZ$, in square meters?

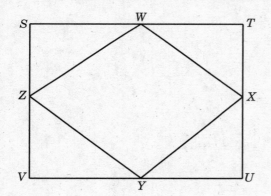

A. $2\sqrt{32}$

B. 18

C. $16\sqrt{2}$

D. 32

E. $32\sqrt{2}$

50. Which of the following is equivalent to 1?

F. $(\tan \theta)(\sin \theta)$

G. $\dfrac{\tan \theta}{\cot \theta}$

H. $\dfrac{\sin \theta}{\cos \theta}$

J. $(\sin \theta)(\cos \theta)$

K. $(\tan \theta)\left(\dfrac{\cos \theta}{\sin \theta}\right)$

DO YOUR FIGURING HERE.

Practice Test 2

GO ON TO THE NEXT PAGE. • 165

51. The graph of the equation $y = -x - 3$ such that $0 \leq x \leq 5$ is shown below. Which of the following statements is (are) true?

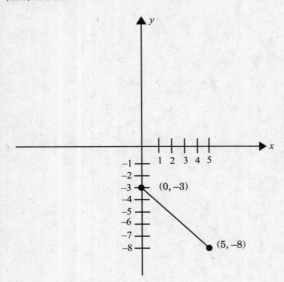

DO YOUR FIGURING HERE.

I. The graph has constant slope -2.

II. The range of the graph can be written as $-8 \leq y \leq -3$.

III. The polynomial $y = -x - 3$ has a zero of $x = -3$.

A. I only
B. I and II only
C. II and III only
D. I, II, and III
E. None are true

52. Tom went to the grocery store to buy milk and bread. Three loaves of bread and two gallons of milk would cost $15.50. Three gallons of milk and two loaves of bread would cost $17.25. How much would 1 loaf of bread and 1 gallon of milk cost?

F. $6.00
G. $6.15
H. $6.25
J. $6.45
K. $6.55

53. Which of the following is the set of all real numbers y such that $y - 4 < y - 6$?

A. The set containing all real numbers
B. The set containing all positive real numbers
C. The set containing all negative real numbers
D. The empty set
E. The set containing only zero

GO ON TO THE NEXT PAGE.

54. Which of the following graphs represents $|x| \le 6$?

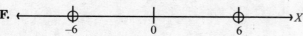

DO YOUR FIGURING HERE.

55. A function A is defined as follows:

for $n > 0$, $A(n) = 2x^3 - x^2 + 18x + 2$

for $n < 0$, $A(n) = -2x^3 + x^2 - 18x - 2$

What is the value of $A(-3)$?

A. -115
B. -75
C. 75
D. 89
E. 115

56. If $\sin\theta = \dfrac{7}{9}$ and $0 \le \theta \le \dfrac{\pi}{6}$, then $\cos\theta = ?$

F. $\dfrac{32}{81}$

G. $\dfrac{4\sqrt{2}}{9}$

H. $\dfrac{\sqrt{2}}{3}$

J. $\dfrac{4\sqrt{2}}{3}$

K. $\dfrac{2}{9}$

Practice Test 2

57. Which of the following is the graph of $y = \dfrac{4x^2 + x}{x}$, in the standard (x, y) coordinate plane?

DO YOUR FIGURING HERE.

A.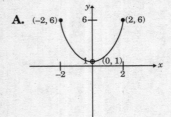

B.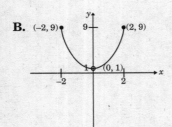

C.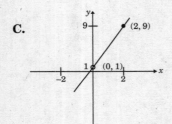

D.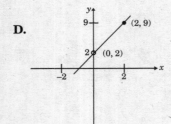

E.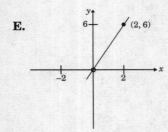

GO ON TO THE NEXT PAGE.

58. Which system of inequalities is represented by the shaded region of the graph below?

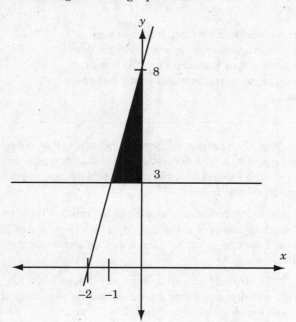

F. $y \le 5x + 8$ and $y \ge 3$

G. $y \ge 5x + 8$ and $y \ge 3$

H. $y \le 5x + 8$ and $y \ge 5$

J. $y \ge 8x + 8$ and $y \ge 5$

K. $y \le 8x + 8$ and $y \le 3$

59. Consider the functions $a(x) = \sqrt{x+2}$ and $b(x) = x^2 + 5x + c$. In the standard (x,y) coordinate plane, $y = a(b(x))$ passes through $(10,15)$. What is the value of c?

A. 24

B. 36

C. $\sqrt{37}$

D. 73

E. 75

60. Which of the following quadratic equations has solutions $z = 9f$ and $z = -15g$?

F. $z^2 + z(15g - 9f) - 135fg = 0$

G. $z^2 - z(15g + 9f) + 135fg = 0$

H. $z^2 - 135fg = 0$

J. $z^2 + z(15g + 9f) - 135fg = 0$

K. $z^2 + gz - 135fg = 0$

END OF TEST 2.
STOP! DO NOT TURN THE PAGE UNTIL TOLD TO DO SO.
DO NOT RETURN TO THE PREVIOUS TEST.

READING TEST

35 Minutes—40 Questions

DIRECTIONS: On this test, you will have 35 minutes to read four passages and answer 40 questions (ten questions on each passage). Each set of ten questions appears directly after the relevant passage. You should select the answer choice that best answers the question. There is no time limit for work on the individual passages, so you can move freely between the passages and refer to each as often as you'd like.

Passage I

Ivan Dmitritch lived with his family on a modest income and was very satisfied with his life.

"I forgot to look at the newspaper today to check the winning lottery numbers," his wife said to him as she
5 cleared the table.

"Hasn't your ticket expired?"

"No, I bought it Tuesday."

"What is the number?"

"Series 9,499, number 26."

10 Ivan had no faith in lottery luck, but he passed his finger downwards along the column of numbers. And immediately, as though in mockery of his skepticism, his eye was caught by the figure 9,499! Unable to believe his eyes, he hurriedly dropped the paper on his knees without
15 looking to see the number of the ticket, and, just as though someone had splashed him with cold water, he felt an agreeable chill in the pit of the stomach; tingling and terrible and sweet!

"Marsha, 9,499 is there!" he said in a hollow voice.

20 "And the number of the ticket?"

"It is our series," said Ivan, after a long silence. "So there is a probability that we have won. It's only a probability, but there it is!"

"Well, now look!"

25 "Wait a little. We have plenty of time to be disappointed. The prize is $750,000. What if we really have won?"

The husband and wife began laughing and staring at one another in silence. The possibility of winning
30 bewildered them; they could not have said, could not have dreamed, what they both needed that money for, what they would buy, where they would go.

Ivan, holding the paper in his hand, walked several times from corner to corner, and only when he had
35 recovered from the first impression began dreaming a little.

"And if we have won," he said, "why, it will be a new life, it will be a transformation! The ticket is yours, but if it were mine I would buy a bigger house with new furniture,
40 pay debts, and travel."

And pictures came crowding in his mind of lying on a beach thinking of nothing, and feeling all over that he doesn't need to go to the office today, tomorrow, or the day after.

45 "Yes, it would be nice to buy a new house," said his wife, also dreaming, and from her face it was evident that she was enchanted by her thoughts.

Ivan pictured autumn with its rains and cold evenings when he would take long walks outside before coming
50 home and stretching out on the sofa for a nap.

Except that autumn weather is cloudy and gloomy. It rains day and night, the bare trees weep, and the wind is damp and cold. There is nowhere to walk, and you can't go out for days. It is dreary!

55 Ivan stopped and looked at his wife.

"I should travel overseas, you know, Marsha," he said.

And he began thinking how nice autumn would be in the South of France.

"I should certainly travel overseas too," his wife said.
60 "But look at the number of the ticket!"

"Wait, wait!"

He walked about the room and went on thinking. It occurred to him: what if his wife really did travel? Ivan imagined his wife complaining that trains made her head
65 ache, or that she had spent too much money.

"She would begrudge me every cent," he thought, with a glance at his wife. "The lottery ticket is hers, not mine."

Ivan thought of her wretched relatives, who would come crawling about as soon as they heard of the winning
70 ticket. They would begin whining like beggars and fawning upon them with oily, hypocritical smiles.

And his wife's face, too, struck him as repulsive and hateful. Anger surged up in his heart against her, and he thought malignantly:

GO ON TO THE NEXT PAGE.

75 "If she won the lottery, she would give me a hundred dollars, and put the rest away under lock and key."

And he looked at his wife, not with a smile now, but with hatred. She glanced at him too, and also with hatred and anger. She had her own daydreams, her own plans, 80 her own reflections; she understood perfectly well what her husband's dreams were. She knew who would be the first to try and grab her winnings.

"It's very nice making daydreams at other people's expense!" is what her eyes expressed. "No, don't you dare!"

85 Her husband understood her look; hatred began stirring again in his breast, and in order to annoy his wife he glanced quickly, to spite her, at the fourth page on the newspaper and read out triumphantly:

"Series 9,499, number 46! Not 26!"

90 Hatred and hope both disappeared at once, and it began immediately to seem to Ivan and his wife that their rooms were dark and small and that the evenings were long and wearisome.

1. As it is used in (line 74), the word *malignantly* most nearly means:

　A. unsteadily.
　B. fearfully.
　C. certainly.
　D. cruelly.

2. Which of the following can be reasonably inferred from the passage?

　F. Marsha has never purchased a lottery ticket.
　G. Ivan has never purchased a lottery ticket.
　H. Marsha purchases a lottery ticket every week.
　J. Ivan purchases a lottery ticket every week.

3. According to the passage, Ivan attributes which of the following characteristics to Marsha's relatives?

　A. Greediness and insincerity
　B. Misery and hostility
　C. Impoverishment and hopefulness
　D. Shame and disgrace

4. According to the passage, why does Ivan dream of traveling instead of taking long walks in his village?

　F. He does not want his wife to travel alone.
　G. He wants to travel overseas with his wife.
　H. He dislikes the cold weather in the village.
　J. He dislikes the walking paths in the village.

5. It can reasonably be inferred from the conclusion of the passage (lines 90–93) that after Ivan and Marsha imagine what their life would be like if they had won the lottery:

　A. they will likely soon purchase another lottery ticket.
　B. they are relieved that they can return to normal.
　C. their real life seems lackluster by comparison.
　D. they both regret that Marsha purchased the lottery ticket.

6. According to the passage, Ivan becomes concerned about his wife traveling because:

　F. Marsha would become tired and ill.
　G. Marsha would worry and complain.
　H. Marsha would spend too much money.
　J. Marsha would want to visit her relatives.

7. It can reasonably be inferred from this passage that the reason Ivan does not immediately read the winning lottery number is to:

　A. provide himself the opportunity to imagine living a different existence.
　B. elevate Marsha's sense of anticipation and excitement about the ticket.
　C. delay the disappointment he will feel when the number is not theirs.
　D. encourage Marsha to dream about what they could do with the money.

8. According to the narrator, how does Ivan's attitude about his life change as a result of the incident with the lottery ticket?

　F. Ivan's attitude about his life remains the same throughout the passage.
　G. Ivan's opinion about his life changes from tolerance to dissatisfaction.
　H. Ivan's opinion about his life changes from contentment to displeasure.
　J. Ivan's attitude about his life changes from aversion to acceptance.

9. The passage suggests that the thought of winning the lottery introduces which of the following elements to the marriage of Ivan and Marsha?

　A. Cruelty
　B. Distrust
　C. Indifference
　D. Aggression

10. According to the passage, both Ivan and Marsha agree that the first way to spend the lottery money is to:

　F. buy new furniture.
　G. travel abroad.
　H. pay off debts.
　J. buy a new house.

GO ON TO THE NEXT PAGE. • 171

Passage II

SOCIAL SCIENCE: This passage is adapted from the article "A Study of Bluegrass Music" by Albert Haas.

Without a doubt, Bill Monroe established a new musical genre in 1939 when he formed his band, Bill Monroe and the Blue Grass Boys. Although elements of folk, blues, ragtime, and jazz can be heard in the music,
5 bluegrass is considered an extension of country music. Bluegrass differs from its musical cousin because of unique vocal harmonies, the use of acoustic stringed instruments, and a driving sound.

A heavy reliance on a variety of acoustic instruments
10 and the absence of electric instruments allows bluegrass artists to create unique sounds. What instruments should be used to produce true bluegrass music is a source of debate among fans, musicians, and historians. Bill Monroe's band was the first to play the non-traditional
15 country music, and the new music was dubbed "bluegrass" after Monroe's Blue Grass Boys, which he named after his home state of Kentucky. Some bluegrass purists believe that a band should not be categorized as bluegrass unless it uses the same five instruments as Monroe's band:
20 mandolin, fiddle, guitar, banjo, and upright bass. Despite the controversy, bluegrass bands often add an accordion, harmonica, piano, or washboard to the standard mix.

In addition to relying on a variety of stringed instruments, bluegrass music distinguishes itself from
25 other music genres through vocal harmonies and song selections. Bluegrass typically features two, three, or four part harmony, as well as the "high lonesome" vocal solo that involves singing over the main melody. Bluegrass songs have roots in gospel music, work songs, country, and
30 blues and can be traced to Scottish and Irish immigrants who settled in Appalachia. While bluegrass is clearly not folk music in regards to tempo, many bluegrass songs are narratives about heartbreak and loneliness.

Bill Monroe and the Blue Grass Boys appeared at the
35 Grand Ole Opry in 1939, but not until after World War II did the genre truly take off. During the war, recording artists were unable to produce records due to rationing, so enjoyment of the new sound was limited to live concerts. Another important event occurred in the mid 1940s—Earl
40 Scruggs became one of the Blue Grass Boys. The 21-year-old banjo prodigy from North Carolina had a unique three-finger picking style that energized audiences and created the authoritative sound of bluegrass. Although Scruggs was not the first banjo player to use a three-finger roll,
45 he made the technique so famous that it is now known as "Scruggs style."

With the addition of Scruggs, the Blue Grass Boys had all the ingredients that characterize the genre, including fast paced tempos, complicated vocal harmonies,
50 and skilled instrumentalists who would demonstrate their amazing abilities during solos on mandolin, banjo, and fiddle. Instrumental solos illustrate the connection between bluegrass and jazz. In both styles, each instrument is given the chance to play the melody and
55 improvise with the main tune, while the other instruments provide back-up.

Within bluegrass music, there are three different sub-genres: traditional bluegrass, progressive bluegrass, and bluegrass gospel. As might be anticipated, traditional
60 bluegrass musicians follow the lead established by Bill Monroe by playing folk songs and using only acoustic instruments. Although traditional bluegrass bands occasionally alter the way in which they play the standard instruments, by using more than one fiddle or guitar,
65 for example, for the most part the style mirrors that established in the mid 1940s. Ricky Skaggs and his band Kentucky Thunder are a modern example of a Grammy Award winning band that plays traditional bluegrass music.

70 In contrast to traditional bluegrass, progressive bluegrass bands incorporate electric instruments and rock and roll songs into the bluegrass style. Progressive bluegrass gained attention during the 1960s and 1970s, when bands such as Earl Scruggs's Foggy Mountain Boys
75 performed their own versions of Bob Dylan songs and included a saxophone player on duets. Alison Krauss, an American bluegrass-country singer, performs progressive bluegrass music with her band Union Station; Krauss's popularity has renewed interest in the genre.

80 Finally, while many bluegrass musicians include gospel music in their repertoire, Bluegrass gospel has become a distinctive style of its own. Lyrics focus on Christian faith and include three- or four-part harmony singing with subdued instruments in the background as well as a
85 cappella choruses.

Over the last decade, bluegrass music has enjoyed a revival with the help of Hollywood and Nashville. Bluegrass music was featured on the soundtracks of the popular films *O Brother, Where Art Thou?* and *Cold Mountain*. A number
90 of mainstream country musicians, such as Dolly Parton and Patty Loveless, have released bluegrass albums that received positive receptions from critics and fans. While the specific elements of bluegrass music vary, the legacy of Bill Monroe can still be heard today.

11. According to the passage, Bill Monroe and the Blue Grass Boys were unable to sell albums during World War II because:

    A. most of the band members had enlisted in the military.

    B. Earl Scruggs had not joined the band, so bluegrass was not popular yet.

    C. the rationing of materials prevented albums from being produced.

    D. the government limited the sale of nonessential items.

12. Use of the word *legacy* (line 93) to describe Bill Monroe indicates the author's:

    F. idea that Monroe fails to receive enough credit for his contributions.

    G. feelings of gratitude for Monroe's willingness to create a new genre.

    H. notion that Monroe was a controversial figure in the world of music.

    J. belief that Monroe represents the beginning of bluegrass music.

13. According to the passage, which of the following combinations of instruments characterizes bands that play traditional bluegrass music?

    A. Harmonica, fiddle, guitar, accordion, and saxophone

    B. Upright bass, fiddle, banjo, harmonica, and piano

    C. Fiddle, mandolin, guitar, upright bass, and banjo

    D. Banjo, electric guitar, fiddle, and mandolin

14. It may reasonably be inferred from the passage that Earl Scruggs left the Blue Grass Boys in order to:

    F. experiment with new bluegrass styles.

    G. write his own gospel lyrics and melodies.

    H. produce music for movie soundtracks.

    J. establish a new banjo picking style.

15. According to the passage, bluegrass music contains elements of all of the following musical genres EXCEPT:

    A. blues.

    B. classical.

    C. country.

    D. ragtime.

16. The passage suggests that musicians such as Alison Krauss have created a renewed interest in bluegrass music because:

    F. the singer and her band have earned Grammy Awards.

    G. elements of rock and roll music are incorporated into her style.

    H. acoustic instruments are limited in progressive bluegrass bands.

    J. country music is losing popularity, and people are intrigued by bluegrass.

17. The passage indicates that jazz and bluegrass are alike in that they both:

    A. emphasize songs with fast-paced tempos and three- or four-part harmonies.

    B. present opportunities for improvisation when guest musicians join bands for a set.

    C. offer the chance for musicians to demonstrate their instrumental skills through solos.

    D. include complicated harmonies and melodies that require exceptional musical abilities.

18. The passage indicates that "Scruggs style" refers to which of the following?

    F. The way that Earl Scruggs energized the audience

    G. The way that Earl Scruggs changed the sound of bluegrass

    H. The way that Earl Scruggs used three fingers to play banjo

    J. The way that Earl Scruggs played rock and roll songs on the banjo

19. According to the passage, Bill Monroe and the Blue Grass Boys would be categorized as:

    A. progressive bluegrass.

    B. traditional bluegrass.

    C. bluegrass gospel.

    D. country bluegrass.

20. Which of the following questions is NOT answered by information in the passage?

    F. How have folk songs influenced bluegrass?

    G. How has traditional bluegrass changed?

    H. What makes bluegrass gospel unique?

    J. When was the first bluegrass album recorded?

GO ON TO THE NEXT PAGE. • 173

Passage III

HUMANITIES: This passage is adapted from the book *The Story of My Life* by Helen Keller.

When the time of daisies and buttercups came, Miss Sullivan took me by the hand across the fields to the banks of the Tennessee River where I had my first lesson about nature. I learned how the sun and the rain help every
5 tree grow, how birds build their nests, and how squirrels and deer find food and shelter. As my knowledge of things grew, I felt more delighted about the world I was in. Long before I learned to do arithmetic, Miss Sullivan taught me to find beauty in the fragrant woods and in every blade of
10 grass.

About this time I had an experience which taught me that nature is not always kind. One day my teacher and I were returning from a nature walk. As we headed home, the weather grew warm and sultry, which required us to
15 rest periodically under shade trees. A short distance from home, we stopped under a wild cherry tree, which was so easy to climb that with my teacher's assistance I was able to scramble to a seat in the branches. It was so cool up in the tree that Miss Sullivan suggested that we eat lunch
20 there, if I promised to keep still while she went to the house for a picnic.

Suddenly a change passed over the tree while all the sun's warmth left the air. I knew the sky was black because all the heat, which meant light to me, had died
25 out of the atmosphere. A strange odor came up from the earth; I knew it was the aroma that always precedes a thunderstorm. A nameless fear clutched at my heart; I felt absolutely alone, cut off from my friends and the firm earth. The immense, the unknown, enveloped me.
30 I remained still and expectant as a chilling terror crept over me. I longed for Miss Sullivan's return, but above all things, I wanted to get down from that tree.

There was a moment of sinister silence followed by a stirring of the leaves. A shiver ran through the tree, and
35 the wind sent forth a blast that would have knocked me off if had I not clung to the branch. The tree swayed and strained, and the small twigs snapped and fell around me in showers. A wild impulse to jump seized me, but terror held me back. I crouched down in the fork of the tree as
40 the branches lashed around me. I felt the intermittent jarring that came now and then, as if something heavy had fallen and the shock had traveled up until it reached the limb I sat on. It worked my suspense up to the highest point, and just as I was thinking the tree and I would fall
45 down together, my teacher seized my hand and helped me down. I clung to her, trembling with joy to feel the earth under my feet once more. I had learned a new lesson—that

nature "wages open war against her children, and under softest touch hides treacherous claws."

50 After this experience it was a long time before I climbed another tree since the mere thought filled me with terror. But one beautiful spring morning when I was alone in the house, I became aware of a wonderful subtle fragrance in the air. I stood up and instinctively
55 stretched out my hands; it seemed as if the spirit of spring had passed through the house. I recognized the odor of the mimosa blossoms, so I felt my way to the end of the garden, knowing that the mimosa tree was near the fence where the path turns. Yes, there it was, all quivering in
60 the warm sunshine, its blossom-laden branches almost touching the long grass. Was there ever anything so exquisitely beautiful in the world before! I made my way through a shower of petals to the great trunk and for one minute stood irresolute before putting my foot in the
65 broad space between the forked branches and pulling myself up into the tree. I had some difficulty holding on because the branches were large and the bark hurt my hands. However, I had a delicious sense that I was doing something unusual and wonderful, so I kept on climbing
70 higher and higher until I reached a little seat which somebody had built there so long ago that it had become part of the tree itself. I sat there for a long, long time, feeling like a fairy on a rosy cloud. After that I spent many happy hours in my tree of paradise, thinking fair thoughts
75 and dreaming bright dreams.

21. Which of the following statements best describes the structure of this passage?

   A. It primarily consists of an event that occurred to the narrator and the interesting fact about nature that she learned as a result.

   B. It describes an incident that had an emotional effect on the narrator and how she later overcame her fears.

   C. It illustrates the narrator's attitude about a frightening event in her life and contrasts it with the objective perspective of her teacher.

   D. It begins with a description of the relationship she developed with her teacher and concludes with how the relationship made her strong.

22. At the end of the fourth paragraph (lines 47–49), the narrator's attitude about nature is apparently one of:

   F. watchful concern.

   G. reckless panic.

   H. mild disinterest.

   J. simple pleasure.

23. According to the third paragraph (lines 22–32), the narrator first realized a storm was approaching based on:

   A. the smell in the air.

   B. a change in temperature.

   C. a change in cloud color.

   D. the leaves blowing around.

24. As it is used in the fifth paragraph (line 64), the word *irresolute* most nearly means:

   F. determined.

   G. restrained.

   H. doubtful.

   J. restless.

25. It can reasonably be inferred from the passage that Miss Sullivan:

   A. believed that teaching the narrator about academic subjects was secondary to encouraging an appreciation for nature.

   B. disregarded the narrator's fears by forcing her to spend time outside alone learning how to get from place to place.

   C. thought that the narrator's fears were foolish and encouraged the narrator to prove her strength by climbing trees.

   D. felt that the narrator was unable to learn academic subjects and instead should spend time becoming familiar with her surroundings.

26. The narrator indicates that during the storm she was primarily concerned with:

   F. being hit by a branch.

   G. falling to the ground.

   H. being struck by lightning.

   J. not knowing how to return home.

27. It can reasonably be inferred from the passage that the narrator has which of the following characteristics?

   A. Sensitive hands and skin

   B. Discriminating taste buds

   C. A keen sense of direction

   D. A heightened sense of smell

28. It can reasonably be inferred that when the narrator writes about feeling "like a fairy on a rosy cloud" (line 73), she most likely means that she:

   F. imagines that she can accomplish anything now that she is strong.

   G. experiences an exciting sensation from doing something dangerous.

   H. feels pleased with herself for no longer being afraid of climbing.

   J. has a joyful sense of freedom and beauty as she sits high in the air.

29. According to the passage, the narrator appreciates which of the following aspects of the cherry tree as she sits in its branches?

   A. The feel of the petals

   B. The shade of the leaves

   C. The sound of the wind

   D. The smell of the blossoms

30. The main theme of this passage concerns the:

   F. difficulties of being different from others and the hardships that are often involved.

   G. process of growing up and finding great pleasure in activities that were once frightening.

   H. problems the narrator has with fears of being alone and of being unable to care for herself.

   J. ability to learn from frightening experiences and deal with a variety of challenging situations.

Passage IV

NATURAL SCIENCE: This passage is adapted from the article "Wind Energy and the Environment" by Carlos Fitzhugh.

Fields of large white turbines rise out of the ground along the open highways of California, Texas, and New York. Each turning blade silently promises a source of clean and free electricity as well as the hope of a reduction
5　in fossil fuel dependence. Governments around the world, including the United States, have promoted the construction of wind farms by giving subsidies to private wind energy companies. However, wind power may not be living up to its pristine image, as indicated by the rising
10　number of opponents concerned about the environmental impact of wind farms. While wind farms offer a clean source of energy that creates no air pollution and uses no water, they damage the environment in more subtle ways.

Turbines convert the kinetic energy in wind into
15　mechanical energy. Old-fashioned windmills used the energy of the wind to pump water or grind stones, but modern turbines direct the collected energy into rotors that produce electricity. Wind results from the sun shining unevenly on the earth, which occurs somewhere every day
20　due to constant temperature fluctuations; therefore, wind should provide a constant supply of energy.

In order to generate a significant amount of electricity, wind energy developers use a large number of sizeable turbines, which creates an environmental eyesore.
25　Turbines used on wind farms vary in size and power ratings, but many of them have rotor diameters over 200 feet resting on equally sized towers. Such turbines measure over 400 feet from base to blade tip. Before erecting such a considerable turbine, a large hole must
30　be dug and a concrete foundation poured to support the structure. The amount of concrete required for turbine foundations at a wind farm in Wales, England, required the developer to build a concrete factory on site, which is not an uncommon occurrence.

35　Acres of wind turbines in the middle of nowhere may not damage the visual appeal of an area, but what about wind farms along coast lines? A proposed 130-turbine windmill farm off the shores of Cape Cod faces opposition from many Massachusetts residents including Senator
40　Ted Kennedy. With a footprint of 25 square miles, Cape Wind would be visible from Cape Cod and Martha's Vineyard—vacation destinations dependent on tourists seeking tranquil views of the ocean, not a horizon littered with turbines. Tourists hoping to sail Nantucket Sound
45　would be forced to navigate around the unsightly towers, and local realtors worry about property values declining.

In addition to disrupting the visual appearance of an area, wind turbines disturb the environment for native plants and animals. While some wind farms are built on
50　flat ranch land, others are erected on mountain ridges. For example, a Pennsylvania wind plant has turbines resting on foundations that stretch over 30 feet into the bedrock. Blasting holes into a mountainside ultimately leads to erosion, water flow disturbance, the demise of plants, and
55　the disruption of animal habitats. Moreover, wind farms require the construction of access roads, power lines, and transformers, all of which impact the surrounding environment. The habitats of woodland animals are physically disturbed by the construction of wind farms,
60　especially those built on heavily wooded mountain ridges.

Not only do wind farms displace wildlife, they also harm birds and bats that mistakenly fly into turbine blades. One of the oldest wind farms in the U.S. is located in Altamont Pass, California, one hour east of San
65　Francisco. The Altamont wind farm consists of 4,800 wind turbines and was built in 1981 in response to federal and state legislation enacted after energy prices skyrocketed in the 1970s. The wind turbines at Altamont Pass are located on a major bird migratory route and are in an area with
70　the world's largest population of breeding golden eagles. A report issued in 2003 estimated that over 1,000 birds were being killed every year by the Altamont Pass turbines.

Reports further indicate that wind farms in West Virginia, Pennsylvania, and Maryland are to blame for
75　a reduction in the number of migrating bats in the area. Although uncertain why bats are flying into the turbines, researchers suspect that the creatures may be drawn to the spinning motion of the blades. Another theory suggests that bats are attracted to the once wooded mountaintops
80　cleared for the placement of numerous wind turbines because the open space makes finding insects easier. Whether birds and bats are attracted to the motion of the turbines or fail to see the large white structures remains a mystery, but the fact is clear that birds, bats, and other
85　wildlife are negatively affected by wind farms.

Wind farms appear to be a benign method of gathering electricity, but the land, animal habitats, birds, and bats destroyed by acres of wind turbines raise many questions about wind power as an environmentally friendly energy
90　source.

　　　　　　　　　　　　GO ON TO THE NEXT PAGE.

31. It can be inferred from paragraph 3 (lines 22–34), that the power generated by a wind turbine mostly depends on the:

 A. air temperature.
 B. size of the turbine.
 C. speed of the wind.
 D. location of the turbine.

32. According to the fourth paragraph, the greatest concern of people opposed to Cape Wind is the impact of the wind farm on the:

 F. local fishing industry.
 G. noise level in Cape Cod.
 H. scenic charm of the area.
 J. aquatic wildlife in Nantucket Sound.

33. According to the passage, which of the following correctly states the environmental concern about Altamont Pass?

 A. The wind farm is located in an area attractive to bats and birds searching for insects and trying to nest.
 B. The numerous turbines take up so much land that native animals are becoming extinct due to a lack of habitat space.
 C. The wind farm is situated in a heavily traveled bird migration path and is also near important breeding grounds.
 D. The turbines on the aging wind farm are beginning to deteriorate and have become too expensive to maintain.

34. The passage suggests that windmills differ from wind turbines in that windmills:

 F. generate a manual activity from kinetic electricity.
 G. convert wind energy into a manual activity.
 H. generate kinetic energy from the wind.
 J. convert kinetic energy into electricity.

35. It is reasonable to infer from the passage that the wind energy industry has benefited the most from:

 A. environmental activists calling for a reduction in greenhouse gases.
 B. electrical energy consultants advocating alternative energy sources.
 C. global predictions regarding increasing demands for energy.
 D. federal government concerns about increasing energy costs.

36. According to the passage, all of the following are potential problems associated with building wind farms on mountainsides EXCEPT:

 F. disruption of creeks and rivers.
 G. removal of trees and plants.
 H. displacement of animals.
 J. contamination of soil.

37. Based on the passage, which of the following statements, if true, would most WEAKEN the idea that wind farms "damage the environment"(lines 11–13)?

 A. Wind energy benefits society by providing a reliable and efficient source for electricity.
 B. Wind farms resolve the problem of the world's decreasing energy supply because nature provides an endless amount of wind.
 C. Wind farms produce energy quickly, and the cost of wind energy is competitive with that of coal-powered plants.
 D. Wind energy does not emit pollutants into the air or toxic waste into the water supply, so its effect on nature is minimal.

38. According to the passage, which of the following theories may explain why birds and bats fly into wind turbines?

 F. The suction pulls them toward the blades.
 G. The white structures are difficult for them to see.
 H. The turbine blades attract insects for them to eat.
 J. They are attracted to the noise of the spinning blades.

39. It can be reasonably inferred that one of the author's concerns about the construction of windmill farms, even those located on flat, open spaces, is the:

 A. additional damage caused by the need for readily available concrete.
 B. displacement of birds and bats accustomed to building nests nearby.
 C. pollution of underground water supplies caused by digging turbine holes.
 D. excessive erosion caused by large trucks carrying heavy turbine equipment.

40. According to the passage, it is the opinion of wind energy advocates that wind farms provide:

 F. an inexpensive substitute for fossil fuels.
 G. a way to maximize solar cell technology.
 H. the least intrusive use of kinetic energy.
 J. a safe alternative to nuclear power.

END OF TEST 3.
STOP! DO NOT TURN THE PAGE UNTIL TOLD TO DO SO.
DO NOT RETURN TO A PREVIOUS TEST.

SCIENCE TEST

35 Minutes—40 Questions

DIRECTIONS: This test contains seven passages, each accompanied by several questions. You should select the answer choice that best answers each question. Within the total allotted time for the Subject Test, you may spend as much time as you wish on each individual passage. Calculator use is not permitted.

Passage I

CITATION: Khomenko IA, Ivanova AR, Chakina NP, Skriptunova EN, Zavyalova AA (2007). Freezing precipitation in Russia and the Ukraine. *Advances in Geosciences* 10: 25–29.

Freezing precipitation (FP), which causes icing of the parked, taking-off, or landing aircraft and subsequently produces glaze, is one of the weather phenomena that is most dangerous for aviation. FP caused several fatal accidents in Russia and the Ukraine in the 1990s, which led to public demand that protection against icing be improved.

The amount of freezing precipitation is heavily dependent upon surface temperature in a particular region. In this report, conditions associated with FP at 8 Russian airports and 4 Ukrainian airports are studied. Figure 1 shows the distribution of FP cases based on surface air temperature.

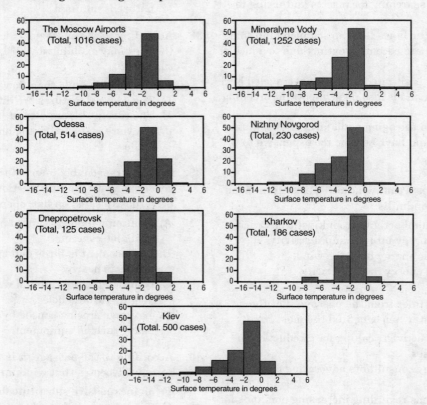

Figure 1

GO ON TO THE NEXT PAGE.

Surface wind direction also has an impact on the freezing-precipitation cases at airports. In Table 1, the Russian and Ukrainian FP cases are further classified into the number of cases (n.c.) that occurred when the wind blew in a particular direction.

	Moscow		Min. Vody		Nizhmi Novg.		Odessa		Kiev	
	n.c	%	n.c.	%	n.c.	%	n.c.	%	n.c.	%
N	38	3.7	10	0.8	29	6.4	141	29.3	19	3.8
NE	18	1.8	72	5.8	32	7.1	164	34.0	53	10.6
E	74	7.3	901	72.0	27	6.0	84	17.5	102	20.4
SE	162	15.9	139	11.1	46	10.2	7	1.5	77	15.4
S	215	21.2	8	0.6	135	29.9	7	1.5	61	12.2
SW	246	24.2	4	0.3	105	23.2	6	1.2	37	7.4
W	209	20.6	39	3.1	47	10.4	22	4.6	69	13.8
NW	54	5.3	13	1.0	21	4.6	48	10.0	46	9.2
Calm	—	—	66	5.3	10	2.2	2	0.4	36	7.2
Total	1016	100	1252	100	452	100	481	100	500	100

Table 1

1. According to Figure 1, when the surface air temperature was between −2° and 0°, which two areas had the highest percentage of reported FP cases?
   A. The Moscow Airports and Kiev
   B. Dnepropetrovsk and Kharkov
   C. Odessa and Dnepropetrovsk
   D. Kiev and Kharkov

2. According to Table 1, the greatest number of freezing-precipitation cases in Nizhny Novgorod occurs when the surface wind blows in which direction?
   F. S
   G. NW
   H. E
   J. SW

3. According to Table 1, which of the following statements is true about freezing-precipitation cases in Odessa?
   A. The greatest number of FP cases is observed when surface winds blow north.
   B. There are no recorded FP cases when surface winds are calm.
   C. There are as many FP cases when surface winds blow southeast as when they blow south.
   D. The smallest number of FP cases is observed when surface winds blow northwest.

4. A pilot receives information that she will be landing in a city where there were approximately 10 observations of freezing precipitation when the surface temperature measured between 0° and 2°. According to the information in Figure 1, the pilot could be landing in:
   F. Odessa.
   G. Kharkov.
   H. Kiev.
   J. Mineralnye Vody.

5. Which of the following statements best describes the implications of the data in Figure 1?
   A. When the surface temperature is higher than 0° C, it's safer to fly into Odessa than it is to fly into Kiev.
   B. The Moscow airports receive twice as much freezing precipitation as the Mineralnye Vody airport.
   C. At these airports, chances of freezing precipitation increase as the surface temperature decreases.
   D. At these airports, protection against icing is particularly important when the surface temperature is between −2° and 0° C.

Passage II

CITATION: Sayer EJ, Powers JS, Tanner EVJ (2007). Increased Litterfall in Tropical Forests Boosts the Transfer of Soil CO_2 to the Atmosphere. *PLoS* ONE 2(12): e1299.

Aboveground litter production in forests is likely to increase as a result of elevated atmospheric carbon dioxide (CO_2) concentrations, rising temperatures, and changing rainfall patterns. Because litterfall represents a major pathway for carbon and nutrients between vegetation and soil, it seems likely that changes in aboveground litter production will have consequences for the belowground carbon balance. This balance is particularly important in the tropics, because tropical forests store nearly 30% of the Earth's soil carbon.

Study 1

Fifteen 2,025-square-meter plots were established in an old-growth tropical forest in 2001. In 2003, all 15 plots were trenched to a depth of 0.5 meter in order to minimize water movement through the root network. Beginning in January 2003, the litter (including thick branches) was raked up once a month, resulting in the litter-removal plots (L– plots). The removed litter was immediately spread on five other plots, approximately doubling the monthly litterfall (L+ plots). The remaining five plots were left as control plots (CT plots).

In the first study, scientists measured the differences in soil respiration (CO_2 efflux) between the litter treatments and the controls in the tropical rainforest. The differences are calculated as a percentage of the average respiration of the control plots for each month. The study began in May 2004 and ended in July 2007. The gray bars represent L+ plots, while the white bars represent L– plots.

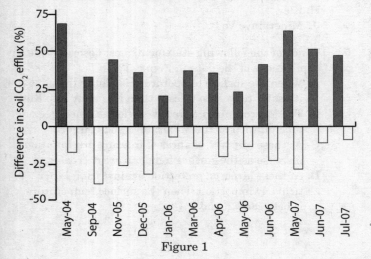

Figure 1

Study 2

In the second study, scientists measured the fine root *biomass* (living matter) in the plots' soil in 2004 and 2006. The results are shown in grams of biomass per square millimeter.

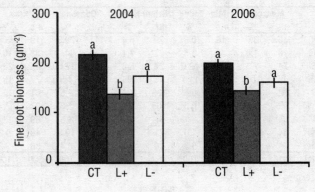

Figure 2

GO ON TO THE NEXT PAGE.

6. In April 2006, the soil CO_2 efflux in the litter-removal plots was:
    F. equal to the CO_2 efflux in the control plots.
    G. approximately 40 percent greater than the CO_2 efflux in the control plots.
    H. approximately 20 percent less than the CO_2 efflux in the control plots.
    J. approximately 5 percent less than the CO_2 efflux in the control plots.

7. According to Figure 2, the amount of fine root biomass was greatest in:
    A. the litter-addition plots.
    B. the control plots.
    C. the litter-removal plots.
    D. the control plots in 2004, but the litter-removal plots in 2006.

8. The data in Figure 1 support which of the following statements about the differences in CO_2 efflux between litter-treatment plots and control plots in the tropical rainforest?
    F. The difference in CO_2 efflux among all plots depended on the volume of the fine root biomass.
    G. The difference in CO_2 efflux between litter-addition plots and control plots is the same as the difference in CO_2 efflux between litter-removal plots and control plots.
    H. The difference in CO_2 efflux between litter-addition plots and control plots was greater than the difference in CO_2 efflux between litter-removal plots and control plots.
    J. The difference in CO_2 efflux between litter-removal plots and control plots was greater than the difference in CO_2 efflux between litter-addition plots and control plots.

9. In which timeframe did the difference in CO_2 efflux in the litter-addition plots change the most?
    A. Between June 2007 and July 2007
    B. Between December 2005 and January 2006
    C. Between May 2004 and September 2004
    D. Between March 2006 and April 2006

10. Which of the following conclusions about fine root biomass is consistent with the results shown in Figure 2?
    F. Total fine root biomass decreased significantly between May 2004 and May 2006.
    G. Total fine root biomass increases as litterfall on rainforest soil increases.
    H. Total fine biomass increased significantly between May 2004 and May 2006.
    J. Total fine root biomass decreases as litterfall on rainforest soil increases.

11. An unclassified plot of rainforest soil produced the greatest amount of CO_2 efflux in May 2004. This same plot yielded between 100 and 200 g/m^{-2} of fine root biomass in both 2004 and 2006. According to Figures 1 and 2, which of the following could scientists conclude about the unclassified plot?
    A. The unclassified plot is a control plot.
    B. The unclassified plot is a litter-addition plot.
    C. The unclassified plot is a litter-removal plot.
    D. The unclassified plot has a greater fine root biomass yield than other plots.

Passage III

CITATION: Schmidt NM, Asferg T, Forchhammer MC (2004). Long-term patterns in European brown hare population dynamics in Denmark: effects of agriculture, predation and climate. *BMC Ecology* 4:15.

In Denmark, harvest records indicate a significant decline European brown hare numbers. This decline is often attributed to agricultural practice. The amount of both uncultivated and semi-cultivated land in Denmark has been reduced dramatically, owing to the general intensification of agriculture. The brown hare is an herbivore that depends upon winter cereals, root crops, and other plant forms for survival. Figure 1 shows the total areas of seven crop categories in Denmark from 1955 to 2000.

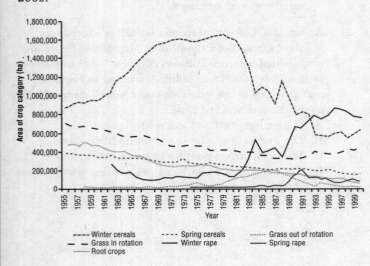

Figure 1

Researchers also studied the brown-hare population in Denmark from 1955 to 2000. Figure 2 and 3 show the shifts in hare population in the towns of Viborg and Ringkøbing.

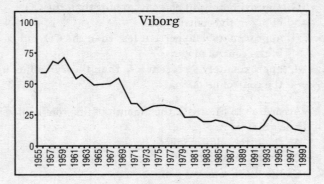

Figure 2

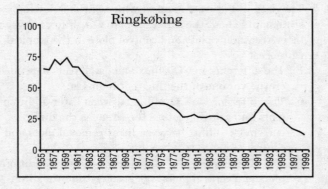

Figure 3

GO ON TO THE NEXT PAGE.

12. According to Figures 2 and 3, the hare population in Viborg and Ringkøbing can best be described as:
    F. in constant decline.
    G. in steady decline, with occasional increases.
    H. steadily increasing.
    J. slowly increasing, with occasional decreases.

13. According to Figure 2, during which year was the hare population in Ringkøbing at its highest?
    A. 1955
    B. 1960
    C. 1988
    D. 1995

14. Researchers discovered that, during a certain time period, a destructive fungus attacked the winter cereal crop. According to the information in Figure 1, this most likely happened:
    F. before 1955.
    G. between 1963 and 1967.
    H. between 1977 and 1979.
    J. between 1981 and 1984.

15. According to the data in all three figures, what most likely happened around 1995?
    A. The hare population increased, leading to an increase in root crops.
    B. The hare population increased, leading to an increase in the winter cereal crop.
    C. Root crops increased, leading to an increase in the hare population.
    D. The winter cereal crop increased, leading to an increase in the hare population.

16. Red foxes prey upon brown hares. If a researcher discovered that the red fox population was at its peak in the 1960s, which of the following questions would this information answer?
    F. Why did the amount of grass in rotation slowly decline throughout the 1960s?
    G. Why did the brown hare population suddenly increase in the mid-1990s?
    H. Why did the brown hare population decrease in the 1960s even though the winter cereal crop was at its peak?
    J. Why did the red fox population suddenly increase in the 1960s even though there weren't many brown hares?

Passage IV

CITATION: So P-W, Yu W-S, Kuo Y-T, Wasserfall C, Goldstone AP, et al. (2007). Impact of resistant starch on body fat patterning and central appetite regulation. *PLoS ONE 2*(12): e1309.

The link between obesity, *adipose* (fatty tissue) distribution, and premature mortality is one of the most enduring observations in the field of nutrition. Adipose tissue patterning has a major influence on the risk of developing chronic disease. There is evidence that changes in carbohydrate consumption have contributed to an increase in obesity. The following studies were performed to investigate the impact of resistant starch (RS) on adipose tissue in mice.

Study 1

For eight weeks, forty mice were put on a diet supplemented with either the high resistant starch (HRS) or the readily digestible, low resistant starch (LRS). The food intake of both groups of mice is displayed in Figure 1. The mice in both groups were weighed during each of the eight weeks. The weight (in grams) of the HRS-intake mice and the LRS-intake mice are displayed in Figure 2.

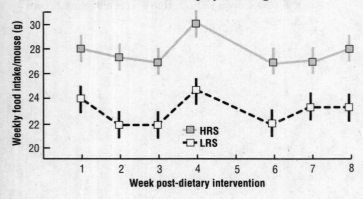

Figure 1

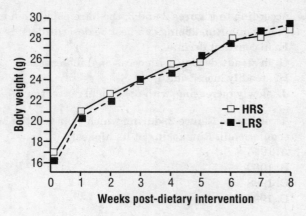

Figure 2

Study 2

In addition to measuring the weight of the mice, researchers measured the adiposity percentage in both groups. Figure 3 shows the results of these measurements.

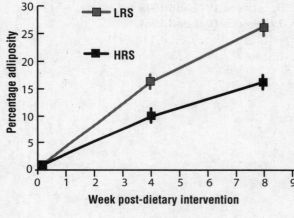

Figure 3

GO ON TO THE NEXT PAGE.

17. According to Figure 1, during which week did mice in both groups consume the most food?
    A. Week 1
    B. Week 2
    C. Week 4
    D. Week 8

18. According to Figure 3, which group of mice had the highest percentage of adiposity, and during which week?
    F. Mice on the LRS diet during Week 8
    G. Mice on the HRS diet during Week 8
    H. Mice on the LRS diet during Week 1
    J. Mice on the HRS diet during Week 4

19. Based on the information in Figure 1 and Figure 2, one can conclude that a mouse on the HRS diet:
    A. has a greater body weight than a mouse on the LRS diet, despite consuming similar amounts of food each week.
    B. has a body weight very similar to a mouse on the LRS diet, despite consuming a significantly smaller amount of food each week.
    C. has a smaller body weight than a mouse on the LRS diet, despite consuming similar amounts of food each week.
    D. has a body weight very similar to a mouse on the LRS diet, despite consuming a significantly greater amount of food each week.

20. During Week 2, a mouse consumes approximately 28 grams of food, and its adiposity percentage is around 5 percent. This mouse:
    F. weighs around 26 grams.
    G. weighs around 30 grams.
    H. is on the HRS diet.
    J. is on the LRS diet.

21. Which of the following assumptions was made in the design of both studies?
    A. Mice prefer diets high in HRS to diets high in LRS.
    B. At the beginning of the study, all forty mice had similar body weights and adiposity percentages.
    C. The reactions of mice to LRS and HRS diets are not representative of other species.
    D. At the beginning of the study, all forty mice had different body weights and adiposity percentages.

22. The results from which of the studies, if either, support the conclusion that an LRS diet is healthier than an HRS diet?
    F. Study 1 only
    G. Study 2 only
    H. Studies 1 and 2
    J. Neither study supports this conclusion.

Passage V

Scientists, politicians, and heads of corporations frequently debate the advantages and disadvantages of biotechnology. One of the biggest biotechnology debates surrounds genetically modified organisms (GMOs). The Cartagena Protocol, an international agreement on biotechnology and biosafety, allows nations to ban the import of GMOs if they feel the products are unsafe. Opponents of this protocol say that GMOs are safe and the Cartagena Protocol is unnecessary. Supporters of the Cartagena Protocol say that GMOs are often bad for the environment and for society. Both arguments are presented below.

The Anti-Cartagena Protocol Argument

Global fears about genetically modified organisms are largely unfounded and overblown. In order for participating nations to agree on the elements of the Cartagena Protocol, there must be many meetings and debates. This is a waste of time, particularly when the time and money would be better spent teaching farmers in the developing world how to benefit from GMOs.

GMO technology is already widely accepted and utilized. According to the International Service for the Acquisition of Agri-Biotech Applications, 8.5 million farmers in 21 countries grow genetically modified crops. Ninety percent of those farmers reside in poor, developing countries. They would not use GMO technology if it didn't benefit them. Additionally, farmers who grow genetically modified crops can reduce the use of harmful farm chemicals and increase their crop yields. This increased yield is vital for developing, rural economies. Instead of spending time and money debating the details of the Cartagena Protocol, we should focus our resources where they will do the most good: with the food growers of the world.

The Pro-Cartagena Protocol Argument

The production of genetically modified organisms is dangerous for the environment and for the stability of developing-world economies. For this reason, the Cartagena Protocol is very important. Modern biotechnology creates unnecessary risks, particularly when we examine its impact on the environment. More than 50 percent of the United States' soybean crop is genetically engineered to withstand being sprayed by herbicide (weed killer). Because of this, herbicide is sprayed in greater quantities. Some biotech companies produce plants that can create their own insecticides. The insecticide is so plentiful in these plants that, over time, the insects it targets will develop a resistance to it. Clearly, these herbicide-producing plants create more problems than they solve. Finally, the patents for most genetically modified organisms are owned by biotechnology corporations. This means that the farmers who grow the genetically modified crops do not have the right to save and replant seeds. In effect, without the Cartagena Protocol in place, large biotechnology firms will have control over food resources in developing nations.

23. The Anti-Cartagena Protocol Argument would be most strengthened by finding that genetically modified crops:

A. increase the number of herbicide-resistant weeds.

B. pass environmental safety tests worldwide.

C. provide financial stability for large biotech corporations.

D. are more difficult to grow than traditional crops.

24. Supporters of both the Anti-Cartagena Protocol Argument and the Pro-Cartagena Protocol Argument would agree that the Cartagena Protocol:

F. affects the way in which farmers grow their crops.

G. is necessary to protect the rights of farmers in developing nations.

H. is more beneficial for the United States than for developing nations.

J. wastes time and money that could be spent helping farmers.

25. Assuming that the Pro-Cartagena Protocol Argument is correct, which of the following conclusions can be made about genetically modified soybean crops?

A. Genetically modified soybean crops are safe to grow in the United States but harmful to grow in developing nations.

B. Genetically modified soybean crops require a greater financial investment than traditional soybean crops.

C. Genetically modified soybean crops are harmful for the environment, because farmers who grow them are likely to use a greater amount of harmful herbicides.

D. Genetically modified soybean crops provide an economic boost to farmers in developing nations.

26. Which of the following questions is raised by the Anti-Cartagena Protocol Argument, but NOT answered in the passage?

F. Are genetically modified crops grown more frequently in industrialized or developing nations?

G. What are the advantages of saving and replanting seeds?

H. How does growing genetically modified crops reduce the use of harmful farm chemicals?

J. Why is the United States' soybean crop being sprayed with large amounts of herbicide?

27. If it was discovered that crops in developing nations failed when farmers did not save and replant seeds, how would this discovery affect the arguments, if at all?

A. It would have no effect on either argument.

B. It is consistent with the Anti-Cartagena Protocol Argument only.

C. It is consistent with both arguments.

D. It is consistent with the Pro-Cartagena Protocol Argument only.

28. Based on both arguments, genetically modified organisms:

F. are only useful in developing nations.

G. have a significant impact on the world's food supply.

H. pose a serious threat to the environment.

J. lead to economic stability in rural economies.

29. The Pro-Cartagena Protocol Argument predicts that plants capable of producing their own insecticide will

A. prevent farmers in developing nations from replanting seeds.

B. reduce farmers' dependence on harmful chemicals.

C. lead to an increase in the insecticide-resistant insect population.

D. pose health risks to humans who consume them.

Practice Test 2

Passage VI

CITATION: Knudsen BM, Harris NRP, Andersen SB, Christiansen B, Larsen N, Rex M, Naujokat B (2004). Extrapolating future Arctic ozone losses, *Atmospheric Chemistry and Physics:* 1849–1856.

The *stratosphere* (the second layer of the Earth's atmosphere) has been cooling for decades. Additionally, some measurements suggest that the amount of water vapor in the stratosphere is increasing, leading to an increase in polar stratospheric clouds (PSCs). Both of these factors tend to increase the ozone depletion. However, researchers disagree about the manner and rate in which ozone depletion will occur. Different climate models yield different results.

Figure 1 shows a strong correlation between an increase in PSCs and an increase ozone depletion. The data in the legend represents the total Northern Hemisphere ozone depletion in metric tons (Mt) from 1992 to 2000.

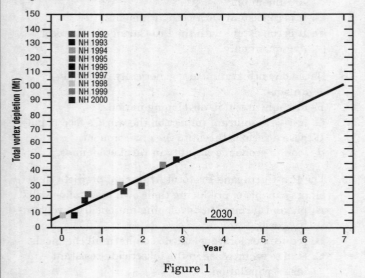

Figure 1

Figure 2 represents a longer-term approach to ozone-depletion research. The figure charts ozone depletion in metric tons (Mt) from 1970 onward.

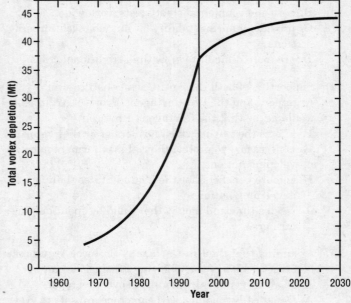

Figure 2

GO ON TO THE NEXT PAGE.

30. According to Figure 1, during which year were approximately 20 metric tons of ozone depleted in the Northern Hemisphere?

F. 1992
G. 1993
H. 1994
J. 1996

31. According to Figure 2, during which decade did ozone depletion increase the most?

A. 1960s
B. 1970s
C. 1980s
D. 1990s

32. Which of the following statements best describes the major difference between Figure 1 and Figure 2?

F. Figure 1 predicts a steady, consistent increase in ozone depletion, while Figure 2 predicts the depletion rate will slow down significantly around the year 2010.
G. Figure 1 predicts a rapid rise in ozone depletion around the year 2030, while Figure 2 predicts a steady decline in ozone depletion.
H. Figure 1 predicts a steady decrease in ozone depletion, while Figure 2 predicts the depletion rate will increase significantly around the year 2010.
J. Figure 1 predicts no increase in ozone depletion, while Figure 2 predicts the depletion rate will continue steadily through the year 2010.

33. The researchers who created Figure 1 examined Figure 2. How would these researchers most likely explain the decrease in total ozone depletion beginning around 2010?

A. The temperature of the stratosphere will decrease around 2010.
B. The total area of polar stratospheric clouds will begin to decrease around 2010.
C. The total amount of water vapor in the atmosphere will increase around 2010.
D. The total area of polar stratospheric clouds will begin to increase around 2010.

34. The success of the Montreal Protocol, an international treaty that aims to stop the production of environment-endangering chemicals, should lead to decreasing amounts of ozone-depleting substances in the future. This, in turn, would lead to decreased ozone depletion if other factors remained unchanged. Which of the following statements is true?

F. Figure 1 reflects the goals of the Montreal Protocol.
G. Figure 2 reflects the goals of the Montreal Protocol.
H. Both Figure 1 and Figure 2 reflect the goals of the Montreal Protocol.
J. Neither Figure 1 nor Figure 2 reflects the goal of the Montreal Protocol.

Passage VII

CITATION: Hurst BS, Bhojwani JT, Marshburn PB, Papadakis MA, Loeb TA, Matthews ML (2005). Low-dose aspirin does not improve ovarian stimulation, endometrial response, or pregnancy rates for in vitro fertilization. *Journal of Experimental & Clinical Assisted Reproduction* 2: 8.

Aspirin has been utilized as a potential therapy to assist in the success of in vitro fertilization (IVF). The drug has been shown to increase blood flow in the uterus. As a result, clinicians have hypothesized that aspirin can increase the thickness of the endometrium, or uterine lining, thereby increasing the rates of implantation, pregnancy, and live births during IVF procedures. Two experiments were conducted by scientists to determine the effect of aspirin on the success of IVF.

Experiment 1

Scientists collected data on 316 subjects who underwent IVF cycles during a specified time period. Subjects in the experimental group received 80 mg of aspirin per day throughout their entire IVF cycles. Subjects in the control group received no aspirin during the course of their IVF cycles. Table 1 summarizes the demographic characteristics of both groups studied.

Characteristic	Experimental Group	Control Group
Number of subjects	72 (23%)	244 (77%)
Age	34 years	34 years
Previously pregnant	7 (10%)	39 (16%)
Prior IVF	32%	22%
Basal FSH (mIU/mL)	7 ± 2	7 ± 8

Table 1

The scientists determined the maximum thickness of the endometrial linings of all subjects in the experimental and control groups. The results are shown in Table 2.

Characteristic	Experimental Group	Control Group
Maximum endometrial thickness (mm)	12 ± 2	12 ± 2

Table 2

Experiment 2

Scientists recorded the number of embryos transferred to subjects in the experimental and control groups of Experiment 1 during their IVF cycles. They then measured and recorded the implantation, pregnancy, and live birth rates for these same subjects. The results are shown in Table 3. Implantation occurs when the embryo successfully attaches to the endometrium.

Characteristic	Experimental Group	Control Group
Embryos transferred	4 ± 1	3 ± 1
Implantation rate	21%	30%
Pregnancy rate	48%	57%
Live birth rate	29%	41%

Table 3

GO ON TO THE NEXT PAGE.

35. In Experiment 1, by how many millimeters did the maximum endometrial thickness differ between the subjects who received aspirin and the subjects who received no aspirin?
A. 0
B. 1
C. 3
D. 12

36. Do the results of Experiment 2 support the hypothesis that aspirin treatment increases the pregnancy rate of women who undergo IVF procedures?
F. Yes; the pregnancy rate for subjects who took aspirin was higher than the live birth rate of the subjects who took aspirin.
G. Yes; although subjects who took aspirin had fewer embryos transferred, their pregnancy rate was higher than that of the subjects who did not take aspirin.
H. No; the pregnancy rate for subjects who took aspirin was lower than that of the subjects who did not take aspirin.
J. No; the pregnancy rate for subjects who took aspirin remained the same as that for subjects who did not take aspirin.

37. From the results of Experiments 1 and 2, what would one hypothesize, if anything, about the effect of age on the pregnancy rate of women undergoing IVF treatment?
A. The older the patient, the lower the pregnancy rate during IVF treatment.
B. The older the patient, the higher the pregnancy rate during IVF treatment.
C. The age of IVF patients does not affect the pregnancy rate of the patients.
D. No hypothesis can be made because only one age group was tested.

38. Which of the following, if it had occurred, would most likely have supported the conclusion that aspirin treatment increases the success of IVF procedures?
F. The pregnancy rate for the experimental group was 33%.
G. The live birth rate for the experimental group was 60%.
H. The live birth rate for the control group was 60%.
J. The implantation rate for the control group was 21%.

39. In Experiment 1, which of the following factors varied?
A. The IVF history of subjects
B. The pregnancy history of subjects
C. The administration of aspirin to subjects
D. The method of measuring endometrial thickness

40. Based on the results of Experiment 2, if a doctor wishes to improve the chances of a live birth during an IVF cycle, which of the following approaches should be utilized?
F. Exactly four embryos should be transferred during the IVF procedure.
G. Aspirin should be administered only for part of the IVF cycle.
H. Aspirin should be administered in doses of 80 mg per day.
J. Aspirin should not be administered during the IVF cycle.

END OF TEST 4.
STOP! DO NOT RETURN TO ANY OTHER TEST.

WRITING TEST

DIRECTIONS: This test evaluates your writing skills. You will be given thirty (30) minutes to write an original essay. Before you start, read the writing prompt and be sure you understand the task required. Your essay will be scored based on how well you express judgments by taking a clear position on the issue presented; maintain your focus on your argument throughout the entire essay; support your position with logical reasoning and relevant evidence; present your ideas in an organized manner; and demonstrate clear and effective use of language, based on standard written English language conventions.

To plan out your essay, you may use the unlined page provided. You will not be scored on any information written on this unlined page. *Your essay must be written on the lined pages provided.* Your essay will be scored based only on the writing on those lined pages. You may not end up using all of the lined pages provided, but to be sure that you have enough space to complete your essay, do NOT skip any lines. Corrections or additions may be written in neatly between the lines of your essay, but you must NOT include any writing in the margins of the lined pages. *If your essay is illegible, it cannot be scored, so be sure to write or print clearly.*

If you finish your essay early, you may go back and review what you have written. When time is called, stop writing immediately and lay down your pencil.

ACT Assessment Writing Test Prompt

Some public high schools have considered implementing policies that require students to wear uniforms to school. Some people think that requiring uniforms is a good idea because a uniform dress code will help improve student performance in school. Other people think students should not be required to wear uniforms, because they see no relationship between dress code and student performance. In your opinion, should public high schools require students to wear uniforms to school?

Write an essay that develops your position on this question. You may choose to take one of the two viewpoints given, or you may present a different position on this question. Support your position using specific reasons and examples.

Begin WRITING TEST here.

WRITING TEST

Practice Test 2: Answers & Explanations

Question Number	Answer	Right	Wrong	Question Number	Answer	Right	Wrong
	English			38.	J	—	—
1.	B	—	—	39.	B	—	—
2.	J	—	—	40.	G	—	—
3.	C	—	—	41.	D	—	—
4.	J	—	—	42.	H	—	—
5.	B	—	—	43.	C	—	—
6.	F	—	—	44.	H	—	—
7.	A	—	—	45.	D	—	—
8.	H	—	—	46.	G	—	—
9.	A	—	—	47.	D	—	—
10.	J	—	—	48.	H	—	—
11.	C	—	—	49.	C	—	—
12.	G	—	—	50.	J	—	—
13.	B	—	—	51.	B	—	—
14.	H	—	—	52.	G	—	—
15.	B	—	—	53.	C	—	—
16.	G	—	—	54.	H	—	—
17.	D	—	—	55.	B	—	—
18.	G	—	—	56.	J	—	—
19.	A	—	—	57.	D	—	—
20.	J	—	—	58.	H	—	—
21.	C	—	—	59.	C	—	—
22.	G	—	—	60.	J	—	—
23.	D	—	—	61.	D	—	—
24.	H	—	—	62.	H	—	—
25.	D	—	—	63.	B	—	—
26.	H	—	—	64.	G	—	—
27.	B	—	—	65.	D	—	—
28.	F	—	—	66.	H	—	—
29.	C	—	—	67.	C	—	—
30.	J	—	—	68.	G	—	—
31.	C	—	—	69.	A	—	—
32.	J	—	—	70.	F	—	—
33.	B	—	—	71.	D	—	—
34.	F	—	—	72.	H	—	—
35.	A	—	—	73.	B	—	—
36.	H	—	—	74.	J	—	—
37.	B	—	—	75.	C	—	—

Question Number	Answer	Right	Wrong	Question Number	Answer	Right	Wrong
	Mathematics			31.	E	—	—
1.	E	—	—	32.	K	—	—
2.	K	—	—	33.	D	—	—
3.	B	—	—	34.	H	—	—
4.	H	—	—	35.	A	—	—
5.	C	—	—	36.	J	—	—
6.	J	—	—	37.	D	—	—
7.	D	—	—	38.	G	—	—
8.	H	—	—	39.	B	—	—
9.	C	—	—	40.	H	—	—
10.	J	—	—	41.	C	—	—
11.	C	—	—	42.	H	—	—
12.	K	—	—	43.	C	—	—
13.	B	—	—	44.	G	—	—
14.	H	—	—	45.	D	—	—
15.	B	—	—	46.	J	—	—
16.	G	—	—	47.	C	—	—
17.	A	—	—	48.	F	—	—
18.	G	—	—	49.	E	—	—
19.	D	—	—	50.	K	—	—
20.	G	—	—	51.	C	—	—
21.	D	—	—	52.	K	—	—
22.	H	—	—	53.	D	—	—
23.	D	—	—	54.	H	—	—
24.	G	—	—	55.	E	—	—
25.	D	—	—	56.	G	—	—
26.	G	—	—	57.	C	—	—
27.	B	—	—	58.	F	—	—
28.	F	—	—	59.	D	—	—
29.	E	—	—	60.	F	—	—
30.	G	—	—				

Question Number	Answer	Right	Wrong	Question Number	Answer	Right	Wrong
	Reading			21.	B	—	—
1.	D	—	—	22.	F	—	—
2.	G	—	—	23.	B	—	—
3.	A	—	—	24.	H	—	—
4.	H	—	—	25.	A	—	—
5.	C	—	—	26.	G	—	—
6.	G	—	—	27.	D	—	—
7.	A	—	—	28.	J	—	—
8.	H	—	—	29.	B	—	—
9.	B	—	—	30.	G	—	—
10.	J	—	—	31.	B	—	—
11.	C	—	—	32.	H	—	—
12.	J	—	—	33.	C	—	—
13.	C	—	—	34.	G	—	—
14.	F	—	—	35.	D	—	—
15.	B	—	—	36.	J	—	—
16.	G	—	—	37.	D	—	—
17.	C	—	—	38.	G	—	—
18.	H	—	—	39.	A	—	—
19.	B	—	—	40.	F	—	—
20.	J	—	—				

Question Number	Answer	Right	Wrong	Question Number	Answer	Right	Wrong
	Science			21.	B	—	—
1.	B	—	—	22.	J	—	—
2.	F	—	—	23.	B	—	—
3.	C	—	—	24.	F	—	—
4.	H	—	—	25.	C	—	—
5.	D	—	—	26.	H	—	—
6.	H	—	—	27.	D	—	—
7.	B	—	—	28.	G	—	—
8.	H	—	—	29.	C	—	—
9.	C	—	—	30.	H	—	—
10.	J	—	—	31.	C	—	—
11.	B	—	—	32.	F	—	—
12.	G	—	—	33.	B	—	—
13.	B	—	—	34.	G	—	—
14.	J	—	—	35.	A	—	—
15.	D	—	—	36.	H	—	—
16.	H	—	—	37.	D	—	—
17.	C	—	—	38.	G	—	—
18.	F	—	—	39.	C	—	—
19.	D	—	—	40.	J	—	—
20.	H	—	—				

Calculating Your Score

To find your scaled scores for each test, add up the number of questions you answered correctly on each test. That number represents your raw score for the test. Then covert your raw score to a 1–36 score using the table below. To find your Composite Score for the entire exam, add up your scaled scores for all four tests and divide that total by 4. Round off any fractions to the nearest whole number.

Keep in mind that this score is just a rough estimate. The only completely accurate predictors of your current scoring level are the scoring scales provided with official ACT materials, so make sure you practice with them in the week or two before the test to gauge where you stand.

Scaled Score	Raw Scores				Scaled Score
	Test 1	Test 2	Test 3	Test 4	
	English	Mathematics	Reading	Science	
36	75	60	38–40	40	36
35	73–74	58–59	37	—	35
34	71–72	56–57	36	39	34
33	70	55	35	—	33
32	69	54	34	38	32
31	68	52–53	—	—	31
30	67	50–51	33	37	30
29	65–66	48–49	32	36	29
28	64	46–47	30–31	35	28
27	62–63	43–45	29	34	27
26	60–61	41–42	28	32–33	26
25	57–59	39–40	27	30–31	25
24	55–56	37–38	26	29	24
23	53–54	35–36	25	27–28	23
22	50–52	33–34	24	25–26	22
21	47–49	31–32	23	23–24	21
20	44–46	30	22	21–22	20
19	42–43	27–29	21	18–20	19
18	39–41	25–26	20	16–17	18
17	37–38	22–24	19	14–15	17
16	34–36	18–21	17–18	13	16
15	30–33	15–17	16	12	15
14	28–29	12–14	14–15	10–11	14
13	26–27	09–11	12–13	09	13
12	24–25	08	10–11	08	12
11	22–23	06–07	08–09	07	11
10	20–21	05	07	06	10
9	18–19	04	06	05	9
8	15–17	—	05	04	8
7	13–14	03	—	03	7
6	10–12	02	04	—	6
5	08–09	—	03	02	5
4	06–07	—	02	—	4
3	04–05	01	—	01	3
2	02–03	—	01	—	2
1	00–01	00	00	00	1

Practice Test 2: Answers & Explanations

ENGLISH

1. B
Basic Grammar and Usage: Subject-Verb Agreement *Easy*

Group is a collective noun, which means that it should be treated as a unit. Since *group* is a singular noun, the verb *live* does not agree. The verb *live* would be appropriate with a plural noun. **C** and **D** are incorrect for the same reason—*do live* and *have lived* agree with plural nouns. The best answer is **B**—*group lives*.

2. J
Sentence Structure: Parallelism *Medium*

Multiple verbs in a sentence should be parallel, which means they should be similarly structured. The verb phrase *are renowned* is not parallel with the second verb of the sentence *proving*. **H** makes the sentence confusing, and **G** fails to make the verbs parallel. **J** is the best answer because the past-tense verb *proved* is joined by the helping verb *have*, which is similar in structure to *are renowned*.

3. C
Style: Word Choice and Identifying Tone *Medium*

It is important to pay close attention to the phrasing of this question. The question asks for the choice that does NOT show exactness. In other words, the best answer here is the worst word choice. *Roughly*, *nearly*, and *approximately* convey the idea that the number of Sherpas living in the Khumbu Valley is an estimate. *Precisely* is the only word that indicates exactness, so **C** is the best answer.

4. J
Style: Redundancy and Wordiness *Medium*

The underlined portion is unnecessary because the first part of the sentence makes it clear that Sherpas live in Nepal. **H** also repeats previously stated information about Nepal. The information in **G** is included in the last part of the sentence, so *of Nepal near the border of China* is also unnecessary. The underlined portion serves no purpose in the sentence and is redundant, so deleting *of Nepal* from the sentence is the best choice.

5. B

Sentence Structure: Sentence Fragments   *Medium*

Due to their physical strength and seeming resistance to cold temperatures is an incomplete sentence when followed by a period, so **A** is wrong. Semicolons are used to separate two complete sentences, so **C** is also wrong. A comma placed after *temperatures* clarifies that the main part of the sentence begins with *Sherpas* and creates a necessary pause, so the best answer is **B**. The lack of any punctuation, as in **D**, creates confusion for the reader.

6. F

Sentence Structure: Comma Splices   *Medium*

Remember that this question asks for which choice is NOT acceptable, so we are looking for a grammatically incorrect choice. The underlined portion is a comma splice, which means that a complete sentence is on both sides of the comma, and the two complete thoughts need to be separated. **G** and **H** are correct because a period or semicolon breaks up the two parts. A colon also works in this case because the second sentence further explains the first. **F** is the correct answer because it includes no punctuation.

7. A

Writing Strategy: Additional Detail and Evidence   *Difficult*

A is correct because some readers may not know about *typical effects of high altitude*, and adding examples of the effects clarifies the meaning. The additional information does not pertain specifically to the *health of Sherpas*, so **B** is wrong. **C** and **D** are incorrect because the phrase is necessary, relates to the essay, and clarifies information.

8. H

Punctuation: Commas   *Easy*

In the original version, the comma after *Goddess Mother* precedes the prepositional phrase *of the Land*, and commas are unnecessary before prepositional phrases. **G** is incorrect because the comma interrupts the phrase *refer to as*. A comma between *Nepalese* and *refer* breaks up the noun and the verb in **J**, and subjects and verbs should not be separated by commas. No commas are necessary in the underlined portion, so the best answer is **H**.

9. A

Organization: Sentence Reorganization   *Difficult*

The original organization of the sentence makes sense in relation to the rest of the paragraph, which indicates that Mount Everest is special to the Nepalese. **B** makes it seem that the Nepalese are *too special for humans to cross*. The placement of *them* in **C** makes it unclear whether *them* refers to *slopes* or *humans*. **D** is wrong because *humans* are described as *too special* rather than the *slopes of Mount Everest*. The best answer is **A**.

10. J

Basic Grammar and Usage: Pronoun-Antecedent Agreement   *Easy*

The singular pronoun *its* does not agree with *Sherpas*, which is a plural noun, so the original version is incorrect. **G** is wrong because *it's* is a contraction of *it is*, which is not a possessive pronoun. *There* indicates the placement of something and shows no possession, so **H** is incorrect. *Their* is the correct answer because *their* is a plural possessive pronoun, which agrees with *Sherpas*.

11. C

Sentence Structure: Sentence Fragments   *Medium*

Because the underlined portion is missing a verb, the original sentence is a fragment. A sentence fragment still exists with the addition of the relative pronoun *which* in **B**. Deleting *often* fails to solve the fragment problem. The subject (*sherpa*) needs to be connected to *used* with a linking verb, such as *is*. **C** is the best way to correct the sentence.

12. G

Basic Grammar and Usage: Comparative and Superlative Modifiers   *Easy*

The *pay* of the Sherpas is being compared to that of another group of guides. When two things are being compared, the comparative form of an adjective is used. The superlative form is used to compare three or more things. *Most highest* is incorrect because a double superlative is being used rather than only one. **J** and **H** are superlative modifiers used to compare three or more things. **G** is the correct answer because *higher* is the comparative form of *high*.

13. B

Sentence Structure: Parallelism   *Medium*

The verbs in the prepositional phrase should all match or be parallel, and the original sentence fails to do that. Only **B** correctly balances the verbs—*carrying*, *establishing*, and *setting*. **D** is incorrect because *carrying* does not match *to establish* and *to set*. **C** is incorrect because *the carrying of* does not match *establishing* and *for setting* because prepositions have been added to *setting* and *carrying*.

14. H

Sentence Structure: Connecting and Transitional Words   *Medium*

Thus suggests that a cause-and-effect relationship exists between farming and mountain climbing, so the original version is wrong. *Nevertheless* suggests that working as *traders and farmers* prevented Sherpas from leading expeditions. Although the sentence is the last one in the passage, it is not summing up the entire passage, and *in conclusion* seems out of place. The preceding sentence in the paragraph describes what Sherpas did before guiding people up mountains, and the transitional word *now* helps illustrate the difference between Sherpas of the past and Sherpas of today.

15. B

Writing Strategy: Additional Detail and Evidence   *Medium*

The sentence explains why Sherpas can climb at high altitudes, which relates to the information presented in the second paragraph. The author states in the second paragraph: *it remains unknown why Sherpas do not feel the typical effects of high altitude*. The other paragraphs do not relate to the physical abilities of Sherpas, so **B** is the best answer.

16. G

Organization: Sentence Reorganization   *Medium*

In the original version, *who lived when I was 16* modifies *an aunt*, which makes it seem as if the aunt were only alive when the author was 16. **H** has a similar problem because *who lived when I was 16* modifies *an aunt* and creates an illogical sentence. **J** is awkwardly worded because *who I had the opportunity to stay with* ends in a preposition. **J** is also confusing because it suggests the aunt only lived in Italy when the author was 16. **G** is the best choice because *when I was 16* modifies *I* and makes it clear that the author was 16 when she visited her aunt in Rome.

17. D

Punctuation: Semicolons   *Medium*

However is a conjunctive adverb separating two complete sentences. *However* should always have a semicolon before it and a comma after it. **A** and **C** are wrong because dashes and commas should not be used before *however*. **B** is tempting, but the semicolon is after *however* instead of before. The correct answer is **D**.

18. G

Organization: Transitions, Topic Sentences & Conclusions   *Difficult*

The focus of the paragraph is on the author's attempt to understand and learn Italian, so **G** is the best topic sentence. Although the author mentions the aunt in the paragraph, she is not the focus. **H** and **J** are incorrect because the statements relate to the aunt rather than learning Italian. **F** relates to *cultural opportunities* instead of language, so it is wrong.

19. A

Style: Word Choice and Identifying Tone   *Medium*

The author learned *important words* from her aunt and extra words while *eavesdropping on conversations*. Although *additional* and *bonus* have similar meanings, *additional* better matches the tone and context of the sentence. *Bonus* typically refers to something extra one person gives to another, and the author took them through the process of eavesdropping. Although the author was not required to learn the Italian phrases, *optional* is not an accurate word choice. Similarly, the author intended to learn the phrases, but the phrases themselves would not be described as *intentional*.

20. J

Sentence Structure: Connecting and Transitional Words   *Medium*

The author first explains how she tried to learn Italian. She then states she had a *hard time* being *understood*. *Yet* is a connecting word that indicates contrasting ideas, so **J** is the correct answer. *While* is a tempting option, but the flow of the sentence is awkward. *So* and *as* suggest a cause-and-effect relationship and create an illogical sentence.

21. C

Basic Grammar and Usage: Verb Tenses   *Easy*

The original version is a fragment because *visitors to Rome having been rewarded* is an incomplete thought. *Were rewarded* suggests that visitors are no longer *rewarded* in Rome. Moreover, the next sentence in the paragraph states *graffiti is everywhere*, using the present tense verb *is*, so *were rewarded* would create confusion for the reader. Deleting the underlined portion creates a sentence fragment, so **D** is incorrect. *Are rewarded* is present tense and consistent with the sentence that follows.

22. G

Punctuation: Commas   *Easy*

The buildings are both *large* and *expensive*. **G** is correct because the necessary comma is between both adjectives. The adverb *very* modifies *large* and should not be followed by a comma, which is the reason **H** is wrong. **J** is incorrect because it lacks a comma between *large* and *expensive*, and it includes an unnecessary comma after *expensive*.

23. D

Style: Redundancy and Wordiness   *Medium*

D is the most concise option, which is often the best choice with style questions. Including *disorderly mess* in the original version is unnecessary because the next sentence describes the traffic scene. Adding *cars and scooters* in **B** merely piles on more unnecessary words. **C** is wordy as well, with the inclusion of *worrisome, disorderly*, and *frightening* even though one of the words would suffice.

24. H

Basic Grammar and Usage: Idioms   *Medium*

An idiomatic phrase typically consists of a verb and a preposition, such as *try to* or *agree with*. *Due to* is idiomatic, so the best answer is **H**. *Due from the* and *due with* are not idiomatic, so **F** and **G** are incorrect. *Due the traffic snarls* does not make sense either, so omitting the underlined portion is incorrect.

25. D

Basic Grammar and Usage: Subject-Verb Agreement   *Medium*

The subject of the sentence is *lifestyle* not *citizens*, which is part of a prepositional phrase. *Lifestyle* does not agree with *appeal*, so **A** is incorrect. Similarly, **B** and **C** are wrong because *are appealing* and *have appealed* are verb phrases intended for plural subjects. The correct answer is **D** because *lifestyle appeals* creates proper agreement between the subject and the verb.

26. H

Sentence Structure: Parallelism   *Medium*

The verbs in a sentence should be similar or parallel in their grammatical form. The original version here creates an unbalanced sentence. *Having a snack on gelato* is confusing and not parallel with *strolling around the city's fountains*, so **G** is wrong. *To snack* does not match the form of *strolling*, so **J** is wrong. **H** creates a matched situation between *strolling* and *snacking*.

27. B

Punctuation: Apostrophes   *Easy*

The singular word *world* needs to show possession of *cities*, which is accomplished with *world's cities*. The lack of an apostrophe in **C** shows no ownership of cities. **A** suggests the existence of more than one world with the placement of an apostrophe after the plural noun *worlds*. **D** incorrectly includes an extra letter *s*.

28. **F**

Style: Redundancy and Wordiness   *Medium*

The original version is the best option because it concisely states the key information without the addition of unnecessary words. The reader can infer that the author *returns home on the airplane*, so there is no need to state the obvious. The reader can also infer that the author will be returning to *family and friends*, so **H** is too wordy. Similarly, the inclusion of *to leave Italy* is unnecessary because the essay has been about the author's time in Italy.

29. **C**

Writing Strategy: Analysis   *Difficult*

The essay is very informal and changing pronouns from first person to third person would make the passage inappropriately formal. Third-person pronouns would not gain any more readers, so **B** is incorrect. **D** is tempting because a sense of intimacy would be lost, but **D** is wrong because the subject matter is not sensitive. The best answer is **C** because losing the first-person pronouns in an autobiographical passage would alter the sense of sharing a personal experience.

30. **J**

Writing Strategy: Big Picture Purpose   *Difficult*

The correct answer is **J** because the focus of the essay is the author's experiences in Rome. **H** is incorrect because the author's language issues are only one aspect of the essay. **F** is incorrect because the author only briefly mentions taking a single *day trip to Venice*. **G** is wrong because the author describes her experiences in Rome, but she does not discuss the benefits of traveling through *small towns*.

31. **C**

Basic Grammar and Usage: Adverbs and Adjectives   *Easy*

In the original version, *dance moves* is modified incorrectly with the adverb *intricately*. *Intricate dance moves* is correct because *intricate* is an adjective describing *dance moves*. *Intricate as a dance move* creates an awkward and confusing sentence structure, so **D** is incorrect. Using the adverb *intricately*, as in **B**, is incorrect because *moves* is a noun not a verb.

32. **J**

Organization: Sentence Reorganization   *Difficult*

The original sentence is confusing and needs to be reorganized. The original sentence and **G** both make it seem as if the audiences, rather than Jolson, were known as the *world's greatest entertainer*. **H** is confusing because Jolson's talents instead of Jolson were given the *greatest entertainer* title. The best answer is **J**, which makes it clear that Jolson is the *greatest entertainer*.

33. **B**

Sentence Structure: Connecting and Transitional Words   *Medium*

The underlined word is connecting the two halves of the compound sentence, and each clause in the sentence relates to Jolson's onstage performances. *Yet* and *although* would be appropriate if information in one clause contrasted with information in the other clause. **A** and **D** are both wrong because *theatrical techniques* and *plea-*

sure in performing are not in disagreement. *Since* is a connecting word used when a cause-effect relationship exists, but no such relationship occurs in the sentence, which makes **C** wrong. *And* is the best choice because the second part of the sentence merely provides additional information to the first part of the sentence.

34. F

Punctuation: Parentheses and Dashes   *Medium*

The original punctuation in the sentence is correct because the author is emphasizing the information after the dash. The phrase *music he greatly admired and respected* cannot stand alone as a complete sentence, which is a requirement for using a period or a semicolon, so **G** and **J** are incorrect. **H** is wrong because a pause is necessary after *blues* but not after *music*.

35. A

Sentence Structure: Connecting and Transitional Words   *Medium*

The question is asking for the answer that is NOT acceptable, or the worst option in the group. The names of the musicians should be preceded by a connecting word or phrase that indicates a list. *Such as*, *including*, and *specifically* would all be acceptable options before a list of names. *Consequently* would not be an appropriate word to show the reader that a list is on the way, so the answer is **A**.

36. H

Organization: Sentence Reorganization   *Difficult*

The original sentence does not flow very smoothly, so it needs reorganization. **G** is wrong because *when he was a child* seems to be modifying *his parents* instead of *Jolson*. **J** is incorrect because *when he was a child* modifies *born* instead of *immigrated*. **H** offers the most logical way to organize the information.

37. B

Style: Redundancy and Wordiness   *Medium*

With style questions, being economical with words is typically the correct choice, unless additional words are necessary to clarify meaning. *Performer* and *entertainer* suggest someone is a *musician, actor, comedian*, and *dancer*, so **A** and **C** are redundant. *Entertainer* and *performer* are synonymous, so **D** is also redundant. **B** is the best answer because it uses the fewest number of words to convey the same information as the other options.

38. J

Sentence Structure: Parallelism   *Medium*

Parallelism refers to words and phrases in a sentence being balanced and presented in a similar manner. The original sentence is not parallel because *singing* is a verb and *bird whistles* is a noun. The opposite occurs in **G** because *songs* is a noun and *bird whistling* is a verb. **H** pairs *singing* with *bird whistles*, which is not parallel. The best answer is **J**, which matches two verbs together—*singing* with *bird whistling*.

39. B

Punctuation: Commas   *Easy*

The author lists a series of three events: *stopped, turned*, and *asked*. A comma should separate each verb and its corresponding prepositional phrases to improve readability. The original version needs revision because a comma does not precede *turned*. **C** is incorrect because a comma does not separate *play* from *turned*, and an unnecessary comma follows *members*. **D** includes no punctuation, which makes the information difficult to process. **B** is the best answer because commas separate each event.

40. **G**

Basic Grammar and Usage: Pronoun-Antecedent Agreement   *Easy*

The underlined pronoun should agree with *members*, which is a plural noun. Since the pronoun *it* is singular and used to refer to things instead of people, **F** is incorrect. *We* would only be used if the passage was written in first person, so **J** is wrong. *Them* is not a subjective pronoun, so **H** would be grammatically incorrect. The best answer is **G** because *they* is a plural pronoun and agrees with *members*.

41. **D**

Style: Word Choice and Identifying Tone   *Medium*

D is the best answer because *delight* expresses the idea that the audience was thrilled that Jolson was performing a *spontaneous one-man show*. *Thunderous encouragement* indicates the audience was cheering and applauding, and *delight* best describes the attitude of the crowd. *Alarm* suggests the audience does not want Jolson to perform, which is not the case because the audience is cheering for Jolson. *Admiration* is a positive word, but it fails to convey the audience's excitement. *Dismay* is wrong because the audience desired Jolson's performance and would not be upset by his antics.

42. **H**

Organization: Transitions, Topic Sentences & Conclusions   *Difficult*

Paragraph 4 describes Jolson's career on Broadway, while paragraph 5 describes his movie career. **H** provides the best transition between the two paragraphs because it connects the information in the fourth paragraph with the information in the fifth paragraph. The original transition is too vague and lacks any connection to paragraph 4, so **F** is incorrect. **G** and **J** are more specific, but they fail to connect the information of the fourth paragraph with the fifth paragraph.

43. **C**

Writing Strategy: Additional Detail and Evidence   *Difficult*

The information about movie reviews and the biographical elements of the storyline are interesting, but **A** and **D** do not provide details that *explain the historical significance of The Jazz Singer*. **B** does not explain why the film is historically relevant. **C** is the best answer because it explains that the film marked a major change in the movie industry because it *ended the days of silent films*.

44. **H**

Organization: Passage Reorganization   *Medium*

Paragraph 3 provides background information about Jolson's youth, so the paragraph belongs earlier in the passage instead of where it is now. It would make no sense to place the paragraph at the end of the passage, so **J** is incorrect. Although many essays begin with where and when a person was born, the first sentence of the third paragraph would make a confusing first paragraph, so **G** is wrong. The first paragraph introduces Jolson to the reader with a brief overview, so it would be logical for the next paragraph to be about Jolson's early years. The third paragraph should be placed after paragraph 1, so **H** is the best answer.

45. D

Writing Strategy: Big Picture Purpose   *Difficult*

A is wrong because the focus of the essay is Jolson's career instead of how working hard leads to success in the entertainment industry. **B** is incorrect because there is no indication that film was more *fulfilling* than Broadway for Jolson. **C** is tempting because the author mentions twentieth-century superstars in paragraph 1; however, the author does not refer to *modern-day celebrities* in the fifth paragraph. The best answer is **D** because the fifth paragraph connects Jolson's appearance in *The Jazz Singer* with changes in the film industry.

46. G

Style: Redundancy and Wordiness   *Medium*

Frustrated, annoyed, aggravated, and *discouraged* are synonyms, so any one of the words will be sufficient. Repeating similar words or including adverbs such as *very* or *extremely* creates wordiness. The best answer is **G**, which concisely conveys the same meaning as the other options.

47. D

Basic Grammar and Usage: Verb Tenses   *Easy*

The first verb in the sentence, *put*, is past tense, so the second verb should be past tense as well to maintain consistency within the sentence. In the original sentence, *will spend* is future tense, so **A** is incorrect. *Was spending* is past progressive, which is used to describe a past action that was occurring when another action took place. Since *put* is clearly past tense, using past progressive seems illogical. *Spends* is present tense, so **C** is wrong. The best answer is **D** because *spent* is past tense.

48. H

Writing Strategy: Additional Detail and Evidence   *Difficult*

F and **G** are incorrect because **F** focuses on the operating system used by Napster, while **G** refers to other *file-sharing networks*. **J** is tempting because it describes why Napster became popular, but the sentence fails to explain the *purpose of Napster*. The best answer is **H** because the sentence further explains how Napster works, which relates directly to the *purpose of Napster*.

49. C

Sentence Structure: Subordinate or Dependent Clauses   *Easy*

The introductory clause begins with *since* and ends with *files*, and a comma is needed to separate it from the rest of the sentence. Only **C** includes the comma in the correct location.

50. J

Sentence Structure: Connecting and Transitional Words   *Easy*

Remember, you are searching for the LEAST acceptable option instead of the best option. The sentence contrasts the idea that even though Napster faced lawsuits, other companies took its place. Connecting words such as *but, however, yet*, and *although* are used to connect contrasting ideas. The least acceptable choice is *since*, which is used to connect cause-and-effect relationships. The best answer is **J**.

51. B

Basic Grammar and Usage: Subject-Verb Agreement   *Medium*

The subject is the plural noun *representatives*, not the singular noun *music industry*. The prepositional phrase *of the recording industry* describes the type of *representatives*, and it separates the subject (*representatives*) from the verb. *Continues* does not agree with *representatives* because *continues* would be appropriate for a singular noun. Similarly, *does continue* and *has continued* are verb phrases intended for singular nouns, so **C** and **D** are wrong. Only **B** provides a verb that agrees with a plural noun—*representatives continue*.

52. G

Style: Redundancy and Wordiness   *Medium*

When *sales are lower than expected*, readers can infer that *money is being lost*, so the original version is unnecessarily wordy. *Sales and profits are taking a downward turn* is wordy, and including both *profits* and *sales* is unnecessary. **J** is wordy because the reader can assume that if *sales of albums have declined* then *profits* will be *hurt*. *Sales are down* saves words and provides the necessary information.

53. C

Organization: Transitions, Topic Sentences & Conclusions   *Difficult*

The main point of the third paragraph is that albums are too expensive, which is why consumers would prefer to download music. **B** and **D** are specific details about Napster that do not relate to the main topic of the paragraph. **A** is tempting because it mentions free downloading, but **A** is still off topic. The best answer is **C** because the sentence addresses the subject of the paragraph.

54. H

Sentence Structure: Connecting and Transitional Words   *Medium*

The author is providing additional examples to illustrate a point. **G** and **J** are incorrect because *in contrast* and *however* are used to contrast different ideas. *Therefore* is incorrect as well because the author is not summarizing. *Similarly* is the best transitional word to show the addition of another point. **H** is the correct answer.

55. B

Punctuation: Commas   *Easy*

The correct answer is **B** because a comma is unnecessary before the conjunction *or* since two independent clauses are not being connected. If *or* were replaced with *and*, it might become more obvious that a comma is unnecessary. Semicolons join independent clauses, so **C** is wrong. The dash would be wrong as well because the author is not trying to emphasize a point.

56. J

Organization: Sentence Reorganization   *Medium*

The adverb *inexpensively* should be near the verb it modifies, *purchased*. In the original version, *inexpensively* follows *albums*, which is confusing, so the sentence should be reorganized. With **G** and **H**, *inexpensively* is still too far away from *purchased*, and the sentence remains awkward. *Fast food can be purchased inexpensively, unlike albums* places the adverb after the verb it is intended to modify, so **J** is the best answer.

57. D

Style: Word Choice and Identifying Tone   *Medium*

The passage indicates that the music industry feels threatened by the downloading trend, and it is highly unlikely that the *recording industry* would be *excited about every new music format. Eager* also suggests pleasure, so **C** is wrong. *Relaxed* fails to convey the idea that executives are concerned, so **B** is wrong. The best word choice is *anxious*, which appropriately describes the worries of recording industry executives in regards to the digital age.

58. H

Punctuation: Semicolons   *Medium*

When related independent clauses are together in one sentence, they may be linked by a semicolon, so **H** is correct. *Before MP3 players, cassette recorders were considered a threat* is the first independent clause. *Before that it was reel-to-reel tape recorders* is the second independent clause. In the original version, a comma is not sufficient to separate the two independent clauses, so **F** is wrong. **G** needs a comma before the conjunction *and* to be correct. Removing the punctuation in **J** creates a run-on sentence.

59. C

Writing Strategy: Analysis   *Difficult*

The word *everyone* is too vague, and the phrase *both fans and musicians* emphasizes the author's argument that downloading can benefit both parties. **A** is wrong because the details are not confusing; in fact, they clarify the meaning of the statement. **B** is incorrect because the information is necessary to emphasize the author's argument. While the author may suggest that *both fans and musicians* would benefit from *a better method of music distribution*, the concept is not *clearly established elsewhere in the essay*.

60. J

Writing Strategy: Big Picture Purpose   *Difficult*

F and **G** are incorrect because the essay does not argue in favor of monitoring the music industry. **H** is tempting but wrong. The essay suggests that the public's demands for downloads will force the practice to continue, but no mention is made of monitoring the business practices of the recording industry. **J** is correct because the main point of the essay is that downloads benefit both fans and producers.

61. D

Sentence Structure: Parallelism   *Medium*

For a sentence to be parallel, words should be in similar grammatical form. In this sentence, the underlined verb should match *playing*, which *to train* does not. Including the preposition *for* makes **B** incorrect because *playing* does not include a preposition. Similarly, *help train* does not balance with *playing*, so **C** is wrong. The best answer is **D** because *playing* and *training* are in the same grammatical form with *-ing* endings.

62. H

Writing Strategy: Analysis   *Difficult*

The additional information provides readers with a visual image of the condition of the shelter, so **H** is the best answer. **F** is wrong because the animals are not being described, only the shelter. The information has not been stated elsewhere, so **G** is wrong. **J** is incorrect because the description is clear and not confusing.

63. B

Sentence Structure: Connecting and Transitional Words   *Easy*

The question asks which option is NOT acceptable, so you should select the worst transitional word. The author is contrasting the two reasons that animals end up in shelters. Sometimes animals are *picked up as strays or rescued from unfit homes*. In other cases, pet owners are *trying to be responsible*. All of the choices except *likewise* are transitional words that help point out the two different reasons that animals go to shelters. *Likewise* is appropriate when a writer needs to indicate a similarity between two ideas or situations.

64. G

Basic Grammar and Usage: Verb Tenses   *Easy*

The author is describing a past event, so a past-tense verb is necessary. In the original version, *arriving* is present tense, and its usage creates an incomplete sentence. *Will arrive* is future tense. **J** is incorrect because *who have arrived* creates a sentence fragment due to the lack of a verb. The best answer is **G** because *arrived* is past tense.

65. D

Organization: Transitions, Topic Sentences & Conclusions   *Difficult*

A and **B** are specific details that fail to smoothly move the reader to the next paragraph. **C** is a little harsher than the previous statements in the second paragraph, and it does not relate to the information in the third paragraph. **D** is the best answer because it wraps up the information in the second paragraph and provides a transition into the discussion about pet ownership in the third paragraph.

66. H

Style: Redundancy and Wordiness   *Medium*

The original underlined portion is both wordy and redundant. *Responsible pet ownership* implies *being able to properly care for dogs and cats*. **G** is too wordy with the inclusion of *dogs, cats, and other animals* when *animals* would encompass all types of pets. Deleting the underlined portion and ending the sentence with *if more people were educated* creates an unclear meaning regarding the type of education required. **H** makes it clear to the reader the type of education that is necessary—*educated about responsible pet ownership*.

67. C

Basic Grammar and Usage: Verb Tenses   *Easy*

Verb tenses within a sentence should remain consistent to avoid confusing the reader. The verb *discover* indicates that a present-tense verb is needed for the underlined portion. *Are making* is present progressive tense, which is used to express events that are currently in progress. The author does not write the sentence or the passage in a way suggesting the events are currently taking place, so *are making* is inappropriate. *Making* creates a confusing sentence, so **B** is wrong. Since *discover* is present tense, *made* is wrong because it is past tense. *Make* is present tense and the correct choice.

68. G

Sentence Structure: Subordinate or Dependent Clauses   *Medium*

The sentence begins with a subordinate clause that ends with *litter*. The main part of the sentence begins with *pet owners*, so a comma needs to separate the clause from the rest of the sentence. **G** correctly punctuates the sentence. The original version lacks a comma after *litter*, so **F** is incorrect. Commas are inserted in the wrong locations for **H** and **J**, so the subordinate clause is not clearly separated from the main sentence.

69. A

Sentence Structure: Connecting and Transitional Words   *Medium*

The author is describing a cause-and-effect relationship between people breeding their pets and puppies and kittens ending up in animal shelters. No change is necessary to the original sentence because the transitional word *consequently* adequately illustrates a cause-effect relationship. *Similarly* is a transition used when another argument is being made that is like a previous one, so **B** is wrong. The transition *furthermore* is used when additional points are being made. *In other words* helps when transitioning into a summary.

70. F

Writing Strategy: Analysis   *Difficult*

G is incorrect because the writer is discussing the problem of people who neglect their animals. **H** is wrong because the essay argues in favor of responsible pet ownership, so the original sentence is not too argumentative. **J** is incorrect because the author is trying to illustrate the living conditions of neglected animals, and the details in the original are necessary to make the sentence have an impact. The best answer is **F** because the author is emphasizing the devastating effects caused by pet owners who fail to take responsibility for their animals.

71. D

Organization: Transitions, Topic Sentences & Conclusions   *Difficult*

The final paragraph reiterates the point that pets need responsible owners because they are living creatures. **A** and **B** do not relate to this main idea of the paragraph. **C** relates to the main idea of the third, rather than final, paragraph and provides too much of a detail for a topic sentence. The best answer is **D**, which introduces the concept that acquiring a pet is a serious commitment.

72. H

Punctuation: Commas   *Easy*

The coordinating adjectives *living* and *breathing* describe the noun *beings*. A comma is necessary between these two adjectives because each one separately modifies *beings*. **G** and **F** are incorrect because a comma should not separate the adjective from the noun. **J** is wrong because it lacks a comma between the adjectives, and it includes an unnecessary comma after *beings*.

73. B

Punctuation: Apostrophes   *Medium*

Owners is a possessive plural noun with ownership of *attitudes*, and **B** provides the correct punctuation. **A** indicates no ownership. *Owner's* shows that only one owner is being discussed rather than multiple pet owners. **D** is incorrect because an extra letter *s* is added after the apostrophe.

74. J

Style: Redundancy and Wordiness   *Medium*

The original construction is too wordy and disturbs the flow of the sentence, so it should be corrected. **G** is redundant because *responsibility* necessarily involves *dedication*. Similarly, **H** does not need to include both *dedication* and *effort* when one of the words would suffice. The best answer is **J**, which concisely states the same information as the other options.

75. C

Writing Strategy: Big Picture Purpose   *Difficult*

The writer does not indicate she adopted an animal, so **A** is wrong. Although the author discusses being a responsible pet owner, she does not offer advice about selecting animals for adoption. **D** is wrong because the author only mentions in the first paragraph what duties she thought she would have, while the rest of the essay focuses on why animals are in shelters. The best answer is **C** because it best describes the focus of the essay, which does not involve animal adoptions.

MATHEMATICS

1. E

Algebra: Writing Expressions and Equations   *Easy*

Naomi decides her babysitting rate by first tripling the number of hours worked. In other words, she multiplies w by 3. She then adds 9. Only answer **E** represents this expression.

2. K

Pre-Algebra: Percentages, Fractions & Decimals   *Easy*

Find the total amount of sugar needed by adding $2\frac{1}{3}$ cups and $3\frac{4}{5}$ cups together. To do this, first find a common denominator. The least common denominator in this instance is 3(5), or 15. Multiply the fractional part of $2\frac{1}{3}$ by $\frac{5}{5}$ to convert $\frac{1}{3}$ to a common denominator. The resulting fraction is $\frac{5}{15}$. Next, multiply the fractional part of $3\frac{4}{5}$ by $\frac{3}{3}$ to convert $\frac{4}{5}$ to a common denominator. The resulting fraction is $\frac{12}{15}$. To add $2\frac{5}{15}$ and $3\frac{12}{15}$, we first add 2 and 3, and then we add $\frac{5}{15}$ and $\frac{12}{15}$. The result is $5\frac{17}{15}$, or $6\frac{2}{15}$. **J** is definitely a distracter. You will get this incorrect answer if you add the whole numbers, then add the numerators and denominators separately: $\frac{1}{3}+\frac{3}{5}$.

3. **B**

Plane Geometry: Polygons *Easy*

The question is asking for the perimeter of the playground. Find the perimeter of a rectangle by using the following formula:

$$P = 2(l + w)$$

The perimeter of this playground is:

$$P = 2(30 + 18)$$
$$= 60 + 36$$
$$= 96$$

D represents the area of the playground, not the perimeter.

4. **H**

Pre-Algebra: Mean, Median & Mode *Easy*

We are looking for the average number of passengers who rode the commuter train each day. First, add the daily passenger totals together:

$$212 + 280 + 299 + 301 + 313 = 1,405$$

Then, find the average by dividing the total number of passengers by the number of days:

$$\frac{1,405}{5} = 281$$

The average number of passenger is 281. **F** reflects the range of passengers rather than the mean. **J** represents the median of the passengers rather than the mean.

5. **C**

Algebra: Simplification *Easy*

Take the following steps to simplify the expression:

$$3(4a - 3) + 5(6a + 4) = (3 \times 4a) - (3 \times 3) + (5 \times 6a) + (5 \times 4)$$
$$= 12a - 9 + 30a + 20$$
$$= 42a + 11$$

6. **J**

Pre-Algebra: Number Problems *Easy*

Sam's Sporting Goods sells 20 tennis balls for $13, which is $\frac{\$13}{20}$, or $0.65, per ball. Al's Athletics sells the same type of tennis balls at 15 for $9, which is $\frac{\$9}{15}$, or $0.60, per ball. Al's Athletics offers tennis balls for 5 cents less than Sam's Sporting Goods.

7. **D**

Plane Geometry: Angles and Lines *Easy*

$\overline{XZ}$ is a transversal between the two parallel lines. Therefore, $\angle m$ and $\angle 4$ are alternate interior angles. Alternate interior angles are equal to one another.

8. **H**

Plane Geometry: Polygons   *Easy*

This question asks you to find the perimeter of an 8-sided polygon. To do this, figure out the lengths of the unlabeled sides. It might be helpful to imagine the figure as one big rectangle.

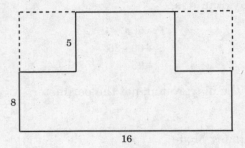

The width of the rectangle is 16 feet, and we can figure out the length of the rectangle by adding 8 feet to 5 feet to get 13 feet. The perimeter of this polygon is equal to:

$$2 \times l + 2 \times w = 2 \times 13 + 2 \times 16$$
$$= 58$$

K represents the area of the polygon, not the perimeter.

9. **C**

Algebra: Substitution   *Easy*

Substitute 12 for $x + y$ in the equation:

$$3(x + y) + \frac{x + y}{3} + (x + y)^3 - 3 = 3(12) + \frac{12}{3} + (12)^3 - 3$$
$$= 36 + 4 + 1,728 - 3$$
$$= 1,765$$

10. **J**

Intermediate Algebra: Exponents and Roots   *Easy*

First, solve $a^2 = 81$ for a:

$$a^2 = 81$$
$$a = \sqrt{81}$$
$$= 9$$

By substituting 9 for a in the original expression, we get:

$$a^3 + \sqrt{a} = 9^3 + \sqrt{9}$$
$$= 729 + 3$$
$$= 732$$

11. **C**

Pre-Algebra: Percentages, Fractions & Decimals   *Easy*

To solve this percentage problem, first calculate the amount of the reduction. We can find this by multiplying $18 by 20%, or 0.20 × 18. The result is $3.60. The question asks for the price of the DVD after the reduction. Find this by subtracting $3.60 from $18. The current price of the DVD is $14.40, because $18.00 − $3.60 = $14.40.

   A represents the amount of the discount only.

12. K

Algebra: Multiplying Binomials   *Easy*

Rewrite this expression in its binomial form: $(5x + 9)(5x + 9)$. When multiplying binomials, remember the acronym FOIL: First, Outer, Inner, Last. Begin by multiplying the first two numbers in each binomial: $(5x)(5x)$. Then multiply the outer numbers: $(5x)(9)$. Next, multiply the inner numbers: $(9)(5x)$. Finally, multiply the last numbers: $(9)(9)$. The result is $25x^2 + 45x + 45x + 81 = 25x^2 + 90x + 81$.

13. B

Algebra: Solving Linear Equations   *Easy*

The first step is to find a common denominator for the fractions:

$$\frac{1}{5}d + \frac{1}{3}d = 2$$

$$\frac{3}{15}d + \frac{5}{15}d = 2$$

Then, simplify the equation and solve for d:

$$\frac{8}{15}d = 2$$

$$\frac{15}{8} \times \frac{8}{15}d = 2 \times \frac{15}{8}$$

$$d = \frac{30}{8}$$

$$= 3\frac{6}{8}$$

$$= 3\frac{3}{4}$$

14. H

Geometry: Triangles   *Easy*

The third angle must be equal to 180° minus the measurement of the other two angles. A good strategy here is to work backward from the answers. The measurements in **F** are too small. Even if two angles were 40°, the sum of the angles would be only 100°. The measurements in **G** are also too small. If two of the angles were 60°, the sum would be just 140°. **J** and **K** both result in measurements that are too large. **H** works perfectly, because 35° + 35° + 110° = 180°.

15. B

Pre-Algebra: Number Problems   *Medium*

Ilya can only order whole cases of pie crusts. Each case contains 12 boxes of pie crusts, with 3 pie crusts in each box. The number of pie crusts in each case is:

$$12 \times 3 = 36$$

If Ilya ordered 9 cases, she would have 324 pie crusts, which falls short of her need for 350 pie crusts. To receive 350 pie crusts, Ilya needs to order 10 cases of pie crusts.

   E represents the approximate number of boxes, not cases, that Ilya would need to order.

16. G

Plane Geometry: Triangles   *Medium*

Set up a ratio to solve this problem. Use the corresponding sides of each triangle to set up the following ratio: $\frac{11}{9} = \frac{16}{t}$, where t is the length of the longest side of the second triangle. Cross multiply to find that $11x = 144$. Then, divide by 11 to get ≈ 13.1 cm.

17. A

Pre-Algebra: Percentages, Fractions & Decimals   *Medium*

You might find it helpful to solve this fraction problem algebraically. We can say that a is the number that is added to the numerator and the denominator. We want to find the number a that solves the equation $\frac{9+a}{11+a} = \frac{2}{3}$. Start by cross multiplying:

$$\frac{9+a}{11+a} = \frac{2}{3}$$
$$3(9+a) = 2(11+a)$$
$$27+3a = 22+2a$$
$$a = -5$$

Alternately, you can work backward from the answers. Check each one to see if it works. If you're not totally comfortable with algebra, this alternative option might be preferable.

18. G

Pre-Algebra: Percentages, Fractions & Decimals   *Medium*

To solve this problem, you may want to make up numbers. Imagine that each T-shirt costs $5. Find the regular price of all 5 T-shirts:
$$5 \times \$5 = \$25$$
The fifth T-shirt is free, so find the sale price:
$$4 \times \$5 = \$20$$
The sale price is $\frac{20}{25}$, or 80%, of the original price. The discount is 20%.

19. D

Plane Geometry: Triangles   *Medium*

The diagonal, d, forms the hypotenuse of a right triangle with legs of length 36 feet and 48 feet. To find the measure of d, use the Pythagorean theorem:

$$a^2 + b^2 = c^2$$
$$36^2 + 48^2 = c^2$$
$$1{,}296 + 2{,}304 = c^2$$
$$3{,}600 = c^2$$
$$\sqrt{3{,}600} = c$$
$$60 = c$$

20. G

Plane Geometry: Polygons   *Medium*

To find the height of the trapezoid, draw lines from the base of the trapezoid to its opposite side:

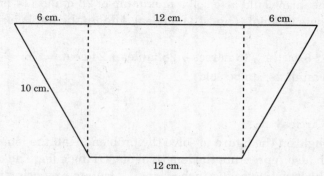

Drawing the lines divides the trapezoid into two triangles and a rectangle. We can find the height of the triangles—and therefore the trapezoid—by using the Pythagorean theorem. The length of the hypotenuse is 10 centimeters, and the length of one of the sides is 6 centimeters. Plug these into the formula:

$$a^2 + b^2 = c^2$$
$$a^2 + 6^2 = 10^2$$
$$a^2 + 36 = 100$$
$$a^2 + 36 - 36 = 100 - 36$$
$$a^2 = 64$$
$$a = 8$$

The height of the trapezoid is 8 centimeters. Put the numbers into the formula:

$$A = \frac{1}{2}h(b_1 + b_2)$$
$$A = \frac{1}{2} \times 8 \times (24 + 12)$$
$$A = 4 \times (36)$$
$$A = 144$$

21. D

Plane Geometry: Three Dimensions   *Medium*

Write the edge length of the small cube as s. The volume of the small cube is s^3. The large square box has edges that are 4 times as long as the edges of the small square box, so we can write its edges as $4s$. The volume of the large box can be written as $(4s)^3 = (4)(4)(4)(s)(s)(s) = 64s^3$, which is 64 times the size of the small cube with volume s^3.

22. H

Intermediate Algebra: Absolute Value Equations and Inequalities   *Medium*

You could work backward from the answers to solve this problem. **F** would be $|-2 - 4|$, which simplifies to $|-6|$, which has an absolute value of 6. This number is too large. **G** satisfies the equation but does not represent the *maximum* amount: $|2 - 4|$ simplifies to an absolute value of 2. **H** also satisfies the equation, plus it is the maximum amount: $|6 - 4|$ simplifies to an absolute value of 2. **J** and **K** are both too large to satisfy the equation.

23. D

Pre-Algebra: Number Problems   *Medium*

The maximum number of cattle that can be sold is 8: 4 males and 4 females. There-fore, exactly 16 horses will be sold, 8 males and 8 females.

In addition, the farm could also sell a maximum of 28 mules (14 males and 14 females) and 24 goats (12 males and 12 females). Add up the totals for all four types of livestock:

$$8 \text{ cattle} + 16 \text{ horses} + 28 \text{ mules} + 24 \text{ goats} = 76$$

A maximum of 76 animals can be sold.

24. G

Plane Geometry: Circles   *Medium*

Use the right triangle on the figure to solve the problem. Half the length of the chord is 16 inches, which also represents the length of one triangle leg. The other leg is 7 inches long, and the hypotenuse is r inches long. Calculate r by using the Pythago-rean theorem:

$$r^2 = 16^2 + 7^2$$
$$r^2 = 305$$
$$r = \sqrt{305}$$

Multiply $\sqrt{305}$ by 2 to find the diameter. To the nearest tenth of an inch, the diameter of the circle is 34.9 inches.

25. D

Pre-Algebra: Probabilities   *Medium*

To solve a probability problem, divide the number of favorable outcomes by the total number of possible outcomes. There are a total of 26 (10 + 8 + 8) socks in the drawer, so the number of possible outcomes is 26. The number of favorable outcomes is 18, because there are 10 red socks and 8 white socks (10 + 8 = 18). Therefore, the prob-ability of a selected sock NOT being blue is $\frac{10+8}{10+8+8} = \frac{18}{26} = \frac{9}{13}$.

A represents the probability of choosing a blue sock.

26. G

Algebra: Solving Linear Equations   *Medium*

Substitute 95 for F to get $95 = \frac{3}{4}H + 5$. Then, subtract 5 from both sides for the result to get $90 = \frac{3}{4}H$. Multiply both sides by $\frac{4}{3}$ to find the answer: 120.

27. B

Plane Geometry: Circles   *Medium*

Line segment RT represents a diagonal of $QRST$, and it also represents the diam-eter of the circle. If the circle is 264 inches in diameter, then its radius is $\frac{264}{2}$, or 132 inches. Convert this length into feet: $\frac{132}{12} = 11$. The radius is therefore 11 feet. Substitute 11 feet for r in the formula for the circumference of the circle:

$$C = 2\pi r$$
$$= 2\pi(11)$$
$$= 22$$

28. F

Coordinate Geometry: Slope   *Medium*

Rewrite each equation in slope-intercept form: $y = mx + b$

F is the only equation that results in a slope of 8:

$$16x - 2y + 9 = 0$$
$$-2y = -16x - 9$$
$$y = 8x + \frac{9}{2}$$

29. E

Pre-Algebra: Number Problems   *Medium*

Plug in the information from the question to find the answer:

$$\text{Mon} + \text{Weds} + \text{Fri} + \text{Sat} + \text{Sun} = 6(\$7.00) + 4(\$9.25) + 3(\$7.00) + 6(\$7.00) + 8(\$8.50)$$
$$= \$42.00 + \$37.00 + \$21.00 + \$42.00 + \$68.00$$
$$= \$210.00$$

The total charged was \$210.00.

30. G

Pre-Algebra: Number Properties   *Medium*

The sum of two negative numbers will always be a negative number. The difference of two negative numbers could be negative or positive, but it will always be larger than the sum of those two numbers. For instance, if $a = -7$ and $b = -5$, then $a + b = -12$, and $a - b = -2$. If $a = -1$ and $b = -2$, then $a + b = -3$, and $a - b = 1$. If the two numbers are fractions, the statement still holds true. If $a = -\frac{1}{2}$ and $b = -\frac{1}{4}$, then $a + b = -\frac{3}{4}$ and $a - b = -\frac{1}{4}$. **G** is correct.

F is incorrect, because two negative numbers multiplied together will always have a positive product. **H** is incorrect, because the question doesn't tell us whether a or b is the larger number, so we can't know which squared value will be greater. **J** is incorrect, because if $a = -1$ and $b = -3$, then $a - b$ would equal 2. **K** is also incorrect, because if a and b both equal -1, then both ab and $\frac{a}{b}$ would equal 1.

31. E

Intermediate Algebra: Exponents and Roots   *Medium*

To raise a power to another power, multiply the exponents:

$$(3a^2b^4)^3 = 3^3 \times (a^2)^3 \times (b^4)^3$$
$$= 27 \times (a^{2\times3}) \times (b^{4\times3})$$
$$= 27a^6b^{12}$$

32. **K**

Algebra: Inequalities   *Medium*

To simplify matters, subtract 14 from both sides to get $-3x \leq 7 - 14$. Then divide both sides by -3 to solve for x. When dividing an inequality by a negative number, always reverse the direction of the inequality sign:

$$-3x \leq 7 - 14$$
$$-3x \leq -7$$
$$x \geq \frac{7}{3}$$

33. **D**

Geometry: Polygons   *Medium*

We find the area of a parallelogram by multiplying base times height, or bh. Here, base $\overline{WZ} = 6 + 12 = 18$ cm. The height is 8 cm. Calculate the area by multiplying 18×8. The result is 144. **E** is incorrect because it represents the product of the two side lengths: 10×18.

34. **H**

Intermediate Algebra: Exponents and Roots   *Medium*

We know that $x^4 = y$, so $y^3 = (x^4)^3$. This means that $z = y^3$ equates to $z = (x^4)^3$, which is equal to $z = x^{4 \times 3}$, or x^{12}.

35. **A**

Algebra: Writing Expressions and Equations   *Medium*

If $s\%$ of the doctors perform at least one type of specialized surgery, then $(100 - s)\%$ do not. We can write the total number of doctors who do not perform any type of specialized surgery as $\frac{(100 - s)d}{100}$.

36. **J**

Algebra: Writing Expressions and Equations   *Medium*

You may find it useful to write out equations. Let a be the larger number and b the smaller number. The first sentence states that the larger of two numbers exceeds 3 times the smaller number by 4. We can write this as:

$$a = 3b + 4$$

The second sentence states that the sum of 3 times the larger number and 4 times the smaller number is 82. We can write this as:

$$3a + 4b = 82$$

Next, substitute the value of a into the equation:

$$3(3b + 4) + 4b = 82$$

37. **D**

Plane Geometry: Circles   *Medium*

First, determine the area of the two circles. Let r represent the radius of the smaller circle. The area of the smaller circle is $A = \pi r^2$. The radius of the larger circle is 7 centimeters longer than the radius of the smaller circle. So, the radius of the larger circle can be represented by $r + 7$. Find the area of the larger circle:

$$A = \pi(r + 7)^2$$
$$= \pi(r + 7)(r + 7)$$
$$= \pi(r^2 + 14r + 49)$$
$$= \pi r^2 + 14\pi r + 49\pi$$

We know that the area of the smaller circle is πr^2. Subtract this from the area of the larger circle:

$$\pi r^2 + 14\pi r + 49\pi - \pi r^2 = 14\pi r + 49\pi$$
$$= \pi(14r + 49)$$

38. G

Pre-Algebra: Percentages, Fractions & Decimals   *Medium*

Let's write an expression to solve this problem. Let s be Rodrigo's sales in 2005. His sales in 2006 would be $1.2 \times s$. His sales in 2007 would be $1.15(1.2 \times s)$. This simplifies to $1.38s$ and represents an increase of 38% from 2005 to 2007.

39. B

Pre-Algebra: Mean, Median & Mode   *Medium*

Remember that the median is the number whose value is in the middle of the numbers in a data set. It may help to write out the numbers in this set: 40, 40, 37, 40, 40. The number in the middle is 37.

   If you selected **A**, you selected the range, not the median. If you selected **C**, you probably averaged the numbers together to find the mean. If you chose **D**, you selected the mode (the number that appears the most often in a data set), not the median.

40. H

Trigonometry: SOHCAHTOA   *Medium*

Draw a vertical line from (5, 5) to the x-axis to create a right triangle.

$$\tan \theta = \frac{\text{opposite}}{\text{adjacent}}$$
$$\frac{5}{5} = 1$$

41. C

Coordinate Geometry: Parallel and Perpendicular   *Medium*

Parallel lines have the same slope. So, a line that is parallel to $y = -9x + 3$ will also have a slope of $m = -9$. All of the answer choices are written in the form $y = mx + b$. Skimming down the choices, we see that only **C** and **D** have slopes of -9. **A**, **B**, and **E** can be eliminated.

   Try out the given coordinate in the equations for **C** and **D**, to see which equation is correct. The equation for **C** is $y = -9x - 41$. Substitute -5 for x and 4 for y in this equation:

$$y = -9x - 41$$
$$(4) = -9(-5) - 41$$
$$4 = 45 - 41$$
$$4 = 4$$

The coordinate $(-5, 4)$ works in this equation, so **C** is correct.

42. **H**

Intermediate Algebra: Matrices   *Medium*

To determine the matrix product, multiply each of the values in the left matrix by each of the values in the right matrix. The matrix product will contain 9 values, so **F**, **G**, and **J** can be eliminated.

Start with $3c$ at the top of the left matrix. Multiply $3c$ by each value in the right matrix. Then start a new line, and multiply $5c$ by each value in the right matrix. Finally, start a third line, and multiply $-c$ by 3, -6, and 4. Here's what the multiplication looks like:

$$\begin{bmatrix} 3c \\ 5c \\ -c \end{bmatrix} \begin{bmatrix} 3 & -6 & 4 \end{bmatrix} = \begin{bmatrix} (3c \times 3) & (3c \times -6) & (3c \times 4) \\ (5c \times 3) & (5c \times -6) & (5c \times 4) \\ (-c \times 3) & (-c \times -6) & (-c \times 4) \end{bmatrix}$$

$$= \begin{bmatrix} 9c & -18c & 12c \\ 15c & -30c & 20c \\ 3c & 6c & -4c \end{bmatrix}$$

H is correct. If you chose **K**, you multiplied correctly, but you placed the terms incorrectly in the matrix.

43. **C**

Coordinate Geometry: Conic Sections   *Medium*

The parabola is upside down, so there will be a negative value for x^2 in the equation. Thus, **A**, **D**, and **E** can be eliminated. Further, when you multiply the first term of **B**, it too has a positive value for x^2. Therefore, we can eliminate **B** and choose **C** as the correct answer.

44. **G**

Pre-Algebra: Multiples, Factors & Primes   *Medium*

You may find it helpful to write out all of the odd numbers between 20 and 40 (even numbers are never prime), and then circle the prime numbers. The prime numbers in this set are 23, 29, 31, and 37. The sum of these numbers is $23 + 29 + 31 + 37 = 120$, so **G** is correct.

45. **D**

Trigonometry: Solving Triangles   *Medium*

Find the cos of $\angle E$:

$$\cos E = \frac{\text{hypotenuse}}{\text{adjacent}}$$

$$= \frac{a}{3}$$

46. J

Plane Geometry: Angles and Lines   *Medium*

Add the two angles and set them equal to 180°. Then solve for x:

$$8x + 12 + 4x = 180$$
$$12x + 12 = 180$$
$$12x + 12 - 12 = 180 - 12$$
$$12x = 168$$
$$x = 14$$

Substitute 14 for x into the value of the larger angle:

$$8x + 12 = 8(14) + 12$$
$$= 124$$

The larger angle measures 124°.

If you chose **G**, you probably determined the value of x, not $8x + 12$. If you chose **H**, you probably determined the value of the smaller angle, $4x$.

47. C

Coordinate Geometry: Distance and Midpoints   *Medium*

Use the distance formula:

$$d = \sqrt{(x_2 - x_1)^2 + (y_2 - y_1)^2}$$

Label the coordinates as $x_1, x_2, y_1,$ and y_2. Substitute the values into the distance formula:

$$= \sqrt{(2 - (-5))^2 + (6 - 8)^2}$$
$$= \sqrt{(7)^2 + (-2)^2}$$
$$= \sqrt{49 + 4}$$
$$= \sqrt{53}$$

48. F

Coordinate Geometry: Equation of a Line   *Medium*

Plug the point $(-8, 47)$ into the equation $y = sx + 4$:

$$47 = -8x + 4$$
$$47 - 4 = -8x$$
$$43 = -8x$$
$$-\frac{43}{8} = x$$

The lines $y = sx + 4$ and $y = -7x - 9$ intersect at $(-8, 47)$ when $s = -\frac{43}{8}$.

49. E

Plane Geometry: Polygons   *Medium*

All of the corner triangles in this figure are right triangles, because they share an angle with the square. Both legs of each triangle are 8 inches long, because they are half the length of the side of the square. We can use the Pythagorean theorem to find the hypotenuse of these triangles: $\sqrt{8^2 + 8^2} = 8\sqrt{1^2 + 1^2} = 8\sqrt{2}$. There are 4 of these right triangles, so multiply $8\sqrt{2}$ by 4 to get $4 \times 8\sqrt{2} = 32\sqrt{2}$ square meters.

If you selected **D**, you probably assumed that the perimeter of the inner square was half the perimeter of the outer square.

50. K

Trigonometry: Trigonometric Identities   *Medium*

Convert $\tan\theta$ to its trigonometric identity: $\tan\theta = \dfrac{\sin\theta}{\cos\theta}$. Next, multiply $\dfrac{\sin\theta}{\cos\theta}$ by $\dfrac{\cos\theta}{\sin\theta}$.
Since the two fractions are reciprocals, their product equals 1:

$$\left(\tan\theta\right)\left(\frac{\cos\theta}{\sin\theta}\right) = \left(\frac{\sin\theta}{\cos\theta}\right)\left(\frac{\cos\theta}{\sin\theta}\right)$$

$$= \frac{\sin\theta \times \cos\theta}{\sin\theta \times \cos\theta}$$

$$= 1$$

51. C

Coordinate Geometry: Graphing Equations   *Medium*

The graph has a slope of -1, which can be found by using the slope formula:

$$m = \frac{y_2 - y_1}{x_2 - x_1}$$

$$= \frac{-8 - (-3)}{5 - 0}$$

$$= \frac{-8 + 3}{5}$$

$$= \frac{-5}{5}$$

$$= -1$$

Thus, the slope given is not correct. The range is correct (look at the minimum and maximum y-values). The polynomial does have a zero of $x = -3$. To see if -3 is a zero, substitute -3 into the equation $-x - 3$:

$$-x - 3$$
$$-\left(-3\right) - 3 = 0$$

Only II and III are correct.

52. K

Intermediate Algebra: Systems of Equations   *Medium*

Set up equations to represent the problem:

$$3b + 2m = 15.50$$
$$2b + 3m = 17.25$$

Multiply each side by a number that will cancel out one of the variables. For example:

$$(2)(3b + 2m) = 15.50(2)$$
$$(-3)(2b + 3m) = 17.25(-3)$$

Now, write the two new equations:

$$6b + 4m = 31$$
$$-6b - 9m = -51.75$$

Add the two equations:

$$-5m = -20.75$$
$$m = 4.15$$

Substitute the value of m back into one of the original equations to find the value of b. For example:

$$3b + 2(4.15) = 15.50$$
$$3b + 8.30 = 15.50$$
$$3b = 7.20$$
$$b = 2.40$$

Add the two amounts together to get the total cost:

$$\$4.15 + \$2.40 = \$6.55$$

53. D

Algebra: Inequalities   *Medium*

Solve the inequality:

$$y - 4 < y - 6$$
$$y - 4 + 4 < y - 6 + 4$$
$$y < y - 2$$
$$y - y < y - y - 2$$
$$0 < -2$$

Since $0 < -2$ is never true, there is not a solution for y. Thus, the empty set is the solution set.

54. H

Coordinate Geometry: Number Lines and Inequalities   *Medium*

Look for the graph that shows an absolute distance from 0 of less than 6 or exactly 6 units.

55. E

Intermediate Algebra: Functions   *Difficult*

The value of $n = -3$ meets the criterion for the second definition, $n < 0$.

Substitute -3 for n in the equation, $A(n) = -2x^3 + x^2 - 18x - 2$:

$$A(n) = -2x^3 + x^2 - 18x - 2$$
$$= -2(-3)^3 + (-3)^2 - 18(-3) - 2$$
$$= -2(-27) + 9 + 54 - 2$$
$$= 54 + 9 + 54 - 2$$
$$= 115$$

56. G

Trigonometry: Trigonometric Identities   *Difficult*

One way to solve this problem is to use the trigonometric identity $\sin^2\theta + \cos^2\theta = 1$. You're given that $\sin\theta = \frac{7}{9}$. Plug in $\frac{7}{9}$ for $\sin\theta$ in the equation:

$$\sin^2\theta + \cos^2\theta = 1$$

$$\left(\frac{7}{9}\right)^2 + \cos^2\theta = 1$$

$$\cos^2\theta = 1 - \left(\frac{7}{9}\right)^2$$

$$\cos^2\theta = 1 - \frac{49}{81}$$

$$\cos^2\theta = \frac{32}{81}$$

You're almost there! Take the square root of both sides:

$$\cos^2\theta = \frac{32}{18}$$

$$\sqrt{\cos^2\theta} = \sqrt{\frac{32}{81}}$$

$$\cos\theta = \frac{\sqrt{16 \times 2}}{9}$$

$$= \pm\frac{4\sqrt{2}}{9}$$

The value for $\cos\theta$ is $\frac{4\sqrt{2}}{9}$, since $\cos\theta > 0$.

57. C

Coordinate Geometry: Conic Sections   *Difficult*

Rewrite the equation $y = \frac{4x^2 + x}{x}$ in factored form:

$$y = \frac{x(4x+1)}{x}$$

$$y = 4x + 1$$

The equation is a linear function, so **A** and **B** can be eliminated. The equation indicates a shift upward of 1 unit, so **D** and **E** can be eliminated. **C** is the only graph that is linear, shifted upward 1 unit, and has a point at (2, 9), which is a point on the line. This point can be checked by plugging 2 in for x and 9 in for y.

58. F

Coordinate Geometry: Number Lines and Inequalities   *Difficult*

Using the endpoints of the shaded region, (0, 8) and (–2, 0), write an equation for the first line, $y = 5x + 8$. Also write a simple equation for the second line, $y = 3$. An examination of the shaded portion reveals that y is greater than 3, which eliminates choices **H**, **J**, and **K**. Further, if we look at point (0, 8) the shaded region is all below this point, so we want y to be *less than or equal to* $5x + 8$. This makes **F** the correct answer.

59. D

Intermediate Algebra: Functions   *Difficult*

Find the composition of $a(b(x))$:

$$a(b(x)) = a(x^2 + 5x + c) = \sqrt{x^2 + 5x + c + 2}$$

Plug $x = 10$ into the function:

$$= \sqrt{10^2 + 5(10) + c + 2}$$
$$= \sqrt{100 + 50 + c + 2}$$
$$= \sqrt{152 + c}$$

The value of $a(b(x)) = y$, so substitute $y = 15$ into the composition of $\sqrt{152 + c}$:

$$15 = \sqrt{152 + c}$$

The value of c that makes the equation true is 73:

$$15 = \sqrt{152 + 73}$$
$$15 = \sqrt{225}$$
$$15 = 15$$

60. F

Intermediate Algebra: Quadratic Equations   *Difficult*

Set both quadratic equations equal to 0:

$$z - 9f = 0 \text{ and } z + 15g = 0$$

Multiply the binomials and set equal to 0:

$$(z - 9f)(z + 15g) = 0$$
$$z^2 + 15gz - 9fz - 135fg = 0$$
$$z^2 + z(15g - 9f) - 135fg = 0$$

READING

---

1. D

Prose Fiction: Vocabulary in Context   *Medium*

Anger surged up in his heart against her indicates that Ivan is feeling hateful toward his wife, so *malignantly* must be a negative word. *Unsteadily* and *certainly* have no negative connotations, so **A** and **C** are incorrect. Although *fearfully* is tempting, strongly charged context words such as *repulsive*, *hatred*, and *anger* indicate that *cruelly* is the correct answer.

2. G

Prose Fiction: Inference   *Medium*

The passage indicates that Marsha purchased the ticket, but it is unknown how often she buys them, which makes **F** and **H** incorrect. The text also indicates that Ivan *had no faith in lottery luck*, so **J** is incorrect. The best answer is **G** because Ivan's apparent disdain for the lottery suggests he has never purchased a ticket before.

3. A

Prose Fiction: Specific Detail   *Medium*

Ivan describes Marsha's relatives as *wretched* and expects them to begin *whining like beggars and fawning upon them with oily, hypocritical smiles*, which indicates **A** is the best answer. Although the relatives may show characteristics of misery, impoverishment, and shame, only *greediness and insincerity* indicates the dishonesty suggested by *fawning* and *oily, hypocritical smiles*.

4. H

Prose Fiction: Specific Detail   *Easy*

Ivan remembers that *autumn weather is cloudy and gloomy* in his village, so he decides he should travel *instead of taking long walks*. **J** is incorrect because it is the gloominess and dampness that Ivan dislikes rather than the walking. Ivan changes his mind about walking in wet weather prior to thinking of his wife traveling, so the best answer is **H**.

5. C

Prose Fiction: Inference   *Medium*

The passage tells us that after the experience of dreaming about being wealthy, Ivan and Marsha negatively viewed the reality of their life. Their rooms seemed *dark and small*, and the evenings seemed *long and wearisome*. This description suggests that their reality seemed dreary in comparison to the life they dreamed about. **B** is incorrect because Ivan and Marsha seem let down instead of relieved. **A** and **D** are incorrect because it is too much of a stretch to conclude that they will soon buy another ticket or that they regret having this one.

6. G

Prose Fiction: Specific Detail   *Medium*

Ivan worries that if Marsha travels she will complain *that trains made her head ache, or that she had spent too much money*, so **G** is the best answer. **F** is tempting because of the reference to headaches in the text, but the narrator does not indicate that Marsha is ill. Ivan does not think Marsha will spend too much money, only that she would *worry* that she had spent too much money. **J** is wrong because Ivan is concerned about Marsha's relatives visiting them, not the other way around.

7. A

Prose Fiction: Inference   *Medium*

Ivan asks Marsha, *"What if we really have won?"* However, Ivan does not specifically show an interest in keeping his wife in suspense, so **B** is wrong. **C** is tempting because Ivan tells Marsha that they *have plenty of time to be disappointed*, but the passage focuses on Ivan's thoughts about what could happen if they won the money. **D** is incorrect, because Ivan does not directly encourage Marsha to dream, and the narrator makes it clear that Ivan is the one *dreaming a little*. Marsha periodically interrupts her husband's thoughts to find out the winning number, but Ivan continues to *imagine living a different existence*, so the best answer is **A**.

8. H

Prose Fiction: Specific Detail   *Difficult*

The first paragraph indicates that Ivan is *very satisfied with his life*, so **J** is incorrect because *aversion* means *hatred*. **G** is also incorrect because *tolerance* suggests that Ivan accepts his life but is unhappy about it. The last sentence of the passage states that Ivan now considers evenings at home *long and wearisome*, so **F** is wrong because Ivan is not comfortable anymore. The best answer is **H** because Ivan's attitude about his life has changed from satisfaction at the beginning of the story to dissatisfaction at the end.

9. B

Prose Fiction: Inference   *Medium*

A and **D** are incorrect because both Marsha and Ivan keep their hateful thoughts to themselves. **C** is wrong because both Marsha and Ivan are worried about the thoughts and plans of the other. The best answer is **B** because both individuals imagine negative behaviors on the part of the other, which suggests they do not trust each other.

10. J

Prose Fiction: Specific Detail   *Easy*

J is the best answer because both Ivan and Marsha agree that *it would be nice to buy a new house. I would buy a bigger house with new furniture, pay debts, and travel* describes the order of priorities for Ivan, so **F**, **G**, and **H** are incorrect.

11. C

Social Science: Cause-Effect   *Medium*

As stated in the fourth paragraph, *recording artists were unable to produce records due to rationing* during the war, so the best answer is **C**. The author does not describe band members who had *enlisted in the military*, so **A** is wrong. Similarly, no mention is made of limitations on *nonessential items*, so **D** is incorrect. **B** is incorrect because bluegrass was becoming popular before Scruggs joined the band in the 1940s.

12. J

Social Science: Purpose   *Difficult*

The author begins and ends the passage with a sentence about Monroe being the one to begin bluegrass music, so the best answer is **J**. The author does not suggest that Monroe was not given *enough credit* or was a *controversial figure*, so **F** and **H** are incorrect. **G** is too emotional to fit the factual tone of the passage.

13. C

Social Science: Specific Detail   *Medium*

The traditional bluegrass instruments, as first played by the Blue Grass Boys, are fiddle, mandolin, upright bass, and banjo, so **C** is correct. According to the passage, progressive bluegrass bands often include some of the nontraditional instruments like electric guitar, saxophone, piano, and harmonica.

14. F

Social Science: Inference   *Medium*

The author does not indicate that Scruggs produced music for soundtracks or wrote gospel lyrics, so **G** and **H** are untrue. Scruggs established his picking style before joining Monroe's band, so **J** is wrong. Scruggs's band played progressive bluegrass music, so **F** is the best answer.

15. B

Social Science: Specific Detail   *Easy*

The author states in the opening paragraph that *although elements of folk, blues, ragtime, and jazz can be heard in the music, bluegrass is considered an extension of country music.* The answer is **B** because classical has not had an impact on bluegrass according to the text.

16. G

Social Science: Cause-Effect   *Medium*

The author writes that Ricky Skaggs earned a Grammy Award, but there is no textual evidence indicating Alison Krauss earned a Grammy. The passage does not include information about *country music losing popularity*, so **J** is incorrect. **H** is false because electric instruments are used more frequently by progressive bluegrass bands, but no suggestion is made that acoustic instruments are *limited*. The seventh paragraph states that *progressive bluegrass bands incorporate electric instruments and rock and roll songs into the bluegrass style* and that *Krauss's popularity has renewed interest in the genre.* The best answer is **G**.

17. C

Social Science: Comparison   *Medium*

C is correct because the author states in the fifth paragraph that *instrumental solos illustrate the connection between bluegrass and jazz. Fast-paced tempos and complicated harmonies* are related to bluegrass music not jazz, so **A** and **D** are incorrect. The author does not address improvisation, so **B** is wrong.

18. H

Social Science: Specific Detail   *Easy*

The author writes in the fourth paragraph that Scruggs made the three-finger picking style *so famous that it is now known as "Scruggs style."* Although **F**, **G**, and **J** are true statements, they do not explain the meaning of *Scruggs style*.

19. B

Social Science: Specific Detail   *Easy*

The sixth paragraph states that *traditional bluegrass musicians follow the lead established by Bill Monroe by playing folk songs and using only acoustic instruments.* The correct answer is **B**, since progressive bluegrass, bluegrass gospel, and country gospel are spin-offs of the traditional bluegrass style that Monroe originated.

20. J

Social Science: Specific Detail   *Medium*

Remember, the question is asking which question is NOT answered by information in the passage. The author describes the influence of folk songs on bluegrass in the third paragraph. In the sixth paragraph, the author discusses the way traditional blue-grass has changed. The eighth paragraph focuses on the unique qualities of bluegrass gospel. The author does not discuss when the first bluegrass album was recorded, so the answer is **J**.

21. B

Humanities: Structure and Organization   *Difficult*

B is the best answer because the passage describes how a young Helen Keller was frightened when she was sitting alone in a tree during a storm. The passage ends with Keller overcoming her fears by climbing a tree. **A** is tempting, but what Keller learns about nature is more emotional than factual. **C** is incorrect because the passage is autobiographical without input from other sources. **D** is wrong because Keller focuses more on the tree incident than on her relationship with her teacher.

22. F

Humanities: Point of View and Tone   *Difficult*

Keller writes at the end of the fourth paragraph that *"nature wages open war against her children, and under softest touch hides treacherous claws."* Keller's frightening experience teaches her to be cautious with nature because it can change from beautiful to ugly very quickly, so **F** is the best answer. **G** is too extreme because in the fifth paragraph she only mentions that she has not climbed a tree and never indicates being panicked by nature. **H** and **J** do not address Keller's concerns, so they are both wrong as well.

23. B

Humanities: Specific Detail   *Easy*

Keller first realized the storm was coming when *the sun's warmth left the air*. The aroma and blowing leaves were noticeable afterward. Keller is blind, so she cannot see the clouds change color.

24. H

Humanities: Vocabulary in Context   *Medium*

Before stepping onto the tree, Keller *for one minute stood irresolute*, which suggests she is uncertain or *doubtful*. If she had been *determined* or *restless*, she would not have waited for one minute, so **F** and **J** are incorrect. Although she is hesitant about climbing, *restrained* suggests she is calming herself down, and there is no indication she is upset.

25. A

Humanities: Inference   *Medium*

A is correct because in the first paragraph, Keller writes that *long before I learned to do arithmetic, Miss Sullivan taught me to find beauty in the fragrant woods and in every blade of grass*. Although **D** is tempting, the narrator never suggests she is unable to learn math, only that Miss Sullivan wants to teach her first about nature. **B** and **C** are incorrect because Keller never says anything negative about her teacher.

26. G

Humanities: Specific Detail   *Easy*

Keller does not write about *being struck by lightning* or *not knowing how to return home*, so **H** and **J** are wrong. Although the narrator describes the branches breaking, being hit does not seem to be a primary concern for Keller. The narrator considers jumping down but states that *terror held me back*, which means the best answer is **G**.

27. D

Humanities: Inference   *Medium*

When Keller is in the tree the first time, she describes *the aroma that always precedes a thunderstorm*. Later, she is drawn to the mimosa tree by the *wonderful subtle fragrance in the air*, so the best answer is **D**. Although she is sensitive to the feel of the bark on her hands and is able to find the tree in the yard, Keller describes her sense of smell in more detail throughout the passage. Keller never mentions her sense of taste.

28. J

Humanities: Inference   *Medium*

J is the best answer because Keller writes in the last sentence of the passage that she enjoyed *thinking fair thoughts and dreaming bright dreams* while sitting in her *tree of paradise*. Although Keller thinks she is doing something *unusual and wonderful* by climbing the tree, she does not indicate it is dangerous. **F** and **H** are incorrect because no mention is made of her previous fear of climbing or a sense of strength, only the happiness she feels while in the tree.

29. B

Humanities: Specific Detail   *Medium*

The narrator writes in paragraph 2 that it was *cool up in the tree*, so the best answer is **B**. The narrator describes the petals and blossoms when she climbs the mimosa tree at the end of the passage, so **A** and **D** are incorrect. The narrator does not like the wind blowing while she sits in the cherry tree during the storm, so **C** is wrong.

30. G

Humanities: Main Idea, Argument & Theme   *Medium*

G summarizes how Keller's first experience in a tree was frightening, but sitting in a tree was pleasurable when Keller was older. **F** is too broad of a statement for the narrow subject of the passage. **H** is incorrect because it was nature, not being *alone*, which frightened Keller. **J** is close but wrong because the limited subject matter of the passage does not focus on a *variety of challenging situations*.

31. B

Natural Science: Inference   *Medium*

Paragraph 3 states that *turbines used on wind farms vary in size and power ratings*, so it can be inferred that the larger the size, the higher the power rating. Air temperature affects wind speed, so **A** is incorrect. If a turbine does not have a high enough power rating, neither its location nor the wind speed will generate additional power. The best answer is **B**.

32. H

Natural Science: Specific Detail   *Easy*

The primary assertion of the fourth paragraph is that Cape Wind will damage the *visual appeal* of the Cape Cod area, so **H** is correct. The author does not mention the noise associated with Cape Wind or the effects on aquatic wildlife, so **G** and **J** are incorrect. The author writes that *tourists hoping to sail Nantucket Sound would be forced to navigate around the unsightly towers*, but no mention is made of the fishing industry.

33. C

Natural Science: Specific Detail   *Easy*

Paragraph 6 states that Altamont Pass is *located on a major bird migratory route* and is near *the world's largest population of breeding golden eagles*. The number of birds killed by the turbines raises environmental concerns, so **C** is the correct answer. **A** and **B** relate to concerns associated with other windmill farms, but not Altamont Pass. The author does not address the deterioration of turbines and ensuing maintenance costs, so **D** is wrong.

34. G

Natural Science: Comparison   *Difficult*

The second paragraph states that *windmills used the energy of the wind to pump water or grind stones, but modern turbines direct the collected energy into rotors that produce electricity*, which means the best answer is **G**. *Turbines convert the kinetic energy in wind into mechanical energy* rules out **J** as the correct answer. **H** is wrong because kinetic energy is in the wind, so a turbine cannot *create* the kinetic energy, only *convert* it. Although windmills are used for manual activities, kinetic energy is the source, not kinetic electricity.

35. D

Natural Science: Inference   *Difficult*

A, **B**, and **C** are plausible reasons for the wind industry to benefit. However, the only idea suggested by the passage is *government concerns about increasing energy costs*. The author states in the opening paragraph that *governments around the world . . . have promoted the construction of wind farms by giving subsidies to private wind energy companies*.

36. J

Natural Science: Specific Detail   *Medium*

With this EXCEPT question, the answer will be the one that cannot be supported by information in the passage. The author describes in the fifth paragraph the way mountainside windmill farms cause *water flow disturbance, the demise of plants, and the disruption of animal habitats*, so **F**, **G**, and **H** are incorrect. Although the author mentions soil erosion being a result of turbine construction, the text does not refer to *soil contamination*. The correct answer is **J**.

37. D

Natural Science: Strengthen/Weaken   *Difficult*

The passage asserts that wind farms have a negative effect on the environment, especially animals and their habitats. **D** asserts that wind energy is clean and thus better for the environment. Although **A**, **B**, and **C** offer arguments in favor of wind energy, **D** more specifically addresses environmental concerns.

38. G

Natural Science: Specific Detail   *Medium*

The seventh paragraph describes the different theories regarding the number of bird and bat deaths associated with turbines, and **G** is the correct answer as indicated by the last sentence of the paragraph. **H** is tempting because *the open space makes finding insects easier*. **J** is also tempting, but only the *spinning motion of the blades* attracts birds and bats—not the noise of the blades. The author does not discuss *suction*, so **F** is incorrect.

39. A

Natural Science: Inference   *Medium*

The author notes in the third paragraph that turbine farms require large amounts of concrete and often necessitate onsite concrete factories. Given that the author is concerned about the environmental impact of wind farms, readers can assume that the construction of a concrete factory would damage the surrounding area. **D** is tempting because the author mentions that trucks require roads, which further affect the environment, but no mention is made of *erosion* caused by trucks. The author does not discuss the water supply, and the concern with birds regards their flight patterns instead of their nesting locations. The best answer is **A**.

40. F

Natural Science: Specific Detail   *Easy*

The author does not mention *nuclear power* or *solar cell technology*, so **J** and **G** are incorrect. Although turbines convert kinetic energy into mechanical energy, the process would not be described as *intrusive*. **F** is correct because the author writes in the first paragraph that people perceive wind energy as *clean and free electricity* and that wind energy promises *the hope of a reduction in fossil fuel dependence*.

SCIENCE

1. B

Data Representation: Read the Chart   *Easy*

Figure 1 shows that when the temperature was between −2° and 0°, Dnepropetrovsk and Kharkov had the highest percentage of reported cases (both areas reported nearly 60% of FP cases at these temperatures).

2. F

Data Representation: Read the Chart   *Easy*

The greatest number of FP cases reported in Nizhny Novgorod is 135, so **F** is the correct answer. The second-smallest number of cases was reported when the wind blew NW, so **G** is not correct. The number of cases in **H** is also very small. **J** represents the second-greatest number of FP cases reported in Nizhny Novgorod, but this question is asking for the greatest.

3. C

Data Representation: Use the Chart   *Medium*

In Odessa, there are 7 FP cases when the wind blows southeast, and there are also 7 FP cases when the wind blows south. This means that **C** is the correct answer. The greatest number of FP cases is observed when the winds blow northeast, not north, so **A** is incorrect. **B** is incorrect because there are 2, not 0, recorded FP cases when winds are calm. Finally, the smallest number of FP cases is observed when the winds are calm, not when they blow northwest, so **D** is incorrect.

4. H

Data Representation: Use the Chart   *Medium*

According to the information in Figure 1, there were approximately 10 observations of FP in Kiev when the surface temperature measured between 0° and 2°. The correct answer is **H**. None of the measurements on the Odessa bar graph or the Kharkov bar graph represent 10 observations, so **F** and **G** are incorrect. In Mineralnye Vody, there were approximately 10 observations of FP when the temperature measured between –6° and –4°, so **J** is also incorrect.

5. D

Data Representation: Use the Chart   *Difficult*

Across all of these Russian and Ukrainian regions, the greatest number of FP observations were recorded when the surface temperature was between –2° and 0°, so the correct answer is **D**. **A** is not backed up by the data, because there is a greater amount of precipitation in Odessa than in Kiev when the temperature is higher than 0°. **B** and **C** are also unsupported by the data.

6. H

Research Summary: Read the Chart   *Easy*

In Figure 1, the white bars represent the CO_2 efflux in the litter-removal plots. By reading the chart, we find that in April 2006, CO_2 efflux in the litter-removal plots was approximately 20 percent less than the CO_2 efflux in the control plots. The correct choice is **H**. **F** is not represented by any of the bars in the graph. **G** describes the bar representing the litter-addition plot in April 2006. **J** describes the bar representing the CO_2 efflux from the litter-removal plot in January 2006.

7. B

Research Summary: Read the Chart   *Easy*

In both 2004 and 2006, the amount of fine root biomass was greatest in the control plots, so the correct answer is **B**. **A**, **C**, and **D** represent a misreading of the data in the figure.

8. H

Research Summary: Use the Chart   *Medium*

According to Figure 1, the difference in CO_2 efflux between litter-addition plots and control plots was greater than the difference in CO_2 efflux between litter-removal plots and control plots. The correct answer is **H**. **F** brings in information from Figure 2, which the question does not address. **G** is not reflected in the data. **J** has it backward.

9. C

Research Summary: Read the Chart   *Medium*

CO_2 efflux dropped by nearly 40 percent between May 2004 and September 2004. This represents the biggest difference in CO_2 efflux in the litter-addition plots. The drop between June 2007 and July 2007 was approximately 10 percent, so **A** is not correct. The drop between December 2005 and January 2006 and between March 2006 and April 2006 was around 25 percent, so neither **B** nor **D** is correct.

10. J

Research Summary: Use the Chart   *Medium*

The data in Figure 2 show that as litterfall (L+) increases, total fine root biomass decreases. This means the correct answer is **J**. There was not a significant decrease in total fine root biomass between May 2004 and May 2006, so **F** is incorrect. **G** has it backward—total fine root mass *decreases*, not increases, as litterfall on rainforest soil increases. There was not a significant increase in total fine root biomass between May 2004 and May 2006, so **H** is incorrect.

11. B

Research Summary: Use the Chart   *Difficult*

This question requires you to use both figures. By looking at Figure 1, we see that the greatest amount of CO_2 efflux in May 2004 was produced by litter-addition plots. By looking at Figure 2, we see that litter-addition plots yielded between 100 and 200 g/m^{-2} of fine root biomass in both 2004 and 2006. Therefore, the correct answer is **B**. **A** and **C** do not meet both criteria of the question, and **D** misses the mark entirely.

12. G

Data Representation: Read the Chart   *Easy*

The line graphs that represent the hare population in Viborg and Ringkøbing depict a steady decline with occasional increases. **G** is correct. Because there are several spikes, we cannot describe the population as "in constant decline," so **F** is incorrect. The population is definitely on the downward climb, so neither **H** nor **J** can be correct.

13. B

Data Representation: Read the Chart   *Easy*

The hare population in Ringkøbing was at its highest in 1960, so **B** is correct. **A, C,** and **D** represent a misreading of the data.

14. J

Data Representation: Use the Chart   *Medium*

We can assume that if a destructive fungus attacked the winter cereal crop, many acres of the crop were lost. This happened between 1981 and 1984, so the correct answer is **J**. No data on winter cereals exist prior to 1960, so **F** is not correct. There was an increase in the winter cereal crop between 1963 and 1967 and between 1977 and 1979, so **G** and **H** are incorrect.

15. D

Data Representation: Use the Chart   *Medium*

This question requires the use of both figures. In 1995, the brown hare population spiked, as did the winter cereal crop. Because brown hares depend on winter cereals to survive, we can conclude that the winter cereal crop increased, leading to an increase in hare population. The correct answer is **D**. Root crops did not increase in 1995, so neither **A** nor **C** can be correct. **B** has the relationship between the hares and the winter cereal crop backward.

16. **H**

Data Representation: Use the Chart   *Difficult*

This question introduces information that is not included in either figure. The increase in the red fox population explains why the brown hare population decreased, even though the winter cereal crop was at its peak. The correct answer is **H**. **F** is not relevant to the situation. **G** addresses an event that occurs three decades later. **J** contradicts the new data introduced by the question.

17. **C**

Research Summary: Read the Chart   *Easy*

Mice in both the HRS group and the LRS group consumed the most food during Week 4, so the correct answer is **C**. The mice consumed a smaller amount of food in Weeks 1, 2, and 8 than they did in Week 4, so **A**, **B**, and **D** are all incorrect.

18. **F**

Research Summary: Read the Chart   *Easy*

Mice on the LRS diet have greater adiposity than mice on the HRS diet. The LRS mice had the highest percentage of adiposity during Week 8, so **F** is correct. **G** and **J** are incorrect because they address HRS mice. **H** addresses LRS mice, but they had the *lowest* level of adiposity, not the highest, during Week 1.

19. **D**

Research Summary: Use the Chart   *Medium*

Figure 1 shows that there is very little difference in the body weights of mice on the LRS diet and mice on the HRS diet. Figure 2 shows that the mice in the HRS group consume more food per week than the mice in the LRS group. Therefore, the correct answer is **D**. Mice on the HRS diet do not have a greater body weight than mice on the LRS diet, so **A** in incorrect. Mice on the HRS diet consume more food, not less, than mice on the LRS diet, so **B** is not correct either. Finally, **C** is incorrect because mice on the HRS diet have similar body weights to mice on the LRS diet.

20. **H**

Research Summary: Use the Chart   *Medium*

This question requires using Figure 1 and Figure 3. A mouse on the HRS diet consumes 28 grams of food and has an adiposity percentage of around 5 percent in Week 2, so the correct answer is **H**. The data in Figure 2 are not relevant to this question, so **F** and **G** are both incorrect. **J** has it backward.

21. **B**

Research Summary: Take the Next Step   *Difficult*

The results of this study would not have much meaning if the mice all had different body weights and adiposity percentages. All forty mice needed to have highly similar weights and adiposity percentages. The correct answer is **B**. **A** is not relevant to the study. **C** is incorrect because the study has implications for human health. **D** is the opposite of the correct answer.

22. J

Research Summary: Use the Chart   *Difficult*

The data show that the LRS diet leads to higher body weight and greater adiposity percentages. This means that an LRS diet is *not* healthier than an HRS diet, so the correct answer is **J**. **F**, **G**, and **H** represent a misinterpretation of the data.

23. B

Conflicting Viewpoints: Detail   *Easy*

One of the arguments made by people who support the Cartagena Protocol is that genetically modified crops pose environmental dangers. The Anti-Cartagena Protocol Argument would be most strengthened by finding that genetically modified crops pass environmental-safety tests worldwide, so **B** is correct. **A**, **C**, and **D** weaken the Anti-Cartagena Protocol Argument rather than strengthen it.

24. F

Conflicting Viewpoints: Comparison   *Easy*

Supporters of both arguments would agree that the Cartagena Protocol affects the way in which farmers grow their crops, so the correct answer is **F**. Only supporters of the Pro-Cartagena Protocol Argument would agree with **G**, and only supporters of the Anti-Cartagena Protocol Argument would agree with **J**. Neither group mentions **H** in its argument.

25. C

Conflicting Viewpoints: Inference   *Medium*

The Pro-Cartagena Protocol Argument describes the disadvantages of genetically modified soybean crops. Chief among those disadvantages is the crops' resistance to harmful herbicides, so the correct answer is **C**. The argument does not make a distinction between places where the crops are or are not safe to grow, so **A** is incorrect. **B** is incorrect because the argument does not state whether genetically modified soybean crops are more or less expensive than traditional soybean crops. **D** is an argument that could be made by supporters of the Anti-Cartagena Protocol Argument.

26. H

Conflicting Viewpoints: Detail   *Medium*

The Anti-Cartagena Protocol Argument states that *farmers who grow genetically modified crops can reduce the use of harmful farm chemicals*, but it does not explain how this occurs. The correct answer is **H**. **F** is answered by the passage. **G** and **J** are addressed by the Pro-Cartagena Protocol Argument, not the Anti-Cartagena Protocol Argument.

27. D

Conflicting Viewpoints: Inference   *Medium*

The Pro-Cartagena Protocol Argument specifically mentions farmers losing the right to save and replant seeds, so **D** is the correct answer. The discovery is not consistent with the Anti-Cartagena Protocol Argument, so **B** and **C** are incorrect. The discovery definitely *would* have an impact on the Pro-Cartagena Protocol Argument, so **A** is also incorrect.

28. G

Conflicting Viewpoints: Comparison   *Medium*

Both arguments emphasize genetically modified organisms' impact on the world's food supply, so **G** is correct. Neither argument says that GMOs are only useful in developing nations, so **F** is incorrect. **H** is incorrect because it is only supported by the Pro-Cartagena Protocol Argument. **J** is incorrect because it is only supported by the Anti-Cartagena Protocol Argument.

29. C

Conflicting Viewpoints: Detail   *Difficult*

The Pro-Cartagena Protocol Argument warns against genetically modified plants capable of producing their own insecticide, because such plants will lead to an increase in the insecticide-resistant insect population. **C** is correct. **A** is a concern raised by Pro-Cartagena Protocol Argument, but it has nothing to do with insecticide-producing plants. **B** is the *opposite* of the Pro-Cartagena Protocol Argument. **D** is not addressed by the passage.

30. H

Data Representation: Read the Chart   *Easy*

Use the legend to answer this question. Approximately 20 metric tons of ozone were depleted in the Northern Hemisphere in 1994, so the correct answer is **H**. In 1992, 1993, and 1996, more than 20 metric tons of ozone were depleted, so **F**, **G**, and **J** are all incorrect.

31. C

Data Representation: Read the Chart   *Easy*

Looking at Figure 2, we see that the steepest increase in ozone depletion took place in the 1980s. This means the correct answer is **C**. The incline was not as steep in the 1960s and 1970s, so **A** and **B** are incorrect. The incline begins to taper off in the 1990s, so **D** is also incorrect.

32. F

Data Representation: Use the Chart   *Medium*

Figure 1 uses the correlation between the increase in PSCs and the loss of ozone to predict a steady, consistent increase. Figure 2 predicts the depletion rate will slow down significantly around the year 2010. The correct answer is **F**. Neither figure predicts a steady decline in ozone depletion, so **G** and **H** are both incorrect. Figure 1 predicts a consistent increase in ozone depletion, so **J** is incorrect.

33. B

Data Representation: Use the Chart   *Medium*

This question requires an understanding of both graphs. The researchers who created Figure 1 based their prediction on the correlation between an increase in PSCs and a decrease in ozone. They would credit the decrease in total ozone depletion a decrease in the total area of PSCs, so the correct answer is **B**. The cooling of the stratosphere leads to an *increase* in ozone depletion, so **A** is incorrect. **C** and **D** also have it backward—an increase in water vapor and in PSCs would lead to an *increase*, not a decrease, in ozone depletion.

34. **G**

Data Representation: Use the Chart   *Difficult*

Figure 2 reflects the goals of the Montreal Protocol, because the line's trajectory reflects a decrease in ozone-depletion rate after the year 2000. This means that the correct answer is **G**. Figure 1 shows a steady increase in ozone depletion, which does not reflect the goals of the Montreal Protocol, so **F** is incorrect. Because only Figure 2 reflects the goals of the Montreal Protocol, **H** and **J** are incorrect.

35. **A**

Research Summary: Read the Chart   *Easy*

Table 2 shows identical measurements for subjects in both the experimental and control groups. Therefore, the difference in the maximal endometrial thickness between the subjects in the two groups is 0.

36. **H**

Research Summary: Use the Chart   *Medium*

Table 3 shows that the pregnancy rate for those who took aspirin (the experimental group) was 48%. By contrast, the pregnancy rate for those who did not take aspirin (the control group) was 57%. Subjects who did not take aspirin had a higher pregnancy rate than did the subjects who took aspirin. So, the results of Experiment 2 do not support the hypothesis that aspirin treatment increases pregnancy rates during IVF. **H** is correct.

F is incorrect because it does not compare results between the experimental group and the control group. **G** is the opposite of the correct answer. The experimental group had more embryos transferred and a lower pregnancy rate than did the control group. **J** is incorrect because the pregnancy rate in the control group was 9 percentage points less than the pregnancy rate in the experimental group.

37. **D**

Research Summary: Use the Chart   *Medium*

Table 1 shows the ages of women in both the experimental and control groups during the study. Women in both groups were 34 years old. The age of the subjects did not vary, so no conclusion can be drawn from these experiments regarding the effect of age on pregnancy rates during IVF.

38. **G**

Research Summary: Use the Chart   *Medium*

In both experiments, the experimental groups consisted of subjects who took aspirin. The control groups contained subjects who took no aspirin. If the experimental group had shown a live birth rate of 60%, this rate would have exceeded the live birth rate for the control group. Such a result would have supported the conclusion that aspirin treatment increases IVF success, since more live births would have occurred among those subjects who took aspirin.

F and **H** are incorrect because both would have made aspirin look even less effective in assisting IVF. **J** is incorrect because an implantation rate of 21% for the control group would have equaled the implantation rate of the experimental group. This equal rate would not have supported the conclusion that aspirin improves IVF success.

39. C

Research Summary: Read the Chart   *Medium*

The first paragraph of the passage states that the purpose of the experiments was to determine the effect of aspirin on IVF success. In Experiment 1, the only difference between the two groups studied was that one group received aspirin and the other group did not. Thus, aspirin administration was the independent variable, or the factor that varied, in Experiment 1.

A and **B** are incorrect because although these characteristics are presented in Table 1, they are given only as part of the background summary for the subjects studied. The experiment itself did not test the role of IVF history or pregnancy history on IVF success. **D** is incorrect, because the passage does not indicate that different methods were used to measure endometrial thickness.

40. J

Research Summary: Use the Chart   *Medium*

Table 3 shows that the live birth rate was higher for women who did not receive aspirin than for those who did receive aspirin in Experiment 2. Thus, based on the results of this experiment alone, it would be more likely for a woman to have a live birth if she did not receive aspirin during her IVF cycle. The results of Experiment 2 suggest that the chances of a live birth during IVF will increase if aspirin is not administered.

F is incorrect because Experiment 2 does not provide any data about the effect of embryo transfer on live birth rates. It provides data on how many embryos were transferred to subjects in the two test groups, but it does not investigate the effect of the number of embryos on live births. **H** is the opposite of the correct answer, because Table 3 shows that subjects who were given aspirin had a lower live birth rate than did subjects in the control group. **G** is also incorrect because the study does not suggest that partial administration of aspirin would improve live birth rates. It does not assess the effect of partial administration of aspirin but rather the effect of aspirin administered throughout the entire IVF cycle.

ACT Practice
Test 3

DIRECTIONS: The ACT consists of tests in four separate subject areas: English, Mathematics, Reading, and Science. These four tests measure skills learned through high school coursework that are relevant to success in college. *YOU MAY USE CALCULATORS ON THE MATHEMATICS TEST ONLY.*

Each test contains a set of numbered questions. The answer choices for each question are lettered. On your answer sheet, you will find rows of ovals that are numbered to match the questions. Each oval contains a letter to correspond to a particular answer choice.

Choose the best answer for each question. Then, on your answer sheet, find the row of ovals that is numbered the same as the question. Find the oval containing the letter of your chosen answer, and fill in this oval completely. You must use a soft lead pencil for this purpose, and your marks must be heavy and black. *BALLPOINT PENS SHOULD NOT BE USED TO FILL IN THE ANSWER SHEET.*

Fill in only one answer choice oval for each question. If you wish to change an answer, make sure that your original answer is thoroughly erased before marking the new one. After filling in your answer, double-check to be sure that you have marked the row of ovals that corresponds to the question number being answered.

Responses will be scored only if they are marked on your answer document. Your score for each test is determined by the number of questions answered correctly during the testing period. Your score will NOT be reduced if you choose an incorrect answer. *FOR THIS REASON, IT IS ADVANTAGEOUS FOR YOU TO ANSWER EVERY QUESTION, EVEN IF YOU GUESS ON SOME QUESTIONS.*

You may work on a test ONLY when the test supervisor gives you permission to do so. If you finish a test before the end of the time allowed, use any remaining time to review questions that you are unsure about. You are permitted to review ONLY your answers for the test on which you are currently working. You may NOT look back to a test you have already completed, and you may NOT continue on to another test. If you do so, you will be disqualified from the examination.

When the end of each test is announced, put your pencil down immediately. You are NOT permitted to fill in or change ovals for a test after the end of that test has been called. If you do so, for any reason, you will be disqualified from the examination.

You may not fold or tear the pages of your test.

DO NOT TURN TO THE FIRST TEST
UNTIL YOU ARE TOLD TO DO SO.

ACT Practice Test 3: Answer Sheet

TEST 1

1 Ⓐ Ⓑ Ⓒ Ⓓ	16 Ⓕ Ⓖ Ⓗ Ⓙ	31 Ⓐ Ⓑ Ⓒ Ⓓ	46 Ⓕ Ⓖ Ⓗ Ⓙ	61 Ⓐ Ⓑ Ⓒ Ⓓ
2 Ⓕ Ⓖ Ⓗ Ⓙ	17 Ⓐ Ⓑ Ⓒ Ⓓ	32 Ⓕ Ⓖ Ⓗ Ⓙ	47 Ⓐ Ⓑ Ⓒ Ⓓ	62 Ⓕ Ⓖ Ⓗ Ⓙ
3 Ⓐ Ⓑ Ⓒ Ⓓ	18 Ⓕ Ⓖ Ⓗ Ⓙ	33 Ⓐ Ⓑ Ⓒ Ⓓ	48 Ⓕ Ⓖ Ⓗ Ⓙ	63 Ⓐ Ⓑ Ⓒ Ⓓ
4 Ⓕ Ⓖ Ⓗ Ⓙ	19 Ⓐ Ⓑ Ⓒ Ⓓ	34 Ⓕ Ⓖ Ⓗ Ⓙ	49 Ⓐ Ⓑ Ⓒ Ⓓ	64 Ⓕ Ⓖ Ⓗ Ⓙ
5 Ⓐ Ⓑ Ⓒ Ⓓ	20 Ⓕ Ⓖ Ⓗ Ⓙ	35 Ⓐ Ⓑ Ⓒ Ⓓ	50 Ⓕ Ⓖ Ⓗ Ⓙ	65 Ⓐ Ⓑ Ⓒ Ⓓ
6 Ⓕ Ⓖ Ⓗ Ⓙ	21 Ⓐ Ⓑ Ⓒ Ⓓ	36 Ⓕ Ⓖ Ⓗ Ⓙ	51 Ⓐ Ⓑ Ⓒ Ⓓ	66 Ⓕ Ⓖ Ⓗ Ⓙ
7 Ⓐ Ⓑ Ⓒ Ⓓ	22 Ⓕ Ⓖ Ⓗ Ⓙ	37 Ⓐ Ⓑ Ⓒ Ⓓ	52 Ⓕ Ⓖ Ⓗ Ⓙ	67 Ⓐ Ⓑ Ⓒ Ⓓ
8 Ⓕ Ⓖ Ⓗ Ⓙ	23 Ⓐ Ⓑ Ⓒ Ⓓ	38 Ⓕ Ⓖ Ⓗ Ⓙ	53 Ⓐ Ⓑ Ⓒ Ⓓ	68 Ⓕ Ⓖ Ⓗ Ⓙ
9 Ⓐ Ⓑ Ⓒ Ⓓ	24 Ⓕ Ⓖ Ⓗ Ⓙ	39 Ⓐ Ⓑ Ⓒ Ⓓ	54 Ⓕ Ⓖ Ⓗ Ⓙ	69 Ⓐ Ⓑ Ⓒ Ⓓ
10 Ⓕ Ⓖ Ⓗ Ⓙ	25 Ⓐ Ⓑ Ⓒ Ⓓ	40 Ⓕ Ⓖ Ⓗ Ⓙ	55 Ⓐ Ⓑ Ⓒ Ⓓ	70 Ⓕ Ⓖ Ⓗ Ⓙ
11 Ⓐ Ⓑ Ⓒ Ⓓ	26 Ⓕ Ⓖ Ⓗ Ⓙ	41 Ⓐ Ⓑ Ⓒ Ⓓ	56 Ⓕ Ⓖ Ⓗ Ⓙ	71 Ⓐ Ⓑ Ⓒ Ⓓ
12 Ⓕ Ⓖ Ⓗ Ⓙ	27 Ⓐ Ⓑ Ⓒ Ⓓ	42 Ⓕ Ⓖ Ⓗ Ⓙ	57 Ⓐ Ⓑ Ⓒ Ⓓ	72 Ⓕ Ⓖ Ⓗ Ⓙ
13 Ⓐ Ⓑ Ⓒ Ⓓ	28 Ⓕ Ⓖ Ⓗ Ⓙ	43 Ⓐ Ⓑ Ⓒ Ⓓ	58 Ⓕ Ⓖ Ⓗ Ⓙ	73 Ⓐ Ⓑ Ⓒ Ⓓ
14 Ⓕ Ⓖ Ⓗ Ⓙ	29 Ⓐ Ⓑ Ⓒ Ⓓ	44 Ⓕ Ⓖ Ⓗ Ⓙ	59 Ⓐ Ⓑ Ⓒ Ⓓ	74 Ⓕ Ⓖ Ⓗ Ⓙ
15 Ⓐ Ⓑ Ⓒ Ⓓ	30 Ⓕ Ⓖ Ⓗ Ⓙ	45 Ⓐ Ⓑ Ⓒ Ⓓ	60 Ⓕ Ⓖ Ⓗ Ⓙ	75 Ⓐ Ⓑ Ⓒ Ⓓ

TEST 2

1 Ⓐ Ⓑ Ⓒ Ⓓ Ⓔ	13 Ⓐ Ⓑ Ⓒ Ⓓ Ⓔ	25 Ⓐ Ⓑ Ⓒ Ⓓ Ⓔ	37 Ⓐ Ⓑ Ⓒ Ⓓ Ⓔ	49 Ⓐ Ⓑ Ⓒ Ⓓ Ⓔ
2 Ⓕ Ⓖ Ⓗ Ⓙ Ⓚ	14 Ⓕ Ⓖ Ⓗ Ⓙ Ⓚ	26 Ⓕ Ⓖ Ⓗ Ⓙ Ⓚ	38 Ⓕ Ⓖ Ⓗ Ⓙ Ⓚ	50 Ⓕ Ⓖ Ⓗ Ⓙ Ⓚ
3 Ⓐ Ⓑ Ⓒ Ⓓ Ⓔ	15 Ⓐ Ⓑ Ⓒ Ⓓ Ⓔ	27 Ⓐ Ⓑ Ⓒ Ⓓ Ⓔ	39 Ⓐ Ⓑ Ⓒ Ⓓ Ⓔ	51 Ⓐ Ⓑ Ⓒ Ⓓ Ⓔ
4 Ⓕ Ⓖ Ⓗ Ⓙ Ⓚ	16 Ⓕ Ⓖ Ⓗ Ⓙ Ⓚ	28 Ⓕ Ⓖ Ⓗ Ⓙ Ⓚ	40 Ⓕ Ⓖ Ⓗ Ⓙ Ⓚ	52 Ⓕ Ⓖ Ⓗ Ⓙ Ⓚ
5 Ⓐ Ⓑ Ⓒ Ⓓ Ⓔ	17 Ⓐ Ⓑ Ⓒ Ⓓ Ⓔ	29 Ⓐ Ⓑ Ⓒ Ⓓ Ⓔ	41 Ⓐ Ⓑ Ⓒ Ⓓ Ⓔ	53 Ⓐ Ⓑ Ⓒ Ⓓ Ⓔ
6 Ⓕ Ⓖ Ⓗ Ⓙ Ⓚ	18 Ⓕ Ⓖ Ⓗ Ⓙ Ⓚ	30 Ⓕ Ⓖ Ⓗ Ⓙ Ⓚ	42 Ⓕ Ⓖ Ⓗ Ⓙ Ⓚ	54 Ⓕ Ⓖ Ⓗ Ⓙ Ⓚ
7 Ⓐ Ⓑ Ⓒ Ⓓ Ⓔ	19 Ⓐ Ⓑ Ⓒ Ⓓ Ⓔ	31 Ⓐ Ⓑ Ⓒ Ⓓ Ⓔ	43 Ⓐ Ⓑ Ⓒ Ⓓ Ⓔ	55 Ⓐ Ⓑ Ⓒ Ⓓ Ⓔ
8 Ⓕ Ⓖ Ⓗ Ⓙ Ⓚ	20 Ⓕ Ⓖ Ⓗ Ⓙ Ⓚ	32 Ⓕ Ⓖ Ⓗ Ⓙ Ⓚ	44 Ⓕ Ⓖ Ⓗ Ⓙ Ⓚ	56 Ⓕ Ⓖ Ⓗ Ⓙ Ⓚ
9 Ⓐ Ⓑ Ⓒ Ⓓ Ⓔ	21 Ⓐ Ⓑ Ⓒ Ⓓ Ⓔ	33 Ⓐ Ⓑ Ⓒ Ⓓ Ⓔ	45 Ⓐ Ⓑ Ⓒ Ⓓ Ⓔ	57 Ⓐ Ⓑ Ⓒ Ⓓ Ⓔ
10 Ⓕ Ⓖ Ⓗ Ⓙ Ⓚ	22 Ⓕ Ⓖ Ⓗ Ⓙ Ⓚ	34 Ⓕ Ⓖ Ⓗ Ⓙ Ⓚ	46 Ⓕ Ⓖ Ⓗ Ⓙ Ⓚ	58 Ⓕ Ⓖ Ⓗ Ⓙ Ⓚ
11 Ⓐ Ⓑ Ⓒ Ⓓ Ⓔ	23 Ⓐ Ⓑ Ⓒ Ⓓ Ⓔ	35 Ⓐ Ⓑ Ⓒ Ⓓ Ⓔ	47 Ⓐ Ⓑ Ⓒ Ⓓ Ⓔ	59 Ⓐ Ⓑ Ⓒ Ⓓ Ⓔ
12 Ⓕ Ⓖ Ⓗ Ⓙ Ⓚ	24 Ⓕ Ⓖ Ⓗ Ⓙ Ⓚ	36 Ⓕ Ⓖ Ⓗ Ⓙ Ⓚ	48 Ⓕ Ⓖ Ⓗ Ⓙ Ⓚ	60 Ⓕ Ⓖ Ⓗ Ⓙ Ⓚ

TEST 3

1 Ⓐ Ⓑ Ⓒ Ⓓ	9 Ⓐ Ⓑ Ⓒ Ⓓ	17 Ⓐ Ⓑ Ⓒ Ⓓ	25 Ⓐ Ⓑ Ⓒ Ⓓ	33 Ⓐ Ⓑ Ⓒ Ⓓ
2 Ⓕ Ⓖ Ⓗ Ⓙ	10 Ⓕ Ⓖ Ⓗ Ⓙ	18 Ⓕ Ⓖ Ⓗ Ⓙ	26 Ⓕ Ⓖ Ⓗ Ⓙ	34 Ⓕ Ⓖ Ⓗ Ⓙ
3 Ⓐ Ⓑ Ⓒ Ⓓ	11 Ⓐ Ⓑ Ⓒ Ⓓ	19 Ⓐ Ⓑ Ⓒ Ⓓ	27 Ⓐ Ⓑ Ⓒ Ⓓ	35 Ⓐ Ⓑ Ⓒ Ⓓ
4 Ⓕ Ⓖ Ⓗ Ⓙ	12 Ⓕ Ⓖ Ⓗ Ⓙ	20 Ⓕ Ⓖ Ⓗ Ⓙ	28 Ⓕ Ⓖ Ⓗ Ⓙ	36 Ⓕ Ⓖ Ⓗ Ⓙ
5 Ⓐ Ⓑ Ⓒ Ⓓ	13 Ⓐ Ⓑ Ⓒ Ⓓ	21 Ⓐ Ⓑ Ⓒ Ⓓ	29 Ⓐ Ⓑ Ⓒ Ⓓ	37 Ⓐ Ⓑ Ⓒ Ⓓ
6 Ⓕ Ⓖ Ⓗ Ⓙ	14 Ⓕ Ⓖ Ⓗ Ⓙ	22 Ⓕ Ⓖ Ⓗ Ⓙ	30 Ⓕ Ⓖ Ⓗ Ⓙ	38 Ⓕ Ⓖ Ⓗ Ⓙ
7 Ⓐ Ⓑ Ⓒ Ⓓ	15 Ⓐ Ⓑ Ⓒ Ⓓ	23 Ⓐ Ⓑ Ⓒ Ⓓ	31 Ⓐ Ⓑ Ⓒ Ⓓ	39 Ⓐ Ⓑ Ⓒ Ⓓ
8 Ⓕ Ⓖ Ⓗ Ⓙ	16 Ⓕ Ⓖ Ⓗ Ⓙ	24 Ⓕ Ⓖ Ⓗ Ⓙ	32 Ⓕ Ⓖ Ⓗ Ⓙ	40 Ⓕ Ⓖ Ⓗ Ⓙ

TEST 4

1 Ⓐ Ⓑ Ⓒ Ⓓ	9 Ⓐ Ⓑ Ⓒ Ⓓ	17 Ⓐ Ⓑ Ⓒ Ⓓ	25 Ⓐ Ⓑ Ⓒ Ⓓ	33 Ⓐ Ⓑ Ⓒ Ⓓ
2 Ⓕ Ⓖ Ⓗ Ⓙ	10 Ⓕ Ⓖ Ⓗ Ⓙ	18 Ⓕ Ⓖ Ⓗ Ⓙ	26 Ⓕ Ⓖ Ⓗ Ⓙ	34 Ⓕ Ⓖ Ⓗ Ⓙ
3 Ⓐ Ⓑ Ⓒ Ⓓ	11 Ⓐ Ⓑ Ⓒ Ⓓ	19 Ⓐ Ⓑ Ⓒ Ⓓ	27 Ⓐ Ⓑ Ⓒ Ⓓ	35 Ⓐ Ⓑ Ⓒ Ⓓ
4 Ⓕ Ⓖ Ⓗ Ⓙ	12 Ⓕ Ⓖ Ⓗ Ⓙ	20 Ⓕ Ⓖ Ⓗ Ⓙ	28 Ⓕ Ⓖ Ⓗ Ⓙ	36 Ⓕ Ⓖ Ⓗ Ⓙ
5 Ⓐ Ⓑ Ⓒ Ⓓ	13 Ⓐ Ⓑ Ⓒ Ⓓ	21 Ⓐ Ⓑ Ⓒ Ⓓ	29 Ⓐ Ⓑ Ⓒ Ⓓ	37 Ⓐ Ⓑ Ⓒ Ⓓ
6 Ⓕ Ⓖ Ⓗ Ⓙ	14 Ⓕ Ⓖ Ⓗ Ⓙ	22 Ⓕ Ⓖ Ⓗ Ⓙ	30 Ⓕ Ⓖ Ⓗ Ⓙ	38 Ⓕ Ⓖ Ⓗ Ⓙ
7 Ⓐ Ⓑ Ⓒ Ⓓ	15 Ⓐ Ⓑ Ⓒ Ⓓ	23 Ⓐ Ⓑ Ⓒ Ⓓ	31 Ⓐ Ⓑ Ⓒ Ⓓ	39 Ⓐ Ⓑ Ⓒ Ⓓ
8 Ⓕ Ⓖ Ⓗ Ⓙ	16 Ⓕ Ⓖ Ⓗ Ⓙ	24 Ⓕ Ⓖ Ⓗ Ⓙ	32 Ⓕ Ⓖ Ⓗ Ⓙ	40 Ⓕ Ⓖ Ⓗ Ⓙ

ENGLISH TEST

45 Minutes—75 Questions

DIRECTIONS: There are five passages on this test. You should read each passage once before answering the questions on it. In order to answer correctly, you may need to read several sentences beyond the question.

There are two question formats within the passages. In one format, you will find words and phrases that have been underlined and assigned numbers. These numbers will correspond with sets of alternative words/phrases given in the right-hand column of the test booklet. From the sets of alternatives, choose the answer choice that works best in context, keeping in mind whether it employs standard written English, whether it gets across the idea of the section,

and whether it suits the tone and style of the passage. You will usually be offered the option "NO CHANGE," which you should choose if you think the version found in the passage is best.

In the second format, you will see boxed numbers referring to sections of the passage or to the passage as a whole. In the right-hand column, you will be asked questions about or given alternatives for the sections marked by the boxes. Choose the answer choice that best answers the question or completes the section. After choosing your answer choice, fill in the corresponding bubble on the answer sheet.

Passage I

Johannes Brahms: Musical Genius

[1]

German pianist Johannes Brahms is perhaps best known for *Brahms' Lullaby*, which was written for a friend <u>which</u> had recently given birth to a son.

1.

   A. NO CHANGE
   B. she who
   C. whom
   D. who

[2]

Born in 1833, Brahms showed musical promise from a <u>very, early age,</u> and his father, also a musician, made certain that his son received a proper musical education.

2.

   F. NO CHANGE
   G. very early age,
   H. very early, age,
   J. very early age

Because Brahms was a <u>student of classical music he tended</u> to create his arrangements in a more conservative style,

3.

   A. NO CHANGE
   B. student of classical music, he tended
   C. student, of classical music, he tended
   D. student of classical music he tended,

a technique that was increasingly disappearing as new musicians attempted to break fresh ground in <u>musical composition methods by establishing new arrangement styles</u>. Despite his more traditional approach, Brahms

4.

   F. NO CHANGE
   G. musical composition methods.
   H. how they arranged new styles of music.
   J. composing music with their own original methods.

GO ON TO THE NEXT PAGE.

<u>has gained</u> acclaim from his fans as the next Beethoven,
₅

a compliment not bestowed on his contemporary peers.

Unwittingly, the comparison to Beethoven may have stifled

<u>Brahms</u> growth as a musician and caused many brilliant
₆

works to be lost. It is believed that Brahms was such a

perfectionist that he refused to publish anything before he

was completely satisfied. [7] <u>Although,</u> Brahms destroyed
₈

many of his earliest compositions.

[3]

    <u>In his youth,</u> Brahms played piano at local bars to earn
₉

money for his family, but later the musical prodigy became

a brilliant orchestra composer and <u>he toured as a concert</u>
₁₀

<u>pianist.</u> Brahms's most well-known pieces include some
₁₀

of the following <u>compositions</u> *Ein deutsches Requiem* (A
₁₁

German Requiem), *Symphony No. 1 in C minor, Op. 68,*

Variations and Fugue on a Theme by Handel, and *Academic*

Festival Overture.

5. **A.** NO CHANGE
   B. gains
   C. gained
   D. will gain

6. **F.** NO CHANGE
   G. Brahm
   H. Brahm's
   J. Brahms's

7. The writer is considering revising "such a perfectionist that he refused to publish anything before he was completely satisfied" to read "a perfectionist." That revision would cause the sentence to lose primarily:
   A. descriptive details that explain Brahms's personality.
   B. unimportant information that clutters the essay.
   C. specific details that raise questions about Brahms.
   D. redundant information that is addressed elsewhere.

8. **F.** NO CHANGE
   G. Finally,
   H. As a result,
   J. For instance,

9. Which of the transitions provides the most effective link from paragraph 2 to paragraph 3?
   A. NO CHANGE
   B. During his career,
   C. At some time in his life,
   D. After achieving fame,

10. **F.** NO CHANGE
   G. a touring concert pianist.
   H. was playing piano in touring concerts.
   J. had played as a touring concert pianist.

11. **A.** NO CHANGE
   B. compositions.
   C. compositions;
   D. compositions:

[4]

Before his death in 1897, Brahms <u>decided to settle in Vienna,</u> and in sharp contrast to his beautiful
compositions, Brahms was perceived as a grouch by the locals. [13] To his close friends, <u>in other words,</u> Brahms
was both loyal and generous. Fame brought fortune to Brahms, who <u>graciously</u> gave away much of his earnings
to family members and anonymously supported aspiring musicians.

12. **F. NO CHANGE**
   G. settled in Vienna,
   H. settled down in the city of Vienna,
   J. made a decision to settle in the city of Vienna,

13. With the intention of adding more information, the writer is considering inserting at this point the following true statement:

   While he welcomed the company of children, Brahms seemed to find most adults irritating and did not hide his disdain.

   Should the writer insert the new sentence here? Why or why not?
   A. Yes, because the sentence supports the author's opinion that Brahms was strange and eccentric.
   B. Yes, because the sentence gives the reader interesting information about the personality of Brahms.
   C. No, because the sentence provides irrelevant details that are not important enough to include.
   D. No, because the sentence provides contradictory information about the character of Brahms.

14. **F. NO CHANGE**
   G. however,
   H. therefore,
   J. for example,

15. **A. NO CHANGE**
   B. (Place underlined word after *fortune*)
   C. (Place underlined word after *Brahms*)
   D. (Place underlined word after *earnings*)

GO ON TO THE NEXT PAGE.

Passage II

Vaccines and Public Health

[1]

To prevent the spread of contagious diseases like chicken pox and whooping cough, many school districts require that students be vaccinated. However, some parents refuse to <u>comply to</u> vaccination policies and do not
16
immunize their children for religious or ethical reasons. [17]

Some scientists contend that this puts communities at risk for a resurgence of diseases once thought <u>surrendered</u>.
18

[2]

Despite the drastic reduction of common childhood <u>illnesses, such as, smallpox,</u> measles, and diphtheria
19
due to vaccinations, many parents question the validity and safety of immunizations. While some <u>vaccination critics and</u>
20
<u>opponents</u> express concern over possible side effects,
20
others argue that immunizations are ineffective. Both beliefs sharply contrast with those held by the mainstream medical community.

16. **F.** NO CHANGE
    G. comply by
    H. comply for
    J. comply with

17. The writer is thinking of revising the second part of the preceding sentence to read:

    do not immunize their children.

    If this revision were made, the sentence would primarily lose:
    A. relevant information about one side of the vaccination controversy.
    B. unnecessary and controversial information about people's beliefs.
    C. details about vaccination critics that are explained later in the essay.
    D. essential details that support those in favor of requiring vaccinations.

18. **F.** NO CHANGE
    G. devastating.
    H. adaptable.
    J. eradicated.

19. **A.** NO CHANGE
    B. illnesses, such as smallpox,
    C. illnesses such as, smallpox,
    D. illnesses, such as smallpox

20. **F.** NO CHANGE
    G. vaccination critics
    H. critical vaccination opponents
    J. oppositional vaccination critics

[3]

Health risks from vaccinations are rare, and improvements over the years have <u>made immunizations safer and reduced</u> possible side effects. <u>In addition,</u> the argument that the increase in childhood vaccinations explains a rise in cases of autism has been investigated, and no link has been found.

[4]

Critics assert that vaccines are ineffective. However, over the last forty years, several countries have faced disease outbreaks after vaccination rates decreased. For example, between 1999 and 2000 <u>there was an outbreak of measles that occurred in Ireland</u> after vaccination levels dropped. Over 300 measles cases were reported, <u>yet</u> at least three Irish children died.

[5]

<u>A vaccination issue was raised in Indiana after an incident took place in 2005.</u> A non-vaccinated teenager traveled overseas, where she contracted measles. <u>After</u>

<u>returning, to Indiana the teen</u> came into contact

21. **A.** NO CHANGE
    B. made immunizations safer and are reducing
    C. been making immunizations safer and reduced
    D. made immunizations safer and will be reducing

22. Which of the following alternatives to the underlined portion would be LEAST acceptable?
    F. Moreover,
    G. Furthermore,
    H. So,
    J. Also,

23. **A.** NO CHANGE
    B. an outbreak of measles occurred throughout Ireland
    C. a measles outbreak occurred in Ireland
    D. a measles outbreak occurred

24. **F.** NO CHANGE
    G. and
    H. so
    J. but

25. Which choice would most effectively and appropriately lead the reader from the topic of paragraph 4 to that of paragraph 5?
    A. NO CHANGE
    B. Measles broke out in Indiana in 2005 after numerous non-vaccinated individuals made contact with an exposed individual.
    C. During 2005, Indiana suffered through an outbreak of measles.
    D. Similarly, a measles outbreak occurred in Indiana in 2005.

26. **F.** NO CHANGE
    G. After returning, to Indiana, the teen
    H. After returning to Indiana, the teen,
    J. After returning to Indiana, the teen

<u>for religious reasons with a group of people who had not</u>
₂₇

<u>been vaccinated.</u> As a result, 34 people contracted the
₂₇

disease.

[6]

Vaccination programs across the country <u>has</u>
₂₈

eliminated or reduced many diseases. While domestic

immunization rates are fairly high, it is important to

remember that diseases still exist in the world, and deadly

outbreaks can occur unless everyone takes preventive

action. ⟨29⟩ ⟨30⟩

---

27. **A.** NO CHANGE
   B. with a group of people who had not been vaccinated for religious reasons.
   C. with a group of people and for religious reasons had not been vaccinated.
   D. and for religious reasons had not been vaccinated with a group of people.

28. **F.** NO CHANGE
   G. has been
   H. have
   J. is

29. Upon reviewing this essay and realizing that some information has been left out, the writer composes the following sentence, incorporating the missing information:

Vaccination opponents suggest that improved sanitation, hygiene, and dietary habits are the reasons why certain diseases are no longer a problem.

The most logical and effective place to add this sentence would be after the first sentence of paragraph:
   A. 1
   B. 3
   C. 4
   D. 6

30. Suppose the writer had chosen to write an essay indicating that vaccinations are necessary to control contagious diseases. Would this essay fulfill the writer's goal?
   F. No, because the writer disagrees with the notion that vaccinations are the reason for fewer contagious diseases.
   G. No, because the writer believes that the side effects caused by vaccinations are not worth the minimal reduction in contagious diseases.
   H. Yes, because the writer illustrates the damage done by contagious diseases when people are not vaccinated.
   J. Yes, because the writer suggests that scientific advancements have created better vaccinations to fight contagious diseases.

Passage III

Family Changes

[1]

When my parents divorced, I was furious with my father for moving out <u>yet</u> angry at my mother for dating
₃₁
someone else before giving Dad an opportunity to change.

Mom said Dad needed to <u>make many changes to himself</u>
₃₂
before she would consider <u>reconciling,</u> Dad said
₃₃
the same thing about her. As I heard those comments, I knew Mom and Dad would probably never resolve their differences.

[2]

Immediately after their divorce, my parents sent my younger sister and me to counseling, which was helpful. 34
Mom and Dad reassured us that nothing my sister or I did caused the divorce, and although I was old enough to know that, I think my sister was comforted.

[3]

<u>For the past 11 years,</u> my sister and I have lived
₃₅

---

31. **A.** NO CHANGE
B. but
C. and
D. although

32. **F.** NO CHANGE
G. make numerous changes in his life
H. change his ways
J. change

33. **A.** NO CHANGE
B. reconciling and
C. reconciling;
D. reconciling

34. With the intention of adding more information, the writer is considering inserting at this point the following true statement:

The counselor specialized in children whose parents were going through divorce, and my best friend had recently seen the same counselor after his parents broke up.

Should the writer insert the new sentence here? Why or why not?
F. Yes, because the sentence confirms that counseling was unsuccessful at minimizing the author's guilt.
G. Yes, because the sentence gives the reader some valid information about the benefits of counseling.
H. No, because the sentence provides irrelevant information that does not relate to the essay's main topic.
J. No, because the sentence provides information that contradicts the main argument established in the essay.

35. Which of the transitions provides the most effective link from paragraph 2 to paragraph 3?
A. NO CHANGE
B. During the years since the divorce,
C. That difficult time was 11 years ago, and
D. Since my parents divorced 11 years ago,

GO ON TO THE NEXT PAGE.

with my mom. Dad <u>visited</u> on <u>weekends or we go to his</u>
₃₆ ₃₇

<u>house, which</u> is weird because he remarried three years
₃₇

ago. I don't think his new wife likes me very much because

<u>I've heard her say I cause trouble.</u>
₃₈

[4]

I often wish my parents could have <u>faced their problems,</u>
₃₉

<u>be open to settling their issues,</u> and stayed together.
₃₉

Adjusting to living with <u>only one parent and being without</u>
₄₀

<u>our father</u> has not been too difficult for my sister
₄₀

because she and Mom can talk about girl stuff. However,

I wish I could see my father more than just a few times a

month.

[5]

One <u>aspect positive</u> of the new living arrangements
₄₁

<u>are</u> my mother's new husband, Rob. Rob takes me to
₄₂

36. F. NO CHANGE
G. visits
H. will visit
J. was visiting

37. A. NO CHANGE
B. weekends, or we go to his house, which
C. weekends, or we go to his house which
D. weekends or we go to his house which

38. Given that all the choices are true, which one gives the most specific details about the father's new wife to the reader at this point in the essay?
F. NO CHANGE
G. of comments she has made.
H. of how she acts around me.
J. I've spent time with her.

39. A. NO CHANGE
B. faced their problems, settle their issues,
C. faced their problems, settled their issues,
D. been facing their problems, settling their issues,

40. F. NO CHANGE
G. our mother and not our father
H. only one parent
J. our divorced mother

41. A. NO CHANGE
B. positive aspect
C. aspect, it is positive
D. positively aspect

42. F. NO CHANGE
G. have been
H. were
J. is

basketball games and invites me on fishing trips. Since
43
I dislike fishing, I sometimes go anyway to spend time with

Rob. I realize that my three step-siblings are in a similar

predicament because they never wanted their parents to

divorce either. While none of us can change the actions of

our parents, the new relationships that are being created by
44
the situation can all be made the best by us. 45
44

43. **A.** NO CHANGE
    B. Nevertheless,
    C. When
    D. Although

44. **F.** NO CHANGE
    G. the situation that has created the new relationships can be made the best by all of us.
    H. we can all make the best of the situation and the new relationships that have been created.
    J. the best can be made out of what we have created by the new relationships and the situation.

45. Suppose the writer's goal had been to write a brief essay focusing on a specific moment from his childhood. Would this essay successfully fulfill this goal?
    A. Yes, because the essay refers to the many activities the author enjoyed as a child.
    B. Yes, because the essay details the author's emotions after his parents' divorce.
    C. No, because the essay frequently refers to the author's relationship with his parents.
    D. No, because the essay describes how his family situation changed over the years.

GO ON TO THE NEXT PAGE.

Passage IV

Rabbits in Australia

[1]

Farmers around the world can commiserate about droughts, blights, and insects, but only Australian farmers consider rabbits their primary enemies. Australias' rabbits <u>Australias' rabbits</u>
46
leave the soil <u>exposed to nature's elements of wind and</u>
47
<u>rain and susceptible</u> to erosion by eating native plants,
47
tree bark, and seedlings. Feral rabbits are to blame for a reduction in plant species and Australian mammals. <u>Small</u>
48
<u>native animals eventually die and force the abundant</u>
48
<u>rabbits from their homes and habitats.</u> <u>Moreover,</u>
48   49

rabbits <u>devouring</u> the food and grasses intended
50
for livestock, which further frustrates local farmers and ranchers.

[2]

Although rabbits were brought to Australia by the first settlers in 1788, the current overpopulation is blamed on Thomas Austin. The landowner enjoyed rabbit hunting so much that he asked his nephew to acquire 24 rabbits and 5 hares from England in 1859. Hoping to establish a local <u>population for hunting purposes, Austin,</u> released the
51

46. **F.** NO CHANGE
    G. Australia's rabbits'
    H. Australia's rabbits
    J. Australias rabbits

47. **A.** NO CHANGE
    B. exposed
    C. open to the elements of nature
    D. exposed to wind, rain, and extreme temperatures

48. **F.** NO CHANGE
    G. The abundant rabbits, forced from their homes and habitats by small native animals, eventually die.
    H. Forced from their homes and habitats by the abundant rabbits, small native animals eventually die.
    J. The abundant rabbits force small native animals from their homes and habitats and eventually die.

49. Which of the following alternatives to the underlined portion would NOT be acceptable?
    A. Meanwhile,
    B. Furthermore,
    C. In addition,
    D. Also,

50. **F.** NO CHANGE
    G. will devour
    H. devoured
    J. devour

51. **A.** NO CHANGE
    B. population for hunting purposes, Austin
    C. population, for hunting purposes Austin
    D. population for hunting purposes Austin

GO ON TO THE NEXT PAGE. • 255

rabbits onto his <u>property, and</u> neighboring landowners
52

soon followed suit.

[3]

A combination of the prolific nature of rabbits, mild

winters, and the conversion of woodlands into farmland

created an ideal setting for the bunnies. The weather

enabled the rabbits to breed year-round. Local farms

provided the nourishment the small mammals needed

to <u>succeed.</u> The rabbit population reached plague
53

proportions by 1890 when approximately 36 million rabbits

were found in one area of New South Wales, which is

located in the southeast part of Australia. 54 55

52. F. NO CHANGE
   G. property and
   H. property; and
   J. property,

53. A. NO CHANGE
   B. recover.
   C. improve.
   D. thrive.

54. The writer is thinking of revising the preceding sentence to read:

   The rabbit population reached plague proportions by 1890 when approximately 36 million rabbits were found in one area of New South Wales.

   If this revision were made, the sentence would primarily lose:
   F. confusing details about Australia that are presented elsewhere in the passage.
   G. descriptive details that provide the reader with insight about the geography of Australia.
   H. unimportant information that only serves to distract the reader from the main idea.
   J. relevant details that provide the reader with a better appreciation of the situation.

55. Which of the following sentences, if added here, would most effectively lead the reader from paragraph 3 to paragraph 4?
   A. A pest-exclusion fence was constructed in the 1880s to protect sheep from dingoes, although rabbits were still Australia's biggest pest.
   B. Frustrated farmers trapped or killed as many rabbits as possible, but the effect was minimal.
   C. The soil damaged by the burrowing rabbits takes hundreds of years to restore, and increased housing demands have worsened the situation.
   D. Thomas Austin never anticipated that a few rabbits from Europe would devastate Australia.

GO ON TO THE NEXT PAGE.

[4]

Current methods for eliminating the large-eared pests include <u>destroyed burrows, poisoning, rabbit-proof fences,</u> <u>and hunting.</u> Attempts have been made over the years to biologically control rabbits by releasing rabbit fleas infected with the myxoma virus, which is <u>fatal for many</u> <u>rabbits.</u> The virus was released in the 1950s, but the surviving rabbits developed a resistance to the disease.

<u>While</u> feral rabbits are blamed for millions of dollars in crop damage every year, the farmers of Australia will continue searching for a solution to <u>its</u> rabbit problem. 60

56. F. NO CHANGE
G. destroyed burrows, poison, rabbit-proof fencing, and hunts.
H. destroying burrows, poison, rabbit-proof fences, and hunts.
J. destroying burrows, poisoning, rabbit-proof fencing, and hunting.

57. A. NO CHANGE
B. fatal and deadly for many rabbits.
C. deadly for many rabbits but not others.
D. lethal for some rabbits and harmless for others.

58. F. NO CHANGE
G. Although
H. Since
J. After

59. A. NO CHANGE
B. our
C. whose
D. their

60. Suppose the writer had decided to write a short essay illustrating why small farms in Australia are on the decline. Would this essay successfully fulfill the assignment?
F. Yes, because the essay describes how rabbits have been a long-term problem for Australian farmers.
G. Yes, because the essay shows how the rabbit population is responsible for the small number of Australian farms.
H. No, because the essay indicates that small Australian farms are on the rise despite the problem with rabbits.
J. No, because the essay focuses on the problems caused to Australian farms by the rabbit population.

Passage V

Emeril Lagasse—Bam!

[1]

Whether he is spicing up a dish or introducing a new ingredient, Emeril Lagasse cannot keep from saying "Bam" or "Kick it up a notch." If you haven't watched Emeril in action on his successful Food Network show. Then you
[61]
have probably seen his picture on cookbooks or on one of his signature cooking products. As one of the most popular
[62]
chefs in the world, Emeril Lagasse, is hard to miss.
[62]

[2]

[1] In 1978, Lagasse graduated from the Johnson & Wales University College of Culinary Arts before heading to Paris and Lyon, where he perfected the art of French cuisine. [2] The young Emeril's Portuguese mother, Hilda, lay the
[63]
cooking foundation for the future chef. [64] [3] Emeril was born in 1959, in Fall River, Massachusetts, and named after his father.

[3]

Once he returned home to the United States, Emeril
[65]
honed his craft in such cities as New York, Boston, and

61. **A.** NO CHANGE
    B. show, and then
    C. show; then
    D. show, then

62. **F.** NO CHANGE
    G. popular chefs in the world, Emeril Lagasse
    H. popular chefs, in the world, Emeril Lagasse,
    J. popular chefs in the world Emeril Lagasse

63. **A.** NO CHANGE
    B. laid
    C. lain
    D. was laying

64. Which of the following sequences of sentences makes Paragraph 2 most logical?
    F. NO CHANGE
    G. 1, 3, 2
    H. 3, 1, 2
    J. 3, 2, 1

65. Which transition provides the most effective link from Paragraph 2 to Paragraph 3?
    A. NO CHANGE
    B. In the United States,
    C. It was later in time when
    D. After moving back,

GO ON TO THE NEXT PAGE.

Philadelphia before accepting the position of head chef at Commander's Palace in New Orleans. For seven years, Emeril helped the Palace uphold its status legend as an upscale restaurant, he created a name for himself in the culinary world. During his time in New Orleans, Emeril fell in love with the Cajun and Creole cooking styles so very popular in the Crescent City. The spiciness of Cajun and Creole foods often provide the inspiration for many of Emeril's spicy recipes.

[4]

Today, Emeril owns 10 renowned restaurants in: New Orleans, Las Vegas, Orlando, Miami, and Atlanta, all of which have been reviewed in national publications. Emeril's restaurants are just one portion of his multimillion-dollar empire which also boasts a mainstay on the Food Network with cooking tools with Emeril's name, top-selling books, and highly rated television programs. With more

66. F. NO CHANGE
G. status legendary
H. legendary status
J. status as a legend

67. Which of the following alternatives to the underlined portion would NOT be acceptable?
A. restaurant, and he
B. restaurant; he
C. restaurant he
D. restaurant. He

68. F. NO CHANGE
G. that have become popular
H. popular
J. popular and well liked

69. A. NO CHANGE
B. provides
C. are providing
D. have provided

70. Three of these choices indicate that Emeril's recipes were full of flavor and seasonings. Which choice does NOT do so?
F. NO CHANGE
G. zesty
H. fiery
J. healthy

71. A. NO CHANGE
B. restaurants in New Orleans, Las Vegas, Orlando
C. restaurants in New Orleans, Las Vegas, Orlando,
D. restaurants, in New Orleans, Las Vegas, Orlando

72. F. NO CHANGE
G. multimillion-dollar empire which, also,
H. multimillion-dollar empire, which, also
J. multimillion-dollar empire, which also

73. A. NO CHANGE
B. highly rated television programs, cooking tools with Emeril's name, and top-selling books, which have been a mainstay on the Food Network.
C. cooking tools with Emeril's name, top-selling books, and highly rated television programs that have made him a mainstay on the Food Network.
D. top-selling books, highly rated television programs, and cooking tools with Emeril's name, which have made him a mainstay on the Food Network.

than 85 million fans watching his shows, it likely seems

likely that Emeril will be "kicking it up a notch" for a long

time to come. 74 75

74. The writer is considering revising "will be 'kicking it up a notch' for a long time to come" to read "will be successful for a long time to come." That revision would cause the sentence to lose primarily:
F. a reference to details in the introductory paragraph.
G. a characterizing detail about the essay's subject.
H. information about Emeril's personality on TV.
J. information about Emeril's cooking techniques.

75. Suppose the writer had been assigned to write a short essay about a famous individual who overcame adversity. Would this essay fulfill the assignment, and why?
A. No, because the essay mostly focuses on Emeril's popularity on the Food Network.
B. No, because the essay primarily describes how Emeril became a successful chef.
C. Yes, because the essay describes the difficulties faced by Emeril as a young chef.
D. Yes, because the essay provides information about the hard work required of Emeril.

END OF TEST 1.
STOP! DO NOT TURN THE PAGE UNTIL TOLD TO DO SO.

MATHEMATICS TEST

60 Minutes—60 Questions

DIRECTIONS: After solving each problem, pick the correct answer from the five given and fill in the corresponding oval on your answer sheet. Solve as many problems as you can in the time allowed. Do not worry over problems that take too much time; skip them if necessary and return to them if you have time.

Calculator use is permitted on the test. Calculators can be used for any problem on the test, though calculators may be more harm than help for some questions.

Note: Unless otherwise stated on the test, you should assume that:

1. Figures accompanying questions are not drawn to scale.

2. Geometric figures exist in a plane.

3. When given in a question, "line" refers to a straight line.

4. When given in a question, "average" refers to the arithmetic mean.

---

1. Raul sells tickets for popular Broadway musicals. He charges $28.00 for each ticket and also adds a $3.50 service fee for each ticket purchased. Which of the following expresses the total cost of buying *t* tickets from Raul?

   A. $24.50*t*
   B. $31.50*t*
   C. $28.00*t* + $3.50
   D. $28.00 + $3.50*t*
   E. $98.00*t*

2. If 16 cupcakes cost $24, what is the price of 3 cupcakes?

   F. $0.50
   G. $1.50
   H. $3.00
   J. $4.50
   K. $6.00

3. If $a + 4$, what is the value of $\frac{a^2 - 2}{a + 3}$?

   A. $\frac{3}{7}$
   B. $\frac{6}{7}$
   C. 1
   D. $1\frac{3}{7}$
   E. 2

4. Which of the following lists all of the positive factors of 12?

   F. 1, 12
   G. 2, 4
   H. 1, 2, 6, 12
   J. 2, 3, 4, 6
   K. 1, 2, 3, 4, 6, 12

DO YOUR FIGURING HERE.

5. Over 7 days, the daily totals of cars that passed through the Serand Toll Plaza were 193, 146, 783, 225, 456, 299, and 348. How many cars passed through the toll plaza, on average, each day?

   F. 185
   G. 271
   H. 299
   J. 308
   K. 350

DO YOUR FIGURING HERE.

6. What is the measure of ∠Y in quadrilateral WXYZ?

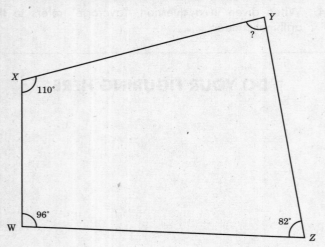

   F. 60°
   G. 72°
   H. 88°
   J. 90°
   K. 101°

7. What is the measure of angle r shown in the figure below?

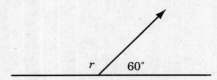

   A. 36°
   B. 72°
   C. 108°
   D. 120°
   E. 160°

8. The expression $w[(x + y) - z]$ is equivalent to:

   F. $wx - wy + wz$
   G. $wx + wy - wz$
   H. $wx - wy + z$
   J. $wx + y + wz$
   K. $wx + wy + z$

GO ON TO THE NEXT PAGE.

9. What is the value of $|5 + a|$ if $a = -8$?

    A. −13

    B. −3

    C. 1

    D. 3

    E. 13

10. Ms. Haskins just sold her house. After giving 20% of the house's sale price to her real estate agent, Ms. Haskins has $90,000. For what price did Ms. Haskins's house sell?

    F. $108,000

    G. $112,500

    H. $118,750

    J. $122,000

    K. $129,750

11. For all q, $(5q - 2)^2 = ?$

    A. $25q + 4$

    B. $25q^2 + 4$

    C. $25q^2 - 4$

    D. $25q^2 - 10q + 4$

    E. $25q^2 - 20q + 4$

12. The shadow cast by a 24-foot-tall flagpole is 16 feet. What is the length, in feet, of the shadow cast by a 6-foot-tall person at the same time of day?

    F. 2

    G. 3

    H. 4

    J. 5

    K. 6

DO YOUR FIGURING HERE.

13. Yolanda volunteers at an animal shelter. During the shelter's yearly fundraiser, she takes donations over the phone during a five-hour shift. Each point on the graph below represents the amount of money that Yolanda raises during each hour of her shift. What is the average amount that she raises per hour during her shift?

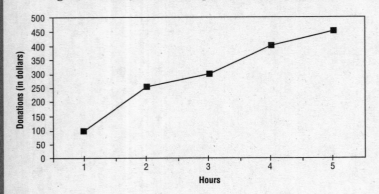

A. $150
B. $200
C. $275
D. $300
E. $350

DO YOUR FIGURING HERE.

14. The expression $(a^9)^6$ is equivalent to:

F. a^{15}
G. a^{54}
H. $15a^3$
J. $15a^{54}$
K. $54a$

15. A triangle has two sides in a ratio of 2:3. The length of the remaining side is 12 centimeters. If the perimeter of the triangle is 82 centimeters, what is the length, in centimeters, of the *shortest* side?

A. 6
B. 12
C. 18
D. 28
E. 42

16. Which of the following expressions is equivalent to

$$(19r^4 - 12r) + (2rs^3 - 4s^3) + (3rs^3 + 7r^4 - 4r)?$$

F. $19r^4 - 25rs^3 - 14s^3$
G. $26r^3 - 2r + 4s^3$
H. $31r^5 - 2rs^6 - 10r^6s^3$
J. $26r^4 - 16r + 5rs^3 - 4s^3$
K. $12r^4 - 8r + 5rs^3$

GO ON TO THE NEXT PAGE.

17. If $4\frac{3}{4} = a + 2\frac{7}{10}$, then $a = ?$

    A. $\frac{19}{20}$

    B. $1\frac{13}{15}$

    C. $2\frac{1}{20}$

    D. $3\frac{4}{5}$

    E. $7\frac{9}{20}$

DO YOUR FIGURING HERE.

18. A wheel of cheese is divided into 5 wedges, as shown in the figure below, where AD and BE are straight lines. If the central angle of Wedge 1 measures 35°, and the central angle of Wedge 3 measures 60°, what is the measure of the central angle of Wedge 5?

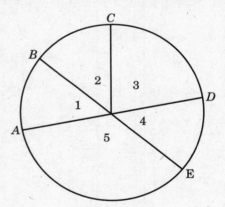

    F. 85°
    G. 95°
    H. 116°
    J. 130°
    K. 145°

19. A rectangle measures 63 meters by 45 meters. What is the length, in meters, of the diagonal of the rectangle?

    A. 36
    B. $\sqrt{2,025}$
    C. $\sqrt{5,994}$
    D. 72
    E. 108

20. Nina has a number cube with faces numbered 1 to 6. She rolls the cube eight times. If the results are as shown below, what is the probability that Nina will roll a 4 on her next roll?

$$1, 6, 2, 2, 3, 4, 5, 6$$

F. 0

G. $\dfrac{1}{2}$

H. $\dfrac{1}{6}$

J. $\left(\dfrac{1}{4}\right)^2$

K. 1

21. In the (x, y) coordinate plane, what is the slope of the line that is perpendicular to the line whose equation is $x + 5y = 30$?

A. $-\dfrac{1}{5}$

B. $\dfrac{1}{5}$

C. 1

D. 3

E. 5

22. In the figure below, $WXYZ$ is a rhombus with four sides of equal length. Diagonals WY and ZX bisect each other. If WY measures 16 centimeters and ZX measures 12 centimeters, what is the perimeter of the polygon in centimeters?

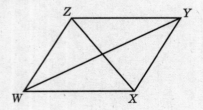

F. 10
G. 40
H. 56
J. 60
K. 78

GO ON TO THE NEXT PAGE.

23. In an essay-writing competition, 1 male student and 1 female student will be awarded first-place prizes. If 175 males and 225 females enter the competition, how many different 2-person combinations of 1 male and 1 female are possible?

    A. 50
    B. 400
    C. 1,275
    D. 7,875
    E. 39,375

24. In the triangle below, if the measure of ∠AGB is 100°, then w = ?

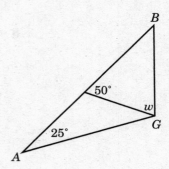

    F. 20°
    G. 35°
    H. 55°
    J. 75°
    K. 130°

25. A family rented a moving truck for $41.50 per day and $0.25 per mile. How many miles did the family drive the truck if they spent $185.50 on the rental and used the truck for one day?

    A. 475
    B. 500
    C. 532
    D. 576
    E. 600

26. Which of the following is the equation of the line with y-intercept (0, 3) and x-intercept (−1, 0)?

    F. $y = \frac{1}{3}x$
    G. $y = 3x + 3$
    H. $y = -3x + 3$
    J. $y = -2x + 2$
    K. $y = -\frac{1}{3}x + 3$

DO YOUR FIGURING HERE.

27. If $a = 5$, $b = 7$, $c = \dfrac{1}{4}$, and $d = -3$, $\left(\dfrac{a-b}{c}\right) - \left(\dfrac{b}{d+a}\right) =$

DO YOUR FIGURING HERE.

    A. −4

    B. $-4\dfrac{1}{2}$

    C. $-11\dfrac{1}{2}$

    D. $-12\dfrac{3}{4}$

    E. −17

28. What is the radius of the circle with equation $(x + 5)^2 + (y - 4)^2 = 5$ in the standard (x, y) coordinate plane?

    F. 2

    G. $\sqrt{5}$

    H. 4

    J. 5

    K. $5\sqrt{2}$

29. In the standard (x, y) coordinate plane, the midpoint of JK is $\left(\dfrac{5}{2}, 3\right)$ and K is located at $(4, 5)$. Which of the following represents point J?

    A. (−7, 4)
    B. (1, 1)
    C. (3, 2)
    D. (6, 3)
    E. (5, 4)

30. If the area of circle P shown below is 72π centimeters squared, what is the length, in centimeters, of PQ?

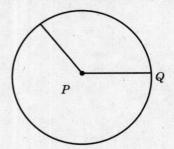

    F. $\sqrt{6}$
    G. $6\sqrt{2}$
    H. $7\sqrt{7}$
    J. 18
    K. 36

GO ON TO THE NEXT PAGE.

31. For all pairs of real numbers C and D where $C = 4D - 8$, $D = ?$

DO YOUR FIGURING HERE.

    A. $\dfrac{C}{8} + 4$

    B. $\dfrac{C}{4} + 8$

    C. $\dfrac{C}{8} - 4$

    D. $\dfrac{C - 8}{4}$

    E. $\dfrac{C + 8}{4}$

32. If $\dfrac{2}{3}x < 1$, what is the set of all possible values of x?

    F. $x > -\dfrac{2}{3}$

    G. $x > \dfrac{3}{2}$

    H. $x > \dfrac{2}{3}$

    J. $x < \dfrac{3}{2}$

    K. $x < -\dfrac{3}{2}$

33. In the standard (x, y) coordinate plane, what is the distance between the points $(6, -1)$ and $(22, -7)$?

    A. $2\sqrt{7}$

    B. 8

    C. $2\sqrt{55}$

    D. $2\sqrt{73}$

    E. 48

34. Annie's office uses a faxing service. The service charges $0.25 per page for domestic faxes sent between 8 a.m. and 5 p.m. Monday through Friday and all day Sunday; $0.75 per page for international faxes sent between 8 a.m. and 5 p.m. Monday through Friday and all day Sunday; $1.20 per page for domestic faxes sent after 5 p.m. Monday through Saturday; and $1.80 per page for international faxes sent after 5 p.m. Monday through Saturday. The table below shows the time and quantity of faxes sent by Annie's office in one week.

Day	Time	Type of Fax	Number of Pages
Monday	4:00 p.m.	international	6
Tuesday	7:15 p.m.	domestic	8
Wednesday	2:30 p.m.	domestic	3
Friday	8:30 p.m.	international	7
Sunday	9:00 p.m.	international	4

How much money did Annie's office spend on international faxes during the week shown?

F. $12.75
G. $20.10
H. $24.30
J. $30.60
K. $39.10

35. How many prime numbers are there between 12 and 35?

A. 3
B. 5
C. 6
D. 7
E. 8

DO YOUR FIGURING HERE.

270 •

GO ON TO THE NEXT PAGE.

36. A large college campus has the shape and dimension in blocks shown in the figure below. Each point represents a campus building. A student who lives in a dorm located at point Z attends class in a building at point X. Assuming the student cannot cut across campus to get to class, what is the minimum number of blocks the student must travel to get from point Z to X?

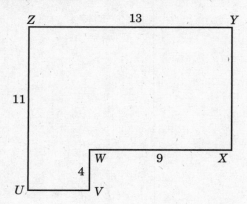

DO YOUR FIGURING HERE.

F. 13 blocks
G. 20 blocks
H. 24 blocks
J. 28 blocks
K. 33 blocks

37. Which of the following statements is NOT true about the arithmetic sequence 3, 7, 11, 15, 19, ...?

A. The seventh term in the sequence is 27.
B. The common ratio of consecutive terms is 4.
C. The sum of the first six terms in the sequence is 78.
D. The ninth term in the sequence is 35.
E. The common difference of consecutive terms is 4.

Practice Test 3

38. In triangle JKL, $\tan L = \dfrac{2}{3}$ and $\overline{LK} = 6$ ft. What is the measure of $\overline{JK}$ in feet?

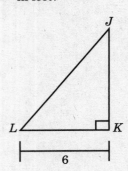

F. 4

G. 8

H. $\dfrac{3}{4}$

J. 3

K. $\dfrac{1}{2}$

39. Which of the following lines goes through $(2, -1)$ and is perpendicular to $y = 3x - 7$?

A. $y = \dfrac{1}{3}x + \dfrac{1}{3}$

B. $y = \dfrac{2}{3}x - \dfrac{1}{7}$

C. $y = -\dfrac{1}{3}x + \dfrac{2}{7}$

D. $y = 3x - 7$

E. $y = -\dfrac{1}{3}x - \dfrac{1}{3}$

40. There are 724 people in an apartment building. Of those people, approximately $\dfrac{2}{9}$ live in two-bedroom apartments and approximately $\dfrac{1}{3}$ of those who live in two-bedroom apartments have fireplaces in both bedrooms. Which of the following is the closest estimate of how many people in the apartment building live in two-bedroom apartments with fireplaces in both bedrooms?

F. 40

G. 54

H. 98

J. 161

K. 241

GO ON TO THE NEXT PAGE.

41. Which of the following equations could represent the parabola graphed below?

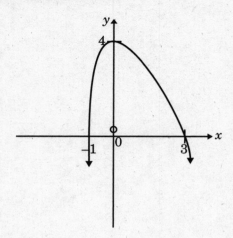

A. $y = (x + 2)(x - 2)$
B. $y = -x(x - 2) + 4$
C. $y = x(x + 2) + 4$
D. $y = -x(x + 2) - 4$
E. $y = x^2 - 2x - 4$

42. In the figure below, $\sin \theta = ?$

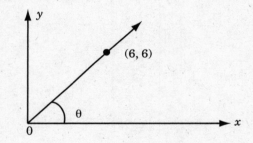

F. $\dfrac{\sqrt{2}}{2}$

G. 1

H. 2

J. $\dfrac{6\sqrt{2}}{3}$

K. $\dfrac{\sqrt{2}}{3}$

43. If $x^2 + 8 = 6x$, what are the possible values of x?

A. $(-4, -2)$

B. $(1, -8)$

C. $\left(\sqrt{2}, -\sqrt{2}\right)$

D. $(2, -2)$

E. $(4, 2)$

44. If 85% of a number is 340, what is 130% of the number?

    F. 360

    G. 480

    H. 520

    J. 640

    K. 730

DO YOUR FIGURING HERE.

45. What is the total surface area, in square inches, of the rectangular box shown below?

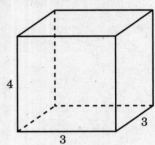

    A. 24

    B. 36

    C. 66

    D. 80

    E. 120

46. The definition of $\csc \theta$ = ?

    F. $\dfrac{1}{\tan \theta}$

    G. $\dfrac{1}{\cos \theta}$

    H. $\dfrac{1}{\sin \theta}$

    J. $\dfrac{1}{\sin^2 \theta}$

    K. $\dfrac{1}{\tan^2 \theta}$

47. In rectangle $WXYZ$ shown below, $\tan a$ = ?

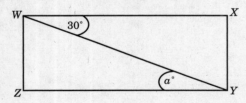

    A. $\dfrac{\sqrt{3}}{3}$

    B. $\dfrac{1}{2}$

    C. $\dfrac{\sqrt{3}}{2}$

    D. $\sqrt{2}$

    E. 2

GO ON TO THE NEXT PAGE.

DO YOUR FIGURING HERE.

48. What is the value of h for which the lines $y = hx - 3$ and $y = x + 4$ intersect at the point $(3, 7)$ in the standard (x, y) coordinate plane?

   F. -2

   G. $\dfrac{6}{7}$

   H. $\dfrac{3}{2}$

   J. 2

   K. $\dfrac{10}{3}$

49. Which inequality represents the number line graph shown below?

   A. $-1 \le x \ge 6$
   B. $-1 \le x \le 6$
   C. $-1 \ge x \le 6$
   D. $-1 > x \le 6$
   E. $-1 \ge x \ge 6$

50. An electronics store sells DVD and VHS movies. Four DVDs and three VHSs would cost $109.93. Four VHSs and three DVDs would cost $99.93. How much would 1 DVD and 1 VHS cost?

   F. $28.50
   G. $29.03
   H. $29.53
   J. $29.98
   K. $29.99

51. How many diagonals does the hexagon below have?

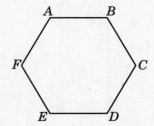

   A. 3
   B. 6
   C. 9
   D. 18
   E. 36

GO ON TO THE NEXT PAGE. • 275

52. If $f(x) = x^2 - 7$ and $g(x) = x + 2$, which of the following shows the value of $f(g(x))$?

   F. $x^2 + 7x + 13$
   G. $x^2 - 3x + 2$
   H. $x^2 + 2x - 4$
   J. $x^2 + 3$
   K. $x^2 + 4x - 3$

53. Allen plans to plant a circular garden in the center of a rectangular plot of land, which measures 14 yards by 18 yards. What is the largest area of the circular flowerbed that Allen can plant?

   A. 38π
   B. 43π
   C. 49π
   D. 81π
   E. 224π

54. If $|a + b| = 15$ and $|-c| = 15$, then which of the following MUST be true?

   I. $|c| > -a$

   II. $|c| = |b - a|$

   III. $|a + b| = c$

   F. III only
   G. I and II only
   H. II and III only
   J. I, II, and III
   K. None of the statements must be true.

55. Lines A, B, C, and D are intersecting lines contained within a plane. Each line intersects every other line, and each line crosses the other at only one point. What is the maximum number of points at which the four lines intersect?

   A. 1
   B. 2
   C. 4
   D. 6
   E. 7

56. Karla drove for 12 hours at a speed of y miles per hour (mph) and 10 more hours at an increased speed of 70 mph. If the average speed for her whole trip was 65 mph, which equation could be used to find y?

   F. $y + 70 = 2(70)$
   G. $y + 10(70) = 22(65)$
   H. $12y - 10(70) = 65$
   J. $12y + 10(70) = 22(65)$
   K. $12y + 10(65) = 2(65)$

DO YOUR FIGURING HERE.

GO ON TO THE NEXT PAGE.

57. Sisters Jaclyn and Nicole have toy boxes in the shape of cubes. The edges of Jaclyn's toy box are exactly 50% longer than the edges of Nicole's toy box. The volume of Jaclyn's box is how many times the volume of Nicole's box?

    A. 2
    B. 3.375
    C. 5.5
    D. 8.275
    E. 25

58. Furniture sales at Fantasy Designs decreased by 40% from April to May and by 65% from May to June. By what percent did their furniture sales decrease from April to June?

    F. 21%
    G. 39%
    H. 79%
    J. 112%
    K. 114%

59. What is the value of $\log_n (cd)^2$ if $\log_n c = a$ and $\log_n d = b$?

    A. $2ab$
    B. $a + b$
    C. $2a + b$
    D. $2a + 2b$
    E. $4ab$

DO YOUR FIGURING HERE.

60. A function g is an even function if and only if $g(-x) = g(x)$ for every value of x in the domain of g. Which of the functions graphed in the standard (x, y) coordinate plane below is an even function?

DO YOUR FIGURING HERE.

F.
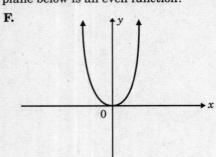

G.
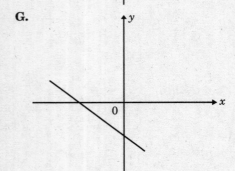

H.
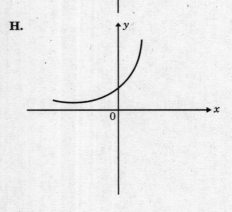

GO ON TO THE NEXT PAGE.

DO YOUR FIGURING HERE.

J.

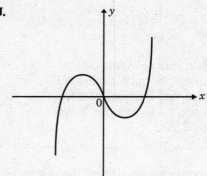

K.

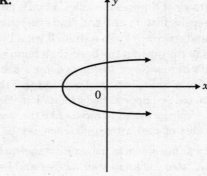

END OF TEST 2.
STOP! DO NOT TURN THE PAGE UNTIL TOLD TO DO SO.
DO NOT RETURN TO THE PREVIOUS TEST.

READING TEST

35 Minutes—40 Questions

DIRECTIONS: On this test, you will have 35 minutes to read four passages and answer 40 questions (ten questions on each passage). Each set of ten questions appears directly after the relevant passage. You should select the answer choice that best answers the question. There is no time limit for work on the individual passages, so you can move freely between the passages and refer to each as often as you'd like.

Passage I

PROSE FICTION: This passage is adapted from a short story titled "Leave It to Winter" by Charles Adelman, from his book *Rites of Passage*.

I was waiting for winter to take it all. Sweep everything clean, just like that, with its bustling storms and unpredictability. I knew I was taking a bit of a risk, leaving things to chance, but I still had some sense of
5 adventure, and besides—it was a calculated risk. Winter usually did erase the fall.

Every November, storm by storm, snowflake by snowflake, the memories of autumn faded defenselessly in winter's grip. Yellow leaves turned to brown and
10 then disappeared, indiscernible beneath the frost. Soon the pageantry of bitter cold was all that held anyone's attention. All remnants of the fall forgotten, winter would settle in.

It was the laughter that always got to me. For some
15 reason, I had the least tolerance for that. Walking through St. Anthony's campus, conveniently unavoidable on the short route to where I worked, I seemed to be able to focus on nothing *but* the laughter and socializing. Fine young men and women strode by in droves, passing away what
20 would probably be the most important four years of their lives without so much as a moment's thought. For them, the fall only existed for the purpose of being taken for granted. The perfect start to each new school year slipped by unnoticed between the jokes, the gossip, and the fun.

25 I didn't have the right to resent them, I knew; they had nothing to do with the fact that my path had been chosen so carefully for me. It wasn't the least bit their fault, in fact, that my path had been chosen for me and not by me. Perhaps I had no one to blame about that but myself, for
30 giving in. What a tired story it is to rant on about how you never really wanted to run your father's poultry business and you certainly never intended to do so, but you just wound up there out of a profound sense of obligation or some sort of "moral duty." Yes, I admit—I ran that tired
35 story over and over again in my head, practically on a daily basis, especially in the fall. I kept replaying the story but it was also the truth, and a truth I didn't know how to evade.

Though no one in my family took the idea seriously, I had always wanted to be a professor. A history professor, to
40 be exact: a professor of European studies. I had a profound passion for European history and had read everything I could get my hands on since I was a child. It got a little hard to explain to the guys on the basketball team what that copy of Joll's *Europe Since 1870* was doing stuck in
45 my gym bag. After a while, I stopped explaining. I think the stopping started as I approached graduation, when the idea of attending college began to recede like the waning tide, and the reality of work after high school set in.

"Jeremy," my father spoke to me over his spectacles at
50 the dinner table, "son, you know your mother and I want what is best for you. Leaving the poultry business in your hands is all we ever considered. It's a reputable way to make a living. You should be proud to carry on the family name in this town."

55 And I was proud—I just wasn't happy. It was during fall that I noticed it most. Fall was back-to-school time, when all of the St. Anthony's students were perusing the local stores, shopping for new clothes and school supplies. I thought of the carts we'd fill up every September at the
60 local office supply store: binders, notebooks, loose leaf paper, folders, pencils, and pens. For certain years, in math, I'd get a compass or protractor or whatever special gadget was needed for the subject at hand. These days, since graduation, September had been like any other nondescript
65 month for me. Walk across the campus at St. Anthony's to the corner of Fleet and Wayne; open the shop and stash the cash for the day in the cash box. September could have been December or March or July, for all that it mattered. No school supplies, no new classes, and nothing to choose.

70 So I resented the coeds for having the life that I wanted but had opted against. I resented them, and I rejected fall. I couldn't wait for winter to literally bury it under a mound of snow. Once November hit, and the storms began, everything would change. The weather would become
75 formidable, and seriousness would set in. The excitement of the new school year would be over at last. This year, like every year, I would welcome the changing season and wait. "Leave it to winter," I'd tell myself. "Winter will take care of it." Then I'd watch as the impinging cold moved in and
80 whisked all the reminders away.

GO ON TO THE NEXT PAGE.

1. The passage indicates that the narrator would most likely be interested in which of the following subjects?

    A. Geometry
    B. French history
    C. Russian literature
    D. American history

2. Which of the following can be reasonably inferred about Jeremy's family?

    F. Jeremy's parents disagreed about what their son should do.
    G. Jeremy's father could not afford to send his son to college.
    H. Jeremy's family business is in financial trouble.
    J. Jeremy's parents did not attend college.

3. At the time of the events in the story, the narrator is most likely:

    A. an adolescent thinking about a recent conversation with his father about plans to work in the family business.
    B. an adult walking through a college campus reflecting on how the plans for his life have changed.
    C. an adolescent looking around a college campus with hopes of enrolling after he graduates from high school.
    D. an adult trying to determine whether he should leave the family business to attend college.

4. The narrator claims that he eagerly anticipates autumn turning into winter because:

    F. autumn reminds him of the pleasures associated with the beginning of a new school semester.
    G. winter provides him the opportunity to reflect on the choices he has made in his life and the changes he will make.
    H. autumn is a busy and noisy time as students return to campus and prepare for their classes.
    J. winter snowstorms break up the monotony of his life and remind him that seasonal change can be exciting.

5. Which of the following best describes Jeremy's opinion of the students at St. Anthony's?

    A. They are unable to succeed in college because they gossip and socialize too much.
    B. They enjoy shopping for new school supplies more than they enjoy learning.
    C. They ignore the seasons because they are too absorbed in their schoolwork.
    D. They cannot appreciate college because they are too interested in having fun.

6. Which of the following best describes Jeremy's nature as it is presented in the passage?

    F. Irrational and bitter
    G. Infuriated and resentful
    H. Responsible yet frustrated
    J. Appreciative and vindictive

7. According to the passage, why are months no longer significant to the narrator?

    A. Jeremy's life does not vary because his job remains the same no matter the month.
    B. Jeremy's attention is on fall and winter, and spring and summer do not matter to him.
    C. Jeremy's path through campus does not change because it is the fastest route to work.
    D. Jeremy's decisions about work, school, and life are not dependent on the calendar.

8. It can reasonably be inferred that the yellow leaves mentioned in the second paragraph (lines 7–13) are symbolic of Jeremy's:

    F. honor and duty.
    G. hopes and dreams.
    H. guilt and resentment.
    J. youth and innocence.

9. We may reasonably infer from details in the passage that Jeremy believes:

    A. winter will ease the pain of autumn because it has done so in the past.
    B. autumn will be less difficult next year because painful memories are fading.
    C. winter is the best season because storms make life exciting and unpredictable.
    D. autumn will be more difficult every year because winter never helps with the pain.

10. According to the passage, the narrator relinquishes his dreams while:

    F. talking to his friends, when he realizes no one understands or cares about his unique interests.
    G. working at his family's business, when he no longer sees September as a special month.
    H. speaking with his father, when he learns what the family expects of Jeremy after graduation.
    J. walking to work, when he decides that he should make the most of the life that he has chosen.

Passage II

SOCIAL SCIENCE: This passage is adapted from Kathleen Kellett's "Uncovering the Unconscious: Freud's Innovative Contributions to Dream Analysis."

The origins and meanings of dreams have fascinated people since prehistoric times. In classical antiquity, the ancients regarded dreams not as products of the dreaming mind but as divine revelations from gods or demons.
5 Centuries later, Aristotle theorized that dreams were created by the mental activity of the sleeper, his mind engaged in the process of dreaming. The subject of possible derivations and interpretations of dreams has continued to captivate and perplex more modern thinkers such as
10 Sigmund Freud. In his seminal work, *The Interpretation of Dreams*, Freud revolutionized the manner in which dreams could be scrutinized and analyzed. In this controversial writing, Freud attributed the construction of dreams to three essential factors: displacement, condensation, and
15 secondary revision.

Freud posited that the first necessary element in the construction of an individual's dream was *displacement*. He believed that each person dreamt about thoughts and events from the previous day. Occasionally, nightmares
20 resulted because the events of the day had acutely affected the dreamer. Because a person's disturbing thoughts may have prevented him or her from resting, and because a person required sleep to perform even the most basic functions of daily existence, Freud surmised that the
25 dreamer must remove unacceptable or upsetting material from his dreams and displace it with more tranquil thoughts. For example, one of Freud's patients reported a vision involving a hotel where many of his acquaintances received accommodations either on the first floor (up above)
30 or the ground floor (down below). Freud suggested that the higher and lower levels represented in the patient's dream masked his fears about the dangers of intimacy with a woman of an "inferior social class" with whom he had established a close relationship. Following the
35 displacement of this anxiety-producing thought, Freud's patient spent an uneventful night dreaming about trivial situations. In this manner, displacement allows one to obtain his or her imperative amount of rest by resolving the traumas of the previous day.

40 Another method Freud examined as fundamental to the construction of dreams was *condensation*. Most individual's dreams, he reasoned, are brief and meager in comparison to the plethora of thoughts preceding the dream. The source for material found in dreams was
45 derived from a person's experiences and reminiscences throughout the day; however, the proportion of these thoughts recollected in the dream was usually minute.

Moreover, the harder a person attempted to analyze his or her dream, the more he or she appeared to have forgotten
50 it. Freud attributed the relative brevity of a person's dream to the reflections prefacing it, or condensation. For example, Freud discussed a vision in which he pictured a man with a yellow beard, sharing characteristics of both his Uncle Joseph and his friend, Dr. R. He was puzzled by
55 this dream because he held his friend in high repute in contrast to his Uncle Joseph, a criminal whose activities had alienated his family. When Freud pondered the content of the dream further, he realized that numerous thoughts had merged together to form the composite
60 figure in his vision, including recent disturbing news about his uncle, his apprehension regarding a promotion, and fear that his friend, Dr. R., would receive the coveted position instead of himself. Therefore, Freud explained condensation as a process of the unconscious mind during
65 the formation of dreams in which a variety of pre-dream thoughts were reduced into a "condensed" version.

Freud described a final procedure as necessary to the formation of dreams which he termed *secondary revision*. He theorized that secondary revision fused the distorted
70 and fragmented thoughts contained in one's dreams into an intelligible whole. This process served to fill in the gaps occurring in a typical dream, connecting these vague images into a pleasant story. As a result, the dream was coherent, its context lacking absurdity. For instance,
75 one dream that fascinated Freud involved a patient who recalled visions from the previous evening which included exiting a crowded dinner party, encountering a woman carrying a child, and responding "I will" to an officer who had arrested him. Through the process of secondary
80 revision, the dreamer consciously gathered these detached ideas and congregated them into a logical sequence, which Freud could analyze effectively as representing a fantasy of marriage. Through this method of secondary revision, Freud deduced that a person rearranges his assorted
85 recollections to amalgamate the "missing parts" of a dream and render it both rational and significant.

Although *The Interpretation of Dreams* was written nearly a century ago, the material presented remains influential. Freud's innovative ideas concerning the
90 process of dream analysis initiated the practice of psychoanalysis. The same censoring agents predominating dream interpretation—condensation, displacement, and secondary revision—continue to be applied in current psychoanalytic theory. Freud's research provides indelible
95 insight into the structures, functions, and hidden characteristics of the unconscious mind.

GO ON TO THE NEXT PAGE.

11. The main function of the fifth paragraph (lines 87–96) in relation to the passage as a whole is to:

   A. emphasize the author's point that dream interpretation remains both controversial and intriguing.
   B. suggest that Freud's dream research inadvertently supports the dubious field of psychoanalysis.
   C. point out that Freud's dream research is relevant to modern psychiatry methods and assessments.
   D. establish that the author believes that Freud's categories for dream interpretation should be reevaluated.

12. The passage indicates that condensation, displacement, and secondary revision are alike in that they all:

   F. are essential components to the assembly of an individual's dreams.
   G. enable people to assemble incoherent thoughts into sensible dreams.
   H. are elements that vary between individuals depending on experiences.
   J. weaken the strength of a person's dream by working simultaneously.

13. As it is used in line 42, the term *meager* most nearly means:

   A. flawed.
   B. limited.
   C. restrained.
   D. miserable.

14. Which of the following questions is NOT answered by information in the passage?

   F. Why do dreams seem logical when people are having them?
   G. What causes some people to have nightmares?
   H. What did people believe about dreams before Freud?
   J. Why was Freud's research considered controversial?

15. The failure of most people to recall their own dreams is most likely a result of:

   A. excessive attempts to interpret the meaning of their dreams.
   B. unsuccessful efforts at remembering the minor details of their dreams.
   C. an illogical sequence of events in their dreams that is difficult to remember.
   D. confusing details added by the subconscious that clutter their dreams.

16. According to the passage, which of the following occurs during displacement?

   F. Individuals replace convoluted dreams with lucid ones.
   G. Patients are able to sleep soundly and be well rested for work.

H. Traumatic ideas are exchanged for insignificant thoughts.
   J. Confusing dreams are analyzed and assessed when the patient awakens.

17. According to the passage, the process of condensation involves:

   A. reorganizing the sequence of events in a dream to create a logical story that appears to be subconsciously realistic.
   B. reducing the numerous thoughts and actions from a person's day into symbols representative of the deepest concerns.
   C. omitting the day's emotional events from the subconscious and creating a dream from only the most frivolous activities.
   D. minimizing the significance of disturbing thoughts and activities during the day by avoiding deep sleep.

18. It may reasonably be inferred from the passage that Freud believes:

   F. people bury thoughts deep in their minds, and dreams provide an outlet for emotions to come to the surface.
   G. regularly assessing thoughts and emotions before going to sleep prevents nightmares from occurring.
   H. individuals dream about all of their activities and thoughts that occurred during the day but only remember small parts.
   J. constantly analyzing dreams allows individuals to recall more specific details that can be used for psychiatric treatment.

19. As it is used in line 85, the word *amalgamate* most nearly means:

   A. dissolve.
   B. separate.
   C. expand.
   D. combine.

20. As indicated in the passage, the patient described in lines 27–37 suffered from nightmares for which of the following reasons?

   F. He was trying to determine whether or not to marry a woman.
   G. He was concerned about his social standing being lowered.
   H. He was worried about the hotel in which he was staying.
   J. He was hoping to improve his social status through marriage.

Passage III

HUMANITIES: This passage is adapted from Matthew Lang's "Anguished Emotion: Elements of Gothic Literature in Edgar Allan Poe's 'The Fall of the House of Usher.'"

Edgar Allan Poe's unsettling story "The Fall of the House of Usher" recounts the events leading to the deaths of the last two remaining members of the Usher family. Written in 1839, the story is an important example of
5 Gothic fiction. During the late 18th century, Gothic fiction developed out of the larger Romantic movement characterized by appreciation for the imagination, subjective experience, and freedom of expression. Gothic fiction combined these Romantic ideals with aspects of
10 horror, including mystery and violence, to induce strong emotions in the reader. Through his masterful use of Gothic fiction elements, including ominous settings, supernatural events, and psychological terror, Poe engages his readers and creates an enduring tale of suspense and
15 madness.

Poe's descriptions of the House of Usher's decaying exterior hint at the problems inside its doors and foreshadow the events to follow. The story begins with the narrator traveling to the home of his childhood
20 friend, Roderick Usher, after Usher writes to him describing his fragile health and beseeching him to visit and provide comfort. Upon his arrival, the narrator reveals his uneasiness, commenting, "I know not how it was—but, with the first glimpse of the building, a sense
25 of insufferable gloom pervaded my spirit." As he examines the mansion before him, his feelings of apprehension grow stronger. He reports, "I looked upon the scene before me . . . upon the bleak walls—upon the vacant eye-like windows— upon a few rank white trunks of decayed trees—with an
30 utter depression of soul which I can compare to no earthly sensation."

When he enters the Usher home, the narrator again feels the same chilling emotion. He recalls, "Feeble gleams of encrimsoned light made their way through the
35 trellised panes, and served to render sufficiently distinct the more prominent objects around; Dark draperies hang upon the walls." An atmosphere of gloom pervades the house and mirrors the physical and mental disintegration of its inhabitants. He continues, "I felt that I breathed
40 an atmosphere of sorrow. An air of stern, deep, and irredeemable gloom hung over and pervaded all."

Another element of Gothic fiction, the exploration of supernatural events, is also woven throughout the story. For example, Lady Madeline Usher, Roderick Usher's
45 twin, is seemingly able to feel Roderick's physical and mental pain. Like her brother, Madeline has been afflicted all her life with an illness that has caused her body to slowly deteriorate. Both Madeline and Roderick are sick with undiagnosed conditions and have highly sensitized
50 reactions to both their own afflictions and those of their sibling. Roderick is constantly unnerved about Madeline's illness and acts evasively when the narrator questions him about its origins.

Sinister noises that plague Roderick and the narrator
55 also convey a sense of the supernatural since they seem to transcend the laws of nature. The narrator reports, "Here again I paused abruptly, and now with a feeling of wild amazement—for there could be no doubt whatever that, in this instance, I did actually hear . . . a low and apparently
60 distant, but harsh, protracted and most unusual screaming or grating sound." These inexplicable noises occur night after night, seem to have no basis in reality, and underlie the gloom of the Usher house.

Poe's fascination with the unconscious mind and
65 the experience of mental anguish also contribute to the story's effectiveness. The frightening events that occur after Madeline's burial lead to the final unraveling of the Ushers' physical and mental states. One fateful night, during a raging storm, Roderick taps on the narrator's
70 door and enters the room shaking and upset. While the narrator gently reads to him in an attempt to calm his nerves, Roderick yells, "Not hear it? Yes, I hear it, and have heard it. Long—long—long—many minutes, many hours, many days, have I heard it. . . ."

75 Roderick's psychological upset continues to escalate as the story races to its chilling end. He raves, "Said I not that my senses were acute? . . . Madman! I tell you that she now stands without the door." After this terrifying declaration by Roderick, the narrator sees Madeline enter
80 the bedroom, and he flees in fear.

As the narrator escapes the death and intrigue of the Usher estate, he turns his back to see the great walls of the mansion crumbling in a pile of dust and debris, symbolizing the destruction of the Usher family. Featuring
85 elements of Gothic fiction, Poe's enduring story continues to interest readers today with its exploration of the unconscious mind and the fragility of human life.

21. According to the passage, "The Fall of the House of Usher" is an example of Gothic literature because it is:

   A. rational, horrifying, and imaginative.
   B. suspenseful, creative, and emotional.
   C. solemn, expressive, and inspirational.
   D. reflective, exciting, and comforting.

22. Which of the following statements from the passage suggests that setting is essential to the tone established in "The Fall of the House of Usher"?

   F. "One fateful night, during a raging storm, Roderick taps on the narrator's door and enters the room shaking and upset."
   G. "Roderick is constantly unnerved about Madeline's illness and acts evasively when the narrator questions him about its origins."
   H. "Poe's descriptions of the House of Usher's decaying exterior hint at the problems inside its doors and foreshadow the events to follow."
   J. "Poe's fascination with the unconscious mind and the experience of mental anguish also contribute to the story's effectiveness."

23. Based on the passage, Poe was inspired to write "The Fall of the House of Usher" because of his interest in:

   A. emotional distress.
   B. physical destruction.
   C. personal relationships.
   D. mysterious illnesses.

24. The main function of the fifth paragraph (lines 54–63) in relation to the passage as a whole is to:

   F. redirect the passage toward a discussion of Poe's development of Roderick as an unstable character throughout the story.
   G. establish the passage's claim that "The Fall of the House of Usher" uses supernatural elements to convey Poe's disdain for Romantic literature.
   H. emphasize the passage's point that "The Fall of the House of Usher" should be characterized as Gothic literature because of its mystic elements.
   J. shift the passage's focus toward a discussion of psychological distress as characterized by Roderick and Madeline.

25. It can reasonably be inferred from the passage that the narrator in "The Fall of the House of Usher":

   A. is called to the house to provide medical treatment.
   B. has known Roderick for a brief amount of time.
   C. is romantically interested in Madeline.
   D. has never visited Roderick before.

26. According to the passage, modern readers enjoy "The Fall of the House of Usher" because the story:

   F. studies the causes of stressful family relationships.
   G. examines the precarious nature of human existence.
   H. illustrates the detrimental effects of a solitary existence.
   J. incorporates suspenseful moments into a tale of romance.

27. The author's attitude toward the use of Gothic elements in "The Fall of the House of Usher" can best be characterized as:

   A. slight aversion.
   B. elated fascination.
   C. sincere admiration.
   D. passionate obsession.

28. According to the author, at what point does the narrator in "The Fall of the House of Usher" first feel uneasy about visiting Roderick?

   F. When he notices the dark, closed window curtains
   G. When he realizes that Madeline is extremely ill
   H. When he and Roderick hear strange noises
   J. When he sees the dying trees in the yard

29. Which of the following can be reasonably inferred from the passage about the Usher family?

   A. Madeline and Roderick lost their parents to psychological diseases that could not be diagnosed or treated.
   B. The Ushers prefer to isolate themselves from the rest of society in order to protect their many secrets.
   C. Madeline and Roderick are the last surviving members of the once wealthy Usher family.
   D. The Ushers suffer from unspecified hereditary illnesses that have run in their family for generations.

30. What does the passage indicate about the relationship between Madeline and Roderick?

   F. Madeline and Roderick share such a close connection with each other that they physically hurt when the other is suffering.
   G. Madeline suffers from an unknown disease, and Roderick tries to protect his twin sister from excessive pain.
   H. Madeline is so disturbed by Roderick's physical pain that she falsely believes she also suffers from the same ailment.
   J. Madeline and Roderick comfort each other through their physical problems and enjoy an especially close sibling bond.

Passage IV

NATURAL SCIENCE: This passage is adapted from an article titled "Babies, Bottles, and Bisphenol A: The Story of a Scientist-Mother" by Aimee Quitmeyer and Rebecca Roberts (© 2007 by PLoS Biology).

My 11-month-old daughter loves her baby bottles and sippy cups. But as I sit and watch her drink from them, I cringe, because I happen to be a scientist who studies a chemical found in those bottles and cups. I also know that
5 some scientific research suggests that exposure to that compound, called bisphenol A (BPA), is detrimental to good health—something I can't help but think about as I watch my daughter use her sippy cup as a teething ring.

In 1952, chemists working with BPA discovered that it
10 could help form a hard, clear plastic called polycarbonate. Polycarbonates make such products as compact discs, sunglasses, bicycle helmets, water and milk bottles, baby bottles, food storage containers, tableware, plastic windows, bullet-resistant laminate, cell phones, car
15 parts, toys, and some medical devices such as incubators, dialysis machines, and blood oxygenators. BPA is also used to make certain resins that are commonly found in the linings of food cans to prevent corrosion, and it is present in some polyvinyl chloride (PVC) plastic products,
20 in white dental fillings, dental sealants, and in some flame retardants. In keeping with its widespread applications, BPA ranks among the highest-volume chemicals manufactured worldwide, with an annual production in 2003 of about 13 billion kilograms.

25 BPA has been shown to leach from water bottles and food cans into the packaged foodstuffs. It then enters the body through the digestive tract when those foods are consumed. The level of BPA released from plastic depends on the age and wear of the plastic and on exposure to heat.
30 For example, one study showed that small levels of BPA leached from baby bottles subjected to simulated normal uses, including boiling, washing with a bottle brush, and dishwashing. Plastic tableware (such as those used in some schools) was also found to release BPA into hot
35 vegetable soup. Older, worn bottles and bowls released BPA more readily than newer products. BPA is also present in rivers and streams and in drinking water, presumably due to leaching from plastic items in landfills. A survey by the Centers for Disease Control and Prevention found that
40 approximately 95% of Americans have detectable levels of BPA in their bodies.

Naturally, the prevalence of human exposure leads to questions about safety and health. Although the plastic industry continues to assert that BPA is safe,
45 the chemical's endocrine-disrupting properties raise concern about its potential to cause harm. BPA exposure affects the hormonal system, in particular, the pathway involving estrogen; its effects have been studied on cells, tissues, and whole organisms. In adult male mice and rats,
50 effects of BPA exposure—abnormal sperm and reduced fertility—were reversed when exposure stopped. Of the few human epidemiological studies, one revealed a relationship between BPA exposure and repeated miscarriage. Additionally, BPA causes a human breast cancer cell line
55 to proliferate, indicating that estrogen-sensitive tissues and cells in the body may react similarly.

At this point, you might be wondering why this is the first time you've ever heard of BPA. The information is out there but it is a puzzle to get through. Early studies
60 indicated that BPA did not leach or leached in very small amounts from plastic products, including baby bottles. These studies are often referred to by those in the chemical industry, such as the American Plastics Council, who have a vested interest in maintaining the use of BPA
65 in plastics production, to verify the safety of the products. However, since 1999 many studies have shown that BPA leaches from products at levels known to cause health effects in animals. Earlier studies on BPA exposure also tended to find little resulting adverse health effects, yet
70 these studies were often using doses that were higher than those now regarded as being in an environmentally relevant range—that is, the low doses that humans are exposed to regularly and that fit within the so-called "low-dose theory" that claims that lower doses can be more
75 harmful than higher doses. These were the main studies initially used by the EPA to determine the "safe" level of BPA exposure and that are often referenced to attest to the safety of BPA.

In the meantime, what is the scientist-mother to do?
80 The mother in me still waits anxiously for the regulatory agencies and the legislature to catch up with the research on BPA that the scientist in me appreciates. I have switched my brand of sippy cups to one that doesn't contain BPA (a quick internet search will yield many
85 sites describing these and other BPA-free baby products). Nevertheless, while I feel proactive as I watch my daughter happily drink her water, I still cringe a little bit when she drops the sippy cup, toddles over to her toy bin, and starts to gnaw on her plastic turtle instead.

31. According to the passage, why do the majority of Americans have noticeable levels of BPA in their bodies?

   A. Plastic items intended for small children contain BPA, which can never be flushed from the body.
   B. BPA used in canned goods seeps into food items and is absorbed by the body once the food is consumed.
   C. Plastic manufacturers have dumped BPA into rivers, and the contaminated water has ended up in bottled water.
   D. Older plastic materials that contain high amounts of BPA are being recycled and used in plastic bottles and tableware.

32. It can reasonably be inferred that one of the functions of the last sentence (lines 86–89) is to:

   F. point out that the harmful effects of BPA are realized by only scientists like herself who understand the chemical's toxicity.
   G. illustrate the author's alarm about her daughter's safety in regards to the prevalence of BPA.
   H. suggest that people should be as angry as she is about the use of BPA in children's products.
   J. emphasize the author's belief that people should be moderately concerned about the effects of BPA.

33. According to the author, all of the following attributes of food containers affect the quantity of BPA transferred from plastic EXCEPT:

   A. temperature.
   B. cleanliness.
   C. quality.
   D. age.

34. It is reasonable to conclude from the passage that chemical companies that manufacture BPA have:

   F. monetary reasons for supporting the results of BPA studies done before 1999.
   G. ethical reasons for supporting the results of EPA surveys and assessments.
   H. financial reasons for supporting the results of BPA studies done after 1999.
   J. publicity reasons for supporting the results of CDC surveys and assessments.

35. Based on information in the passage, which of the following situations might cause BPA to be released?

   A. Cleaning a baby bottle with hot water
   B. Storing canned goods in a pantry
   C. Serving cereal in a plastic bowl
   D. Drinking water from a plastic bottle

36. The passage indicates that BPA may have harmful effects on the human body because:

   F. contact increases estrogen production and activity.
   G. exposure disturbs hormones related to fertility.
   H. consumption triggers fat-cell activity and obesity.
   J. exposure causes cancer in male rats and mice.

37. According to the passage, the baby product industry has responded to BPA concerns by:

   A. supporting legislation to ban BPA from items intended for small children.
   B. labeling items with health warnings about the compound's possible risks.
   C. urging the EPA and other legislative agencies to study the hazards of BPA.
   D. offering alternative products for consumers concerned about the compound.

38. According to the fifth paragraph (lines 57–78), studies indicate that low doses of BPA, as compared to high doses of BPA, are:

   F. equally harmful.
   G. less harmful.
   H. more harmful.
   J. not harmful.

39. Based on the passage, which of the following statements, if true, would most WEAKEN the argument that BPA poses a health concern?

   A. Multiple studies have found a correlation between an increased likelihood of developing type 2 diabetes and BPA consumption.
   B. Blood levels of women with fertility problems have been shown to have high percentages of BPA.
   C. The BPA danger level designated by the Environmental Protection Agency (EPA) has been modified three times over the last ten years.
   D. Recent studies indicate that the human body neutralizes and flushes out BPA at a faster rate than rats and mice.

40. It is reasonable to infer from the passage that which of the following industries would be the most negatively affected by restrictions on polycarbonates?

   F. Furniture
   G. Construction
   H. Food and beverage
   J. Information technology

END OF TEST 3.
STOP! DO NOT TURN THE PAGE UNTIL TOLD TO DO SO.
DO NOT RETURN TO THE PREVIOUS TEST.

SCIENCE TEST

35 Minutes—40 Questions

DIRECTIONS: This test contains seven passages, each accompanied by several questions. You should select the answer choice that best answers each question. Within the total allotted time for the subject test, you may spend as much time as you wish on each individual passage. Calculators use is not permitted.

Passage I

Citation: Nagy S, Rychlicki S, Siemek J (2006). Impact of inactive hard-coal mines processes in Silesian Coal Basin on greenhouse gases pollution. *Acta Geologica Polonica 56*(2): 221–228.

Greenhouse gases are significantly more abundant in Poland than in neighboring European nations. These gases absorb red-wavelength radiation, which results in higher air temperatures and increased amounts of ozone. An excess of ozone has a negative influence on the state of forests and vegetation, and may also cause a smog formation around urban areas. Among the greenhouse gases are: water steam, ozone, carbon dioxide (CO_2), nitrogen oxide (N_2O), methane (CH_4), fluorohydrocarbons (HFC), carbon perfluorides (PFC-CF_4, C_2F_6, C_4H_{10}), sulphur and fluoride SF_6 compounds and aerosols. By converting emitted gas weights to equivalent $MtCO_2$[1] (million tons of CO_2), a potential of greenhouse gases can be determined. Table 1 shows Poland's total emission of greenhouse gases for the years 1988–2002. (NE means "not estimated.")

	Year								
Gas	**1988**	**1990**	**1992**	**1994**	**1995**	**1996**	**1998**	**2000**	**2002**
CO_2	476.6	380.7	371.6	371.6	348.2	372.5	337.4	314.8	308.3
CH_4	66.0	58.8	52.0	51.8	51.6	47.3	49.0	45.9	37.8
N_2O	21.8	19.4	15.6	15.6	16.7	16.7	16.0	23.9	22.6
HFCs	NE	NE	NE	NE	0.02	0.07	0.22	0.89	1.26
PFCs	NE	NE	NE	NE	0.82	0.77	0.81	0.72	0.27
SF_6	NE	NE	NE	NE	0.00	0.00	0.01	0.02	0.02
Total $MtCO_2$	**564.4**	**458.9**	**439.2**	**439.8**	**417.34**	**437.34**	**403.44**	**386.23**	**370.25**

Table 1

GO ON TO THE NEXT PAGE.

Pollution in Poland is concentrated in the area of the Upper Silesian Coal Basin (USCB). The analysis of methane (CH_4) emissions caused by coal mines leads to the conclusion that almost all of the methane produced in Poland comes from the USCB. Since 1990, industry in Poland has been modernized and restructured. As a result, many coal mines have shut down. Table 2 shows the methane produced by Polish coal mines between 1989 and 2003.

Year	Number of methane-bearing mines	Absolute methane release rate (cubic meters/minute)
1989	55	1,989.6
1990	55	1,881.5
1991	54	1,577.7
1992	54	1,613.6
1993	54	1,483.9
1994	52	1,431.0
1995	48	1,418.0
1996	44	1,400.2
1997	43	1,504.7
1998	43	1,453.6
1999	43	1,436.1
2000	41	1,470.0
2001	38	1,440.2
2002	38	1,455.6
2003	36	1,522.5

Table 2

1. According to Table 1, emissions of nitrogen oxide in Poland were lowest in:
   A. 1988 and 1990.
   B. 1992 and 1994.
   C. 1994 and 1995.
   D. 2000 and 2002.

2. According to Table 2, the number of coal mines in Poland decreased most significantly during which five-year span?
   F. Between 1989 and 1993
   G. Between 1992 and 1996
   H. Between 1997 and 2001
   J. Between 1999 and 2003

3. Which of the following lists Poland's greenhouse gases from the lowest to highest amount of contributed pollution for the year 1996?
   A. CO_2, CH_4, N_2O, HFCs
   B. N_2O, HFCs, CO_2, CH_4
   C. HFCs, N_2O, CH_4, CO_2
   D. HFCs, CO_2, N_2O, CH_4

4. Based on the information presented and the data in Table 1, during which year did Polish forests and vegetation face the most danger from greenhouse gases?
   F. 1988
   G. 1992
   H. 1996
   J. 2002

5. According to Table 2, which of the following is true about the relationship between the number of coal mines in Poland and the amount of methane produced?
   A. Both the number of coal mines and the amount of methane produced decreased from year to year.
   B. As the number of coal mines increased, the amount of methane produced also increased.
   C. As the number of coal mines decreased, the amount of methane produced increased.
   D. The number of coal mines decreased steadily, but the amount of methane produced increased in certain years.

Passage II

Citation: Gonzalez H, Tarras-Wahlberg N, Strömdahl B, Juzeniene A, Moan J, Larkö O, Rosén A, Wennberg A (2007). Photostability of commercial sunscreens upon sun exposure and irradiation by ultraviolet lamps. *BMC Dermatology*, 7:1.

Sunscreens are widely used to reduce exposure to harmful ultraviolet (UV) radiation. However, some sunscreens are *photounstable* (subject to change upon exposure to light). Photounstable sunscreens break down upon exposure to UV rays, making them less effective than photostable sunscreens. The following experiments exposed seven brands of sunscreen to both natural UV radiation (UVnat) and artificial UV exposure (UVart). The results of both experiments are recorded in Figure 1.

Experiment 1

The goal of this experiment was to measure photostability in sunscreens exposed to natural UV radiation (UVnat), which includes UVB, UVA1, and UVA2 rays. Samples of each of the seven sunscreens were weighed and placed between two plates of curved, polished quartz. Then, the samples were placed outside when the weather was sunny. At several intervals during the experiment, researchers measured the area under the curve (AUC) of each sample. Each sunscreen's photostability was measured using an AUC Index (AUCI), which is equal to AUC_{after}/AUC_{before}. Researchers considered the sunscreen photostable if its AUCI was higher than 0.8. In Figure 1, AUCI is referred to as "absorbance."

Experiment 2

The goal of this experiment was to measure photostability in sunscreens exposed to artificial UV radiation (UVart), which includes UVB, UVA1, and UVA2 rays. The procedure of this experiment was very similar to that of Experiment 1. Samples of each of the seven sunscreens were weighed and placed between two plates of curved, polished quartz. Then, the samples were exposed to UV radiation by a radiation-producing machine called UVASUN 2000. At several intervals during the experiment, researchers measured the area under the curve (AUC) of each sample. Each sunscreen's photostability was measured using an AUC Index (AUCI), which is equal to AUC_{after}/AUC_{before}. Researchers considered the sunscreen photostable if its AUCI was higher than 0.8. In Figure 1, AUCI is referred to as "absorbance."

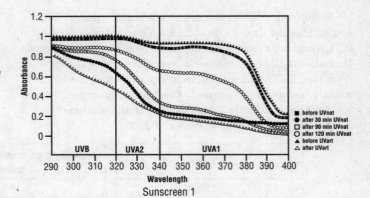

Sunscreen 1

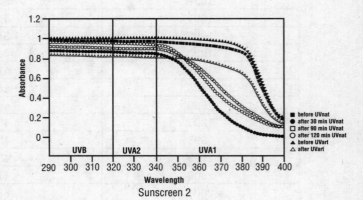

Sunscreen 2

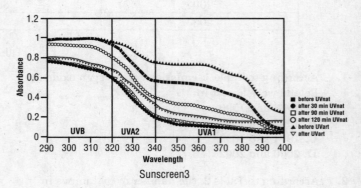

Sunscreen3

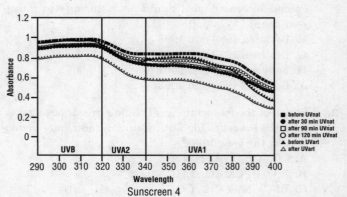

Sunscreen 4

GO ON TO THE NEXT PAGE.

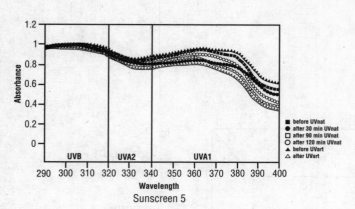

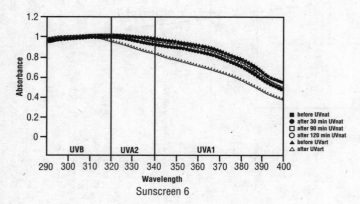

Figure 1

6. According to the figure, *Sunscreen 4 was the most photostable:*

  F. after 30 minutes of exposure to natural UV radiation.

  G. after 90 minutes of exposure to natural UV radiation.

  H. before being exposed to natural UV radiation.

  J. before being exposed to artificial UV radiation.

7. According to the figure, the most photounstable sunscreen is:

  A. Sunscreen 2, before exposure to artificial UV radiation.

  B. Sunscreen 1, after 90 minutes of exposure to natural UV radiation

  C. Sunscreen 6, after 30 minutes of exposure to natural UV radiation.

  D. Sunscreen 3, after 120 minutes of exposure to natural UV radiation.

8. After exposure to artificial UV radiation at a wavelength of 340 nm, the absorbance of Sunscreen 6 is approximately:

  F. 0.9

  G. 0.7

  H. 0.6

  J. 0.4

9. Michael plans to spend 90 minutes on a sunny beach. He will be exposed to UVB, UVA2, and UVA1 rays, and he wants to use a sunscreen with an absorbance of 0.4 or greater. Which sunscreen should Michael NOT take to the beach?

  A. Sunscreen 3

  B. Sunscreen 4

  C. Sunscreen 5

  D. Sunscreen 6

10. Which of the following conclusions about the photostability of sunscreen is consistent with the results shown in Figure 1?

  F. In general, a sunscreen is more photostable when it is exposed to UVA1 rays than when it is exposed to UVB rays.

  G. In general, a sunscreen's photostability decreases as its UV exposure reaches 400 nm.

  H. In general, a sunscreen is more photostable after being exposed to artificial UV radiation.

  J. In general, a sunscreen's photostability increases as its UV exposure reaches 400 nm.

11. The researchers who created this study recommend that sunscreen manufacturers mark the photostability of their product on its label to help consumers make the most appropriate choice of sunscreen. Which of the following assumptions is required to make this suggestion?

  A. All sunscreen manufacturers will increase UVA protection in their products.

  B. All sunscreen manufacturers will use a standardized method to measure photostability.

  C. All sunscreen manufacturers will use different methods to measure photostability.

  D. All sunscreen manufacturers will decrease UVA protection in their products.

Practice Test 3

Passage III

A *spectroscope* is a device used to analyze the different wavelengths of light contained in a light beam (Figure 1). The dotted arrows show the direction of light as it travels into the spectroscope and to the viewer's eye.

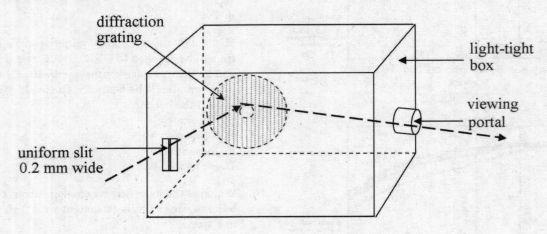

Figure 1

The spectroscope spreads out the colors of light on the visible spectrum so they appear individually as spectral lines. Each color corresponds to a different wavelength of light, measured in nanometers (nm). Figure 2 shows the wavelength ranges for different colors of visible light. Table 1 shows the colors visible in the spectra displayed by the spectroscope when directed at different light sources.

Figure 2

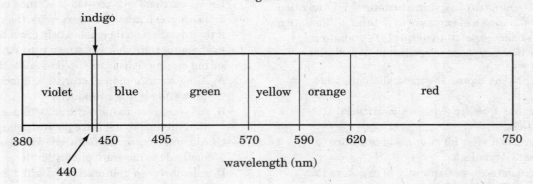

Colors Visible in Spectrum							
Source	Violet	Indigo	Blue	Green	Yellow	Orange	Red
Sun	x	x	x	x	x	x	x
Fluorescent light			x	x			
Neon light						x	x
Yellow-green LED				x	x	x	x
Red laser diode							x

Table 1

GO ON TO THE NEXT PAGE.

Figures 3 and 4 show graphical representations of the spectra displayed when the spectroscope was directed at two of the light sources listed in Table 1. Figure 3 shows the spectrum displayed by Source A. Figure 4 shows the spectrum displayed by Source B. The higher intensity wavelengths in the graphs indicate the colors seen in the spectra.

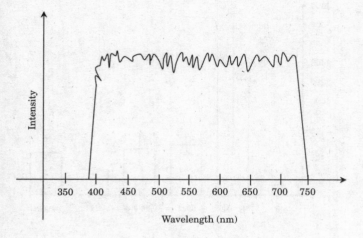

Figure 3

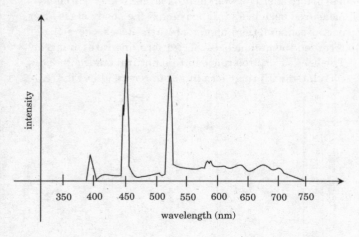

Figure 4

12. According to Figure 2, a wavelength of 445 nm represents which of the following colors?
    F. Red
    G. Green
    H. Indigo
    J. Blue

13. Based on the information in Figure 2 and Table 1, a wavelength of 580 nm would be displayed in the color spectrum of which of the following light sources?
    A. Red laser diode
    B. Fluorescent light
    C. Neon light
    D. Yellow-green LED

14. Spectral lines with a wavelength of 393 nm are due to the presence of the substance calcium. Based on the data in Figure 2 and Table 1, calcium is most likely present in which of the following?
    F. The sun
    G. Yellow-green LED
    H. Red laser diode
    J. Fluorescent light

15. Based on the information presented, Source B is most likely:
    A. the sun.
    B. a fluorescent light.
    C. a yellow-green LED.
    D. a neon light.

16. Based on the information presented, when a spectroscope is used to view the sun, the resulting spectrum displays:
    F. a color pattern highly similar to that of a red laser diode.
    G. the colors violet and blue at higher levels of intensity than red and orange.
    H. all colors of the visible light spectrum with relatively equal intensity.
    J. the colors blue and green at higher levels of intensity than other colors in the spectrum.

Passage IV

Citation: Raine N, Chittka L (2007). The adaptive significance of sensory bias in a foraging context: floral colour preferences in the bumblebee. *PLoS ONE* 2(6): e556.

Bees are constantly exposed to stimuli that vary widely in significance. They use their senses to determine which stimuli are most important in *foraging* (finding food). The flower choices of pollinating bees represent a good model system in which to study the adaptive role of sensory bias in the context of foraging. Different flower colors appear to be linked to the reliability of finding high nectar rewards. In these studies, newly emerged bees that have never seen flowers show distinct biases toward certain colors.

Experiment 1

Nine bumblebee colonies (colonies A through I) were raised in a laboratory setting. Worker bees were not exposed to flowers before the beginning of this experiment—in other words, they were completely "color-naïve." First, bees were placed in a flight box with 16 colorless flowers. The flowers were filled with a sucrose solution. Whenever bees visited these flowers, they were rewarded with the solution. Next, the 16 colorless flowers were replaced by 16 flowers that did not contain any sucrose solution. Of these flowers, 8 were violet (also called "UV-blue") and 8 were blue. The bees' preference for violet flowers is shown in Figure 1. In this figure, the thick horizontal line in each box represents the colony average.

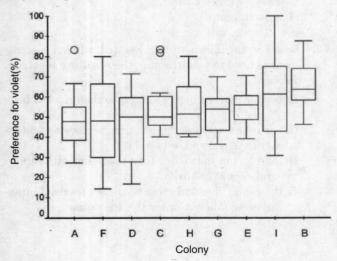

Figure 1

Experiment 2

The same nine bumblebee colonies (colonies A through I) were then placed in a natural environment. The colonies had access to multiple flower species in bloom in dry grassland, forest, and farmland. First, researchers measured the nectar production rates in various colors of flowers. The results are in Figure 2.

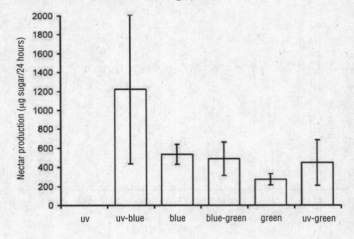

Figure 2

Researchers measured the empty body mass of each bee before that bee went out to forage. The researchers measured each bee's full body mass (i.e., body mass after nectar consumption) upon its return. Researchers also recorded the bumblebees' nectar foraging rate (in mg/hr). The bees' color preference in this natural environment is correlated with their foraging rate recorded in Figure 3.

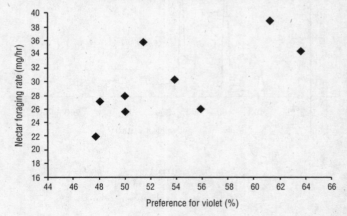

Figure 3

GO ON TO THE NEXT PAGE.

17. According to Figure 1, which colony of bees, on average, had the greatest preference for violet?
  A. Colony B
  B. Colony D
  C. Colony F
  D. Colony I

18. According to Figure 3, what is the approximate nectar foraging rate of bees that prefer violet flowers 56 percent of the time?
  F. 38 mg/hr
  G. 34 mg/hr
  H. 30 mg/hr
  J. 26 mg/hr

19. According to Figure 2, the amount of nectar produced by violet (UV-blue) flowers is:
  A. slightly greater than the amount of nectar produced by UV-green flowers.
  B. equal to approximately 500 μ sugar/24 hours.
  C. equivalent to more than twice the nectar produced by the blue and blue-green flowers combined.
  D. equal to approximately 900 μ sugar/24 hours.

20. Based on the information in Figure 1 and Figure 3, one can conclude that the bumblebees in Colony B:
  F. had a lower nectar foraging rate, on average, than the bumblebees in Colony E.
  G. had a higher nectar foraging rate, on average, than the bumblebees in Colony F.
  H. have a greater preference for blue flowers than for violet flowers.
  J. had greater success foraging in the flight box than foraging in the natural environment.

21. Which of the following conclusions is supported by all three figures?
  A. Flowers with the greatest nectar production attract the highest percentage of bumblebees.
  B. Bumblebees would be attracted to violet flowers even if they did not produce nectar.
  C. Bumblebees have an easier time finding nectar in laboratory environments than they do in natural environments.
  D. There is no correlation between the color of flowers and bumblebees' foraging habits.

22. The results from which experiment, if either, support the conclusion that bumblebees prefer violet (UV blue) flowers?
  F. Experiment 1 only
  G. Experiment 2 only
  H. Experiment 1 and 2
  J. Neither experiment supports this conclusion.

Passage V

Citation: Levine M, Adida B, Mandl K, Kohane I, Halamka J (2007). What are the benefits and risks of fitting patients with radiofrequency identification devices? *PLoS Med 4*(11): e322.

In 2004, the United States Food and Drug Administration approved a radio frequency identification device (RFID) that is implanted under the skin of patients and that stores the patient's medical identifier. When a scanner is passed over the device, the identifier is displayed on the screen of an RFID reader. An authorized health professional can then use the identifier to access the patient's clinical information, which is stored in a separate database. Such RFID devices may have many medical benefits, but critics of the technology have raised several concerns, including the risk of the patient's identifying information being used for nonmedical purposes.

RFID Implantation Invades Privacy

The American Medical Association (AMA) recommends that patients should be told of "medical uncertainties associated with [RFID] devices." However, doctors must understand that RFID devices have an impact upon patients' privacy that extends far beyond the medical arena. With an implanted RFID device, individuals can be tracked surreptitiously by anyone using a generic RFID reader. Consequently, RFID devices have been aptly described as "a kind of license plate for people." If such devices become widely deployed, they may provide an incentive for both well- and ill-intentioned parties to set up readers for these "license plates." Because the RFID identifier is of no medical significance, it is not protected by the Health Insurance Portability and Accountability Act (HIPAA), and there are no laws that regulate how and by whom it can be read.

As personalized medicine incorporates a wider range of advanced technologies, these sorts of "crossover consequences" will become more frequent. Given the importance of privacy in health care, the AMA should set a strong, privacy-friendly precedent with its RFID recommendation. There are many applications of RFID technology that can improve health care, but the implantation of these devices into patients merits a healthy dose of skepticism.

RFID Devices Lead to Patient Freedom

The RFID chip holds 16-digit code, which is used to point to a Web site containing personal health records. The Web site requires a username and password, ensuring appropriate security. Since we have no universal health identifier in the U.S., there is no simple way to uniquely identify a patient at all sites of care. The result is a fractured medical record scattered in hospital, laboratory, and pharmacy, and emergency sites. The implanted RFID devices enable patients to establish health care identities. This patient-controlled record is available to treating clinicians in the case of emergency via the implanted device.

It is a personal choice whether or not to be fitted with an RFID device, but for some patients such a record has value. For example, such devices may be particularly helpful for a patient with Alzheimer's disease who cannot give a history. Implantation of RFID devices could be considered a tool that empowers patients unable to communicate by serving as a source of identity and a link to a personal health record.

GO ON TO THE NEXT PAGE.

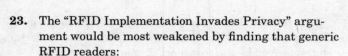
23. The "RFID Implementation Invades Privacy" argument would be most weakened by finding that generic RFID readers:
    A. can be purchased for a small amount of money.
    B. cannot decipher the 16-number code on medical RFID devices.
    C. are compatible with a number of RFID devices, including medical-data chips.
    D. can store large amounts of information.

24. Proponents of both arguments would agree that RFID devices:
    F. change the way in which patients and doctors access medical data.
    G. pose a significant security risk to those who have the devices implanted.
    H. allow patients greater control over their medical records.
    J. are not affordable options for most elderly patients.

25. Assuming that the "RFID Implementation Invades Privacy" argument is the most valid, which of the following conclusions can be made about RFID devices?
    A. The AMA will prohibit the use of RFID devices in American medical practices.
    B. RFID devices would be far more secure if they had a 24-number code.
    C. RFID devices are completely inappropriate for use with Alzheimer's patients.
    D. Physicians should not offer patients the option of an RFID device without first warning them of potential risks.

26. If it was discovered that RFID devices allowed patients to be treated more quickly in emergency situations, how would this discovery affect the arguments, if at all?
    F. It would have no effect on either argument.
    G. It would strengthen the "RFID Devices Lead to Patient Freedom" argument only.
    H. It is consistent with both arguments.
    J. It would strengthen the "RFID Implantation Invades Privacy" argument only.

27. Which of the following questions is raised by the "RFID Implantation Invades Privacy" argument but NOT answered in the passage?
    A. Why aren't RFID devices covered by the Health Insurance Portability and Accountability Act (HIPAA)?
    B. Why should the AMA change its recommendation regarding RFID devices?
    C. What is the incentive for people to surreptitiously steal information from RFIDs?
    D. How do RFID devices help patients who have Alzheimer's disease?

28. Based on both arguments, RFID devices:
    F. are equipped with effective security features.
    G. can be described as "license plates for people."
    H. allow clinical access to an individual's medical data.
    J. should require strict oversight by the AMA.

29. The "RFID Devices Lead to Patient Freedom" argument says that RFID devices can:
    A. provide organization for once-scattered patient medical records.
    B. reduce patients' need to visit a doctor on a regular basis.
    C. pose a substantial risk to the security of patient medical records.
    D. use voice-recognition software to record patient histories.

Passage VI

Citation: Rapp D (2006). Radiation effects and shielding requirements in human missions to the Moon and Mars. *MARS: The International Journal of Mars Science and Exploration* 2: 46–71.

Radiation in space poses a threat to humans embarked on missions to the Moon or Mars. From the standpoint of radiation protection for humans in interplanetary space, the two endangering sources of radiation for lunar and Mars missions are 1) GCR (heavy ions of the galactic cosmic rays) and 2) SPE (sporadic production of energetic protons from large particle events). GCR particles deliver much smaller amounts of radiation than SPE particles do. Table 1 shows the allowable radiation exposure for astronauts. This is the amount of exposure astronauts can receive without experiencing negative health effects. In the table, BFO stands for "blood-forming organ" (i.e., heart, kidneys, liver, etc.). Radiation is measured in cSv, or dose unit.

Period of Exposure	BFO Dose Equivalent (cSv)	Ocular Lens Dose Equivalent (cSv)	Skin Dose Equivalent (cSv)
30 Days	25	100	150
1 Year	50	200	300
Astronaut's Career		400	600

Table 1

To be protected from radiation in space, astronauts need sufficient shielding. The effectiveness of any shield material is characterized by the transport of energetic particles within the shield. Figure 1 displays a comparison of the shielding effectiveness of various materials. The 5-cm dose equivalent rate represents the amount of radiation that would enter an astronaut's body after moving through the shield and through layers of skin.

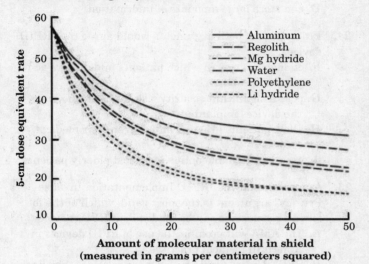

Figure 1

GO ON TO THE NEXT PAGE.

30. According to Table 1, how much radiation can an astronaut's skin be exposed to over her career, without any negative health effects?
    F. 300 cSv
    G. 400 cSv
    H. 600 cSv
    J. 1,000 cSv

31. According to Figure 1, which material is most effective in shielding astronauts from high doses of radiation?
    A. Aluminum
    B. Regolith
    C. Polyethylene
    D. Lithium hydride

32. Some astronauts and aerospace engineers have complained about the heavy, inflexible nature of aluminum shielding. Considering the information in the passage and the data in Table 1 and Figure 1, when would it be appropriate to use lighter, more flexible polyethylene shielding?
    F. On a year-long mission where astronauts are exposed only to GCR-particle radiation
    G. On a 30-day mission where astronauts are exposed only to GCR-particle radiation
    H. On a year-long mission where astronauts are exposed only to SPE-particle radiation
    J. On a 30-day mission where astronauts are exposed only to SPE-particle radiation

33. According to Figure 1, a regolith shield at 10 g/cm² protects an astronaut from approximately:
    A. 10 cSv/year of radiation
    B. 30 cSv/year of radiation
    C. 40 cSv/year of radiation
    D. 60 cSv/year of radiation

34. An aerospace engineer is designing a new type of shield for astronauts. The engineer wants the shield amount to be 20 g/cm² and to protect astronauts from radiation levels of 30 cSv/year or higher. Which materials could the engineer use to make the shield?
    F. Aluminum only
    G. Magnesium hydride, regolith, or aluminum
    H. Regolith or aluminum
    J. Polyethylene or lithium hydride

Passage VII

Citation: Egwaikhide P, Akporhonor E, Okieiman F (2007). Effect of coconut fiber filler on the cure characteristics of physico-mechanical and swelling properties of natural rubber vulcanizates. *International Journal of Physical Sciences* 2(2): 39–46.

The search for means and methods of improving the properties and processing of rubber dates back more than a century. One way to extend the service life of rubber is to incorporate *additives* (materials that ensure easy processing, reduce cost of product, and enhance service properties) into the polymer. In the rubber industry, one common additive is carbon black. Carbon black is derived from petro-chemical sources; however, and unstable oil prices have led to the search for additives from other sources. One possible filler is coconut fiber. In the following experiments, researchers compared the effectiveness of coconut fiber to the effectiveness of carbon black.

Experiment 1

Researchers compared the tensile strength of rubber mixed with coconut fiber to the tensile strength of rubber mixed with carbon black. Tensile strength measures the stress required to elongate (stretch) rubber to its breaking point. The results are shown in Figure 1. The amount of carbon-black filler and coconut-fiber filler is measured in parts per hundred (phr).

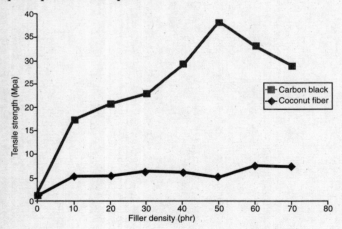

Figure 1

Experiment 2

Figure 2 shows the results for a hardness test, in which researchers compared the relative resistances of rubber mixed with coconut fiber and rubber mixed with carbon black. Rubber's hardness is its capability to resist indentation by a specified weight.

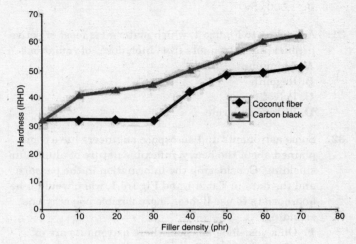

Figure 2

GO ON TO THE NEXT PAGE.

35. In Experiment 1, what was the approximate tensile strength of rubber with 50 phr coconut fiber?
    A. 35 Mpa
    B. 20 Mpa
    C. 15 Mpa
    D. 5 Mpa

36. According to the data in Experiment 2, which rubber mixture had the greatest hardness?
    F. Rubber with 10 phr coconut fiber
    G. Rubber with 10 phr carbon black
    H. Rubber with 70 phr coconut fiber
    J. Rubber with 70 phr carbon black

37. Both of the experiments support which of the following conclusions?
    A. Rubber with high levels of coconut-fiber filler has greater hardness but less tensile strength than rubber with high levels of carbon black.
    B. Carbon black is a more effective filler for rubber than coconut fiber.
    C. Rubber with high levels of coconut-fiber filler has greater tensile strength but less hardness than rubber with high levels of carbon black.
    D. Coconut fiber is a more effective filler for rubber than carbon black.

38. The data in Experiment 1 support the hypothesis that carbon black:
    F. is most effective in rubber at a ratio of 50 phr.
    G. provides less tensile strength at 10 phr than does coconut fiber at 10 phr.
    H. provides ten times as much strength at 20 phr than does coconut fiber at 20 phr.
    J. yields only a slightly greater amount of tensile strength than coconut fiber.

39. In which scenario might rubber mixed with coconut-fiber filler be preferable to rubber mixed with carbon-black filler?
    A. A ball manufacturer wants a rubber that will bounce off of any surface.
    B. An eraser manufacturer wants a rubber that will not snap when a person presses down on the eraser.
    C. A dog-toy manufacturer wants a rubber that will give way when a dog chews it.
    D. A tire manufacturer wants a rubber that will retain its shape on rough roads.

40. During the course of the experiment, a rubber mixture loses its label. A researcher tests the mixture and finds that its tensile strength is approximately 20 Mpa, and its hardness is approximately 40 IRHD. Which of the following statements is correct?
    F. The mixture is 10 phr carbon black.
    G. The mixture is 15 phr coconut fiber.
    H. The mixture is 20 phr carbon black.
    J. The mixture is 40 phr coconut fiber.

END OF TEST 4.
STOP! DO NOT RETURN TO ANY OTHER TEST.

WRITING TEST

DIRECTIONS: This test evaluates your writing skills. You will be given thirty (30) minutes to write an original essay. Before you start, read the writing prompt and be sure you understand the task required. Your essay will be scored based on how well you express judgments by taking a clear position on the issue presented; maintain your focus on your argument throughout the entire essay; support your position with logical reasoning and relevant evidence; present your ideas in an organized manner; and demonstrate clear and effective use of language, based on standard written English language conventions.

To plan out your essay, you may use the unlined page provided. You will not be scored on any information written on this unlined page. *Your essay must be written on the lined pages provided.* Your essay will be scored based only on the writing on those lined pages. You may not end up using all of the lined pages provided, but to be sure that you have enough space to complete your essay, do NOT skip any lines. Corrections or additions may be written in neatly between the lines of your essay, but you must NOT include any writing in the margins of the lined pages. *If your essay is illegible, it cannot be scored, so be sure to write or print clearly.*

If you finish your essay early, you may go back and review what you have written. When time is called, stop writing immediately and lay down your pencil.

ACT Assessment Writing Test Prompt

Some public high schools have considered implementing policies that require students to complete a course in basic financial management before graduating. Some people think that requiring a basic financial management course is a good idea because it helps prepare students for the real world. Other people think students should not be required to take a class on financial management, because high school courses should be devoted to core subjects such as English and Math. In your opinion, should public high schools require students to complete a financial management class before graduation?

Write an essay that develops your position on this question. You may choose to take one of the two viewpoints given, or you may present a different position on this question. Support your position using specific reasons and examples.

Begin WRITING TEST here.

WRITING TEST

Practice Test 3: Answers & Explanations

Question Number	Answer	Right	Wrong	Question Number	Answer	Right	Wrong
	English			38.	F	—	—
1.	D	—	—	39.	C	—	—
2.	G	—	—	40.	H	—	—
3.	B	—	—	41.	B	—	—
4.	G	—	—	42.	J	—	—
5.	C	—	—	43.	D	—	—
6.	J	—	—	44.	H	—	—
7.	A	—	—	45.	D	—	—
8.	H	—	—	46.	H	—	—
9.	A	—	—	47.	B	—	—
10.	G	—	—	48.	H	—	—
11.	D	—	—	49.	A	—	—
12.	G	—	—	50.	J	—	—
13.	B	—	—	51.	B	—	—
14.	G	—	—	52.	F	—	—
15.	A	—	—	53.	D	—	—
16.	J	—	—	54.	H	—	—
17.	A	—	—	55.	B	—	—
18.	J	—	—	56.	J	—	—
19.	B	—	—	57.	A	—	—
20.	G	—	—	58.	H	—	—
21.	A	—	—	59.	D	—	—
22.	H	—	—	60.	J	—	—
23.	C	—	—	61.	D	—	—
24.	G	—	—	62.	G	—	—
25.	D	—	—	63.	B	—	—
26.	J	—	—	64.	J	—	—
27.	B	—	—	65.	A	—	—
28.	H	—	—	66.	H	—	—
29.	C	—	—	67.	C	—	—
30.	H	—	—	68.	H	—	—
31.	C	—	—	69.	B	—	—
32.	J	—	—	70.	J	—	—
33.	C	—	—	71.	C	—	—
34.	H	—	—	72.	J	—	—
35.	D	—	—	73.	C	—	—
36.	G	—	—	74.	F	—	—
37.	C	—	—	75.	B	—	—

Question Number	Answer	Right	Wrong	Question Number	Answer	Right	Wrong
	Mathematics			31.	E	—	—
1.	B	—	—	32.	J	—	—
2.	J	—	—	33.	D	—	—
3.	E	—	—	34.	G	—	—
4.	K	—	—	35.	C	—	—
5.	K	—	—	36.	G	—	—
6.	G	—	—	37.	B	—	—
7.	D	—	—	38.	F	—	—
8.	G	—	—	39.	E	—	—
9.	D	—	—	40.	G	—	—
10.	G	—	—	41.	B	—	—
11.	E	—	—	42.	F	—	—
12.	H	—	—	43.	E	—	—
13.	D	—	—	44.	H	—	—
14.	G	—	—	45.	C	—	—
15.	B	—	—	46.	H	—	—
16.	J	—	—	47.	A	—	—
17.	C	—	—	48.	K	—	—
18.	K	—	—	49.	B	—	—
19.	C	—	—	50.	J	—	—
20.	H	—	—	51.	C	—	—
21.	E	—	—	52.	K	—	—
22.	G	—	—	53.	C	—	—
23.	E	—	—	54.	K	—	—
24.	J	—	—	55.	D	—	—
25.	D	—	—	56.	J	—	—
26.	G	—	—	57.	B	—	—
27.	C	—	—	58.	H	—	—
28.	G	—	—	59.	D	—	—
29.	B	—	—	60.	F	—	—
30.	G	—	—				

Question Number	Answer	Right	Wrong	Question Number	Answer	Right	Wrong
Reading				21.	B	—	—
1.	B	—	—	22.	H	—	—
2.	J	—	—	23.	A	—	—
3.	B	—	—	24.	H	—	—
4.	F	—	—	25.	D	—	—
5.	D	—	—	26.	G	—	—
6.	H	—	—	27.	C	—	—
7.	A	—	—	28.	J	—	—
8.	G	—	—	29.	C	—	—
9.	A	—	—	30.	F	—	—
10.	F	—	—	31.	B	—	—
11.	C	—	—	32.	J	—	—
12.	F	—	—	33.	B	—	—
13.	B	—	—	34.	F	—	—
14.	J	—	—	35.	A	—	—
15.	A	—	—	36.	G	—	—
16.	H	—	—	37.	D	—	—
17.	B	—	—	38.	H	—	—
18.	F	—	—	39.	D	—	—
19.	D	—	—	40.	H	—	—
20.	G	—	—				

Question Number	Answer	Right	Wrong	Question Number	Answer	Right	Wrong
Science				21.	A	—	—
1.	B	—	—	22.	H	—	—
2.	G	—	—	23.	B	—	—
3.	C	—	—	24.	F	—	—
4.	F	—	—	25.	D	—	—
5.	D	—	—	26.	G	—	—
6.	H	—	—	27.	C	—	—
7.	D	—	—	28.	H	—	—
8.	F	—	—	29.	A	—	—
9.	A	—	—	30.	H	—	—
10.	G	—	—	31.	A	—	—
11.	B	—	—	32.	G	—	—
12.	H	—	—	33.	C	—	—
13.	D	—	—	34.	G	—	—
14.	F	—	—	35.	D	—	—
15.	B	—	—	36.	J	—	—
16.	H	—	—	37.	B	—	—
17.	A	—	—	38.	F	—	—
18.	J	—	—	39.	C	—	—
19.	C	—	—	40.	H	—	—
20.	G	—	—				

Calculating Your Score

To find your scaled scores for each test, add up the number of questions you answered correctly on each test. That number represents your raw score for the test. Then covert your raw score to a 1–36 score using the table below. To find your Composite Score for the entire exam, add up your scaled scores for all four tests and divide that total by 4. Round off any fractions to the nearest whole number.

Keep in mind that this score is just a rough estimate. The only completely accurate predictors of your current scoring level are the scoring scales provided with official ACT materials, so make sure you practice with them in the week or two before the test to gauge where you stand.

Scaled Score	Raw Scores				Scaled Score
	Test 1	Test 2	Test 3	Test 4	
	English	Mathematics	Reading	Science	
36	75	60	38–40	40	36
35	73–74	58–59	37	—	35
34	71–72	56–57	36	39	34
33	70	55	35	—	33
32	69	54	34	38	32
31	68	52–53	—	—	31
30	67	50–51	33	37	30
29	65–66	48–49	32	36	29
28	64	46–47	30–31	35	28
27	62–63	43–45	29	34	27
26	60–61	41–42	28	32–33	26
25	57–59	39–40	27	30–31	25
24	55–56	37–38	26	29	24
23	53–54	35–36	25	27–28	23
22	50–52	33–34	24	25–26	22
21	47–49	31–32	23	23–24	21
20	44–46	30	22	21–22	20
19	42–43	27–29	21	18–20	19
18	39–41	25–26	20	16–17	18
17	37–38	22–24	19	14–15	17
16	34–36	18–21	17–18	13	16
15	30–33	15–17	16	12	15
14	28–29	12–14	14–15	10–11	14
13	26–27	09–11	12–13	09	13
12	24–25	08	10–11	08	12
11	22–23	06–07	08–09	07	11
10	20–21	05	07	06	10
9	18–19	04	06	05	9
8	15–17	—	05	04	8
7	13–14	03	—	03	7
6	10–12	02	04	—	6
5	08–09	—	03	02	5
4	06–07	—	02	—	4
3	04–05	01	—	01	3
2	02–03	—	01	—	2
1	00–01	00	00	00	1

Practice Test 3: Answers & Explanations

ENGLISH

---

1. D

Basic Grammar and Usage: Pronoun-Antecedent Agreement   *Easy*

The underlined portion should be a pronoun that agrees with the antecedent *friend*. **A** is wrong because the pronoun *which* is used for animals or things, not people. **B** inserts an unnecessary pronoun *she*, which serves no purpose. **C** is incorrect because *whom* is an object pronoun. The subject pronoun *who* is the appropriate pronoun to use for a person, so **D** is correct.

2. G

Punctuation: Commas   *Easy*

The original sentence is incorrect because a comma should not separate the adverb *very* and the adjective *early*. **H** is incorrect because the comma between *early* and *age* is unnecessary. **J** is wrong because a comma is needed after *age* and before *and* to separate the two parts of the compound sentence. **G** is the best answer since *age* is accurately modified by *very early*.

3. B

Sentence Structure: Subordinate or Dependent Clauses   *Medium*

Because Brahms was a student of classical music is a dependent clause that needs to be separated from the main part of the sentence by a comma, which means **B** is the correct answer. **C** includes an unnecessary comma after *student*. Both **A** and **D** fail to include a comma after *music*, and a comma after the verb *tended* in **D** is unnecessary.

4. G

Style: Redundancy and Wordiness   *Medium*

The underlined portion includes many redundancies, so the sentence needs to be revised. *Composition* and *arrangement* are synonymous, and *arrangement* is used earlier in the sentence. In addition, *break fresh ground* eliminates the need for the phrase *establishing new arrangement styles*. **J** is wrong because *break fresh ground* and *own original methods* are similar in meaning. *New* and *arranged* are in the first part of the sentence, so **H** is incorrect. **G** is the most free of redundancies and clearly conveys the author's meaning.

5. C

Basic Grammar and Usage: Verb Tenses *Easy*

A past-tense verb is necessary, since the sentence discusses what happened to Brahms in the past. The original version needs to be revised because *has gained* is present perfect tense. **B** is incorrect because *gains* is a present-tense verb. **D** is also wrong because *will gain* is future tense.

6. J

Punctuation: Apostrophes *Easy*

Since *Brahms* is a name that ends in the letter *s*, the possessive is shown by adding an apostrophe plus the letter *s*. The underlined portion contains no apostrophe, so **F** is incorrect. **H** misspells the composer's name by placing the apostrophe after the letter *m*. **G** fails to indicate any possession, but it needs to be clarified that *growth as a musician* refers to Brahms. The best choice is **J**, which correctly includes an apostrophe plus *s* (*Brahms's*) to indicate possession.

7. A

Writing Strategy: Analysis *Difficult*

Since the information about Brahms being a perfectionist is not mentioned elsewhere in the essay, **D** is incorrect. The information is important to the essay because it explains the meaning of perfectionist in regards to Brahms, so **B** is wrong. The details do not raise questions about the composer; rather, they provide readers with insight into his personality.

8. H

Sentence Structure: Connecting and Transitional Words *Medium*

The sentence is explaining what occurred *as a result* of Brahms's perfectionism, so **H** is the best answer. *Finally* would be acceptable if the author was making a list of various points to support an argument, which is not the case. Similarly, the author is not presenting examples, so **J** is incorrect. A contrast of two ideas is not being made, so *although* does not make sense.

9. A

Organization: Transitions, Topic Sentences & Conclusions *Medium*

D is incorrect because Brahms would not have *played piano at local bars to earn money for his family* if he had already become famous. The transitional phrases *during his career* and *at some time in his life* are both rather vague. A more specific phrase is necessary to clarify that the first part of the sentence is about Brahms's youth, while the second part is about what occurred *later* in his career. No change is required because *in his youth* creates a clear transition between paragraph 2 and paragraph 3.

10. G

Sentence Structure: Parallelism *Medium*

The underlined portion should be parallel with *became a brilliant orchestra composer*. Including *he* before *toured* creates an unbalanced sentence, so **F** is wrong. The verb phrases in **H** and **J** are different from the past-tense verb *became*, so those choices are both incorrect. **G** creates balance by matching the noun phrase *a touring concert pianist* with *a brilliant orchestra composer*..

11. D

Punctuation: Colons   *Easy*

A period after *compositions* would make the list of composition titles a sentence fragment, so **B** is wrong. **C** is incorrect because semicolons separate two independent clauses, and the list of compositions cannot stand alone as a complete sentence. *Brahms's most well-known pieces include some of the following compositions* introduces the list of piano pieces. A colon is necessary before a series of items introduced by an independent clause, so **D** is the best answer.

12. G

Style: Redundancy and Wordiness   *Medium*

The underlined portion is unnecessarily wordy because it includes two prepositional phrases: *to settle* and *in Vienna*. **J** is wordier than the original, and it offers no additional, relevant information. **H** is incorrect because *in the city of* is unnecessary: Readers can infer that Vienna is a city if they do not already know that fact. **G** is the best answer because it concisely states where Brahms lived when he grew old.

13. B

Writing Strategy: Additional Detail and Evidence   *Difficult*

The author does not express an opinion in the essay, so **A** is wrong. Enjoying children and disliking adults may be unique, but it does not contradict information presented in the essay, which means **D** is wrong. **C** is incorrect because the details relate to the reason locals thought Brahms was grumpy. The best answer is **B** because the information provides interesting details about Brahms's personality.

14. G

Sentence Structure: Connecting and Transitional Words   *Medium*

The sentence contrasts how Brahms's friends enjoyed the composer unlike the locals described in the previous sentence. A transitional word that indicates contrasting opinions is needed, so *however* is the best choice. *Therefore* is used to indicate a conclusion has been reached, while *for example* is used to illustrate a point. The author is not rephrasing information, so *in other words* does not make sense in the sentence.

15. A

Organization: Sentence Reorganization   *Medium*

Graciously describes how Brahms gave away his money, so it should be as close as possible to what it modifies. Even if *graciously* modified *brought*, placing the adverb near *fortune* or *Brahms* would be too far away. Similarly, placing the adverb next to *earnings* makes the sentence confusing because of the adverb's distance from the verb. The original wording of the sentence places *graciously* near *gave away*, so no changes to the sentence are required.

16. J

Basic Grammar and Usage: Idioms   *Easy*

Idioms are forms of speech that do not follow any specific rules. The underlined portion is an example of an incorrect idiom. *Comply with* is idiomatic, so **J** is the correct answer. *Comply to*, *comply by*, and *comply for* are not idiomatic, so **F**, **G**, and **H** are incorrect.

17. A

Writing Strategy: Analysis   *Difficult*

Information that explains why some people do not immunize their children is important in understanding both sides of the argument, so **A** is the best answer. Although
controversy may surround those who oppose vaccinations for religious reasons, the
information itself is not controversial, which makes **B** incorrect. While the example of
the Indiana outbreak mentions that people refused vaccinations for religious purposes, no elaboration is provided, which eliminates **C**. The deleted portion does not relate
to vaccination proponents, so **D** is wrong.

18. J

Style: Word Choice and Identifying Tone   *Medium*

The phrase *puts communities at risk for a resurgence of diseases* indicates that
diseases may be returning that people *once thought* were gone. Diseases do not sur-
render, so **F** is wrong. **H** is incorrect because people did not think the diseases had
adapted or changed but rather that they were no longer a threat. Although it would
be *devastating* if the diseases returned, **G** does not make sense in the sentence. Disease outbreaks were *devastating* in the past, and they would be *devastating* today.
Eradicated is the best choice because the diseases were once thought to be under
control but now have the potential to return because of people not being vaccinated.

19. B

Punctuation: Commas   *Medium*

A series of diseases is being listed, so a comma is necessary after *smallpox*, which
rules out **D**. *Such as* serves the same function as a preposition, so a comma after *such
as* would be incorrect. However, a comma is necessary before *such as* to set off the list
of diseases. Both **C** and **D** are incorrect because unnecessary commas are inserted
after *such as*. **B** is correct because a comma is placed before *such as* to set off the list,
and a comma is inserted after *smallpox* to separate the list of diseases.

20. G

Style: Redundancy and Wordiness   *Medium*

The underlined portion is redundant because *critics* and *opponents* have the same
basic meaning. Since *opponents* are typically *critical* of an idea, **H** is redundant as
well. Similarly, *critics* of vaccines would be *oppositional*, so **J** is redundant. **G** is more
concise than the other options, and it conveys the same amount of information.

21. A

Sentence Structure: Parallelism   *Medium*

The verbs in the sentence should both have the same tense for the sentence to be parallel and grammatically balanced. The original version is correct because *made* and
reduced are both past-tense verbs that work with *have* to create present perfect verb
phrases. In **B**, *made* is past tense and *are reducing* is present progressive, so balance
is not created. Similarly, different tenses of *made* and *reduced* are used in both **C** and
D, which disrupts the flow of the sentence.

22. H

Sentence Structure: Connecting and Transitional Words   *Medium*

Remember, this question is asking for the LEAST acceptable transitional word. The
author is making an additional point about the safety of vaccinations. *Moreover*,

furthermore, and *also* are all transitions that are used when a writer needs to transition between one reason and another. **H** would be an ineffective transition because *so* suggests that there is a cause-effect relationship between the *investigation* into *autism cases* and vaccination *improvements over the years*.

23. **C**

Style: Redundancy and Wordiness   *Medium*

The inclusion of *there was* and *that occurred* in **A** makes it a wordy alternative. *Of measles* and *throughout* make **B** wordy as well. Although **D** is the shortest option, the omission of the outbreak's location makes the sentence confusing. A reader would not realize until the next sentence that the outbreak occurred in Ireland. The most logical and concise version of the underlined portion is **C**.

24. **G**

Sentence Structure: Connecting and Transitional Words   *Medium*

The author is stating two related facts, and it would be incorrect to use *yet* or *but* because they are connecting words used to contrast information. **H** might be tempting, but the conjunction creates an illogical statement: *Over 300 measles cases were reported, so at least three Irish children died.* The best way to connect the two facts is with the conjunction *and*: *Over 300 measles cases were reported, and at least three Irish children died.*

25. **D**

Organization: Transitions, Topic Sentences & Conclusions   *Difficult*

D best connects the topic from the fourth paragraph (a measles outbreak in Ireland) with the topic from the fifth paragraph (a measles outbreak in Indiana). Using the transition *similarly* enables readers to draw an immediate connection between the two paragraphs. Although the statements presented in **A** and **C** are general enough to be topic sentences for the fifth paragraph, they fail to flow from the third paragraph. **B** repeats information found later in the paragraph and does not relate to the fourth paragraph.

26. **J**

Sentence Structure: Subordinate or Dependent Clauses   *Medium*

After returning to Indiana is a subordinate clause and needs to be separated from the main part of the sentence by a comma, as is done in **J**. **F** incorrectly separates two prepositional phrases with a comma and does not insert one after *Indiana*. Similarly, **G** includes a comma between *returning* and *to*, although the comma after *Indiana* is correct. The illogical placement of a comma between *teen* and *came*—the subject and verb—makes **H** an incorrect choice.

27. **B**

Organization: Sentence Reorganization   *Difficult*

The underlined portion is confusing because *for religious reasons* is modifying *contact* instead of *vaccinated*. **C** and **D** make it seem as if the teen did not get vaccinated because she had interacted with the group. **B** makes it clear that the exposed girl interacted with people who had chosen not to be vaccinated *for religious reasons*.

28. H

Basic Grammar and Usage: Subject-Verb Agreement   *Easy*

The subject of the sentence is the plural noun *programs*, and the helping verb *has* is appropriate for singular nouns. **G** and **J** are also verbs used with singular nouns, so they are incorrect. The best answer is **H** because *have* is used with plural nouns—*programs have*.

29. C

Writing Strategy: Additional Detail and Evidence   *Difficult*

The additional information is too specific for the general information presented in the introductory and concluding paragraphs, so **A** and **D** are wrong answers. The third paragraph provides arguments in favor of vaccinations, but the additional sentence is an argument used by critics of vaccines. The sentence is best suited for the fourth paragraph, which discusses the various arguments used by vaccination opponents.

30. H

Writing Strategy: Big Picture Purpose   *Difficult*

The last paragraph counters **F**, and the third paragraph refutes **G**. Although the progress made in vaccinations is mentioned in the third paragraph, **J** fails to address why vaccines are necessary for disease control. The best answer is **H** because the author illustrates what occurred in Ireland and Indiana when vaccination rates were at a low point.

31. C

Sentence Structure: Connecting and Transitional Words   *Easy*

The writer feels *furious* with his mother and *angry* with his father. Since there is little difference between the emotions, contrasting words, such as *yet, but*, and *although* would not be logical. The two similar ideas need to be connected by the conjunction *and*, which means **C** is the best answer.

32. J

Style: Redundancy and Wordiness   *Medium*

The most concise option, **J**, works the best in this sentence. Additional words, such as *his ways, in his life*, and *to himself*, merely clutter the sentence. *Dad needed to change* conveys the same idea to readers as the other options, and it does so in a more concise manner.

33. C

Punctuation: Semicolons   *Medium*

The original sentence structure and punctuation create a comma splice, which occurs when two independent clauses are joined with only a comma. **C** is the best answer because semicolons are a correct way to connect two complete sentences. **B** needs a comma after *reconciling* to be correct. The lack of any punctuation in **D** creates a run-on sentence.

34. H

Writing Strategy: Additional Detail and Evidence   *Difficult*

Although the sentence relates to the subject of counseling, the mention of the author's friend is irrelevant, so **H** is the best answer. **J** is incorrect because the essay is not argumentative. **G** is wrong because the sentence does not relate to the benefits of counseling. Although guilt is mentioned in the previous sentence, the new sentence does not address the author's guilt, which means **F** is incorrect.

35. D

Organization: Transitions, Topic Sentences & Conclusions *Medium*

Both **A** and **C** are too vague because the divorce is not specifically addressed. Although **B** refers to the divorce, no specific time period is included, making it difficult for the reader to know the amount of time that has passed. **D** includes information about the divorce and the time period and provides an effective transition between the second and third paragraphs.

36. G

Basic Grammar and Usage: Verb Tenses *Easy*

The first two paragraphs of the passage are reflections of past events, so the author uses past-tense verbs. However, the third paragraph depicts current events, so present-tense verbs are appropriate. *Visited* is past-tense, so the underlined portion should be revised. *Will visit* is future tense, so **H** is incorrect. *Was visiting* is past progressive tense, which means **J** is wrong. *Visits* is a present-tense verb, so **G** is the best answer.

37. C

Punctuation: Commas *Medium*

Two commas are required in the underlined portion: one before the conjunction *or* and one before the pronoun *which*. The phrase *which is weird* is not part of the main sentence, so it needs to be set off with a comma. Since the sentence is compound, a comma is needed before *or* to separate each half. Only **B** places two commas in the correct locations.

38. F

Writing Strategy: Additional Detail and Evidence *Medium*

The underlined portion requires no changes because it provides the most specific details about why the author thinks his stepmother dislikes him. *Comments* and *how she acts* are too vague and do not offer specific evidence of a strained relationship. Similarly, **J** does not provide proof of any aversion toward the author.

39. C

Sentence Structure: Parallelism *Medium*

Parallelism requires that the verbs in the sentence be in the same grammatical form for good sentence flow. The verbs in the underlined portion should match the past-tense verb *stayed* at the end of the sentence. **A** is wrong because *be open to settling* does not match *faced* and *stayed*. **B** is incorrect because *settle* is present tense, while *faced* and *stayed* are past tense. **D** is incorrect because *been facing* and *settling* are not parallel with *stayed*. Only **C** structures the verbs in the same fashion.

40. H

Style: Redundancy and Wordiness *Medium*

F is redundant because *being without our father* repeats the idea of *living with only one parent*. **G** is too wordy because it includes *our mother* and *our father*. Including *divorced* in **J** repeats information presented earlier in the passage. Typical of many style questions, the best answer is the most concise one, **H**.

41. B

Basic Grammar and Usage: Adverbs and Adjectives *Easy*

Aspect is a noun, and *positive* is its modifying adjective. **B** is correct because the adjective should be before the noun it modifies. An adverb, *positively*, should not modify a noun, so **D** is wrong. The structure of **C** incorrectly creates a separate sentence: *it is positive*. **A** reverses the noun and adjective, so **B** is the best answer.

42. J

Basic Grammar and Usage: Subject-Verb Agreement *Easy*

The singular subject of the sentence is *aspect*, and the plural noun *arrangements* is part of a prepositional phrase. The underlined verb should agree with *aspect* rather than *arrangements* even though the prepositional phrase *of the new living arrangements* separates the noun from the verb. The verbs in **F**, **G**, and **H** all agree with plural nouns, so those choices would create a grammatically incorrect sentence. Only **J** agrees with the singular noun: *aspect is*.

43. D

Sentence Structure: Connecting and Transitional Words *Medium*

The original sentence is illogical because it suggests the author goes fishing because he dislikes it. Similarly, **C** is illogical and awkward. *Nevertheless* indicates a contrast, but its use creates an independent clause resulting in a comma splice: *nevertheless, I dislike fishing*. **D** is correct because the connecting word, *although*, alerts the reader to the two contrasting ideas of the sentence. *Although* the author dislikes fishing, he goes fishing with Rob to spend time with his stepfather.

44. H

Organization: Sentence Reorganization *Difficult*

The original version indicates that the *relationships can all be made the best*, which is confusing and illogical. **F** is confusing because it seems that only the *situation* can be improved rather than the *relationships*. **J** awkwardly uses *best* as the subject. **J** incorrectly indicates that the author created the *situation* and the *new relationships*. **H** is the clearest and most logical arrangement.

45. D

Writing Strategy: Big Picture Purpose *Difficult*

The best answer is **D** because the essay focuses on how divorce affected the author's family structure. **A** and **B** are incorrect because the author does not describe any enjoyable activities, and the author's anger is only mentioned in the first sentence of the essay. The author only briefly mentions his relationship with his parents in the fourth paragraph, so **C** is wrong.

46. H

Punctuation: Apostrophes *Easy*

Australia possesses the *rabbits*, so an apostrophe is necessary before the letter *s* in *Australia* to indicate ownership, which makes **H** correct. **F** is incorrect because an apostrophe after the *s* suggests that more than one *Australia* exists. An apostrophe after the *s* in the plural *rabbits* suggests the rabbits have possession of something, but that is not the case in this sentence. The lack of punctuation in **J** fails to indicate ownership.

47. **B**

Style: Redundancy and Wordiness   *Medium*

Including *nature's elements of wind and rain* in the original version creates a wordy sentence, so a change is required. **D** is even wordier than the original with the inclusion of *wind, rain, and extreme temperatures*. Although **C** is slightly more concise, the phrase *open to the elements of nature* is a long way of saying *exposed*. **B** is the best option.

48. **H**

Organization: Sentence Reorganization   *Difficult*

The original version needs reorganization because it sounds like the *small native animals* force out the rabbits, instead of vice versa. The organization of **G** suggests a similar situation. The location of *and eventually die* at the end of the **J** suggests the rabbits die instead of the small native animal, which cannot be true based on the overpopulation of rabbits. *Small native animals eventually die* because of the *abundant rabbits*, so **H** is the most logical answer.

49. **A**

Sentence Structure: Connecting and Transitional Words   *Medium*

Remember, this question is asking for the transitional word that would NOT fit the sentence. The author is providing an additional example of the problems caused by feral rabbits. **B**, **C**, and **D** are transitional words used when making additional points. *Meanwhile* is a transitional word used to indicate the passage of time, so *meanwhile* would not be a logical choice for this particular sentence.

50. **J**

Basic Grammar and Usage: Verb Tenses   *Easy*

F needs a helping verb to make sense: *are devouring*. The verb *frustrates* indicates the sentence is taking place in the present, so the present-tense verb *devour* works best. **G** is future tense, and the passage indicates rabbits are a current problem. Similarly, **H** fails to work because *devoured* is a past-tense verb.

51. **B**

Sentence Structure: Subordinate or Dependent Clauses   *Medium*

Hoping to establish a local population for hunting purposes is a dependent clause that introduces the main part of the sentence. Therefore, the clause needs to be set apart with a comma before *Austin*, as in choice **B**. Placing a comma after *Austin* separates the subject (*Austin*) from the verb (*released*), so **A** is wrong. A comma should not be placed before a prepositional phrase like *for hunting purposes*, so **C** is wrong. **D** is incorrect because the required comma before *Austin* has been omitted.

52. **F**

Punctuation: Commas   *Easy*

No changes need to be made to the original sentence because the comma followed by *and* correctly separates the two parts of the compound sentence. **G** is wrong because a comma does not precede the conjunction. **H** would be a correct alternative if the conjunction *and* were deleted. Semicolons can stand alone when joining independent clauses; they do not need conjunctions. **J** creates a comma splice with the omission of the conjunction.

53. D

Style: Word Choice and Identifying Tone   *Medium*

The sentence indicates that the rabbits were able to receive the *nourishment* they needed from the food on *local farms*. As a result, the *rabbit population reached plague proportions*. *Thrive* is the best choice to describe how the rabbits were able to flourish and grow in number, so **D** is correct. *Improve* and *recover* suggest that something had been wrong with the rabbits before they discovered the food on farms, but this suggestion is not supported by the passage. Although the rabbits grew in number, *succeed* suggests they had a plan they were trying to accomplish, which is doubtful.

54. H

Writing Strategy: Analysis   *Difficult*

Eliminating the information about the location of New South Wales makes little impact on the passage, so **G** and **J** are wrong. The information about the location of New South Wales is not mentioned elsewhere in the passage, so **F** is incorrect. The best answer is **H** because the information is not important, and it distracts from the main point of the sentence, which is that the rabbit problem was becoming severe.

55. B

Organization: Transitions, Topic Sentences & Conclusions   *Difficult*

C and **D** can be eliminated because neither statement addresses rabbit-control measures, which are the focus of the fourth paragraph. **A** addresses the problems caused by wild dingo dogs, not rabbits. **B** describes how farmers attempted to control the initial population problem, which transitions into the discussion in the next paragraph about modern pest-control methods.

56. J

Sentence Structure: Parallelism   *Medium*

Parallelism occurs when verbs are in the same tense, and the underlined portion is not parallel. *Destroyed* is past tense while *poisoning* and *hunting* are present tense, so the sentence needs revision. **G** is not parallel because *destroyed* and *hunts* are not the same verb tense. Similarly, *destroying*, *poison*, and *hunts* in **H** do not balance. The best answer is **J** because all of the verbs are present tense: *destroying, poisoning, fencing,* and *hunting.*

57. A

Style: Redundancy and Wordiness   *Medium*

Fatal, deadly, and *lethal* are synonyms, so it is redundant to include more than one of these words in the underlined portion. **C** and **D** are wordy because of the inclusion of *for some, for many,* and *for others*. The most concise version is the original; no changes to the sentence are necessary.

58. H

Sentence Structure: Connecting and Transitional Words   *Medium*

The first part of the sentence establishes a cause, and the second part establishes the effect. *Since* feral rabbits damage crops, farmers *will continue searching for a solution*. *While* and *after* are transitions used to show the passage of time, so **F** and **J** are incorrect. *Although* is a contrasting transition, so it would be a poor choice for a cause-effect relationship.

59. D

Basic Grammar and Usage: Pronoun-Antecedent Agreement   *Easy*

The underlined pronoun needs to agree with *farmers*, so **D** is the correct answer. **A** would be correct if *Australia* were the subject, but *Australia* is part of a prepositional phrase explaining the location of the farmers. **B** is wrong because the author has not written the essay in first person. *Whose* would be illogical, so **C** is wrong.

60. J

Writing Strategy: Big Picture Purpose   *Difficult*

The essay does not indicate that Australian farms are on the decline, only that they are losing a great deal of money because of the rabbit problem. **F** and **G** are incorrect because these statements affirm that small farms in Australia are struggling. **H** is wrong because no indication is given that Australian farms are on the rise. **J** is correct because the topic of the essay is how and why rabbits are a major problem in Australia.

61. D

Sentence Structure: Sentence Fragments   *Easy*

If you haven't watched Emeril in action on his successful Food Network show is not a complete sentence, so a period after *show* creates a sentence fragment. A semicolon would be acceptable if two complete thoughts were on each side, but this is not the case. **B** creates an illogical sentence. Placing a comma between *show* and *then* converts a sentence fragment into an introductory clause, so **D** is the best answer.

62. G

Sentence Structure: Subordinate or Dependent Clauses   *Medium*

As one of the most popular chefs in the world is a dependent clause. Since the main part of the sentence begins with *Emeril*, a comma is necessary between *world* and *Emeril* to separate the two parts of the sentence. **F** is wrong because a comma separates the subject (*Emeril Lagasse*) from the verb (*is*). Commas should not be inserted before prepositional phrases, so **H** is wrong. **J** lacks all punctuation, so it is unclear where the main part of the sentence begins.

63. B

Basic Grammar and Usage: Verb Tenses   *Easy*

The verb in the underlined portion should be a past-tense form of *lay*, which means to place something down. *Laid* is the past-tense form of *lay*, so **B** is correct. *Lay* and *lain* are forms of *lie*, which means to rest or recline. Because the author is describing events that were completed in the past, the progressive verb *was laying*, in **D**, is wrong.

64. J

Organization: Paragraph Reorganization   *Difficult*

The order of events should be arranged from earliest to most recent, but the original paragraph organization ends with Emeril's birth. **G** also begins with the most recent event, so it is incorrect. **H** and **J** both begin with information on Emeril's birth; however, **H** is confusing because a leap is made from birth to college without any information in between. Only **J** presents the information in a logical chronological sequence.

65. A

Organization: Transitions, Topic Sentences & Conclusions   *Medium*

The original sentence does not need reorganization because the underlined portion makes it clear that Emeril returned to the United States after spending time in Europe. The third paragraph discusses his activities while in the United States, so *once he returned home to the United States* is a good introduction to the paragraph. **B** fails to draw a clear connection between Emeril's experience in Europe with his work in *New York, Boston, and Philadelphia*. The use of *later* in choice **C** is vague. It is unclear from **D** where Emeril has moved, so **A** is the best choice.

66. H

Basic Grammar and Usage: Adverbs and Adjectives   *Easy*

Legendary is an adjective describing the type of *status* that *Commander's Palace in New Orleans* maintained. Adjectives come before the words they modify, so **H** is the correct answer. **F** is confusing because both *status* and *legend* are nouns. **J** creates an awkward sentence flow with *status as a legend as an upscale restaurant*.

67. C

Sentence Structure: Comma Splices   *Medium*

Remember, this question is asking for the option that would be grammatically incorrect. Two complete thoughts are on each side of *restaurant*, and a comma alone between the two parts creates a comma splice. Comma splices are corrected by using a comma-conjunction combination, inserting a semicolon, or separating the two independent clauses with a period. **C** is grammatically incorrect, and therefore the best answer, because removing the comma creates a run-on sentence.

68. H

Style: Redundancy and Wordiness   *Medium*

So very makes the underlined portion wordy without providing relevant information, so **F** is incorrect. The phrase *that have become popular* adds unnecessary words, so **G** is wrong. *Popular* and *well liked* have the same meaning, making **J** redundant and wordy. **H** is the most concise and clear option provided.

69. B

Basic Grammar and Usage: Subject-Verb Agreement   *Easy*

The subject of the sentence is the singular noun *spiciness*. **A**, **C**, and **D** are verbs that agree with plural nouns instead of singular nouns. **B** is the correct answer because *provides* agrees with *spiciness*: *spiciness provides*.

70. J

Style: Word Choice and Identifying Tone   *Medium*

Spicy, *zesty*, and *fiery* all convey the basic idea that Emeril's food is full of flavor. The first part of the sentence states that the *spiciness of Cajun and Creole foods* influences Emeril's recipes. No textual evidence suggests the chef's recipes are *healthy*, although they may be. Moreover, the question is asking for the terms that indicate *flavor* and *seasonings*. **J** does NOT fit this description.

71. C

Punctuation: Commas   *Easy*

Commas are needed to provide separation between items in the series of city names. The colon in the original version is inappropriate because it divides the preposition (*in*) from the series of cities, so **A** is wrong. A comma should follow *Orlando* because the list of cities continues, so **B** and **D** are wrong. **D** also includes an inappropriate comma before the preposition *in*. The correct answer is **C** because it only includes commas between *New Orleans, Las Vegas*, and *Orlando*.

72. J

Punctuation: Commas   *Easy*

The main part of the sentence ends with *empire*; the rest of the sentence is a clause that needs to be set apart with a comma before *which*. **F** lacks any comma for separation. **G** has commas around *also*, which does not need to be set apart. **H** includes an unnecessary comma after *which*, so **J** is correct.

73. C

Organization: Sentence Reorganization   *Medium*

Mainstay on the Food Network describes Emeril's television programs. Only **C** correctly places this phrase near *television programs*. The organization of **A** suggests that Emeril's *multimillion-dollar empire* is a *mainstay on the Food Network*. With **B**, *books* are the *mainstay*. **D** organizes the sentence so that Emeril's *cooking tools* are the *mainstay*, which is also incorrect.

74. F

Writing Strategy: Analysis   *Difficult*

Kicking it up a notch is mentioned in the opening paragraph and using this phrase in the conclusion helps bring the passage full circle. Therefore, **F** is the best answer. The phrase does not necessarily provide information about Emeril's *personality* or *cooking techniques*, so **H** and **J** are incorrect. Although Emeril says *kicking it up a notch* frequently during his shows, the phrase does not necessarily provide an insightful detail to the reader about Emeril, which means **G** is incorrect.

75. B

Writing Strategy: Big Picture Purpose   *Difficult*

While Emeril probably had difficulties on his road to success, the essay does not address the adversities he faced. Although Emeril's popularity on the Food Network is discussed, that is not the primary focus of the essay, which makes **A** incorrect. **B** is the best answer because the essay describes the path Emeril took in becoming a chef.

MATHEMATICS

1. B
Algebra: Writing Expressions and Equations *Easy*

Raul adds $3.50 to every $28.00 ticket he sells, so each ticket t costs $31.50. The cost of buying a ticket from Raul can be expressed as $31.50t$.

If you selected **A**, you probably subtracted $3.50 from $28.00 rather than adding it. If you selected **C**, you probably thought that Raul charged the $3.50 service fee for the entire transaction, regardless of how many tickets were purchased.

2. J
Pre-Algebra: Number Problems *Easy*

There are 16 cupcakes, and they cost $24 total, so each cupcake costs:

$$\frac{\$24}{16} = \$1.50$$

The question asks for the price of 3 cupcakes:

$$\$1.50 \times 3 = \$4.50$$

If you chose **F**, you probably found the cost of $\frac{1}{3}$ of a cupcake, not 3 cupcakes. If you chose **G**, you probably found the cost of 1 cupcake and then stopped.

3. E
Algebra: Substitution *Easy*

This is a substitution problem, so substitute 4 for a:

$$\frac{4^2 - 2}{4 + 3} = \frac{16 - 2}{7}$$
$$= \frac{14}{7}$$
$$= 2$$

4. K
Pre-Algebra: Multiples, Factors & Primes *Easy*

The positive factors of 12 are all numbers that, when multiplied together, equal 12. Here are each of the factors in equation form:

$$1 \times 12 = 12$$
$$2 \times 6 = 12$$
$$3 \times 4 = 12$$

5. K
Pre-Algebra: Mean, Median & Mode *Easy*

To find the average, add up the numbers you are given: 193 + 146 + 783 + 225 + 456 + 299 + 348 = 2,450. Next, divide that sum by the number of terms you are given, 7:

$$2,450 \div 7 = 350$$

K is the correct answer. **H** is incorrect because it represents the median of the daily totals, not the average.

6. G

Plane Geometry: Polygons   *Easy*

To solve this problem, you need to know that the sum of the measures of all four interior angles in a quadrilateral is always 360°. First, add up the three given angles:

$$96° + 110° + 82° = 288°$$

Then subtract 288° from 360° to find the measurement of the missing angle:

$$360° − 288° = 72°$$

7. D

Plane Geometry: Angles and Lines   *Easy*

Angle r is supplementary to the angle marked 60°. Supplementary angles add up to 180°. To find the measure of angle r, subtract 60° from 180°:

$$180° − 60° = 120°$$

8. G

Algebra: Simplification   *Easy*

Multiply w by $(x + y) − z$ to find an equivalent, simplified expression. The simplification is $w(x) + w(y) − w(z) = wx + wy − wz$.

9. D

Pre-Algebra: Absolute Value Simplification and Substitution   *Easy*
Substitute −8 for a:

$$|5 + -8|$$
$$= |5 - 8|$$
$$= |-3|$$
$$= 3$$

10. G

Pre-Algebra: Percentages, Fractions & Decimals   *Easy*

If Ms. Haskins gave her real estate agent 20% of the house's sale price, that means Ms. Haskins kept 80% of that price. We can find the house's price by setting up an expression:

$$.80x = \$90,000$$

Now, solve for x:

$$\frac{.80x}{.80} = \frac{\$90,000}{.80}$$
$$= \$112,500$$

The selling price of the house was $112,500.

11. E

Algebra: Multiplying Binomials *Easy*

The power 2 indicates that this question is asking you to multiply binomials. We can rewrite the expression as:

$$(5q-2)(5q-2)$$

When you multiply a binomial, remember the acronym FOIL: First, Outer, Inner, Last. Perform your multiplication in that order:

$$\begin{aligned} \text{First + Outer + Inner + Last} &= (5q \times 5q) + (5q \times -2) + (-2 \times 5q) + (-2 \times -2) \\ &= 25q^2 - 10q - 10q + 4 \\ &= 25q^2 - 20q + 4 \end{aligned}$$

If you chose **B**, you probably thought that $(5q-2)(5q-2)$ was equal to $(5q)^2 + (-2)^2$.

12. H

Pre-Algebra: Ratios and Proportions *Easy*

To solve this problem, set up a proportion. Let s represent the length of the person's shadow:

$$\begin{aligned} \frac{24}{16} &= \frac{6}{s} \\ 24s &= 16 \times 6 \\ 24s &= 96 \\ s &= 4 \end{aligned}$$

The shadow is 4 feet long, so **H** is correct.

13. D

Pre-Algebra: Mean, Median & Mode *Easy*

Read the chart to find the amount of money donated each hour. Then add the amounts together:

$$\$100 + \$250 + \$300 + \$400 + \$450 = \$1,500$$

To find the average, divide the total amount of money donated by the number of hours:

$$\frac{\$1,500}{5} = \$300$$

E is incorrect because it represents the range of amounts donated rather than the average.

14. G

Intermediate Algebra: Exponents and Roots *Easy*

To find the equivalent of $(a^9)^6$, multiply the exponents:

$$a^{9 \times 6} = a^{54}$$

A is incorrect, because the exponents are added rather than multiplied.

15. **B**

Plane Geometry: Triangles   *Medium*

The perimeter of the triangle is 82 centimeters. This is the length of the triangle's three sides added together. Because one side is 12 centimeters long, the other sides together must be equal to 82 − 12, or 70.

To find the values of the other sides, whose ratio is 2:3, we can write an equation:

$$2x + 3x = 70$$
$$5x = 70$$
$$x = 14$$

So the sides are 2(14) = 28 centimeters, and 3(14) = 42 centimeters long.
The sides of the triangle are 12, 28, and 42. The shortest side is 12.

16. **J**

Algebra: Simplification   *Medium*

Combine like terms and simplify:

$$(19r^4 - 12r) + (2rs^3 - 4s^3) + (3rs^3 + 7r^4 - 4r) = (19r^4 + 7r^4) + (-12r - 4r) + (2rs^3 + 3rs^3) - 4s^3$$
$$= (26r^4) + (-16r) + (5rs^3) - 4s^3$$
$$= 26r^4 - 16r + 5rs^3 - 4s^3$$

J is the correct answer.

17. **C**

Algebra: Solving Linear Equations   *Medium*

Solve the equation by first finding a common denominator:

$$4\frac{3}{4} = a + 2\frac{7}{10}$$
$$4\frac{15}{20} = a + 2\frac{14}{20}$$

Now, solve for a:

$$4\frac{15}{20} = a + 2\frac{14}{20}$$
$$4\frac{15}{20} - 2\frac{14}{20} = a + 2\frac{14}{20} - 2\frac{14}{20}$$
$$2\frac{1}{20} = a$$

18. **K**

Plane Geometry: Angles and Lines   *Medium*

Wedges 1, 2, and 3 are adjacent to each other along a straight line, which has a measure of 180°. The measure of the central angle of Wedge 2 = 180° − 35° − 60° = 85°.

The central angle of Wedge 5 is a vertical angle to the central angle formed by Wedges 2 and 3. Vertical angles are congruent, so Wedge 5 measures the same as the central angles of Wedges 2 and 3 combined. The central angle of Wedge 5 measures 85° + 60°, or 145°.

19. C

Geometry: Triangles   *Medium*

You can use the Pythagorean theorem to find the length of a diagonal. The sides of a rectangle are the legs of the right triangle, and the diagonal is its hypotenuse. The following figure helps you visualize this:

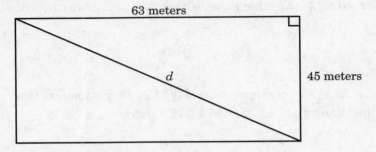

Insert the values into the Pythagorean theorem:

$$d^2 = 63^2 + 45^2$$
$$d = \sqrt{5{,}994}$$

E is incorrect because it represents 63 and 45 added together.

20. H

Pre-Algebra: Probability   *Medium*

This question looks trickier than it actually is. The chance of a 6-sided number cube landing on any number is *always* 1 out of 6, regardless of how many times the die is rolled. The correct answer is **H**.

21. E

Coordinate Geometry: Parallel and Perpendicular Lines   *Medium*

Perpendicular lines have slopes that are negative reciprocals of one another. So, we are looking for the negative reciprocal of the slope of the given line.

To first determine the slope of the given line, put the equation in the form $y = mx + b$:

$$x + 5y = 30$$
$$5y = -x + 30$$
$$y = \frac{-x + 30}{5}$$
$$y = -\frac{1}{5}x + 6$$

The slope of the given line is $-\frac{1}{5}$. The negative reciprocal of $-\frac{1}{5}$ is 5.

22. G

Plane Geometry: Polygons   *Medium*

Diagonals *WY* and *ZX* bisect each other, creating four identical triangles with interior legs of 6 centimeters and 8 centimeters, as shown here:

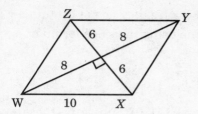

You might recognize a special right triangle, with legs in a ratio of 6-8-10. Or, you can use the Pythagorean theorem to find the length of the missing sides:

$$a^2 + b^2 = c^2$$
$$6^2 + 8^2 = c^2$$
$$36 + 64 = c^2$$
$$100 = c^2$$
$$c = 10$$

The sides of the rhombus are 10 centimeters, so the perimeter is 40.

23. E

Pre-Algebra: Number Problems *Medium*

There are 175 male students who could be awarded a first-place prize. For each of those 175 male students, there are 225 female students who could also be awarded a first-place prize. We multiply 175×225 to find 39,375 possible pairs.

24. J

Plane Geometry: Triangles *Medium*

The measures of the interior angles of a triangle add up to 180°. We are given the measures of $\angle BAG$ and $\angle AGB$. This lets us find the measure of $\angle ABG$:

$$180° - 100° - 25° = 55°$$

Use this information to find the value of w:

$$180° - 50° - 55° = 75°$$

25. D

Pre-Algebra: Number Problems *Medium*

Set up an equation representing the rental. Let m represent the number of miles driven:

$$41.50 + 0.25m = 185.50$$
$$0.25m = 185.50 - 41.50$$
$$0.25m = 144$$
$$m = 576$$

The family was able to drive 576 miles for a total cost of $185.50.

26. G

Coordinate Geometry: Graphing Equations *Medium*

The y-intercept of an equation is represented by the variable b in the following formula:

$$y = mx + b$$

F and **J** can be eliminated because they do not contain a y-intercept of $b = 3$. Next, find the slope of the line using the slope formula:

$$m = \frac{y_2 - y_1}{x_2 - x_1}$$

Let $(x_1, y_1) = (0, 3)$, and $(x_2, y_2) = (-1, 0)$. Substitute these coordinates into the slope formula:

$$m = \frac{0 - 3}{-1 - 0}$$
$$= \frac{-3}{-1}$$
$$= 3$$

This line also has a slope of 3. So, the coefficient m must equal 3. The only remaining choice with a slope of $m = 3$ is **G**, $y = 3x + 3$.

27. C

Algebra: Substitution   *Medium*

Substitute in the values given for the variables and solve:

$$\frac{a - b}{c} - \frac{b}{d + a} = \frac{(5) - (7)}{\frac{1}{4}} - \frac{(7)}{(-3) + (5)}$$

$$= \frac{-2}{\frac{1}{4}} - \frac{7}{2}$$

$$= -2(4) - \frac{7}{2}$$

$$= -8 - 3\frac{1}{2}$$

$$= -11\frac{1}{2}$$

28. G

Coordinate Geometry: Conic Sections   *Medium*

The equation for a circle is always given in the following form:

$$(x - h)^2 + (y - k)^2 = r^2$$

In that standard formula, r represents the radius of the circle. Compare the standard formula to the equation given in the question:

$$(x + 5)^2 + (y - 4)^2 = 5$$

In this case, r is equal to 5. To find the radius, create an equation and take the square root of both sides:

$$r = 5$$
$$r = \sqrt{5}$$

29. B

Coordinate Geometry: Distance and Midpoints   *Medium*

Plug the given coordinates into the midpoint formula:

$$\left(\frac{5}{2}, 3\right) = \left(\frac{x_1 + 4}{2}, \frac{y_1 + 5}{2}\right)$$

Solve for x_1, the x-coordinate of point J:

$$\frac{5}{2} = \frac{x_1 + 4}{2}$$
$$10 = 2(x_1 + 4)$$
$$10 = 2x_1 + 8$$
$$10 - 8 = 2x_1$$
$$2 = 2x_1$$
$$x_1 = 1$$

Solve for y_1, the y-coordinate of point J:

$$3 = \frac{y_1 + 5}{2}$$
$$3 = \frac{y_1 + 5}{2}$$
$$6 = y_1 + 5$$
$$1 = y_1$$

The coordinates of point J are (1, 1).

30. G

Plane Geometry: Circles   *Medium*

To solve this question, use the formula for the area of a circle, $A = \pi r^2$. Substitute in 72π for the area:

$$A = \pi r^2$$
$$72\pi = \pi r^2$$
$$72 = r^2$$

Now take the square root of both sides of the equation, to find r:

$$72 = r^2$$
$$\sqrt{72} = \sqrt{r^2}$$
$$r = \sqrt{36 \times 2}$$
$$= 6\sqrt{2}$$

31. E

Algebra: Solving Linear Equations   *Medium*

Solve the equation $C = 4D - 8$ by first adding 8 to both sides. The result is $C + 8 = 4D$.

Next, divide both sides by 4 to find D: $\frac{C + 8}{4} = D$.

32. J

Algebra: Inequalities   *Medium*

This question is asking you to solve an inequality. Here are the steps we take to find the set of all possible values of x:

$$\frac{2}{3}x < 1$$

$$\frac{3}{2} \times \frac{2}{3}x < 1 \times \frac{3}{2}$$

$$x < \frac{3}{2}$$

G is incorrect because the direction of the inequality sign has changed. When dividing by a positive number, the direction of the inequality sign stays the same. It's only when you divide by a *negative* number that the direction of the inequality sign changes.

33. D

Coordinate Geometry: Distance and Midpoints   *Medium*

Use the formula for the distance between points in a coordinate plane:

$$d = \sqrt{(x_2 - x_1)^2 + (y_2 - y_1)^2}$$

Let $(x^1, y^1) = (6, -1)$ and $(x^2, y^2) = (22, -7)$. Substitute these coordinates into the formula and simplify:

$$d = \sqrt{(22 - 6)^2 + (-7 + 1)^2}$$
$$d = \sqrt{(16)^2 + (-6)^2}$$
$$d = \sqrt{256 + 36}$$
$$d = \sqrt{292}$$
$$d = \sqrt{73 \times 4}$$
$$d = 2\sqrt{73}$$

34. G

Pre-Algebra: Number Problems   *Medium*

Annie's office sent 6 international faxes at $0.75 apiece at 4:00 p.m. Monday, 7 international faxes at $1.80 apiece at 8:30 p.m. Friday, and 4 international faxes at $0.75 on Sunday. We can write the following expression: 6($0.75) + 7($1.80) + 4($0.75). This simplifies to $4.50 + $12.60 + $3.00 = $20.10.

If you chose **F**, you probably multiplied all 17 international prices by the lowest domestic price, $0.75. If you chose **H**, you probably forgot to use the lower Sunday rate when multiplying the cost of Sunday's international faxes.

35. C

Pre-Algebra: Multiples, Factors & Primes   *Medium*

List out the numbers between 12 and 35. To find the primes, first eliminate even numbers, since they can all be divided by 2 and another number. Next, eliminate any multiples of 3, 5, or 7. The remaining numbers are prime numbers:

13, 17, 19, 23, 29, 31

36. G

Plane Geometry: Polygons *Medium*

Find the missing length, $\overline{YX}$, by subtracting 4 (the length of $\overline{WV}$) from 11 (the length of $\overline{ZU}$). The minimum number of blocks is 20. The student travels 13 blocks from point Z to point Y and then travels 7 more blocks from point Y to point X.

J is incorrect because it represents the distance the student would travel from point Z to point U to point V to point W to point X.

37. B

Intermediate Algebra: Series *Medium*

When you see a series question, it's always a good idea to expand the sequence by a few terms. Let's expand this sequence to 10 terms: 3, 7, 11, 15, 19, 23, 27, 31, 35, 39.

We can now see that the seventh term is 27 and the ninth term is 35, so we know that neither **A** nor **D** is correct. Additionally, $3 + 7 + 11 + 15 + 10 + 23 = 78$, so **C** is not correct either. By testing a few numbers, we find that the ratio between consecutive numbers is not 4. The ratio of consecutive terms is defined by $\frac{a_i + 1}{a_i}$ for all i. For the first two terms, the ratio is $\frac{7}{3}$, or $2\frac{1}{3}$. For the second and third term, the ratio is $\frac{11}{7}$, or approximately 1.57. Therefore, the statement in **B** is not true about this sequence.

38. F

Trigonometry: Solving Triangles *Medium*

Find the opposite side using the tangent formula:

$$\tan L = \frac{\text{opposite}}{\text{adjacent}}$$

$$\frac{2}{3} = \frac{\text{opposite}}{6}$$

$$3x = 12$$

$$x = 4$$

39. E

Coordinate Geometry: Parallel and Perpendicular *Medium*

Use the point-slope formula and multiply the slope by the negative reciprocal, $m = -\frac{1}{3}$:

$$y - y_1 = m(x - x_1)$$

$$y + 1 = -\frac{1}{3}(x - 2)$$

$$y + 1 = -\frac{1}{3}x + \frac{2}{3}$$

$$y = -\frac{1}{3}x + \frac{2}{3} - 1$$

$$y = -\frac{1}{3}x - \frac{1}{3}$$

40. G

Pre-Algebra: Percentages, Fractions & Decimals   *Medium*

First, find the approximate number of people who live in two-bedroom apartments:

$$\frac{2}{9}(724) \approx 161$$

Approximately 161 people live in two-bedroom apartments. Now, find the number of people who live in two-bedroom apartments and have fireplaces in both bedrooms:

$$\frac{1}{3}(161) \approx 54$$

Approximately 54 people in the apartment building live in two-bedroom apartments and have fireplaces in both bedrooms. **J** is incorrect because it represents the number of people who live in two-bedroom apartments.

41. B

Coordinate Geometry: Conic Sections   *Medium*

The downward parabola indicates a negative x^2, so **A**, **C**, and **E** can be eliminated. **D** can be eliminated because the graph doesn't shift to the left 2 units. Remember $(x + 2)$ indicates a shift to the left 2 units.

42. F

Trigonometry: SOHCAHTOA   *Medium*

Draw a vertical line from $(6, 6)$ to the x-axis to create a right triangle. Doing so, you can see that the side adjacent to θ is 6, the side opposite θ is 6, and the hypotenuse is $6\sqrt{2}$. Sin $\theta = \dfrac{\text{opposite}}{\text{hypotenuse}}$, or $\dfrac{6}{6\sqrt{2}} = \dfrac{6\sqrt{2}}{12} = \dfrac{\sqrt{2}}{2}$.

43. E

Intermediate Algebra: Quadratic Equations   *Medium*

Set the equation equal to 0:

$$x^2 + 8 = 6x$$
$$x^2 + 8 - 6x = 0$$

Rewrite equation in descending order:

$$x^2 - 6x + 8 = 0$$

Factor the equation to solve:

$$(x - 2)(x - 4) = 0$$

Set both factors equal to 0:

$$(x - 2) = 0 \quad (x - 4) = 0$$
$$x = 2 \qquad x = 4$$

44. H

Pre-Algebra: Percentages, Fractions & Decimals   *Medium*

Set up an equation to determine the original number, represented by x. We know that

85% of x equals 340, so write this in equation form:

$$.85x = 340$$
$$x = \frac{340}{.85}$$
$$= 400$$

The original number is therefore 400. Now calculate 130% of 400:

$$1.3 \times 400 = 520$$

45. C

Plane Geometry: Three Dimensions   *Medium*

We find the surface area of the rectangular box by adding up the areas of all six sides. In this problem, the top and bottom both have an area of 9, and the 4 sides each have an area of 12. The equation looks like this: 2(9) + 4(12) = 66.

If you selected **B**, you probably multiplied 4 × 3 × 3. If you selected **D**, you probably calculated the total perimeter instead of the total surface area.

46. H

Trigonometry: Trigonometric Identities   *Medium*

According to the definition of csc θ:

$$\text{Csc } \theta = \frac{\text{hypotenuse}}{\text{opposite}}$$

The definition of sin θ states:

$$\text{Sec } \theta = \frac{\text{opposite}}{\text{hypotenuse}}$$

The functions csc and sin are reciprocals of one another. Thus csc θ also equals $\frac{1}{\sin \theta}$.

47. A

Trigonometry: SOHCAHTOA   *Medium*

In the figure, the two marked angles are congruent. They represent opposite interior angles of parallel lines crossed by a transversal. Therefore, $\angle a$ measures 30°. This tells us that $\angle ZWY$ measures 60°, and we have a 30-60-90 triangle.

In a 30-60-90 triangle, the sides of the triangle are in a ratio of $1 : \sqrt{3} : 2$. The tangent of the angle measuring 30° equals $\frac{\text{opposite}}{\text{adjacent}}$, or $\frac{1}{\sqrt{3}}$, which is expressed as $\frac{\sqrt{3}}{3}$.

48. K

Coordinate Geometry: Equation of a Line   *Medium*

Substitute the values (3, 7) for x and y in the equation and solve for h:

$$y = hx - 3$$
$$(7) = h(3) - 3$$
$$7 + 3 = h(3)$$
$$10 = h(3)$$
$$\frac{10}{3} = h$$

49. B

Coordinate Geometry: Number Lines and Inequalities   *Medium*

The number line shows that x is greater than or equal to –1 and less than or equal to 6.

50. J

Intermediate Algebra: Systems of Equations   *Medium*

Set up equations to represent the problem:

$$4d + 3v = 109.93$$
$$3d + 4v = 99.93$$

Multiply each side by a number that will cancel out one of the variables. For example:

$$(3)(4d + 3v) = 109.93(3)$$
$$(-4)(3d + 4v) = 99.93(-4)$$

Now, write the two new equations:

$$12d + 9v = 329.79$$
$$-12d - 16v = -399.72$$

Add the two equations:

$$-7v = -69.93$$
$$v = 9.99$$

Substitute the value of v back into one of the original equations to find the value of d. For example:

$$4d + 3(9.99) = 109.93$$
$$4d + 29.97 = 109.93$$
$$4d = 79.96$$
$$d = 19.99$$

Add the two amounts together to get the total cost:

$$\$9.99 + \$19.99 = 29.98$$

51. C

Plane Geometry: Polygons   *Medium*

A hexagon has 9 diagonals. This question is tricky because you might be tempted to count each vertex twice. For this reason, **D** is the most common wrong answer. Remember, though, that this method counts each diagonal twice (for example, it considers $\overline{AC}$ and $\overline{CA}$ to be two separate diagonals, when in reality they are the same).

To check your work on questions like this, try drawing the diagonals on the figure, as shown.

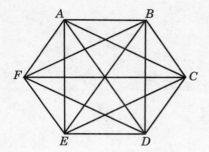

52. **K**

Intermediate Algebra: Functions *Medium*

Replace $g(x)$ with $x + 2$ and find the value of the function $f(x + 2)$:

$$f(x) = x^2 - 7$$
$$f(x + 2) = (x + 2)^2 - 7$$
$$= x^2 + 4x + 4 - 7$$
$$= x^2 + 4x - 3$$

53. **C**

Plane Geometry: Polygons *Medium*

Allen's plot of land has a total area of 14 by 18 yards, or $14 \times 18 = 252$ yards. The area of the flowerbed must fit within that space. The diameter of the flowerbed can be at most 14 yards, because this is the smallest dimension of the garden.

If the diameter of the flowerbed is 14 yards, then its radius is 7 yards. Use the area formula to determine the area of the flowerbed:

$$A = \pi r^2$$
$$A = \pi(7^2)$$
$$A = 49\pi$$

54. **K**

Intermediate Algebra: Absolute Value Equations and Inequalities *Difficult*

Pick numbers for a, b, and c when considering each of the Roman numeral options. Statement I might be false, because c could be a negative number. That eliminates **G** and **J**. Statement II might also be false—for instance, if $c = 15$, $a = 7$, and $b = 8$. That eliminates **H**.

Statement III could be false as well, if $c = 15$ and $a = -15$. In that case, $|c|$ would equal $-a$.

55. **D**

Plane Geometry: Angles and Lines *Difficult*

A is incorrect because although the lines could intersect at a single point while still meeting the rules, this represents the minimum number of points at which the lines could intersect. The maximum number of intersection points is 6, as shown in the following figure.

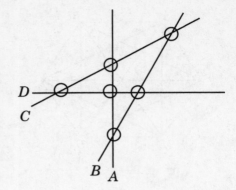

56. **J**

Algebra: Writing Expressions and Equations   *Difficult*

The expression for number of hours and speed traveled during each hour would be represented by 12y + 10(70). The unknown speed, y, is multiplied by the number of hours driven at that speed, which is 12. Since Karla drives an additional 10 hours, those hours are added and then multiplied by a rate of 70 mph. By knowing the average speed for the whole trip, you can multiply the number of total hours by the average speed to find the sum of the mph, or 22(65). Setting these two expressions equal to one another, we have: 12y + 10(70) = 22(65).

57. **B**

Plane Geometry: Three Dimensions   *Difficult*

Let s represent the edge of the smaller toy box, which belongs to Nicole. The volume of Nicole's box is therefore s3.

The edges of Jaclyn's box are 50% longer than those of Nicole's box, so the edges of Jaclyn's box can be represented as 1.5s. Determine the volume of Jaclyn's box:

$$V = 1.5s \times 1.5s \times 1.5s$$
$$= 3.375s^3$$

The volume of Jaclyn's toy box is 3.375 times greater than the volume of Nicole's toy box.

58. **H**

Pre-Algebra: Percentages, Fractions & Decimals   *Difficult*

Start with a concrete number to use as an example. Say that Fantasy Designs sold $1,000 worth of furniture in April. In May, sales decreased by 40%, or $400. So, the store sold $600 of furniture in May.

From May to June, sales decreased another 65%. Determine 65% of $600:

$$600 \times .65 = \$390$$

The store made only $600 − $390, or $210 in sales in June. Overall, their sales decreased from $1,000 in April to $210 in June. That's a decrease of $790, or 79%.

59. D

Intermediate Algebra: Logarithms   *Difficult*

The expression $\log_n (cd)2$ can be written in the following format:

$$\log_n (cd)^2 = 2\log_n (cd)$$
$$= 2(\log_n c + \log_n d)$$

The question tells us that $\log_n c = a$ and $\log_n d = b$. Substitute a and b into the equation:

$$2(\log_n c + \log_n d) = 2(a+b)$$
$$= 2a + 2b$$

60. F

Intermediate Algebra: Functions   *Difficult*

In the graph of an even function, the parabola will be symmetric around the y-axis. **F** is the only parabola that is symmetric around the y-axis. **K** is incorrect because its parabola is symmetric around the x-axis.

READING

1. B

Prose Fiction: Specific Detail   *Easy*

The narrator states in the fifth paragraph that he has *a profound passion for European history*, so the correct answer is **B**. The narrator specifies European history, so **C** and **D** are incorrect. The narrator indicates he enjoyed buying special math tools but not that he was fond of math, which means **A** is incorrect.

2. J

Prose Fiction: Inference   *Medium*

The passage provides no indication that the family is struggling financially, so **G** and **H** are incorrect. **F** is wrong because the father states in the sixth paragraph that *leaving the poultry business in your hands is all we ever considered*. The same statement supports **J** as the correct answer because Jeremy's parents have never considered that Jeremy would go to college—only that he should take over the family business. If Jeremy's parents had attended college, they would most likely encourage Jeremy to do the same. Similarly, Jeremy indicates that no one understands his passion for history, which suggests his friends and family are not college educated.

3. B

Prose Fiction: Specific Detail   *Easy*

The passage indicates that Jeremy is already working, which suggests he has graduated from high school, so **A** and **C** are incorrect. The narrator does not suggest that he will leave the family business, so **D** is wrong. As Jeremy walks through the campus, he thinks about how his *path had been chosen for me and not by me*, so the best answer is **B**.

4. F

Prose Fiction: Cause-Effect   *Medium*

The text does not suggest that Jeremy will be making any changes, so **G** is wrong. Jeremy dislikes the laughter and noise on campus during the fall because it reminds him of what he is missing, which means **H** is incorrect. Jeremy looks forward to the storms because the weather will force students to stay inside and get serious about school. Fall reminds the narrator of the pleasures of preparing for school, so now he wants winter to come to help him forget what he is missing.

5. D

Prose Fiction: Specific Detail   *Medium*

The narrator states in the third paragraph that for the college students *the fall only existed for the purpose of being taken for granted*, which suggests **D** is the best answer. The narrator does not indicate the students will be unsuccessful, so **A** is incorrect. The narrator enjoys shopping for new school supplies, but the text only indicates that the students shop, not that they enjoy it. Although the narrator states that once winter arrives *seriousness* will set in, the passage does not suggest that the students ignore the seasons.

6. H

Prose Fiction: Character   *Medium*

Bitter and *infuriated* are too harsh, since Jeremy never seems extremely angry about his chosen path. Although Jeremy wants winter to arrive to help him forget what he is missing, he is not *vindictive* or hateful toward the students, which means **J** is wrong. Jeremy acts *responsibly* by taking over the family business, yet he is *frustrated*, as indicated when he states he is *proud* but not *happy*.

7. A

Prose Fiction: Specific Detail   *Medium*

A is the best answer because the author writes in the seventh paragraph that *September could have been December or March or July, for all that it mattered. No school supplies, no new classes, and nothing to choose.* Although the focus of the passage is Jeremy's obsession with fall and winter, this is only because fall reminds him of school. **C** and **D** are distractors.

8. G

Prose Fiction: Inference   *Difficult*

The first sentence of the second paragraph describes how *the memories of autumn faded defenselessly in winter's grip*, and throughout the passage it becomes clear that Jeremy dislikes fall because it reminds him of the hopes and dreams of college that he once had. Although Jeremy is honorable for taking over the family business, his honor has not *disappeared* like the leaves. Jeremy does not feel guilty, so **H** is incorrect. The narrator makes it clear that he made the decision to work and cannot blame anyone else, so he was not innocent. **G** is correct because *yellow leaves* represent autumn and the start of a new semester.

9. A

Prose Fiction: Inference   *Medium*

Winter usually did erase the fall suggests that Jeremy has previously experienced painful thoughts in the fall and that winter helps make them fade away. **B** and **D** are wrong because the narrator gives no indication that fall will be any more or less painful next year. Jeremy likes the winter because the *bustling storms and unpredictability* help him forget about college, not because his life becomes exciting.

10. F

Prose Fiction: Specific Detail   *Medium*

After giving up on explaining why he likes history, the narrator indicates in the fifth paragraph that *the idea of attending college began to recede like the waning tide, and the reality of work after high school set in. The reality of work after high school* indicates that Jeremy has already spoken to his father but continued to hope for college, so **H** is wrong. Jeremy does not dream of college once he is working—he wants to forget about it, which means **G** and **J** are wrong.

11. C

Social Science: Purpose   *Medium*

The fifth paragraph draws a connection between Freud's century-old work and *current psychoanalytic theory*. No textual evidence suggests that psychoanalysis is a questionable field, so **B** is incorrect. **D** is wrong because the author indicates that Freud's categories are still used. **A** is incorrect because the purpose of the passage is to provide an overview of Freud's method of interpreting dreams, not describe the controversy of dream interpretation.

12. F

Social Science: Comparison   *Medium*

F is correct because the author states in the first paragraph that *Freud attributed the construction of dreams to three essential factors: displacement, condensation, and secondary revision.* **H** and **J** are both distractors, and **G** only applies to secondary revision.

13. B

Social Science: Vocabulary in Context   *Medium*

Context clues in the sentence indicate that *meager* is used in contrast to *plethora*, which means *surplus. Flawed* and *miserable* are alternate meanings for *meager*, but the use of the word *minute* in the next sentence confirms that *limited* is the best answer. **A** is a distractor.

14. J

Social Science: Specific Detail   *Medium*

The fourth paragraph addresses **F**. The author describes the causes of nightmares in paragraph 2, so we can eliminate **G**. The opening paragraph mentions historical beliefs about dreams, so **H** can also be eliminated. Although the first paragraph describes Freud's book as *controversial writing*, the author does not provide an explanation for the controversy. This makes **J** the best answer.

15. A

Social Science: Cause-Effect   *Medium*

A is correct because the third paragraph states that *the harder a person attempted to analyze his or her dream, the more he or she appeared to have forgotten it.* **B** is incorrect because people do not totally forget their dreams when they forget a few details. Similarly, **C** and **D** may be true, but the text does not indicate that strange sequences or odd details are the cause of forgotten dreams.

16. H

Social Science: Specific Detail   *Easy*

The author explains displacement in the second paragraph, which states that a person *must remove unacceptable or upsetting material from his dreams and displace it with more tranquil thoughts.* Although the second paragraph indicates that poor sleep prohibits people from performing *even the most basic functions of daily existence*, **G** fails to address what occurs during displacement, even though it is mentioned as a result of displacement. **F** is incorrect because most dreams are confusing rather than clear. **J** has no relationship to displacement, so **H** is correct.

17. B

Social Science: Specific Detail   *Easy*

B provides the best summary of condensation, which is described in the third paragraph as *a process of the unconscious mind during the formation of dreams in which a variety of pre-dream thoughts were reduced into a "condensed" version.* **A** describes secondary revision. **C** relates to the idea of displacement rather than condensation. The author does not discuss the avoidance of deep sleep, so **D** is incorrect.

18. F

Social Science: Inference   *Difficult*

G is countered by information about displacement that suggests people should think of tranquil ideas to prevent nightmares. **H** is incorrect because the third paragraph states that people dream about a *minute* amount of the activities that occur in a day. Although Freud assessed patients through their dreams, the third paragraph states that *the harder a person attempted to analyze his or her dream, the more he or she appeared to have forgotten it.* **F** best summarizes Freud's belief as implied by his analysis of a patient described in the fourth paragraph.

19. D

Social Science: Vocabulary in Context   *Medium*

The context clues indicate that a person *rearranges* his *recollections* to create a dream that is *rational and significant. Dissolve* and *expand* do not fit because the thoughts are being moved around, not destroyed or made larger. **B** is incorrect because the *missing parts* are being brought together, not taken apart. **D** is the best answer because a person rearranges his or her thoughts to create what seems to be a rational dream.

20. G

Social Science: Specific Detail   *Easy*

The dream involved the floors in a hotel, which represented the patient's social standing, so **H** is wrong. Another patient, described in the fourth paragraph, had a *fantasy* *of marriage*, so **F** and **J** are incorrect. **G** is correct because the passage indicates that the patient had nightmares because he had *fears about the dangers of intimacy with a woman of an "inferior social class."*

21. B

Humanities: Specific Detail   *Medium*

B is correct because the first paragraph states that Gothic authors combined the *imagination, subjective experience, and freedom of expression* of Romanticism with *aspects of horror, including mystery and violence, to induce strong emotions in the reader.* Gothic literature is not *rational, inspirational*, or *comforting*, so **A, C**, and **D** are all incorrect.

22. H

Humanities: Inference   *Medium*

Although **F** makes reference to the setting, Roderick's demeanor is the focus of the quotation presented here. Similarly, **G** describes Roderick, while **J** focuses on the subject of Poe's story instead of the setting. **H** is the best answer because *Poe's descriptions of the House of Usher's decaying exterior* makes it clear that setting plays a major role in the story.

23. A

Humanities: Specific Detail   *Easy*

The first sentence of the sixth paragraph states that Poe was fascinated with *the unconscious mind and the experience of mental anguish*, so **A** is the best answer. Although physical destruction, personal relationships, and mysterious illnesses are elements found in "The Fall of the House of Usher," the author clearly indicates that the basis of the story stems from Poe's interest in the emotional distress of individuals.

24. H

Humanities: Purpose   *Medium*

In the fourth paragraph, the author discusses how Poe's story includes *another element of Gothic fiction, the exploration of supernatural events*. The function of the fifth paragraph is to provide additional examples in support of the same idea, so **H** is the correct answer. Although the author discusses Roderick in the fifth paragraph, Roderick's character illustrates how Poe conveys *a sense of the supernatural*, so **F** and **J** are incorrect. **G** is wrong because Gothic literature includes elements of Romantic literature, as explained in the first paragraph.

25. D

Humanities: Inference   *Medium*

The author does not indicate that the narrator provides medical assistance to Roderick or Madeline, and the second paragraph states that Roderick asked his friend to *visit and provide comfort*. The narrator is the *childhood friend* of Roderick, so **B** is wrong. **C** is wrong because the text provides no evidence of a relationship between the narrator and Madeline. The narrator's shock at the state of the Usher home suggests he had never visited.

26. **G**

Humanities: Specific Detail   *Easy*

The last sentence of the passage states that readers enjoy Poe's story today because of its *exploration of the unconscious mind and the fragility of human life*. Although the story involves the solitary life of a brother and sister, **F** and **H** fail to explain why the story remains popular. **J** is wrong because "The Fall of the House of Usher" is not a romantic tale, although it has elements of Romanticism, a literary movement described in the first paragraph.

27. **C**

Humanities: Point of View and Tone   *Medium*

In the first paragraph, the author describes the way Poe uses Gothic elements as *masterful*, which suggests **C** is the best answer. **B** and **D** are too extreme for the tone of the passage. **A** is incorrect because the author does not indicate he finds the Gothic elements disturbing.

28. **J**

Humanities: Specific Detail   *Easy*

According to the second paragraph, the narrator first feels a sense of gloom about the house when he sees the outside, including the *few rank white trunks of decayed trees*. **F**, **G**, and **H** all add to the narrator's discomfort, but **J** occurs first.

29. **C**

Humanities: Inference   *Difficult*

The last paragraph states that the collapse of the Usher house symbolized *the destruction of the Usher family*, which suggests Madeline and Roderick were the last of the Ushers. The narrator describes the Usher house as a *mansion*, but its state of disrepair and the lack of servants in the home suggest the money is gone. **A** and **D** could be true since both Madeline and Roderick are mentally ill; however, the passage does not indicate the illness caused the death of their parents or has been in the family for generations. **B** is wrong because the narrator receives an invitation to the home.

30. **F**

Humanities: Specific Detail   *Medium*

F is the best answer because the fourth paragraph states that *Madeline and Roderick are sick with undiagnosed conditions and have highly sensitized reactions to both their own afflictions and those of their sibling*. This statement also contradicts the assertions made in **G** and **H**. The text does not suggest that the siblings comfort each other, so **J** is also wrong.

31. **B**

Natural Science: Specific Detail   *Easy*

The first two sentences of the third paragraph describe how BPA used to line cans seeps into food, which then ends up in people's digestive systems. No textual evidence suggests that BPA always remains in the body, so **A** is wrong. BPA found in rivers may be the result of plastic bottles that have leached. The author does not indicate that older plastic containers with BPA are being recycled, so **D** is incorrect.

32. J

Natural Science: Purpose   *Medium*

The author realizes that her daughter is chewing on a plastic turtle that contains BPA, and through the act of cringing, the author indicates *moderate concern*, not *alarm* or *anger*. **F** is suggested earlier in the passage but not in the last sentence. The best answer is **J** because the author's actions suggest some level of concern regarding BPA.

33. B

Natural Science: Specific Detail   *Medium*

The author states in the third paragraph that *the level of BPA released from plastic depends on the age and wear of the plastic and on exposure to heat*. Cleanliness of a container does not affect the amount of BPA that leaches out, so **B** is the answer.

34. F

Natural Science: Inference   *Difficult*

The second paragraph states that *BPA ranks among the highest-volume chemicals manufactured worldwide,* so it can be inferred that if BPA were shown to be harmful a great deal of money would be lost by these firms. The fifth paragraph states that pre-1999 studies showed *that BPA did not leach or leached in very small amounts from plastic products*. These two statements indicate that **F** is the best answer. Post-1999 studies showed higher amounts of BPA leaching out, so **H** is wrong. **J** is incorrect because CDC studies showed that most people have BPA in their bodies. **G** is wrong because the text only briefly mentions the EPA.

35. A

Natural Science: Specific Detail   *Easy*

A is correct because the author states in the third paragraph that *small levels of BPA leached from baby bottles subjected to simulated normal uses, including boiling, washing with a bottle brush, and dishwashing.* Although plastic bowls, canned goods, and plastic bottles may contain BPA, the acts of storing, serving, and drinking will not force the release of BPA in the same way that high temperatures will.

36. G

Natural Science: Cause-Effect   *Medium*

The fourth paragraph explains the possible connection between BPA and the hormonal system, so **G** is the best answer. Fat-cell activity is not mentioned, so **H** is incorrect. The author indicates that BPA may disrupt estrogen but not increase it, so **F** is wrong. Exposure was found to affect the sperm and fertility of male rats and mice, so **J** is incorrect.

37. D

Natural Science: Specific Detail   *Medium*

The author writes in the last paragraph that *BPA-free baby products* are now available, so **D** is the correct answer. Although concerned parents may be pushing for legislation and warning labels, the text does not indicate that the baby product industry has been behind such activism.

38. H

Natural Science: Comparison *Medium*

According to the *low-dose theory* described in the fifth paragraph, *lower doses can be more harmful than higher doses*. Therefore, **H** is the correct answer.

39. D

Natural Science: Strengthen/Weaken *Difficult*

A and **B** support the argument that BPA poses a health risk. **C** is a neutral statement that neither strengthens nor weakens the argument. The fourth paragraph describes studies performed on rats and mice that indicated BPA caused *abnormal sperm and reduced fertility*. If **D** is true, then BPA would be less harmful to humans than rodents.

40. H

Natural Science: Inference *Medium*

The majority of the passage focuses on BPA in plastic food and beverage containers, so **H** is the best answer. Although plastic windows, parts, and compact discs contain polycarbonates, the impact on the furniture, construction, and information technology would be minimal in comparison to the food and beverage industry, which relies on plastic containers.

SCIENCE

1. B

Data Representation: Read the Chart *Easy*

Table 1 shows that nitrogen oxide (N_2O) levels were lowest in the years 1992 and 1994. N_2O levels were not at their lowest in 1988 and 1990, nor were they at their lowest during 1994 and 1995, so neither **A** nor **C** is correct. N_2O levels were at their *highest* during 2000 and 2002, so **D** is also incorrect

2. G

Data Representation: Read the Chart *Easy*

The number of coal mines in Poland decreased most significantly between 1992 and 1996. During this five-year span, the number of coal mines dropped from 54 to 44, so the correct answer is **G**. Between 1989 and 1993, the number of coal mines dropped insignificantly (from 55 to 54), so **F** is not correct. Between 1997 and 2001, the number of coal mines dropped from 43 to 38, so **H** is not correct. Between 2000 and 2002, the number of coal mines dropped from 38 to 36, making **J** incorrect as well.

3. C

Data Representation: Use the Chart *Medium*

This question requires you to examine Table 1 and place Poland's greenhouse gases in *increasing* order of contributed pollution. The correct answer is **C**: HFCs, N_2O, CH_4, CO_2. **A** gets it backward by listing Poland's greenhouse gases in *decreasing* order of contributed pollution. **B** and **D** are also out of order.

4. F

Data Representation: Use the Chart   *Medium*

According to the information in the passage, greenhouse gases contribute to increased amounts of ozone, and excess ozone has a negative influence on the state of forests and vegetation. According to Table 1, greenhouse-gas emissions were highest in 1988 (at 564.4 $MtCO_2^1$). The total greenhouse-gas emissions in 1992, 1996, and 2002 were all lower than 564.4 $MtCO_2^1$.

5. D

Data Representation: Use the Chart   *Difficult*

According to Table 2, the number of coal mines in Poland decreased steadily over the years. However, there was some flux in absolute methane release rate (for example, the release rate decreased between 1990 and 1991, then increased between 1991 and 1992). The correct answer is **D**. **A** is only half right: The number of coal mines decreases from year to year, but the amount of methane produced does not. **B** is incorrect because the number of coal mines did not increase between 1989 and 2003. **C** represents a relationship that is not supported by the data.

6. H

Research Summary: Read the Chart   *Easy*

The higher a sunscreen's absorbance is, the more photostable it is. The graph for Sunscreen 4 shows that this sunscreen was the most photostable (absorbent) before it was exposed to natural UV radiation, so the correct answer is **H**. Sunscreen 4 lost photostability after 30 minutes of exposure to natural UV radiation, so **F** is incorrect. The sunscreen lost even *more* photostability after 90 minutes, so **G** is incorrect as well. **J** is also incorrect, because Sunscreen 4 was more photostable before its exposure to natural UV radiation than before its exposure to artificial UV radiation.

7. D

Research Summary: Read the Chart   *Easy*

After 120 minutes of exposure to natural UV radiation, Sunscreen 3 had an absorbance that dipped below 0.2. This makes Sunscreen 3 the most photounstable, so the correct answer is **D**. None of the other sunscreens have such a low absorbance after the specified intervals to natural UV radiation.

8. F

Research Summary: Read the Chart   *Medium*

Examine the chart for Sunscreen 6. At 340 nm, this sunscreen's absorbance rate is approximately 0.9. The correct answer is **F**. The rates in **G**, **H**, and **J** are too low to be correct.

9. A

Research Summary: Use the Chart   *Medium*

Michael is going to spend 90 minutes on a sunny beach. In other words, he will be spending 90 minutes exposed to natural UV radiation. He wants a sunscreen with absorbance that will never drop below 0.4. Michael should NOT take Sunscreen 3 to the beach, because its absorbance drops below 0.4 when exposed to UVA1 rays. The correct answer is **A**. Sunscreens 4, 5, and 6 all have absorbencies of 0.4 or greater after 90 minutes of natural UV ray exposure.

10. G

Research Summary: Use the Chart   *Difficult*

Looking at all six of the sunscreen graphs, we see that each product's photostability decreases as its UV exposure reaches 400 nm. Therefore, the correct answer is **G**. **F** is incorrect because the sunscreens are *less* photostable when exposed to UVA1 rays. **H** is not supported by the data. **J** is the opposite of the correct answer.

11. B

Research Summary: Take the Next Step   *Difficult*

For a label describing photostability to be useful, all sunscreen manufacturers would need to use a standardized method to measure photostability. **C** gets it backward: It wouldn't be useful at all for sunscreen manufacturers to use different methods to measure photostability. An increase in UVA protection may lead to greater photostability, but this is not what the question is asking, so **A** is incorrect. **D** also misses the point of the question (and decreasing UVA protection would likely have a detrimental effect on a sunscreen's photostability).

12. H

Data Representation: Read the Chart   *Easy*

Figure 2 shows that the color indigo has a wavelength of slightly less than 450 nm. Indigo is therefore most likely to be the color with a wavelength of 445 nm. **J** is incorrect, because blue has a wavelength of 450 to 495 nm.

13. D

Data Representation: Read the Chart   *Medium*

Table 2 reveals that yellow light has a wavelength of 570 to 590 nm. So, light with a wavelength of 580 nm is yellow light. Table 1 shows that the color yellow is displayed in the spectra produced by two sources: the sun and a yellow-green LED. The sun is not present among the answer choices, so **D** is correct.

14. F

Data Representation: Use the Chart   *Medium*

Figure 2 shows that a wavelength of 393 nm is seen as the color violet. This means that when violet is seen in the color spectrum, it reflects the presence of calcium in the light source. Table 1 shows that violet light is visible in the color spectrum produced by the sun. **F** is therefore correct. **G**, **H**, and **J** are incorrect because, according to Table 1, violet is not present in the spectra produced by these sources.

15. B

Data Representation: Handle Graphs   *Difficult*

The passage explains that Source B is the light source used to create the graph in Figure 4. Figure 4 shows the color spectrum displayed by Source B. The graph contains two spikes: one at about 450 nm and one at about 525 nm. According to Figure 2, 450 nm is blue light, and 525 nm is green light.

These are the only two spikes in the graph, so blue and green are the only two colors that can be seen in the spectrum of Source B. We're therefore looking for a light source that contains only blue and green spectral lines. According to Table 1, fluorescent light contains only blue and green colors in its spectrum. **B** is therefore correct.

A is incorrect because the sun contains all colors of visible light in its spectrum. **C** and **D** are incorrect because yellow-green LEDs and neon lights contain colors other than blue and green in their spectra.

16. H

Data Representation: Handle Graphs   *Difficult*

Table 1 shows that the sun contains all of the colors of visible light in its color spectrum. **F** can be eliminated, because the spectrum of the sun displays all colors, and the spectrum of the red laser diode displays only red.

Figure 3 reflects the spectrum of a light source that contains all colors of visible light, ranging from about 380 to 750 nm. According to Figure 2, this range of wavelengths includes all of the colors from violet through red. The only light source in Table 1 that displays all colors in its spectrum is the sun, so Figure 3 reflects the spectrum of the sun.

Figure 3 shows all of the wavelengths appearing at the same level of intensity, so **H** is correct. **G** and **J** are incorrect, because Figure 3 does not show any wavelengths displayed at a higher intensity than others.

17. A

Research Summary: Read the Chart   *Easy*

The passage states that the thick horizontal line in each box in Figure 1 represents the colony average. Colony B had the greatest preference for violet, at slightly more than 60 percent. The correct answer is **A**. **B**, **C**, and **D** all point to colonies with violet preferences lower than 60 percent, so none of those answers can be correct.

18. J

Research Summary: Read the Chart   *Easy*

Bees that prefer violet flowers 56 percent of the time have a nectar foraging rate of approximately 26 mg/hr. The foraging rates in **F**, **G**, and **H** are all too high to be correct.

19. C

Research Summary: Use the Chart   *Medium*

Violet (UV-blue) flowers produce approximately 1,200 μ sugar every 24 hours. This is equivalent to more than twice the nectar produced by the blue flowers (which produce approximately 500 μ sugar/24 hours) and the blue-green flowers (which produce slightly less than 500 μ sugar/24 hours) combined. The correct answer is **C**. The amount of nectar produced by violet flowers is significantly greater than the amount of nectar produced by UV-green flowers, so **A** is incorrect. Violet flowers produce 1,200 μ sugar/24 hours, not 500 μ sugar/24 hours, so **B** is also incorrect. **D** provides an incorrect rate as well.

20. G

Research Summary: Use the Chart   *Medium*

This question requires Figure 1 and Figure 3. Figure 1 shows that bumblebees in Colony B had the greater preference for violet flowers than the bees in Colony F. Figure 3 shows that bees with the greater preference for violet flowers typically have the higher nectar foraging rate. The correct answer, therefore, is **G**. The bees in Colony B have a greater preference for violet flowers than the bees in Colony E, so choice

F is incorrect. **H** is incorrect because there is no evidence that the bees in Colony B prefer blue flowers. Neither the passage nor the figures imply that the bumblebees in Colony B had greater success foraging in the flight box than foraging in the natural environment, so **J** is incorrect as well.

21. A

Research Summary: Use the Chart   *Difficult*

Figures 1, 2, and 3 all support the conclusion that flowers with the greatest nectar production (in other words, violet flowers) attract the highest percentage of bumblebees. There is no evidence that bumblebees would be attracted to violet flowers that did not produce nectar, so **B** is incorrect. The passage does not state whether bumblebees have an easier time finding nectar in the lab than in the natural environment, so we cannot assume that **C** is correct. Finally, **D** is incorrect because there is a clear correlation between the color of flowers and bees' foraging habits.

22. H

Research Summary: Use the Chart   *Difficult*

Both experiments support this conclusion, so the correct answer is **H**. **F**, **G**, and **J** represent a misreading of the data.

23. B

Conflicting Viewpoints: Detail   *Easy*

One of the arguments made by those who support the "RFID Implementation Invades Privacy" argument is that the devices' information can be surreptitiously accessed by generic RFID readers. If the 16-number code on medical RFID devices could not be deciphered, this argument would not be relevant, so the correct answer is **B**. **A** and **C** would strengthen the "RFID Implementation Invades Privacy" argument, not weaken it. **D**, while true, would neither weaken nor strengthen the argument.

24. F

Conflicting Viewpoints: Comparison   *Easy*

Supporters of both arguments would agree that RFID devices change the way in which patients and doctors access medical data. **G** is supported only by the "RFID Implementation Invades Privacy" argument, and **H** is supported only by the "RFID Devices Lead to Patient Freedom" argument. **J** is not addressed by either argument.

25. D

Conflicting Viewpoints: Inference   *Medium*

The "RFID Implementation Invades Privacy" argument states that *doctors must understand that RFID devices have an impact on patients' privacy that extends far beyond the medical arena.* Proponents of this argument believe that the decision to implant an RFID device should not be taken lightly and would therefore support **D**. **A** is too extreme: Supporters of the "RFID Implementation Invades Privacy" argument want the AMA to revise its recommendation about RFID devices, not prohibit them entirely. The passage makes no mention of how to improve upon the devices' security, so **B** is incorrect. **C** is incorrect because this argument does not include any mention of Alzheimer's patients.

26. G

Conflicting Viewpoints: Inference   *Medium*

This discovery would strengthen the "RFID Devices Lead to Patient Freedom" argument, which states that RFID devices make patient records available to clinicians in the case of an emergency. Because the finding would have an effect on the "RFID Devices Lead to Patient Freedom" argument, **F** cannot be correct. The finding would not strengthen the "RFID Implementation Invades Privacy" argument, which takes a skeptical view of RFID implantation, so neither **H** nor **J** can be correct.

27. C

Conflicting Viewpoints: Detail   *Medium*

The "RFID Implementation Invades Privacy" argument states that "ill-intentioned" people might steal information from RFID devices, but it never states *why* people would want to steal this information. The argument explains why the devices aren't covered by HIPAA (they're not considered to be of *medical significance*), so **A** is incorrect. The argument exists to let the AMA know why it should change its recommendation, so **B** cannot be correct. Use of RFID devices with Alzheimer's patients is mentioned only in the "RFID Devices Lead to Patient Freedom" argument, so **D** is incorrect.

28. H

Conflicting Viewpoints: Comparison   *Medium*

Both arguments explain that RFID devices allow clinical access to an individual's medical data, so **H** is correct. Only the "RFID Devices Lead to Patient Freedom" argument states that the devices are secure, making **F** incorrect. Only the "RFID Implementation Invades Privacy" argument describes RFID devices as *license plates for people* and encourages stricter oversight by the AMA, so both **G** and **J** are incorrect.

29. A

Conflicting Viewpoints: Detail   *Difficult*

The "RFID Devices Lead to Patient Freedom" argument states that RFID devices solve the problem of *fractured medical records* and *enable patients to establish health care identities*. The argument never states that RFID devices reduce a patient's need to see a doctor on a regular basis, so **B** is incorrect. The "RFID Implementation Invades Privacy" argument discusses risks posed by RFID devices, so **C** is incorrect. Neither argument makes any mention of voice-recognition software, so **D** is incorrect.

30. H

Data Representation: Read the Chart   *Easy*

Table 1 shows that an astronaut's skin can safely be exposed to 600 cSv over his or her career. **F** presents the amount of radiation an astronaut's skin can safely be exposed to *annually*, so it is incorrect. **G** presents the amount of radiation an astronaut's ocular lens can safely be exposed to over his or her career. **J** is not represented by any of the data in the table.

31. A

Data Representation: Read the Chart   *Easy*

Figure 2 indicates that aluminum is the most effective material for shielding astronauts from high doses of radiation. Regolith is slightly less effective than aluminum, so **B** is incorrect. Polyethylene and lithium hydride are far less effective against high doses of radiation than aluminum is, so **C** and **D** are both incorrect as well.

32. G
Data Representation: Use the Chart   *Medium*

The passage states that GCR particles release much smaller amounts of radiation than SPE particles do. If an astronaut embarked on a relatively short mission and was exposed only to these less-harmful particles, he could use a lighter, more flexible shield. Therefore, the correct answer is **G**. **F** is incorrect because annual exposure levels are higher than 30-day exposure levels. SPE particles release large amounts of radiation, so neither **H** nor choice **J** can be correct.

33. C
Data Representation: Read the Chart   *Medium*

A regolith shield at 10 g/cm^2 protects an astronaut from approximately 40 cSv/year of radiation, so the correct answer is **C**. The radiation amounts in **A** and **B** are too small, and the radiation amount in **D** is too large.

34. G
Data Representation: Use the Chart   *Difficult*

Use Figure 1 to answer this question. The engineer has the option of using magnesium hydride, regolith, or aluminum, because all of these materials can protect against radiation levels of 30 cSv/year or higher at a shield amount of 20 g/cm^2. The correct answer is **G**. **F** neglects to include magnesium hydride and regolith. **H** neglects to include magnesium hydride. **J** lists materials that could not protect against radiation levels of 30 cSv/year or higher at a shield amount of 20 g/cm^2.

35. D
Research Summary: Read the Chart   *Easy*

The approximate tensile strength for rubber with 50 phr coconut fiber is 5 Mpa. If you selected **A**, you probably found the tensile strength for rubber with 50 phr carbon black. **B** and **C** are also too high.

36. J
Research Summary: Read the Chart   *Easy*

The mixture with the greatest hardness is rubber with 70 phr carbon black. **F** represents a rubber mixture with a low hardness level, as does **G**. **H** gets the parts per hundred correct but includes the wrong filler material.

37. B
Research Summary: Use the Chart   *Medium*

In both experiments and at all mixture ratios, carbon black proved to be a more effective filler overall than coconut fiber. Because carbon black has greater tensile strength *and* greater hardness, **A** and **C** cannot be correct. **D** gets it backward.

38. F

Research Summary: Use the Chart   *Medium*

Rubber mixed with 50 phr carbon black has the greatest tensile strength, so **F** is the correct answer. The tensile strength of carbon black is never less than the tensile strength of coconut fiber, so **G** is incorrect. Rubber mixed with 20 phr carbon black is approximately 4, not 10, times stronger than rubber mixed with 20 phr coconut fiber, so **H** is incorrect. **J** is incorrect because carbon black yields a much greater tensile strength than coconut fiber.

39. C

Research Summary: Use the Chart   *Medium*

The passage explains that a rubber's hardness describes its capability to resist indentation. Only option **C** presents a scenario in which someone would *want* rubber that has little resistance. The ball manufacturer, eraser manufacturer, and tire manufacturer would all want rubber with high levels of hardness and tensile strength.

40. H

Research Summary: Use the Chart   *Difficult*

First, use Figure 1 to find the rubber mixture with a tensile strength of 20 Mpa. Then, use Figure 2 to find the rubber mixture with a hardness of 40 IRHD. In both cases, this rubber mixture is 20 phr carbon black. The correct answer is **H. F**, **G**, and **J** all represent a misreading of the data.

ACT Practice Test 4

DIRECTIONS: The ACT consists of tests in four separate subject areas: English, Mathematics, Reading, and Science. These four tests measure skills learned through high school course-work that are relevant to success in college. *YOU MAY USE CALCULATORS ON THE MATHEMATICS TEST ONLY.*

Each test contains a set of numbered questions. The answer choices for each question are lettered. On your answer sheet, you will find rows of ovals that are numbered to match the questions. Each oval contains a letter to correspond to a particular answer choice.

Choose the best answer for each question. Then, on your answer sheet, find the row of ovals that is numbered the same as the question. Find the oval containing the letter of your chosen answer, and fill in this oval completely. You must use a soft lead pencil for this purpose, and your marks must be heavy and black. *BALLPOINT PENS SHOULD NOT BE USED TO FILL IN THE ANSWER SHEET.*

Fill in only one answer choice oval for each question. If you wish to change an answer, make sure that your original answer is thoroughly erased before marking the new one. After filling in your answer, double-check to be sure that you have marked the row of ovals that corresponds to the question number being answered.

Responses will be scored only if they are marked on your answer document. Your score for each test is determined by the number of questions answered correctly during the testing period. Your score will NOT be reduced if you choose an incorrect answer. *FOR THIS REASON, IT IS ADVANTAGEOUS FOR YOU TO ANSWER EVERY QUESTION, EVEN IF YOU GUESS ON SOME QUESTIONS.*

You may work on a test ONLY when the test supervisor gives you permission to do so. If you finish a test before the end of the time allowed, use any remaining time to review questions that you are unsure about. You are permitted to review ONLY your answers for the test on which you are currently working. You may NOT look back to a test you have already completed, and you may NOT continue on to another test. If you do so, you will be disqualified from the examination.

When the end of each test is announced, put your pencil down immediately. You are NOT permitted to fill in or change ovals for a test after the end of that test has been called. If you do so, for any reason, you will be disqualified from the examination.

You may not fold or tear the pages of your test.

DO NOT TURN TO THE FIRST TEST
UNTIL YOU ARE TOLD TO DO SO.

ACT Practice Test 4: Answer Sheet

TEST 1

1 Ⓐ Ⓑ Ⓒ Ⓓ	16 Ⓕ Ⓖ Ⓗ Ⓙ	31 Ⓐ Ⓑ Ⓒ Ⓓ	46 Ⓕ Ⓖ Ⓗ Ⓙ	61 Ⓐ Ⓑ Ⓒ Ⓓ
2 Ⓕ Ⓖ Ⓗ Ⓙ	17 Ⓐ Ⓑ Ⓒ Ⓓ	32 Ⓕ Ⓖ Ⓗ Ⓙ	47 Ⓐ Ⓑ Ⓒ Ⓓ	62 Ⓕ Ⓖ Ⓗ Ⓙ
3 Ⓐ Ⓑ Ⓒ Ⓓ	18 Ⓕ Ⓖ Ⓗ Ⓙ	33 Ⓐ Ⓑ Ⓒ Ⓓ	48 Ⓕ Ⓖ Ⓗ Ⓙ	63 Ⓐ Ⓑ Ⓒ Ⓓ
4 Ⓕ Ⓖ Ⓗ Ⓙ	19 Ⓐ Ⓑ Ⓒ Ⓓ	34 Ⓕ Ⓖ Ⓗ Ⓙ	49 Ⓐ Ⓑ Ⓒ Ⓓ	64 Ⓕ Ⓖ Ⓗ Ⓙ
5 Ⓐ Ⓑ Ⓒ Ⓓ	20 Ⓕ Ⓖ Ⓗ Ⓙ	35 Ⓐ Ⓑ Ⓒ Ⓓ	50 Ⓕ Ⓖ Ⓗ Ⓙ	65 Ⓐ Ⓑ Ⓒ Ⓓ
6 Ⓕ Ⓖ Ⓗ Ⓙ	21 Ⓐ Ⓑ Ⓒ Ⓓ	36 Ⓕ Ⓖ Ⓗ Ⓙ	51 Ⓐ Ⓑ Ⓒ Ⓓ	66 Ⓕ Ⓖ Ⓗ Ⓙ
7 Ⓐ Ⓑ Ⓒ Ⓓ	22 Ⓕ Ⓖ Ⓗ Ⓙ	37 Ⓐ Ⓑ Ⓒ Ⓓ	52 Ⓕ Ⓖ Ⓗ Ⓙ	67 Ⓐ Ⓑ Ⓒ Ⓓ
8 Ⓕ Ⓖ Ⓗ Ⓙ	23 Ⓐ Ⓑ Ⓒ Ⓓ	38 Ⓕ Ⓖ Ⓗ Ⓙ	53 Ⓐ Ⓑ Ⓒ Ⓓ	68 Ⓕ Ⓖ Ⓗ Ⓙ
9 Ⓐ Ⓑ Ⓒ Ⓓ	24 Ⓕ Ⓖ Ⓗ Ⓙ	39 Ⓐ Ⓑ Ⓒ Ⓓ	54 Ⓕ Ⓖ Ⓗ Ⓙ	69 Ⓐ Ⓑ Ⓒ Ⓓ
10 Ⓕ Ⓖ Ⓗ Ⓙ	25 Ⓐ Ⓑ Ⓒ Ⓓ	40 Ⓕ Ⓖ Ⓗ Ⓙ	55 Ⓐ Ⓑ Ⓒ Ⓓ	70 Ⓕ Ⓖ Ⓗ Ⓙ
11 Ⓐ Ⓑ Ⓒ Ⓓ	26 Ⓕ Ⓖ Ⓗ Ⓙ	41 Ⓐ Ⓑ Ⓒ Ⓓ	56 Ⓕ Ⓖ Ⓗ Ⓙ	71 Ⓐ Ⓑ Ⓒ Ⓓ
12 Ⓕ Ⓖ Ⓗ Ⓙ	27 Ⓐ Ⓑ Ⓒ Ⓓ	42 Ⓕ Ⓖ Ⓗ Ⓙ	57 Ⓐ Ⓑ Ⓒ Ⓓ	72 Ⓕ Ⓖ Ⓗ Ⓙ
13 Ⓐ Ⓑ Ⓒ Ⓓ	28 Ⓕ Ⓖ Ⓗ Ⓙ	43 Ⓐ Ⓑ Ⓒ Ⓓ	58 Ⓕ Ⓖ Ⓗ Ⓙ	73 Ⓐ Ⓑ Ⓒ Ⓓ
14 Ⓕ Ⓖ Ⓗ Ⓙ	29 Ⓐ Ⓑ Ⓒ Ⓓ	44 Ⓕ Ⓖ Ⓗ Ⓙ	59 Ⓐ Ⓑ Ⓒ Ⓓ	74 Ⓕ Ⓖ Ⓗ Ⓙ
15 Ⓐ Ⓑ Ⓒ Ⓓ	30 Ⓕ Ⓖ Ⓗ Ⓙ	45 Ⓐ Ⓑ Ⓒ Ⓓ	60 Ⓕ Ⓖ Ⓗ Ⓙ	75 Ⓐ Ⓑ Ⓒ Ⓓ

TEST 2

1 Ⓐ Ⓑ Ⓒ Ⓓ Ⓔ	13 Ⓐ Ⓑ Ⓒ Ⓓ Ⓔ	25 Ⓐ Ⓑ Ⓒ Ⓓ Ⓔ	37 Ⓐ Ⓑ Ⓒ Ⓓ Ⓔ	49 Ⓐ Ⓑ Ⓒ Ⓓ Ⓔ
2 Ⓕ Ⓖ Ⓗ Ⓙ Ⓚ	14 Ⓕ Ⓖ Ⓗ Ⓙ Ⓚ	26 Ⓕ Ⓖ Ⓗ Ⓙ Ⓚ	38 Ⓕ Ⓖ Ⓗ Ⓙ Ⓚ	50 Ⓕ Ⓖ Ⓗ Ⓙ Ⓚ
3 Ⓐ Ⓑ Ⓒ Ⓓ Ⓔ	15 Ⓐ Ⓑ Ⓒ Ⓓ Ⓔ	27 Ⓐ Ⓑ Ⓒ Ⓓ Ⓔ	39 Ⓐ Ⓑ Ⓒ Ⓓ Ⓔ	51 Ⓐ Ⓑ Ⓒ Ⓓ Ⓔ
4 Ⓕ Ⓖ Ⓗ Ⓙ Ⓚ	16 Ⓕ Ⓖ Ⓗ Ⓙ Ⓚ	28 Ⓕ Ⓖ Ⓗ Ⓙ Ⓚ	40 Ⓕ Ⓖ Ⓗ Ⓙ Ⓚ	52 Ⓕ Ⓖ Ⓗ Ⓙ Ⓚ
5 Ⓐ Ⓑ Ⓒ Ⓓ Ⓔ	17 Ⓐ Ⓑ Ⓒ Ⓓ Ⓔ	29 Ⓐ Ⓑ Ⓒ Ⓓ Ⓔ	41 Ⓐ Ⓑ Ⓒ Ⓓ Ⓔ	53 Ⓐ Ⓑ Ⓒ Ⓓ Ⓔ
6 Ⓕ Ⓖ Ⓗ Ⓙ Ⓚ	18 Ⓕ Ⓖ Ⓗ Ⓙ Ⓚ	30 Ⓕ Ⓖ Ⓗ Ⓙ Ⓚ	42 Ⓕ Ⓖ Ⓗ Ⓙ Ⓚ	54 Ⓕ Ⓖ Ⓗ Ⓙ Ⓚ
7 Ⓐ Ⓑ Ⓒ Ⓓ Ⓔ	19 Ⓐ Ⓑ Ⓒ Ⓓ Ⓔ	31 Ⓐ Ⓑ Ⓒ Ⓓ Ⓔ	43 Ⓐ Ⓑ Ⓒ Ⓓ Ⓔ	55 Ⓐ Ⓑ Ⓒ Ⓓ Ⓔ
8 Ⓕ Ⓖ Ⓗ Ⓙ Ⓚ	20 Ⓕ Ⓖ Ⓗ Ⓙ Ⓚ	32 Ⓕ Ⓖ Ⓗ Ⓙ Ⓚ	44 Ⓕ Ⓖ Ⓗ Ⓙ Ⓚ	56 Ⓕ Ⓖ Ⓗ Ⓙ Ⓚ
9 Ⓐ Ⓑ Ⓒ Ⓓ Ⓔ	21 Ⓐ Ⓑ Ⓒ Ⓓ Ⓔ	33 Ⓐ Ⓑ Ⓒ Ⓓ Ⓔ	45 Ⓐ Ⓑ Ⓒ Ⓓ Ⓔ	57 Ⓐ Ⓑ Ⓒ Ⓓ Ⓔ
10 Ⓕ Ⓖ Ⓗ Ⓙ Ⓚ	22 Ⓕ Ⓖ Ⓗ Ⓙ Ⓚ	34 Ⓕ Ⓖ Ⓗ Ⓙ Ⓚ	46 Ⓕ Ⓖ Ⓗ Ⓙ Ⓚ	58 Ⓕ Ⓖ Ⓗ Ⓙ Ⓚ
11 Ⓐ Ⓑ Ⓒ Ⓓ Ⓔ	23 Ⓐ Ⓑ Ⓒ Ⓓ Ⓔ	35 Ⓐ Ⓑ Ⓒ Ⓓ Ⓔ	47 Ⓐ Ⓑ Ⓒ Ⓓ Ⓔ	59 Ⓐ Ⓑ Ⓒ Ⓓ Ⓔ
12 Ⓕ Ⓖ Ⓗ Ⓙ Ⓚ	24 Ⓕ Ⓖ Ⓗ Ⓙ Ⓚ	36 Ⓕ Ⓖ Ⓗ Ⓙ Ⓚ	48 Ⓕ Ⓖ Ⓗ Ⓙ Ⓚ	60 Ⓕ Ⓖ Ⓗ Ⓙ Ⓚ

TEST 3

1 Ⓐ Ⓑ Ⓒ Ⓓ	9 Ⓐ Ⓑ Ⓒ Ⓓ	17 Ⓐ Ⓑ Ⓒ Ⓓ	25 Ⓐ Ⓑ Ⓒ Ⓓ	33 Ⓐ Ⓑ Ⓒ Ⓓ
2 Ⓕ Ⓖ Ⓗ Ⓙ	10 Ⓕ Ⓖ Ⓗ Ⓙ	18 Ⓕ Ⓖ Ⓗ Ⓙ	26 Ⓕ Ⓖ Ⓗ Ⓙ	34 Ⓕ Ⓖ Ⓗ Ⓙ
3 Ⓐ Ⓑ Ⓒ Ⓓ	11 Ⓐ Ⓑ Ⓒ Ⓓ	19 Ⓐ Ⓑ Ⓒ Ⓓ	27 Ⓐ Ⓑ Ⓒ Ⓓ	35 Ⓐ Ⓑ Ⓒ Ⓓ
4 Ⓕ Ⓖ Ⓗ Ⓙ	12 Ⓕ Ⓖ Ⓗ Ⓙ	20 Ⓕ Ⓖ Ⓗ Ⓙ	28 Ⓕ Ⓖ Ⓗ Ⓙ	36 Ⓕ Ⓖ Ⓗ Ⓙ
5 Ⓐ Ⓑ Ⓒ Ⓓ	13 Ⓐ Ⓑ Ⓒ Ⓓ	21 Ⓐ Ⓑ Ⓒ Ⓓ	29 Ⓐ Ⓑ Ⓒ Ⓓ	37 Ⓐ Ⓑ Ⓒ Ⓓ
6 Ⓕ Ⓖ Ⓗ Ⓙ	14 Ⓕ Ⓖ Ⓗ Ⓙ	22 Ⓕ Ⓖ Ⓗ Ⓙ	30 Ⓕ Ⓖ Ⓗ Ⓙ	38 Ⓕ Ⓖ Ⓗ Ⓙ
7 Ⓐ Ⓑ Ⓒ Ⓓ	15 Ⓐ Ⓑ Ⓒ Ⓓ	23 Ⓐ Ⓑ Ⓒ Ⓓ	31 Ⓐ Ⓑ Ⓒ Ⓓ	39 Ⓐ Ⓑ Ⓒ Ⓓ
8 Ⓕ Ⓖ Ⓗ Ⓙ	16 Ⓕ Ⓖ Ⓗ Ⓙ	24 Ⓕ Ⓖ Ⓗ Ⓙ	32 Ⓕ Ⓖ Ⓗ Ⓙ	40 Ⓕ Ⓖ Ⓗ Ⓙ

TEST 4

1 Ⓐ Ⓑ Ⓒ Ⓓ	9 Ⓐ Ⓑ Ⓒ Ⓓ	17 Ⓐ Ⓑ Ⓒ Ⓓ	25 Ⓐ Ⓑ Ⓒ Ⓓ	33 Ⓐ Ⓑ Ⓒ Ⓓ
2 Ⓕ Ⓖ Ⓗ Ⓙ	10 Ⓕ Ⓖ Ⓗ Ⓙ	18 Ⓕ Ⓖ Ⓗ Ⓙ	26 Ⓕ Ⓖ Ⓗ Ⓙ	34 Ⓕ Ⓖ Ⓗ Ⓙ
3 Ⓐ Ⓑ Ⓒ Ⓓ	11 Ⓐ Ⓑ Ⓒ Ⓓ	19 Ⓐ Ⓑ Ⓒ Ⓓ	27 Ⓐ Ⓑ Ⓒ Ⓓ	35 Ⓐ Ⓑ Ⓒ Ⓓ
4 Ⓕ Ⓖ Ⓗ Ⓙ	12 Ⓕ Ⓖ Ⓗ Ⓙ	20 Ⓕ Ⓖ Ⓗ Ⓙ	28 Ⓕ Ⓖ Ⓗ Ⓙ	36 Ⓕ Ⓖ Ⓗ Ⓙ
5 Ⓐ Ⓑ Ⓒ Ⓓ	13 Ⓐ Ⓑ Ⓒ Ⓓ	21 Ⓐ Ⓑ Ⓒ Ⓓ	29 Ⓐ Ⓑ Ⓒ Ⓓ	37 Ⓐ Ⓑ Ⓒ Ⓓ
6 Ⓕ Ⓖ Ⓗ Ⓙ	14 Ⓕ Ⓖ Ⓗ Ⓙ	22 Ⓕ Ⓖ Ⓗ Ⓙ	30 Ⓕ Ⓖ Ⓗ Ⓙ	38 Ⓕ Ⓖ Ⓗ Ⓙ
7 Ⓐ Ⓑ Ⓒ Ⓓ	15 Ⓐ Ⓑ Ⓒ Ⓓ	23 Ⓐ Ⓑ Ⓒ Ⓓ	31 Ⓐ Ⓑ Ⓒ Ⓓ	39 Ⓐ Ⓑ Ⓒ Ⓓ
8 Ⓕ Ⓖ Ⓗ Ⓙ	16 Ⓕ Ⓖ Ⓗ Ⓙ	24 Ⓕ Ⓖ Ⓗ Ⓙ	32 Ⓕ Ⓖ Ⓗ Ⓙ	40 Ⓕ Ⓖ Ⓗ Ⓙ

ENGLISH TEST

45 Minutes—75 Questions

DIRECTIONS: There are five passages on this test. You should read each passage once before answering the questions on it. In order to answer correctly, you may need to read several sentences beyond the question.

There are two question formats within the passages. In one format, you will find words and phrases that have been underlined and assigned numbers. These numbers will correspond with sets of alternative words/phrases given in the right-hand column of the test booklet. From the sets of alternatives, choose the answer choice that works best in context, keeping in mind whether it employs standard written English, whether it gets across the idea of the section,

and whether it suits the tone and style of the passage. You will usually be offered the option "NO CHANGE," which you should choose if you think the version found in the passage is best.

In the second format, you will see boxed numbers referring to sections of the passage or to the passage as a whole. In the right-hand column, you will be asked questions about or given alternatives for the sections marked by the boxes. Choose the answer choice that best answers the question or completes the section. After choosing your answer choice, fill in the corresponding bubble on the answer sheet.

Passage I

Falling Asleep

[1]

Although narcolepsy is one of the most prevalent sleep

<u>disorders and affects 1 in 2,000 people the chronic</u>
[1]

<u>condition,</u> often goes undiagnosed. Many people <u>assumed</u>
[1]   [2]

that excessive daytime sleepiness does not suggest a

physiological problem, so they disregard the symptoms.

Studies have shown that an average of 14 years <u>pass</u>
[3]

between the onset of narcolepsy and an accurate diagnosis.

1. **A.** NO CHANGE
   B. disorders and affects 1 in 2,000 people the chronic condition
   C. disorders and affects 1 in 2,000 people, the chronic condition
   D. disorders, and affects 1 in 2,000 people the chronic condition,

2. **F.** NO CHANGE
   G. who assume
   H. were assuming
   J. assume

3. **A.** NO CHANGE
   B. passes
   C. are passing
   D. have passed

GO ON TO THE NEXT PAGE.

[2]

Defined as a neurological disorder characterized by recurrent and uncontrollable bouts of deep sleep, narcolepsy is <u>a serious problem that is often mocked in films and television shows.</u> While nighttime sleep patterns are
4
often erratic for narcoleptics, it is <u>daytime sleeping habits</u> that distinguish narcolepsy from insomnia. Narcoleptics
5
may nap without warning for a few seconds or for thirty minutes several times every day, even while working or driving. <u>In conclusion,</u> narcoleptics often suffer from
6
hallucinations <u>while trying to fall asleep at night and when</u>
7
<u>they are awake they experience sudden muscle weakness.</u>
7
Many narcoleptics also experience sleep paralysis, which is the inability to move or talk soon after waking up.

[3]

<u>Scientists, who suspect genetics are to blame for the</u>
8
<u>causes of narcolepsy, remain largely unknown.</u> At present,
8
no cure exists for the <u>disorder, however;</u> options are
9
available to help narcoleptics gain control of their sleep

4. Which choice best leads the reader into the subject matter of paragraph 2?
   F. NO CHANGE
   G. a lifelong condition that requires constant assessment.
   H. also typically confused with insomnia.
   J. a difficult problem to diagnose.

5. A. NO CHANGE
   B. habitual, daytime sleeping
   C. sleeping in daytime habits
   D. sleeping daytime habits

6. F. NO CHANGE
   G. Consequently,
   H. On the other hand,
   J. In addition,

7. A. NO CHANGE
   B. while falling asleep and sudden muscle weakness while awake.
   C. when they try falling asleep and sudden muscle weakness when they are awake.
   D. when going to sleep and sudden, unexpected muscle weakness when awake.

8. F. NO CHANGE
   G. The causes of narcolepsy remain largely unknown, but scientists suspect genetics are to blame.
   H. Scientists, who remain largely unknown, suspect genetics are to blame for the causes of narcolepsy.
   J. According to scientists, genetics are suspected to be the blame for the unknown causes of narcolepsy.

9. A. NO CHANGE
   B. disorder, however,
   C. disorder, however
   D. disorder; however,

habits. Prescription medications can <u>alleviate and lessen some of the symptoms of narcolepsy.</u>[10] [11] In addition to being prescribed medications, narcoleptics are advised to make behavioral changes, like scheduling naps to avoid

unplanned ones. Narcoleptics should also stay away from stimulants, <u>such as caffeine alcohol and nicotine, which</u>[12] can interfere with nighttime sleep patterns.

[4]

Narcolepsy symptoms typically arise in individuals <u>of</u>[13] the ages of 10 and 25. Those who are undiagnosed

for too long may experience <u>academic problems, personal,</u>[14] and professional difficulties. Being aware of the signs of narcolepsy is the first step to managing the often frightening condition. With a timely diagnosis and proper medical treatment, narcoleptics can live long and fruitful lives. [15]

10. **F.** NO CHANGE
 G. lessen some of the symptoms faced on a daily basis by narcoleptics.
 H. alleviate some of the symptoms.
 J. medically lessen some symptoms.

11. With the intention of adding more information, the writer is considering inserting at this point the following true statement:

 > Stimulants help narcoleptics stay awake, and antidepressants reduce the frequency of hallucinations and muscle weakness.

 Should the writer insert the new sentence here? Why or why not?
 A. Yes, because the sentence gives the reader some relevant information about the benefits of medicating narcoleptics.
 B. Yes, because the sentence confirms the belief that narcoleptics should use prescription medications to control their symptoms.
 C. No, because the sentence provides incidental details that are not of sufficient relevance for inclusion.
 D. No, because the sentence offers important details that would be more appropriate in another paragraph.

12. **F.** NO CHANGE
 G. such as, caffeine, alcohol, and nicotine which
 H. such as caffeine, alcohol, and nicotine, which
 J. such as caffeine, alcohol and nicotine which

13. **A.** NO CHANGE
 B. between
 C. from
 D. in

14. **F.** NO CHANGE
 G. problems in academics, and who have personal,
 H. academic, personal troubles,
 J. academic, personal,

15. Suppose the writer had been assigned to write a short essay illustrating the dangers of narcolepsy. Would this essay successfully fulfill the assignment?
 A. Yes, because the essay mentions the problems faced by narcoleptics.
 B. Yes, because the essay describes how narcoleptics can injure themselves.
 C. No, because the essay addresses other issues related to narcolepsy.
 D. No, because the essay focuses only on treatment options for narcoleptics.

Passage II

Frederick Douglass: An Educated Man

[1]

Most people today cannot fathom the idea of being treated

as <u>property; no</u> better than livestock or a bag of flour.
16

However, in the 1860s, slavery was prevalent throughout

the United States. One of the most accomplished slaves

to emerge from the bonds of slavery <u>was</u> Frederick
17

Douglass, <u>whom</u> later became a famous author, orator,
18

and abolitionist.

[2]

Born into <u>slavery in 1818, in Maryland Douglass</u>
19

changed owners several times before being given to Hugh

Auld when Douglass was 12. Auld's wife, Sophia, changed

Douglass's life when she taught him beginning reading

skills. Eventually, armed with some basic knowledge,

Douglass was able to teach himself how to read at higher

levels. [20]

16. **F.** NO CHANGE
    G. property. No
    H. property—no
    J. property! No

17. **A.** NO CHANGE
    B. are
    C. were
    D. have been

18. **F.** NO CHANGE
    G. which
    H. who
    J. and

19. **A.** NO CHANGE
    B. slavery in 1818 in Maryland, Douglass
    C. slavery, in 1818 in Maryland Douglass
    D. slavery in 1818 in Maryland Douglass,

20. Which of the following sentences, if added here, would
    most effectively lead the reader from paragraph 2 to
    paragraph 3?
    F. Sophia Auld introduced Douglass to the sounds of
    the alphabet, and Douglass was able to progress
    from that point.
    G. Douglass's reading abilities improved as a result of
    his interaction with local white children and also
    through his own independent studies to develop his
    literacy.
    H. Before becoming the slave of Hugh Auld, Douglass
    spent time working at Wye House, a large planta-
    tion in Maryland.
    J. Children in the town who went to school proved to
    be a source of education for the young Frederick.

[3]

At that time, Douglass's reading abilities signifies a
remarkable achievement. Plantation owners feared slaves

would learn to read, but education had the potential

to make slaves dissatisfied with their lives, which might

possibly result in a revolt. Hugh Auld was particularly

upset that his wife had taught Douglass to read because

such activities were deemed illegal.

[4]

As a teenager, Douglass moved to a new plantation owned

by a vicious and cruel man who was named Edward

Covey. Covey prided himself on "breaking" slaves, which

meant that he beat them into submission. As expected,

Douglass received many thrashings, but at one point the

young slave fought back and defeated Covey, who never

struck Douglass again. 26

21. A. NO CHANGE
B. is signifying
C. have signified
D. signified

22. F. NO CHANGE
G. since
H. yet
J. and

23. A. NO CHANGE
B. well
C. could
D. OMIT the underlined portion.

24. F. NO CHANGE
G. (Place the underlined text before *Hugh Auld*)
H. (Place the underlined text after *upset*)
J. (Place the underlined text after *that*)

25. A. NO CHANGE
B. cruel slave owner who was named
C. man who was vicious and cruel,
D. vicious man named

26. At this point, the writer is considering adding the following true sentence:

Covey's plantation was appropriately named Mount Misery, and it changed hands several times since the era of slavery.

Should the writer make this addition?
F. Yes, because pointing out the coincidence of Douglass suffering in a place named Mount Misery provides an interesting anecdote related to his suffering.
G. Yes, because the information provides interesting information about the history of Douglass's former plantation.
H. No, because the additional detail distracts the reader from the main focus of the essay.
J. No, because the essay does not explain how Douglass was able to escape from Covey.

　　　　　　　　　　GO ON TO THE NEXT PAGE.

[5]

Eventually, Douglass's freedom was purchased, and

he wrote <u>his famous autobiography A Narrative</u>
                                    27

of the Life of Frederick Douglass, an American Slave.

For a self-taught man, Douglass penned an amazing

autobiography that vividly portrays slave life. 28 Douglass's

other accomplishments include becoming a renowned

abolitionist speaker, an ordained minister, a world traveler,

a newspaper publisher, and <u>besides being a</u> U.S.
                                        29

marshal. 30

27. **A.** NO CHANGE
    B. his famous, autobiography *A Narrative*
    C. his famous autobiography, *A Narrative*
    D. his famous autobiography, *A Narrative,*

28. The writer is considering revising "an amazing auto-
    biography that vividly portrays slave life" to read "an
    amazing autobiography." That revision would cause
    the sentence to lose primarily:
    F. the writer's personal opinion about Douglass's life.
    G. confusing details that create an awkward sentence.
    H. relevant information about Douglass's accomplish-
    ments.
    J. clarifying details regarding the focus of Douglass's
    book.

29. **A.** NO CHANGE
    B. a
    C. along with being
    D. also being a

30. Suppose the writer had been assigned to write a brief
    essay about the history of slavery in the United States.
    Would this essay successfully fulfill that goal?
    F. No, because the essay focuses on only the experi-
    ences of one former slave.
    G. No, because the essay describes how the education
    of slaves ended slavery.
    H. Yes, because the essay describes how slaves were
    able to win their freedom.
    J. Yes, because the essay traces the history of slavery
    through the life of one slave.

Passage III

Tractor Joy Riding

[1]

When I was a child, I used to visit my uncle's farm during summer vacations. I loved riding horses, <u>running</u>
31
barefoot through miles of cornfields, and wasting summer days fishing at the catfish pond. My uncle was <u>usually</u>
32
busy tending to the animals or planting crops, so I spent a great deal of time with my cousin, Jacob.

[2]

Aside from all the fun I had, I became very familiar with the importance of farm safety. The big wakeup call occurred when I was <u>14, Jacob</u> was 16. Jacob <u>has been</u> helping in the
33   34
fields, and after driving the tractor into the barn, he fell

from the seat. Fortunately, the tractor engine was turned off, <u>but</u> Jacob's injuries were limited to a few bruises
35
and some sore ribs. I have always suspected that Jacob was so stunned by the quickness of the event that he became <u>extreme cautious</u> afterward.
36

31. **A.** NO CHANGE
    B. how I ran
    C. to run
    D. would run

32. Three of these choices indicate that the uncle was busy with farm work on a regular basis. Which choice does NOT do so?
    F. NO CHANGE
    G. often
    H. seldom
    J. frequently

33. **A.** NO CHANGE
    B. 14 Jacob
    C. 14 and Jacob,
    D. 14, and Jacob

34. **F.** NO CHANGE
    G. had been
    H. will be
    J. is

35. **A.** NO CHANGE
    B. so
    C. since
    D. while

36. **F.** NO CHANGE
    G. extreme caution
    H. extremely cautious
    J. extremely cautiously

        GO ON TO THE NEXT PAGE.

[3]

If you live in a farming community or have ever visited

a rural <u>area. In</u> the summer, you have probably seen
₃₇

young kids driving tractors. We never thought <u>honestly</u>
₃₈

much about playing around on the tractors until Jacob's

accident. That summer, my <u>cousins' fall and my uncle's</u>
₃₉

subsequent safety talk taught me that <u>they</u> should not
₄₀

be treated as toys. We haven't had any injuries since then,

unless you count the time I got a fishing hook stuck in my

finger while trying to wrestle "my big catch"—a bunch of

seaweed.

[4]

My uncle <u>is using</u> Jacob's fall to teach us the importance
₄₁

of staying alert to danger, even on a seemingly innocuous

farm. We did not go out of our way to seek <u>danger but</u>
₄₂

we weren't always careful when climbing on <u>mechanical</u>
₄₃

<u>farm equipment and tractors.</u> My uncle later reinforced
₄₃

37. **A.** NO CHANGE
B. area; in
C. area, in
D. area in

38. **F.** NO CHANGE
G. (Place after *never*)
H. (Place after *much*)
J. (Place after *around*)

39. **A.** NO CHANGE
B. cousin's fall and my uncles'
C. cousin's fall and my uncle's
D. cousins' fall and my uncles'

40. **F.** NO CHANGE
G. it
H. such big things
J. tractors and other farm equipment

41. **A.** NO CHANGE
B. used
C. will use
D. has been using

42. **F.** NO CHANGE
G. danger; but,
H. danger, but
J. danger but,

43. **A.** NO CHANGE
B. farm machinery and equipment.
C. farm equipment.
D. mechanical farm tools like tractors, combines, and
plows.

his safety tips by grounding us for a month for what he

described as "tractor joy riding." [44] [45]

44. The writer is considering revising "for what he described as 'tractor joy riding'" to read "for fooling around with the tractor." That revision would cause the sentence to lose primarily:
   F. details supporting the fact that the uncle is serious about tractor safety.
   G. information about the cousins' inability to follow directions.
   H. a humorous description that provides relevant details about the incident.
   J. confusing details that create an awkward and confusing sentence.

45. For the sake of logic and coherence, paragraph 4 should be:
   A. placed where it is now.
   B. placed after paragraph 1.
   C. placed after paragraph 2.
   D. OMITTED, because the passage primarily focuses on the fun aspects of riding tractors.

GO ON TO THE NEXT PAGE.

Passage IV

Measuring National Wealth

[1]

When it comes to measuring the national wealth of a country, some might be tempted to think in terms of the supply of dollars that a nation possesses. National <u>wealth</u> <u>however,</u> is not defined in terms of the amount of money that a nation prints. Instead, it is defined in terms of the real goods and services <u>manufactured and produced in a</u> <u>country.</u>

[2]

Money cannot be used as a measure of national <u>wealth.</u> <u>Because</u> it only has value when accepted as a medium of exchange. <u>In fact,</u> it is possible for a nation's monetary supply to have no value, if people aren't willing to receive that money in payment for goods sold. At times, in certain <u>nations histories,</u> the value of money has dropped because individuals within the society refused to trade in the national currency. Under these <u>circumstances the</u> <u>coins or currency notes</u> used by the country <u>becomes</u> worthless pieces of metal or paper, like trinkets from a Cracker Jack box.

46. **F.** NO CHANGE
    G. wealth; however,
    H. wealth, however,
    J. wealth, however

47. **A.** NO CHANGE
    B. produced by the country.
    C. made and produced by a country's workers and businesses.
    D. produced by local and national companies in a country.

48. **F.** NO CHANGE
    G. wealth—because
    H. wealth; because
    J. wealth because

49. **A.** NO CHANGE
    B. In short,
    C. Nonetheless,
    D. Regardless,

50. **F.** NO CHANGE
    G. nation's histories,
    H. nations' histories,
    J. nations' history's,

51. **A.** NO CHANGE
    B. circumstances, the coins or currency notes
    C. circumstances, the coins, or currency notes,
    D. circumstances the coins, or currency notes,

52. **F.** NO CHANGE
    G. is becoming
    H. has become
    J. become

[3]

[1]<u>At least fifteen member countries of the European</u>
                                                    53

<u>Union have adopted the euro as a common currency.</u> [2]
                                                    53

<u>During a given year, national output is computed by adding</u>
                                                    54

<u>up the one way value of what a country produces.</u> [3]Annual
                                                    54

national output can be measured in terms of Gross National

Product (GNP) and Gross Domestic Product (GDP). [4]GNP,

the older measure, <u>is considering</u> all of the goods and
                        55

services produced by the citizens of a country, regardless

of where those individuals reside, whether they live in

the United States or abroad. 56 [5]<u>In contrast,</u> GDP
                                                    57

53. Which choice would most effectively and appropriately
lead the reader from the topic of paragraph 2 to that of
paragraph 3?
A. NO CHANGE
B. During times of recession, economic activity de-
clines as indicated by high rates of employment,
rising prices of goods, and low profits.
C. A nation's wealth is instead defined in terms of its
national output of goods and services.
D. The foreign-exchange rate between the currencies
of two nations indicates the value of one currency in
terms of the other.

54. F. NO CHANGE
G. What a country produces during a given year is one
way in which national output and value is computed and added up.
H. One way in which national output is computed is
by adding up the value of what a country produces
during a given year.
J. National output is computed one way during a
given year by adding up the value of what a country
produces.

55. A. NO CHANGE
B. has considered
C. will consider
D. considers

56. The writer is considering revising "regardless of where
those individuals reside, whether they live in the
United States or abroad" to read "regardless of where
those individuals reside." That revision would cause
the sentence to lose primarily:
F. redundant information that creates an awkward
sentence.
G. important information that supports the author's
argument.
H. details that provide a logical transition to the next
sentence.
J. relevant details that clarify the author's explanation of output.

57. Which of the following alternatives to the underlined
portion would be LEAST acceptable?
A. Therefore,
B. On the other hand,
C. On the contrary,
D. However,

 GO ON TO THE NEXT PAGE.

accounts for all goods and services produced within the

territorial boundaries of the nation. [58]

[4]

By <u>assessing</u> a country's wealth in terms of its total
59

national output, we get a sense of the true value of that

country's economic capacity. It would be much more difficult

for a country to double its national output than it would

be for the government to simply double its production of

currency. [60]

58. The writer is considering adding the following true statement to this paragraph:

> The country of origin of a firm is disregarded when calculating GDP.

Should the sentence be added to this paragraph, and if so, where should it be placed?
F. Yes, after sentence 3.
G. Yes, after sentence 4.
H. Yes, after sentence 5.
J. The sentence should NOT be added.

59. **A.** NO CHANGE
B. securing
C. obtaining
D. ignoring

60. Suppose the writer had been assigned to write a short essay about the difficulties of comparing the wealth of the United States with that of other nations. Would this essay successfully fulfill the assignment?
F. Yes, because the essay shows how to compare GDP with GNP to determine the overall wealth of developing countries.
G. Yes, because the essay argues that the wealth of the United States vastly overshadows the wealth of smaller nations.
H. No, because the essay focuses on how a nation's economic wealth is measured through productivity rather than money.
J. No, because the essay asserts that comparing the wealth of multiple nations is simple once currency is removed from the equation.

Passage V

Dissension in Oraibi

[1]

[1]The town of Oraibi, Arizona, is reputed to be the oldest continuously inhabited town in the United States. [2] Dissension began not long after the formation of a Hopi Indian Reservation in Oraibi in 1882. [3]Five years after <u>the formation, development, and establishment of a reservation,</u> the first school was opened in Keams
61

Canyon. [4]By 1890, when only a few Hopi children were attending the school, a local agent wrote to the Commissioner of Indian Affairs in Washington <u>better</u>
62
urging relations with the Hopi. [5]<u>As a result,</u> a trip
63
to Washington was arranged for some of the Hopi village leaders.

[2]

[1]<u>One</u> was Lololma of the Bear Clan from Oraibi, the
64
undisputed leader and spokesman of the Hopi people. 65

61. **A.** NO CHANGE
B. the formation of a Hopi reservation establishment,
C. establishing and creating a Hopi reservation,
D. the reservation was established,

62. **F.** NO CHANGE
G. (Place before *school*)
H. (Place before *relations*)
J. (Place before *Hopi*)

63. Which of the following alternatives to the underlined portion would be the LEAST acceptable?
A. So,
B. Yet,
C. For this reason,
D. Consequently,

64. Which of the transitions provides the most effective link from paragraph 1 to paragraph 2?
F. NO CHANGE
G. The representative
H. One of the Hopis
J. One of those chosen for the trip

65. The writer is considering revising "Lololma of the Bear Clan from Oraibi, the undisputed leader and spokesman of the Hopi people" to read "Lololma of the Bear Clan from Oraibi." That revision would cause the sentence to lose primarily:
A. an explanation of why Lololma was chosen as leader of the Bear Clan.
B. background information about the leadership structure of the Bear Clan.
C. details about Lololma that provide the reader with information about his position in the tribe.
D. information about Lololma's role with the Bear Clan that is presented later in the passage.

GO ON TO THE NEXT PAGE.

[2]At the meeting with the Commissioner of Indian Affairs, Lololma and the other Hopi leaders voiced its concern
66

about Navajo encroachment upon their territory. [3]They describe Navajo attacks as the main reason why they
67

refused to send their children to the agency school.

[4] Representatives of the Commission of Indian Affairs, a
68

government agency, convinced Lololma that the Hopi
68

reservation would be protected against Navajo trespassers.

[5]In turn, Lololma promised cooperation with the government commission in every respect.

[3]

After the meeting in Washington, Lololma returned to
69

Oraibi, which was founded in 1100. He sent his own
69

male family members to the school, moved from Oraibi, and
70

encouraged others to move from the mesas as well. Such
70

moves were proposed to help protect the perimeters of the

Hopi reservation; and Hopis would be more spread out
71

instead of clustered at the top of the mesas.

66. F. NO CHANGE
G. his
H. their
J. ones

67. A. NO CHANGE
B. are describing
C. do describe
D. described

68. F. NO CHANGE
G. The government representatives
H. Commission of Indian Affairs representatives
J. The people representing the government agency

69. Given that all of the choices are true, which one would most effectively introduce this paragraph?
A. NO CHANGE
B. After Lololma returned to Oraibi, he began demonstrating evidence of his cooperation as an example for others to follow.
C. The name Hopi translates to "the Peaceful People," and Lololma tried to uphold his heritage.
D. Lololma went back to his home in Oraibi where non-Indian influences were making an impact on the Hopi culture.

70. F. NO CHANGE
G. moving from Oraibi, and encouraging
H. he then moved from Oraibi to encourage
J. moves from Oraibi, and encourages

71. A. NO CHANGE
B. reservation, Hopis
C. reservation; Hopis
D. reservation and Hopis

[4]

In Oraibi, the opposition to Lololma's plan was fairly

immediate. Two factions developed, referred to as the

Friendlies and the Hostiles. The Hostile group was led by

Lomahokenna head of the Spider Clan, and Yukioma,
72

from the Fire Clan. Lololma's Bear Clan had traditionally

been a rival of the Spider Clan, but the rift followed a
73

division that had been established generations before. 74 75

72. **F.** NO CHANGE
   G. Lomahokenna head of the Spider Clan
   H. Lomahokenna, head of the Spider Clan
   J. Lomahokenna, head of the Spider Clan,

73. **A.** NO CHANGE
   B. so
   C. yet
   D. then

74. To explain how the Hopi in Oraibi were affected by the establishment of a reservation, the writer is considering adding the following sentence to the essay:

   Hopi children were exposed to outsiders, such as missionaries, who encouraged the children to attend school.

   If added, this sentence would most logically be placed after:
   F. sentence 3 in paragraph 1.
   G. sentence 5 in paragraph 1.
   H. sentence 2 in paragraph 2.
   J. sentence 4 in paragraph 2.

75. Suppose the writer had chosen to write a brief essay about a conflict between the American government and Native Americans. Would this essay successfully fulfill the writer's goal?
   A. Yes, because the essay explains why the Navajo and Hopi joined forces against the American government.
   B. Yes, because the essay describes how outside influences created tension among the Hopi, Navajo, and American settlers.
   C. No, because the essay presents the theories of how Oraibi has survived so long despite tribal wars.
   D. No, because the essay describes the disagreement within the Hopi tribe regarding how to handle the Navajo.

END OF TEST 1.
STOP! DO NOT TURN THE PAGE UNTIL TOLD TO DO SO.

MATHEMATICS TEST

60 Minutes—60 Questions

DIRECTIONS: After solving each problem, pick the correct answer from the five given and fill in the corresponding oval on your answer sheet. Solve as many problems as you can in the time allowed. Do not worry over problems that take too much time; skip them if necessary and return to them if you have time.

Calculator use is permitted on the test. Calculators can be used for any problem on the test, though calculators may be more harm than help for some questions.

Note: Unless otherwise stated on the test, you should assume that:

1. Figures accompanying questions are not drawn to scale.
2. Geometric figures exist in a plane.
3. When given in a question, "line" refers to a straight line.
4. When given in a question, "average" refers to the arithmetic mean.

---

1. Marta is riding the Whirly-Gig, a carnival ride that spins in clockwise circles. When the ride began, Marta was facing south. Five seconds later, the ride had rotated 90° and she was facing west. At this rate, how many degrees will the Whirly-Gig rotate in 15 seconds?
   A. 90°
   B. 180°
   C. 210°
   D. 270°
   E. 360°

2. What is the value of the expression $m \times (m-3)^3$ for $m = 5$?
   F. 8
   G. 15
   H. 20
   J. 40
   K. 60

3. At the first meeting of a bird watcher's organization, the education director gave a talk on 4 different bird species. At each meeting after the first, the director discussed exactly 6 different species. In the first 15 meetings, how many birds did the director discuss?
   A. 60
   B. 84
   C. 88
   D. 90
   E. 94

DO YOUR FIGURING HERE.

4. In the figure below, if $c = 75$, then $d = ?$

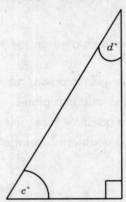

DO YOUR FIGURING HERE.

F. 5
G. 15
H. 35
J. 80
K. 105

5. Reina has earned the following scores on five 100-point history tests: 94, 81, 88, 94 and 93. She wants her average test grade to be 90. What score must Reina earn on the sixth and final test to earn this average?
A. 89
B. 90
C. 93
D. 94
E. Reina cannot earn an average of 90.

6. In t hours, a jet fighter plane can travel 2,450 miles. Which of the following expresses r, the rate of the airplane, in miles per hour?

F. $\dfrac{t}{2,450+t}$

G. $2,450t$

H. $\dfrac{2,450}{t}$

J. $2,450t - 1$

K. $t + 2,450$

GO ON TO THE NEXT PAGE.

7. B and C represent points on the number line, m, shown below. If $8 < B < C$, which of the following must also be true?

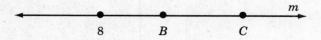

8   B   C

A. $C < 8$
B. $B < 9$
C. $B + C > 8$
D. $B = C + 1$
E. $B = C - 1$

8. An architect designs a museum in the shape of the diagram shown below. Each of the dimensions is given in feet. If all of the walls meet at right angles, what is the area, in square feet, of the museum?

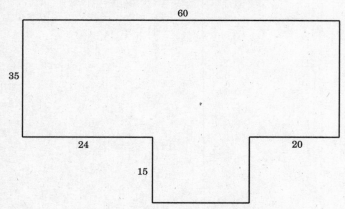

F. 240
G. 2,100
H. 2,340
J. 2,500
K. 3,000

9. Lowry College has a current enrollment of 500 students. If the college's enrollment increases by 35% next year, what will be the total number of students enrolled?

A. 175
B. 250
C. 325
D. 675
E. 790

10. Which of the following is equivalent to $4a(a^2b + 4ab^2)$?

F. $16a^4b^4$
G. $20a^5 + b^3$
H. $4a^3b + 8a^2b^2$
J. $4a^2b + 16a^2b^2$
K. $4a^3b + 16a^2b^2$

11. Harold's grandfather owns a boat that is 45 feet long. Harold wants to build a model that is $\frac{1}{30}$ the length of his grandfather's boat. How long should Harold's model boat be, in feet?

    A. $1\frac{1}{2}$

    B. $1\frac{17}{30}$

    C. $1\frac{3}{4}$

    D. $2\frac{1}{30}$

    E. $2\frac{1}{10}$

DO YOUR FIGURING HERE.

12. Milo is creating a rectangular quilt from fabric squares. The quilt will measure 36 inches long by 42 inches wide, and each quilting square is 2 inches long by 2 inches wide. What is the minimum number of fabric squares that Milo needs for the quilt?

    F. 39
    G. 156
    H. 244
    J. 378
    K. 1,512

13. Of the 900 students at a college, 360 are liberal arts majors. If one of the students is randomly selected from the college, what is the probability that the person selected will NOT be a liberal arts major?

    A. $\frac{1}{8}$

    B. $\frac{2}{5}$

    C. $\frac{3}{7}$

    D. $\frac{3}{5}$

    E. $\frac{2}{3}$

GO ON TO THE NEXT PAGE.

14. The chart below shows the favorite books of English students at Roosevelt High School.

Book Title	Grade level	Number of Students
The Great Gatsby	Sophomore Junior Senior	28 39 31
Of Mice and Men	Sophomore Junior Senior	44 30 46
Farewell to Arms	Sophomore Junior Senior	56 32 47
Catcher in the Rye	Sophomore Junior Senior	33 40 38

What is the average number of students per grade level whose favorite book is *A Farewell to Arms*?
F. 32
G. 33
H. 45
J. 47
K. 52

15. Which of the following represents the unique prime factors of 964?
A. 2, 3, 7
B. 2, 241
C. 2, 7, 121
D. 2, 5, 41
E. 3, 49, 57

16. If $3\frac{5}{6} = a + 2\frac{1}{3}$, then $a = $?

F. $1\frac{1}{2}$

G. $1\frac{2}{3}$

H. $2\frac{3}{4}$

J. $5\frac{2}{6}$

K. $6\frac{1}{6}$

17. In the figure below, lines r and s are parallel. Transversals t and u intersect to form an angle of measure $a°$, and 2 other angle measures are 110° and 70°. What is the value of a?

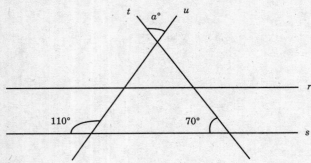

DO YOUR FIGURING HERE.

A. 40°
B. 55°
C. 70°
D. 80°
E. 88°

18. Which of the following is NOT a factor of $a^2 - 5$?

F. $a - \sqrt{5}$

G. $a + \sqrt{5}$

H. 25

J. $a^2 - 5$

K. 1

19. A pizza is $\frac{3}{16}$ pepperoni, $\frac{3}{8}$ mushroom, and $\frac{1}{4}$ olive. The remainder of the pizza is onion. What fraction of the pizza is onion?

A. $\frac{1}{8}$

B. $\frac{3}{16}$

C. $\frac{1}{4}$

D. $\frac{3}{8}$

E. $\frac{5}{16}$

20. If $x = -4$, and $y = 1$, what is the value of a^{x-y}?

F. -5

G. $5a$

H. $-4a - 1$

J. $\frac{1}{a^5}$

K. $-3a$

21. At an amusement park, game winners can trade tickets for prizes. All of the prizes are equal in value. The tickets can be redeemed only as follows: 50 tickets for 1 prize, 175 tickets for 5 prizes, or 325 tickets for 10 prizes. If Esther wishes to redeem her tickets for exactly 24 prizes, what is the minimum number of tickets she must trade in?

    A. 650
    B. 825
    C. 850
    D. 1,075
    E. 1,400

22. What is the value of $f(3)$ if $f(x) = 2x + 4$?

    F. 10
    G. 12
    H. 14
    J. 23
    K. 26

23. The number of minutes of talk time provided by a telephone card, m, varies directly with the price, p, of the card. If a card costing $50.00 provides 600 minutes of talk time, what price will be charged for a card that provides 840 minutes of talk time?

    A. $12
    B. $48
    C. $60
    D. $70
    E. $84

24. The staff at an animal shelter plans to select 1 cat and 1 dog to photograph for their annual fundraising poster. There are 60 cats and 43 dogs at the shelter. How many different combinations of 1 cat and 1 dog are possible?

    F. 78
    G. 103
    H. 250
    J. 2,580
    K. 4,029

25. In the standard (x, y) coordinate plane, what is the slope of the line joining the points $(2, 4)$ and $(3, 7)$?

    A. $\dfrac{1}{3}$
    B. $\dfrac{11}{5}$
    C. 3
    D. 5
    E. $7\dfrac{1}{2}$

DO YOUR FIGURING HERE.

26. In the figure below, $\overline{MN} = \overline{NO}$ and $\overline{OP} = 4$. What is the length of $\overline{MP}$?

A. 8
B. 10
C. 12
D. 16
E. Cannot be determined from the given information

27. Mark is visiting the World's Largest Sandbox. The informational sign next to the sandbox says that it holds 12,000 cubic feet of sand. If the sand is spread evenly throughout the sandbox depicted below, about how many feet deep would the layer of sand be?

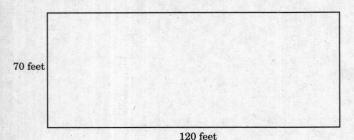

A. Less than 1
B. Between 1 and 1.5
C. Between 1.5 and 2
D. Between 2 and 2.5
E. Between 2.5 and 3

28. $(p^2 + 3p - 5) + (2p^2 - 3p + 5)$ is equivalent to:

F. $3p^2$
G. $3p^2 - 6p$
H. $3p^2 - 10$
J. $3p^2 - 6p^2 - 10$
K. $3p^2 + 6p^2 - 10$

DO YOUR FIGURING HERE.

GO ON TO THE NEXT PAGE.

29. Figure *PQRST* shown below is a regular pentagon, with sides of equal length and congruent interior angles. If $\overline{CR}$ bisects $\angle QRS$, what is the measure of a?

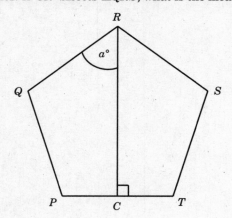

DO YOUR FIGURING HERE.

A. 54°
B. 108°
C. 172°
D. 204°
E. 540°

30. 175 is $\frac{7}{18}$ of what number?

F. 30
G. 68
H. 74
J. 225
K. 450

31. In the standard (x, y) coordinate plane, line $\overline{AB}$ passes through points $A(1, 11)$ and $B(-2, -10)$. What is the *y*-intercept of $\overline{AB}$?

A. $(0, 12)$
B. $\left(0, \frac{32}{3}\right)$
C. $(0, 7)$
D. $\left(0, \frac{21}{4}\right)$
E. $(0, 4)$

32. For all pairs of real numbers a and b, if $a = 8b - 3$, then $b = ?$

F. $\frac{a}{3} + 8$

G. $\frac{a}{8} + 3$

H. $\frac{a + 3}{8}$

J. $\frac{a + 8}{3}$

K. $8a - 3$

GO ON TO THE NEXT PAGE. • 379

33. Wendy plans to travel from Plantville to Wright City. To get to Wright City, she must drive north from Plantville to Brighton 220 miles. Then, at Brighton, she must drive east for 160 miles to Wright City. If Wendy could drive directly from Plantville to Wright City along a single straight road, what would be the shortest possible length of the trip?

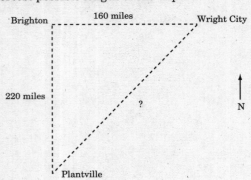

A. $\sqrt{74,000}$
B. 300
C. $\sqrt{90,600}$
D. 380
E. 420

34. In the right triangle shown below, if $\sin \theta = \dfrac{3}{12}$, then $\cos \theta = ?$

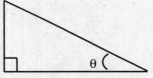

F. $\dfrac{4}{3}$

G. $2\sqrt{3}$

H. $3\sqrt{5}$

J. $\dfrac{\sqrt{13}}{12}$

K. $\dfrac{\sqrt{15}}{4}$

35. In the x, y coordinate plane, what is the slope of the line that is parallel to the line whose equation is given by $2x + 4y = 24$?

A. 2

B. $\dfrac{1}{2}$

C. 0

D. $-\dfrac{1}{2}$

E. -4

DO YOUR FIGURING HERE.

36. The solution set of $\sqrt{a+2} \geq 3$ is the set of all real numbers a such that:

F. $a \geq 2$
G. $a \geq 5$
H. $a \geq 7$
J. $a \geq 13$
K. $a \geq 15$

DO YOUR FIGURING HERE.

37. In the coordinate plane, the graph of $y = x^2 - 144$ crosses the x-axis at which of the following points?

A. 9 and −16
B. 12 and −12
C. 12 and −2
D. 2 and −2
E. 16 and −9

38. A farmer wants to know how much grain a particular grain silo can hold. The interior radius of the silo is 6 feet. The height of the silo is 30 feet. Which of the following is closest to the grain silo's volume, in cubic feet?

F. 960
G. 1,800
H. 2,450
J. 2,800
K. 3,400

39. The table below shows the number of seats that Lowell Theater sold for the first 9 nights of its new play.

Night	1	2	3	4	5	6	7	8	9
Seats	293	267	293	245	222	208	276	289	243

Which night represents the median number of seats sold in the first 9 nights?

A. 2
B. 4
C. 6
D. 7
E. 9

40. $\left(\dfrac{3}{4}a + b\right)^2 = ?$

F. $\dfrac{9}{16}a^2 - b^2$

G. $\dfrac{3}{4}a^2 + ab + b^2$

H. $\dfrac{9}{16}a^2 + \dfrac{6}{4}ab + b^2$

J. $a^2 + b^2$

K. $a^2 + ab + b^2$

Practice Test 4

41. If $0 \leq \theta \leq 90$ and $\sin^2 \theta + \cos^2 \theta = 1$, what is $\cos \theta$ if $\sin \theta = \frac{3}{4}$?

A. $4\sqrt{7}$

B. $4\sqrt{3}$

C. 2

D. $\frac{\sqrt{7}}{4}$

E. $\sqrt{3}$

42. What is the matrix product $\begin{bmatrix} 3 & 0 & 7 \end{bmatrix} \begin{bmatrix} x \\ 7 \\ 5x \end{bmatrix}$?

F. $[0]$

G. $\begin{bmatrix} 3x & 0 & 7x \end{bmatrix}$

H. $\begin{bmatrix} 3x & 0 & 7x \\ 21 & 0 & 49 \\ 15x & 0 & 35x \end{bmatrix}$

J. $\begin{bmatrix} 3x & 21 & 15x \end{bmatrix}$

K. $\begin{bmatrix} 3x & 21 & 15x \\ 0 & 0 & 0 \\ 7x & 49 & 35x \end{bmatrix}$

43. The point $(-4, 1)$ is a point on a line shown in the standard coordinate plane below. Which of the following is another point on the line through the point $(-4, 1)$ with a slope of -6?

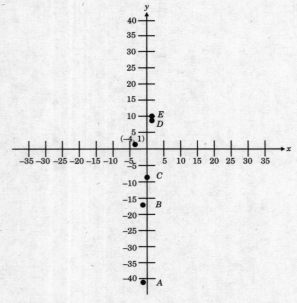

A. $(-2, -42)$

B. $(-1, -17)$

C. $(0, -8)$

D. $(1, 8)$

E. $(2, 10)$

DO YOUR FIGURING HERE.

GO ON TO THE NEXT PAGE.

44. Two squares have areas in a ratio of 9:16. Which of the following could be the lengths of the sides of the two squares?

F. 2:8
G. 3:6
H. 3:9
J. 6:12
K. 9:12

45. Which of the following is the midpoint of the line segment joining (8, 4) and (−2, 2)?

A. (6, 2)
B. (10, 2)
C. (6, 6)
D. (3, 3)
E. (5, 3)

46. What is the value of u for which the lines $y = ux + \dfrac{1}{2}$ and $y = x + 4$ intersect at the point (2, 6) in the standard coordinate plane?

F. $\dfrac{7}{6}$

G. 2

H. $\dfrac{9}{4}$

J. $\dfrac{11}{4}$

K. 3

47. In triangle ABC below, if $\overline{AC}$ measures $10\sqrt{3}$ and $\overline{BD}$ bisects $\overline{AC}$, what is the measure of $\angle DAB$?

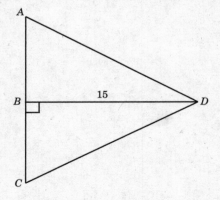

A. $2\sqrt{2}$
B. 5
C. $5\sqrt{3}$
D. 7
E. 10

DO YOUR FIGURING HERE.

48. The number 16 has how many positive integer factors?
    F. 5
    G. 6
    H. 8
    J. 10
    K. 11

DO YOUR FIGURING HERE.

49. In the table shown below, the top row of numbers represent values of x, and the bottom row represents values of y. For all values $x < 10$, the sum of the y values in the first x columns is equal to $x + 7$. For all values $x \geq 10$, the sum of the values in the first x columns is equal to $x + 9$. What is the y value for the column $x = 12$?

x	1	2	3	4	5	6
y	8	1	1	1	1	1

    A. 0
    B. 1
    C. 2
    D. 3
    E. 21

50. Marlon practices riding his unicycle in a parking lot that is 40π feet long. He rides his unicycle the length of the lot exactly 3 times. How many revolutions does his unicycle wheel make if the diameter of the wheel is 1.5 feet?
    F. 26.7
    G. 80
    H. 105π
    J. 160
    K. 376.8

51. For all integers a and b such that $a < 1 < b$, which of the following must be true?
    A. $a \div b$ is negative
    B. $a \times b$ is positive
    C. $b - a > a - b$
    D. $a - b$ is odd
    E. $a^2 + b^2$ is even

52. If $\cos \theta = -\dfrac{1}{6}$ and $\leq \theta \leq \dfrac{4}{3}$, then $\sin \theta = ?$

    F. $\pm\dfrac{\sqrt{35}}{6}$

    G. -1

    H. $\dfrac{\sqrt{35}}{6}$

    J. 5

    K. $\dfrac{2\sqrt{3}}{6}$

GO ON TO THE NEXT PAGE.

53. In $\triangle XYZ$ show below, if $r = 50°$ and $\overline{XY} = 10$ centimeters, which of the following expressions could be used to calculate the length, in centimeters, of $\overline{YZ}$?

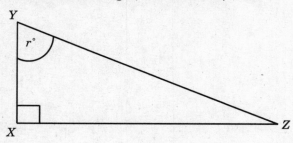

A. $\dfrac{10}{\tan 40°}$

B. $10 \cos 40°$

C. $10 \cos 50°$

D. $\dfrac{10}{\cos 40°}$

E. $\dfrac{10}{\cos 50°}$

54. Which of the following graphs represents $2|x| \geq 6$?

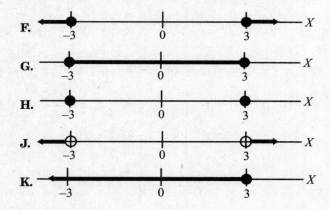

55. If $g(x) = \sqrt{x+2}$, then $g(x+s) = ?$

A. $\sqrt{x+s+2}$

B. $\sqrt{x+2}+s$

C. $x+2+s$

D. x^2+s

E. $\sqrt{s+2}+x$

Practice Test 4

Practice Test 4

56. Which of the following quadratic equations has solutions $x = 4a$ and $x = -7b$?

   F. $x^2 + x(7b + 4a) - 28ab = 0$
   G. $x^2 + x(4a - 7b) + 28ab = 0$
   H. $x^2 - 28ab = 0$
   J. $x^2 - x(4a - 7b) + 28ab = 0$
   K. $x^2 + x(7b - 4a) - 28ab = 0$

57. In the standard (x, y) coordinate plane, the vertices of the square below have coordinates $(0, 0)$, $(4, 0)$, $(4, 4)$, and $(0, 4)$. Which of the following equations represents the equation of the circle inscribed in the square?

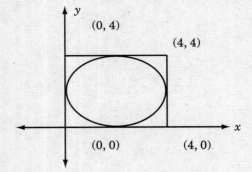

   A. $(x - 2)^2 + (y - 2)^2 = 2$
   B. $(x + 2)^2 - (y + 2)^2 = 2$
   C. $(x - 4)^2 + (y - 4)^2 = 16$
   D. $(x - 2)^2 + (y - 2)^2 = 4$
   E. $(x + 4)^2 - (x + 4)^2 = 16$

GO ON TO THE NEXT PAGE.

58. Points F, G, H, and K are points located on the unit circle shown below. The center is labeled N. Measuring $\angle GNK$ in the direction of the arrow shown reveals a measure of $a°$. Likewise, measuring $\angle GNH$ in the direction of the arrow shown reveals a measure of $b°$. Both $a°$ and $b°$ are negative. Lengths of arc FG and arc HK are congruent. Based on the direction of the arrow shown, what is the measure of $\angle GNF$?

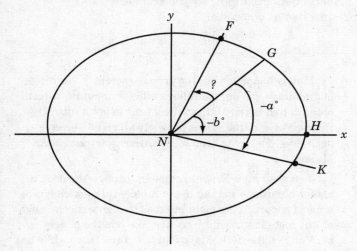

DO YOUR FIGURING HERE.

F. $b°$

G. $b° + a°$

H. $-b° + a°$

J. $b° - a°$

K. $a°$

59. If $r = 3z - 4$ and $s = 7 - z$, which of the following expresses s in terms of r?

A. $s = 7 - 12r$

B. $s = \dfrac{25 - r}{3}$

C. $s = 3 - r$

D. $s = 5 - r$

E. $s = \dfrac{17 - r}{3}$

60. What is the real value of y in the equation $\log_3 21 - \log_3 7 = \log_6 y$?

F. 0

G. 7

H. 14

J. 126

K. 147

END OF TEST 2.
STOP! DO NOT TURN THE PAGE UNTIL TOLD TO DO SO.
DO NOT RETURN TO THE PREVIOUS TEST.

READING TEST

35 Minutes—40 Questions

DIRECTIONS: On this test, you will have 35 minutes to read four passages and answer 40 questions (ten questions on each passage). Each set of ten questions appears directly after the relevant passage. You should select the answer choice that best answers the question. There is no time limit for work on the individual passages, so you can move freely between the passages and refer to each as often as you'd like.

Passage I

PROSE FICTION: This passage is adapted from a short story titled "In Case of Fire" by Gordon Randall Garrett.

In his office apartment, Bertrand Malloy leafed casually through the files of the four new men who had been assigned to him. They were typical of the kind of men who were sent to him, he thought. Which meant, as usual, 5 that they were atypical.

Take this first one, for instance. Looking at his psychological analysis, Malloy could see that the man wasn't technically insane; he could be as lucid as the next man most of the time. But he was overly suspicious that 10 every man's hand was turned against him.

Number two suffered from some sort of emotional block that left him continually struggling with one dilemma or another. He was psychologically incapable of making a decision if he were faced with two or more possible 15 alternatives of any major importance.

Before he could get to number three, Malloy sighed and pushed the files away from him. No two people were alike, and yet there sometimes seemed to be an eternal sameness about everyone.

20 It was Bertrand Malloy's job to keep the production output high for the war effort. The job would have been a cinch in the right circumstances; a staff of top-rate men could have handled it without half trying. But Malloy didn't have top-rate men. They couldn't be spared from 25 work that required their total capacity. So Malloy was stuck with the others—not the worst ones, of course; but all the same, not top-rate.

The mental disabilities were harder to deal with than the physical handicaps, but not totally impossible. Malloy 30 didn't like to stop at merely thwarting mental quirks; he liked to find places where a person's mental quirks were *useful*. His assistant Miss Drayson was a case in point. She was uncommunicative. She liked to gather in information, but she found it difficult to give it up once it was in her 35 possession.

Malloy had made her his private secretary. Nothing— but *nothing*—got out of Malloy's office without his direct order. It had taken Malloy a long time to get it into Miss Drayson's head that it was perfectly all right—even 40 desirable—for her to keep secrets from everyone except Malloy.

Just then Miss Drayson came in through the door, a rather handsome woman in her middle thirties, clutching a file of papers in her right hand as though someone might 45 at any instant snatch it from her. She laid the papers carefully on the desk. Malloy let her stand there while he picked up the file. She wanted to know what his reaction was going to be; it didn't matter because no one would ever find out from her what he had done unless she was ordered 50 to tell someone.

He read the first paragraph, and his eyes widened involuntarily.

"Armistice," he said in a low whisper. "There's a chance that the war may be over."

55 "Yes, sir," said Miss Drayson in a hushed voice.

Malloy read the whole thing through, fighting to keep his emotions in check. Miss Drayson stood there calmly, her face a mask; her emotions were a secret.

Finally, Malloy looked up. "I'll let you know as soon as 60 I reach a decision, Miss Drayson. I think I hardly need say that no news of this is to leave this office."

"Of course not, sir."

There was going to be an armistice conference to finalize the details of the peace settlement. Each side 65 had to get a delegation to the conference within the three-day limit or lose what might be a vital point in the negotiations. And that was where Bertrand Malloy came in: He had been appointed as a representative to the conference. He looked up at the ceiling again. "What *can* I 70 do?" he said softly.

On the second day after the arrival of the news about the armistice, Malloy made his decision. He flipped on his intercom and said: "Miss Drayson, get hold of Kylen Braynek. I want to see him immediately."

75 "Yes, sir," Miss Drayson replied. Braynek arrived in a flash.

Kylen Braynek was a smallish man with mouse-brown hair that lay flat against his skull, and hard, penetrating, dark eyes that were shadowed by heavy, protruding brows.
80 Malloy asked him to sit down and went through the explanation of the peace conference.

"Naturally, they'll be trying to trick you every step of the way," Malloy went on. "They're shrewd and underhanded; we'll simply have to be more shrewd and
85 more underhanded. Your job will be to find the loopholes they're laying out for themselves and plug them. Don't antagonize them, but don't baby them, either."

"They won't get anything by me, Mr. Malloy."

1. Which of the following best describes the relationship between Miss Drayson and Mr. Malloy?

  A. Mr. Malloy provides Miss Drayson a job because he needs to monitor her behavior.

  B. Miss Drayson hides her thoughts and emotions from everyone except Mr. Malloy.

  C. Mr. Malloy employs Miss Drayson because she is able to maintain confidentiality.

  D. Miss Drayson practices her communication skills by working with Mr. Malloy.

2. The passage establishes that most of the people who work for Mr. Malloy have which of the following traits?

  F. Physical strengths that allow them to perform extraordinary feats

  G. Intellectual skills that make it difficult for them to work in typical jobs

  H. Physical disabilities that prevent them from being employed elsewhere

  J. Psychological difficulties that prevent them from working in normal jobs

3. It can most be reasonably inferred from Mr. Malloy's reaction to the armistice news that he feels:

  A. frightened about what he needs to do.

  B. indifferent about the peace settlement.

  C. excited that the war may soon be over.

  D. confused about the decision he must make.

4. Which of the following best describes the way the first paragraph (lines 1–5) functions in the passage?

  F. It illustrates that Mr. Malloy has a job that requires him to be clever and secretive.

  G. It reveals that Mr. Malloy has a job that requires him to work with unusual people.

  H. It suggests that Mr. Malloy feels uneasy about most of the people sent to work for him.

  J. It reveals that Mr. Malloy thinks his job is too difficult because of the staff he receives.

5. It can logically be inferred from the passage that Mr. Malloy sends Kylen Braynek to the conference because:

  A. Mr. Malloy is unsure of his own ability to succeed at the conference.

  B. Mr. Malloy does not know what to do at the conference.

  C. Kylen Braynek has had experience with peace agreements.

  D. Kylen Braynek feels confident about his speaking abilities.

6. It can reasonably be inferred from the conversation between Mr. Malloy and Kylen Braynek that Mr. Malloy:

  F. anticipates the conference to go smoothly.

  G. worries that the opposition will outwit them.

  H. has studied the opposition and their tactics.

  J. has negotiated many peace agreements.

7. According to the passage, what is the reason that Mr. Malloy does not employ top-rate men?

  A. Mr. Malloy prefers to hire average workers with good attitudes that want to be useful.

  B. They were needed by other divisions that required high levels of productivity.

  C. Mr. Malloy prefers to hire low-achievers whom he can encourage to be productive.

  D. They were needed at the armistice conference to facilitate agreements.

8. Which of the following best describes what Kylen Braynek is supposed to do at the conference?

  F. To monitor the opposition and prevent deception

  G. To anger the opposition and obstruct an agreement

  H. To assist the opposition and promote an agreement

  J. To provoke the opposition and discover inconsistencies

9. It can most reasonably be inferred from the passage that Miss Drayson was:

  A. pleased about the news regarding the peace agreement.

  B. unaware of the armistice until Mr. Malloy told her.

  C. often reprimanded for leaking secret information.

  D. aware of the peace agreement before Mr. Malloy.

10. As it is used in the passage, the word *thwarting* (line 30) most nearly means:

  F. supporting.

  G. promoting.

  H. changing.

  J. hindering.

Passage II

SOCIAL SCIENCE: This passage is adapted from an essay titled "Education in Individual Development" by Carol Frye Lassiter.

Mandatory school attendance was first established in the United States in the state of Massachusetts, with the passing of the compulsory attendance law in 1852. Six decades later, by 1918, all U.S. states had passed
5 similar laws. These laws have served to make education an institution in the United States, at least for children of a certain age. But the compulsory nature of school attendance does not offer much to clarify the purposes for which education should be provided to our young
10 people. This discussion has been left to the philosophers, politicians, and idealists of our age.

Indeed, overlapping views can be seen in the works of many noted public leaders, who argue that education ultimately serves the purpose of making an individual
15 a better citizen of society. Martin Luther King Jr. put it simply in his essay "The Purpose of Education," when he argued that education should serve the twin goals of intellect formation and societal development. "It seems to me that education has a two-fold function to perform in the
20 life of man and in society," King wrote, "the one is utility and the other is culture." King believed that the role of education was to help individuals become both intelligent and moral. He described "intelligence plus character" as the ultimate end that education should seek.

25 Philosopher John Dewey, writing years before King, agreed in principle that education should serve the purpose of making individuals upstanding members of society. He then emphasized that different cultures would achieve this end result in different ways. "The purpose
30 of education has always been to everyone, in essence, the same," Dewey argued in 1934. In brief, he explained, its goal was to help young people develop "in an orderly, sequential way" into individuals who could participate in society. Because of this reality, Dewey noted, different
35 countries would produce different educational programs designed to serve the goals of their particular cultures. "Any education," Dewey contended, "is . . . an outgrowth of the needs of the society in which it exists."

Eleanor Roosevelt also shared Dewey's and King's
40 sentiments, writing as Dewey's contemporary in the 1930s. In her "Good Citizenship: The Purpose of Education," she makes it clear that she supports a societally oriented perspective on education rather than the traditional view. Conventional wisdom was based, Roosevelt noted, on the
45 rather limited belief that education was designed to help students acquire knowledge, read books, and learn facts.

Her view, by contrast, supported the notion advocated by the Archbishop of New York that "the true purpose of education is to produce citizens." She would undoubtedly
50 have agreed with Dr. King that intelligence, defined in terms of knowledge of facts, by itself was not enough. As King pointed out, "the most dangerous criminal may be the man gifted with reason, but with no morals."

While the view of education as intricately connected
55 with citizenship does not deny the value of individuality, its focus on the larger societal outcome downplays the importance of the role of education as a tool for individual growth. This aspect of learning is key for the individual as a unique self, regardless of whether he or she upholds
60 the mores of a specific society. A more effective way to put this point would be to describe the role of education as not to teach people what to think, but to teach people *how* to think, and how to express their beliefs compellingly.

King himself touched on this idea when he mentioned
65 that education should help an individual to more efficiently achieve legitimate life goals. Roosevelt also argued that the study of academic subjects itself would lead individuals to develop prudent judgment in real-life situations. "The child taking Latin and mathematics," she wrote, "is also
70 learning invaluable lessons in citizenship." She noted that such studies required both concentration and accuracy—skills which, if developed, would help the individual deal with difficult situations later in life. In terms of character building, Roosevelt believed, the harder it was to learn a
75 subject, the greater would be the "sense of self-mastery and perseverance" that individuals would develop as a result.

Whether or not classes taught in school provide direct training for real-life decision-making, the education process can nonetheless teach the individual important
80 perceptual skills essential to later growth. These skills can serve to help students develop the tools, or building blocks, needed for creativity. This view has more empowering implications than an approach that focuses on the importance of education primarily for its citizenship value.

85 True education, the kind that develops the "character" which Dr. King spoke about, goes beyond emphasizing cultural participation and encourages human progress and innovation. Inevitably this progress will involve challenges to the ruling ideologies, producing paradigm shifts which
90 let the dominant factions know their "time" is at an end. The ultimate goal for teachers within such a person-centered system would be to assist their students—quite literally—in eventually making them obsolete. Only such a non-egoistic view of the instructor's role can hope to
95 cultivate the crowning achievement of effective education: to encourage individual and societal growth by enriching the self.

GO ON TO THE NEXT PAGE.

11. The passage indicates that King, Dewey, and Roosevelt are alike in that they all asserted that the goal of education should be to:

    A. encourage individuals to seek additional instruction and personal growth.
    B. promote values related to citizenship, sincerity, and cultural change.
    C. develop well-rounded citizens who are intellectual and ethical.
    D. motivate students to seek inner growth and spirituality.

12. It can most reasonably be inferred from the passage that the author believes that the purpose of education should be to develop:

    F. citizens who are educated in the beliefs and attitudes of their society.
    G. individuals who are well-educated enough to find meaningful employment.
    H. people who are well versed in Latin and mathematics
    J. moral individuals who are motivated to improve themselves and society.

13. The main function of the seventh paragraph (lines 77–84) in relation to the passage as a whole is to:

    A. contrast the author's beliefs about the purpose of education with those held by Roosevelt, King, and Dewey.
    B. shift focus from the beliefs held by Roosevelt, King, and Dewey about the purpose of education to the opinion of the author.
    C. redirect the passage toward a discussion of flaws in the current American education system.
    D. emphasize the passage's point that the purpose and value of education varies from culture to culture.

14. According to the first paragraph of the passage (lines 1–11), compulsory attendance laws:

    F. require children to begin school by at least first grade.
    G. have been enforced for over sixty years in the United States.
    H. clarify the goals of each state's education system.
    J. have been established in every state in the United States.

15. One of the main points that the author seeks to make in the passage is that society:

    A. requires an education system to reduce the dependency on teachers by inspiring individuals to be self-motivated.
    B. expects individuals to be educated, moral, and productive in order to maximize wealth and prosperity.
    C. depends on the intelligence, character, and creativity of its citizens in order to function at the highest level.
    D. relies on the education system to develop individuals who intellectually understand the needs of the community.

16. According to the passage, why did Dewey believe that the methods of educating young people should not be the same in every society?

    F. A culture determines the characteristics an individual needs to function in that society.
    G. Governments cannot comprehend the specific educational needs of different cultures.
    H. Individuals determine how they fit into society and the education they need to do so.
    J. Governments guide the cultural and educational needs of individuals in society.

17. It can most reasonably be inferred from the passage that the Archbishop of New York believed that the education system was:

    A. focusing its efforts on morality and traditional subjects.
    B. teaching factual information to students instead of values.
    C. teaching students how to be innovative and creative.
    D. focusing its efforts on job skills instead of thinking skills.

18. According to the passage, Roosevelt believed that students benefit from enrollment in difficult classes by learning how to:

    F. improve their social skills.
    G. manage their time wisely.
    H. deal with failure in life.
    J. handle tough obstacles.

19. It can most reasonably be inferred from the passage that the "traditional view" of education as mentioned in paragraph 4 (lines 39–53):

    A. shifted in the United States after the critical writings of Roosevelt and Dewey were published.
    B. is defended by King in his essay as the best way to promote an educated citizenry.
    C. continues to dominate the education system in most societies, including the United States.
    D. is supported by the author as the most beneficial way of educating individuals.

20. According to the fifth paragraph (lines 54–63), an important aspect of education is to:

    F. provide relevant information to people.
    G. teach individuals how to analyze and convey information.
    H. instill appropriate societal values on individuals.
    J. encourage the development of a social conscience.

Passage III

HUMANITIES: This passage is adapted from Elizabeth Haas's "Bequeathed Burdens and Limited Legacies: The Development of the Self in Toni Morrison's *Sula*."

In an interview recorded in Charles Ruas's "Conversations with American Writers," Toni Morrison expresses her convictions regarding the pervasive and continuing effects of child-parent relationships. She
5 believes that in many cases, lack of interest or outright cruelty shown by children's parents has a negative, irrevocable influence on their future development. Toni Morrison's novel *Sula* explores the ramifications of effective or detrimental relationships between parents
10 and their children, centering on mother-daughter relationships that she feels are the mainstay of the black community. Her examination of two close friends, Nel and Sula, and their relationships to and formations by their vastly dissimilar mothers, allows Morrison to probe each
15 woman's resulting lifestyle and the type of selfhood it grants her.

Early in the novel, Morrison describes Helene Wright (Nel's mother) and the circumstances surrounding her birth and childhood. She describes Helene's
20 Creole mother, a prostitute in New Orleans, as well as Helene's grandmother, who "rescues" Helene from this unwholesome atmosphere to bring her up in a more pious manner. Morrison relates, "The grandmother took Helene away from the soft lights and flowered carpets of the
25 Sundown House and raised her under the doleful eyes of a multicolored Virgin Mary, counseling her to be constantly on guard for any sign of her mother's wild blood." Helene's continual surveillance of her own daughter Nel for any signs of unruly behavior proves successful, for "the girl
30 became obedient and polite. Any enthusiasms that little Nel showed were calmed by the mother until she drove her daughter's imagination underground." These attempts to suppress her history shape Helene's existence, and eventually Nel's as well.

35 Morrison's interest in the socialization patterns within mother-daughter relationships permeates the novel and is the focus of a pivotal scene in which Helene and Nel take a train trip to New Orleans following the death of Helene's grandmother. When Nel and her
40 mother board the segregated train and walk through the section allocated for whites only, they are confronted by an irritated white conductor who is placated by words of apology and an unexpected smile from Helene. Nel is shocked at her first real glimpse of racism and the ability
45 of the white conductor to humiliate her mother. Morrison

relates, "If this tall, proud woman, this woman who was very particular about her friends, who slipped into church with unequaled elegance, who could quell a roustabout with a look, if she were really custard, then there was
50 a chance that Nel was too." The sense of fear connected with this incident, combined with her mother's repeated discouragement of Nel's expressions of individuality, solidifies Nel's acceptance of a narrowed life with limited options that her friend Sula finds impossible to embrace.

55 One of the few stands that Nel does make, however, is her decision to befriend Sula despite her mother's objections. The friendship between Sula and Nel develops as a comforting remedy for both girls' incessant loneliness. Whereas Nel's solitude developed as she "sat on the steps
60 of her back porch surrounded by the high silence of her mother's incredibly orderly house," Sula's isolation is the result of being "wedged into a household of throbbing disorder constantly awry with things, people, voices and the slamming of doors," where she is somehow lost in
65 the shuffle. While Nel's worldview is shaped by her strict upbringing, Sula's sense of self is a product of her mother's indifference. Sula's mother and her grandmother, Eva, are fond of men and delight in entertaining them. Eva challenges men intellectually—they visit her to argue
70 about politics or to play checkers. Her grandmother also takes in boarders, newlyweds, and homeless children, which adds to the general chaos of the household and diminishes Sula's importance in the family. Morrison examines Sula's lack of a strong, meaningful bond with
75 other members of her family, describing Sula as having "no center, no speck around which to grow."

Just as Nel's train trip with her mother marks a crucial step in the development of her sense of self, Sula's defining moment also occurs during her childhood, when she
80 overhears an ill-fated conversation in which her mother states, "I love Sula. I just don't like her." The attitudes exhibited by Sula's mother are quite different from the conservative views held by members of the community. Morrison explores the result of Sula's mother's actions,
85 noting, "outside the house, where children giggled about underwear, the message was different. So she watched her mother's face and the faces of the men when they opened the pantry door and made up her own mind." Far from the carefully monitored childhood that shaped Nel's
90 conventional beliefs, Sula's childhood was undirected and unsupervised, forcing her to make her own decisions and to draw her own conclusions about the choices available to her as a black woman in the 1920s and 1930s.

Practice Test 4

21. Which of the following statements best describes the structure of this passage?

    A. It consists mainly of a story about two friends of Toni Morrison who are strongly affected by the relationships they form with their mothers.

    B. It begins and ends with an analysis of the importance of parent-child bonding and the negative impact of poor family relationships.

    C. It compares and contrasts the childhood experiences of two fictional characters as they grow up in the South.

    D. It contains a personal anecdote from the author about the experiences of two of her friends as they struggled to bond with their mothers.

22. It can most reasonably be inferred from the passage that Toni Morrison believes:

    F. dysfunctional parent-child relationships impact young children and lead to generations of issues that cannot be overcome.

    G. healthy family relationships are essential to the transformation of young people into confident, productive adults.

    H. strained relationships between mothers and daughters are too often blamed for problems in black communities.

    J. children that are too closely supervised by their parents are unable to freely express themselves and gain self-esteem.

23. As it is used in paragraph 2 (line 22), the word *pious* most nearly means:

    A. structured.

    B. pleasant.

    C. healthy.

    D. moral.

24. According to the passage, which of the following issues best explains why Nel and Sula become friends?

    F. Loneliness and isolation

    G. Racism and segregation

    H. Abusive relationships

    J. Low self-esteem

25. It can most reasonably be inferred from the passage that Helene's grandmother:

    A. prevented Nel from being rebellious like Helene and Helene's mother.

    B. assisted Helene by raising Nel in a religious home free of harmful influences.

    C. changed the course of Nel's life by raising Helene in a religious environment.

    D. angered her own daughter by taking Helene away from a life of prostitution.

26. Based on the passage, which of the following pairs of words best describes Sula's mother?

    F. Strict and regimented

    G. Cruel and unwavering

    H. Uncaring and impulsive

    J. Intellectual and intolerant

27. The author develops the fourth paragraph (lines 55–76) mainly through:

    A. a detailed description of how Helene interferes with the budding friendship between Nel and Sula.

    B. an analysis of the psychological issues faced by Sula as a result of the uncaring atmosphere in which she is raised.

    C. an explanation of how Nel and Sula grow close to each other and help each other work through family issues.

    D. a comparison of the experiences of Nel and Sula as they struggle through difficulties associated with their families.

28. According to the passage, which of the following is most affected by the family experiences of both Nel and Sula?

    F. Goals and plans for the future

    G. Abilities to develop relationships

    H. Methods of dealing with racism

    J. Attitudes toward authority figures

29. It can reasonably be inferred from the passage that before the train incident described in the third paragraph (lines 35–54) Nel believed that:

    A. racism and segregation did not exist.

    B. her mother was strong and confident.

    C. she was different from her mother.

    D. she had few opportunities in her life.

30. The passage indicates that in her book *Sula*, Toni Morrison does which of the following?

    F. She explores the childhood experiences of both Nel and Sula.

    G. She primarily describes the relationship between Nel and Sula.

    H. She analyzes the family history of Sula, Nel, and their mothers.

    J. She traces the lives of Nel and Sula from childhood to adulthood.

Passage IV

NATURAL SCIENCE: This passage is adapted from an article titled "Untapped Bounty: Sampling the Seas to Survey Microbial Biodiversity" by Liza Gross (© 2007 by PLoS Biology).

Most of what we know about the biochemical diversity of microbes comes from the tiny fraction studied in lab investigations. Not until scientists discovered that they could use molecular sequences to identify species and
5 determine their evolutionary heritage, or phylogeny, did it begin to become apparent just how diverse microbes are. We now know that microbes are the most widely distributed organisms on earth, having adapted to environments as diverse as boiling sulfur pits and the
10 human gut. Accounting for half of the world's biomass, microbes provide essential services to the ecosystem by cycling the mineral nutrients that support life on earth. Marine microbes remove so much carbon dioxide from the atmosphere that some scientists see them as a potential
15 solution to global warming.

Yet even as scientists describe seemingly endless variations on the cosmopolitan microbial lifestyle, the concept of a bacterial species remains elusive. Some bacterial species (such as anthrax) appear to have little
20 genetic variation, while in others (such as *Escherichia coli*), individuals can have completely different sets of genes, challenging scientists to explain the observed diversity.

The emerging field of environmental genomics aims to capture the full measure of microbial diversity by trading
25 the lens of the microscope for the lens of *genomics*, which involves the study of genes. By recovering communities of microbial genes where they live, environmental genomics avoids the need to take cultures of uncooperative organisms. By linking microbial gene data to details such
30 as the pH, salinity, and water temperature of the collection sites, environmental genomics sheds light on the biological processes encoded in the genes.

The largest environmental genomics dataset collected so far comes from the *Sorcerer II* expedition, named after
35 a yacht that was transformed into a marine research vessel by researcher J. Craig Venter. In a pilot study of the Sargasso Sea, Venter and his team identified 1.2 million genes and inferred the presence of at least 1,800 bacterial species. But the diversity of the data imposed
40 new challenges on existing genome assembly methods and other analysis techniques. The researchers next designed the *Sorcerer II* Global Ocean Sampling (GOS) expedition to see if collecting more samples would improve their assembly and lead to a better estimate of the number and
45 diversity of microbial genes in the oceans.

Now, in three new studies, Venter's team has combined the expedition's latest bounty with the data from the Sargasso Sea pilot study. The result is a geographically diverse environmental genomic dataset of 6.3 billion base
50 pairs—twice the size of the human genome. In the first study, researchers Rusch and Halpern et al. attempt to describe the immense amount of microbial diversity in the seas and to determine how—or if—that diversity is structured and what might be shaping that structure.
55 In the second study, Shibu Yooseph et al. examine the millions of proteins in the GOS sequences to see if we're close to discovering all the proteins in nature. In the third study, Kannan and Manning et al. classify thousands of kinases (enzymes) into 20 distinct families, revealing their
60 structural and functional diversity.

The *Sorcerer II* expedition was inspired by the British *Challenger* expedition (1872–1876), a pioneering oceanography research project that discovered nearly 5,000 new marine species. Its gun stations replaced
65 with research stations, the *Challenger* circumnavigated the oceans, stopping every 320 kilometers to recover specimens from bottom, intermediate, and surface depths of the ocean. At each stop, the crew recorded the location of the ship, the process used to extract the sample, the
70 depth of the sample, and several observations related to water and atmospheric conditions. The *Sorcerer II* followed a sampling schedule similar to that of the *Challenger*, traveling nearly 9,000 kilometers to collect samples of microbial marine life and record the water's location,
75 depth, pH, salinity, and temperature.

The *Sorcerer II* crew collected samples from surface waters of diverse, mostly marine aquatic environments. The samples were collected between August 2003 and May 2004 during a six-leg journey that followed a path
80 from northeastern Canada to the South Pacific Gyre. Venter's crew collected microbial samples by pumping 200 liters of surface seawater through a series of increasingly fine filters. The samples were then labeled, frozen, and sent back to the lab of the J. Craig Venter Institute in
85 Maryland.

Altogether, the *Sorcerer II* studies reveal the power of environmental genomics to capture the true measure of microbial diversity by uncovering genomic differences that would not have been apparent using traditional
90 approaches. The breadth of this newly revealed diversity may come as a surprise to even inveterate microbe hunters.

31. It can most reasonably be inferred from the passage that prior to environmental genomics, studying microbes involved:

A. using microscopes to analyze diversity within the natural environment of the microbes.

B. analyzing small sample sizes with limited information about the living conditions of the microbes.

C. assessing changes in the environment of the microbes to evaluate variations within the organisms.

D. collecting large samples from the ocean and storing them for long-term microbial studies.

32. With which of the following statements would the author most likely agree?

F. Collecting samples of oceanic microbes provides scientists with the opportunity to better understand the function of microbes in the world.

G. The field of environmental genomics holds the potential to reverse the false hypotheses made through traditional scientific methodology.

H. Gathering microbial gene data from the world's oceans will provide scientific support to the theory of global warming.

J. Studies of the Sargasso Sea imply that the majority of the world's proteins have been detected and categorized.

33. According to the passage, environmental genomics may provide more accurate information to scientists than other methods by:

A. allowing the opportunity to analyze communities of microbial genes in new environments.

B. altering the water and air temperatures of microbial genes by freezing group samples from the ocean.

C. assessing the function of oceanic microbial genes as they acclimate to laboratory conditions.

D. providing the chance to study groups of microbial genes in their normal living conditions.

34. The passage indicates that an important function of land and marine microbes is to:

F. invade other organisms and spread disease.

G. serve as a potential solution to global warming.

H. transfer nutrients throughout the natural world.

J. reproduce rapidly and freely exchange genes.

35. The word *elusive* in paragraph 2 (line 18) most nearly means:

A. skillful at avoiding capture.

B. based on a deception.

C. difficult to define.

D. possible to touch.

36. It can most reasonably be inferred from the passage that Venter's initial study of the Sargasso Sea was:

F. successful because of the discovery of numerous new genes and bacterial species.

G. problematic because of insufficient analysis methods and inadequate samples.

H. beneficial because of improved assembly methods and estimation techniques.

J. challenging because of imprecise assessments of the water's depth, pH, and salinity.

37. According to the passage, all of the following could possibly be learned through environmental genomics EXCEPT:

A. The number of base pairs in the human genome

B. The evolutionary relationships between species

C. The genetic coding of oceanic microorganisms

D. The structural and functional range of microbes

38. One of the main points of the sixth paragraph (lines 61–75) is that:

F. The *Challenger* expedition was the first one to study microbial life in the Sargasso Sea.

G. The *Sorcerer II* followed the route of the *Challenger* in order to assess oceanic microbial changes.

H. Venter and his crew collected thousands of water samples in order to determine changes in the global climate.

J. Venter is not the first person to investigate the activity of microbes in the world's oceans.

39. According to the passage, the significant difference between anthrax and *Escherichia coli* is that only one:

A. is a discernible viral species.

B. has limited genetic deviations.

C. is an organism living in the sea.

D. has emerging microbial genes.

40. According to information in the fifth paragraph (lines 46–60), Venter is using his collection of genomic data to study which of the following?

I. How enzymes are structured

II. How proteins are classified

III. What affects the structure of microbes

F. I only

G. III only

H. I and II only

J. I and III only

END OF TEST 3.
STOP! DO NOT TURN THE PAGE UNTIL TOLD TO DO SO. DO NOT RETURN TO A PREVIOUS TEST.

SCIENCE TEST

35 Minutes—40 Questions

DIRECTIONS: This test contains seven passages, each accompanied by several questions. You should select the answer choice that best answers each question. Within the total allotted time for the Subject Test, you may spend as much time as you wish on each individual passage. Calculator use is not permitted.

Passage I

Citation: Bruzgul J, Long W, Hadly E (2005). Temporal response of the tiger salamander (*Ambystoma tigrinum*) to 3,000 years of climactic variation. BMC *Ecology* 5: 7.

Amphibians are sensitive indicators of environmental conditions and show measurable responses to changes in precipitation and temperature. This study analyzes a 3,000-year fossil record of the tiger salamander (*Ambystoma tigrinum*), a species that is able to choose different lifestyles in response to different environmental conditions. Many tiger salamanders are *paedomorphic*, which means that they may undergo an aquatic (water-dwelling) larval stage and then metamorphose into terrestrial (land-dwelling) adults. Tiger salamanders' body sizes also vary in response to environmental conditions. Researchers divided the 3,000-year fossil record into six intervals. Interval C is the Medieval Warm Period (MWP), a climactic anomaly when the salamanders' environment was unusually warm and dry.

Figure 1 shows the tiger salamanders' body size index for each of the six time intervals (E is the earliest, and A is the most recent). The dark bars represent paedomorphic adults, and the light bars represent terrestrial adults.

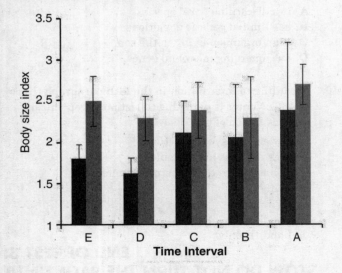

Figure 1

Figure 2 depicts the percentage of paedomorphic tiger salamanders in each time interval.

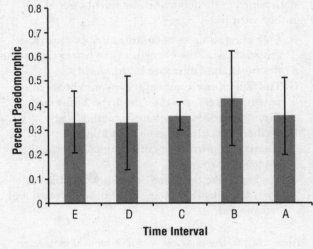

Figure 2

GO ON TO THE NEXT PAGE.

1. According to Figure 1, during which two time intervals did terrestrial tiger salamanders have the greatest body size index?
   A. Interval A and Interval C
   B. Interval A and Interval E
   C. Interval D and Interval E
   D. Interval B and Interval D

2. According to Figure 2, what percentage of the tiger salamander population was paedomorphic during the Medieval Warm Period?
   F. Slightly less than 0.2
   G. Slightly less than 0.4
   H. Slightly less than 0.5
   J. Slightly less than 0.6

3. According to Figures 1 and 2, what percentage of the tiger salamander population had a body size index of 1.5 during Interval D?
   A. Slightly greater than 0.6
   B. Slightly greater than 0.4
   C. Slightly greater than 0.3
   D. Slightly greater than 0.2

4. The size of paedomorphic adults in a tiger salamander population depends on the health of the pond system. In other words, paedomorphic tiger salamanders thrive when ponds are clean and plentiful. According to the data in Figure 1, during which time interval was the pond system the least healthy?
   F. Interval A
   G. Interval B
   H. Interval C
   J. Interval D

5. Which of the following hypotheses is most strongly supported by the data in Figure 2?
   A. The percentage of paedomorphic individuals in the total tiger salamander population varies little from one time interval to the next.
   B. The percentage of paedomorphic individuals in the total tiger salamander population varies greatly from one time interval to the next.
   C. The body size index of terrestrial tiger salamanders is always greater than the body size index of paedomorphic tiger salamanders.
   D. The percentage of paedomorphic individuals in the total tiger salamander population increased most significantly during the Medieval Warm Period.

Practice Test 4

Passage II

Citation: Tommerdahl M, Tannan V, Zachek M, Holden J, Favorov O (2007). Effects of stimulus-driven synchronization on sensory perception. *Behavioral and Brain Functions* 3: 61.

The following experiments attempt to assess human beings' temporal order judgment (TOJ) and temporal discrimination thresholds (TDT). TOJ is a measure obtained from determining the minimal inter-stimulus interval (the time between the two stimuli) necessary for each subject to detect the order in which the stimuli were delivered. A subject's TDT is his or her ability to detect the presence of multiple stimuli.

Three different conditions of TOJ and TDT assessment were performed. In the first condition (the control), there was no simultaneous stimulation. In the second and third conditions, a 25 Hz or a 200 Hz simultaneous stimulation was delivered, respectively.

Experiment 1 (TOJ Assessment)

Twenty subjects were studied, and each subject underwent 20 trials. Two probe tips were positioned at one of three sets of stimulus sites: 1) 30 mm apart on the *hand dorsum* (back of hand), 2) on the tips of the second and third *digits* (fingers) of the same hand, and 3) on the tips of the second digit of both hands. Two pulses were delivered to the skin and separated by an inter-stimulus interval (ISI) of 150 milliseconds. The subject was then asked to identify the skin site that received the first stimulus. For the remaining trials, the ISI between the two pulses was modified based on subject response. Figures 1, 2, and 3 show subjects' TOJ performance under the three conditions.

Experiment 2 (TDT Assessment)

This experiment measured TDT. Twenty subjects were studied, and each subject underwent 20 trials. The probe positioning was the same as in Experiment 1. Two pulses were delivered either at the same time or separated by the ISI. Subject response was not dependent on the order of which two stimuli were delivered, but rather on whether the pulses were felt to be simultaneous or not. Figures 1, 2, and 3 show subjects' TDT performance under the three conditions.

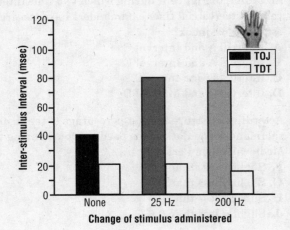

Figure 1

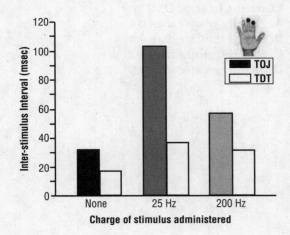

Figure 2

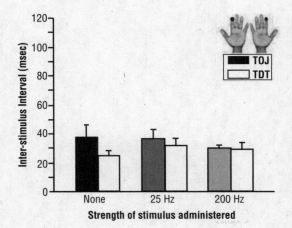

Figure 3

GO ON TO THE NEXT PAGE.

6. According to Figure 2, how long was the inter-stimulus interval for the TDT control?
    F. Approximately 10 msec
    G. Approximately 20 msec
    H. Approximately 35 msec
    J. Approximately 40 msec

7. The data in Figures 1, 2, and 3 support which of the following hypotheses?
    A. Subjects take more time to recognize the presence of multiple stimuli than they do to identify the locations of those stimuli.
    B. Subjects take less time to recognize the presence of multiple stimuli than they do to identify the locations of those stimuli.
    C. Subjects take less time to locate stimuli on the hand dorsum than they do to locate stimuli on the second digit of each hand.
    D. Subjects take more time to locate stimuli on the second digit of each hand than they do to locate stimuli on the second and third digit of the same hand.

8. According to Figures 1, 2, and 3, which TOJ assessment scenario required the longest inter-stimulus interval?
    F. 200 Hz delivered to two points on the hand dorsum
    G. 200 Hz delivered to the tips of the second digit of both hands
    H. 25 Hz delivered to the tips of the second and third digits of the same hand
    J. 25 Hz delivered to the tips of the second digit of both hands

9. In Figure 1, the inter-stimulus interval for the 25 Hz TOJ assessment is nearly:
    A. 4 times as long as the inter-stimulus interval for the 25 Hz TDT assessment.
    B. 2 times as long as the inter-stimulus interval for the 25 Hz TDT assessment.
    C. ½ as long as the inter-stimulus interval for the 25 Hz TDT assessment.
    D. ¼ as long as the inter-stimulus interval for the 25 Hz TDT assessment.

10. Which of the following conclusions is accurate based on the data in Figure 3?
    F. When stimulus points are on different hands, the TDT inter-stimulus interval is half as long as the TOJ inter-stimulus symbol.
    G. When stimulus points are on different hands, the TDT inter-stimulus interval is greater than the TOJ stimulus interval.
    H. When stimulus points are on different hands, it is more difficult to distinguish between stimuli.
    J. When stimulus points are on different hands, it is easier to distinguish between stimuli.

11. The researchers who created these experiments want to add a fourth test scenario: delivering 200 Hz to the third digit on each hand. According to the data in Figure 3, what is a reasonable estimate for the inter-stimulus interval in the TOJ assessment?
    A. 10 seconds
    B. 30 seconds
    C. 55 seconds
    D. 70 seconds

Passage III

Citation: Groneberg-Kloft B, Kraus T, van Mark A, Wagner U, Fischer A (2006). Analysing the causes of chronic cough: relation to diesel exhaust, ozone, nitrogen oxides, sulphur oxides and other environmental factors. *Journal of Occupational Medicine and Toxicology* 1: 6.

Air pollution remains a leading cause of many respiratory diseases, including chronic cough. In industrialized and developing nations, pollutants such as dust and common cigarette smoke may be responsible for the development of chronic cough in both children and adults. Often, chronic cough is not paid much attention, even though it can lead to decreased lung function and other severe problems. A valuable way to quantify the amount of research being done on particular pollutants is to collect all of the relevant medical literature. Researchers used the online medical library PubMed to find the number of articles available about various cough-related topics.

Figure 1 shows the results of a PubMed search for the term "cough" and different environmental factors.

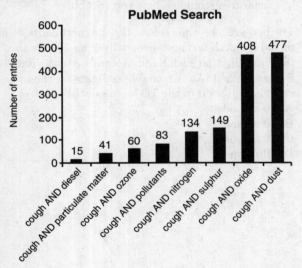

PubMed Search

Figure 1

Figure 2 shows the frequency of studies related to cough and environmental factors as assessed by a PubMed search for the terms "cough" and "environmental" and different publication dates.

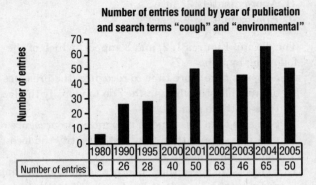

Number of entries found by year of publication and search terms "cough" and "environmental"

	1980	1990	1995	2000	2001	2002	2003	2004	2005
Number of entries	6	26	28	40	50	63	46	65	50

Figure 2

GO ON TO THE NEXT PAGE.

12. According to Figure 1, the greatest number of entries resulted following which two PubMed searches?
    F. "cough AND oxide" and "cough AND dust"
    G. "cough AND diesel" and "cough AND particulate matter"
    H. "cough AND diesel" and "cough AND dust"
    J. "cough AND nitrogen" and "cough AND sulphur"

13. According to Figure 2, the total number of published studies related to cough and environmental factors between 2004 and 2005 was:
    A. 130
    B. 115
    C. 65
    D. 50

14. According to the data in Figure 2, which of the following statements is true?
    F. More patients complained of chronic cough in 2004 than in any other year.
    G. Harmful environmental factors decreased between 2002 and 2003.
    H. Articles linking environmental factors to cough appeared more frequently in 2004 than in any other year in the graph's range.
    J. Articles linking environmental factors to cough were not published prior to 1980.

15. Which of the following hypotheses is most strongly supported by the data in Figure 1?
    A. Chronic cough is not caused by diesel pollution.
    B. The link between dust and chronic cough is strong enough to warrant frequent study.
    C. Medical interest in the correlation between environmental factors and chronic cough has increased steadily over the years.
    D. Chronic cough results far more frequently from exposure to sulphur than from exposure to nitrogen.

16. Which of the following statements, if true, supports the trend displayed in Figure 2?
    F. After 1980, medical writers lost interest in studying the correlation between environmental factors and chronic cough.
    G. After 1980, a steadily increasing number of medical writers began exploring the link between environmental factors and chronic cough.
    H. After 1980, medical advances helped to decrease the number of chronic-cough cases in industrialized and developing nations.
    J. After 1980, individuals exposed to excessive cigarette smoke began developing chronic cough.

Passage IV

Vacuum filtration is a process that enables rapid filtration and isolation of pure solids. Scientists conducted two studies to analyze the characteristics of certain solids.

Study 1

A vacuum filtration apparatus was set up as shown in Figure 1 below. A flat-bottomed porcelain funnel, known as a Buchner funnel, was attached to a heavy-wall suction filtration flask with a rubber stopper. A piece of filter paper was placed in the Buchner funnel over the hole in the bottom of the funnel and wetted with a solvent. The filtration flask was then connected via thick-wall rubber tubing to a second flask, known as a safety trap. The safety trap was also connected with rubber tubing to a vacuum device. The safety trap served to prevent water from backing up into the filtration flask after the vacuum was turned off.

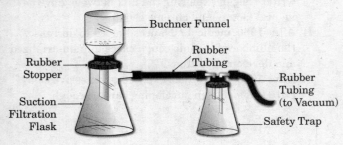

Figure 1

Different solutions were combined and filtered through the apparatus to produce crystallized solids. The results are shown in Table 1.

Combination	Catalyst	Product(s)
Ethanol + Distilled water	N/A	Alum
Iron (III) chloride + Potassium ferrocyanide	N/A	Prussian blue
Salicylic acid + Acetic anhydride	Phosphoric acid	Aspirin + Acetic acid
Calcium chloride + Sodium carbonate	N/A	Sodium chloride + Calcium carbonate
Aniline + Acetic anhydride	N/A	Acetanilide + Acetic acid

Table 1

Study 2

A purity check of the solids was conducted by examining the melting points of each solid. The melting point of a substance is the temperature at which the substance changes from a solid to a liquid. Crystalline substances that are pure will melt at a very specific temperature that typically varies less than 1°C. When impurities are present in a substance, the substance will melt over a range of temperatures instead of a sharp melting point. By comparing the melting ranges of each isolated solid with the known melting points of the pure substances, the scientists were able to determine the purity of their isolated solids.

Table 2 shows the results of Study 2. Table 3 shows the reference melting points for the pure solids produced in Study 1.

Solid	Melting Point (° C)
Alum	91 – 94
Prussian Blue	Decomposed
Aspirin	135 – 138
Sodium Chloride	799 – 801
Acetanilide	114

Table 2

Solid	Purity	Melting Point (° C)
Alum	98.00%	92
Prussian Blue	99.90%	Decomposes
Aspirin	99.00%	136
Sodium Chloride	99.99%	801
Acetanilide	99.95%	113 – 115

Table 3

GO ON TO THE NEXT PAGE.

17. According to the results of Study 1, phosphoric acid was used as a catalyst in the production of:
A. acetic anhydride.
B. sodium chloride.
C. aspirin.
D. acetanilide.

18. According to the results of Study 1, acetic acid is produced in reactions involving which of the following solutions?
F. Acetic anhydride
G. Iron (III) chloride
H. Sodium carbonate
J. Ethanol

19. According to Study 2, compared with the melting points for pure substances, the melting points for the solids isolated in Study 1 are:
A. always larger temperature ranges.
B. always exact temperatures.
C. always smaller temperature ranges.
D. sometimes larger temperature ranges and sometimes exact temperatures.

20. Based on the results of Study 2, which of the following conclusions can be draw about the purity level of the alum isolated in Study 1?
F. It is greater than 98%.
G. It is less than 98%.
H. It is less than 92%.
J. The purity level cannot be determined from the information given.

21. According to the results of Study 2, the purity level of the acetanilide isolated in Study 1 is closest to that of which of the following pure solids listed in Table 3?
A. Sodium chloride
B. Aspirin
C. Alum
D. Prussian blue

22. According to Study 2, which of the following most likely lists the purity levels of three of the solids isolated in Study 1 in order from *lowest* to *highest*?
F. Sodium chloride, alum, Prussian blue
G. Acetanilide, aspirin, sodium chloride
H. Alum, aspirin, sodium chloride
J. Aspirin, sodium chloride, alum

Passage V

Citation: Fisk NM, Roberts IAG, Markwald R, Mironov V (2005). Can routine commercial cord blood banking be scientifically and ethically justified? *PLoS Med* 2(2): e44.

Umbilical cord blood can be collected and stored frozen for years. A well-accepted use of cord blood is as an alternative to bone marrow as a source of transplantation to siblings or to unrelated recipients. However, private banks are now open that offer expectant parents the option to pay a fee for the chance to store cord blood for possible future use by that same child. Scientists disagree about whether this for-profit service is ethical.

Private Banking Is Unethical

No one disputes the merit of public cord blood banking, in which women selflessly donate umbilical cord blood (UCB). The validity of directed UCB storage in "low risk" families, however, has been widely challenged. First, UCB is very unlikely ever to be used. The probability of needing an *autologous* (one's own blood) transplant is less than one in 20,000. Even in the uncommon event of a requirement for autologous stem cells, failure to store UCB is unlikely to be disastrous; stem cells could still be harvested from bone marrow.

Second, there are important moral issues. The persuasive promotional materials of commercial UCB banks target parents at a vulnerable time. Even at a typical cost of several thousand dollars, how could any responsible parent fail to provide for their child's future by preserving "something that may conceivably save his or her life"? Such banks use the promise of "helping children" to disguise a commercial project.

Third, collection imposes a considerable logistic burden on the obstetrician. A large volume of blood has to be collected from the umbilical vessels, requiring multiple syringes under aseptic technique. This may distract professionals from their primary task of caring for the mother and baby at this risky time.

Private Banking Is Necessary

Stem cells may potentially be used in life-saving therapies for degenerative diseases or injuries. While stem cells can come from many sources, our viewpoint is that UCB is an important source of stem cells that can be used as an immediate alternative for bone marrow transplantation and for engineering healthy new cells and tissues.

To fully realize this potential will require collection and banking of UCB cells, which are harvested without pain from structures that are normally discarded after birth. We realize that UCB banking has sparked controversy. Critics of routine banking question its cost-to-benefit ratio, citing doubts about the clinical relevance of cord stem cells or the likelihood that they will ever be used. Other critics argue that embryonic stem cells (ESCs) are the better option.

The "usefulness" of UCB cells is not merely theoretical. These cells can develop into liver, kidney, brain, bone, and cardiac muscle cells. While the chance of a donor benefiting may presently be low, this does not automatically mean that another member of society could not benefit. For people with genetic diseases or cancers, the chances of finding an immune-tolerant donor match would obviously be increased by the expansion of cord blood sampling. Also, at the pace that stem cell research is moving, perhaps there will be new uses for UCB cells in the next decade. Importantly, unlike bone marrow, an increase in UCB samples will enhance availability for every ethnic group for tissue matching. What is certain is that no one has a second chance to collect their cord blood.

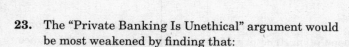
23. The "Private Banking Is Unethical" argument would be most weakened by finding that:
    A. the probability of needing an autologous transplant is actually one in 60,000.
    B. hospitals rely upon the availability of public cord blood banking.
    C. private UCB banks charge between $4,000 and $6,000 for banking.
    D. certain life-saving therapies can only be carried out with UCB cells.

24. Proponents of both arguments would agree that UCB banking:
    F. increases the amount of available stem cells.
    G. distracts medical professionals from important obstetric tasks.
    H. is a better alternative to bone-marrow harvesting.
    J. is widely misunderstood by the general population.

25. Assuming that the "Private Banking Is Necessary" argument is more valid, which of the following conclusions can be made about private UCB banks?
    A. Private UCB banks are better equipped than public UCB banks.
    B. Private UCB banks may charge high fees, but their services are necessary to maintain an abundant supply of UCB cells.
    C. Private UCB banks take advantage of families' emotions during particularly vulnerable times.
    D. Private UCB banks protect medical professionals from birth-related liabilities.

26. If it was discovered that the stem cells in bone marrow were more universally effective than the stem cells in UCB, how would this discovery affect the arguments, if at all?
    F. It would have no effect on either argument.
    G. It would weaken the "Private Banking Is Necessary" argument only.
    H. It is consistent with both arguments.
    J. It would weaken the "Private Banking Is Unethical" argument only.

27. Which of the following questions is raised by the "Private Banking is Necessary" argument but NOT answered in the passage?
    A. Why do critics argue that embryonic stem cells are a better option than UCB cells?
    B. What sorts of cells can UCB cells develop into?
    C. In what way are UCB cells more beneficial than bone-marrow cells?
    D. What is the procedure for donating UCB cells to a public bank?

28. Based on both arguments, stem cells:
    F. are too expensive to harvest.
    G. should not be handled by a for-profit business.
    H. contribute to life-saving therapies.
    J. are most effective when derived from UCB.

29. The "Private Banking Is Unethical" argument implies that:
    A. UCB cells are a better match for various ethnic groups than bone-marrow cells are.
    B. patients cannot be effectively treated with UCB cells from private banks.
    C. the emphasis on collecting UCB in the delivery room could put mother and baby at risk.
    D. all new mothers should be required to donate UCB cells to public banks.

Passage VI

Citation: Company J, Puig P, Sardà F, Palanques A, Latasa M, Scharek R (2008). Climate influence on deep sea populations. *PLoS ONE* 3(1): e1431.

The well-being of animals dwelling in the vast expanses of the deep-sea realm mainly relies on particles sinking from the *euphotic layer* (the uppermost layer of the ocean), where primary production is generally low. Despite this scenario of low productivity, the deep sea sustains surprisingly large biomasses of fish. However, the increase of deep-sea fisheries has often led to a depletion of these stocks after only a few years of exploitation. Mediterranean fisheries are considered to be particularly susceptible to overexploitation. Surprisingly, Mediterranean stocks have not collapsed. One of the most striking examples of this paradox is the Mediterranean deep-sea shrimp *Aristeus antennatus*.

A climate-driven phenomenon called *cascading* (water falling over the ocean shelf) influences the ecology of this deep-sea population of shrimp. Figure 1 shows a long-term analysis of *Aristeus antennatus* landings in four major Mediterranean harbors. The dashed lines indicate years when strong cascading events occurred.

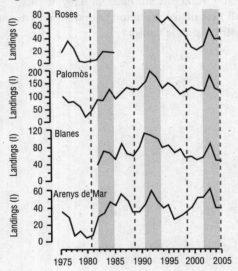

Figure 1

Figure 2 shows the evolution of the *Aristeus antennatus* population structure. This is an estimation of the abundance of small (solid line) and large (dotted line) individuals found in the annual landings at the four studied harbors. Again, the dashed lines indicate years when strong cascading events occurred. Individuals are counted in increments of 1 million ($N \times 10^6$).

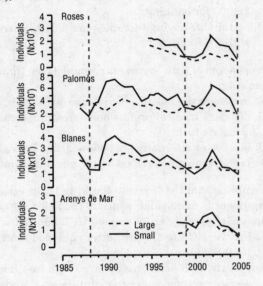

Figure 2

GO ON TO THE NEXT PAGE.

30. According to Figure 1, approximately how many *Aristeus antennatus* landings occurred at the Arenys de Mar harbor in 1999?
    F. 20
    G. 30
    H. 40
    J. 50

31. According to Figure 2, approximately how many large individuals landed at the Blanes harbor in 1990?
    A. 0.5 million
    B. 1 million
    C. 1.5 million
    D. 2 million

32. According to Figure 1, during which time frame did annual *Aristeus antennatus* landings spike at all four harbors?
    F. Between 2000 and 2005
    G. Between 1995 and 2000
    H. Between 1985 and 1990
    J. Between 1975 and 1980

33. Based on the data in Figure 1 and Figure 2, we can conclude that:
    A. three to five years after a strong cascading event, the *Aristeus antennatus* population decreases.
    B. three to five years after a strong cascading event, the *Aristeus antennatus* population increases.
    C. strong cascading events have an effect on the size of individual *Aristeus antennatus*, but not on the size of the overall population.
    D. strong cascading events have no effect on *Aristeus antennatus*.

34. Fisheries use annual landing data in order to predict the year's fishing haul. Which of the following represents the time frame where the smallest fishing haul would be likely?
    F. Between 1975 and 1977
    G. Between 1980 and 1982
    H. Between 1991 and 1993
    J. Between 2001 and 2003

Passage VII

Citation: Sridach W, Hodgson K, Nazhad M (2006). Biodegradation and recycling potential of barrier coated paperboards. Bio Resources 2 (2), 179–192.

Paper and paperboard are by far the most prevalent sources of packing material the world over. Global production of paper for wrapping, packing, corrugated boxes, and other containers increased 75 percent over just the past 5 years. This rapid growth in paper packaging has also had the effect of exacerbating solid waste handling problems. Disposal of paper products in landfill sites can lead to emissions of greenhouse gases. As a result, the management of this waste has become one of the more pressing issues of the modern age. The following experiments were developed from the premise that an accelerated biodegradation rate for commercial barrier coated boards could be achieved if pretreatment was done prior to the biodegradation stage.

Experiment 1

The materials used were folding boxboards. The boxboards were 1) bleached, uncoated paperboard; 2) paperboard coated on one side with polyethylene (1S); 3) paperboard coated on both sides with polyethylene (2S); and 4) commercial liquid packaging board (LPK). The biodegradation potential of the samples was estimated by burying the boards in soil and monitoring changes in weight as a function of burial time. The results are displayed in Figure 1.

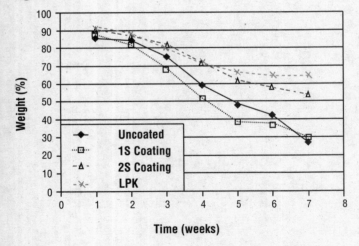

Figure 1

Experiment 2

Using the same types of folding boxboards, researchers monitored the changes in the *tensile strength* of the samples by burying the boards in soil and monitoring changes. Tensile strength measures the amount of stress required to pull something until it breaks. The results are displayed in Figure 2.

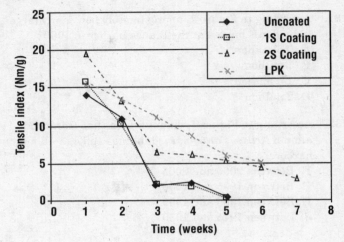

Figure 2

GO ON TO THE NEXT PAGE.

35. In week 4 of Experiment 1, of the paperboard coated on two sides, what percentage of its original weight remained?
   A. Approximately 80%
   B. Approximately 70%
   C. Approximately 60%
   D. Approximately 50%

36. According to the data in Experiment 2, during which time frame did the paperboard coated on one side lose the most tensile strength?
   F. Between Weeks 4 and 5
   G. Between Weeks 3 and 4
   H. Between Weeks 2 and 3
   J. Between Weeks 1 and 2

37. Both of the experiments support which of the following conclusions?
   A. Uncoated paperboard biodegrades more quickly than any of the other sample boards.
   B. The most substantial biodegradation takes place between Weeks 3 and 4.
   C. Uncoated and one-side-coated paperboard biodegrade more quickly than two-side-coated paperboard and commercial liquid packaging board.
   D. The most substantial biodegradation takes place following Week 7.

38. The data in Experiment 1 support the hypothesis that commercial liquid packaging board:
   F. is the least biodegradable material in the experiment.
   G. is the most biodegradable material in the experiment.
   H. loses 50% of its original weight by Week 7.
   J. loses 50% of its original weight by Week 5.

39. In which scenario might two-side-coated paperboard be preferable to uncoated paperboard?
   A. A shipping manager wants boxes that will biodegrade quickly.
   B. A pizza company wants boxes made of all-natural materials.
   C. A landfill manager wants boxes that will break down quickly.
   D. A moving company wants boxes that will withstand exposure to natural elements.

40. After 5 weeks, a piece of paperboard has a tensile index of 5 Nm/g and is approximately 60% its original weight. This is:
   F. uncoated paperboard.
   G. one-side-coated paperboard.
   H. two-side-coated paperboard.
   J. commercial liquid packaging board.

END OF TEST 4.
STOP! DO NOT RETURN TO ANY OTHER TEST.

Practice Test 4

WRITING TEST

DIRECTIONS: This test evaluates your writing skills. You will be given thirty (30) minutes to write an original essay. Before you start, read the writing prompt and be sure you understand the task required. Your essay will be scored based on how well you express judgments by taking a clear position on the issue presented; maintain your focus on your argument throughout the entire essay; support your position with logical reasoning and relevant evidence; present your ideas in an organized manner; and demonstrate clear and effective use of language, based on standard written English language conventions.

To plan out your essay, you may use the unlined page provided. You will not be scored on any information written on this unlined page. *Your essay must be written on the lined pages provided.* Your essay will be scored based only on the writing on those lined pages. You may not end up using all of the lined pages provided, but to be sure that you have enough space to complete your essay, do NOT skip any lines. Corrections or additions may be written in neatly between the lines of your essay, but you must NOT include any writing in the margins of the lined pages. *If your essay is illegible, it cannot be scored, so be sure to write or print clearly.*

If you finish your essay early, you may go back and review what you have written. When time is called, stop writing immediately and lay down your pencil.

ACT Assessment Writing Test Prompt

Many entering college students consider using their high school advanced placement credits to complete college in three years instead of four. Some people think that completing college more quickly is a good idea because they think students will benefit from the reduction in college tuition. Other people think students should not complete college in three years, because students will lose the personal growth opportunities that a four-year education provides them and, as a result, will not benefit from the experience. In your opinion, should college students use their high school advanced placement credits to graduate in three years?

Write an essay that develops your position on this question. You may choose to take one of the two viewpoints given, or you may present a different position on this question. Support your position using specific reasons and examples.

Begin WRITING TEST here.

WRITING TEST

Practice Test 4: Answers & Explanations

Question Number	Answer	Right	Wrong	Question Number	Answer	Right	Wrong
	English			38.	G	—	—
1.	C	—	—	39.	C	—	—
2.	J	—	—	40.	J	—	—
3.	B	—	—	41.	B	—	—
4.	H	—	—	42.	H	—	—
5.	A	—	—	43.	C	—	—
6.	J	—	—	44.	H	—	—
7.	B	—	—	45.	C	—	—
8.	G	—	—	46.	H	—	—
9.	D	—	—	47.	B	—	—
10.	H	—	—	48.	J	—	—
11.	A	—	—	49.	A	—	—
12.	H	—	—	50.	H	—	—
13.	B	—	—	51.	B	—	—
14.	J	—	—	52.	J	—	—
15.	C	—	—	53.	C	—	—
16.	H	—	—	54.	H	—	—
17.	A	—	—	55.	D	—	—
18.	H	—	—	56.	F	—	—
19.	B	—	—	57.	A	—	—
20.	G	—	—	58.	H	—	—
21.	D	—	—	59.	A	—	—
22.	G	—	—	60.	H	—	—
23.	D	—	—	61.	D	—	—
24.	F	—	—	62.	H	—	—
25.	D	—	—	63.	B	—	—
26.	H	—	—	64.	J	—	—
27.	C	—	—	65.	C	—	—
28.	J	—	—	66.	H	—	—
29.	B	—	—	67.	D	—	—
30.	F	—	—	68.	G	—	—
31.	A	—	—	69.	B	—	—
32.	H	—	—	70.	F	—	—
33.	D	—	—	71.	C	—	—
34.	G	—	—	72.	J	—	—
35.	B	—	—	73.	B	—	—
36.	H	—	—	74.	F	—	—
37.	D	—	—	75.	D	—	—

Question Number	Answer	Right	Wrong	Question Number	Answer	Right	Wrong
	Mathematics			31.	E	—	—
1.	D	—	—	32.	H	—	—
2.	J	—	—	33.	A	—	—
3.	C	—	—	34.	J	—	—
4.	G	—	—	35.	D	—	—
5.	B	—	—	36.	H	—	—
6.	H	—	—	37.	B	—	—
7.	C	—	—	38.	K	—	—
8.	H	—	—	39.	A	—	—
9.	D	—	—	40.	H	—	—
10.	K	—	—	41.	D	—	—
11.	A	—	—	42.	H	—	—
12.	J	—	—	43.	B	—	—
13.	D	—	—	44.	K	—	—
14.	H	—	—	45.	D	—	—
15.	B	—	—	46.	J	—	—
16.	F	—	—	47.	C	—	—
17.	A	—	—	48.	F	—	—
18.	H	—	—	49.	B	—	—
19.	B	—	—	50.	G	—	—
20.	J	—	—	51.	C	—	—
21.	C	—	—	52.	F	—	—
22.	F	—	—	53.	E	—	—
23.	D	—	—	54.	F	—	—
24.	J	—	—	55.	A	—	—
25.	C	—	—	56.	K	—	—
26.	E	—	—	57.	D	—	—
27.	B	—	—	58.	H	—	—
28.	F	—	—	59.	E	—	—
29.	A	—	—	60.	F	—	—
30.	K	—	—				

Question Number	Answer	Right	Wrong	Question Number	Answer	Right	Wrong
	Reading			21.	C	—	—
1.	C	—	—	22.	G	—	—
2.	J	—	—	23.	D	—	—
3.	D	—	—	24.	F	—	—
4.	G	—	—	25.	C	—	—
5.	A	—	—	26.	H	—	—
6.	H	—	—	27.	D	—	—
7.	B	—	—	28.	F	—	—
8.	F	—	—	29.	B	—	—
9.	D	—	—	30.	J	—	—
10.	J	—	—	31.	B	—	—
11.	C	—	—	32.	F	—	—
12.	J	—	—	33.	D	—	—
13.	B	—	—	34.	H	—	—
14.	J	—	—	35.	C	—	—
15.	C	—	—	36.	G	—	—
16.	F	—	—	37.	A	—	—
17.	B	—	—	38.	J	—	—
18.	J	—	—	39.	B	—	—
19.	C	—	—	40.	J	—	—
20.	G	—	—				

Question Number	Answer	Right	Wrong	Question Number	Answer	Right	Wrong
	Science			21.	A	—	—
1.	B	—	—	22.	H	—	—
2.	G	—	—	23.	D	—	—
3.	C	—	—	24.	F	—	—
4.	J	—	—	25.	B	—	—
5.	A	—	—	26.	G	—	—
6.	G	—	—	27.	A	—	—
7.	B	—	—	28.	H	—	—
8.	H	—	—	29.	C	—	—
9.	A	—	—	30.	H	—	—
10.	J	—	—	31.	C	—	—
11.	B	—	—	32.	F	—	—
12.	F	—	—	33.	B	—	—
13.	B	—	—	34.	G	—	—
14.	H	—	—	35.	B	—	—
15.	B	—	—	36.	H	—	—
16.	G	—	—	37.	C	—	—
17.	C	—	—	38.	F	—	—
18.	F	—	—	39.	D	—	—
19.	D	—	—	40.	H	—	—
20.	G	—	—				

Calculating Your Score

To find your scaled scores for each test, add up the number of questions you answered correctly on each test. That number represents your raw score for the test. Then covert your raw score to a 1–36 score using the table below. To find your Composite Score for the entire exam, add up your scaled scores for all four tests and divide that total by 4. Round off any fractions to the nearest whole number.

Keep in mind that this score is just a rough estimate. The only completely accurate predictors of your current scoring level are the scoring scales provided with official ACT materials, so make sure you practice with them in the week or two before the test to gauge where you stand.

Scaled Score	Raw Scores				Scaled Score
	Test 1	Test 2	Test 3	Test 4	
	English	Mathematics	Reading	Science	
36	75	60	38–40	40	36
35	73–74	58–59	37	—	35
34	71–72	56–57	36	39	34
33	70	55	35	—	33
32	69	54	34	38	32
31	68	52–53	—	—	31
30	67	50–51	33	37	30
29	65–66	48–49	32	36	29
28	64	46–47	30–31	35	28
27	62–63	43–45	29	34	27
26	60–61	41–42	28	32–33	26
25	57–59	39–40	27	30–31	25
24	55–56	37–38	26	29	24
23	53–54	35–36	25	27–28	23
22	50–52	33–34	24	25–26	22
21	47–49	31–32	23	23–24	21
20	44–46	30	22	21–22	20
19	42–43	27–29	21	18–20	19
18	39–41	25–26	20	16–17	18
17	37–38	22–24	19	14–15	17
16	34–36	18–21	17–18	13	16
15	30–33	15–17	16	12	15
14	28–29	12–14	14–15	10–11	14
13	26–27	09–11	12–13	09	13
12	24–25	08	10–11	08	12
11	22–23	06–07	08–09	07	11
10	20–21	05	07	06	10
9	18–19	04	06	05	9
8	15–17	—	05	04	8
7	13–14	03	—	03	7
6	10–12	02	04	—	6
5	08–09	—	03	02	5
4	06–07	—	02	—	4
3	04–05	01	—	01	3
2	02–03	—	01	—	2
1	00–01	00	00	00	1

Practice Test 4:
Answers & Explanations

ENGLISH

1. C

Sentence Structure: Subordinate or Dependent Clauses   *Medium*

The main part of this sentence begins with *the chronic condition*. *Although narcolepsy is one of the most prevalent sleep disorders and affects 1 in 2,000 people* is a dependent clause. The two parts need to be separated with a comma after *people*, so **C** is the correct answer. **A** divides the subject (*condition*) from the verb phrase (*often goes undiagnosed*.) The lack of punctuation in **B** makes it difficult to tell where the main part of the sentence begins. **D** includes two unnecessary commas.

2. J

Basic Grammar and Usage: Verb Tenses   *Easy*

The verbs *does suggest* and *disregard* are present tense, so the present-tense verb *assume* is the correct answer. **G** creates an awkward and ungrammatical sentence structure. **F** is incorrect because *assumed* is past tense. *Were assuming* is a past progressive tense verb, so **H** is wrong.

3. B

Basic Grammar and Usage: Subject-Verb Agreement   *Easy*

Since the plural noun *years* is part of a prepositional phrase, the underlined verb should agree with the singular noun *average*: *average passes*. **A** is incorrect because the verb *pass* agrees with *years* rather than *average*. Similarly *are passing* and *have passed* are verb phrases that agree with plural nouns instead of singular nouns, so **C** and **D** are incorrect.

4. H

Organization: Transitions, Topic Sentences & Conclusions   *Difficult*

The second sentence of the second paragraph explains the difference between narcolepsy and insomnia. *Also typically confused with insomnia* provides a bridge to the information presented in the rest of the second paragraph. Although **F, G,** and **J** are all true statements, none of them relates to the information about insomnia presented in the paragraph.

5. A

Basic Grammar and Usage: Adverbs and Adjectives   *Easy*

No change is required because the underlined portion is grammatically correct as written with *daytime* describing the type of *sleeping habits*. **B** makes the last part of the sentence ungrammatical. **C** and **D** are incorrect because *daytime* should modify *sleeping* instead of *habits*.

6. J

Sentence Structure: Connecting and Transitional Words   *Medium*

The author goes on to discuss another characteristic of narcolepsy, so **J** most appropriately indicates that another point is being made. A cause-effect relationship is not being discussed, so **G** is incorrect. Similarly, a contrast is not being made, which means **H** is also incorrect. **F** might be an attractive answer, but the last sentence of the second paragraph describes an additional characteristic of narcolepsy, which means the underlined portion should not be a transition used for concluding information.

7. B

Style: Redundancy and Wordiness   *Medium*

Both **A** and **C** are wordy with the inclusion of *when they*. *Sudden* and *unexpected* have the same meaning, so **D** includes redundancies. **B** conveys the same amount of information as the other options but in a more economical manner. If a sentence can be written more concisely without losing its core meaning, then revision is appropriate.

8. G

Organization: Sentence Reorganization   *Difficult*

The organization of **F** and **H** suggests that the *scientists* are *unknown* rather than the *causes of narcolepsy*. **J** is illogically organized and confusing. **G** clearly presents the idea that scientists believe genetics may play a role in the *causes of narcolepsy*.

9. D

Punctuation: Semicolons   *Easy*

When *however* is used to join two independent clauses, it must be preceded by a semicolon and followed by a comma. **A** reverses the punctuation order. **B** and **C** fail to include both the semicolon and the comma. Only **D** follows the rules of punctuating *however*.

10. H

Style: Redundancy and Wordiness   *Medium*

Alleviate and *lessen* have the same meaning, so the original sentence is redundant and in need of correction. Including *faced on a daily basis by narcoleptics* in **G** is unnecessary and wordy. **J** is redundant because *prescription medications* is the subject of the sentence, so using the word *medically* is redundant Therefore, the best answer is **H**.

11. A

Writing Strategy: Additional Detail and Evidence   *Difficult*

The author is describing narcolepsy treatment options in the paragraph, so the sentence should be added because it provides relevant information about the medical options available to narcoleptics. **C** and **D** are incorrect because the additional details relate to the information presented in the paragraph. The author does not assert that medication is necessary, so **B** is incorrect.

12. H

Punctuation: Commas   *Easy*

The underlined portion lacks commas separating the three different stimulants listed, so **F** is incorrect. A comma should not be placed after *such as* because *such as* acts as a preposition so **G** is wrong. **G** also lacks a comma setting off the phrase *which can interfere with nighttime sleep patterns*. **J** is wrong because it lacks a comma before *which*. **H** is the clearest answer because commas have been inserted between all the stimulants listed and before *which*.

13. B

Style: Word Choice and Identifying Tone   *Medium*

The author is discussing the age range when *narcolepsy symptoms typically arise in individuals*. Since symptoms appear anywhere in the range of 10 years old and 25 years old, the best word to choose is *between*. *In* and *of* suggest that symptoms occur either at 10 or 25, so **A** and **D** are wrong. *From* is confusing because it fails to clarify an age range, and it suggests that symptoms may appear in someone older than 25.

14. J

Sentence Structure: Parallelism   *Medium*

J is the best answer because *academic, personal*, and *professional* act as adjectives describing *difficulties* in a parallel and balanced form. The underlined portion should match the structure of *professional difficulties*. No balance occurs with the way **F**, **G**, and **H** are constructed. Balancing similar words and phrases in a sentence improves readability.

15. C

Writing Strategy: Big Picture Purpose   *Difficult*

A and **B** are wrong because the main point of the essay is not the dangers of narcolepsy. The essay provides an overview of the disorder, which includes mentioning what problems narcoleptics face and what treatment options are available. The essay only briefly mentions that narcoleptics sometimes fall asleep while driving. Therefore, the best answer is **C**.

16. H

Punctuation: Parentheses and Dashes   *Easy*

No better than livestock or a bag of flour is explaining *property*, and it should be set apart for emphasis with a dash. *No better than livestock or a bag of flour* is not an independent clause, so both a period and a semicolon would be incorrect. Although *most people today cannot fathom the idea of being treated as property* may seem like it needs emphasis with an exclamation mark, doing so leaves *no better than livestock or a bag of flour* standing alone, which it cannot.

17. A

Basic Grammar and Usage: Subject-Verb Agreement *Easy*

The underlined verb (*was*) correctly agrees with *one*, the singular subject of the sentence. Despite the fact that four prepositional phrases—*of the most accomplished slaves to emerge from the bonds of slavery*—stand between *one* and *was*, the verb must agree with the subject of the sentence and not with the subject of a prepositional phrase. The correct answer is **A** because *are*, *were*, and *have been* would only be appropriate with plural subjects.

18. H

Sentence Structure: Connecting and Transitional Words *Medium*

The underlined word is introducing a clause—*later became a famous author, orator, and abolitionist*. *Which* is used with things rather than people, so **G** is incorrect. **J** creates a confusing sentence. *Whom* is an object pronoun, while *who* is a subject pronoun. **H** is correct because *who* is the subject of the clause and *became* is the verb.

19. B

Sentence Structure: Subordinate or Dependent Clauses *Medium*

Born into slavery in 1818 in Maryland is a dependent clause, and the main part of the sentence begins with *Douglass*. A comma is necessary between *Maryland* and *Douglass* to indicate a separation between the two parts of the sentence, which means **B** is the correct answer. The original version is incorrect because it lacks a comma after *Maryland* and includes an unnecessary one after *1818*. Similarly, **C** fails to separate the subordinate clause from the rest of the sentence with a comma and incorrectly inserts a comma before the prepositional phrase *in 1818*. The comma in **D** separates the subject (*Douglass*) from the verb (*changed*).

20. G

Organization: Transitions, Topic Sentences & Conclusions *Difficult*

The author discusses how Douglass learned to read in paragraph 2, and paragraph 3 focuses on the fears related to slaves becoming educated. **H** does not relate to reading, while **F** repeats information already mentioned in the second paragraph. **J** is tempting because the children may have taught Frederick to read better; however, the sentence does not specify how they were a *source of education*. **G** most clearly states how Douglass's reading improved and provides an easy transition into the third paragraph.

21. D

Basic Grammar and Usage: Verb Tenses *Easy*

Maintaining the consistency of verb tenses is important so that readers are not confused about the time of the described actions. The phrase *at that time* indicates that the author is referring to past events. The past-tense verb *signified* is the best choice. **A** and **B** are present tense, and **C** is present perfect tense.

22. G

Sentence Structure: Connecting and Transitional Words *Medium*

The second part of the sentence explains why *plantation owners feared slaves would learn to read*. The connecting word *since* is the best choice for clarifying the relationship between the two parts of the sentence. **F** and **H** would be used to contrast information. The connecting word *and* would be appropriate if two nonrelated ideas needed to be connected.

23. D

Style: Redundancy and Wordiness   *Medium*

Might and *possibly* are synonymous, so there is no reason to include both to describe *result*. *Might* and *could* are both helping verbs, so including both to modify *result* would be ungrammatical, as well as unnecessary. The underlined portion should be omitted since *which might result in a revolt* is clear without the addition of extra words.

24. F

Organization: Sentence Reorganization   *Medium*

Particularly describes how *upset* Auld was. Adverbs are typically placed before the words they modify. Therefore, this sentence is correct as it stands, and the best answer is **F**.

25. D

Style: Redundancy and Wordiness   *Medium*

Vicious and *cruel* are synonyms, so it is redundant to include both in the same sentence. **B** is wordy with the inclusion of *who was named* rather than just *named*. **B** also includes *owner* when *owned* was used earlier in the sentence—a redundancy. Therefore, the best answer is **D** because it concisely states the necessary information.

26. H

Writing Strategy: Additional Detail and Evidence   *Difficult*

Although the name of the plantation and the information about the number of times it has changed owners may be interesting, these details do not relate to the main topic of the essay. The essay does not describe how Douglass was able to escape from Covey, so **J** is incorrect. Therefore, the best answer is **H**.

27. C

Punctuation: Commas   *Easy*

A pause in the form of a comma is needed after *autobiography* to set the title apart from the rest of the sentence, so **C** is correct. **B** is wrong because a comma should not separate an adjective from the noun it modifies. **D** is wrong because a comma would be unnecessary between *narrative* and the prepositional phrase *of the life*.

28. J

Writing Strategy: Analysis   *Difficult*

A is incorrect because the omitted information relates to Douglass's book rather than his life. Including the information does not make the sentence awkward, so **G** is wrong. The omitted information does not describe Douglass's accomplishments, although the sentence that follows describes his many interests. Therefore, the best answer is **J** because the additional information specifies the topic of Douglass's book.

29. B

Sentence Structure: Parallelism   *Medium*

Each of Douglass's accomplishments is preceded by *a* or *an*, so *U.S. marshal* should also be preceded by an article for the sentence to be balanced and parallel. **A**, **C**, and **D** are unnecessarily wordy and create an unparallel construction, so **B** is the best answer.

30. F

Writing Strategy: Big Picture Purpose   *Difficult*

The essay focuses on the life of Frederick Douglass, so **F** is the correct answer. Although the education of slaves is discussed in the essay, the main point was how education helped Frederick Douglass. **H** is incorrect because the essay only mentions that Douglass was eventually freed, and no mention is made of how all slaves earned freedom. **J** may be tempting because the essay focuses on the life of one slave; however, the history of the slave trade is not discussed in the essay.

31. A

Sentence Structure: Parallelism   *Medium*

The original sentence is parallel because the very *running* is in the same *-ing* form as *riding* and *wasting*. Structuring all the verbs and verb phrases in a similar form improves readability, so the original sentence is correct as it stands. **B**, **C**, and **D** are incorrect, because they do not maintain parallelism in the sentence.

32. H

Style: Word Choice and Identifying Tone   *Medium*

Usually, *often*, and *frequently* all indicate that the author's uncle was regularly busy doing chores around the farm. The answer is **H** because *seldom* implies that the uncle was rarely busy with farm work. The misuse of words can alter the meaning of a written piece, so word choice is an important aspect of writing.

33. D

Sentence Structure: Comma Splices   *Medium*

A comma splice occurs when only a comma joins two independent clauses. A comma splice exists in the original sentence between *14* and *Jacob*. Removing the comma does not repair the problem; it creates a run-on sentence, which means **B** is wrong. **C** incorrectly puts a comma between Jacob and his age. The correct answer is **D** because it repairs the comma splice with a conjunction and a comma.

34. G

Basic Grammar and Usage: Verb Tenses   *Easy*

The author is describing a past event, as indicated by the preceding sentence: *The big wakeup call occurred when I was 14*. It is important to remain consistent with verb tenses to prevent confusion. Since the author is describing Jacob's fall from the tractor, a past-tense verb is necessary for the underlined portion. *Has been* is present perfect tense, so **F** is incorrect. **J** is present tense, while **H** is future tense. Only **G** provides a past-tense verb.

35. B

Sentence Structure: Connecting and Transitional Words   *Medium*

The sentence illustrates a cause-effect relationship: Because the tractor was off, Jacob had few injuries. **B** best connects the cause with the effect. *But* is used to contrast information, which is why the original sentence needs revision. *While* is used to show the passage of time, so **D** is incorrect. Although *since* is a transitional word that indicates a cause-effect relationships, its placement in the sentence creates an illogical structure. *Since* would be correct if placed at the beginning of the sentence: *Since the tractor was turned off, Jacob's injuries were limited to a few bruises and some sore ribs.*

36. H

Basic Grammar and Usage: Adverbs and Adjectives   *Medium*

J is incorrect because *cautiously* is an adverb, which is ungrammatical after a being verb (*became*). Similarly, **G** is wrong because *caution* is a noun. **F** fails to work because *extreme* is an adjective, and adverbs modify adjectives. The correct answer is **H** because *cautious* describes Jacob's behavior, and *extremely* describes the degree of caution.

37. D

Sentence Structure: Sentence Fragments   *Medium*

If you live in a farming community or have ever visited a rural area is not a complete thought, so the fragment needs correction. A semicolon would be incorrect because both sides of a semicolon should include independent clauses. **C** is wrong because commas are unnecessary before prepositional phrases, such as *in the summer*. The best way to correct the fragment is with **D**, which combines the fragment with the next sentence.

38. G

Organization: Sentence Reorganization   *Medium*

The current placement of *honestly* creates an awkward sentence, so the adverb should be moved elsewhere. Placing adverbs near the words they modify creates clarity for the reader. In this sentence, *honestly* should be near *thought*. **H** and **J** place the adverb too far from the verb *thought*. **G** is the best answer because *we never honestly thought* allows the adverb to precede the verb it modifies.

39. C

Punctuation: Apostrophes   *Easy*

The author discusses one cousin and one uncle. The apostrophe punctuation in **C** is the only one that indicates singular possession for both the cousin and the uncle. The punctuation in **A** indicates more than one cousin fell, rather than only one. Similarly, **B** and **D** suggest that more than one uncle is on the farm, which is incorrect. With **A**, **B**, and **D**, the misplacement of an apostrophe suggests a change in the number of people involved, which may lead to reader confusion.

40. J

Style: Ambiguous Pronoun References   *Medium*

It is unclear what the author means by the pronoun *they*. They could refer to many things, such as the author's family, the farm equipment, or the *safety talk*. Ambiguous pronoun references create problems for readers, so this sentence should be revised for clarity. *It* and *such big things* are still vague and fail to clarify the author's meaning. **J** makes the author's idea clear, and it makes sense in the context of the paragraph.

41. B

Basic Grammar and Usage: Verb Tenses   *Easy*

The entire passage is about an experience that occurred in the past. Therefore, all of the verbs should be past tense to convey the idea that the author is writing about when he was young. The events are not currently taking place, so present-tense verbs such as *is using* and *has been using* are incorrect for this sentence. Future tense would be illogical, so **C** is wrong. Only **B** is a past-tense verb.

42. H

Punctuation: Commas   *Easy*

The sentence is compound, which means it is composed of two independent clauses that have the ability to stand on their own as simple sentences. A comma should precede the coordinating conjunction (*but*), so **F** is wrong. A semicolon would be acceptable only if the conjunction were omitted, which explains why **G** is wrong. **J** inserts the comma after the conjunction, which is incorrect. **H** is correct because the comma is located between the first independent clause and the conjunction.

43. C

Style: Redundancy and Wordiness   *Medium*

Tractors are types of *mechanical farm equipment*, so the original version is redundant. Similarly, *farm machinery* and *equipment* are synonymous, so it is redundant to include both in **B**. It is unnecessary to list different types of mechanical farm tools, so **D** is redundant as well. **C** conveys the same idea as the other options but with fewer words.

44. H

Writing Strategy: Analysis   *Difficult*

Both sentence options present the same basic information, so **G** is incorrect. **F** is wrong because the author explains the uncle's punishment in the first part of the sentence. Changing the second part of the sentence does not affect that information. The details actually provide a clear picture of what the boys were doing, so **J** is incorrect. The phrase *tractor joy riding* is somewhat humorous, and it provides readers with an understanding of the cousins' activities.

45. C

Organization: Passage Reorganization   *Difficult*

The current organization of the passage is confusing, and the passage lacks a clear conclusion. The fourth paragraph, which describes what happened to the boys after Jacob's fall, should be placed after paragraph 2. The last sentence of paragraph 3 makes it clear that the third paragraph is the conclusion of the essay. The paragraph serves a purpose in the essay by relating Jacob's accident with what the cousins learned from their uncle about tractor safety. The author refers to the *safety talk* in the third paragraph, so omitting the fourth paragraph would make the passage confusing.

46. H

Punctuation: Commas   *Medium*

However is a conjunctive adverb that needs to be set off from the rest of the sentence by commas on each side, so **H** is the correct answer. **F** and **J** include only one comma. **G** is wrong because a semicolon is needed before *however* only when it is joining two independent clauses.

47. B

Style: Redundancy and Wordiness   *Medium*

The underlined portion needs to be changed because *manufactured* and *produced* are synonymous. Similarly, **C** is incorrect because *made* and *produced* are redundant. Including both *national* and *country* in **D** seems redundant as well. **B** concisely conveys the same information as the other options without being repetitive.

48. J

Sentence Structure: Sentence Fragments   *Easy*

A period after *wealth* creates a sentence fragment beginning with *because*, so **F** is incorrect. Dashes are typically used to set off information that needs to be emphasized, so **G** is wrong. **H** is wrong since semicolons are used to connect independent clauses, and *because it only has value when accepted as a medium of exchange* cannot stand on its own. **J** combines the dependent clause with the first sentence and eliminates the sentence fragment.

49. A

Sentence Structure: Connecting and Transitional Words   *Medium*

A is the best answer because the transitional phrase *in fact* is appropriate when introducing examples. The sentence further explains the value of money, which was the subject of the previous sentence. *In short* is used for summarizing, so **B** is incorrect. *Nonetheless* and *regardless* are transitional phrases used for contrasting or restricting clauses.

50. H

Punctuation: Apostrophes   *Medium*

Nations' is the correct way of indicating the plural possessive form of *nation*. The *histories* belong to many *nations*, but in the original version, there is no apostrophe to indicate ownership. If only one nation's history was the focus, then **G** would be correct; however, the use of *certain* to describe nations indicates more than one nation has a history. **J** is wrong because *history* possesses nothing—*certain nations* possess *histories*.

51. B

Sentence Structure: Subordinate or Dependent Clauses   *Medium*

The main part of the sentence begins with *the coins*, and *under these circumstances* is a dependent clause. **B** correctly includes a comma to indicate the beginning of the sentence. **A** lacks any punctuation to separate the dependent clause from the main sentence. **C** includes unnecessary commas after *coins* and *notes*, while **D** is missing the comma after *circumstances* and includes unnecessary commas.

52. J

Basic Grammar and Usage: Subject-Verb Agreement   *Easy*

The plural subject of the sentence, *coins*, and the underlined verb, *becomes*, are not in agreement. **G** and **H** are verb phrases intended for singular nouns rather than plural nouns. **J** is the correct answer because it creates agreement between the subject and the verb: *coins become*.

53. C

Organization: Transitions, Topic Sentences & Conclusions   *Difficult*

The second and third sentences of the third paragraph describe how a nation's output is calculated, and **C** mentions *national output*. **A** may fit with the information in the second paragraph but not the third. The essay does not discuss *exchange rates* or *recessions*, so **B** and **D** are wrong.

54. H

Organization: Sentence Reorganization   *Difficult*

H logically and clearly states the information about calculating *national output*. The phrase *one way value* makes **F** confusing. **G** is awkward and illogical. **J** is confusing because the phrase *computed one way during a given year* suggests that the method used to calculate national output varies during the year.

55. D

Basic Grammar and Usage: Verb Tenses   *Easy*

Present tense is the best choice for the underlined portion, so **D** is the correct answer. **A** implies that the GNP is actively thinking about *goods and services* much like a person would think about something. The author writes the essay in present tense, so future tense, **C**, is incorrect. Although the author refers to GNP as *the older measure*, no indication is given that GNP is no longer used, which means **B** is wrong.

56. F

Writing Strategy: Analysis   *Difficult*

It is redundant to state *whether they live in the United States or abroad* because readers can infer the information from the preceding phrase: *regardless of where those individuals reside*. **H** is wrong because the extra details do not transition to the next sentence about GDP. The additional information is about calculating GNP not output, so **J** is incorrect. **G** is wrong because the author is not making an argument, only explaining how GNP is calculated.

57. A

Sentence Structure: Connecting and Transitional Words   *Medium*

The underlined portion tells you that a contrast is being made, and **B**, **C**, and **D** are all transitions used for making contrasts. *Therefore* is used to summarize a point, so **A** is the LEAST acceptable choice and the correct answer.

58. H

Writing Strategy: Additional Detail and Evidence   *Difficult*

The sentence should be added to the paragraph because it further explains GDP, so **J** is incorrect. Since GDP is not explained until the end of the paragraph, the new sentence should be placed after the fifth sentence, which is **H**. The third sentence is introducing the idea of GNP and GDP to the reader. The additional detail is too specific for insertion after sentence 3 because the concepts of GNP and GDP have not been explained at that point. GNP is the subject of Sentence 4, so the additional detail would be out of place after the fourth sentence.

59. A

Style: Word Choice and Identifying Tone   *Medium*

No change is necessary because the word *assessing* best conveys the author's idea that analyzing a country's *total national output* offers a *sense* of a country's *value*. Maintaining safety or *securing* wealth does not relate to the subject, so **B** is incorrect. Since the passage is about determining a nation's value, the author would not suggest *ignoring* a *country's wealth*. In the context of the sentence, a nation's wealth cannot be *obtained*, but it should be *assessed* or *considered*.

60. H

Writing Strategy: Big Picture Purpose   *Difficult*

Developing countries are not discussed in the essay, so **F** is wrong. **G** is incorrect because the essay is not argumentative. Although the author explains how currency is not used to determine a nation's wealth, **J** is wrong because comparing the wealth of nations is not asserted to be simple. **H** provides the best summary of the essay's purpose.

61. D

Style: Redundancy and Wordiness   *Medium*

D is the most concise option available, which in many cases is the best answer. *Formation, development*, and *establishment* are synonymous, so it is redundant to include all of them in **A**. *Establishing* and *creating* are also redundant in **C**. *Reservation establishment* is redundant, and **B** is wordy as well.

62. H

Organization: Sentence Reorganization   *Easy*

Better urging creates a confusing sentence, so a change is necessary. Since the author only describes one school, **G** is incorrect. Placing *better* before *Hopi* does not make sense, which means **J** is wrong. The agent is *urging better relations*, so **H** is correct.

63. B

Sentence Structure: Connecting and Transitional Words   *Medium*

As a result indicates that a cause-effect relationship exists between concerns about school attendance and the trip to Washington. *So, for this reason*, and *consequently* are transitions that express a cause-effect relationship. **B** is the correct answer because *yet* is a transition used to contrast information, so it would be the LEAST acceptable alternative.

64. J

Organization: Transitions, Topic Sentences & Conclusions   *Medium*

The last sentence of the first paragraph explains how Hopi leaders would be traveling to Washington, and **J** provides the best transition into the second paragraph by referring to the trip. **F**, **G**, and **H** fail to connect the two paragraphs very well because they do not mention the Washington trip. The last sentence of the first paragraph and the first sentence of the second paragraph flow smoothly together, which makes the information coherent to readers.

65. C

Writing Strategy: Analysis   *Difficult*

The details do not explain why Lololma was chosen as leader, only that he was the leader, which makes **A** wrong. **B** is wrong because the information does not explain the leadership structure of the tribe. The author does not present the information later in the passage, so **D** is wrong. **C** is the best answer because the information explains Lololma's role with the tribe.

66. H

Basic Grammar and Usage: Pronoun-Antecedent Agreement   *Easy*

The underlined possessive pronoun should agree with its antecedent, *Lololma and the other Hopi leader*. Since a group of people is the subject, *its, ones*, and *his* would be inappropriate. The correct answer is **H** because *their* agrees with the plural subject.

67. D

Basic Grammar and Usage: Verb Tenses   *Easy*

The past-tense verb *refused* in the last part of the sentence indicates that the underlined verb should be past tense, so **D** is correct. *Describe, are describing*, and *do describe* are present-tense verbs, so **A**, **B**, and **C** are incorrect. Maintaining the consistency of verb tenses in a passage helps the reader understand the time of the events described and eliminates confusion.

68. G

Style: Redundancy and Wordiness   *Medium*

Earlier in the paragraph, it was established that the Hopi were meeting with the Commissioner of Indian Affairs, so it is redundant to repeat the name of the agency in **F** and **H**. **J** is wordy in comparison to **G**, which conveys the same meaning more concisely. *The people representing the government agency* can be reduced to *the government representatives* without losing anything except clutter.

69. B

Organization: Transitions, Topic Sentences & Conclusions   *Difficult*

A and **D** are tempting because they mention Lololma returning to Oraibi. However, the second sentence of the paragraph specifies Lololma's actions, and **A** and **D** fail to transition into the information of the second sentence. **C** is a distractor that does not relate to the topic of the paragraph. The third paragraph discusses the changes that took place after Lololma met with government officials, and **B** best addresses the paragraph's focus.

70. F

Sentence Structure: Parallelism   *Medium*

No changes need to be made to the underlined portion because the verbs are past tense like *sent*, so the sentence is parallel. The verbs in **G** and **J** are not past-tense, so they do not match the past tense verb *sent*. **H** creates a comma splice with the addition of *he then moved* and no conjunction. Therefore, **F** is the correct answer.

71. C

Punctuation: Semicolons   *Easy*

Two independent clauses have been joined, so a semicolon is an appropriate punctuation to use. Semicolons do not need conjunctions, so **A** is wrong. **B** creates a comma splice, which means that the independent clauses are weakly separated by only a comma instead of a comma with a conjunction. **D** needs a comma before the conjunction to be correct.

72. J

Punctuation: Commas   *Easy*

Head of the Spider Clan renames *Lomahokenna*, so it needs to be set apart with two commas, as in **J**. The second part of the compound sentence begins after *Clan*, so it would be wrong to leave off the second comma, which explains why **H** is incorrect.

73. B

Sentence Structure: Connecting and Transitional Words   *Easy*

The phrases *traditionally been a rival* and *established generations before* indicate that a relationship exists between the two events. *But* and *yet* are words used to show contrast, not connections. *Then* indicates a passage of time, so **D** is wrong. The best connecting word is *so*, which helps the reader understand the cause-effect relationship between the rivalry and the *rift*.

74. F

Writing Strategy: Additional Detail and Evidence   *Difficult*

The third sentence of the first paragraph states when the first school opened, which would be an appropriate location for the new detail about missionaries encouraging Hopi children to attend school. Sentence 5 of the first paragraph relates to a meeting between Hopi leaders and government officials, so the detail would be out of place in that location. The second paragraph focuses on the meeting between government officials and the Hopi regarding issues with the Navajo, so **H** and **J** would be incorrect.

75. D

Writing Strategy: Big Picture Purpose   *Difficult*

The Navajo and Hopi are rivals, so **A** is incorrect. Although outside influences affected the Hopi, the author does not discuss American settlers in the essay. The author does not mention tribal wars either, so **C** is wrong. The best answer is **D** because much of the essay describes the disagreement within the Hopi tribe regarding how to handle issues with the Navajos.

MATHEMATICS

1. D

Plane Geometry: Circles   *Medium*

The ride turns 90° every 5 seconds. You might want to set this up algebraically:

$$\frac{90°}{5 \text{ seconds}} = \frac{x°}{15 \text{ seconds}}$$
$$5x = 1,350$$
$$x = 270$$

2. J

Algebra: Substitution   *Easy*

This is a substitution question. Substitute 5 for m:

$$5 \times (5 - 3)^3$$
$$= 5 \times (2)^3$$
$$= 5 \times 8$$
$$= 40$$

3. C

Intermediate Algebra: Series   *Easy*

This is a series question. We find the answer by adding together the number of birds presented at each meeting:

$$4 + (6 \times 14) = 4 + 84$$
$$= 88$$

Altogether, 88 birds were discussed over the 15 meetings.

4. G

Plane Geometry: Triangles   *Easy*

The sum of the interior angles of a triangle is always 180°. To find the value of d, subtract 75° and 90° from 180°:

$$180° - 90° - 75° = 15°$$

5. B

Pre-Algebra: Mean, Median & Mode   *Easy*

Reina needs a certain score on her sixth history test to earn a 90 average. First, find her point total on the first five tests by adding 94, 81, 88, 94, and 93. The sum is 450. To average 90 on six tests, Reina needs to earn 540 total points. The score she needs on the sixth and final test is the difference between 540 and 450, or 90.

If you chose **C**, you selected the median of Reina's first five test scores. If you chose **D**, you selected the mode.

6. H

Algebra: Writing Expressions and Equations   *Easy*

To solve this problem, start with the distance formula:

$$\text{distance} = \text{rate} \times \text{time}$$

$$\text{rate} = \frac{\text{distance}}{\text{time}}$$

Now, plug in the values you know. The total distance is 2,450 miles. The time is given just as the variable t:

$$\text{rate} = \frac{2,450}{t}$$

7. C

Pre-Algebra: Number Properties   *Easy*

The question tells us that $C > B$, and that $B > 8$. Since both B and C are greater than 8, the sum $B + C$ must also be greater than 8.

B is incorrect because the question does not provide any information regarding the distance between B and 8. Point B could possibly lie one unit from 8 or many units from 8.

8. H

Plane Geometry: Polygons   *Easy*

Divide the figure into two rectangles, as shown below:

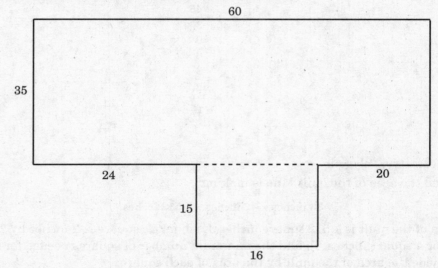

Calculate the area of each rectangle. The larger rectangle measures 60 by 35 feet. The area of the larger rectangle is therefore $60 \times 35 = 2,100$ square feet.

For the smaller rectangle, we are given a height of 15 feet. Its width can be determined by taking the full width of the larger rectangle, 60 feet, and subtracting 24 and 20:

$$60 - 24 - 20 = 16 \text{ feet}$$

The area of the smaller rectangle is therefore $15 \times 16 = 240$ square feet. Adding up the areas of both rectangles, we get:

$$2,100 + 240 = 2,340 \text{ ft}^2$$

9. D

Pre-Algebra: Percentages, Fractions & Decimals   *Easy*

To determine the number of additional students, multiply 500 by 35%:

$$500 \times 0.35 = 175$$

Then add this number to the current enrollment: 500 + 175 = 675. **A** is incorrect because it represents the number of additional enrollees, not the total student population.

10. K

Algebra: Simplification   *Easy*

This is a simplification question. Here are the steps we take to simplify the expression:

$$4a(a^2b + 4ab^2) = (4a \times a^2b) + (4a \times 4ab^2)$$
$$= 4a^3b + 16a^2b^2$$

11. A

Pre-Algebra: Ratios and Proportions   *Medium*

To find the answer, we multiply the length of Harold's grandfather's boat by $\frac{1}{30}$:

$$45 \times \frac{1}{30} = \frac{45}{30}$$
$$= \frac{9}{6}$$
$$= \frac{3}{2}$$
$$= 1\frac{1}{2}$$

12. J

Plane Geometry: Polygons   *Easy*

First, find the area of the quilt Milo is making:

$$36 \text{ inches} \times 42 \text{ inches} = 1,512 \text{ inches}^2$$

The area of the quilt is 1,512 square inches. Each fabric square is 2 inches by 2 inches, or 4 square inches. To find the minimum number of squares needed for the quilt, divide the area of the quilt by the area of each square:

$$\frac{1,512}{4} = 378$$

K is incorrect because it represents the area of the quilt. **G** is incorrect because it represents the perimeter of the quilt.

13. D

Pre-Algebra: Probability   *Easy*

To solve this problem, first determine the number of college students who are NOT liberal arts majors: 900 − 360 = 540. The chance that a student will not be a liberal arts major is therefore $\frac{540}{900}$ or $\frac{3}{5}$.

B is incorrect because it represents the probability that a person chosen at random WILL be a liberal arts major.

14. H

Pre-Algebra: Mean, Median & Mode   *Easy*

To find the average (or mean) number of students per grade level whose favorite book is *A Farewell to Arms*, add the number of sophomores, juniors, and seniors together: $56 + 32 + 47 = 135$. Then, divide this sum by 3 to find the average: $\frac{135}{3} = 45$.

J is incorrect because it represents the median, not the mean.

15. B

Pre-Algebra: Multiples, Factors & Primes   *Medium*

To solve this problem, factor 964 into its prime factors:
$$964 = 2 \times 482$$
$$= 2 \times 2 \times 241$$

The number 241 is prime, so the number cannot be factored any further. **C** and **E** can be eliminated, because 121 and 49 are not prime numbers.

16. F

Algebra: Solving Linear Equations   *Medium*

Solve the equation for a:
$$3\frac{5}{6} = a + 2\frac{1}{3}$$
$$a = 3\frac{5}{6} - 2\frac{1}{3}$$
$$= (3 - 2) + \left(\frac{5}{6} - \frac{1}{3}\right)$$
$$= 1 + \left(\frac{10}{12} - \frac{4}{12}\right)$$
$$= 1\frac{6}{12}$$
$$= 1\frac{1}{2}$$

17. A

Plane Geometry: Angles and Lines   *Medium*

Angle a has a vertical angle that also measures $a°$. Note how the vertical angle is part of a larger triangle. The larger triangle has a second angle measuring 70°. It also has a third angle that lies on a straight line with the angle measuring 110°.

First, find the value of the third angle. Subtract 110° from 180°:
$$180° - 110° = 70°$$

So, the larger triangle is an isosceles triangle. It has two angles measuring 70°, and a third angle measuring $a°$.

The three angles of this large triangle must add up to 180°. To find the value of a, set up an equation:
$$a + 70° + 70° = 180°$$
$$a + 140° = 180°$$
$$a = 180° - 140°$$
$$a = 40°$$

18. H

Algebra: Multiplying Binomials   *Medium*

To find the factors, use the reverse FOIL method:

$$(a - \sqrt{5})(a + \sqrt{5})$$

25 is not a factor.

19. B

Pre-Algebra: Percentages, Fractions & Decimals   *Medium*

Call the fraction that is onion x. If we add up the fractions of the pizza we are given, they will total 1 pizza. So let's set up an equation:

$$\frac{3}{16} + \frac{3}{8} + \frac{1}{4} + x = 1$$

Find a common denominator between 16, 8, 4, and 1 so that we can add the fractions. The least common denominator is 16. Multiply the numerator and denominator of each fraction by the factor you need to get the common denominators of 16:

$$\frac{3}{16} + \frac{3}{8}\left(\frac{2}{2}\right) + \frac{1}{4}\left(\frac{4}{4}\right) + x = \frac{1}{1}\left(\frac{16}{16}\right)$$

Next, simplify the equation:

$$\frac{3}{16} + \frac{6}{16} + \frac{4}{16} + x = \frac{16}{16}$$

$$\frac{13}{16} + x = \frac{16}{16}$$

Subtract $\frac{13}{16}$ from both sides:

$$x = \frac{16}{16} - \frac{13}{16}$$

$$x = \frac{3}{16}$$

Since x represents the fraction that is onion, it is $\frac{3}{16}$.

20. J

Intermediate Algebra: Exponents and Roots   *Medium*

Substitute the values of –4 for and 1 for x and y in the equation:

$$a^{x-y} = a^{(-4)-1}$$

$$= a^{-5}$$

$$= \frac{1}{a^5}$$

F can be eliminated, because no value is given for a.

21. C

Pre-Algebra: Number Problems — *Medium*

The minimum number of tickets that must be redeemed for exactly 24 prizes is 850. Esther would redeem 650 tickets for 2 sets of 10 prizes and 200 tickets for 4 individual prizes.

B is incorrect because tickets can only be traded for single prizes or sets of 5 or 10 prizes.

22. F

Intermediate Algebra: Functions — *Medium*

To find the value of the function, replace x with 3:

$$f(x) = 2x + 4$$
$$= 2(3) + 4$$
$$= 6 + 4$$
$$= 10$$

23. D

Intermediate Algebra: Relationships — *Medium*

Let k represent the constant of variation. Set up the equation of variation: $m = kp$. Substitute 600 for m and \$50.00 for p and solve for k:

$$m = kp$$
$$600 = k(\$50.00)$$
$$12 = k$$

Now that you know the constant k, set up the equation again and solve for p:

$$m = kp$$
$$840 = (12)p$$
$$\$70.00 = p$$

24. J

Intermediate Algebra: Series — *Medium*

The staff may choose from among 60 cats and 43 dogs. To determine the total number of possible combinations, multiply the total number of cats and dogs together. Since only 1 cat and 1 dog can be selected, there are $60 \times 43 = 2{,}580$ possible combinations.

25. C

Coordinate Geometry: Slope — *Medium*

Use the slope formula:

$$m = \frac{y_2 - y_1}{x_2 - x_1}$$

Let $(x_1, y_1) = (2, 4)$ and $(x_2, y_2) = (3, 7)$. Substitute these coordinates into the slope formula and simplify:

$$m = \frac{y_2 - y_1}{x_2 - x_1}$$
$$m = \frac{7 - 4}{3 - 2}$$
$$m = \frac{3}{1}$$
$$m = 3$$

26. **E**

Plane Geometry: Angles and Lines   *Medium*

On this number line, we know the length of segment OP. We also know that $\overline{MN}$ and $\overline{NO}$ are equal to each other. However, we don't have enough information to calculate the length of $\overline{MP}$. For this we'd need to know the length of $\overline{MN}$ or $\overline{NO}$, or at least something about the relationship between those two segments and $\overline{MP}$. The question doesn't give us that, so the most we can determine is that $\overline{MP} = 2\overline{MN} + 4$.

27. **B**

Plane Geometry: Three Dimensions   *Medium*

This question is asking you to find volume. To find the uniform depth of the 12,000 cubic feet of sand in the sandbox with dimensions 120 feet by 70 feet, use the formula for the volume of a rectangular solid, which is $V = lwh$. Substitute the numbers provided:

$$12,000 = 120(70)(h)$$
$$12,000 = 8,400h$$
$$h = \frac{12,000}{8,400}$$
$$h \approx 1.43$$

The answer is between 1 and 1.5 feet. **A** is incorrect because it represents the result when 8,400 is divided by 12,000 rather than the other way around.

28. **F**

Algebra: Simplification   *Medium*

This question asks you to simplify. First, combine like terms:

$$(p^2 + 3p - 5) + (2p^2 - 3p + 5) = (p^2 + 2p^2) + (3p - 3p) + (-5 + 5)$$

Next, perform the addition:

$$(p^2 + 2p^2) + (3p + -3p) + (-5 + 5) = 3p^2 + 0 + 0$$
$$= 3p^2$$

If you selected one of the other answer choices, you probably made a mistake involving one of the negative signs.

29. **A**

Plane Geometry: Polygons   *Medium*

The sum of the interior angles of a regular polygon is determined using the following formula:

$$180°(n - 2)$$

In the formula, n represents the number of sides of the polygon. A pentagon has 5 sides, so the sum of its interior angle measures $180°(5 - 2) = 540°$. There are 5 interior angles, so each angle measures $540° \div 5 = 108°$.

We're told that $\overline{CR}$ bisects $\angle QRS$, so $\angle a$ will equal half the measure of $\angle QRS$. The measure of $\angle a$ is therefore $108° \div 2$, or $54°$.

30. K

Pre-Algebra: Percentages, Fractions & Decimals   *Medium*

Set up an equation to solve for the missing number. Let x represent the missing number:

$$175 = \frac{7}{18}x$$

$$\frac{175}{\frac{7}{18}} = \frac{\frac{7}{18}x}{\frac{7}{18}}$$

$$175\left(\frac{18}{7}\right) = x$$

$$25 \times 18 = x$$

$$450 = x$$

31. E

Coordinate Geometry: Equation of a Line   *Medium*

The y-intercept represents the point at which a line crosses the y-axis. Use the given points to determine the equation of the line. First, determine the slope of the line. Let $(1, 11)$ represent (x_1, y_1) and $(-2, -10)$ represent (x_2, y_2):

$$m = \frac{y_2 - y_1}{x_2 - x_1}$$

$$= \frac{(-10) - (11)}{(-2) - (1)}$$

$$= \frac{-21}{-3}$$

$$= 7$$

The slope of the line is 7. Substitute 7 for m in the slope-intercept equation of the line:

$$y = mx + b$$

$$y = 7x + b$$

Now we have the equation of the line, where b represents the y-intercept. That's the coordinate we're looking for. Plug one of the coordinates into the equation to solve for b. Let's use $(1, 11)$:

$$y = 7x + b$$

$$11 = 7(1) + b$$

$$11 - 7 = b$$

$$4 = b$$

The y-intercept of the line is 4. The line crosses the y-axis at the point $(0, 4)$.

32. H

Algebra: Solving Linear Equations   *Medium*

We can take the following steps to solve for b:

$$a = 8b - 3$$

$$a + 3 = 8b$$

$$\frac{a + 3}{8} = \frac{8b}{8}$$

$$\frac{a + 3}{8} = b$$

G is incorrect because the 3 is not divided by 8.

33. A

Plane Geometry: Triangles   *Medium*

Because this is a right triangle, we can use the Pythagorean theorem to solve the problem:

$$a^2 + b^2 = c^2$$
$$220^2 + 160^2 = c^2$$
$$48,400 + 25,600 = c^2$$
$$74,000 = c^2$$
$$\sqrt{74,000} = c$$

34. J

Trigonometry: SOHCAHTOA   *Medium*

You are told that $\sin \theta = \dfrac{3}{12}$. The sine of angle θ is the ratio of the side opposite θ and the hypotenuse. This means that the side opposite θ is 3, and the hypotenuse is 12.

The cosine of angle θ is the ratio of the side adjacent to θ and the hypotenuse. To find $\cos \theta$, you must solve for the length of b using the Pythagorean theorem:

$$a^2 + b^2 = c^2$$
$$3^2 + b^2 = 12^2$$
$$9 + b^2 = 144$$
$$b^2 = 144 - 9$$
$$b^2 = 135$$
$$b = \sqrt{135}$$
$$b = \sqrt{9 \times 15}$$
$$b = 3\sqrt{15}$$

In this problem, the side adjacent to θ is $3\sqrt{15}$ and the hypotenuse is 12, so $\cos \theta = \dfrac{3\sqrt{15}}{12}$, or $\dfrac{\sqrt{15}}{4}$.

35. D

Coordinate Geometry: Parallel and Perpendicular Lines   *Medium*

First, determine the slope by putting the equation in $y = mx + b$ form:

$$2x + 4y = 24$$
$$4y = -2x + 24$$
$$y = \dfrac{-2x + 24}{4}$$
$$y = -\dfrac{1}{2}x + 6$$

The slope of the given line is $-\dfrac{1}{2}$, and we're looking for a slope that is parallel.

Parallel lines have the same slope.

36. H

Algebra: Inequalities   *Medium*

The first step to take is solving $\sqrt{a + 2} \geq 3$. To do this, square both sides of the inequality:

$$\sqrt{a+2} \geq 3$$
$$\left(\sqrt{a+2}\right)^2 \geq 3^2$$
$$a+2 \geq 9$$
$$a \geq 7$$

37. **B**

Coordinate Geometry: Conic Sections   *Medium*

When the graph crosses the *x*-axis, this means that *y* will equal 0. Substitute 0 for *y* in the equation. Then factor the equation and solve for *x*.

$$y = x^2 - 144$$
$$x^2 - 144 = 0$$
$$(x+12)(x-12) = 0$$

Set each factor equal to 0 and solve:

$$\begin{array}{ccc} x+12 = 0 & & x-12 = 0 \\ x = -12 & \text{or} & x = 12 \end{array}$$

The solutions are 12 and −12, which represent the points at which the graph crosses the *x*-axis.

38. **K**

Plane Geometry: Three Dimensions   *Medium*

The silo is a cylinder. The volume of a cylinder is the area of the circular end multiplied by the cylinder's height. The area of an end is:

$$\pi \times 6^2 = 36\,\pi \text{ square feet}$$

Therefore, the volume of the cylinder is

$$36\pi \times 30 = 1,080(3.14)$$
$$\approx 3,391.2$$

Among the choices, this answer is closest to 3,400 cubic feet.

39. **A**

Pre-Algebra: Mean, Median & Mode   *Medium*

The *median* of a set of terms is the middle number when the terms are placed in order from smallest to largest. In this set, there are nine terms. So, we're looking for the fifth largest term in the set.

Place the terms in numerical order:

$$208, 222, 243, 245, 267, 276, 289, 293, 293$$

The number 267 is the middle term, the fifth largest. The 267 tickets were sold on night 2.

40. H

Algebra: Multiplying Binomials   *Medium*

Multiply the binomials:

$$\left(\frac{3}{4}a+b\right)^2 = \left(\frac{3}{4}a+b\right)\left(\frac{3}{4}a+b\right)$$

$$= \left(\frac{9}{16}a^2 + \frac{3}{4}ab + \frac{3}{4}ab + b^2\right)$$

$$= \left(\frac{9}{16}a^2 + \frac{6}{4}ab + b^2\right)$$

41. D

Trigonometry: Trigonometric Identities   *Medium*

Substitute $\frac{3}{4}$ for $\sin\theta$ in the equation $\sin^2\theta + \cos^2\theta = 1$ and solve for $\cos\theta$:

$$\sin^2\theta + \cos^2\theta = 1 \text{ Trigonometric identity given}$$

$$\left(\frac{3}{4}\right)^2 + \cos^2\theta = 1 \text{ Substitute}$$

$$\frac{9}{16} + \cos^2\theta = 1 \text{ Simplify}$$

$$\cos^2\theta = \frac{7}{16} \text{ Subtract}$$

$$\cos\theta = \pm\frac{\sqrt{7}}{4} \text{ Take the square root of both sides}$$

Since you are given $0 \le \theta \le 90$, choose the positive value, since the cosine is positive in the first quadrant.

42. H

Intermediate Algebra: Matrices   *Medium*

Follow the operations shown below to write the product of the two matrices:

$$\begin{bmatrix} 3 & 0 & 7 \end{bmatrix}\begin{bmatrix} x \\ 7 \\ 5x \end{bmatrix} = \begin{bmatrix} (3\times x) & (0\times x) & (7\times x) \\ (3\times 7) & (0\times 7) & (7\times 7) \\ (3\times 5x) & (0\times 5x) & (7\times 5x) \end{bmatrix}$$

$$= \begin{bmatrix} 3x & 0 & 7x \\ 21 & 0 & 49 \\ 15x & 0 & 35x \end{bmatrix}$$

K is incorrect because it presents the terms in the incorrect order.

43. B

Coordinate Geometry: Graphing Equations   *Medium*

Plug the point $(-4, 1)$ into the slope-intercept form of the equation:

$$y = mx + b$$
$$1 = -6(-4) + b$$
$$1 = 24 + b$$
$$1 - 24 = b$$
$$-23 = b$$

Now, rewrite the slope-intercept form of the equation:

$$y = -6x - 23$$

Check each ordered pair to see which one makes the equation true.

44. K

Plane Geometry: Polygons   *Medium*

The two squares have areas in a ratio of 9:16. If the smallest square has an area of 9, its side could measure 3, since $3 \times 3 = 9$. The larger square could have a side that measures 4, since $4 \times 4 = 16$.

However, ratios don't give us definite measures—they only give *relative* measures. The smallest lengths of the squares could be 3 and 4, but the lengths could also be larger. The lengths must always be multiples of 3 and 4. Scanning down the answer choices, we see that the only ratio that contains multiples of 3 and 4 is **K**, 9:12.

Double-check to see if side lengths of 9 and 12 would produce areas in a ratio of 3:4. A square with side length 9 would have an area of 81, and a square with side length 12 would have an area of 144. The ratio 81:144 reduces to 9:16, so these side lengths could work.

45. D

Coordinate Geometry: Distance and Midpoints   *Medium*

Use the midpoint formula:

$$d = \frac{x_1 + x_2}{2}, \frac{y_1 + y_2}{2}$$

$$= \frac{8 + (-2)}{2}, \frac{4 + 2}{2}$$

$$= \frac{6}{2}, \frac{6}{2}$$

$$= (3, 3)$$

46. J

Coordinate Geometry: Equation of a Line   *Medium*

Plug the point (2, 6) into the equation:

$$y = ux + \frac{1}{2}$$

$$6 = 2u + \frac{1}{2}$$

$$6 - \frac{1}{2} = 2u$$

$$\frac{11}{2} = 2u$$

$$\frac{11}{4} = u$$

The lines $y = ux + \frac{1}{2}$ and $y = x + 4$ intersect at $(2, 6)$ when $u = \frac{11}{4}$.

47. C

Plane Geometry: Triangles   *Medium*

You are given that $\overline{AC}$ measures $10\sqrt{3}$ and $\overline{BD}$ bisects $\overline{AC}$, which means that $\overline{AB}$ measures $5\sqrt{3}$. Use the Pythagorean theorem to determine the length of hypotenuse $\overline{AD}$:

$$a^2 + b^2 = c^2$$
$$\left(\overline{AB}\right)^2 + \left(\overline{BD}\right)^2 = \left(\overline{AD}\right)^2$$
$$\left(5\sqrt{3}\right)^2 + \left(15\right)^2 = \left(\overline{AD}\right)^2$$
$$\left(25 \times 3\right) + \left(225\right) = \left(\overline{AD}\right)^2$$
$$\left(75\right) + \left(225\right) = \left(\overline{AD}\right)^2$$
$$300 = \left(\overline{AD}\right)^2$$

Take the square root of both sides to determine the measure of $\overline{AD}$:

$$\left(\overline{AD}\right)^2 = 300$$
$$\overline{AD} = \sqrt{300}$$
$$= \sqrt{100 \times 3}$$
$$= 10\sqrt{3}$$

The measure of $\overline{AD}$ is $10\sqrt{3}$, which gives us three sides of the triangle as follows: $5\sqrt{3}$, 15, and $10\sqrt{3}$. These three sides are in the ratio 1, $\sqrt{3}$, and 2. To double-check this, calculate $5\sqrt{3} \times \sqrt{3}$, which works out to 15. This means we're dealing with a 30-60-90 triangle:

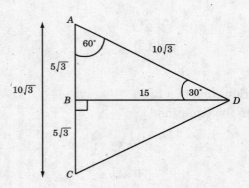

In this case, $\angle DAB$ is the angle opposite the second largest leg. That means $\angle DAB$ measures 60°. **C** is correct.

48. F

Pre-Algebra: Multiples, Factors & Primes   *Medium*

The number 16 can be factored into the following positive integer pairs: 16 × 1, 8 × 2, and 4 × 4. Of these, 5 numbers are unique positive integer factors: 1, 2, 4, 8, and 16.

49. **B**

Pre-Algebra: Number Problems *Medium*

You are told that for all values $x < 10$, the sum of the y values in the first x columns is equal to $x + 7$. This means that for every column x, the y values in the preceding columns add up to $x + 7$. For instance, the y values in the first 2 columns add up to $2 + 7$, or 9:

$$8 + 1 = 9$$

The y values in the first 6 columns add up to $6 + 7$, or 13:

$$8 + 1 + 1 + 1 + 1 + 1 = 13$$

For all values $x \geq 10$, the sum of the y values in the first x columns is increased to $y + 9$. This means that the y values in the first 10 columns add up to $10 + 9$, or 19. The y values in the first 11 columns add up to $11 + 9$, or 20, and the y values in the first 12 columns add up to $12 + 9$, or 21.

Complete the table for the x values 7 through 9. In each column, the preceding y values must add up to $x + 7$:

x	1	2	3	4	5	6	7	8	9	10	11	12
y	8	1	1	1	1	1	1	1	1			

Now complete the table for the x values 10 through 12. In each column, the preceding y values must add up to $x + 9$:

x	1	2	3	4	5	6	7	8	9	10	11	12
y	8	1	1	1	1	1	1	1	1	3	1	1

The y value for the column $x = 12$ is 1. Thus, the first 12 y values add up to $12 + 9$, or 21:

$$8 + 1 + 1 + 1 + 1 + 1 + 1 + 1 + 3 + 1 + 1 = 21$$

50. **G**

Plane Geometry: Circles *Medium*

The question tells you that the diameter of the unicycle wheel is 1.5 feet. This means that the circumference of the wheel is $C = \pi d$, or 1.5π.

Marlon travels the length of the parking lot 3 times, which is a total distance of 120π feet. To find the number of revolutions, divide 120π feet by the circumference of the wheel:

$$120\pi \text{ feet} \div 1.5\pi \text{ feet} = 80 \text{ revolutions}$$

51. **C**

Pre-Algebra: Number Properties *Medium*

Pick numbers for a and b. When picking numbers for integers, always try 0 and negative numbers. **A** is incorrect if $a = 0$, because 0 divided by any number equals 0. **B** is incorrect if a is a negative number. **D** is incorrect if $a = -1$ and $b = 3$. **E** is incorrect if $a = 0$ and $b = 3$.

The only expression that must be true is $b - a > a - b$. Regardless of the numbers chosen, $b - a$ will always be positive, and $a - b$ will always be negative.

52. F

Trigonometry: Trigonometric Identities

Medium

Find $\sin\theta$:

$$\sin^2\theta + \cos^2\theta = 1$$
$$\sin^2\theta + (-\frac{1}{6})^2 = 1$$
$$\sin^2\theta + (\frac{1}{36}) = 1$$
$$\sin^2\theta = 1 - (\frac{1}{36})$$
$$\sin^2\theta = \frac{36}{36} - \frac{1}{36}$$
$$\sin^2\theta = \frac{35}{36}$$
$$\sin\theta = \pm\frac{\sqrt{35}}{6}$$

53. E

Trigonometry: Solving Triangles

Medium

This problem can be solved using the cosine formula. The cosine of an angle equals $\frac{\text{adjacent}}{\text{hypotenuse}}$. In this case, the measure of the side adjacent to $\angle r$ is given as 10 centimeters, and r is given as 50°. We are looking for an expression that represents the length of the hypotenuse. Plug the values you know into the cosine formula:

$$\cos 50° = \frac{\text{adjacent}}{\text{hypotenuse}}$$
$$\cos 50° = \frac{10}{\text{hypotenuse}}$$

Now, solve for the value of the hypotenuse:

$$\text{hypotenuse}(\cos 50°) = 10$$
$$\text{hypotenuse} = \frac{10}{\cos 50°}$$

E gives the expression for the length of $\overline{YZ}$, the hypotenuse of the triangle.

54. F

Coordinate Geometry: Number Lines and Inequalities

Medium

Solve the inequality:

$$2|x| \geq 6$$
$$|x| \geq 3$$

Look for the graph that shows an absolute distance from 0 of greater than or equal to 3 units.

55. A
Intermediate Algebra: Functions   *Difficult*

Substitute $(x + s)$ for x in the function $g(x) = \sqrt{x + 2}$:

$$= \sqrt{x + s + 2}$$

56. K
Intermediate Algebra: Quadratic Equations   *Difficult*

These two solutions work for the equation $(x - 4a)(x + 7b)$. Remember, you can check your work by substituting $4a$ in for x and substituting $-7b$ in for x. This yields the equation $x^2 + (-4a + 7b)x + (-4a)(7b) = 0$, which simplifies to $x^2 + x(7b - 4a) - 28ab = 0$.

57. D
Coordinate Geometry: Conic Sections   *Difficult*

The diameter of the inscribed circle is 4, so the radius is 2. Thus the center is (2, 2). Plug this information into the equation of a circle:

$$\left(x - h\right)^2 + \left(y - k\right)^2 = r^2$$
$$\left(x - 2\right)^2 + \left(y - 2\right)^2 = 4$$

58. H
Plane Geometry: Circles   *Difficult*

Due to the lengths of arcs FG and HK being congruent, it is true that $\angle GNF$ and $\angle HNK$ are congruent. We can find $\angle HNK$ by subtracting $-b°$ from $-a°$. Thus, $\angle HNK = -a° + b°$. Since $\angle GNF$ is positive and goes counterclockwise, you simply negate the measure of $\angle HNK$. So, $-(-a° + b°) = a° - b°$, or $-b° + a°$.

59. E
Algebra: Solving Linear Equations   *Difficult*

You are asked to solve for s in terms of r. This question will involve manipulating equations. Start by solving the first equation for z:

$$r = 3z - 4$$
$$r + 4 = 3z$$
$$\frac{r + 4}{3} = z$$

The value of z is $\frac{r + 4}{3}$. Plug this value in for z in the second equation:

$$s = 7 - z$$
$$s = 7 - \left(\frac{r + 4}{3}\right)$$
$$s = \frac{21}{3} - \left(\frac{r + 4}{3}\right)$$
$$s = \frac{21 - r - 4}{3}$$
$$s = \frac{17 - r}{3}$$

B is incorrect because it involves adding $21 + 4$ in the numerator instead of subtracting $21 - 4$. When you see equations at the end of the section, there will probably be some detailed math involved, so be sure to work carefully.

60. **F**

Intermediate Algebra: Logarithms   *Difficult*

Solve:

$$\log_3 21 - \log_3 7 = \frac{\log_3 21}{\log_3 7}$$
$$= \log_3 3$$
$$= 1$$

Setting $\log_6 y = 1$, $y = 0$ is the value that makes the equation true, since $6^0 = 1$.

READING

---

1. **C**

Prose Fiction: Specific Detail   *Easy*

The sixth paragraph describes Miss Drayson as uncommunicative and as a person who does not reveal information once she has it, so **C** is the best choice. Miss Drayson does not communicate with Mr. Malloy or show her emotions, so **B** and **D** are incorrect. The text does not indicate that Mr. Malloy needs to monitor Miss Drayson, only that her *mental quirks* are useful to him.

2. **J**

Prose Fiction: Specific Detail   *Easy*

The sixth paragraph indicates that Mr. Malloy's employees have *mental quirks*, so **J** is the best answer. **F** and **G** are incorrect because Malloy's workers are not especially strong or intelligent. **H** is tempting because the first sentence of paragraph 6 states that *mental disabilities were harder to deal with than the physical handicaps*. Although this suggests that Malloy may have some employees with physical disabilities, all of the ones described in the passage seem to have mental problems.

3. **D**

Prose Fiction: Inference   *Medium*

When Malloy receives the news, the passage states that he fights *to keep his emotions in check,* which rules out **B**. Malloy never expresses fear or excitement about the peace agreement, much like his assistant. Malloy seems confused about who to send and asks himself what he should do. Moreover, it takes Malloy two days to decide which man to send, so the best answer is **D**.

4. **G**

Prose Fiction: Purpose   *Medium*

The first paragraph describes how the employees of Malloy are *atypical*, so the best answer is **G**. **F** is wrong because the narrator does not reveal until later in the passage that Malloy needs to keep the activities of his office undercover. Similarly, the narrator reveals later that Malloy does not consider his job a *cinch* because of his staff. No indication is given that Malloy feels awkward working with people who have psychological problems, so **H** is incorrect.

5. A

Prose Fiction: Cause-Effect   *Difficult*

Malloy tells Braynek what to do when he is at the conference, so **B** cannot be correct.
There is no evidence in the passage to support **C**, so it should also be eliminated.
Although Braynek exhibits confidence through the last sentence of the paragraph,
the passage does not give us reason to believe that his confidence is due to his speaking abilities, so **D** can be crossed off. **A** is the best answer because when Malloy finds
out he is supposed to go to the conference he looks *up at the ceiling* and quietly asks
himself, "What *can* I do?" This suggests he feels uncertain and uncomfortable about
attending the meeting, although it is unclear why.

6. H

Prose Fiction: Inference   *Difficult*

Malloy does not necessarily think the conference will go smoothly or else he would
not provide Braynek with so much information. Malloy seems prepared but not
worried, so **G** is not the best answer. Although Malloy is knowledgeable, no indication
is given that he has negotiated agreements, which means **J** is also incorrect. Malloy
provides a great deal of tactical information to Braynek about the opposing side's
likely tactics, so **H** is the best answer.

7. B

Prose Fiction: Specific Detail   *Medium*

The fifth paragraph indicates that Malloy did not have top-rate men because *they
couldn't be spared from work that required their total capacity*, so the best answer is
B. Although the passage states that Malloy likes to utilize the *mental quirks* of his
employees to make them *useful*, his employees are not average or low achieving, so **A**
and **C** are incorrect. Malloy sends one of his men to the conference, so **D** is wrong.

8. F

Prose Fiction: Specific Detail   *Easy*

Paragraph 19 describes Braynek's mission, which involves finding and plugging
loopholes, not antagonizing the opposition, and he should be more *shrewd and
underhanded* than them. **F** best summarizes Braynek's job. **G** and **H** are incorrect
because it is unclear from the text whether Malloy wants the agreement to take
place. **J** is wrong because Braynek is told not to *antagonize* anyone.

9. D

Prose Fiction: Inference   *Medium*

A is incorrect because according to the passage Miss Drayson's *emotions were a secret*.
C is wrong because *nothing...got out of Malloy's office without his direct order*. **D** is
the best answer because when Miss Drayson enters Malloy's office she waits to see
his reaction as if she knows what is in the letter.

10. J

Prose Fiction: Vocabulary in Context   *Medium*

Supporting and *promoting* do not make sense in the context of the paragraph, since
these quirks clearly have some disadvantages. The rest of the sentence goes on to

contrast how Molloy takes advantage of his employees' mental quirks, rather than *thwarting* them, so we need a word with the opposite sense from "takes advantage" or "uses." This makes **J** the best answer.

11. C

Social Science: Comparison   *Medium*

King, Dewey, and Roosevelt all believed that the education system should produce individuals who are both intelligent and moral because one aspect without the other was of little value to society. **B** is only partially correct because cultural change was not a specified goal for King, Dewey, or Roosevelt. **A** and **D** may result from being intelligent and moral, but **C** most clearly states the assertions of King, Dewey, and Roosevelt.

12. J

Social Science: Inference   *Medium*

The author indicates in the last paragraph that education should *encourage individual and societal growth by enriching the self*, which indicates **J** is the best answer. **F**, **G**, and **H** mention details from the passage; however, details such as finding employment or learning Latin are too narrow to represent the author's viewpoint.

13. B

Social Science: Purpose   *Medium*

Prior to the seventh paragraph, the author discusses the beliefs of King, Roosevelt, and Dewey, but the rest of the passage focuses more on the author's opinion about the purpose of education, which makes **B** correct. **A** is wrong because the author's beliefs do not differ greatly from those of Roosevelt, King, and Dewey. The author does not discuss **C**. **D** is a minor point made in the passage but not the main idea.

14. J

Social Science: Specific Detail   *Easy*

The author does not mention a specific age in the first paragraph, so **F** is incorrect. **G** is wrong because the laws were passed in 1918. The author indicates that school attendance laws do not address the goals of education, so **H** is wrong. **J** is the correct answer because *all U.S. states* have attendance laws.

15. C

Social Science: Main Idea, Argument & Theme   *Medium*

A is a minor point made at the end of the passage, so it does not qualify is a "main point." **B** is incorrect because the author does not discuss wealth and prosperity as the goals of education. **D** is tempting but no mention is made of developing good citizens, which is a key point of the passage. **C** is the best answer because intelligence and character are the main goals of education, and the author adds in the last paragraph that *true education… goes beyond emphasizing cultural participation and encourages human progress and innovation.*

16. F

Social Science: Specific Detail *Medium*

According to the third paragraph, Dewey believed that *different countries would produce different educational programs designed to serve the goals of their particular cultures*, so the best answer is **F**. No mention is made of government's role in education, so **G** and **J** are incorrect. **H** is wrong because Dewey emphasizes how culture influences the way individuals learn to fit into society.

17. B

Social Science: Inference *Medium*

The fourth paragraph indicates that the archbishop and Roosevelt agreed that schools are helping *students acquire knowledge, read books, and learn facts* when they should also be producing good citizens, which makes **A** wrong and **B** correct. The author does not discuss **C** and **D** in paragraph 4.

18. J

Social Science: Specific Detail *Easy*

J is the best answer because the sixth paragraph states that tough classes *would help the individual deal with difficult situations later in life.*

19. C

Social Science: Inference *Difficult*

A and **B** are wrong because King argued that the education system should teach values as well as basic knowledge; King's writings were published after similar writings from Roosevelt and Dewey. The last paragraph indicates the author hopes that the *ruling ideologies* will soon realize that their *"time" is at an end*, so **D** is wrong. The same statement from the author suggests that the traditional view of education has not changed, so **C** is the correct answer.

20. G

Social Science: Specific Detail *Medium*

The last sentence of paragraph 5 supports **G** by stating that the purpose of education is *not to teach people what to think, but to teach people <u>how</u> to think, and how to express their beliefs compellingly.* **F** and **H** are important aspects of education but not key points in the fifth paragraph. Paragraph 5 makes no mention of developing a social conscience, so **J** is wrong.

21. C

Humanities: Structure and Organization *Medium*

A and **D** are incorrect because Sula and Nel are characters in Morrison's book. **B** might be tempting, but although the passage begins with a statement about the importance of family bonding, it does not end with one. **C** best describes the structure of the passage.

22. G

Humanities: Inference   *Difficult*

Although the first paragraph makes it clear that Morrison believes poor bonding between a parent and child negatively affects children, **F** is wrong because the author does not indicate that the problems cannot be overcome. The first paragraph states that *mother-daughter relationships…are the mainstay of the black community*, but **H** is wrong because the text does not mention problems in the black community. Although the passage suggests that Helene drives *her daughter's imagination underground* due to close supervision, **J** is too broad and not indicated in the passage. **G** is the best answer because the author states in paragraph 1 that Morrison *believes that in many cases, lack of interest or outright cruelty shown by children's parents has a negative, irrevocable influence on their future development.*

23. D

Humanities: Vocabulary in Context   *Medium*

Context clues indicate that *pious* is opposite of *unwholesome*, so *moral* is the best choice. Helene may have lived in a more *structured*, *pleasant*, and *healthy* environment because of the increased morality in her life. However, **D** is the most precise answer available.

24. F

Humanities: Specific Detail   *Easy*

The author states in the fourth paragraph that the *friendship between Sula and Nel develops as a comforting remedy for both girls' incessant loneliness*, so **F** is the correct answer. Although the girls face problems related to segregation and poor self-esteem, these are not the specified reasons the girls become close. The text does not indicate abuse of either girl, so **H** is incorrect.

25. C

Humanities: Inference   *Medium*

Only Helene's mother was rebellious, so **A** is incorrect. The text does not make it clear whether Helene and her grandmother raised Nel together, so **B** is wrong. The author does not suggest that Helene's mother was angry about losing her daughter, so **D** is wrong. **C** is the best answer because the description of the Virgin Mary suggests that Helene's grandmother was devout. Moreover, the last sentence of the second paragraph suggests that *attempts to suppress* the *history* of Helene influenced how Helene raised Nel.

26. H

Humanities: Specific Detail   *Medium*

Sula's mother is *indifferent* about her daughter according to the text, and she and Eva take strangers into their home, which suggests they are *impulsive*. Nel's mother is strict and regimented, so **F** is wrong. Although Sula's mother and grandmother enjoy having intellectual conversations with men, the chaos in the home suggests they are tolerant of different types of people. Sula's mother does not intentionally hurt Sula, so **G** is wrong.

27. D

Humanities: Structure and Organization   *Medium*

The fourth paragraph mainly describes the family experiences of both Nel and Sula, so the best choice is **D**. Only the first sentence mentions that Helene tried to stop the friendship of Nel and Sula, so **A** is incorrect. The author describes the issues faced by Sula in her home but presents no analysis of psychological problems. The paragraph only mentions that the girls helped each other, and it primarily focuses on why each felt lonely within their own families, but it does not mention that they helped each other work through family issues, which means **C** is wrong.

28. F

Humanities: Specific Detail   *Medium*

The last sentence of the third paragraph explains that the incident on the train *solidifies Nel's acceptance of a narrowed life with limited options*. The last sentence of the fifth paragraph explains that Sula's upbringing forced her to *draw her own conclusions about the choices available to her as a black woman in the 1920s and 1930s*. The best answer is **F** because the childhood experiences of both girls greatly affected their outlook on the future. **G**, **H**, and **J** are incorrect because there is no textual evidence to support the idea that both girls have long-term issues with relationships, racism, or authority figures.

29. B

Humanities: Inference   *Medium*

Before showing fear to the white conductor, Nel viewed Helene as a *tall, proud woman*. Nel worries that if her strong mother shows fear then she might, too, so **B** is the best answer. *Nel is shocked at her first real glimpse of racism*, but the text does not state she denied its existence. **C** is wrong because Nel worries that if her mother *were really custard, then there was a chance that Nel was too*. **D** is incorrect because after the incident she views her life as *narrowed*, so Nel most likely believed the opposite before the problem on the train.

30. J

Humanities: Specific Detail   *Easy*

J is correct because the first paragraph states that Morrison examines the mother-daughter relationship that each girl experiences and *each woman's resulting lifestyle and the type of selfhood it grants her*. Although the passage only focuses on the childhood experiences and history of the girls, the novel follows them through adulthood, which means **F** and **H** are wrong. **G** is wrong because the girls' relationship is only one element of the novel.

31. B

Natural Science: Inference   *Medium*

In the opening sentence, the author states that scientists have gathered information about microbes through *lab investigations*, and environmental genomics has advanced the idea of studying microbes in their environment. In the third paragraph, the author writes that *environmental genomics aims to capture the full measure of microbial diversity by trading the lens of the microscope for the lens of genomics*. In the same paragraph the author goes on to explain that environmental genomics involves *recovering communities of microbial genes where they live* and that *environmental genomics avoids the need to take cultures of uncooperative organisms*. It can be inferred that prior to environmental genomics, scientists were only able to analyze isolated samples, so **B** is the best answer. The natural environment was not part of the equation prior to environmental genomics, so **A** and **C** are wrong. The author describes a large sample taken during the *Sorcerer II* expedition, which involved environmental genomics, so **D** is wrong.

32. F

Natural Science: Point of View and Tone   *Difficult*

The author states in the last paragraph that oceanic studies *reveal the power of environmental genomics to capture the true measure of microbial diversity*, which implies she would agree with **F**. Although the author suggests environmental genomics is better than traditional methods, the author provides no textual evidence of false hypotheses. The first paragraph mentions microbes being a possible solution to global warming, but no other mention is made of the subject, which means **H** is incorrect. In paragraph 5, the author questions whether all the proteins have been found, so **J** is incorrect.

33. D

Natural Science: Specific Detail   *Easy*

D is supported by information in the third paragraph. The author states in the third paragraph that *environmental genomics avoids the need to take cultures of uncooperative organisms* because groups of microbial genes are taken along with the water in which they live. **B** may be tempting because the author describes freezing samples; however, no mention is made of changing water and air temperatures. No textual evidence supports the idea of genes becoming acclimated or studying them in different environments, so **A** and **C** are incorrect.

34. H

Natural Science: Specific Detail   *Easy*

The first paragraph indicates that the function of microbes is *cycling the mineral nutrients that support life on earth*, so **H** is the best answer. The author does not state that microbes spread disease or reproduce rapidly, so **F** and **J** are incorrect. **G** refers to marine microbes rather than all microorganisms.

35. C

Natural Science: Vocabulary in Context   *Medium*

The second sentence of paragraph 2 describes the variations in microbes and how the differences challenge *scientists to explain the observed diversity*. **A** is tempting because it is an alternate definition of *elusive*, but the context points to **C** as the best answer. The text does not suggest that microbes can be touched or that scientists are being deceptive, so **B** and **D** are incorrect.

36. G

Natural Science: Inference   *Medium*

Although scientists identified many genes and bacterial species, it is unknown whether the genes and species were new ones, which means **F** is incorrect. **H** is wrong because the team revised the assembly methods in the second study, not the first one. The text does not indicate that scientists had faulty measurements, so **J** is wrong. **G** is the best answer because the data collected *imposed new challenges on existing genome assembly methods and other analysis techniques.*

37. A

Natural Science: Specific Detail   *Medium*

A is the best answer because the number of base pairs in the human genome is already known according to paragraph 5. **B** is wrong because the author writes that environmental genomics enables scientists to *identify species and determine their evolutionary heritage.* **C** is incorrect because the author writes in paragraph 3 that *by linking microbial gene data to details such as the pH, salinity, and water temperature of the collection sites, environmental genomics sheds light on the biological processes encoded in the genes.* **D** is wrong because a study by Kannan and Manning revealed the *structural and functional diversity* of microbes.

38. J

Natural Science: Main Idea, Argument & Theme   *Medium*

The sixth paragraph describes the expedition of the *Challenger* to point out that studying oceanic microbes is not a new idea, so **J** is the best answer. The *Challenger* was not limited to the Sargasso Sea, so **F** is wrong. **G** and **H** are incorrect because assessing changes in global climate and microbes were not specified as goals of Venter's expedition.

39. B

Natural Science: Comparison   *Medium*

The second paragraph supports **B** by explaining how anthrax has *little genetic variation*, unlike *Escherichia coli.* **A** is incorrect because anthrax is a *bacterial species*, not viral. The author only describes anthrax and *E. coli* in the second paragraph, and no textual evidence supports either **C** or **D**.

40. J

Natural Science: Specific Detail   *Medium*

Although Venter's team is studying *the millions of proteins in the GOS sequences to see if we're close to discovering all the proteins in nature*, no textual evidence indicates the way proteins are classified is a focus. *How enzymes are structured* is supported by the last sentence of the paragraph, and *what affects the structure of microbes* is supported by the study by Rusch and Halpern. Therefore, the best answer is **J**. **F**, **G**, and **J** represent a misreading of the data.

SCIENCE

1. B

Data Representation: Read the Chart   *Easy*

According to Figure 1, tiger salamanders' body size indexes were greatest during Interval A and Interval E. That makes **B** the correct answer. **A** represents the intervals when paedomorphic, not terrestrial, tiger salamanders' body indexes were greatest. **C** represents a misreading of the data. **D** represents the intervals when the tiger salamanders' body size indexes were at their smallest, not their greatest.

2. G

Data Representation: Read the Chart   *Easy*

The passage tells us that Interval C is the Medieval Warm Period. Looking at Interval C in Figure 2, we see that slightly less than 0.4 percent of the salamander population was paedomorphic. The correct answer is **G**. The percentage in **F** is too small, and the percentages in **H** and **J** are too large.

3. C

Data Representation: Use the Chart   *Medium*

This question requires the use of both figures. First, look at Figure 1 to confirm that it was the paedomorphic salamanders that had a body size index of 1.5 in Interval D. Then, look at Figure 2 to see the percent of paedomorphosis during Interval D. The correct answer is **C**. The percentages in choices **A** and **B** are too large, and the percentage in choice **D** is too small.

4. J

Data Representation: Use the Chart   *Medium*

The question tells us that paedomorphic tiger salamanders thrive when the pond system is healthy. Therefore, we can assume that the salamanders don't do as well when the pond system is unhealthy. The paedomorphic tiger salamanders' body size index was at its smallest during Interval D, so the correct answer is **J**. **F**, **G**, and **H** all represent intervals when the paedomorphic salamanders' body index was higher than in Interval D, so none of those choices can be correct.

5. A

Data Representation: Use the Chart   *Medium*

According to the data in Figure 2, the percentage of paedomorphic individuals in the total tiger salamander population varies little from one time interval to the next (the greatest jump is less than 0.2 percent). Therefore, the correct answer is **A**. **B** is the exact opposite of the correct answer. **C** is a hypothesis suggested by Figure 1, not Figure 2. The paedomorphic salamander population increased most significantly in Interval B, so **D** is not correct.

6. G

Research Summary: Read the Chart   *Easy*

According to Figure 2, the inter-stimulus interval for the TDT control is approximately 18 seconds. The correct answer is **G**. **F** is too short, and **H** and **J** are both too long.

7. B

Research Summary: Use the Chart   *Easy*

This question requires you to come to a conclusion based on all three figures. In each figure, the TDT inter-stimulus intervals are significantly shorter than the TOJ inter-stimulus intervals. This means that subjects take less time to recognize the presence of multiple stimuli than they do to identify the locations of those stimuli. (Remember that the definitions of TDT and TOJ are given in the passage.) The correct answer is **B**. **A** is the exact *opposite* of the correct answer. Neither **C** nor **D** is supported by the data.

8. H

Research Summary: Read the Chart   *Medium*

The TOJ assessment scenario in which 25 Hz was delivered to the tips of the second and third digits of the same hand was the scenario with the longest inter-stimulus interval. This means that **H** is the correct answer. **F**, **G**, and **J** all represent scenarios with shorter inter-stimulus intervals than the scenario in **H**.

9. A

Research Summary: Use the Chart   *Medium*

Looking at Figure 1, we see that the inter-stimulus interval for the 25 Hz TOJ assessment was approximately 80 msec. This is nearly four times as long as the inter-stimulus interval for the 25 Hz TDT assessment, which was approximately 20 seconds. The correct answer is **A**. **B** and **C** represent an incorrect reading of the data. **D** is the exact *opposite* of the correct answer.

10. J

Research Summary: Use the Chart   *Difficult*

The data in Figure 3 show that, when stimulus points are on different hands, the inter-stimulus intervals for the TOJ and TDT assessments are quite similar to one another. Additionally, each of the inter-stimulus intervals for the TOJ assessment is relatively short. This means that it is easier to distinguish between stimuli when the stimulus points are on different hands, and **J** is the correct answer. **F** is not supported by the data in Figure 3, nor is choice **G**. **H** gets it backward: It's easier, not more difficult, to distinguish between stimuli on different hands.

11. B

Research Summary: Take the Next Step   *Difficult*

We can answer this question based on what we have learned from the experiments and the figures. Thanks to the data in Figure 3, we know that inter-stimulus intervals are relatively short when the stimuli are on different hands. Delivering 200 Hz to the third digit on each hand will likely have an effect similar to delivering 200

Hz to the second digit of each hand. When 200 Hz is delivered to the second digit of each hand, the inter-stimulus interval is approximately 35 seconds. That means the best estimate for this new test scenario is 30 seconds, and **B** is correct. **A** is too short to be correct, and **C** and **D** are both too long.

12. F

Data Representation: Read the Chart *Easy*

In this study, the two PubMed searches that resulted in the greatest number of entries were searches for "cough AND oxide" and "cough AND dust." The correct answer is **F**. **G**, **H**, and **J** all represent searches that did not yield as many results as the searches for "cough AND oxide" and "cough AND dust."

13. B

Data Representation: Read the Chart *Easy*

The total number of published studies related to cough and environmental factors in 2004 was 65. In 2005, 50 such articles were published. The total number of published studies for both years is 115, making **B** the correct choice. **A** is too large to be correct. **C** and **D** represent the number of published studies in 2004 and 2005, respectively, not the total number of published studies for those two years.

14. H

Data Representation: Use the Chart *Medium*

In 2004, 65 articles linking environmental factors to cough appeared in the PubMed database. This is a greater amount of articles than in any other year on the graph, so the correct answer is **H**. We do not know if more patients complained of chronic cough in 2004 than in any other year, so **F** cannot be correct. The number of *articles* about cough and environmental factors decreased between 2002 and 2003, but that doesn't mean that harmful environmental factors decreased, so **G** is incorrect. This particular study searched articles back to 1980, but that doesn't mean there weren't articles on the topic prior to 1980, so **J** is incorrect as well.

15. B

Data Representation: Use the Chart *Medium*

The PubMed search resulted in 477 entries for "cough AND dust," so it makes sense to hypothesize that the link between dust and chronic cough is strong enough to warrant frequent study. The correct answer is **B**. There are only 15 articles about cough and diesel, but that does not mean that chronic cough isn't caused by diesel pollution—so **A** is incorrect. **C** is supported by the data in Figure 2, but this question is asking about Figure 1. The assumption in **D** cannot be verified, as the graph deals with published articles, not with the chronic-cough cases themselves.

16. G

Data Representation: Use the Chart *Medium*

Figure 2 shows a steadily increasing number of articles published between 1980 and 2005. This trend reflects the fact that a steadily increasing number of medical writers began exploring the link between environmental factors and chronic cough, so the correct answer is **G**. **F** is the exact *opposite* of the correct answer. **H** is in no way supported by the data in Figure 2, nor is choice **J**.

17. C

Research Summary: Read the Chart   *Easy*

Table 1 shows that phosphoric acid was used as a catalyst to produce aspirin. **A** is incorrect, because acetic anhydride was used in the original reaction along with phosphoric acid, but it was not the product of the reaction. **B** and **D** are incorrect because Table 1 shows that catalysts were not used in the production of sodium chloride and acetanilide.

18. F

Research Summary: Read the Chart   *Easy*

Table 1 shows that acetic acid was produced in two different reactions, both involving acetic anhydride. **F** is therefore correct. **G**, **H**, and **J** can be eliminated, because the combinations involving these solutions did not produce acetic acid.

19. D

Research Summary: Use the Chart   *Medium*

Table 2 shows that the melting points for the solids isolated in Study 1 generally reflect larger ranges than the melting points given for the pure solids in Table 3. However, the melting point for acetanilide in Table 2 is an exact temperature, whereas the melting point for pure acetanilide is given as a temperature range in Table 3. Therefore, the results of Study 2 show both larger temperature ranges and an exact temperature, so **D** is correct.

20. G

Research Summary: Use the Chart   *Medium*

Study 2 explains that when impurities are present in a substance, the substance will melt over a range of temperatures instead of a sharp melting point. Table 3 shows the melting point of alum as 92°C. This melting point is accurate when alum is 98.00% pure. Table 2 shows the melting range of the isolated alum as 91°–94°C. The fact that the alum displays a melting range shows that it is less pure than the alum in Table 3, which has an exact melting point.

   Since the alum in Table 3 is 98.00% pure, the alum isolated in Study 1 must be less than 98.00% pure. **K** is incorrect because although the exact purity of the isolated alum cannot be determined, it can be concluded that this alum is less pure than the alum in Table 3.

21. A

Research Summary: Use the Chart   *Medium*

Table 2 shows the melting point of the isolated acetanilide as 114°. This temperature is more precise than the temperature range given in Table 3 for 99.95% pure acetanilide. We can conclude, therefore, that the isolated acetanilide is at least 99.95% pure.

   In terms of the purity levels reflected in Table 3, sodium chloride is the closest to 99.95%. Table 3 shows the purity level of sodium chloride as 99.99%, so **A** is correct. **D** is incorrect because the purity level of Prussian blue is 99.90%, which is a 0.05% difference from the purity level of the isolated acetanilide.

22. H

Research Summary: Use the Chart   *Difficult*

Table 3 shows these four substances in increasing order of purity: alum, aspirin, acetanilide, and sodium chloride. Table 2 shows that alum and aspirin each have a melting range of 4°, and sodium chloride has a melting range of 3°. Thus, these three solids are less pure than the reference solids shown in Table 3. Isolated alum is less than 98.00% pure, isolated aspirin is less than 99.00% pure, and isolated sodium chloride is less than 99.99% pure. Though we cannot be sure of the exact purity level of the isolated substances, this ordering of their purity is most likely to be accurate, so **H** is correct.

    G is incorrect, because acetanilide is the most pure of all of the isolated substances, since it has an exact melting point that lies within the melting range given for acetanilide in Table 3. Its purity is at least 99.95%, so it will have a greater purity than alum or aspirin.

23. D

Conflicting Viewpoints: Detail   *Easy*

One of the claims made by the "Private Banking Is Unethical" argument is that therapies can be carried out with a variety of stem cells, including those from bone marrow. The argument would be weakened by the finding that certain life-saving therapies can only be carried out with UCB cells, so the correct answer is **D**. **A** would *strengthen* the "Private Banking Is Unethical" argument. **B** is not addressed in the passage, so it doesn't serve to weaken or strengthen the argument. **D**, like choice **A**, would strengthen the argument.

24. F

Conflicting Viewpoints: Comparison   *Easy*

Supporters of both arguments would agree that UCB banking, whether public or private, increases the amount of available stem cells. The correct answer is **F**. Only supporters of the "Private Banking Is Unethical" argument would agree with **G**. Only supporters of the "Private Banking Is Necessary" argument would agree with **H**. **J** is not addressed by either passage.

25. B

Conflicting Viewpoints: Inference   *Medium*

The "Private Banking Is Necessary" argument doesn't deny that private UCB banks are costly, but it does emphasize that the banks' services are necessary to maintain an abundant supply of UCB cells. The correct answer is **B**. Nothing in the passage implies that private UCB banks are better equipped than public UCB banks, so **A** is incorrect. **C** is an argument made by the "Private Banking Is Unethical" argument, not the "Private Banking Is Necessary" argument. **D** is not addressed in the passage.

26. G

Conflicting Viewpoints: Inference   *Medium*

This discovery would weaken the "Private Banking Is Necessary" argument, which states that UCB cells are superior to bone-marrow cells since they enhance availability for every ethnic group for tissue matching. The correct answer is **G**. Because the finding would have an effect on the "Private Banking Is Necessary" argument, **F** cannot be correct. The finding would not weaken the "Private Banking Is Unethical" argument, which vouches for the usefulness of bone marrow, so neither **H** nor **J** can be correct.

27. A

Conflicting Viewpoints: Detail *Medium*

The "Private Banking Is Necessary" argument mentions that *other critics argue that embryonic stem cells (ESCs) are the better option*, but it never states *why* these critics think that. The correct answer is **A**. The argument gives a list of cells that UCB cells can develop into, so **B** is incorrect. The argument gives a reason (usefulness among all ethnic groups) that UCB cells are more beneficial than bone-marrow cells, so **C** is incorrect. The passage does not raise the question in **D**.

28. H

Conflicting Viewpoints: Comparison *Medium*

Both arguments state that stem cells contribute to life-saving therapies, so **H** is correct. Neither argument states that stem cells are too expensive to harvest, making **G** incorrect. Only the "Private Banking Is Unethical" argument says stem cells should not be handled by a for-profit business, so **G** is incorrect. **J** is a statement made only by the "Private Banking Is Necessary" argument.

29. C

Conflicting Viewpoints: Detail *Difficult*

The "Private Banking Is Unethical" argument says that collecting UCB *may distract professionals from their primary task of caring for the mother and baby at this risky time*. **C** is the correct answer. **A** is a claim made by the "Private Banking Is Necessary" argument, not the "Private Banking Is Unethical" argument. Neither argument implies the statements made in **B** and **D**.

30. H

Data Representation: Read the Chart *Easy*

According to Figure 1, there were approximately 40 *Aristeus antennatus* landings at the Arenys de Mar harbor in 1999. The correct answer is **H**. The number of landings in **F** and **G**—20 and 30—are too low to be correct. The number of landings in **J** is too high.

31. C

Data Representation: Read the Chart *Easy*

Looking at Figure 2, we see that approximately 1.5 million large individuals landed at the Blanes harbor in 1990. This means that the correct answer is **C**. **A** is too small to be correct. **B** is closer to the number of *small* individuals that landed at the Blanes harbor than the number of large individuals. **D** is too large to be correct.

32. F

Data Representation: Read the Chart   *Medium*

The data in Figure 1 show that annual *Aristeus antennatus* landings spiked at all four harbors during the same time frame. That time frame was between 2000 and 2005, so the correct answer is **F**. Between 1995 and 2000, landings gradually decreased at all harbors except Arenys de Mar (where there was a slight increase), so **G** is incorrect. All harbors except for Roses (for which there is no 1985–1990 data available) saw decreases in *Aristeus antennatus* between 1985 and 1990, so **H** is incorrect. Palamós and Arenys de Mar saw decreases between 1975 and 1980, Roses saw an increase and then a decrease, and there is no 1975–1980 data available for Blanes. This means that **J** is incorrect, too.

33. B

Data Representation: Use the Chart   *Medium*

Both Figure 1 and Figure 2 show population increases in *Aristeus antennatus* three to five years after a strong cascading event. The correct answer is **B**. A gets it backward: The population doesn't *decrease* three to five years after a strong cascading event. Strong cascading events do have a definite effect on the size of the overall *Aristeus antennatus* population, so **C** is incorrect. Both figures show the clear impact of strong cascading events on *Aristeus antennatus*, so **D** is incorrect as well.

34. G

Data Representation: Use the Chart   *Difficult*

Use Figure 1 to answer this question. Between 1980 and 1982, the *Aristeus antennatus* population was very low. This would result in a small haul for the fisheries, so **G** is correct. The populations in the time frames presented in **F**, **H**, and **J** are all larger than the population between 1980 and 1982, so none of these answer choices is correct.

35. B

Research Summary: Read the Chart   *Easy*

In Week 4 of Experiment 1, approximately 70% of the double-side-coated paperboard's original weight remained. The correct answer is **B**. A is too high to be correct, and **C** and **D** are both too low.

36. H

Research Summary: Read the Chart   *Easy*

Looking at Figure 2, we see that the most significant drop in the one-side-coated paperboard's tensile strength occurred between Weeks 2 and 3. The correct answer is **H**. The changes between Weeks 4 and 5, Weeks 3 and 4, and Weeks 1 and 2 were much more subtle, meaning that **F**, **G**, and **J** are all incorrect.

37. C

Research Summary: Use the Chart   *Medium*

Both experiments support the conclusion that uncoated and one-side-coated paperboard biodegrade more quickly than two-side-coated paperboard and commercial liquid packaging board. The correct answer is **C**. Uncoated paperboard does *not* biode-grade significantly faster than one-side-coated paperboard, making **A** incorrect. The most substantial biodegradation took place between Weeks 2 and 3 in Experiment 2, and the biodegradation in Experiment 1 took place gradually across all seven weeks, so **B** is incorrect. Because there are no data recorded after Week 7, there is no way to know if the most substantial biodegradation took place after this point, so **D** is also incorrect.

38. **F**

Research Summary: Use the Chart   *Medium*

By Week 7, commercial liquid packaging board has lost the least of its original weight, so it is the least biodegradable. **F** is correct. **G** is the *opposite* of the correct answer. Neither **H** nor **J** is supported by the data.

39. **D**

Research Summary: Use the Chart   *Medium*

Someone interested in using a material that can withstand exposure to natural ele-ments would choose two-side-coated paperboard, so **D** is correct. The individuals in **A**, **B**, and **C** would want to select a material that will biodegrade quickly, so those answers are not correct.

40. **H**

Research Summary: Use the Chart   *Difficult*

First, use Figure 2 to find which material had a tensile index of 5 Nm/g in Week 5. That material is two-side-coated paperboard. Now, use Figure 1 to see if two-side-coated paperboard was approximately 60% of its original weight in Week 5. It was, so the correct answer is **H**. **F**, **G**, and **J** represent a misreading of the data.

ACT Practice
Test 5

DIRECTIONS: The ACT consists of tests in four separate subject areas: English, Mathematics, Reading, and Science. These four tests measure skills learned through high school coursework that are relevant to success in college. *YOU MAY USE CALCULATORS ON THE MATHEMATICS TEST ONLY.*

Each test contains a set of numbered questions. The answer choices for each question are lettered. On your answer sheet, you will find rows of ovals that are numbered to match the questions. Each oval contains a letter to correspond to a particular answer choice.

Choose the best answer for each question. Then, on your answer sheet, find the row of ovals that is numbered the same as the question. Find the oval containing the letter of your chosen answer, and fill in this oval completely. You must use a soft lead pencil for this purpose, and your marks must be heavy and black. *BALLPOINT PENS SHOULD NOT BE USED TO FILL IN THE ANSWER SHEET.*

Fill in only one answer choice oval for each question. If you wish to change an answer, make sure that your original answer is thoroughly erased before marking the new one. After filling in your answer, double-check to be sure that you have marked the row of ovals that corresponds to the question number being answered.

Responses will be scored only if they are marked on your answer document. Your score for each test is determined by the number of questions answered correctly during the testing period. Your score will NOT be reduced if you choose an incorrect answer. *FOR THIS REASON, IT IS ADVANTAGEOUS FOR YOU TO ANSWER EVERY QUESTION, EVEN IF YOU GUESS ON SOME QUESTIONS.*

You may work on a test ONLY when the test supervisor gives you permission to do so. If you finish a test before the end of the time allowed, use any remaining time to review questions that you are unsure about. You are permitted to review ONLY your answers for the test on which you are currently working. You may NOT look back to a test you have already completed, and you may NOT continue on to another test. If you do so, you will be disqualified from the examination.

When the end of each test is announced, put your pencil down immediately. You are NOT permitted to fill in or change ovals for a test after the end of that test has been called. If you do so, for any reason, you will be disqualified from the examination.

You may not fold or tear the pages of your test.

DO NOT TURN TO THE FIRST TEST

UNTIL YOU ARE TOLD TO DO SO.

ACT Practice Test 5: Answer Sheet

TEST 1

1 A B C D   16 F G H J   31 A B C D   46 F G H J   61 A B C D
2 F G H J   17 A B C D   32 F G H J   47 A B C D   62 F G H J
3 A B C D   18 F G H J   33 A B C D   48 F G H J   63 A B C D
4 F G H J   19 A B C D   34 F G H J   49 A B C D   64 F G H J
5 A B C D   20 F G H J   35 A B C D   50 F G H J   65 A B C D
6 F G H J   21 A B C D   36 F G H J   51 A B C D   66 F G H J
7 A B C D   22 F G H J   37 A B C D   52 F G H J   67 A B C D
8 F G H J   23 A B C D   38 F G H J   53 A B C D   68 F G H J
9 A B C D   24 F G H J   39 A B C D   54 F G H J   69 A B C D
10 F G H J   25 A B C D   40 F G H J   55 A B C D   70 F G H J
11 A B C D   26 F G H J   41 A B C D   56 F G H J   71 A B C D
12 F G H J   27 A B C D   42 F G H J   57 A B C D   72 F G H J
13 A B C D   28 F G H J   43 A B C D   58 F G H J   73 A B C D
14 F G H J   29 A B C D   44 F G H J   59 A B C D   74 F G H J
15 A B C D   30 F G H J   45 A B C D   60 F G H J   75 A B C D

TEST 2

1 A B C D E   13 A B C D E   25 A B C D E   37 A B C D E   49 A B C D E
2 F G H J K   14 F G H J K   26 F G H J K   38 F G H J K   50 F G H J K
3 A B C D E   15 A B C D E   27 A B C D E   39 A B C D E   51 A B C D E
4 F G H J K   16 F G H J K   28 F G H J K   40 F G H J K   52 F G H J K
5 A B C D E   17 A B C D E   29 A B C D E   41 A B C D E   53 A B C D E
6 F G H J K   18 F G H J K   30 F G H J K   42 F G H J K   54 F G H J K
7 A B C D E   19 A B C D E   31 A B C D E   43 A B C D E   55 A B C D E
8 F G H J K   20 F G H J K   32 F G H J K   44 F G H J K   56 F G H J K
9 A B C D E   21 A B C D E   33 A B C D E   45 A B C D E   57 A B C D E
10 F G H J K   22 F G H J K   34 F G H J K   46 F G H J K   58 F G H J K
11 A B C D E   23 A B C D E   35 A B C D E   47 A B C D E   59 A B C D E
12 F G H J K   24 F G H J K   36 F G H J K   48 F G H J K   60 F G H J K

TEST 3

1 A B C D   9 A B C D   17 A B C D   25 A B C D   33 A B C D
2 F G H J   10 F G H J   18 F G H J   26 F G H J   34 F G H J
3 A B C D   11 A B C D   19 A B C D   27 A B C D   35 A B C D
4 F G H J   12 F G H J   20 F G H J   28 F G H J   36 F G H J
5 A B C D   13 A B C D   21 A B C D   29 A B C D   37 A B C D
6 F G H J   14 F G H J   22 F G H J   30 F G H J   38 F G H J
7 A B C D   15 A B C D   23 A B C D   31 A B C D   39 A B C D
8 F G H J   16 F G H J   24 F G H J   32 F G H J   40 F G H J

TEST 4

1 A B C D   9 A B C D   17 A B C D   25 A B C D   33 A B C D
2 F G H J   10 F G H J   18 F G H J   26 F G H J   34 F G H J
3 A B C D   11 A B C D   19 A B C D   27 A B C D   35 A B C D
4 F G H J   12 F G H J   20 F G H J   28 F G H J   36 F G H J
5 A B C D   13 A B C D   21 A B C D   29 A B C D   37 A B C D
6 F G H J   14 F G H J   22 F G H J   30 F G H J   38 F G H J
7 A B C D   15 A B C D   23 A B C D   31 A B C D   39 A B C D
8 F G H J   16 F G H J   24 F G H J   32 F G H J   40 F G H J

ENGLISH TEST

45 Minutes—75 Questions

DIRECTIONS: There are five passages on this test. You should read each passage once before answering the questions on it. In order to answer correctly, you may need to read several sentences beyond the question.

There are two question formats within the passages. In one format, you will find words and phrases that have been underlined and assigned numbers. These numbers will correspond with sets of alternative words/phrases given in the right-hand column of the test booklet. From the sets of alternatives, choose the answer choice that works best in context, keeping in mind whether it employs standard written English, whether it gets across the idea of the section, and whether it suits the tone and style of the passage. You will usually be offered the option "NO CHANGE," which you should choose if you think the version found in the passage is best.

In the second format, you will see boxed numbers referring to sections of the passage or to the passage as a whole. In the right-hand column, you will be asked questions about or given alternatives for the sections marked by the boxes. Choose the answer choice that best answers the question or completes the section. After choosing your answer choice, fill in the corresponding bubble on the answer sheet.

Passage I

Spaghetti Westerns

[1]

For some people, the film *The Good, the Bad and the Ugly,* starring Clint Eastwood, is primarily bad due to its length, melodrama, and violence. However, the 1966 spaghetti Western is a cult classic for many film lovers and movie fans <u>1</u> including director Quentin Tarantino, who calls it "the best-directed film of all time."

[2]

Nearly 600 Westerns emerged from European movie production companies between 1960 and 1975. The films were dubbed "spaghetti Westerns" because most of <u>it</u> <u>2</u>

1. **A.** NO CHANGE
   B. many film lovers
   C. lots of people who love movies and films
   D. numerous movies lovers and fans

2. **F.** NO CHANGE
   G. which
   H. them
   J. that

GO ON TO THE NEXT PAGE.

hailed from Italian movie studios. ☐3 Most spaghetti

Westerns used locals for the cast and crew typically
_____4_____

filmed on location in Italy or Spain. However, the genre
____4____

attracted notable actors from Hollywood, such as, Clint
_____5_____

Eastwood, Henry Fonda, Charles Bronson, and Jack
____5____

Palance.

3. The writer is thinking of revising the second part of the preceding sentence to read:

The films were dubbed "spaghetti Westerns" by both fans and critics.

If this revision were made, the sentence would primarily lose:
A. descriptive details that clarify the meaning of the term "spaghetti Western."
B. details about spaghetti Westerns that are presented elsewhere in the passage.
C. humorous information about the origin of the term "spaghetti Western."
D. irrelevant information about spaghetti Westerns that clutters the sentence.

4. **F.** NO CHANGE
G. Typically filmed on location in Italy or Spain, locals were used for the cast and crew of most spaghetti Westerns.
H. Most spaghetti Westerns used locals typically filmed on location in Italy or Spain for the cast and crew.
J. Typically filmed on location in Italy or Spain, most spaghetti Westerns used locals for the cast and crew.

5. **A.** NO CHANGE
B. Hollywood such as Eastwood, Henry Fonda
C. Hollywood, such as Eastwood, Henry Fonda,
D. Hollywood, such as Eastwood, Henry, Fonda,

[3]

But why film Westerns in Italy? Europeans immensely
____6____

enjoyed American Westerns. Over the years, European

filmmakers had tried to produce Westerns European
_____7

audiences preferred those made in America. By 1960,
_____7

Hollywood movie studios were making fewer Westerns

because the demands from American audiences had

changed. As a result, European fans had fewer
____8____

American Westerns to watch.

6. Which choice best leads the reader into the subject matter of the third paragraph?
F. NO CHANGE
G. Many Hollywood actors gained international stardom with spaghetti Westerns.
H. American audiences were looking for new movie genres.
J. A typical theme of many spaghetti Westerns was the Mexican Revolution.

7. **A.** NO CHANGE
B. Westerns European audiences had preferred
C. Westerns, European audiences preferred
D. Westerns, but European audiences preferred

8. Which of the following alternatives to the underlined portion would be LEAST acceptable?
F. Consequently,
G. Besides,
H. For this reason,
J. Thus,

[4]

With a limited amount of funding, European producers

once again experimented with the Western genre. The

result was a number of poorly produced films, mainly with
                                                        9

ineffective sound and dubbing problems, that lacked
                9

the style and feel of American Westerns. Over the next

few years, producers (from Germany, Italy, and Spain)
                                            10

began trying to make profitable Westerns, but it was Italian

director Sergio Leone who broke out of the pack.

[5]

Between 1964 and 1966, Leone produced a trilogy of

films: *A Fistful of Dollars*, *For a Few Dollars More*, and *The

Good, the Bad and the Ugly*. Each film featured the up-and-

coming Eastwood as the main character. Leone's combination
                            11

of creative camera angles, showing brutality, and depicting
            12

an immoral cowboy played well with audiences and
        12

spurred the production of similar films. Similarly as
                                            13

everything else, interest eventually in the spaghetti
                            14

Western waned, but the genre's influence remains evident

today. 15

9. **A.** NO CHANGE
B. poor quality films
C. poorly dubbed and insufficiently edited films
D. films that lacked Hollywood quality and

10. **F.** NO CHANGE
G. producers—German, Italian, and Spanish—
H. producers from: Germany, Italy, and Spain,
J. producers from Germany, Italy, and Spain

11. Given that all the choices are true, which one gives the most descriptive details about Eastwood's film character to the reader at this point in the essay?
A. NO CHANGE
B. who was acting in TV shows at the time
C. in the role of the antihero
D. in a leading role

12. **F.** NO CHANGE
G. creative camera angles, brutality, and an immoral cowboy
H. using creative camera angles, the way he showed brutality, and an immoral cowboy
J. creating unique camera angles, brutality, and the depiction of an immoral cowboy

13. **A.** NO CHANGE
B. According with
C. Like as
D. As with

14. **F.** NO CHANGE
G. (Place after *Western*)
H. (Place after *but*)
J. (Place after *influence*)

15. Suppose the writer had been assigned to write a short personal-opinion essay on a particular movie genre. Would this essay fulfill the assignment, and why?
A. Yes, because the essay describes why spaghetti Westerns receive critical acclaim.
B. Yes, because the essay clearly explains why spaghetti Westerns are inferior to American Westerns.
C. No, because the essay is primarily describing the history behind spaghetti Westerns.
D. No, because the essay focuses on the popularity of one spaghetti Western director and his trilogy.

GO ON TO THE NEXT PAGE.

Passage II

The Man Behind General Electric

[1]

While General Electric (GE) may be a household name, Jack Welch <u>completely</u> is not, although the connection
16
between the two is a tight one. A brilliant business strategist, visionary, and leader, Welch <u>works</u> for GE in
17
1960 as an engineer and by 1981 was elected chairman and CEO.

[2]

<u>Because he disliked the company's bureaucratic structure</u>
18
<u>only one year after being hired, Welch considered leaving</u>
18
<u>GE. When</u> he was convinced to stay by an executive
18 19
<u>which</u> saw something special in young Jack. Because
20
of <u>his business acumen Welch rapidly moved</u> up the
21
corporate ladder. By 1972, Welch was vice president of GE, and less than ten years later he became the firm's youngest CEO.

16. **F.** NO CHANGE
    G. probably
    H. thoroughly
    J. apparently

17. **A.** NO CHANGE
    B. began working
    C. is working
    D. who worked

18. **F.** NO CHANGE
    G. Only one year after being hired because he disliked the company's bureaucratic structure, Welch considered leaving GE.
    H. Welch considered leaving GE only one year after being hired because he disliked the company's bureaucratic structure.
    J. Dislike of the company's bureaucratic structure only one year after being hired made Welch consider leaving GE.

19. **A.** NO CHANGE
    B. Moreover,
    C. While
    D. However,

20. **F.** NO CHANGE
    G. who
    H. he who
    J. whom

21. **A.** NO CHANGE
    B. his business acumen Welch rapidly moved,
    C. his business acumen, Welch rapidly moved
    D. his business, acumen Welch rapidly moved

[3]

Welch's business aim was to make GE <u>products, including</u>
                                                                    22
<u>appliances, electronics, and light bulbs,</u> the highest
                             22
ranked ones in their class. To that end, he eliminated the

notorious bureaucracy that he knew was <u>dissolving</u> the
                                                          23
company; Welch never feared cutting costs <u>by reducing the</u>
                                                               24
<u>workforce or to close factories.</u> Because he abolished
                  24
so many jobs, Welch was nicknamed "Neutron Jack."

Welch disliked the pessimistic moniker, which is derived

from a neutron bomb, which eliminates people but leaves

structures intact. ☐25

22. **F.** NO CHANGE
    G. products, including appliances, electronics, and light bulbs
    H. products including appliances, electronics, and light bulbs
    J. products including appliances, electronics, and light bulbs,

23. **A.** NO CHANGE
    B. obscuring
    C. enlarging
    D. harming

24. **F.** NO CHANGE
    G. with a reduction in workforce or closing factories.
    H. by reducing the workforce or closing factories.
    J. with a workforce reduction or to close factories.

25. The writer is considering deleting the following clause from the preceding sentence (placing a period after the word *moniker*):

    which is derived from a neutron bomb, which eliminates people but leaves structures intact.

    Should the writer make this deletion?
    A. Yes, because the information distracts from the characterization of Jack Welch.
    B. Yes, because the information is unrelated to the topic addressed in this paragraph.
    C. No, because the information explains the nickname given to Jack Welch, which might otherwise confuse readers.
    D. No, because the information describes why Jack Welch received the nickname and why he disliked it.

[4]

<u>While he stepped down as CEO in 2000,</u> Welch was
                                          26
nonetheless touted by others for being personable and

accessible. He was very interested in all of <u>GEs workings,</u>
                                                       27
and he did not hesitate to send handwritten memos

to employees who he thought deserved praise or business

guidance. Such personal touches helped to counter his

"Neutron Jack" reputation.

[5]

　　Encouraging Welch to remain with GE proved to be a

profitable move for the company, <u>yet</u> his leadership
                                    28
turned the corporation into a multibillion-dollar entity.

Welch is celebrated in business circles as a revolutionary

leader whose ingenuity completely revamped GE. Today,

executives from an array of industries <u>strives</u> to
                                          29
emulate Welch's formula for creating globally diverse and

profitable businesses. [30]

26. Which of the transitions provides the most effective
    link from paragraph 3 to paragraph 4?
    F. NO CHANGE
    G. Although criticized by some people for his straight-
       forward style,
    H. While many appreciated his frankness,
    J. Although he was occasionally condemned,

27. A. NO CHANGE
    B. GEs' workings,
    C. GEs workings',
    D. GE's workings,

28. F. NO CHANGE
    G. while
    H. since
    J. but

29. A. NO CHANGE
    B. strive
    C. is striving
    D. has strived

30. Suppose the writer had chosen to write a brief essay
    about the business strategies used by a corporation
    to improve profitability. Would this essay successfully
    fulfill the writer's goal?
    F. Yes, because the essay explains the methods used
       by GE executives to make the company more com-
       petitive.
    G. Yes, because the essay describes how Jack Welch
       improved the financial status of GE.
    H. No, because the essay describes the successful ca-
       reer of one GE executive—Jack Welch.
    J. No, because the essay focuses on the mistakes made
       by the bureaucracy of GE before Jack Welch was
       CEO.

Passage III

Rising to the Top

[1]

It's true that we all have to start somewhere, and no one, no matter how great, begins at the top. In fact, one of the most famous painters of the Impressionist period Pierre-Auguste Renoir began at the bottom by painting designs on fine china.

[2]

[1] Renoir was born to working-class French parents in 1841. 32 [2]As a boy, Renoir's penchant for drawing garnered attention in the porcelain factory where he worked. [3]The factory eventually closed, Renoir earned money toiling in a variety of odd jobs. [4]Renoir struggled to earn a living, and there were times in his early career when he could not afford to buy even the most basic art supplies such as paints. 35

31. **A.** NO CHANGE
    B. period, Pierre-Auguste Renoir
    C. period Pierre-Auguste Renoir,
    D. period, Pierre-Auguste Renoir,

32. The writer is considering deleting the following phrase from the preceding sentence:

    to working-class French parents

    If the writer were to make this deletion, the essay would primarily lose:
    F. a reason for Renoir's bitterness toward upper-class society.
    G. specific descriptive information about Renoir's background.
    H. a minor detail that provides no helpful insight about Renoir.
    J. the writer's opinion about Renoir's childhood and family.

33. **A.** NO CHANGE
    B. closed, and Renoir
    C. closed when Renoir
    D. closed so Renoir

34. **F.** NO CHANGE
    G. even paints, which were too expensive for a poor painter.
    H. the most basic essential art supplies like paints.
    J. basic supplies, such as paints.

35. Upon reviewing this paragraph and finding that some information has been left out, the writer composes the following sentence incorporating that information:

    Nothing compared to his passion for painting, and by the late 1850s, Renoir decided to pursue a career as an artist.

    This sentence would most logically be placed after sentence:
    A. 1
    B. 2
    C. 3
    D. 4

GO ON TO THE NEXT PAGE.

[3]

Renowned for his use of light and color, Renoir <u>enjoys</u>₃₆

painting scenes with a forested backdrop. His paintings

were renditions of <u>peoples lives</u>₃₇ as they were going

about <u>their</u>₃₈ personal business. Some of his most well-

known paintings include *Bathers, The Umbrellas,* and *Le*

Moulin de la Galette. In many ways, looking at a Renoir

painting is like taking a sneak peek into the private lives

of various people. <u>In other words, in his career</u>₃₉ Renoir

focused on depicting scenes of his own family life with his

wife and children. Renoir's preference for <u>his paintings</u>₄₀

<u>of individuals in simpler times</u>₄₀ may be a result of his

dislike for the progressive, industrial world, <u>and with that</u>₄₁

Renoir believed robbed people of individuality.

[4]

<u>In 1892 due to the passion he felt for his craft, Renoir</u>₄₂

<u>was a lifelong artist despite being afflicted with rheumatoid</u>₄₂

<u>arthritis.</u>₄₂ While the <u>debilitatingly disease</u>₄₃ restricted

his movements, Renoir managed to continue creating great

36. F. NO CHANGE
   G. has enjoyed
   H. enjoyed
   J. does enjoy

37. A. NO CHANGE
   B. people's lives
   C. people's lives'
   D. peoples' lives

38. F. NO CHANGE
   G. his
   H. its
   J. one's

39. A. NO CHANGE
   B. For this reason in his career,
   C. Later in his career,
   D. That is, in his career

40. F. NO CHANGE
   G. creating paintings of individuals in times that were simple
   H. creating his paintings of individuals in simpler times
   J. painting individuals in simpler times

41. A. NO CHANGE
   B. which
   C. by which
   D. with which

42. F. NO CHANGE
   G. Renoir was a lifelong artist in 1892 despite being afflicted with rheumatoid arthritis due to the passion he felt for his craft.
   H. Due to the passion he felt for his craft, Renoir was a lifelong artist despite being afflicted with rheumatoid arthritis in 1892.
   J. Despite being afflicted with rheumatoid arthritis in 1892 due to the passion he felt for his craft, Renoir was a lifelong artist.

43. A. NO CHANGE
   B. disease, it is debilitating,
   C. debilitating as a disease
   D. debilitating disease

works by strapping a brush to his arm. When Renoir died <u>in</u>
₄₄

<u>1919. He</u> left the world a legacy of beauty. [45]
₄₄

44. **F.** NO CHANGE
   G. in 1919, he
   H. in 1919; he
   J. in 1919, and he

45. Suppose the writer had been assigned to write a brief essay illustrating how Renoir felt about painting. Would this essay successfully fulfill the assignment?
   A. Yes, because the essay indicates that Renoir received encouragement from others about his skills.
   B. Yes, because the essay indicates Renoir's love for painting at different times in his life.
   C. No, because the essay restricts its focus to the subjects of Renoir's most famous paintings.
   D. No, because the essay does not describe how Renoir felt about his artwork or the praise he received.

Passage IV

Hawaiian Paradise

[1]

Last year, for my parents' twentieth wedding anniversary, Dad wanted to do something extraordinary, <u>but</u> he
₄₆
surprised Mom with a family trip to Hawaii.

46. **F.** NO CHANGE
   G. so
   H. since
   J. although

[2]

Despite the excruciatingly long flight that left my legs cramped, the tropical paradise was amazing. We arrived in Honolulu, which is located on the island of Oahu. After checking into our beachfront hotel, my entire family rushed outside to experience the world-famous Waikiki Beach that we had been eagerly <u>imagining.</u> The ocean's water was
₄₇
the bluest I had ever seen. Of <u>course being a Minneapolis</u>
₄₈
<u>native</u> the murky brown water in Midwestern lakes
₄₈
<u>were</u> my only point of comparison; however, I honestly
₄₉
loved ocean blue waters more!

47. **A.** NO CHANGE
   B. observing.
   C. approaching.
   D. anticipating.

48. **F.** NO CHANGE
   G. course, being a Minneapolis native,
   H. course being, a Minneapolis native,
   J. course, being a Minneapolis native

49. **A.** NO CHANGE
   B. was
   C. are
   D. have been

GO ON TO THE NEXT PAGE.

[3]

The pebbly nature of the beach surprised <u>me; I</u> had to
wear flip-flops <u>swimming</u> because of the rocky ocean
floor. Although the roughness of the sand was somewhat
disappointing, I was willing to overlook the island's one tiny
flaw because I was in paradise.

[4]

Probably the most unforgettable experience of the
Hawaiian vacation <u>was most likely visiting</u> the
USS *Arizona* memorial, which marks the place where
Americans first entered World War II. [53] The Japanese
attacked Pearl Harbor on December 7, 1941, and it was a
sobering experience to be in the exact spot where so many
countrymen had defended America. It is definitely a tour I
will always remember.

[5]

Once we <u>return</u> from the national memorial, my family
decided <u>to learn how to surf.</u> While none of us were
skilled enough to enter a surfing competition, we had fun

50. **F.** NO CHANGE
G. me, I
H. me and I
J. me; and I

51. **A.** NO CHANGE
B. in swimming
C. when swimming
D. having swam

52. **F.** NO CHANGE
G. was visiting
H. quite possibly was visiting
J. was in all likelihood our visit to

53. At this point, the writer is considering adding the following sentence:

> The USS *Arizona* was a U.S. Navy battleship that was originally commissioned in 1916 for use in World War I.

Should the writer make this addition?
A. Yes, because the additional detail explains why visiting the memorial was special for the author.
B. Yes, because if readers understand that the battleship was involved in two wars, they will understand the significance of the loss.
C. No, because the information distracts the reader from the focus of the paragraph as well as the passage.
D. No, because the information undermines the writer's argument that the memorial was an incredible experience.

54. **F.** NO CHANGE
G. returned
H. have returned
J. are returning

55. Which wording provides the most effective topic sentence for paragraph 5?
A. NO CHANGE
B. to visit the ocean.
C. to spend more time in the water.
D. to explore the island's coral reefs.

trying to stay on our boards and <u>laughed</u> at each other's
₅₆

antics. My <u>brother, who is younger than me by three years,</u>
₅₇

even managed <u>approximately</u> to ride a wave for five
₅₈

seconds.

[6]

After returning home to <u>cold snowy Minnesota,</u> we
₅₉

were all a little wistful for the days of sand and surf. Our

vacation to paradise was an exceptional experience. ☐60

56. **F.** NO CHANGE
   G. laughing
   H. by laughing
   J. were laughing

57. **A.** NO CHANGE
   B. younger brother, who has blond hair,
   C. brother is younger than me, and he
   D. younger brother

58. **F.** NO CHANGE
   G. (Place after *even*)
   H. (Place after *wave*)
   J. (Place after *for*)

59. **A.** NO CHANGE
   B. cold, snowy, Minnesota
   C. cold, snowy Minnesota,
   D. cold snowy, Minnesota

60. Suppose the writer's goal had been to write a short
   autobiographical essay about an emotional experience.
   Would this essay fulfill the writer's goal?
   F. Yes, because the essay explains why the author was
      emotionally affected by her visit to Pearl Harbor.
   G. Yes, because the essay discusses the impact of the
      surprise trip on the author's mother.
   H. No, because the essay primarily describes a fun
      experience the author had with her family.
   J. No, because the essay describes how other members
      of the author's family felt about the vacation.

GO ON TO THE NEXT PAGE.

Passage V

Sand Painting Ceremonies

[1]

The Navajo belief system centers on the concept of *hózhó*, which can be loosely translated to mean "balance" but also includes the qualities of beauty, goodness, happiness, harmony, and having good health. In the Navajo
61

view, illness represents an upset in the balance of things.

When balance prevails health and harmony abound
62

as well. When a person falls ill however, the illness
63

signals that *hózhó* or balance has been broken and must be restored. Such restoration happens through Navajo healing ceremonies referred to as *chantways*. 64

[2]

Sand paintings are usually created in the home, or *hogan*, of the individual suffering from an illness that is severe
65

enough to warrant a ceremony. The paintings are made
65

61. **A.** NO CHANGE
    B. being in harmony, and having good health.
    C. harmonious, and healthy.
    D. harmony, and health.

62. **F.** NO CHANGE
    G. balance prevails health,
    H. balance prevails, health
    J. balance, prevails health

63. **A.** NO CHANGE
    B. ill; however,
    C. ill, however
    D. ill, however,

64. Which of the following sentences, if added here, would most effectively lead the reader from paragraph 1 to the discussion of sand paintings in the rest of the essay?
    F. One major part of the healing ceremony involves completing a delicate and intricate sand painting.
    G. Also known as dry painting, the art of sand painting is common among Native Americans, Tibetan monks, and Australian Aborigines.
    H. Navajo sand paintings are strictly used for healing purposes, which explains the involvement of the tribe's medicine man.
    J. For healing ceremonies that last many days, a new sand painting is made for each day that passes.

65. **A.** NO CHANGE
    B. illness.
    C. some kind of illness that is unknown to the medicine man.
    D. an illness in his or her home.

by a ceremony leader known as a singer or medicine man, who conducts the ceremony along with his assistants who are training to become medicine men for other tribes. 66

Next, the singer and his assistants place a layer of
67
windblown sand on the ground. They then construct the sand painting while kneeling on this background layer.

[3]

The makers of the sand painting works from the center
68
out, so as not to disturb the delicate design. The sand painting is partially composed of freestyle images, with some measured out by palm and hand widths. Though other colors may be incorporated, the four main colors
69
of white, blue, yellow, and black are always used. These four colors have ritual connections to the four directions of east, west, north, and south, which are important to Navajo ceremonies. 70

66. The writer is considering deleting the following phrase from the preceding sentence (placing a period after the word *assistants*):

> who are training to become medicine men for other tribes.

Should the writer make this deletion?
F. Yes, because the information adds irrelevant details that make the sentence more difficult to read.
G. Yes, because the information is explained in detail later in the essay.
H. No, because the information explains how medicine men learn about sand painting ceremonies.
J. No, because the information describes the role of medicine men in sand painting ceremonies.

67. A. NO CHANGE
B. For example,
C. First,
D. Also,

68. F. NO CHANGE
G. work
H. does work
J. is working

69. A. NO CHANGE
B. other more vibrant and bright colors
C. other colors such as purple, green, orange, and red
D. many different other colors

70. At this point, the writer is considering adding the following sentence:

> Straight lines are made by using a cotton string, and the painting is smoothed by using a wooden bar from a weaver's loom.

Should the writer make this addition?
F. Yes, because the additional detail explains how sand paintings are created with the use of different tools.
G. Yes, because it is important for readers to understand that some sand paintings are made with tools.
H. No, because the information is irrelevant to the focus of the paragraph and should be placed elsewhere in the essay.
J. No, because the essay focuses on the healing benefits of sand paintings rather than how they are constructed.

GO ON TO THE NEXT PAGE.

[4]

<u>After everything is done,</u> the patient sits in the middle
71

of it. <u>Likewise,</u> the singer begins the healing ceremony,
72

following a <u>specific</u> protocol. When the ceremony is
73

complete, the sand painting is <u>destroyed; however, part</u>
74

of the ceremony protocol involves ensuring that sand

paintings are destroyed before dawn of the following day. 75

71. Which of the following provides the most specific transition from paragraph 3 to paragraph 4?
A. NO CHANGE
B. Once it is finished,
C. Later, when everything is finished,
D. After the sand painting is complete,

72. F. NO CHANGE
G. However,
H. Then,
J. So,

73. Three of these choices indicate that all healing ceremonies are conducted in the same manner. Which choice does NOT do so?
A. NO CHANGE
B. particular
C. respectful
D. deliberate

74. F. NO CHANGE
G. destroyed; part
H. destroyed, part
J. destroyed—part

75. Upon reviewing this essay and realizing that some information has been left out, the writer composes the following sentence, incorporating that information:

Navajo believe that physical contact enables the sick person to directly absorb the healing power of the sand painting.

The most logical and effective place to add this sentence would be after the first sentence of paragraph:
A. 1
B. 2
C. 3
D. 4

END OF TEST 1.
STOP! DO NOT TURN THE PAGE UNTIL TOLD TO DO SO.

MATHEMATICS TEST

60 Minutes—60 Questions

DIRECTIONS: After solving each problem, pick the correct answer from the five given and fill in the corresponding oval on your answer sheet. Solve as many problems as you can in the time allowed. Do not worry over problems that take too much time; skip them if necessary and return to them if you have time.

Calculator use is permitted on the test. Calculators can be used for any problem on the test, though calculators may be more harm than help for some questions.

Note: Unless otherwise stated on the test, you should assume that:

1. Figures accompanying questions are not drawn to scale.
2. Geometric figures exist in a plane.
3. When given in a question, "line" refers to a straight line.
4. When given in a question, "average" refers to the arithmetic mean.

---

1. If $a = -4$ and $b = 3$, then $(a + b)^2 = ?$
   A. -7
   B. -1
   C. 1
   D. 7
   E. 49

2. Allegra's age A can be determined by taking half of Nader's age N and subtracting 7. Which of the following expresses an equation for determining Allegra's age?

   F. $A = \dfrac{N - 7}{2}$

   G. $A = \dfrac{N}{2} - 7$

   H. $A = 2N - \dfrac{7}{2}$

   J. $A = 2N - 7$

   K. $A = 2(N - 7)$

3. Mr. Sanchez instructs his class to build a model of a motorcycle. The original motorcycle is 5 feet long by 3 feet high. If the model motorcycle is built exactly to scale, and its length is 10 inches, what is the height of the model, in inches?
   A. 6
   B. 9
   C. 10
   D. 12
   E. 30

DO YOUR FIGURING HERE.

GO ON TO THE NEXT PAGE.

4. Chad has 6 sports video games and 8 adventure video games. He reaches into a drawer and randomly pulls out one video game. What is the probability that Chad pulls out an adventure video game?

F. $\dfrac{3}{14}$

G. $\dfrac{3}{7}$

H. $\dfrac{4}{7}$

J. $\dfrac{9}{14}$

K. $\dfrac{5}{7}$

5. If $n = 3$, then $(2n^2)^4$ is equivalent to which of the following?

A. 6^6
B. 6^8
C. 12^4
D. 18^4
E. 36^4

6. In the figure shown below, line AB is parallel to line CD. Which of the following angles is congruent to angle r?

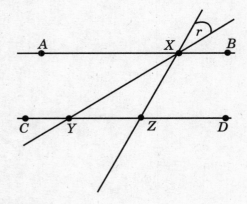

F. $\angle AXY$
G. $\angle XYZ$
H. $\angle YXZ$
J. $\angle BXZ$
K. $\angle XYC$

DO YOUR FIGURING HERE.

7. For a science project, Juanita observes three blooming plants and counts the number of blossoms that appear on each plant over a period of 14 days. There are 10 plants, labeled A through J. Each plant displays the number of blossoms shown in the table below.

Plant	A	B	C	D	E	F	G	H	I	J
No. of Blossoms	9	7	6	2	6	7	4	6	3	2

What is the mode of the number of blossoms displayed by the 10 plants over the 14-day period?

A. 2
B. 5.1
C. 6
D. 7
E. 9

8. If $12p - 7 = 10p + 6$, then $p = $?

F. $\dfrac{2}{13}$

G. $\dfrac{6}{11}$

H. $\dfrac{13}{22}$

J. $2\dfrac{1}{12}$

K. $6\dfrac{1}{2}$

9. The variables x and y represent two integers such that $x < y$. If x is negative, which of the following must be true?

A. The sum $x + y$ is negative.
B. The sum $x + y$ is positive.
C. The product xy is negative.
D. The sum $x + y$ is a fraction.
E. The sum $x + y$ is an integer.

10. What is the value of $|12 - 17 + z|$ if $z = -3$?

F. −8
G. 8
H. 12
J. 15
K. 32

DO YOUR FIGURING HERE.

GO ON TO THE NEXT PAGE.

11. What is the slope of the line through (7, 3) and (12, −6) in the standard (x, y) coordinate plane?

    A. $\dfrac{5}{3}$

    B. $\dfrac{9}{19}$

    C. $\dfrac{3}{5}$

    D. $-\dfrac{5}{9}$

    E. $-\dfrac{9}{5}$

12. Elana and Clark observed a group of birds at an aviary. They counted 5 bluebirds, 6 robins, and 8 hummingbirds. If all of the remaining birds were finches, and finches represented 2 less than half of the total number of birds, how many birds were at the aviary?

    F. 3

    G. $11\dfrac{1}{3}$

    H. 17

    J. 34

    K. 78

13. For all z, $13 - 7(z - 2) = ?$

    A. $-7z + 5$

    B. $-7z - 9$

    C. $-7z + 27$

    D. $6z - 2$

    E. $6z - 20$

DO YOUR FIGURING HERE.

14. The quadrants of the standard (x, y) coordinate plane are shown in the figure below.

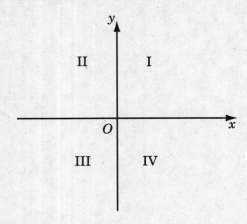

Which of the following points is graphed in quadrant III?

F. $(1, 4)$

G. $(-6, -7)$

H. $-\dfrac{5}{3}, 2$

J. $\dfrac{1}{2}, 12$

K. $(2, -5)$

15. What is the 419th digit after the decimal point in the repeating decimal $0.\overline{91735}$?

A. 9
B. 7
C. 5
D. 3
E. 1

16. Samuel rides his unicycle to his friend Nancy's house, located 2,826 feet away. If the radius of Samuel's unicycle tire is exactly 9 inches, approximately how many rotations does the unicycle make between Samuel's house and Nancy's house?

F. 5
G. 50
H. 86
J. 234
K. 600

DO YOUR FIGURING HERE.

GO ON TO THE NEXT PAGE.

17. For all positive integers j and k, what is the greatest common factor of the 3 numbers $24jk$, $72jk$, and $264jk$?

   A. $9j$
   B. $12k$
   C. jk
   D. $24jk$
   E. $40jk$

18. If $f(x) = 4x^2 - 2x + 6$, then $f(-4) = ?$

   A. -66
   B. -50
   C. 30
   D. 62
   E. 78

19. When $a = \dfrac{3}{4}$, what is the value of $\dfrac{8a - 2}{a}$?

   A. $2\dfrac{3}{4}$
   B. 4
   C. $5\dfrac{1}{3}$
   D. $7\dfrac{1}{3}$
   E. $8\dfrac{2}{3}$

20. In triangle XYZ shown below, $\tan s = ?$

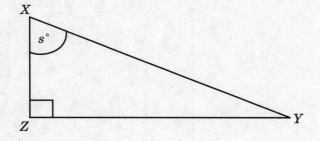

   F. $\dfrac{\overline{XY}}{\overline{YZ}}$
   G. $\dfrac{\overline{YZ}}{\overline{ZX}}$
   H. $\dfrac{\overline{YZ}}{\overline{XY}}$
   J. $\dfrac{\overline{ZX}}{\overline{XY}}$
   K. $\dfrac{\overline{ZX}}{\overline{YZ}}$

DO YOUR FIGURING HERE.

21. Jubilee Events schedules "adventure sessions" that consist of one morning and one afternoon meeting. Each morning or afternoon meeting takes place on any day of the week during a period of four consecutive weeks. The morning and afternoon meetings may take place on the same day, but the morning meeting can not be scheduled on Thursdays. How many different schedules can be created for an "adventure session"?

A. $(4 \times 7)(4 \times 7)$
B. $(4 \times 6)(3 \times 7)$
C. $(3 \times 6)(3 \times 6)$
D. $(3 \times 6)(4 \times 7)$
E. $(4 \times 6)(4 \times 7)$

22. The minute hand of a circular clock moves from 8:00 p.m. to 8:40 p.m. How many degrees does the minute hand travel during this time interval?

F. 195
G. 210
H. 240
J. 270
K. 360

23. Grid lines on the xy-coordinate plane shown below are spaced every $\frac{1}{3}$ unit. What is the slope of line CD?

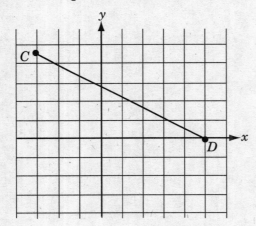

A. $-\frac{3}{5}$

B. $\frac{5}{3}$

C. $-\frac{5}{3}$

D. $\frac{3}{5}$

E. $\sqrt{3^2 + 5^2}$

Practice Test 5

24. A rectangular garden is 4 feet wider than it is long. The garden has an area of 192 feet. How many feet wide is the garden?

    F. 8
    G. 12
    H. 14
    J. 16
    K. 96

25. If $|n + 9| > 27$, then which of the following reflects all possible values of n?

    A. $n \geq -18$
    B. $n > 9$ or $n < -21$
    C. $n > 18$ or $n < -36$
    D. $n > 10$ or $n < -20$
    E. $n < 7$

26. Darris Engines calculates the sales price p, in dollars, of its miniature rocket engines based on the formula $p = 1.57c - \dfrac{3}{2}f + \$265.00$, where c is the cost of materials in dollars and f is a fixed dollar amount. If the fixed dollar amount equals \$5.00, what is the cost of materials for a rocket engine that sells for \$650.00?

    F. \$229.67
    G. \$240.45
    H. \$250.00
    J. \$395.49
    K. \$578.03

27. Two rectangular containers have the same volume. One of the containers is 50 centimeters wide by 40 centimeters long and 27 centimeters tall. What is the approximate height, in centimeters, of the second container if its width is 63 centimeters and its length is 24 centimeters?

    A. 125
    B. 86
    C. 53
    D. 40
    E. 27

28. What are the coordinates of the y-intercept of the line represented by the equation $2x + 6y = 14$?

    F. $0, -\dfrac{1}{3}$

    G. $0, \dfrac{7}{3}$

    H. $(0, 14)$

    J. $-\dfrac{1}{3}, 0$

    K. $(0, 3)$

DO YOUR FIGURING HERE.

29. 150 is $\frac{3}{15}$ of what number?

    A. 30
    B. 100
    C. 450
    D. 750
    E. 810

DO YOUR FIGURING HERE.

> **Use the following information to answer questions 30–32.**

The line segment from point J $(-4, 11)$ to point K $(2, 3)$ is shown in the standard (x, y) coordinate plane below.

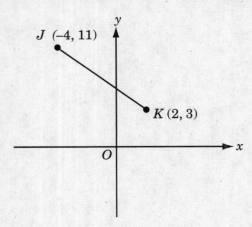

30. If points J and K are 2 vertices of the right triangle $\triangle JKL$, which has a right angle at L, which of the following could be the coordinates of point L?

    F. $(-6, 8)$

    G. $(-4, 3)$

    H. $-\frac{1}{2}, 2$

    J. $(4, 5)$

    K. $(4, -1)$

31. What is the length, in coordinate units, of line segment JK?

    A. $4\sqrt{5}$

    B. $6\sqrt{3}$

    C. 10

    D. $10\sqrt{2}$

    E. 12

GO ON TO THE NEXT PAGE.

32. $\overline{JK}$ is reflected across the x-axis such that point J reflects to point J'. What are the coordinates of point J'?

    F. $(8, 11)$
    G. $(4, 11)$.
    H. $(2, -3)$
    J. $(-4, -8)$
    K. $(-4, -11)$

DO YOUR FIGURING HERE.

33. Which of the following fractions is the largest?

    A. $-\dfrac{3}{2}$

    B. $-\dfrac{1}{4}$

    C. $-\dfrac{5}{7}$

    D. $-\dfrac{8}{14}$

    E. $-\dfrac{9}{28}$

34. In triangle QRS shown below, if $\overline{QR} = 15$ and $\tan q = \dfrac{5\sqrt{7}}{15}$, then $\overline{QS} = ?$

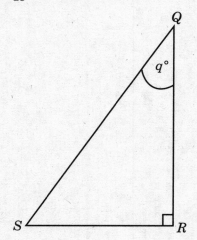

    F. $5\sqrt{7}$

    G. 15

    H. $17\sqrt{3}$

    J. 20

    K. 25

35. Figure *CDEF* shown below is a parallelogram. If $\overline{FG} = \frac{1}{4}\overline{FE}$, then what is the area of $\triangle FCG$?

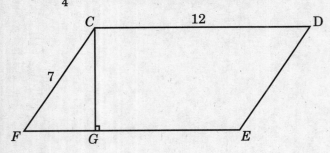

DO YOUR FIGURING HERE.

- **A.** $2\sqrt{10}$
- **B.** $3\sqrt{10}$
- **C.** 10
- **D.** 14
- **E.** $6\sqrt{10}$

36. The solution set of $\sqrt{a+2} \geq 3$ is the set of all real numbers a such that:

- **F.** $a \geq 2$
- **G.** $a \geq 5$
- **H.** $a \geq 7$
- **J.** $a \geq 13$
- **K.** $a \geq 15$

37. Asher and Katya collected egg cartons for a science fair project. Katya collected only $\frac{1}{4}$ as many egg cartons as did Asher. If the two collected 50 cartons altogether, how many did Asher collect?

- **A.** 8
- **B.** 10
- **C.** 16
- **D.** 24
- **E.** 40

38. What value of x will satisfy the equation $0.7(x + 360) = x$?

- **F.** 1,765
- **G.** 840
- **H.** 230
- **J.** 107
- **K.** 84

GO ON TO THE NEXT PAGE.

39. Triangle *ABC* has sides in a ratio of 8:10:12. Triangle *XYZ* is similar to triangle *ABC*, and its shortest side is 10 centimeters long. What is the perimeter, in centimeters, of △*XYZ*?

- **A.** 15
- **B.** 30
- **C.** 37.5
- **D.** 45.3
- **E.** 50

40. If $16 \geq \sqrt{s} \geq 25,$ then which of the following must be true?

- **F.** $256 \geq s \geq 625$
- **G.** $32 \geq s \geq 50$
- **H.** $16 \geq s \geq 25$
- **J.** $4 \geq s \geq 5$
- **K.** $-4 \geq s \geq -5$

41. Which of the following lines goes through the point $(6, 3)$ and is perpendicular to $y = \frac{1}{6}x - 4$?

- **A.** $y = \frac{1}{6}x + 2$
- **B.** $y = -6x - 3$
- **C.** $y = -6x + 39$
- **D.** $y = -\frac{1}{6}x + 4$
- **E.** $y = 6x - 33$

42. The average of a set of 10 integers is 63. If two of the integers in the set are 40 and 60, what is the average of the other 8 integers in the set?

- **F.** 63
- **G.** 66.25
- **H.** 70
- **J.** 71.50
- **K.** 73

43. The point $(6, 10)$ is a point on a line in the standard coordinate plane. Which of the following is another point on the line that passes through the point $(6, 10)$ and has a slope of $\frac{1}{5}$?

- **A.** $(1, 2)$
- **B.** $(2, 3)$
- **C.** $(3, 8)$
- **D.** $3, \frac{47}{5}$
- **E.** $(0, 1)$

DO YOUR FIGURING HERE.

44. Two complementary angles have measurements of $8a$ degrees and $a + 9$ degrees, respectively. What is the measure, in degrees, of the smaller of the two angles?

    F. 9
    G. 18
    H. 24
    J. 30
    K. 72

45. Mrs. Karagrokis has a bucket of 37 carrots to feed to her horses. If there are 15 horses, and each horse gets at least 1 carrot, how many horses could possibly receive 3 carrots?

    I. 9
    II. 11
    III. 12
    A. I only
    B. I and II only
    C. II only
    D. II and III only
    E. I, II, and III

46. If $\tan^2 \theta = \dfrac{\sin^2 \theta}{\cos^2 \theta}$, then $\tan^2 \theta$ is also equivalent to which of the following?

    F. 1
    G. $\cos^2 \theta + 1$
    H. $2\cos^2 \theta$
    J. $\cos^2 \theta$
    K. $\dfrac{1}{\cos^2 \theta} - 1$

47. The rectangular solid shown below has a surface area of 184 square centimeters. What is its height, h, in centimeters?

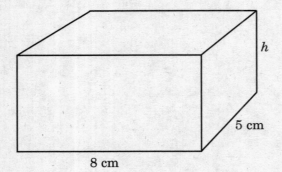

    F. 3.2
    G. 4
    H. 4.6
    J. 11.1
    K. 26

DO YOUR FIGURING HERE.

GO ON TO THE NEXT PAGE.

48. Figure *WXYZ* shown below is a rectangle with diagonals that intersect at point *T*. What is the perimeter of △*XTY*?

DO YOUR FIGURING HERE.

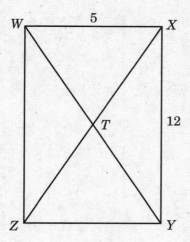

F. 7.5
G. 15
H. 17
J. 25
K. 30

49. If $\sin \theta = \dfrac{y}{z}$ and both *y* and *z* are positive, which of the following reflects the value of $\cos \theta$ if $0 < \theta < \dfrac{\pi}{2}$?

A. $\dfrac{z}{y}$

B. $\dfrac{\sqrt{z^2 - y^2}}{z}$

C. $\dfrac{z}{\sqrt{z^2 - y^2}}$

D. $\dfrac{y}{\sqrt{z^2 - y^2}}$

E. $\dfrac{\sqrt{z^2 - y^2}}{y}$

50. Sharee's Jewelry Co. creates handmade bracelets and necklaces. Two bracelets and four necklaces take 560 minutes to make. Two necklaces and four bracelets take 400 minutes to make. How many minutes does it take to make two bracelets and two necklaces?

F. 40
G. 80
H. 240
J. 320
K. Cannot be determined from the given information

51. Fillmore Elementary School conducted a three-hour bake sale. Five families each brought an equal number of brownies to the bake sale. One-fifth of the brownies were sold in the first hour, one-fifth of the remaining brownies were sold in the second hour, and one-fifth of the remaining brownies were sold in the third hour. If all of the brownies were sold as whole brownies, and 64 brownies remained at the end of the bake sale, how many brownies did each family contribute?

A. 125
B. 100
C. 50
D. 36
E. 25

DO YOUR FIGURING HERE.

52. In figure *JKLON* shown below, all lines meet at right angles. What is the perimeter, in centimeters, of *JKLON*?

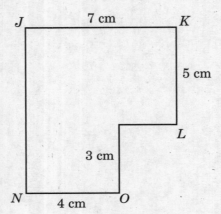

F. 21
G. 24
H. 27
J. 30
K. 38

53. Neera cuts two pieces of felt to serve as coverings for two circular display tables. The felt covers the tops of the tables only, with no fabric hanging over the sides. The radius of the first tabletop is 3 inches. If the area of the second tabletop is exactly two-thirds the area of the first tabletop, what should be the radius, in inches, of the felt cut for the second table covering?

A. $\sqrt{3}$
B. 2
C. $\sqrt{6}$
D. 3
E. 6

54. A *piecewise-defined* function consists of pieces of different functions combined together to form a single function. Which of the following is the graph of the piecewise-defined function $g(x)$ as shown below?

$$g(x) = \begin{cases} x^2 - 1 \text{ for } x < 2 \\ 4 \text{ for } 2 \le x \le 5 \\ x \text{ for } x > 5 \end{cases}$$

DO YOUR FIGURING HERE.

F.

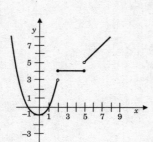

J.

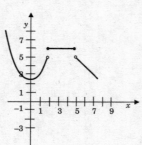

G.

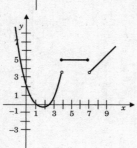

K.

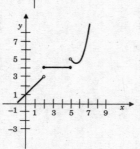

H.

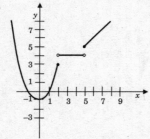

55. What is the value of $r - 8$ if $(x + 4)$ is a factor of $4x^2 + rx - 48$?

A. −4
B. −2
C. 1
D. 2
E. 4

56. If a and b are positive integers, which of the following values of a and b will make the inequality $\dfrac{1}{(2b)^a} > \dfrac{1}{(2a)^b}$ ALWAYS true?

F. $a = b$
G. $a + b > 4$
H. $a > b$
J. $b + a = 3$
K. $a < 4 < b$

57. Which of the following graphs represents the circle with center P and equation $(x - 4)^2 + (y - 5)^2 = 16$?

DO YOUR FIGURING HERE.

A.

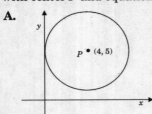

D.

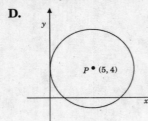

B.

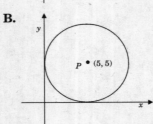

E.

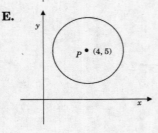

C.

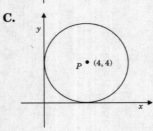

58. Rectangle $ABCD$ shown below has side lengths of a and b centimeters. The rectangle is reflected across $\overline{CD}$, and the images of A and B are represented by A' and B'. Which of the following expressions represents the length, in centimeters, of a diagonal of $A'B'AB$?

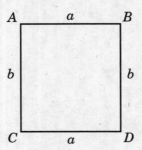

F. $\sqrt{a^2 + b^2}$

G. $a + b$

H. $\sqrt{a^2 + 4b^2}$

J. $\sqrt{a^2 + 2b^2}$

K. $a + 2b$

GO ON TO THE NEXT PAGE.

59. What is the value of $\log_r(12st)^4$ if $\log_r 12s = 12x$ and $\log_r t = y^2$?

   A. $12xy^2$

   B. $4x + 4y$

   C. $12x + y^2$

   D. $48x + 4y^2$

   E. $(12x)^4$

60. Hermann's Investment Advisor online newsletter had 4,700 subscribers on Monday. On Wednesday, Hermann's published a new investment recommendation, and the number of subscribers increased by 35%. On Friday, Hermann's retracted the investment recommendation, and the number of newsletter subscribers then decreased by 40%. What percent of Monday's subscribers were subscribed to the online newsletter on Friday?

   F. 19%

   G. 39%

   H. 60%

   J. 81%

   K. 189%

DO YOUR FIGURING HERE.

END OF TEST 2.
STOP! DO NOT TURN THE PAGE UNTIL TOLD TO DO SO.
DO NOT RETURN TO THE PREVIOUS TEST.

READING TEST

35 Minutes—40 Questions

DIRECTIONS: On this test, you will have 35 minutes to read four passages and answer 40 questions (ten questions on each passage). Each set of ten questions appears directly after the relevant passage. You should select the answer choice that best answers the question. There is no time limit for work on the individual passages, so you can move freely between the passages and refer to each as often as you'd like.

Passage I

PROSE FICTION: This passage is adapted from a book titled *The Haunted Bookshop,* by Christopher Morley.

If you are ever in Brooklyn, New York, hopefully you'll have the chance to visit a quiet side street where there is a very remarkable bookshop.

This bookshop is housed in one of those old New York
5 brownstone buildings that have been the joy of several generations of plumbers and cockroaches. The owner of the shop put a tremendous amount of effort into remodeling the brownstone to make it more suitable for book sales. There is no used bookshop in the world more worthy of respect.

10 It was about six o'clock on one cold November evening, with rain splattering on the pavement, when a young man named Allen Gilbert proceeded along Gissing Street. Gilbert stopped every so often to check the shops' addresses, as though he was unsure of his way. At last, he reached the
15 bookstore. Over the entrance he noticed the sign:

PARNASSUS BOOKS

R. AND H. MIFFLIN

BOOKLOVERS WELCOME!

THIS SHOP IS HAUNTED

20 Gilbert stumbled down the three steps that led into the storefront, turned down his coat collar, and looked around.

The store was very different from the bookstores in which he usually shopped. Two stories of the old house had been converted into one: The lower space was divided into
25 little alcoves, and the upper space showcased a gallery that carried books to the ceiling. The air was heavy with the smells of old paper and leather infused with stale tobacco.

The shop had a warm and comfortable feeling of obscurity. Passing down an aisle between the alcoves,
30 Gilbert could see that some of the compartments were totally dark; in others where lamps were glowing, he could see a table and chairs. In one corner, an elderly gentleman was reading, his face lit up by the sharp glare of electricity.

As Gilbert walked to the back of the shop, the whole
35 environment started to seem more and more surreal. He could hear the rain pelting down on some skylight far overhead, but otherwise the place was completely silent. He began to feel a little agitated, and his throat tightened. Towering above him into the gloom were shelves and
40 shelves of books extending upward toward the roof. Gilbert saw a table with a roll of brown paper and ribbon— evidently where purchases might be wrapped—but there was no sign of a salesperson.

"This place might be haunted," Gilbert thought, "but
45 not by the owners."

Just then, his eyes were caught by a circle of brightness with a curious luster. It was round and white, gleaming in the sheen of a hanging light. Gilbert moved closer and found that it was a bald head.

50 This head sat atop the shoulders of a small, sharp-eyed man, who sat tilted back in a swivel chair in a corner that seemed to be the "nerve center" of the establishment. In front of him was a large desk piled high with books of all sorts amidst newspaper clippings and letters. A cash
55 register was half buried in the mess. The little bald-headed man was chewing on a toothpick and reading a cookbook.

"Excuse me," said Gilbert, "are you the owner?"

Roger Mifflin, owner of Parnassus Books, looked up. Gilbert saw that he had piercing blue eyes, a short red
60 beard, and an air of originality.

"I am," said Mr. Mifflin. "What can I do for you?"

"My name is Allen Gilbert," Gilbert offered. "I represent Grey Matter Advertising. I'd like to talk with you about the possibility of handling your advertising for
65 the shop. With all the competition from other bookstores, you ought to develop a campaign to increase your business."

Mifflin's face beamed. He put down his cookbook and looked up brightly.

70 "Well, thanks for the offer," he said, "but I don't do any advertising."

GO ON TO THE NEXT PAGE.

"What?" Allen asked, incredulously. "That's impossible!" He reacted as if Mifflin had said something indecent.

75 "At least, I don't advertise in the sense that you mean. The advertising that benefits the store the most is handled for me by the best ad writers in the business."

"I suppose you mean Whitewash and Gilt?" said Mr. Gilbert wistfully.

80 "Not at all," Mifflin responded. "The folks who take care of my advertising are Stevenson, Browning, Conrad and Company."

"Hmm," Gilbert looked confounded. "I don't know that agency at all. But I doubt if their ad copy is more effective
85 than ours!"

"I don't think you get what I'm saying. I mean that my advertising is done by the books I sell. If I sell someone a book by Robert Louis Stevenson or Joseph Conrad, and if the book truly moves the customer, that person and
90 that book become my strongest advertisements," Mifflin explained.

Gilbert looked at Mifflin with a baffled expression. He hadn't been prepared for this sort of response!

1. As it is used in line 29, the term *obscurity* refers to the:
   A. way that the bookshop seems unknown to most people because few customers are inside.
   B. manner that the bookshop seems to invite Mr. Gilbert inside with its glowing lamps and comfortable seating.
   C. idea that the bookshop owner wants his shop to remain hidden from only a few booklovers.
   D. way that the bookshop is difficult for Mr. Gilbert to locate because it is concealed from the street.

2. It can reasonably be inferred that the narrator views the bookshop owner with a mixture of:
   F. sadness and apprehension.
   G. admiration and amazement.
   H. impatience and skepticism.
   J. respect and sentimentality.

3. The passage indicates that Mifflin does not want to purchase advertisements from Mr. Gilbert because:
   A. previous advertising campaigns have been unsuccessful.
   B. he is pleased with the firm that takes care of his advertising.
   C. he believes that spending money on advertising is pointless.
   D. he expects the bookshop's reputation to be enough advertisement.

4. Which of the following questions is NOT answered by information in the passage?
   F. What makes Parnassus Books different from other bookstores?
   G. Does Mr. Gilbert ever visit other bookstores in New York?
   H. Has the narrator walked around inside Parnassus Books?
   J. Why is Parnassus Books considered a haunted bookshop?

5. It can most reasonably be inferred that as it is used in line 60, the phrase *air of originality* refers to:
   A. Mr. Gilbert's reaction to the smell in the bookshop.
   B. the strange atmosphere in the bookshop that suggests it is haunted.
   C. Mr. Gilbert's impression of Mifflin as having a unique personality.
   D. the arrogant attitude of Mifflin upon being interrupted by Mr. Gilbert.

6. According to the passage, when Mifflin rejects Mr. Gilbert's suggestion of advertising, Mr. Gilbert is:
   F. stunned.
   G. offended.
   H. irritated.
   J. confused.

7. Which of the following best describes the way the first paragraph (lines 1–3) functions in the passage?
   A. It reinforces the image established by the story's title that the bookshop is haunted but that customers are still welcome to shop.
   B. It reveals that the narrator resides in New York and that he is one of the owners of Parnassus Books.
   C. It suggests that the narrator lives near Parnassus Books and that he frequents the store on a regular basis.
   D. It reveals the narrator's attitude about Parnassus Books and that the bookshop remains in business despite the owner's resistance to Mr. Gilbert's suggestions.

8. Which of the following can most reasonably be inferred from Mr. Gilbert's reaction as he walks through the bookshop in search of Mifflin?
   F. Mr. Gilbert begins to believe that the bookshop is actually haunted.
   G. Mr. Gilbert feels increasingly uncertain about his visit to the bookshop.
   H. Mr. Gilbert begins to relax and enjoy the warm atmosphere in the bookshop.
   J. Mr. Gilbert gradually feels more at ease in the bookshop as he wanders through.

9. The passage states that when Mr. Gilbert visits Parnassus Books:
    A. the elderly man is about to leave because it is late.
    B. Mifflin is busy at his desk counting sales receipts.
    C. Mifflin is the only one working in the store at the time.
    D. the salesperson is busy wrapping a customer's package.

10. Which of the following can be most reasonably inferred about Grey Matter Advertising?
    F. It frequently loses business to Whitewash and Gilt.
    G. It is the top advertising firm in New York City.
    H. It employs the best advertising copywriters.
    J. It recently hired Mr. Gilbert as a salesperson.

Passage II

SOCIAL SCIENCE: This passage is adapted from Jonathon May's "Protests to Progress: A Critique of Working Conditions During the Industrial Revolution."

Published in 1776, Adam Smith's seminal work *Wealth of Nations* promotes the far-reaching benefits of the Industrial Revolution. Starting in Britain during the late 18th and early 19th century, the Industrial Revolution
5 transformed all previous concepts of labor, replacing the former agricultural society based on manual labor with an industrial society reliant on machines and the division of labor. Based on the premise that very large jobs could be subdivided into smaller, distinctive operations in which an
10 individual performs one small part, the division of labor allowed for much greater production of goods and a rapid expansion of economic growth. Smith proposed that the division of labor would create "universal opulence which extends itself to the lowest ranks of the people," and that
15 everyone from factory owners to the working classes would benefit from this increased production. However, many prominent 19th-century thinkers and writers challenged Smith's optimistic notion of the division of labor, arguing that this process not only failed to promote economic
20 equality but also led to a diminishing quality of life for most workers.

Although the Industrial Revolution sparked economic growth and development for Britain, many workers were exploited by the new system and did not share in the
25 newfound wealth. In his treatise, *Past and Present*, 19th-century essayist and historian Thomas Carlyle condemns England for failing to use its rich natural resources to produce universal wealth. Despite increased production resulting from industrialization and the division of labor,
30 he argues, inequality and poverty persist. He laments, "The condition of England…is justly regarded as one of the most ominous…ever seen in this world. England is full of wealth, of produce, to supply for human want of every kind; yet England is dying of starvation."

35   The division of labor, although cost-effective, demanded long, tedious hours of work under stifling working conditions. Nineteenth-century poet William Wordsworth criticizes the weary, unoriginal, and mentally stagnating work inherent to the division of labor in his *Preface
40 to the Lyrical Ballads*. He comments, "a multitude of causes…are now acting with a combined force to blunt the discriminating powers of the mind…to reduce it to a state of almost savage torpor." He also dislikes capitalistic industrialization because the working conditions
45 physically remove most workers from the beauty of nature. Instead, Wordsworth prefers "humble and rustic life" in which "the essential passions of the heart find better soil." Wordsworth's response to the heartless, materialistic conditions prevalent during this time echo Thomas
50 Carlyle's sentiments expressed in *Past and Present*. Carlyle asserts, "Nature's Laws . . . are eternal: her small still voice, speaking from the inmost heart of us, shall not . . . be disregarded."

Likewise, English poet and painter William Blake
55 also discredits Smith's rose-colored predictions regarding the benefits of industrialization. The division of labor, in Blake's opinion, has only led to individual misery and oppression. This rote, tedious, and disheartening work, Blake contends, has caused masses of city workers to
60 feel despondent and hopeless. In his poem *London*, he observes, "I wander through each chartered street/Near where the chartered Thames does flow/And mark in every face I meet/Marks of weakness, marks of woe. In every cry of every Man/In every infant's cry of fear/In every voice,
65 in every ban/The mind-forged manacles I hear." Blake's concern with industrial labor also extended to the tragic plight of child workers who toiled many hours each day for an even lower wage.

Although Smith's optimistic portrayal of capitalistic
70 industrialization provided a solid fundamental analysis of the economic factors involved, he failed to anticipate the human suffering resulting from the reduction of individuals to invisible "hands" lost in the process of production. Philosophers such as Carlyle, along with poets
75 such as Wordsworth and Blake, witnessed the negative effects of industrialization and recognized the essential humanity of all workers.

GO ON TO THE NEXT PAGE.

11. The author suggests that Carlyle and Wordsworth are similar in that they both believe that industrialization:
   A. inhibits laborers from acquiring the wages they actually deserve.
   B. prevents individuals from enjoying the wonders of the natural world.
   C. deepens the societal gap between the wealthy and the impoverished.
   D. provides long-term benefits to the economic strength of a nation.

12. According to the passage, how did the Industrial Revolution affect the way in which tasks were accomplished?
   F. Jobs were assigned to individuals based on their knowledge and skill level.
   G. Farm laborers were replaced with equipment that required fewer workers.
   H. Factory workers acquired skills that enabled them to perform tasks rapidly.
   J. Small, specific jobs were assigned to workers who performed them repeatedly.

13. It can most reasonably be inferred from the passage that Adam Smith assumed that a division of labor would lead to which of the following results?
   A. Better productivity, increased profits for businesses, and better wages for workers
   B. Increased efficiency, higher demand for goods, and lower cost-of-living expenses
   C. Economic equality for laborers, creation of businesses, and better living conditions
   D. Improved labor laws, improved class relations, and increased worker motivation

14. The main function of the second paragraph (lines 22–34) in relation to the passage as a whole is to:
   F. emphasize the validity of Adam Smith's *Wealth of Nations* as it relates to the writings of Carlyle and Wordsworth.
   G. redirect the passage toward a discussion of the impact of the Industrial Revolution on the global economy.
   H. shift the passage toward a discussion of the negative aspects of industrialization and divisions of labor.
   J. establish the passage's claim that industrialization fails to efficiently maximize a society's natural resources.

15. According to the passage, Adam Smith's theory about the Industrial Revolution is:
   A. logical and progressive.
   B. hopeful but unrealistic.
   C. convincing and influential.
   D. promising but unimpressive.

16. As it is used in line 41, the word *blunt* most nearly means to:
   F. withhold.
   G. weaken.
   H. surprise.
   J. necessitate.

17. It is reasonable to infer from the passage that Wordsworth believed the lives of laborers were:
   A. worse when they worked for small wages on farms owned by wealthy landowners.
   B. better after the Industrial Revolution when they earned reasonable wages in factories.
   C. worse after the Industrial Revolution because jobs involved physical strength and challenging tasks.
   D. better when they worked on farms because jobs required being outdoors and using a variety of skills.

18. According to Blake and Carlyle, industrialized England would be described by which of the following phrases?
   F. A wealthy country of miserable workers
   G. A divided nation of wealthy individuals
   H. A communist country of starving people
   J. A prosperous nation of outraged citizens

19. One of the main points that the author seeks to make in the passage is that a division of labor:
   A. negatively affects the economic strength of a nation by relying too heavily on the abilities of unskilled workers.
   B. may diminish the long-term opportunities of laborers by forcing them to perform tedious and meaningless tasks.
   C. separates the rich from the poor, and it encourages businesses to employ children in order to improve profits.
   D. may benefit the economy of a nation, but it harms the well-being of individual workers.

20. According to the passage, which of the following factors does Adam Smith overlook in his advocacy of the division of labor?
   F. People need to be mentally engaged in their daily work.
   G. Individuals are physically unable to perform repetitive tasks.
   H. People need to have important responsibilities at their jobs.
   J. Individuals enjoy interacting with other employees while working.

GO ON TO THE NEXT PAGE. • 501

Passage III

HUMANITIES: This passage is adapted from Joyce Garatty's "Saints, Sages, and Souls: An Overview of the Cao Dai Religion."

Founded less than one hundred years ago in Southeast Asia, Cao Dai (pronounced "cow die") is now the third largest religion in Vietnam, with two to three million followers. Caodaists have a very strong faith in God
5 and believe that their religion, including its teachings, symbolism, and organization, was founded by direct communication with God. "Cao Dai" may be translated to "high place" or "supreme palace" where God reigns, and it is also an abbreviated form of the word *God*, the creator of
10 the universe. Believing that all human life originates from the same source (God), Caodaism promotes harmonious, loving, and just actions towards others, as well as the cultivation of a close relationship with God as a means to eternal salvation. Adherents hope to escape the cycle
15 of birth and death (a belief incorporated from Buddhism) and to live with God in heaven. To achieve these goals, they seek purification through religious beliefs and ethical practices.

Considered a syncretistic or unifying religion, Cao Dai
20 embraces other world religions and stresses one universal God as its common origin. Its followers maintain that various religious doctrines and belief systems throughout the world occurred as a result of geographic separation and not essential theological differences, proposing that
25 "all religions are one." Caodaists combine central tenets of each religious tradition to form their own unique faith. From Buddhism, for example, they borrow the practice of meditation as a way of liberating the mind; from Confucianism, they adopt the ideas of social cohesion and
30 ancestral worship; from Taoism they borrow the concept of the Way, or the path of least resistance; and from Christianity, they accept the teachings of Jesus Christ, emphasizing compassion and forgiveness.

One of the most esoteric Cao Dai beliefs is the worship
35 of sages, including the veneration of Western intellectuals. Practitioners revere great writers, thinkers, and scientists as saints. Known as the Holy See, Cao Dai's holiest temple in Tay Ninh, about fifty-five miles from Ho Chi Minh City, features portraits of prominent Western leaders
40 and thinkers, including William Shakespeare, Thomas Jefferson, Julius Caesar, and Winston Churchill, along with pictures of great religious leaders like Jesus, Buddha, and Lao-tzu (the founder of Taoism). Although Caodaists worship God as the "Supreme Being," they also believe

45 in a holy pantheon with five levels of deities. At the top of the pantheon is Buddha, followed by the Great Immortals (including Confucius and the Chinese poet Li Po), the saints (including famous writers, philosophers, and religious leaders), and venerated spirits or ancestors. The
50 rest of humanity occupies the bottom level of the pantheon.

Cao Dai's religious doctrines exercise great influence on practitioners and their mode of conduct toward both their families and the larger society. Caodaism emphasizes duty toward the self, the family, the society (considered
55 the broader family), and the universal family of humanity. Adherents to the religion follow several fundamental principles common to other world religions: do not kill living beings, do not be dishonest, do not commit adultery, do not overindulge, and do not deal in falsehoods. Each
60 month at both the full moon and the new moon, Caodaists go to temple and abstain from eating meat. Followers observe a vegetarian diet for ten days per month, and those with leadership positions in the church practice vegetarianism at all times. Ethical practices such as
65 vegetarianism, prayer, nonviolence, and veneration of ancestors are all part of the faith and support both a closer relationship with God and the goal of social harmony.

Drawing from the ancient teachings of Confucianism, Cao Dai stresses the attainment of social harmony
70 through performing good works and living a moral life. To this end, Caodaists follow a moral code that emphasizes benevolence both to oneself (through the acquisition of moral knowledge, or distinguishing right from wrong) and to one's fellow human beings (through respect and
75 understanding for all). Righteousness and honesty are expected of Caodaists in their personal lives, as well as in their dealings with family members, coworkers, and the larger society. Practitioners of Cao Dai are encouraged to cultivate the quality of faithfulness and keep their
80 promises to others by carrying out their responsibilities to their children and communities.

Ultimately, Caodaists seek to bring their religious principles and practices into balance, not only to attain a fulfilling life on Earth, but also to advance to the next
85 phase of their spiritual development. By unifying what they define as the three "treasures of nature," including the body, mind, and soul, Caodaists hope to stop the endless cycle of reincarnation and be reunited with God. According to Cao Dai doctrine, there is ultimately but one
90 way to achieve this goal: love and peace. This maxim is reflected in the Caodaist message, "Love is the key to open God's kingdom."

        GO ON TO THE NEXT PAGE.

21. According to the passage, in order to draw closer to God and develop more peaceful relationships with others, followers of Cao Dai should do all of the following EXCEPT:
   A. Attend temple each month
   B. Show respect for ancestors
   C. Regularly participate in prayer
   D. Avoid eating meat for two months

22. It can most reasonably be inferred from the passage that Caodaists:
   F. disdain the attitudes of major religious sects that conflict with the Cao Dai belief system and code of conduct.
   G. evaluate the views and ideas maintained by other religious organizations and sometimes borrow ideas from them.
   H. reveal inconsistencies in the doctrines of the world's largest religions by studying the works and beliefs of scholars.
   J. recognize the discrepancies between the religious doctrines of Cao Dai and those of other world religions and saints.

23. According to the passage, the primary goal for followers of Cao Dai is to:
   A. be reincarnated as a reward for graceful actions toward others.
   B. achieve eternal salvation and avoid continuous reincarnation.
   C. encourage others to convert to the Cao Dai faith.
   D. establish harmonious relationships with all members of society.

24. It can be most reasonably inferred that Caodaists believe which of the following about the relationship between Cao Dai and many other world religions?
   F. Belief in only one God is the original source of all religious faiths.
   G. Geographic proximity promotes religious unity.
   H. A common set of prayers is what unites believers all over the world.
   J. All faiths have faced criticism for their religious doctrines.

25. It can most reasonably be inferred from the passage that one aspect of Cao Dai is that followers uphold the belief that:
   A. sainthood can only be achieved through loving actions and cannot be attained through worldly knowledge.
   B. living a moral life is more important than intellectual accomplishments in regards to earning sainthood.
   C. intelligence is an exceptional characteristic that deserves the highest honor and respect next to the "Supreme Being."
   D. the foundation of modern society depends on intellectuals who maintain moral and ethical standards.

26. As described in the passage, the moral standards of Cao Dai are a way for followers to achieve which of the following?
   F. Holiness
   G. Healing
   H. Peace
   J. Purity

27. According to the passage, Cao Dai fuses together all of the following elements from other religions EXCEPT the concept of:
   A. the lack of any absolute truths (from Taoism).
   B. respecting ancestors (from Confucianism).
   C. showing kindness and mercy (from Christianity).
   D. meditating in order to attain enlightenment (from Buddhism).

28. The passage indicates that Cao Dai emphasizes how problems in society can be overcome if followers:
   F. develop a strong sense of faithfulness, treat others justly, and follow specific guidelines during times of prayer.
   G. persuade others to live moral lives, distinguish right from wrong, and seek out additional knowledge.
   H. maintain a strict ethical code of conduct, show respect toward others, and uphold family responsibilities.
   J. exhibit righteousness in business dealings, provide community support, and experience reality through worship.

29. According to the information presented in the passage about the *holy pantheon* (lines 43–50), which of the following groups of individuals are in the correct order from top to bottom?
   A. Jesus Christ, God, Confucius
   B. Buddha, Thomas Jefferson, Li Po
   C. God, Winston Churchill, Li Po
   D. Buddha, Confucius, Julius Caesar

30. According to the passage, which of the following is credited for the way in which Cao Dai is structured?
   F. The Holy See
   G. Confucianism
   H. The Supreme Being
   J. Buddhism

Passage IV

NATURAL SCIENCE: This passage is adapted from Charlie Malone's "Deconstructing the Damage: How Scientists Use the EF-Scale to Assess and Understand Tornadoes."

Tornadoes, violently rotating columns of air, are a weather phenomenon that many people find both fascinating and terrifying. A tornado's path of destruction can range from slight to horrific. Within the same
5 neighborhood, for example, some homes may be strangely untouched, while others are completely annihilated. Over the years, scientists have studied the mystifying nature of tornadoes and attempted to classify their fluctuating intensity and perplexing array of destruction. During
10 the 1970s, Japanese-American meteorologist Dr. Tetsuya Theodore Fujita developed a system to analyze tornadic wind speed and estimate subsequent damage known as the Fujita Tornado Intensity Scale, or F-Scale.

Since the 1970s, the F-Scale has been the most
15 reliable and widely used scientific tool for analyzing the force of and damage sustained by tornadoes throughout the country. The scale places tornadic wind speeds into progressive categories ranging from F0 (weak tornadoes) to F5 (catastrophic tornadoes). However, in 2007, the
20 National Weather Service, one of six scientific agencies that make up the National Oceanic and Atmospheric Administration (NOAA) of the United States government, formally unveiled the Enhanced Fujita Scale, or EF-Scale. Expanding upon the basic tenets of the original F-Scale,
25 the updated classification system incorporated tornado damage data gathered over the last few decades to make more accurate assessments.

The EF-Scale more closely connects tornadic wind speeds with actual storm destruction, a continuing
30 challenge for scientists plagued by the difficulty of accurately measuring wind speed following a storm's fury. Using enhanced radar data, cycloidal marks (ground swirl patterns), and remote sensing technology from photographs to assess structural and vegetative damage
35 that results from the more than 1200 tornadoes reported in the United States every year, scientists have been able to incorporate the EF-Scale to broaden their damage-perspective lenses and evaluate a more substantial body of relevant data. This data includes factors such as the
40 latitudinal and longitudinal paths of tornadoes and the average and maximum damage produced by tornadoes.

Scientists also take basic construction principles into account when assessing tornado intensities, considering both the structural soundness of affected buildings and
45 the varying degrees of damage. Formerly, when scientists used the now-outdated F-Scale, they primarily assessed post-tornadic structural damage in a very generalized, imprecise manner and failed to consider the size and dimensions of buildings to establish accurate ratings. EF-
50 Scale experts now examine many more types of buildings that sustained light, moderate, or serious damage within a tornado-stricken area, including mobile homes, small farms and farm outbuildings, schools, professional buildings, apartments, heavy timber or steel warehouses,
55 free-standing and transmission towers, and wood or metal buildings.

When a tornado is classified as an EF0 storm, its wind speeds are estimated in the range of 65 to 85 miles per hour. Property destruction is light and normally includes
60 toppled signs; fallen branches and small tree limbs; and mild roof, chimney, gutter, and siding damage. An EF1 tornado's wind speeds are estimated to be between 86–110 miles per hour and typically produce torn roofs (off of mobile homes) and shattered windows. If a tornado's wind
65 speeds reach 111 to 135 miles per hour, it is categorized as an EF2 storm capable of inflicting considerable damage to homes and vegetation—roofs may be ripped from well-constructed houses, home foundations may shift and separate, and well-established trees may be completely
70 uprooted.

As storms increase in size and intensity, so does the severity of the resulting damage. An EF3 tornado generates wind speeds of 136–165 miles per hour, causing massive structural damage to homes and businesses and
75 overturned locomotives and automobiles. When scientists observe even more extensive damage to well-built homes and other structures, the complete destruction of frame houses, and piles of thrown cars, a tornado's wind speeds have reached 166 to 200 miles per hour, an EF4 storm.
80 And if a tornado's strength is catastrophic, obliterating and deforming strong houses, high-rise buildings, and other structures beyond recognition, the tornado is classified as an EF5 with wind speeds in excess of 200 miles per hour. The only tornado in history to measure
85 EF5 occurred on May 4, 2007, in Greensburg, Kansas, producing estimated wind speeds greater than 205 miles per hour and destroying 95 percent of the town.

Tornados continue to be a grave threat across the United States, producing a wide spectrum of structural
90 and vegetative damage that is challenging for scientists to both predict and measure. The original F-Scale and its enhanced version, the EF-Scale, give scientists the best opportunity to assess these storms with newfound accuracy and reliability. Through improved understanding
95 of tornadoes, their powerful and sporadic nature, and their potential to inflict damage, scientists hope to better understand these storms and help protect lives and property in the future.

31. According to the passage, if the only major damage inflicted upon a home by a tornado is a few broken windows, then the storm would most likely be categorized as an:
   A. EF0.
   B. EF1.
   C. EF2.
   D. EF3.

32. It can most reasonably be inferred from the passage that before the F-Scale was developed:
   F. radar data were largely unavailable to meteorologists.
   G. tornadic wind speeds were vastly underestimated.
   H. tornado damages were not averaged every decade.
   J. tornadic intensity had not been correctly categorized.

33. The passage indicates that the EF-Scale, as compared to the F-Scale, designates ratings based on:
   A. more structures of similar sizes.
   B. structures that suffer major damage.
   C. the same types of structures.
   D. a larger range of structures.

34. According to the passage, what is the purpose of the Fujita Scale and the Enhanced Fujita Scale?
   F. Estimate the strength of a tornado based on evaluations of post-storm damages.
   G. Calculate the monetary damage caused by tornados of various strength ratings.
   H. Provide pre-storm warnings to communities based on typical storm patterns.
   J. Examine various levels of destruction caused by high winds and cycloidal marks.

35. The main function of the fifth and sixth paragraphs (lines 57–87) in relation to the passage as a whole is to:
   A. explain how wind speed affects the severity of damage by comparing EF ratings with F-scale ratings.
   B. establish that EF ratings have improved the ability of meteorologists to predict storm damage.
   C. clarify the meaning of EF ratings by describing the destruction caused by various wind speeds.
   D. point out that EF5 tornadoes rarely occur due to improvements in measuring wind speeds.

36. According to the passage, when scientists attempt to determine the EF-Scale classification of a tornado, they consider all of the following factors EXCEPT:
   F. the level of structural damage imposed on a building.
   G. ground swirl patterns located in the storm's vicinity.
   H. the structural stability of buildings hit by tornadoes.
   J. average wind speeds from the National Weather Service.

37. Which of the following findings, if true, would best support the idea that the EF-Scale makes "accurate assessments" (lines 24-26)?
   A. Wind speed measurements taken during a tornado correlate with EF-Scale ratings assigned after a storm.
   B. The average damage of an EF3 storm corresponds to the average damage caused by an F3 storm.
   C. The maximum destruction caused by an EF2 storm includes fallen branches and minor chimney damage.
   D. Radar data used for EF-Scale ratings are consistent with predictions made by the National Weather Service.

38. It may be reasonably inferred from the passage that improving the reliability of tornado ratings involves:
   F. calculating directional paths.
   G. studying a wide range of data.
   H. measuring winds during storms.
   J. using multiple measurement tools.

39. One of the main points that the author seeks to make in the passage is that the EF-Scale:
   A. allows scientists to predict the path and intensity of a tornado before it strikes.
   B. provides scientists with a method of analyzing the unpredictable nature of tornadoes.
   C. enables scientists to measure post-tornadic damage inflicted on farms and buildings.
   D. offers scientists a way to measure tornadic wind speeds from remote locations.

40. According to the passage, why was 2007 a significant year in the study of tornadoes?
   F. The National Weather Service officially implemented the Fujita Scale.
   G. A higher than average number of tornadoes struck communities in the United States.
   H. A tornado with wind speeds over 205 miles per hour destroyed a Midwestern city.
   J. NOAA scientists recorded the first EF6 tornado with winds over 200 miles per hour.

END OF TEST 3.
STOP! DO NOT TURN THE PAGE UNTIL TOLD TO DO SO.
DO NOT RETURN TO A PREVIOUS TEST.

SCIENCE TEST

35 Minutes—40 Questions

DIRECTIONS: This test contains seven passages, each accompanied by several questions. You should select the answer choice that best answers each question. Within the total allotted time for the Subject Test, you may spend as much time as you wish on each individual passage. Calculator use is not permitted.

Passage I

CITATION: Oerlemans J, Dyurgerov M, van de Wal RSW (2007). Reconstructing the glacier contribution to sea-level rise back to 1850. *The Chryosphere* 1: 59–65.

The melting of smaller ice caps and glaciers has been listed as one of the most important processes contributing to sea-level rise. Sea-level rise is a major sign of global warming. In 2005, scientists grouped the world's glaciers into regions and came up with an estimate of glacier contribution to sea-level rise (SL) for the period 1961–2003. Figure 1 shows the results.

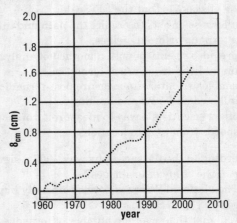

Figure 1

The results in Figure 1 depend upon measuring the mass of glaciers. These mass records cover less than five decades. Glacier *length* records, on the other hand, go back much farther in time and are therefore the only source of observational information from which a sea-level contribution over the past several centuries can be estimated. For Table 2, scientists gathered pre-1950 glacier-length records in 13 different regions. They assigned each region a weight based upon how many of the world's glaciers are in that region.

Area Covered by Glaciers

Region	# of Records	Area (km²)	Weight
Alaska	2	149,600	0.244
Rocky Mountains	28	126,033	0.206
S. Greenland, Iceland	6	87,460	0.143
Jan Mayen, Svalbard	4	92,386	0.151
Alps and Pyrenees	96	2,357	0.004
Caucasus	9	1,456	0.002
Central Asia	18	119,850	0.196
Kamchatka	1	4,300	0.006
Irian Jaya	2	3	0
Central Afric	7	6	0
Tropical Andes	2	2,200	0.004
Southern Andes	10	30,000	0.038
New Zealand	2	1,160	0.002

Table 1

Scientists then compared the glaciers' length over the past 300 years to their length in 1950. The results are displayed in Figure 2.

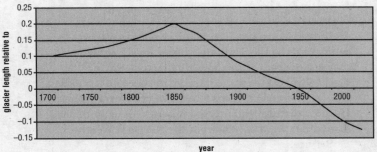

Figure 2

GO ON TO THE NEXT PAGE.

1. According to Figures 1 and 2, what was the relationship between the length of glaciers and the sea level after 1960?
   A. Glacier length increased as the sea level became higher.
   B. Glacier length decreased as the sea level became lower.
   C. Glacier length increased as the sea level became lower.
   D. Glacier length decreased as the sea level became higher.

2. According to Figure 1, by 2015 the sea level will have risen:
   F. 0.4 cm
   G. 1.5 cm
   H. 1.7 cm
   J. 2.0 cm

3. According to Table 1, how many more glacial square kilometers were in the Rocky Mountains than were in the Southern Andes?
   A. 30,000 km^2
   B. 96,033 km^2
   C. 123,833 km^2
   D. 156,033 km^2

4. A scientist wants to add a fourteenth glacial region, Scandinavia, to Table 1. The glacial region in Scandinavia is smaller than the region in Kamchatka but larger than the region in the Alps and Pyrenees. A reasonable estimate of Scandinavia's weight is:
   F. 0.002
   G. 0.005
   H. 0.007
   J. 0.009

5. Based on the information presented and the data in Figure 2, what most likely happened in the years following 1850?
   A. Sea levels lowered worldwide.
   B. More glacial records were discovered.
   C. Scientists began measuring glacial length rather than mass.
   D. There was a significant increase in global warming.

Passage II

Titration experiments are used by scientists to test the pH of different acid and alkali (or base) solutions. The pH of a solution is measured on a scale from 0 to 14. Acids have pH values ranging from 0 to 7, and bases have pH values ranging from 7 to 14. More acidic solutions have pH values closer to 0, while more alkaline solutions have pH values closer to 14. Three experiments were conducted by a scientist to test the pH levels of various solutions.

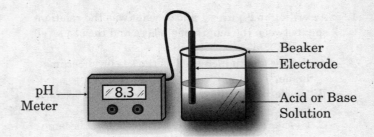

Figure 1

Experiment 1

The pH of 8 acids and 8 bases were tested using a simple pH meter. The acids and bases each had a concentration of 1 mol, and a volume of 25 milliliters (mL). Each solution was placed in a beaker that contained an electrode attached to a simple pH meter, as shown in Figure 1. The results are shown in Table 1.

	Acids			**Bases**		
	Formula	**Name**	**pH**	**Formula**	**Name**	**pH**
Strong	HCl	hydrochloric acid	0	LiOH	lithium hydroxide	14
	HNO_3	nitric acid	0	NaOH	sodium hydroxide	14
	H_2SO_4	sulfuric acid	0	KOH	potassium hydroxide	14
	HBr	hydrobromic acid	0	RbOH	rubidium hydroxide	14
	$HClO_4$	perchloric acid	0	CsOH	cesium hydroxide	14
Weak	HF	hydrofluoric acid	1.59	C_6H_5OH	ammonia	11.62
	CH_3COOH	acetic acid	2.38	$(CH_3CH_2)_2NH$	diethylamine	11.5
	H_3BO_3	boric acid	4.6	NH_3	phenol	9.02

Table 1

Experiment 2

The pH levels of a combined acid-base solution were tested using the apparatus shown in Figure 2. A buret containing 40 mL of a 1 mol strong acid solution was placed over a beaker containing 25 mL of a 1 mol strong base. Acid was added to the base in 1 mL increments, and the pH was measured after each addition of acid. The *equivalence point* was reached when the number of moles of the added solution equaled the number of moles of the solution originally in the beaker. The results are shown in Figure 3.

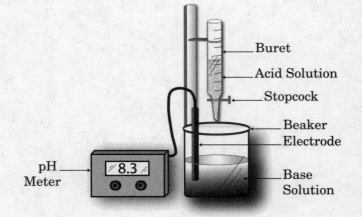

Figure 2

GO ON TO THE NEXT PAGE.

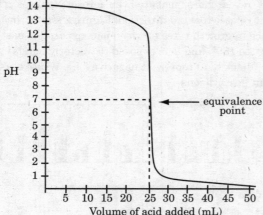

Figure 3

Experiment 3

Using the procedure from Experiment 2, 40 mL of a 1 mol weak acid solution was added to 25 mL of a 1 mol weak base. The results are shown in Figure 4.

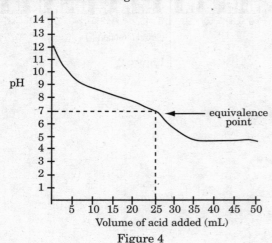

Figure 4

6. According to the results of Experiment 3, the acid-base solution reflected a pH of 7 when approximately how much of the acid was added?
F. 7 mL
G. 10 mL
H. 25 mL
J. 40 mL

7. The pH of an unidentified 1 mol-strong acid solution is tested using the procedure from Experiment 1. Based on the results of Experiment 1, the pH of the unidentified solution is closest to:
A. 0
B. 7
C. 13
D. 14

8. According to the results of Experiment 1, which of the following could have been the acid and base used in Experiment 3?
F. HCl and NaOH
G. CH_3COOH and NH_3
H. HBr and KOH
J. HNO_3 and NH_3

9. Based on the results of Experiment 1, if the scientist wished to conduct a fourth experiment measuring the pH of a solution in which a strong acid is added to a weak base, which of the following procedures would most likely be used?
A. 25 mL of a 1 mol acetic acid solution is added to 25 mL of a 1 mol sodium hydroxide solution.
B. 25 mL of a 1 mol ammonia solution is added to 25 mL of a 1 mol hydrochloric acid solution.
C. 25 mL of a 1 mol hydrobromic acid solution is added to 25 mL of a 1 mol potassium hydroxide solution.
D. 25 mL of a 1 mol perchloric acid solution is added to 25 mL of a 1 mol diethylamine solution.

10. From the results of Experiment 2, what would one hypothesize, if anything, about the effect of adding 15 mL of the original 1 mol strong base to the acid-base solution in the beaker after the initial 40 mL of the strong acid had been added?
F. The pH of the solution in the beaker rises.
G. The pH of the solution in the beaker decreases.
H. The pH of the solution in the beaker first decreases, then rises.
J. The addition pH of the solution in the beaker is not affected.

11. According to the results of Experiments 2 and 3, which of the following conclusions can be made about the magnitude of change in pH that occurs when an acid is added to a base solution?
A. Adding an acid solution to a base solution results in a pH of 7 after the equivalence point of the titration is reached.
B. Adding a strong acid to a strong base causes a steeper drop in pH values near the equivalence point than does adding a weak acid to a weak base.
C. When an acid solution is added to a base solution, the steepest drop in pH values occurs near the equivalence point of the titration.
D. When an acid solution is added to a base solution, the change in pH occurs more slowly the closer the initial pH value is to 14.

Passage III

Citation: Suni T, Kulmala M, Hirsikko A, Bergman T, Laakso L, Aalto P, Leuning R, Cleugh H, Zegelin S, Hughes D, van Gorsel E, Kitchen M, Vana M, Hõrrak U, Mirme S, Mirme A, Sevanto S, Twining J, Tadros C (2008). Formation and characteristics of ions and charged aerosol particles in a native Australian Eucalypt forest. *Atmospheric Chemistry and Physics 8*: 129–139.

Aerosol particles are produced by human activity, but they are also formed naturally in oceans, deserts, and forests. These naturally made aerosol particles are referred to as *biogenic* aerosol. Trees, in particular, are efficient producers of aerosol particles. Determining the magnitude and driving factors of biogenic aerosol production is crucial for future development of climate models. This study examines the production of these particles in an evergreen Eucalyptus forest in Australia.

Researchers measured the average growth rates (GR) in nmh^{-1} of aerosol particles produced in the Eucalyptus forest. From July 2005 until October 2006, researchers measured the growth of negative and positive aerosol ions. (Note that months are represented by numbers rather than words; July is 7, August is 8, and so on.) The results are displayed in Figure 1. Black bars represent ions with starting lengths of 1.3 to 3 nm (small). Gray bars represent ions with starting lengths of 3 to 7 nm (medium). White bars represent ions with starting lengths of 7 to 20 nm (large).

Next, researchers measured the aerosol particles' growth rate as it relates to wind direction. Figure 2 shows the difference in growth rates between ions exposed to easterly winds (0° to 180°) and ions exposed to westerly winds (180° to 360°). Black bars represent negative ions. White bars represent positive ions.

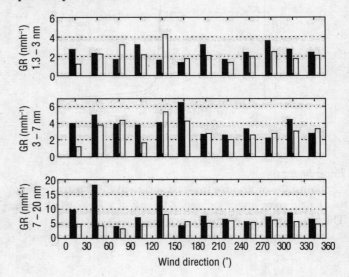

Figure 2

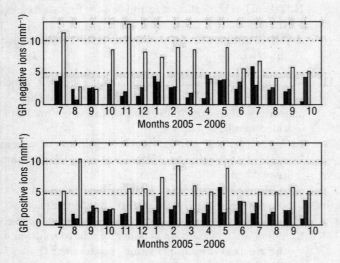

Figure 1

GO ON TO THE NEXT PAGE.

12. According to Figure 1, large negative ions had the greatest growth rate in:
    F. July 2005
    G. September 2005
    H. November 2005
    J. July 2006

13. According to Figure 2, medium positive ions had the smallest growth rate when the wind direction was between:
    A. 0° and 30°
    B. 120° and 150°
    C. 270° and 300°
    D. 330° and 360°

14. According to Figure 1, which of the following statements was true of both negative and positive ions in February 2006?
    F. The growth rate of the medium ions was significantly greater than in January 2006.
    G. The growth rate of the large ions was significantly greater than the growth rate of the small or medium ions.
    H. The growth rate of the small ions was significantly greater than in January 2006.
    J. The growth rate of the large ions was significantly smaller than the growth rate of the small or medium ions.

15. Which of the following hypotheses is most strongly supported by the data in Figure 2?
    A. Regardless of wind direction, the growth rate of small negative ions is greater than the growth rate of large negative ions.
    B. Regardless of wind direction, the growth rate of large positive ions is greater than the growth rate of large negative ions.
    C. On average, the growth rate of large ions is greater in westerly winds than in easterly winds.
    D. On average, the growth rate of medium and large ions is greater in easterly winds than in westerly winds.

16. A researcher indentified an aerosol particle that experiences a growth rate of approximately 15 nmh^{-1} when the wind is blowing at a direction between 120° and 150°. What was the particle's original length?
    F. Between 1.3 and 3 nm
    G. Between 3 and 7 nm
    H. Between 7 nm and 20 nm
    J. The particle's length cannot be determined from these data.

Passage IV

Citation: Mathevon N, Aubin T, Vielliard J, da Silva M, Sebe F, Boscolo D (2008). Singing in the rain forest: how a tropical bird song transfers information. *PLoS ONE 3*(2): e1580.

White-browned warblers' songs are well matched to the acoustic constraints of the rainforest and the ecological requirements of the species. These birds listen to their neighbors' calls to determine whether it is safe to approach. They also make high-pitched contact calls to identify themselves to other birds. Researchers in this experiment measured the white-browned warblers' responses to a variety of natural, synthetic, and altered tones. In each of the experiments, the researchers used 5 tones: a control bird song (control); a synthetic, continuous tone (ptone); a bird song with its FM frequency multiplied by 1.5 (mul1.5); a bird song with its FM frequency divided by 2 (div2); the second half of a bird song (2half); and a bird song without an AM frequency (noAM).

Experiment 1

Recordings of synthetic tones and natural songs were played through a loudspeaker. During playbacks, two observers were hidden a few meters from the loudspeaker. The reaction of the bird was assessed by both observers and the distance at which the bird approached the loudspeaker was visually assessed as being more than 10 meters or less than 10 meters. The results are displayed in Figure 1. Black bars represent a low response (the bird did not approach), light gray bars represent a mixed response (the bird approached but stayed at least 10 meters away), and the dark grays represent a high response (the bird approached and was less than 10 meters from the observers).

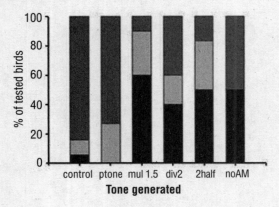

Figure 1

Experiment 2

Researchers assessed variations in the birds' response-call emission rate. The results are displayed in Figure 2. Black bars represent a low response (no change in the emission rate), light gray bars represent a mixed emission rate (weak variation in the emission rate, i.e., up to 3 times the initial calling rate), and dark gray bars represent a high response (strong variation in the emission rate, i.e., more than 3 times the initial calling rate).

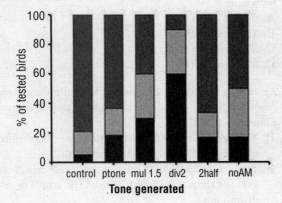

Figure 2

GO ON TO THE NEXT PAGE.

17. According to Figure 1, which tone caused the greatest percentage of birds to stay more than 10 meters away from the researchers?
    A. control
    B. mul1.5
    C. ptone
    D. noAM

18. According to Figure 2, approximately what percentage of tested birds had a high response rate to the control song?
    F. 20%
    G. 40%
    H. 60%
    J. 80%

19. According to Figure 1, among the birds that heard the noAM tone:
    A. 100% approached closer than 10 meters.
    B. approximately 50% approached closer than 10 meters, while the other 50% approached no closer than 10 meters.
    C. approximately 50% approached closer than 10 meters, while the other 50% did not approach at all.
    D. approximately 50% approached no closer than 10 meters, while the other 50% did not approach at all.

20. Based on the information in Figure 1 and Figure 2, one can conclude that the birds:
    F. have the lowest response to the mul1.5 song.
    G. have the highest response to the control song.
    H. do not trust researchers enough to come closer than 10 meters.
    J. have the highest response to the pure, synthetic tone.

21. Which of the following conclusions is supported by Figure 2?
    A. White-browned warblers do not have high responses to songs with altered FM frequencies.
    B. White-browned warblers do not have high responses when exposed to only the second half of a song.
    C. Most white-browned warblers will call at more than 3 times the usual rate if they are played a div2 tone.
    D. Most white-browned warblers will call at more than 3 times the usual rate if they are played a mul1.5 tone.

22. If a researcher wanted a white-browned warbler to approach closer than 10 feet, and then call at less than 3 times the typical emission rate, which series of tones should the researcher play?
    F. control, ptone
    G. mul1.5, div2
    H. control, div2
    J. 2half, control

Passage V

Aspartame is an artificial sweetener found widely in both pharmaceutical and food products, particularly soft drinks. Studies have been conducted on laboratory animals to assess the safety of aspartame for human consumption. Two scientists discuss the relationship between aspartame and cancer in humans.

Scientist 1

A 2007 study conducted at the Cesare Maltoni Cancer Research Center in Italy found statistically significant increases in the incidence of cancer in rats that were given daily doses of aspartame. The study followed a group of 4,000 rats from the 12th day of their fetal lives until their natural deaths. The rats were given doses of aspartame comparable to the average daily intake consumed by humans who drink diet soda on a regular basis. The study found that rats who were fed aspartame displayed a higher incidence of leukemia, lymphoma, and breast cancer than did the control group. The results of this study confirm the findings of a previous study conducted by the same Italian research group.

To assess the safety of food ingredients, the FDA relies on the standard that the ingredient poses "a reasonable certainty of no harm." This standard is called into question with respect to aspartame, given the results of the Italian study. Consumption of aspartame has been demonstrated to cause cancer in doses comparable to that of average human intake, raising serious safety concerns regarding the long-term use of the sweetener.

Scientist 2

The 2007 Maltoni Center study has been cited as evidence of the link between aspartame and cancer, but the study does not provide a basis to justify safety concerns. First, it is questionable whether the study results can be effectively applied to humans. In the research, a statistically significant increase in cancer was found only in those rats that consumed 100 milligrams of aspartame per kilogram of body weight per day. This amount is higher than the amount that some individuals consume on a daily basis. Though the incidence of cancer was also higher in those rats that consumed only 20 milligrams of aspartame per kilogram of body weight daily, this increased incidence was not statistically significant.

Second, and most importantly, conclusions regarding causation cannot be drawn based on findings of correlation alone. The Italian study showed that consumption of aspartame was correlated with increased incidence of certain types of cancer in laboratory animals. The fact that these two factors were present at the same time does not in and of itself demonstrate a causal relationship: correlation is necessary, but not sufficient, to prove causation. A conclusion that aspartame is unsafe for humans is thus unfounded based solely on the evidence from the Italian study.

GO ON TO THE NEXT PAGE.

23. According to Scientist 1, the results of the 2007 Maltoni Center study:
  A. document a relationship between aspartame and thyroid cancer in laboratory rats.
  B. revealed no significant increase in cancer among rats that consumed aspartame.
  C. demonstrate that only male subjects contract cancer from aspartame consumption.
  D. support the results of a prior study conducted by the same set of scientists.

24. A study was conducted that demonstrated an increased incidence of bladder cancer in laboratory rats that were administered aspartame on a daily basis. What conclusion would each scientist most likely draw about the results of this study?
  F. Both Scientist 1 and Scientist 2 would conclude that aspartame consumption causes bladder cancer in rats.
  G. Both Scientist 1 and Scientist 2 would conclude that there is no link between aspartame consumption and bladder cancer in rats.
  H. Scientist 1 would conclude that aspartame consumption causes bladder cancer in rats, and Scientist 2 would not.
  J. Scientist 2 would conclude that aspartame consumption causes bladder cancer in rats, and Scientist 1 would not.

25. According to Scientist 2, the Maltoni Center study revealed an increase in cancer incidence in which of the following groups of rats?
  A. Those that consumed either 100 milligrams or 20 milligrams of aspartame per kilogram of body weight
  B. Only those that consumed 100 milligrams of aspartame per kilogram of body weight
  C. Only those that consumed 20 milligrams of aspartame per kilogram of body weight
  D. None of the groups of rats followed in the study revealed an increase in cancer incidence

26. Based on Scientist 2's explanation, Scientist 2 would most likely argue that the results of an animal study are relevant for humans only if:
  F. the study produces statistically significant findings on all dimensions measured.
  G. the study acknowledges the lack of statistical significance in its findings.
  H. the study focuses on animals whose physiology is most like that of humans.
  J. the conditions of the study mimic conditions that humans actually experience.

27. Both Scientist 1 and Scientist 2 would most likely agree that:
  A. the safety of aspartame should be reconsidered based on the results of the Maltoni Center study.
  B. the Maltoni Center study revealed an increased incidence of cancer in rats that consumed aspartame.
  C. based on the results of the Maltoni Center study, aspartame can be considered safe for human consumption.
  D. aspartame is safe for human consumption only at levels below 100 milligrams per kilogram of body weight.

28. Scientist 2's views differ from that of Scientist 1 in that:
  F. Scientist 2 argues that two factors can occur simultaneously without being causally related.
  G. Scientist 1 argues that the Maltoni Center study did not reveal consistent results with respect to cancer incidence.
  H. Scientist 2 argues that one factor can cause another even if the two are not documented as correlated.
  J. Scientist 1 argues that a food ingredient should be considered safe until it is proven harmful.

29. The Maltoni Center study revealed that in terms of total malignant tumors, only males showed a statistically significant increase in tumor incidence compared to controls. The number of malignant tumors found in females was also higher than the control, but this incidence was not statistically significant. Scientist 2 would most likely view these findings as:
  A. strengthening the conclusion that there is a significant correlation between aspartame consumption and increased incidence of cancer.
  B. weakening the conclusion that where two factors are correlated, a causal connection can be drawn between those factors.
  C. weakening the conclusion that there is a significant correlation between aspartame consumption and increased incidence of cancer.
  D. strengthening the conclusion that where two factors are correlated, a causal connection can be drawn between those factors.

Passage VI

CITATION: Ouni S, Cohen MM Ishak H, Massaro DW (2007). Visual contribution to speech perception: measuring the intelligibility of animated talking heads. *EURASIP Journal on Audio, Speech, and Music Processing.*

Animated agents (sometimes called "talking heads") are becoming increasingly common in research and applications in speech science. Not surprisingly, face-to-face communication is more effective than situations involving just the voice. Given this observation, it is important to evaluate the effectiveness of "talking heads" in terms of the intelligibility of their visible speech. In the following experiments, researchers presented 38 volunteers with a variety of speech scenarios. Test stimuli were 9 consonants and 3 vowels, for a total of 27 consonant-vowel syllables (CVs). The CVs were pronounced at 5 different decibel (dB) levels. Participants were asked to identify the syllables.

Experiment 1

Figure 1 shows the results for a *unimodal auditory* (sound-only) presentation, a *bimodal synthetic face* (an animated agent's entire face), and a *bimodal natural face* (a human speaker's entire face).

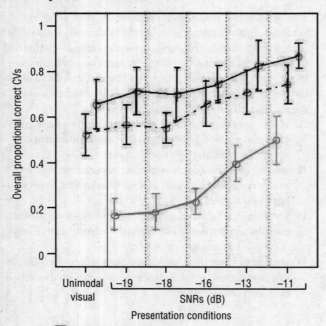

Figure 1

Experiment 2

Figure 2 shows the results for a *unimodal auditory* (sound-only) presentation, *bimodal synthetic lips* (an animated agent's lips only), and a *bimodal synthetic face* (an animated agent's entire face).

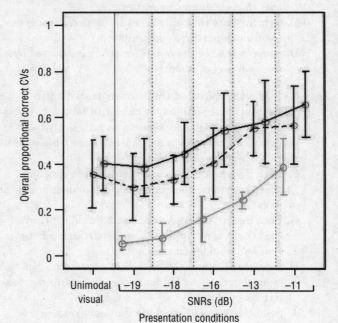

Figure 2

GO ON TO THE NEXT PAGE.

Experiment 3

Figure 3 shows the results for a *unimodal auditory* (sound-only) presentation, *bimodal natural lips* (a human speaker's lips only), and a *bimodal natural face* (a human speaker's entire face).

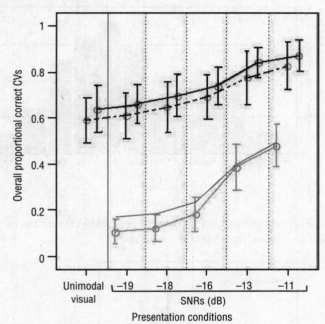

Figure 3

30. In Experiment 2, at which decibel level were the results for the bimodal synthetic lips and the bimodal synthetic face nearly identical?

  F. –13
  G. –15
  H. –18
  J. –19

31. According to the data in Experiment 1, which scenario yielded the greatest proportion of correctly identified CVs?

  A. Bimodal natural face at –11 db
  B. Unimodal auditory presentation at –19 db
  C. Bimodal synthetic face at –13 db
  D. Bimodal natural face at –18 db

32. All three of the experiments support which of the following conclusions?

  F. A bimodal synthetic-face presentation yields a greater proportion of correctly identified CVs than do bimodal synthetic lips or a bimodal natural face.
  G. Synthetic and natural bimodal lips yield a greater proportion of correctly identified CVs than synthetic and natural bimodal faces.
  H. Unimodal auditory presentations always result in the smallest proportion of correctly identified CVs.
  J. Unimodal auditory presentations result in a higher proportion of correctly identified CVs than bimodal face presentations.

33. The data in Experiment 3 support the hypothesis that bimodal natural lips:

  A. yield the same proportion of correctly identified CVs as a bimodal natural face.
  B. yield a much larger proportion of correctly identified CVs than a bimodal natural face.
  C. yield the same proportion of correctly identified CVs as a unimodal auditory presentation.
  D. yield only a slightly smaller proportion of correctly identified CVs than a bimodal natural face.

34. During a unimodal auditory presentation, a participant identified a proportion of 0.2 CVs correctly at –16 db. This participant took part in:

  F. Experiment 1
  G. Experiment 3
  H. Experiment 1 or 3
  J. Experiment 2 or 3

35. A software developer wants to create a highly effective foreign-language tutorial program. Based on the results of the three experiments, what speech scenario should the software developer use?

  A. The software developer should use a unimodal auditory presentation.
  B. The software developer should use the entire face of a human speaker.
  C. The software developer should use just the lips of a human speaker.
  D. The software developer should use the entire face of an animated agent.

Passage VII

CITATION: Wiedinmyer C, Neff JC (2007). Estimates of CO_2 from fires in the United States: implications for carbon management. *Carbon Balance and Management* 2: 10.

Wildfires impact the earth's climate through the direct emission of greenhouse gases, such as CO_2 and methane. Scientists gathered data regarding the role that fire plays in carbon emissions from a number of locations throughout the United States.

Figure 1 shows the average monthly CO_2 emissions in teragrams (Tg) from fires in the lower 48 U.S. states for the five-year period 2002 through 2006.

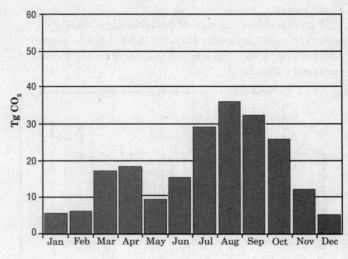

Figure 1

Figure 2 shows the monthly CO_2 emissions from fires in six U.S. states, from 2002 through 2006.

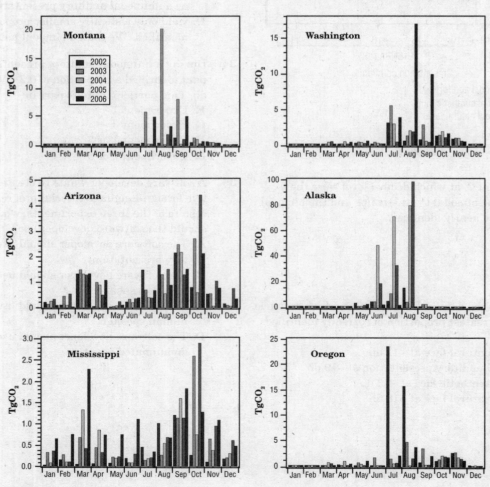

Figure 2

GO ON TO THE NEXT PAGE.

Figure 3 shows the average monthly CO_2 emissions from fires in five U.S. regions over the period 2002 through 2006.

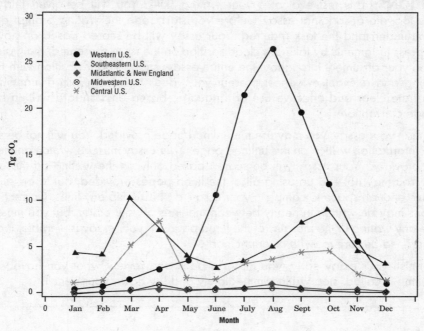

Figure 3

36. According to Figure 1, between 2002 and 2006, total average CO_2 emissions in the United States were closest during which of the following months?

F. June and November

G. April and July

H. August and May

J. January and December

37. An ecologist from the state of Oregon claimed that "Oregon had the greatest summertime emission of CO_2 for any state in the U.S. between 2002 and 2006." Do the data in Figure 2 support this claim?

A. No; Oregon did not have CO_2 emissions during the summers of 2002 through 2006.

B. No; Alaska had a higher summertime emission of CO_2 than Oregon between 2002 and 2006.

C. Yes; Oregon had a peak summertime CO_2 emission of 25 Tg during one year of this period.

D. Yes; Oregon had CO_2 emissions greater than 20 Tg during each summer month of this period.

38. Which of the following descriptions of U.S. fires from 2002 through 2006 is most consistent with the data shown in Figure 1?

F. The United States tends to see large numbers of fires in the southwest and central states during the spring and in the western states during the summer.

G. The incidence of fires is greatest in the United States during the winter months from December through February.

H. U.S. states tend to experience more fires in the month of June than in the month of October.

J. The typical pattern of fire occurrence in the United States starts in the East Coast and gradually spreads westward.

39. According to Figure 3, which of the following lists the U.S. regions in order from *most* to *least* average CO_2 emissions during the month of April for the period 2002 through 2006?

A. Central, Western, Southeastern, Midatlantic, Midwestern

B. Southeastern, Central, Western, Midwestern, Midatlantic

C. Central, Southeastern, Western, Midwestern, Midatlantic

D. Southeastern, Western, Central, Midatlantic, Midwestern

40. Based on the data presented in Figure 2, which of the following was most likely a large fire event that resulted in CO_2 greater than 20 Tg?

F. Cascade Fire in Arizona in August, 2003

G. Treadle Fire in Montana in November, 2005

H. Biscuit Fire in Oregon in July, 2002

J. Sandista Fire in Alaska in May, 2002

END OF TEST 4.
STOP! DO NOT RETURN TO ANY OTHER TEST.

WRITING TEST

DIRECTIONS: This test evaluates your writing skills. You will be given thirty (30) minutes to write an original essay. Before you start, read the writing prompt and be sure you understand the task required. Your essay will be scored based on how well you express judgments by taking a clear position on the issue presented; maintain your focus on your argument throughout the entire essay; support your position with logical reasoning and relevant evidence; present your ideas in an organized manner; and demonstrate clear and effective use of language, based on standard written English language conventions.

To plan out your essay, you may use the unlined page provided. You will not be scored on any information written on this unlined page. *Your essay must be written on the lined pages provided.* Your essay will be scored based only on the writing on those lined pages. You may not end up using all of the lined pages provided, but to be sure that you have enough space to complete your essay, do NOT skip any lines. Corrections or additions may be written in neatly between the lines of your essay, but you must NOT include any writing in the margins of the lined pages. *If your essay is illegible, it cannot be scored, so be sure to write or print clearly.*

If you finish your essay early, you may go back and review what you have written. When time is called, stop writing immediately and lay down your pencil.

ACT Assessment Writing Test Prompt

Many entering college students consider obtaining a part-time job to help meet the cost of attending college. Some people think that holding a part-time job during the first year of college is a good idea because they think students will learn skills necessary for their careers after graduation. Other people think students should not hold part-time jobs during their first year of college, because students will devote less time to their studies and, as a result, will not benefit from the experience. In your opinion, should entering college students hold part-time jobs?

Write an essay that develops your position on this question. You may choose to take one of the two viewpoints given, or you may present a different position on this question. Support your position using specific reasons and examples.

Begin WRITING TEST here.

WRITING TEST

Practice Test 5: Answers & Explanations

Question Number	Answer	Right	Wrong	Question Number	Answer	Right	Wrong
	English			38.	F	—	—
1.	B	—	—	39.	C	—	—
2.	H	—	—	40.	J	—	—
3.	A	—	—	41.	B	—	—
4.	J	—	—	42.	H	—	—
5.	C	—	—	43.	D	—	—
6.	F	—	—	44.	G	—	—
7.	D	—	—	45.	B	—	—
8.	G	—	—	46.	G	—	—
9.	B	—	—	47.	D	—	—
10.	J	—	—	48.	G	—	—
11.	C	—	—	49.	B	—	—
12.	G	—	—	50.	F	—	—
13.	D	—	—	51.	C	—	—
14.	G	—	—	52.	G	—	—
15.	C	—	—	53.	C	—	—
16.	G	—	—	54.	G	—	—
17.	B	—	—	55.	A	—	—
18.	H	—	—	56.	G	—	—
19.	D	—	—	57.	D	—	—
20.	G	—	—	58.	J	—	—
21.	C	—	—	59.	C	—	—
22.	F	—	—	60.	H	—	—
23.	D	—	—	61.	D	—	—
24.	H	—	—	62.	H	—	—
25.	C	—	—	63.	D	—	—
26.	G	—	—	64.	F	—	—
27.	D	—	—	65.	B	—	—
28.	H	—	—	66.	F	—	—
29.	B	—	—	67.	C	—	—
30.	H	—	—	68.	G	—	—
31.	D	—	—	69.	A	—	—
32.	G	—	—	70.	F	—	—
33.	B	—	—	71.	D	—	—
34.	J	—	—	72.	H	—	—
35.	C	—	—	73.	C	—	—
36.	H	—	—	74.	G	—	—
37.	B	—	—	75.	D	—	—

Question Number	Answer	Right	Wrong	Question Number	Answer	Right	Wrong
Mathematics				31.	C	—	—
1.	C	—	—	32.	K	—	—
2.	G	—	—	33.	B	—	—
3.	A	—	—	34.	J	—	—
4.	H	—	—	35.	B	—	—
5.	D	—	—	36.	H	—	—
6.	H	—	—	37.	E	—	—
7.	C	—	—	38.	G	—	—
8.	K	—	—	39.	C	—	—
9.	E	—	—	40.	F	—	—
10.	G	—	—	41.	C	—	—
11.	E	—	—	42.	G	—	—
12.	J	—	—	43.	D	—	—
13.	C	—	—	44.	G	—	—
14.	G	—	—	45.	B	—	—
15.	D	—	—	46.	K	—	—
16.	K	—	—	47.	G	—	—
17.	D	—	—	48.	J	—	—
18.	E	—	—	49.	B	—	—
19.	C	—	—	50.	J	—	—
20.	G	—	—	51.	E	—	—
21.	E	—	—	52.	J	—	—
22.	H	—	—	53.	C	—	—
23.	A	—	—	54.	F	—	—
24.	J	—	—	55.	A	—	—
25.	C	—	—	56.	K	—	—
26.	H	—	—	57.	A	—	—
27.	D	—	—	58.	H	—	—
28.	G	—	—	59.	D	—	—
29.	D	—	—	60.	J	—	—
30.	G	—	—				

Question Number	Answer	Right	Wrong	Question Number	Answer	Right	Wrong
	Reading			21.	D	—	—
1.	A	—	—	22.	G	—	—
2.	G	—	—	23.	B	—	—
3.	D	—	—	24.	F	—	—
4.	J	—	—	25.	C	—	—
5.	C	—	—	26.	J	—	—
6.	F	—	—	27.	A	—	—
7.	D	—	—	28.	H	—	—
8.	G	—	—	29.	D	—	—
9.	C	—	—	30.	H	—	—
10.	F	—	—	31.	B	—	—
11.	B	—	—	32.	J	—	—
12.	J	—	—	33.	D	—	—
13.	A	—	—	34.	F	—	—
14.	H	—	—	35.	C	—	—
15.	B	—	—	36.	J	—	—
16.	G	—	—	37.	A	—	—
17.	D	—	—	38.	G	—	—
18.	F	—	—	39.	B	—	—
19.	D	—	—	40.	H	—	—
20.	F	—	—				

Question Number	Answer	Right	Wrong	Question Number	Answer	Right	Wrong
	Science			21.	A	—	—
1.	D	—	—	22.	H	—	—
2.	J	—	—	23.	D	—	—
3.	B	—	—	24.	H	—	—
4.	G	—	—	25.	A	—	—
5.	D	—	—	26.	J	—	—
6.	H	—	—	27.	B	—	—
7.	A	—	—	28.	F	—	—
8.	G	—	—	29.	C	—	—
9.	D	—	—	30.	F	—	—
10.	F	—	—	31.	A	—	—
11.	B	—	—	32.	H	—	—
12.	H	—	—	33.	D	—	—
13.	A	—	—	34.	H	—	—
14.	G	—	—	35.	B	—	—
15.	D	—	—	36.	J	—	—
16.	H	—	—	37.	B	—	—
17.	B	—	—	38.	F	—	—
18.	J	—	—	39.	C	—	—
19.	C	—	—	40.	H	—	—
20.	G	—	—				

Calculating Your Score

To find your scaled scores for each test, add up the number of questions you answered correctly on each test. That number represents your raw score for the test. Then covert your raw score to a 1–36 score using the table below. To find your Composite Score for the entire exam, add up your scaled scores for all four tests and divide that total by 4. Round off any fractions to the nearest whole number.

Keep in mind that this score is just a rough estimate. The only completely accurate predictors of your current scoring level are the scoring scales provided with official ACT materials, so make sure you practice with them in the week or two before the test to gauge where you stand.

Scaled Score	Raw Scores				Scaled Score
	Test 1	Test 2	Test 3	Test 4	
	English	Mathematics	Reading	Science	
36	75	60	38–40	40	36
35	73–74	58–59	37	—	35
34	71–72	56–57	36	39	34
33	70	55	35	—	33
32	69	54	34	38	32
31	68	52–53	—	—	31
30	67	50–51	33	37	30
29	65–66	48–49	32	36	29
28	64	46–47	30–31	35	28
27	62–63	43–45	29	34	27
26	60–61	41–42	28	32–33	26
25	57–59	39–40	27	30–31	25
24	55–56	37–38	26	29	24
23	53–54	35–36	25	27–28	23
22	50–52	33–34	24	25–26	22
21	47–49	31–32	23	23–24	21
20	44–46	30	22	21–22	20
19	42–43	27–29	21	18–20	19
18	39–41	25–26	20	16–17	18
17	37–38	22–24	19	14–15	17
16	34–36	18–21	17–18	13	16
15	30–33	15–17	16	12	15
14	28–29	12–14	14–15	10–11	14
13	26–27	09–11	12–13	09	13
12	24–25	08	10–11	08	12
11	22–23	06–07	08–09	07	11
10	20–21	05	07	06	10
9	18–19	04	06	05	9
8	15–17	—	05	04	8
7	13–14	03	—	03	7
6	10–12	02	04	—	6
5	08–09	—	03	02	5
4	06–07	—	02	—	4
3	04–05	01	—	01	3
2	02–03	—	01	—	2
1	00–01	00	00	00	1

Practice Test 5: Answers & Explanations

ENGLISH

1. B

Style: Redundancy and Wordiness   *Medium*

The original version is redundant because *film lovers* and *movie fans* have the same meaning. Similarly, **C** includes both *movies* and *films*, which is repetitive. *Lovers* and *fans* are repeated in **D**. **B** conveys the same information as the other options without repeating any words or phrases.

2. H

Basic Grammar and Usage: Pronoun-Antecedent Agreement   *Easy*

The underlined pronoun refers to the plural antecedent *films*, so the two should agree in number. It is a singular pronoun, so the original version needs revision. *Which* and *that* are relative pronouns. *Because most of which* and *because most of that* are illogical and ungrammatical phrases, so **G** and **J** are wrong. *Them* is a plural pronoun that makes a clear reference to *films*, so the best answer is **H**.

3. A

Writing Strategy: Analysis   *Difficult*

B is incorrect because the author does not present any information about the origin of the name spaghetti Western elsewhere in the passage. The information is not particularly funny, so **C** is wrong. The details do not clutter the sentence, so **D** is wrong. Since the information about the origin of the term *spaghetti Western* helps *clarify the meaning of the term*, **A** is the best choice.

4. J

Organization: Sentence Reorganization   *Medium*

The phrase *typically filmed on location in Italy or Spain* describes *spaghetti Westerns*, so the two should be near each other as in **J**. *Typically filmed* modifies *cast and crew* in **F**. In **G** and **H**, *typically filmed* modifies *locals* instead of *spaghetti Westerns*, which makes the meaning of the sentence unclear.

5. C

Punctuation: Commas   *Medium*

A is incorrect because commas should not be placed after *such as*. **B** is incorrect because a comma should be before *such as* and after *Fonda*. **D** is incorrect because *Henry Fonda* is one name. **C** uses commas in the appropriate places.

6. F

Organization: Transitions, Topic Sentences & Conclusions   *Difficult*

The paragraph discusses reasons that Westerns were popular with Europeans, which relates to why the films were made in Italy. No change is necessary because the original sentence asks a question that is answered by details in the paragraph. **G** and **J** are minor details that do not relate to the topic of the paragraph. **H** repeats information presented later in the same paragraph.

7. D

Sentence Structure: Run-On Sentences   *Easy*

The original version lacks a clear break between the first and second parts of the sentence and is a run-on. *Over the years, European filmmakers had tried to produce Westerns, but European audiences preferred those made in America* is a clear and logical sentence. Adding a conjunction and a comma defines the two thoughts that have been combined in this compound sentence, so **D** is the best answer. Adding a comma in **C** creates a comma splice unless a conjunction is added as well. The addition of *had* in **B** creates a confusing sentence and fails to repair the run-on issue.

8. G

Sentence Structure: Connecting and Transitional Words   *Medium*

The question is asking for the LEAST acceptable transitional word, so looking at the original version may provide some clues. *As a result* indicates that a cause-effect relationship exists between *Hollywood movie studios* and the fact that Europeans had *fewer American Westerns to watch. Consequently, for this reason,* and *thus* are also transitional phrases used to show cause and effect, which means any of them would be acceptable options. *Besides* is a transition used when an additional point is being made, so the correct answer is **G**.

9. B

Style: Redundancy and Wordiness   *Medium*

The original version is unnecessarily wordy with the inclusion of *mainly with ineffective sound and dubbing problems. Poorly* and *insufficiently* are redundant in **C**. *Lacked* is used later in the same sentence, so **D** includes a redundancy. *Poor quality films* presents information without repetitive or unnecessary words, so **B** is the best answer. Remember that conciseness is preferred over wordiness with the majority of style questions.

10. J

Punctuation: Parentheses and Dashes   *Medium*

Parentheses are not appropriate in this sentence because the information about where the producers are from is important to the sentence, not supplemental. Similarly, dashes are not necessary because the information does not need emphasis.

Although a list follows the colon in **H**, an independent clause must precede the colon, which it does not. **J** is the best answer because *producers from Germany, Italy, and Spain* is correctly punctuated without unnecessary dashes and parentheses.

11. C

Writing Strategy: Additional Detail and Evidence   *Difficult*

C provides the reader with the most specific information about Eastwood's character. **A** provides no information about Eastwood's film character, so the original version is incorrect. **B** provides irrelevant information about Eastwood's acting career. Eastwood may have played a leading role, but this fails to provide descriptive details about the character. **C** clarifies that Eastwood's character was an *antihero*, which is a specific description.

12. G

Sentence Structure: Parallelism   *Medium*

The original sentence does not flow well because *creative* does not follow the same grammatical form as *showing* and *depicting*. Sentences are awkward when words and phrases are not structured similarly, as with **H** and **J**. *Using*, *the way he showed*, and *an immoral cowboy* are not parallel, which makes **H** very awkward. In **J**, *creating* is a verb, while *brutality* and *depiction* are nouns. **G** is the best answer because the three noun phrases in the series follow a similar format.

13. D

Basic Grammar and Usage: Idioms   *Medium*

Idioms often cause trouble because they follow no specific rules. In the original version, *similarly as* is not idiomatic, although *similar to* is a standard American idiom. *Like as* should be *like with*, so **C** is wrong. *According with* is not a standard idiom, but *according to* is idiomatic. **D** is the correct answer because *as with* provides a proper idiom in standard written English.

14. G

Organization: Sentence Reorganization   *Medium*

The adverb *eventually* should be near the verb it modifies, which is *waned*, so **G** is the best answer. In the original version, *eventually* follows the noun *interest*, which is confusing because adverbs modify adjectives and adverbs. Placing *eventually* after *but* creates an illogical sentence, so **H** is wrong. **J** also creates a confusing and illogical sentence: *the genre's influence eventually remains evident today.*

15. C

Writing Strategy: Big Picture Purpose   *Difficult*

The author does not express a personal opinion in the passage about spaghetti Westerns, so **A** and **B** are incorrect. Although the author discusses the *trilogy* produced by Leone, the movies and their *popularity* are only one element of the essay. The *history behind spaghetti Westerns* is the main topic of the passage, so **C** is the best answer.

16. G

Style: Word Choice and Identifying Tone   *Medium*

The author is contrasting how most people know General Electric but they do not know about Jack Welch. *Completely* is not the best word for the sentence because it suggests that absolutely no one knows about Jack Welch, which is unlikely. *Thoroughly* is illogical in the sentence because it means *deeply*, so **H** is wrong. The author does not provide evidence that Jack Welch is unknown to most people, so it is not *apparent* that the CEO's name is unfamiliar. The name Jack Welch is *probably* unfamiliar to most people, so **G** is the best choice.

17. B

Basic Grammar and Usage: Verb Tenses   *Easy*

Welch's past is being described in the first paragraph, so **B** is correct because *began working* is a past-tense verb phrase. *Works* is present tense, which is confusing since the sentence describes how Welch started working for *GE in 1960 as an engineer.* Similarly, the present-tense verb phrase *is working* doesn't make sense. *Who worked* is wrong because the sentence loses a verb and becomes a fragment.

18. H

Organization: Sentence Reorganization   *Medium*

H logically explains why *Welch considered leaving GE.* **F** and **J** make it sound as if Welch decided he did not like the *company's bureaucratic structure* after one year, rather than decided to quit GE after one year. The organization of **G** indicates that GE hired Welch because of his dislike for the *company's bureaucratic structure*, which is illogical.

19. D

Sentence Structure: Connecting and Transitional Words   *Medium*

When and *while* create sentence fragments, so **A** and **C** are incorrect. The transitional word *moreover* is used when an additional point or example is being provided, which is not the case in this sentence. *However* is the best transitional word to use because the sentence counters the information provided in the previous sentence.

20. G

Basic Grammar and Usage: Pronoun-Antecedent Agreement   *Easy*

The pronoun *which* is used when referring to things, while *who* is used when referring to people, so the original version is incorrect. **H** is wrong because the inclusion of the pronoun *he* serves no purpose in the sentence. The underlined pronoun describes *executive* and needs to be a subjective pronoun instead of an objective pronoun. *Who* is a subjective-case pronoun. *Whom* is a pronoun used for objects.

21. C

Sentence Structure: Subordinate or Dependent Clauses   *Easy*

Because of his business acumen is a dependent clause describing *Welch*, so it needs to be set apart from the main part of the sentence with a comma between *acumen* and *Welch*. The original version includes no comma after the dependent clause, which makes the sentence difficult to understand. The comma after *moved* in **B** comes before a preposition, so **B** is incorrect. The comma between *business* and *acumen* in **D** separates a noun and an adjective.

22. F

Punctuation: Commas   *Medium*

Including appliances, electronics, and light bulbs is a phrase describing *products*, and it needs to be set off with commas on both sides. A comma after *products* and a comma after *bulbs* clarifies to the reader that the types of *products* made by GE include *appliances, electronics, and light bulbs*. **G** lacks a comma after *bulbs*, while **H** lacks the two commas needed on both sides of *including appliances, electronics, and light bulbs*. **J** is missing a comma after *products*, so the best answer is **F**.

23. D

Style: Word Choice and Identifying Tone   *Medium*

The underlined word should help convey the idea that GE's *notorious bureaucracy* was not beneficial to the company, which is why *Welch never feared cutting costs*. We need a negative word, so **C** can be eliminated. *Obscuring* means to make something harder to see, which doesn't convey the idea of "not beneficial." Finally, *dissolving* means to make something disappear into something else, which is not quite the meaning we're looking for. This means that **D**, *harming,* best expresses how *bureaucracy* hurt GE and its ability to make profits.

24. H

Sentence Structure: Parallelism   *Medium*

In the original sentence, *by reducing* and *to close* are not similarly structured, so the sentence is not parallel. *With a reduction* and *closing* are also not in the same grammatical form, so **G** is incorrect. Choice **J** is incorrect because *with a payroll reduction* is unlikely *to close factories*. **H** is the best answer because *by* corresponds with *closing* and *reducing*, which both end in *-ing*.

25. C

Writing Strategy: Analysis   *Difficult*

The information relates to the previous sentence, so **B** is incorrect. Although the information explains why Welch received the nickname, it does not explain why he disliked it, so **D** is wrong. The information provides additional details about Welch, so it does not *distract from the characterization of Jack Welch*. People unfamiliar with the way a neutron bomb works would find the details helpful, so **C** is the best choice.

26. G

Organization: Transitions, Topic Sentences & Conclusions   *Difficult*

F does not relate to content of the second paragraph, so a revision is necessary. **H** is illogical, as the word *nonetheless* indicates a contrast, and **H** does not contrast with what follows. **G** and **J** both relate to the discussion in paragraph 3 as well as to the second part of the sentence. However, **G** is more specific about why people disliked Welch and provides the best transition between the discussion of Neutron Jack in paragraph 3 and the discussion of the friendlier side of Welch in paragraph 4.

27. D

Punctuation: Apostrophes   *Easy*

The *workings* belong to *GE*. An apostrophe needs to be inserted before the *s* in *GEs* to show possession, which means **D** is correct. The original version does not indicate ownership because no apostrophe has been included after *GE*. General Electric is a singular noun. **B** is wrong because an apostrophe after the *s* indicates that more than one *GE* exists. *Workings* owns nothing, so an apostrophe after the *s* in *workings* is inappropriate.

28. H

Sentence Structure: Connecting and Transitional Words   *Medium*

The second part of the sentence explains why *encouraging Welch* was *profitable*. *Since* is the best choice because it helps connect the cause with the effect. Transition words such as *yet* and *but* are used to indicate a contrast, and they are illogical in this sentence. *While* doesn't work because it is used to show the passage of time.

29. B

Basic Grammar and Usage: Subject-Verb Agreement   *Easy*

The plural noun *executives* is the subject, and the singular verb *strives* is not in agreement—*executives strives*. **C** and **D** are also verbs intended for singular subjects. *Executives strive* is the best choice because the subject and verb agree, which makes the meaning of the sentence clear and logical.

30. H

Writing Strategy: Big Picture Purpose   *Difficult*

F and **G** are incorrect because the essay does not primarily describe the *business strategies used by a corporation to improve profitability*, although a brief mention is made about Welch scaling back expenses and jobs. The focus of the essay is Welch, so **H** is the best answer. The author mentions bureaucracy problems at GE, but the main idea of the essay is Welch and not GE's *mistakes*.

31. D

Basic Grammar and Usage: Verb Tenses   *Easy*

Pierre-Auguste Renoir explains who is *one of the most famous painters of the Impressionist period*, and it needs to be set off with commas because it is not part of the main sentence. **A**, **B**, and **C** do not include commas on both sides of *Pierre-Auguste Renoir*. **D** is the correct answer because two commas clarify that Renoir is *one of the most famous painters of the Impressionist period*.

32. G

Writing Strategy: Analysis   *Difficult*

The essay does not indicate that Renoir feels bitter about the *upper class*, so **F** is incorrect. **J** is wrong because the sentence is factual rather than a statement of opinion. The essay's opening paragraph indicates that Renoir had to work his way to the top, and the detail about his parents provides *descriptive information* and *insight* about Renoir's beginnings.

33. B

Sentence Structure: Comma Splices   *Medium*

A comma splice occurs when only a comma separates two independent clauses, as in the original version. *The factory eventually closed* is one independent clause. *Renoir earned money toiling in a variety of odd jobs* is the second independent clause. Adding the conjunction *and* to the comma separating the clauses corrects the problem, so **B** is the best answer. **C** creates an illogical sentence, while **D** needs a comma before *so*.

34. J

Style: Redundancy and Wordiness *Medium*

The original version is wordy. **F** repeats the word *even*, as does **G**. Between **H** and **J**, **J** is the better choice because it is the most economical with words.

35. C

Organization: Paragraph Organization *Difficult*

The first two sentences in the paragraph are about Renoir's childhood, so placing the sentence after that information would be confusing. Since the new sentence regards when Renoir decided to focus on painting, the best location for it is between sentence 3 and sentence 4. Sentence 4 explains that *Renoir struggled* and could not *afford* paints, and the new information would be out of sequence if placed after sentence 4. The new sentence bridges the gap between Renoir working *odd jobs* and his *early career* as a painter, so **C** is the best answer.

36. H

Basic Grammar and Usage: Verb Tenses *Easy*

Since Renoir is no longer living, verbs used to describe his actions should be past tense. Maintaining consistency with verb tenses within paragraphs improves the readability of a text. *Enjoys* and *does enjoy* are present-tense verbs, so **F** and **J** are incorrect. *Has enjoyed* is present-perfect tense, so **G** is incorrect. *Enjoyed* is a past-tense verb, so **H** is correct.

37. B

Punctuation: Apostrophes *Easy*

People own their *lives*, and in the original version, the lack of an apostrophe between *people* and the letter *s* fails to convey ownership. The correct way to show possession is with **B**. The word *lives* does not need an apostrophe because *lives* has no ownership, so **C** is incorrect. **D** is incorrect because *people* is a collective noun that functions as a unit. *People* should be treated as a singular noun without an additional *s* on the end.

38. F

Basic Grammar and Usage: Pronoun-Antecedent Agreement *Easy*

The underlined possessive pronoun refers to *they*. The pronoun *their* correctly agrees with the antecedent *they*, so **F** is the best answer. The writer has not used *one* in the sentence or the passage, so *one's* would be out of place. The underlined word is not referring to Renoir's *personal business*, so *his* is incorrect. **H** is wrong because the pronoun *it* refers to things instead of individuals.

39. C

Sentence Structure: Connecting and Transitional Words *Medium*

In the previous sentences, the author describes the subjects of Renoir's paintings. Renoir's family is another subject, so using *in other words* is an illogical transition. *Later in his career* provides the best transition between the subject matter of Renoir's early work and the *family life* depicted in his later paintings. **D** is wrong because the author is not summarizing but listing an additional point. **B** is illogical because the author is not illustrating a cause-effect relationship between early and later art subjects.

40. J

Style: Redundancy and Wordiness   *Medium*

Renoir's preference for his paintings of individuals in simpler times includes three prepositional phrases making the original version wordy. Similarly, **G** is too wordy—*creating paintings of individuals in times that were simple*. **H** includes only one fewer word than **G**. **J** is the best answer because *creating his paintings* has been reduced to *painting*, which conveys the same information in a more straightforward fashion.

41. B

Sentence Structure: Connecting and Transitional Words   *Easy*

The underlined portion refers to *industrial world*, and the relative pronoun *which* is the best option to clarify the connection for readers. *Renoir believed* the *industrial world robbed people of individuality*. **A**, **C**, and **D** include unnecessary words that make the sentence difficult to understand.

42. H

Organization: Sentence Reorganization   *Medium*

The original organization of the sentence is confusing because it sounds as if Renoir were a *lifelong artist* only *in 1892*. The organization of **G** and **J** creates the false impression that Renoir was *afflicted with rheumatoid arthritis* because of his *passion for art*. **H** logically presents the idea that Renoir was a *lifelong artist* because he had *passion for his craft*.

43. D

Basic Grammar and Usage: Adverbs and Adjectives   *Easy*

Debilitatingly is not a word, so **A** is wrong. *It is debilitating* is a complete sentence, and its placement creates an awkward sentence construction. **C** implies that arthritis is not a disease. **D** correctly places the adjective *debilitating* before the noun it modifies.

44. G

Sentence Structure: Sentence Fragments   *Medium*

When Renoir died in 1919 is not a complete sentence, so the original version creates a sentence fragment. **H** and **J** do not correct the problem because semicolons and comma-conjunction combinations separate independent clauses. **G** correctly repairs the fragment with a comma that separates the clause from the main part of the sentence.

45. B

Writing Strategy: Big Picture Purpose   *Difficult*

B is correct because the author describes how Renoir *struggled* during his early years as a painter and how he fought to continue painting after developing arthritis, which both suggest he loved painting. Although Renoir received praise from others at the china factory, that fact does not illustrate Renoir's feelings about painting. **C** is incorrect because the author only briefly mentions Renoir's most famous paintings. The first sentence of paragraph 4 states that Renoir had a *passion* for his craft, so **D** is incorrect.

46. G

Sentence Structure: Connecting and Transitional Words   *Medium*

The sentence describes a cause-effect relationship. Because *Dad wanted to do something extraordinary, he surprised Mom with a family trip to Hawaii*. The transition word *so* is the best choice to help the reader understand the connection between the two events. *But* and *although* are incorrect because the two events described in the sentence do not contrast with each other. *Since* is a transition used for cause-effect relationships; however, using *since* creates an illogical statement that might work if the sentence were rearranged.

47. D

Style: Word Choice and Identifying Tone   *Medium*

Although the author may have been imagining the beach during the flight, the adverb *eagerly* suggests that the family was looking forward to the beach with excitement and *anticipation*. *Eagerly* would not describe someone *observing* a new place, so **B** is wrong. Similarly, *approaching* describes the family's physical nearness to the beach rather than their emotional excitement.

48. G

Punctuation: Commas   *Medium*

The sentence begins with two different clauses that both need to be set apart from the main section of the sentence that begins with *murky*. In addition, *of course* needs to be separated from *being a Minneapolis native* with a comma, or the sentence will be confusing. **G** correctly includes the two necessary commas, while **J** only includes one. **H** places a comma after *being*, which breaks up the phrase *being a Minneapolis native*.

49. B

Basic Grammar and Usage: Subject-Verb Agreement   *Easy*

The sentence's subject is the singular noun *water*; the plural noun *lakes* is part of a prepositional phrase describing the location of the *water*. *Were*, *are*, and *have been* are verbs that agree with plural nouns. **B** provides the correct answer because *was* agrees with singular nouns—*murky brown water in Midwestern lakes was my only point of comparison.*

50. F

Punctuation: Semicolons   *Medium*

The punctuation in the underlined portion is correct because independent clauses are on each side of the semicolon. **G** creates a comma splice, which occurs when two independent clauses are weakly connected with nothing but a comma. Adding the conjunction *and* would be acceptable if it were preceded by a comma, so **H** and **J** are incorrect.

51. C

Sentence Structure: Connecting and Transitional Words   *Medium*

The conjunction *when* is needed to connect *flip-flops* with *swimming*, so **C** is the correct answer. *When swimming* is an adverb clause that describes under what condition the author *had to wear flip-flops*. The original version is incorrect because it lacks a clear connection between flip-flops and swimming. *I had to wear flip-flops having swam* is illogical, so **D** is wrong. *Swimming* is an action verb, not a noun, so **B**'s *in swimming* does not make sense..

52. G

Style: Redundancy and Wordiness   *Medium*

Probably eliminates the need for *most likely, quite possibly*, and *in all likelihood*. The original version as well as **H** and **J** repeat information previously stated in the sentence. **G** includes no repeated information and includes only the verb phrase—*was visiting*.

53. C

Writing Strategy: Additional Detail and Evidence   *Difficult*

The additional sentence does not relate to the main point of the paragraph or the passage, so **C** is the best answer. The loss of lives on the *Arizona* affects the author and relates to the significance of the memorial, so **A** and **B** are wrong. **D** is incorrect because the additional information does not contradict the author's point that visiting the memorial was *unforgettable*; the information is merely irrelevant.

54. G

Basic Grammar and Usage: Verb Tenses   *Easy*

The author states in the second part of the sentence that *my family decided to try to learn how to surf. Decided* is a past-tense verb, so the underlined verb in the first part of the sentence should be past tense to maintain consistency. *Return* is present tense, so **F** is wrong. *Have returned* is present perfect, which describes an action that began in the past and continues to the present. *Are returning* is present progressive, which describes ongoing actions. *Returned*, which is past tense, is the best choice.

55. A

Organization: Transitions, Topic Sentences & Conclusions   *Medium*

Paragraph 5 focuses on the family's surfing lessons. **A** introduces this topic and provides the most effective introduction to the paragraph. **B, C**, and **D** are wrong choices because they do not specifically mention surfing.

56. G

Sentence Structure: Parallelism   *Medium*

Had fun trying does not match the grammatical form of *laughed*, so the original sentence needs revision. **H** and **J** are also not parallel with *trying* because of the inclusion of *by* and *were*. **G** provides the most balanced option because *we had fun trying* and *laughing* places the two verbs in parallel form.

57. D

Style: Redundancy and Wordiness   *Medium*

A and **B** include irrelevant information about age difference and hair color, which only clutter the sentence with unnecessary words and distract the reader from the main point. **C** creates a compound sentence, which required adding a number of small words such as *is, than*, and *and*. **D** keeps the sentence concise and conveys the same information as **C** without unnecessary wordiness.

58. J

Organization: Sentence Reorganization   *Medium*

Adverbs describe adjectives or verbs, and in this sentence *approximately* should describe the length of time the author's brother *managed to ride a wave. Approximately five seconds* indicates that the exact time is unknown but that it was nearly *five seconds*. Although *managed* is a verb, the phrases *approximately managed* and *managed approximately* are illogical in this sentence. *To ride a wave approximately for five seconds* also seems confusing, so **H** is wrong.

59. **C**

Punctuation: Commas   *Easy*

The main part of the sentence begins after *Minnesota*, so a comma after *Minnesota* is needed to separate the two parts of the sentence. A comma is also necessary between *cold* and *snowy* because they are two separate adjectives describing *Minnesota*. Any other commas are unnecessary, so **C** is the correct answer.

60. **H**

Writing Strategy: Big Picture Purpose   *Difficult*

The correct answer is **H** because the essay is mostly about *a fun experience the author had with her family*. Although the author was emotionally affected by her visit to Pearl Harbor, that experience was only a small part of the essay, which means **F** is wrong. The thoughts and feelings of the author's family members are unknown, so **J** is incorrect. The author mentions in the introduction her father's surprise vacation, but the author does not *discuss the impact of the surprise trip*.

61. **D**

Sentence Structure: Parallelism   *Medium*

All of the listed *qualities* should be in the same grammatical format to be parallel. **A** and **B** are wrong because they include the verbs *having* and *being*. **C** uses the adjectives *harmonious* and *healthy*, which differs from the way the *qualities* are listed as nouns. Therefore, the best answer is **D** because *harmony* and *health* are nouns like *beauty, goodness*, and *happiness*.

62. **H**

Sentence Structure: Subordinate or Dependent Clauses   *Medium*

When balance prevails is a dependent clause, and the main part of the sentence is *health and harmony abound as well*. A comma is needed between *prevails* and *health* to help the reader understand where the dependent clause ends and the sentence begins. The dependent clause is not separated from the main sentence in the original version, so **F** is wrong. **J** is incorrect because the comma is inserted before *prevails* instead of after it. **G** is wrong because a comma is inserted after *health* and not after *prevails*.

63. **D**

Punctuation: Commas   *Medium*

However is a conjunctive adverb. When a conjunctive adverb joins independent clauses, it is preceded by a semicolon and followed by a comma. Otherwise, a conjunctive adverb is separated from the rest of the sentence with a comma on both sides. *When a person falls ill* is a dependent clause, so commas are necessary on both sides of *however* instead of just one side. **B** is wrong because two independent clauses are not on both sides of *however*, which is when a semicolon is necessary.

64. F

Organization: Transitions, Topic Sentences & Conclusions   *Difficult*

The opening paragraph describes healing ceremonies, and the rest of the passage focuses on sand paintings. **F** is the best transitional sentence because it mentions the healing ceremony and introduces the topic of sand paintings. **G**, **H**, and **J** are details about sand paintings, but they do not smoothly introduce the subject of sand paintings to the reader.

65. B

Style: Redundancy and Wordiness   *Medium*

An illness that is severe enough to warrant a ceremony could be reduced to a simpler phrase, so **A** is too wordy. *Some kind of illness that is unknown to the medicine man* is also wordy, so **C** is wrong. **D** is redundant because the first part of the sentence states that the ill person is treated in his or her own home. As with many style questions, the most concise answer, **B**, is the best answer because the other options use too many words to convey very little relevant information.

66. F

Writing Strategy: Analysis   *Difficult*

F is correct because the focus of the paragraph and the passage is sand painting, and information about how medicine men are trained does not relate to the main topic. The information is not provided elsewhere, so **G** is wrong. **H** and **J** are incorrect because the information is irrelevant.

67. C

Sentence Structure: Connecting and Transitional Words   *Medium*

First is the best transitional word for the sentence because the author is explaining the first step of the sand painting process. **A** and **D** are wrong because *next* and *also* suggest that previous steps have been described. The author is not providing an example, so **B** is wrong.

68. G

Basic Grammar and Usage: Subject-Verb Agreement   *Easy*

Makers is the plural subject of the sentence, and the singular noun *painting* is part of a prepositional phrase. The underlined verb should agree with *makers*, and only **G** does: *the makers of the sand painting work from the center out. Works, does work,* and *is working* are verbs for singular nouns.

69. A

Style: Redundancy and Wordiness   *Medium*

B and **D** include redundancies because *vibrant* and *bright* are synonymous and *different* and *other* are synonymous, too. **C** is wordy, since it is unnecessary to list numerous colors for the reader. The original version does not need revision because it conveys the necessary information to readers with two words.

70. F

Writing Strategy: Additional Detail and Evidence   *Difficult*

The additional detail relates to how sand paintings are made, which is the topic of the paragraph, so **H** and **J** are incorrect. **G** is incorrect because the paragraph does not indicate that tools are not used for sand paintings, only that *freestyle images* are *measured out by palm and hand widths*. **F** is the best answer because the additional information further explains to the reader how the paintings are constructed.

71. D

Organization: Transitions, Topic Sentences & Conclusions   *Easy*

The original version and **C** are too vague with the use of *everything*. Similarly, **B** is imprecise because of the use of the pronoun *it*. **D** clearly specifies that sand paintings are the subject of the sentence, which smoothes the transition between the two paragraphs.

72. H

Sentence Structure: Connecting and Transitional Words   *Medium*

The author is describing the steps of the ceremony, and because the second sentence is the second step, the best transitional word is *then*. The author is not comparing or contrasting information, which means *likewise* and *however* would be poor choices. Since the author is not describing a cause-and-effect relationship, **J** is wrong.

73. C

Style: Word Choice and Identifying Tone   *Medium*

Specific, *particular*, and *deliberate* all convey the idea that the ceremonies were performed in a structured manner. Although participants in the ceremony are most likely *respectful*, the term *respectful* means courteous or supportive and does not relate to *all healing ceremonies* being *conducted in the same manner*. Word selection affects the meaning of a sentence and a passage, so care should be taken to understand the various shades of meaning that different words carry.

74. G

Punctuation: Semicolons   *Easy*

The second part of the sentence does not contradict the first, so including *however* is incorrect. A comma without a conjunction creates a comma splice, so **H** is wrong. A dash is used for emphasis and would be inappropriate in this sentence. Two independent clauses have been joined, and a semicolon is the best way to separate the two parts.

75. D

Writing Strategy: Additional Detail and Evidence   *Difficult*

The additional information ties in with the first sentence of the fourth paragraph, which describes how the patient must sit in the middle of the painting. The first paragraph is about healing ceremonies, and the author does not address the topic of sand paintings. The second paragraph may be tempting because the author discusses the patient's home; however, the new sentence relates to physically touching the painting rather than the painting's location. No mention of the patient is made in the first sentence of paragraph 3, so the new detail would not make sense if addd to the third paragraph.

MATHEMATICS

1. C
Algebra: Substitution   *Easy*

Substitute −4 for a and 3 for b into the equation and solve:

$$
\begin{aligned}
(a+b)^2 &= (-4+3)^2 \\
&= (-1)^2 \\
&= (-1) \times (-1) \\
&= 1
\end{aligned}
$$

2. G
Algebra: Writing Expressions and Equations   *Easy*

Take each part of the equation in turn. First, write the expression for half of Nader's age, N:

$$\frac{1}{2}N$$

The expression $\frac{1}{2}N$ can also be written as $\frac{N}{2}$. Next, subtract 7 from $\frac{N}{2}$:

$$A = \frac{N}{2} - 7$$

F is incorrect because the 7 does not need to be divided in half, only Nader's age, N. According to the order of operations, Nader's age is divided in half first, and then 7 is subtracted from that number.

3. A
Pre-Algebra: Ratios and Proportions   *Easy*

Set up a proportion to solve for the height of the model. Let x represent the height of the model:

$$
\begin{aligned}
\frac{5 \text{ feet}}{10 \text{ inches}} &= \frac{3 \text{ feet}}{x \text{ inches}} \\
5x &= 10 \times 3 \\
5x &= 30 \\
x &= \frac{30}{5} \\
x &= 6
\end{aligned}
$$

The height of the model is 6 inches.

4. H
Pre-Algebra: Probability   *Easy*

The probability that the video game chosen will be an adventure video game is the number of favorable outcomes divided by the number of possible outcomes:

$$P = \frac{\text{Favorable outcomes}}{\text{Possible outcomes}}$$

$$= \frac{\text{Number of adventure video games}}{\text{Total number of video games}}$$

$$= \frac{8}{8+6}$$

$$= \frac{8}{14}$$

$$= \frac{4}{7}$$

G is incorrect because it represents the chance of Chad pulling out a sports video game.

5. D

Intermediate Algebra: Exponents and Roots   *Easy*

Use the order of operations to simplify this expression:

$$\left(2n^2\right)^4 = \left(2 \times 3^2\right)^4$$

$$= 2 \times (3 \times 3)^4$$

$$= \left(2 \times 9\right)^4$$

$$= 18^4$$

6. H

Plane Geometry: Angles and Lines   *Easy*

When two lines cross in a plane, their vertical angles are always equal. Angle r is a vertical angle with $\angle$YXZ.

   F and **G** are incorrect because although these angles look equal to angle r, the question gives no information to indicate that they must be equal.

7. C

Pre-Algebra: Mean, Median & Mode   *Easy*

The mode of a set of terms is the term that appears most frequently in the set. In this case, the number 6 appears most often, because there are 3 plants that display 6 blossoms. **C** is correct.

   A is incorrect, because only 2 plants display 2 blossoms. So 2 is not the number that appears most frequently in the set. **B** is incorrect because 5.1 represents the average of the 10 numbers given. **D** is also incorrect, because 7 represents the range of the numbers in the set, or the difference between the largest and smallest term. In this set, the largest number of blossoms is 9 (Plant A), and the smallest number is 2 (Plants D and J), so the range of the set is 7.

8. K

Algebra: Solving Linear Equations *Easy*

Solve for p:

$$12p - 7 = 10p + 6$$
$$12p - 10p = 6 + 7$$
$$2p = 13$$
$$p = \frac{13}{2}$$
$$= 6\frac{1}{2}$$

9. E

Pre-Algebra: Number Properties *Easy*

The question states that x is negative and that y is greater than x. However, we don't know whether y is positive or negative. It could be negative and still be larger than x.

Pick numbers for x and y to determine which statements are false. If $x = -1$ and $y = 2$, then $x + y$ would be positive. **A** is therefore incorrect. If $x = -4$ and $y = -2$, then $x + y$ would be negative. **B** can be eliminated. If $x = -4$ and $y = -2$, then xy would be positive, so **C** is incorrect. The question states that x and y are integers, so $x + y$ cannot be a fraction. It must be a integer, so **E** is correct.

10. G

Pre-Algebra: Absolute Value Simplification and Substitution *Easy*

Substitute -3 for z in this absolute value expression and solve:

$$|12 - 17 + z| = |12 - 17 + (-3)|$$
$$= |-5 + (-3)|$$
$$= |-8|$$
$$= 8$$

The absolute value of -8 is 8, so **G** is correct. **F** is incorrect, because an absolute value is always a positive number.

11. E

Coordinate Geometry: Slope *Easy*

Use the formula for determining the slope of a line:

$$m = \frac{y_2 - y_1}{x_2 - x_1}$$

Substitute $(7, 3)$ for (x_1, y_1) and $(12, -6)$ for (x_2, y_2):

$$m = \frac{y_2 - y_1}{x_2 - x_1}$$
$$= \frac{-6 - 3}{12 - 7}$$
$$= \frac{-9}{5}$$
$$= -\frac{9}{5}$$

12. J

Pre-Algebra: Number Problems   *Easy*

Let x represent the total number of birds at the aviary. The number of finches represents 2 less than half of the birds, or $\frac{x}{2} - 2$. The number of bluebirds, robins, and hummingbirds equals $5 + 6 + 8$, or 19 birds. If you subtract those 19 birds from the total $(x - 19)$, the remaining birds are finches $\frac{x}{2} - 2$. To find the total number of birds, set these two quantities equal and solve for x:

$$x - 19 = \frac{x}{2} - 2$$
$$x - \frac{x}{2} = 19 - 2$$
$$\frac{2x}{2} - \frac{x}{2} = 17$$
$$\frac{x}{2} = 17$$
$$x = 34$$

13. C

Algebra: Simplification   *Easy*

Use the order of operations to simplify this expression. First, multiply 7 by $(z - 2)$:

$$7(z - 2) = 7z - 14$$

Now, add like terms:

$$13 - 7(z - 2) = 13 - (7z - 14)$$
$$= 13 - 7z + 14$$
$$= -7z + 27$$

14. G

Coordinate Geometry: Coordinate Plane   *Easy*

Quadrant III lies in the lower left portion of the coordinate plane. Points in quadrant III will have a negative x-coordinate and a negative y-coordinate. Only $(-6, -7)$ has both a negative x-coordinate and a negative y-coordinate, so **G** is correct.

15. D

Intermediate Algebra: Series   *Medium*

The repeating decimal contains 5 digits. Divide the number 419 by 5. The answer is 83, with a remainder of 4.

This means that the full 5-digit pattern repeats exactly 83 times, plus 4 additional digits. The fourth digit to the right of the decimal point is 3, so the 419th digit after the decimal point is 3.

16. K

Plane Geometry: Circles   *Medium*

First, determine the circumference of the unicycle tire. Use the formula for the circumference of a circle, $C = 2\pi r$. Since the distance to Nancy's house is given in feet, the radius of the tire should also be converted to feet. This will keep the units of distance consistent.

A radius of 9 inches is .75 feet long, so substitute .75 for r in the circumference formula. Use 3.14 for π, since the value of π is approximately 3.14:

$$C \approx 2\pi r$$
$$\approx 2(3.14)(.75)$$
$$\approx 4.71$$

The circumference of the unicycle is approximately 4.71 feet. Divide the circumference into the total distance traveled: 2,826 feet. This will reveal the number of rotations made by the unicycle tire: $2{,}826 \div 4.71 = 600$.

G is incorrect because it reflects the number of rotations when 9 is used for the radius of the unicycle. The radius of the unicycle is 9 inches, but this number must first be converted to feet in order to arrive at the correct answer.

17. **D**

Pre-Algebra: Multiples, Factors & Primes   *Medium*

The number $24jk$ divides evenly into $72jk$ and $264jk$. It divides into $72jk$ exactly 3 times and into $264jk$ exactly 11 times. It also divides into itself 1 time. Therefore, the number $24jk$ is the greatest common factor of the three numbers.

A is incorrect, because $9j$ does not divide evenly into all three numbers, so it is not a factor of all three numbers. **B** and **C** are incorrect, because $24jk$ also divides evenly into all three numbers, and it is greater than $12k$ and jk. **E** is incorrect because $40jk$ is not a factor of any of the three numbers.

18. **E**

Intermediate Algebra: Functions   *Medium*

Substitute $x = -4$ into the function and solve:

$$f(x) = 4x^2 - 2x + 6$$
$$f(-4) = 4\left(-4^2\right) - [2(-4)] + 6$$
$$= 4(16) - (-8) + 6$$
$$= 64 + 8 + 6$$
$$= 78$$

19. **C**

Algebra: Substitution   *Medium*

Substitute $\dfrac{3}{4}$ for a to solve the equation:

$$\frac{8a - 2}{a} = \frac{8\left(\dfrac{3}{4}\right) - 2}{\left(\dfrac{3}{4}\right)}$$

$$= \frac{6 - 2}{\dfrac{3}{4}}$$

$$= 4 \times \frac{4}{3}$$

$$= \frac{16}{3}$$

$$= 5\frac{1}{3}$$

20. G

Trigonometry: SOHCAHTOA   *Medium*

The formula for the tangent of an angle is $\tan = \dfrac{\text{opposite}}{\text{adjacent}}$. For angle s, the opposite side is $\overline{YZ}$, and the adjacent side is $\overline{ZX}$. So, $\tan s$ equals $\dfrac{\overline{YZ}}{\overline{ZX}}$.

H is incorrect because it represents the sine of angle s $\left(\dfrac{\text{opposite}}{\text{hypotenuse}}\right)$, and **J** is incorrect because it represents the cosine of angle s $\left(\dfrac{\text{adjacent}}{\text{hypotenuse}}\right)$.

21. E

Intermediate Algebra: Permutations and Combinations   *Medium*

This is a combination problem. To solve combination problems, multiply the possibilities. The question asks for how many different schedules of one morning meeting and one afternoon meeting can be scheduled. So the answer will be the number of possible morning meetings multiplied by the number of possible afternoon meetings.

Morning sessions cannot be scheduled on Thursdays, so they can only be scheduled on 6 days of each of the 4 consecutive weeks. So the number of possible morning sessions is 4×6.

Afternoon meetings can be scheduled on any day of the week, so they can be scheduled on 7 days of the week for each of the 4 consecutive weeks, or 4×7 possibilities.

Combining the number of possible morning and afternoon sessions gives us $(4 \times 6)(4 \times 7)$, so **E** is the best answer.

22. H

Plane Geometry: Circles   *Medium*

There are 360 degrees in a circle. If the minute hand moved from 8:00 p.m. to 9:00 p.m., or a total of 60 minutes, it would travel a full 360 degrees. It moves less than this distance, however, so **K** can be eliminated.

Set up a proportion that compares the time interval to the number of degrees traveled. If the minute hand travels 360 degrees in 60 minutes, how many degrees does it travel in 40 minutes?

$$\frac{360}{60} = \frac{d}{40}$$
$$60d = 360 \times 40$$
$$60d = 14{,}400$$
$$d = 240$$

The minute hand travels 240 degrees in 40 minutes.

23. A

Coordinate Geometry: Slope   *Medium*

The slope of a line is defined as $\dfrac{\text{rise}}{\text{run}}$. In this case, the line falls down to the right, so the slope will be negative. **B** and **C** can be eliminated. **E** looks fancy, but it can be eliminated as well. It represents a way to find the distance between two points on a line, not the slope of a line.

Find two points that lie squarely on intersections of the grid, as shown in the figure below:

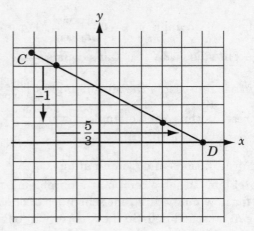

Count the number of units in the rise (−1) and the run $\left(\frac{5}{3}\right)$. Dividing −1 by $\frac{5}{3}$ gives you $-\frac{3}{5}$, so **A** is correct.

24. J

Plane Geometry: Polygons   *Medium*

This is a problem that can be solved by working backward from the answer choices. Start with **H**, the middle choice:

$$14 \times (14 - 4) = 14 \times 10$$
$$= 140$$

This answer is too small, so we know that neither **F** nor **G** will work. Let's test **J**:

$$16 \times (16 - 4) = 16 \times 12$$
$$= 192$$

A garden that is 16 feet wide by 12 feet long would have an area of 192 square feet.

25. C

Intermediate Algebra: Absolute Value Equations and Inequalities   *Medium*

The inequality $|n + 9| > 27$ tells us that the sum $n + 9$ is more than 27 units from 0 on a number line. That means that $n + 9$ can either be greater than 27 or less than −27. If $n + 9 > 27$, then $n > 18$. If $n + 9 < -27$, then $n < -36$.

26. H

Algebra: Solving Linear Equations   *Medium*

Use the information given in the question to solve the equation for c. Substitute $650.00 for p and $5.00 for f:

$$p = 1.57c - \frac{3}{2}f + \$265.00$$

$$\$650.00 = 1.57c - \frac{3}{2}(\$5.00) + \$265.00$$

$$\$650.00 = 1.57c - 1.5(\$5.00) + \$265.00$$

$$\$650.00 = 1.57c - \$7.50 + \$265.00$$

$$\$650.00 = 1.57c + \$257.50$$

$$\$650.00 - \$257.50 = 1.57c$$

$$\$392.50 = 1.57c$$

$$c = \$250.00$$

The cost of the materials is \$250.00.

27. **D**

Plane Geometry: Three Dimensions *Medium*

The containers have the same volume, so first determine this volume using the volume formula. Substitute in the dimensions given for the first container:

$$V = l \times w \times h$$
$$V = 40 \times 50 \times 27$$
$$= 54,000$$

The containers both have a volume of 54,000 cm³. Next, use this value to determine the height of the second container. Substitute the values for the second container into the volume formula:

$$V = l \times w \times h$$
$$54,000 = 24 \times 63 \times h$$
$$54,000 = 1,512h$$
$$\frac{54,000}{1,512} = h$$
$$35.71 \approx h$$

The height of the second container is approximately 35.71 cm. This value is closest to 40 cm.

28. **G**

Coordinate Geometry: Equation of a Line *Medium*

The y-intercept can be determined by putting the equation in the form $y = mx + b$. In this format, m represents the slope of the line, and b represents the y-intercept.

Convert the equation to the form $y = mx + b$:

$$2x + 6y = 14$$
$$6y = -2x + 14$$
$$\frac{6y}{6} = \frac{-2x + 14}{6}$$
$$y = -\frac{2x}{6} + \frac{14}{6}$$
$$y = -\frac{1}{3}x + \frac{7}{3}$$

In this case, $b = \frac{7}{3}$, so the coordinate of the y-intercept is $\left(0, \frac{7}{3}\right)$.

29. D

Pre-Algebra: Percentages, Fractions & Decimals   *Medium*

Set up an equation to solve for the missing number. Let x represent the missing number:

$$150 = \frac{3}{15}x$$
$$150 = \frac{3x}{15}$$
$$150 \times 15 = 3x$$
$$2{,}250 = 3x$$
$$750 = x$$

The number 150 is $\frac{3}{15}$ of 750.

30. G

Coordinate Geometry: Coordinate Plane   *Medium*

Draw two perpendicular lines, one from point J and one from point K, so that they intersect at point L, as shown below.

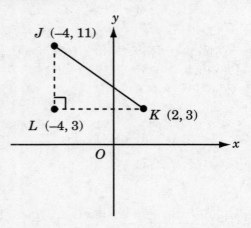

Here the lines are drawn to the left of point K. They intersect at coordinates (–4, 3). The lines could also be drawn to the right of point J, intersecting at coordinates (2, 11). This coordinate is not one of the answer choices, however, so **G** is correct.

31. C

Plane Geometry: Triangles   *Medium*

$\overline{JK}$ forms the hypotenuse of $\triangle JKL$, with legs $\overline{KL}$ and $\overline{JL}$. Count the units in legs $\overline{KL}$ and $\overline{JL}$. $\overline{KL}$ is 6 units long, and $\overline{JL}$ is 8 units, as shown.

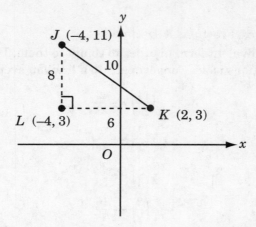

This means that $\triangle JKL$ is a multiple of the Pythagorean triple 3:4:5. The legs will be in a ratio of 3:4:5 each multiplied by 2, or 6:8:10. The length of the hypotenuse $\overline{JK}$ is 10 units.

The distance formula could also be used to solve this problem, but the answer is reached more quickly if you recognize the Pythagorean triple.

32. **K**

Coordinate Geometry: Transformations   *Medium*

Draw a figure that shows $\overline{JK}$ reflected over the x-axis:

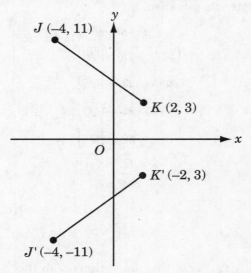

The x-coordinate of point J' is the same as the x-coordinate of point J, –4. The y-coordinate of point J' is the negative of the x-coordinate of point J, because the new line falls below the x-axis. The y-coordinate of point J' is therefore –11.

H is incorrect because it reflects the coordinates of point K'.

33. B

Pre-Algebra: Percentages, Fractions & Decimals   *Medium*

Put the fractions in equivalent form in order to compare them. The least common multiple of all five fractions is 28. Convert each to a fraction over 28:

$$-\frac{3}{2}\left(\frac{14}{14}\right) = -\frac{42}{28}$$

$$-\frac{1}{4}\left(\frac{7}{7}\right) = -\frac{7}{28}$$

$$-\frac{5}{7}\left(\frac{4}{4}\right) = -\frac{20}{28}$$

$$-\frac{8}{14}\left(\frac{2}{2}\right) = -\frac{16}{28}$$

$$-\frac{9}{28} = -\frac{9}{28}$$

The fractions are all negative numbers, so the largest is $-\frac{7}{28}$.

34. J

Trigonometry: Solving Triangles   *Medium*

The formula for the tangent of an angle is "opposite divided by adjacent." If $\tan q = \frac{5\sqrt{7}}{15}$, and adjacent side $\overline{QR} = 15$, this means that opposite side $\overline{SR} = 5\sqrt{7}$. To find the length of $\overline{QS}$, use the Pythagorean theorem:

$$a^2 + b^2 = c^2$$

$$\left(5\sqrt{7}\right)^2 + 15^2 = \left(\overline{QS}\right)^2$$

$$(25 \times 7) + 225 = \left(\overline{QS}\right)^2$$

$$175 + 225 = \left(\overline{QS}\right)^2$$

$$400 = \left(\overline{QS}\right)^2$$

$$\overline{QS} = \sqrt{400}$$

$$\overline{QS} = 20$$

35. B

Plane Geometry: Triangles   *Medium*

If $\overline{FG} = \frac{1}{4}\overline{FE}$, then $\overline{FG} = \frac{1}{4}(12)$, or 3. Use the Pythagorean theorem to find the length of $\overline{CG}$, which represents the height of the triangle:

$$a^2 + b^2 = c^2$$

$$a^2 + 3^2 = 7^2$$

$$a^2 + 9 = 49$$

$$a^2 = 40$$

$$a = \sqrt{4 \times 10}$$

$$a = 2\sqrt{10}$$

The height of the triangle is $2\sqrt{10}$. Plug this value into the formula for the area of a triangle:

$$A = \frac{1}{2}bh$$
$$= \frac{1}{2}3\left(2\sqrt{10}\right)$$
$$= \frac{1}{2}\left(6\sqrt{10}\right)$$
$$= 3\sqrt{10}$$

36. H

Algebra: Inequalities   *Medium*

The first step to take is solving $\sqrt{a+2} \geq 3$. To do this, square both sides of the inequality:

$$\sqrt{a+2} \geq 3$$
$$\left(\sqrt{a+2}\right)^2 \geq 3^2$$
$$a+2 \geq 9$$
$$a \geq 7$$

37. E

Pre-Algebra: Number Problems   *Medium*

Set up an equation to represent the number of egg cartons collected. Katya collected the smaller number of egg cartons. Let x represent the number of cartons that Katya collected. She collected only $\frac{1}{4}$ as many cartons as Asher, so Asher collected 4 times the number of cartons that Katya collected. This means we can represent the number of cartons Asher collected as $4x$.

Add the two values together to provide a total of 50, and solve for x:

$$x + 4x = 50$$
$$5x = 50$$
$$x = 10$$

Katya collected 10 egg cartons, so Asher collected $4 \times 10 = 40$ cartons. **B** is incorrect because it represents the number of egg cartons collected by Katya, not by Asher.

38. G

Algebra: Solving Linear Equations   *Medium*

Solve for x. Start by multiplying 0.7 by $(x + 360)$:

$$0.7(x + 360) = x$$
$$0.7x + 252 = x$$

Next, combine like terms:

$$0.7x + 252 = x$$
$$0.7x - x = -252$$

The x can also be written as $1x$. This will enable you to combine $0.7x - 1x$:

$$0.7x - x = -252$$
$$0.7x - 1x = -252$$
$$-0.3x = -252$$
$$x = \frac{-252}{-0.3}$$
$$x = 840$$

39. C

Plane Geometry: Triangles   *Medium*

This is the type of geometry problem where your algebra skills can come in very handy. Set up a proportion to find the length of the longest side of $\triangle XYZ$:

$$\frac{8}{10} = \frac{12}{x}$$
$$8x = 120$$
$$x = 15$$

The longest side of $\triangle XYZ$ is 15 centimeters, and its shortest side is 10 centimeters. Find the length of the remaining side:

$$\frac{8}{10} = \frac{10}{x}$$
$$8x = 100$$
$$x = 12.5$$

The three sides of $\triangle XYZ$ measure 10, 12.5, and 15 centimeters. The perimeter of the triangle is $10 + 12.5 + 15$, or 37.5 centimeters.

40. F

Intermediate Algebra: Exponents and Roots   *Medium*

Square the inequality to eliminate the radical sign:

$$16 \geq \sqrt{s} \geq 25$$
$$16^2 \geq \left(\sqrt{s}\right)^2 \geq 25^2$$
$$256 \geq s \geq 625$$

41. C

Coordinate Geometry: Parallel and Perpendicular Lines   *Medium*

Perpendicular lines have slopes that are negative reciprocals of one another. To find the negative reciprocal of a number, divide -1 by the number. The negative reciprocal of $\frac{1}{6}$ is -1 divided by $\frac{1}{6}$:

$$\frac{-1}{\frac{1}{6}} = (-1)\left(\frac{6}{1}\right)$$
$$= -6$$

You are looking for a line whose slope is –6. **A**, **D**, and **E** can be eliminated. A line with a slope of $\frac{1}{6}$ would be *parallel* to the line given in the question, not perpendicular to it.

Plug the coordinates (6, 3) into the two remaining equations to see which one fits:

$$y = -6x + 39$$
$$(3) = -6(6) + 39$$
$$3 = -36 + 39$$
$$3 = 3$$

42. **G**

Pre-Algebra: Mean, Median & Mode   *Medium*

Use the formula for determining the average of a set of terms:

$$\text{Average} = \frac{\text{sum of terms}}{\text{number of terms}}$$

In this case, we know that the average of 10 numbers is 63. Substitute these values into the average formula:

$$\text{Average} = \frac{\text{sum of terms}}{\text{number of terms}}$$
$$63 = \frac{\text{sum of terms}}{10}$$

Multiplying 10 by 63, we see that the sum of the 10 original terms is 630. If two integers are subtracted from the total of 630, and those two integers are 40 and 60, then the sum of the remaining 8 integers is 630 – 40 – 60, or 530. To find the average of the remaining 8 terms, divide 530 by 8:

$$\text{Average} = \frac{530}{8}$$
$$= 66.25$$

F can be eliminated because if two terms are taken away from the original 10, and both of these terms are less than 63, the new average is likely to be greater than 63.

43. **D**

Coordinate Geometry: Graphing Equations   *Medium*

You are given the coordinates of one point on the line, and the slope, m, of the line. You can find the equation of the line by determining one more value, the y-intercept. In the slope-intercept form of the equation, $y = mx + b$, the variable b represents the y-intercept. Substitute the values you know into this equation and solve for b:

$$y = mx + b$$
$$10 = \frac{1}{5}(6) + b$$
$$10 = \frac{6}{5} + b$$
$$10 - \frac{6}{5} = b$$
$$\frac{44}{5} = b$$

Now you can write the equation in slope-intercept form:

$$y = \frac{1}{5}x + \frac{44}{5}$$

The equation can be simplified even further to $y = \frac{x + 44}{5}$. Now check each ordered pair to see which one makes the equation true:

$$y = \frac{x + 44}{5}$$

$$\frac{47}{5} = \frac{3 + 44}{5}$$

$$\frac{47}{5} = \frac{47}{5}$$

44. G

Plane Geometry: Angles and Lines   *Medium*

Complementary angles are those whose measurements add up to 90°. Set up an equation to solve for a. Use the angle measurements $8a$ and $a + 9$:

$$8a + (a + 9) = 90$$
$$9a + 9 = 90$$
$$9a = 90 - 9$$
$$9a = 81$$
$$a = 9$$

Though a equals 9, **F** is not the correct answer. The question asks for the value of the smallest angle. The smallest angle is $a + 9$, which measures 18°.

45. B

Pre-Algebra: Number Problems   *Medium*

If there are 15 horses, and each horse receives one carrot, that leaves 22 carrots remaining. An additional 2 carrots could be given to as many as 11 of the horses. Therefore, up to 11 horses could receive 3 carrots.

One way to visualize this is to draw 15 slots for the 15 horses. Place 1 carrot in each slot. Then distribute two additional carrots in as many slots as possible:

1 + 2	1 + 2	1 + 2	1 + 2	1 + 2
1 + 2	1 + 2	1 + 2	1 + 2	1 + 2
1 + 2	1	1	1	1

A is incorrect, because more than 9 of the horses could possibly receive 3 carrots. **D** and **E** are incorrect, because it would not be possible for 12 of the horses to receive 3 carrots each. Roman numerals I and II are the only possibilities, so **B** is correct.

46. K

Trigonometry: Trigonometric Identities   *Medium*

This question requires you to use the trigonometric identity $\sin^2 \theta + \cos^2 \theta = 1$. All of the answer choices are given in terms of $\cos^2 \theta$. Based on the trigonometric identity

$\sin^2 \theta + \cos^2 \theta = 1$, we know that $\sin^2 \theta = 1 - \cos^2 \theta$. Substitute $1 - \cos^2 \theta$ for $\sin^2 \theta$ into the equation given in the question:

$$\begin{aligned}
\tan^2 \theta &= \frac{\sin^2 \theta}{\cos^2 \theta} \\
&= \frac{1 - \cos^2 \theta}{\cos^2 \theta} \\
&= \frac{1}{\cos^2 \theta} - \frac{\cos^2 \theta}{\cos^2 \theta} \\
&= \frac{1}{\cos^2 \theta} - 1
\end{aligned}$$

47. G

Plane Geometry: Three Dimensions   *Medium*

The surface area of a rectangular solid is the sum of the areas of each of its six sides. In this case, the solid has two sides with areas of $8 \times 5 = 40$ cm each, 2 sides with area of $5h$ cm each, and 2 sides with areas of $8h$ cm each. Add these areas together and solve for h:

$$\begin{aligned}
2(8 \times 5) + 2(5h) + 2(8h) &= 184 \\
2(40) + 10h + 16h &= 184 \\
80 + 26h &= 184 \\
26h &= 104 \\
h &= 4
\end{aligned}$$

The height of the rectangular solid is 4 cm.

48. J

Plane Geometry: Polygons   *Medium*

First, find the length of $\overline{XZ}$. This leg is the hypotenuse of a special right triangle with legs measuring 5 and 12 units, respectively. Based on the 5:12:13 Pythagorean triple, the length of diagonal $\overline{XZ}$ must be 13 units.

Since $WXYZ$ is a rectangle, $\overline{XZ}$ and $\overline{WY}$ bisect each other. This means that $\overline{XT}$ equals one-half of $\overline{XZ}$, or 6.5. Since $\overline{XZ}$ and $\overline{WY}$ bisect each other, we also know that $\overline{XT}$ equals $\overline{TY}$. This means that $\overline{TY}$ also equals 6.5. The perimeter of ΔXTY equals $6.5 + 6.5 + 12$, or 25.

49. B

Trigonometry: SOHCAHTOA   *Medium*

The sine of an angle in a right triangle is the length of the opposite side over the hypotenuse. In this case, y represents the length of the side of the triangle that lies opposite angle θ. The hypotenuse of the triangle is represented by z.

Use the Pythagorean theorem to determine the value of the remaining side of the triangle, the side that is adjacent to angle θ:

$$a^2 + b^2 = c^2$$
$$\text{opposite}^2 + \text{adjacent}^2 = \text{hypotenuse}^2$$
$$y^2 + \text{adjacent}^2 = z^2$$
$$\text{adjacent}^2 = z^2 - y^2$$
$$\text{adjacent} = \sqrt{z^2 - y^2}$$

The length of the missing side of the triangle is $\sqrt{z^2 - y^2}$. The formula for the cosine of an angle equals $\dfrac{\text{adjacent}}{\text{hypotenuse}}$, so $\cos\theta = \dfrac{\sqrt{z^2 - y^2}}{z}$.

50. J

Intermediate Algebra: Systems of Equations   *Medium*

Set up two equations. Let bracelets be represented by the variable b, and let necklaces be represented by the variable n. It takes 560 minutes to make two bracelets and four necklaces. So, the first equation is $2b + 4n = 560$.

It takes 400 minutes to make two necklaces and four bracelets. So, the second equation is $4b + 2n = 400$. This gives us a system of equations as follows:

$$2b + 4n = 560$$
$$4b + 2n = 400$$

Multiply the second equation by –2, so you can combine the equations and eliminate the n variable:

$$2b + 4n = 560$$
$$-8b - 4n = -800$$
$$-6b = -240$$
$$b = 40$$

Substitute $b = 40$ into the first equation and solve for n:

$$2b + 4n = 560$$
$$2(40) + 4n = 560$$
$$80 + 4n = 560$$
$$4n = 560 - 80$$
$$4n = 480$$
$$n = 120$$

It takes 120 minutes to make 1 necklace, and 40 minutes to make 1 bracelet. Substitute these values in to determine the time needed to make 2 bracelets and 2 necklaces:

$$2b + 2n = 2(40) + 2(120)$$
$$= 80 + 240$$
$$= 320$$

51. E

Pre-Algebra: Percentages, Fractions & Decimals   *Medium*

This problem can be solved by working backward from the answer choices. Start with the middle answer choice, **C**. If each family contributed 50 brownies, the total number of brownies at the bake sale would have been 250. One-fifth of 250 sold in the first hour is 50, which leaves 200 brownies remaining. One-fifth of 200 brownies sold in the second hour is 40, which leaves 160 remaining. One-fifth of 160 sold in the third hour is 32, which leaves 128 brownies remaining at the end of the bake sale. That number is too large, so try a smaller answer choice.

D states that each family gave 36 brownies, which equals 180 brownies altogether. One-fifth of 180 is 36 brownies sold in the first hour, which leaves 144 remaining. One-fifth of 144 sold in the second hour is 28.8, which means the brownies couldn't have been sold as whole brownies. **D** can be eliminated.

E is the only choice remaining. If each family brought 25 brownies, the bake sale would have started with 125 brownies. One-fifth of 125 sold in the first hour is 25, which leaves 100 remaining. One-fifth of 100 sold in the second hour is 20 brownies, with 80 remaining. One-fifth of 80 sold in the third hour is 16 brownies, with 64 remaining at the end of the bake sale.

52. **J**

Plane Geometry: Polygons   *Medium*

The question states that all lines in the figure meet at right angles. Therefore, we know that $\overline{JN}$ measures 8 centimeters, and the remaining missing side measures 3 centimeters. Add up the lengths: $7 + 5 + 3 + 3 + 4 + 8 = 30$ centimeters.

53. **C**

Plane Geometry: Circles   *Medium*

First, calculate the area of the first tabletop:

$$A = \pi r^2$$
$$= \pi(3)^2$$
$$= 9\pi$$

The area of the first tabletop is 9π, so the area of the second tabletop is $\frac{2}{3} \times 9\pi$, or 6π. To determine the radius of the second tabletop, use the area formula again and work backward:

$$A = \pi r^2$$
$$6\pi = \pi r^2$$
$$\frac{6\pi}{\pi} = \frac{\pi r^2}{\pi}$$
$$r^2 = 6$$
$$r = \sqrt{6}$$

To cover the second tabletop exactly, the radius of the second piece of felt should be $\sqrt{6}$.

54. **F**

Intermediate Algebra: Functions   *Medium*

Look for the graph of each part of the function in the graphs shown. Then, determine whether the conditions are satisfied according to the definitions listed. **F** is the only graph that contains each of the parts of the function shown, with closed circles for the end points of the horizontal line at $2 \leq x \leq 5$ and open circles for the end points of the parabola at $x < 2$ and the diagonal line at $x > 5$.

H is incorrect because although the lines are graphed correctly, the end points are not. **H** contains open circles for the end points of the horizontal line at $2 \leq x \leq 5$ and closed circles for the end points of the parabola at $x < 2$ and the diagonal line at $x > 5$.

55. A

Algebra: Multiplying Binomials   *Difficult*

Factor $4x^2 + rx - 48$ using the reverse FOIL method. If $(x + 4)$ is one of the factors, we know that the first term of the second factor must be $4x$. We also know that the last term of the second factor must be -12, because $4(-12) = -48$. Therefore, the second factor is $(4x - 12)$.

The question asks for the value of $r - 8$. Multiply the two factors together to determine r, the constant on the middle term of the binomial:

$$(x + 4)(4x - 12) = 4x^2 - 12x + 16x - 48$$
$$= 4x^2 + 4x - 48$$

The middle term is $4x$, so $r = 4$. The value of $r - 8$ is -4. **E** is incorrect because it reflects the value of r itself.

56. K

Algebra: Inequalities   *Difficult*

Test out each of the answer choices to determine whether the given inequality remains true. Look for combinations of numbers that would falsify the inequality. **F** is incorrect because if $a = 1$ and $b = 1$, then $\frac{1}{(2 \times 1)^1} = \frac{1}{(2 \times 1)^1}$. **G** is incorrect because if $a = 3$ and $b = 2$, then $\frac{1}{(2 \times 2)^3} < \frac{1}{(2 \times 3)^2}$. **H** is incorrect for the same reason.

J is incorrect because if $a = 1$ and $b = 2$, then $\frac{1}{(2 \times 2)^1} = \frac{1}{(2 \times 1)^2}$. **K** is the only answer choice remaining: If $a = 1, 2$, or 3, and $b \geq 5$, then the given inequality will always be true.

57. A

Coordinate Geometry: Conic Sections   *Difficult*

The equation of a circle is given by the formula $(x - h)^2 + (y - k)^2 = r^2$, where the point (h, k) represents the center of the circle, and r represents the radius. For the equation $(x - 4)^2 + (y - 5)^2 = 16$, we're looking for a circle with center $(4, 5)$. In this case, the value of r^2 is 16, so the correct circle will have a radius of $\sqrt{16}$, or 4.

B, C, and **D** can be eliminated, because they contain incorrect coordinates for the center of the circle, P. **A** and **E** contain the correct center coordinates $(4, 5)$, but only the circle in **A** has a radius of 4. We know this because its x-coordinate is 4, and the circle is tangent to the y-axis. The circle in **E** has a radius of less than 4, so **E** is incorrect.

58. H

Plane Geometry: Polygons   *Difficult*

Reflected over $\overline{CD}$, the new rectangle $A'B'AB$ appears as follows:

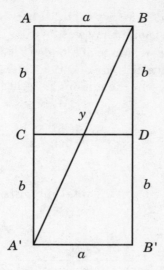

The line marked y represents a diagonal of $A'B'AB$. To find the length of y, use the Pythagorean theorem:

$$\text{side}^2 + \text{side}^2 = \text{hypotenuse}^2$$
$$\left(\overline{A'B'}\right)^2 + \left(\overline{B'B}\right)^2 = y^2$$
$$y^2 = \left(a\right)^2 + \left(2b\right)^2$$
$$y^2 = a^2 + 4b^2$$
$$y = \sqrt{a^2 + 4b^2}$$

K is incorrect because the expression $\sqrt{a^2 + 4b^2}$ cannot be reduced any further.

59. **D**

Intermediate Algebra: Logarithms   *Difficult*

Based on the properties of logarithms, we can write $\log_r(12st)^4$ in the following form:
$$\log_r(12st)^4 = 4\log_r(12st)$$
$$= 4(\log_r 12s + \log_r t)$$

Substitute in $12x$ for $\log_r 12s$ and y^2 for $\log_r t$:

$$4(\log_r 12s + \log_r t) = 4(12x + y^2)$$
$$= 48x + 4y^2$$

60. **J**

Pre-Algebra: Percentages, Fractions & Decimals   *Difficult*

The online newsletter started with 4,700 subscribers on Monday. On Wednesday, the number of subscribers had increased by 35%. Calculate 35% of 4,700:

$$4,700 \times .35 = 1,645$$

Add this value to 4,700 for Wednesday's total subscribers: $4,700 + 1,645 = 6,345$.

On Friday, the number of subscribers decreased by 40%. Calculate 40% of 6,345:

$$6,345 \times .40 = 2,538$$

Subtract this value from 6,345 for Friday's total subscribers: 6,345 − 2,538 = 3,807. The total number of subscribers on Friday was 3,807.

The question asks for the percentage of Monday's subscribers who still subscribed on Friday. To calculate this value, ask the question: 3,807 is what percent of 4,700? Set up an equation. Let x represent the missing percentage:

$$3,807 = x4700$$
$$x = \frac{3,807}{4,700}$$
$$x = .81$$

Friday's subscribers represent 81% of the total subscribed on Monday.

READING

1. A

Prose Fiction: Vocabulary in Context   *Medium*

Obscurity means to be *unknown*. **A** is correct because the store is empty except for one *elderly gentleman*, which suggests that only a few people shop there or that the store is not well known. **B** is wrong because the narrator does not suggest Mr. Gilbert feels welcomed into the shop, only that *the store was very different from the bookstores in which he usually shopped*. The narrator has not introduced Mifflin at this point, so **C** is wrong. Although Mr. Gilbert had some difficulty finding the shop, the interior of the shop is referred to as *obscure* rather than the shop's physical location.

2. G

Prose Fiction: Inference   *Difficult*

In the first two paragraphs, the narrator describes the bookshop as *remarkable* and *worthy of respect*, so it can be inferred that the narrator has a similar opinion of Mifflin. Although Mr. Gilbert seems apprehensive and skeptical about the shop, he is not the narrator, so **F** and **H** are incorrect. While the narrator clearly respects Mifflin, no textual evidence suggests the narrator is sad or sentimental about Mifflin or the bookshop.

3. D

Prose Fiction: Cause-Effect   *Medium*

A and **C** are incorrect because Mifflin gives no indication that he has ever advertised before or that cost is an issue. Although Mifflin states that he uses *the best ad writers in the business*, he later explains that he is referring to the authors of the books that he sells. Mifflin states that *if the book truly moves the customer, that person and that book become my strongest advertisements*, so **D** is correct.

4. J

Prose Fiction: Specific Detail   *Medium*

Remember, this question asks for which information is NOT found in the text. The opening paragraph provides the narrator's impression of Parnassus Books, which answers the question in **H**. **F** and **G** are addressed by the fifth paragraph: *The store was very different from the bookstores in which he usually shopped. Two stories of the old* *house had been converted into one: The lower space was divided into little alcoves, and the upper space showcased a gallery that carried books to the ceiling. Usually shopped* lets the reader know that Mr. Gilbert shops at other bookstores, while the description of Parnassus Books explains how *the store was very different.* Although the store's sign claims the shop is haunted, no textual evidence indicates why, so **J** is the best answer.

5. C

Prose Fiction: Inference   *Medium*

Air of originality refers to Mifflin's character and attitude as observed by Mr. Gilbert, so **C** is the best answer. At this point in the passage, Mr. Gilbert is confronted with Mifflin's appearance, and is no longer concerned with the smell of the bookshop, so **A** is wrong. The narrator is describing Mifflin instead of the store as having *an air of originality*, so **B** is incorrect. Mifflin responds pleasantly to Mr. Gilbert's interruption, so **D** is wrong.

6. F

Prose Fiction: Specific Detail   *Easy*

F is the best answer because Mr. Gilbert responds *incredulously* to Mifflin's statement that he does not advertise. **G** and **H** are tempting because the narrator states that Mr. Gilbert reacts as if Mifflin had *said something indecent*, but that appears to be describing Mr. Gilbert's shock rather than irritation or offense. Although Mr. Gilbert may not understand the reason for Mifflin's statement, Mr. Gilbert is more stunned than confused.

7. D

Prose Fiction: Purpose   *Medium*

D is correct because the narrator indicates his attitude about the bookshop by describing the store as *remarkable*. In addition, the narrator directly invites the reader to visit the store in the first sentence of the passage. The narrator's invitation suggests that Parnassus Books is still in business even though the passage describes a store that has few customers and does not bother with advertising. **A** is wrong because the first paragraph does not refer to the bookshop being haunted. The narrator never suggests he is one of the owners of Parnassus Books, so **B** is wrong. The first paragraph offers no indication of how often the narrator visits Parnassus Books, so **C** is incorrect.

8. G

Prose Fiction: Inference   *Difficult*

In paragraph 7, the narrator describes that Mr. Gilbert *began to feel a little agitated, and his throat tightened* as he walked through the shop, so **G** is the best answer. The narrator describes the shop as having a *warm and comfortable feeling*, but as Mr. Gilbert heads toward the back, his nervousness increases as depicted by his tight throat. Mr. Gilbert's statement that the shop *might be haunted* might make **F** tempting. However, Mr. Gilbert seems to be referring to the fact that he can find no one who works in the shop.

9. C

Prose Fiction: Specific Detail   *Easy*

Although Mr. Gilbert notices a table for wrapping packages, he sees *no sign of a salesperson*, so **C** is correct. The elderly man is reading and shows no sign of leaving, and Mifflin is reading a cookbook at his desk.

10. F

Prose Fiction: Inference   *Medium*

Mr. Gilbert asks *wistfully* if Mifflin uses Whitewash and Gilt when Mifflin states that he uses *the best ad writers in the business*. Mr. Gilbert's disappointment supports the idea that Grey Matter Advertising *frequently loses business to Whitewash and Gilt*. Mr. Gilbert's comment about Whitewash and Gilt suggests that Whitewash and Gilt is the top advertising firm in New York City rather than Grey Matter. It is unknown how long Mr. Gilbert has been working as a *salesperson*, so **J** is wrong. Although Mr. Gilbert *doubts* that another agency has *more effective* ad copy than Grey Matter, Mr. Gilbert never states Grey Matter *employs the best advertising copywriters*.

11. B

Social Science: Comparison   *Medium*

B is correct because the author writes in paragraph 3 that Wordsworth *dislikes capitalistic industrialization because the working conditions physically remove most workers from the beauty of nature* and that Wordsworth's comments *echo Thomas Carlyle's sentiments*. Carlyle and Wordsworth may agree with **A** and **C**, but the author only draws a connection between the two men's attitudes about nature. The text does not support **D**.

12. J

Social Science: Specific Detail   *Medium*

The author writes in the first paragraph that the Industrial Revolution exchanged the *former agricultural society based on manual labor with an industrial society reliant on machines and the division of labor*. The author describes *division of labor* as the idea that *very large jobs could be subdivided into smaller, distinctive operations in which an individual performs one small part*, so **J** is the best answer. The text does not indicate how jobs were assigned, so **F** is incorrect. Although it was hoped that workers would perform jobs quickly, it was because small tasks were assigned, not because of specific skills, which means **H** is false. Although the economy was shifting from agricultural to industrial, the text does not indicate that farm laborers were replaced with farm equipment, which makes **G** wrong.

13. A

Social Science: Cause-Effect   *Medium*

A is the best answer because in paragraph 1 the author writes that Smith proposed *the division of labor allowed for much greater production of goods and a rapid expansion of economic growth* and that *everyone from factory owners to the working classes would benefit from this increased production*. The author does not mention a *higher demand for goods*, the *creation of businesses*, or *labor laws*, so **B**, **C**, and **D** are incorrect.

14. H

Social Science: Purpose   *Medium*

The second paragraph begins the author's discussion of the problems with industrialization as explained by a variety of individuals, so **H** is the best answer. A minor detail of the passage is that England does not utilize its natural resources, so **J** is wrong. **G** is incorrect because the author does not address the global economy. **F** is wrong because the author counters the validity of Smith's claims.

15. **B**

Social Science: Specific Detail   *Easy*

B is correct because throughout the passage the author refers to Smith's ideas as *rose-colored* and *optimistic* while pointing out how Smith *failed to anticipate the human suffering resulting from the reduction of individuals to invisible "hands" lost in the process of production*. **A** and **C** are incorrect because the author stresses the problems with Smith's theory. **D** has a negative tone, but the author does not indicate that anyone viewed Smith's ideas as having potential.

16. **G**

Social Science: Vocabulary in Context   *Medium*

The phrase *reduce it to a state of almost savage torpor* indicates that *blunt* means to weaken or make dull, so **G** is correct. This correctly conveys the meaning of *mentally stagnating* mentioned in the preceding sentence. A *blunt* comment would be described as abrupt or surprising, but that definition does not work in this context, which means **H** is wrong. **F** is tempting, but the *discriminating powers of the mind* are not being withheld as much as they are being *weakened* by a lack of activity. **J** fails to work in the context of the sentence.

17. **D**

Social Science: Inference   *Difficult*

In the third paragraph, the author describes how Wordsworth *dislikes capitalistic industrialization because the working conditions physically remove most workers from the beauty of nature*, which suggests **D** is the best answer. The author describes the tasks of workers as menial rather than challenging, so **C** is incorrect. The author describes the Industrial Revolution as being a time of *heartless, materialistic conditions*, which opposes **A** and **B**.

18. **F**

Social Science: Specific Detail   *Medium*

Blake describes the people in London as *despondent and hopeless* because of the *rote, tedious, and disheartening work* they do. Carlyle writes that *England is full of wealth, of produce, to supply for human want of every kind; yet England is dying of starvation*. **F** best summarizes the attitudes of both Carlyle and Blake. **J** is wrong because neither man describes citizens as *outraged*. Industrialization is capitalistic rather than communistic, so **H** is wrong. **G** is incorrect because not everyone is *wealthy*.

19. **D**

Social Science: Main Idea, Argument & Theme   *Medium*

D best summarizes the main idea of the passage. **C** includes details mentioned in the passage but fails to summarize the idea of the entire passage. The author does not address *long-term opportunities*, so **B** is wrong. **A** is incorrect because the author suggests that a division of labor strengthens the overall economy of a nation.

20. **F**

Social Science: Specific Detail *Easy*

The author writes in the fifth paragraph that Smith *failed to anticipate the human suffering resulting from the reduction of individuals to invisible "hands" lost in the process of production.* According to the author, a division of labor reduces workers to the equivalent of robots, so **F** is the best answer. **G** is incorrect because the author does not claim that workers are physically incapable of doing the same task repeatedly, only that such activities blunt *the discriminating powers of the mind.* Having *important responsibilities* and *interacting with other employees* are not issues that the author mentions in the text.

21. **D**

Humanities: Specific Detail *Medium*

Note that this is an EXCEPT question, so find the activity that Caodaists do not perform. **D** is the best answer because the author explains in the fourth paragraph that Caodaists *observe a vegetarian diet for ten days per month,* and only those *with leadership positions in the church practice vegetarianism at all times.* The author describes praying, attending temple, and respecting elders in paragraph 4.

22. **G**

Humanities: Inference *Medium*

The focus of the second paragraph is how Cao Dai integrates elements of different world religions into its own doctrines, and the third paragraph describes how Caodaists worship intellectuals. **G** is the best answer because Caodaists evaluate and study the views of other religious groups and have taken ideas from those groups. **F** is incorrect because the paragraphs describe what religious elements Cao Dai borrows from other faiths, not what aspects Caodaists dislike. **H** and **J** are wrong because no mention is made of *inconsistencies* or *discrepancies.*

23. **B**

Humanities: Specific Detail *Medium*

The best answer is **B** because the author states in the first paragraph that Caodaism encourages *the cultivation of a close relationship with God as a means to eternal salvation.* According to the sixth paragraph, *Caodaists hope to stop the endless cycle of reincarnation and be reunited with God,* which rules out **A**. **C** is not stated in the passage. **D** is true but is not clearly stated to be the *primary goal for followers of Cao Dai.*

24. **F**

Humanities: Inference *Medium*

The author states in the second paragraph that Caodaists believe that *one universal God* is the *common origin* of all world religions, so **F** is the correct answer. Although **H** and **J** may be true, the author does not address either topic in the passage. **G** is wrong because Caodaists believe geography has caused religions to differ rather than unite.

25. **C**

Humanities: Inference *Difficult*

The third paragraph indicates that Caodaists *revere great writers, thinkers, and scientists as saints,* so **C** is the best answer. Although being loving and peaceful is a key element of Cao Dai, the fact that intellectuals such as Churchill and Shakespeare were made saints without regard to their morality or deeds suggests that intelligence is a characteristic deemed extremely honorable. The author does not present information in the passage regarding **A**, **B**, and **D**.

26. **J**
Humanities: Specific Detail   *Easy*

The author states in paragraph 1 that Caodaists *seek purification through religious beliefs and ethical practices*, so the best answer is **J**. It is not stated in the passage that Caodaists are attempting to achieve *holiness*, *healing*, or *peace* through their *moral standards*, so **F**, **G**, and **H** are incorrect.

27. **A**
Humanities: Specific Detail   *Easy*

Remember three of the choices will be elements from other religions that have been integrated into Cao Dai. The correct answer is the choice that is NOT found in Cao Dai. The author describes in the second paragraph how Confucianism, Christianity, and Buddhism fit into Cao Dai. The author writes in paragraph 2 that *from Taoism they borrow the concept of the Way, or the path of least resistance*; however, having no absolute truths is not addressed in the passage.

28. **H**
Humanities: Specific Detail   *Medium*

H is the best answer because the fifth paragraph describes how *the attainment of social harmony* can be achieved *through performing good works and living a moral life*. **F** is wrong because specific prayer guidelines are not mentioned in the text. Although the author mentions *the acquisition of moral knowledge*, general-purpose knowledge is not mentioned, which means **G** is wrong. No textual evidence supports **J** and *reality through worship*.

29. **D**
Humanities: Specific Detail   *Medium*

D is correct because the third paragraph explains that Buddha is *at the top of the pantheon*, and the next levels include *the Great Immortals* including Confucius, and then saints. **A**, **B**, and **C** list the individuals in the wrong order.

30. **H**
Humanities: Specific Detail   *Easy*

The first paragraph indicates that Caodaists believe their religion's *teachings, symbolism, and organization* were founded by direct communication with God. Later in paragraph 3, the author states that *Caodaists worship God as the "Supreme Being,"* so **H** is the best answer. Confucianism and Buddhism influence the Cao Dai doctrine but not the organization. The Holy See is a temple, so **F** is incorrect.

31. **B**
Natural Science: Specific Detail   *Easy*

B is the best answer because in paragraph 5 the author writes that the typical damage caused by an EF1 tornado is *torn roofs (off of mobile homes) and shattered windows*. EF2 and EF3 storms would cause more damage, while an EF0 storm would be too mild to break windows.

32. J

Natural Science: Inference   *Medium*

The author indicates that *enhanced radar data* make the EF-Scale more accurate than the F-Scale, but no indication is given that radar data were unavailable before the 1970s. The author does not address the issue of underestimating the wind speeds of tornados, so **G** is wrong. Although the author states the EF-Scale *incorporated tornado damage data gathered over the last few decades to make more accurate assessments*, **H** is incorrect because it remains unknown whether *damages* were averaged *every decade before the F-Scale was developed*. The first two sentences of the second paragraph describe how the F-Scale is a *reliable and widely used scientific tool* for categorizing tornadoes, so **J** is the best answer.

33. D

Natural Science: Comparison   *Medium*

The fourth paragraph states that the F-scale *failed to consider the size and dimensions of buildings to establish accurate ratings* whereas the EF-scale considers *many more types of buildings*. This information rules out **A** and **C** and indicates **D** is the best answer. **B** is wrong because both scales considered all types of damage, but building materials and structure are now part of the EF-scale equation.

34. F

Natural Science: Specific Detail   *Medium*

The author writes in the first paragraph that *scientists have studied the mystifying nature of tornadoes and attempted to classify their fluctuating intensity and perplexing array of destruction*, which led to Fujita's *system to analyze tornadic wind speed and estimate subsequent damage*. The author writes in the second paragraph that *the F-Scale has been the most reliable and widely used scientific tool for analyzing the force of and damage sustained by tornadoes throughout the country*, which further supports **F** as the correct answer. Although tornadoes can cause *monetary damage*, the F-Scale and EF-Scale do not calculate tornado costs, so **G** is wrong. The Fujita Scales focus on post-storm analysis, and since tornadoes remain unpredictable, **H** is wrong. Although *levels of destruction* are used to determine EF-Scale ratings, the purpose of the scales is to rate the strength of a tornado.

35. C

Natural Science: Purpose   *Medium*

The fifth and sixth paragraphs describe what the different EF ratings mean in regards to wind speed and typical property damage, so **C** is the best answer. According to the sixth paragraph, EF5 tornadoes are rare but not because of better wind measurements. EF ratings are not compared to F-scale ratings in these paragraphs, so **A** is incorrect. **B** is wrong because no mention is made of damage predictions.

36. J

Natural Science: Specific Detail   *Medium*

Remember to search for the factor NOT considered when determining a tornado's EF-Scale classification. Paragraph 3 indicates that scientists use ground swirl patterns *to assess structural and vegetative damage*, so G is incorrect. The author states in paragraph 4 that *scientists also take basic construction principles into account when assessing tornado intensities, considering both the structural soundness of affected buildings and the varying degrees of damage*, which rules out **F** and **H**. **J** is the best answer because estimating wind speeds is *a continuing challenge for scientists plagued by the difficulty of accurately measuring wind speed following a storm's fury*.

37. A
Natural Science: Strengthen/Weaken   *Difficult*

A is the best answer because if scientists could measure wind speeds during a storm, which is difficult if not impossible, and those measurements matched the EF-Scale ratings, then the EF-Scale would be *accurate*. If the EF-Scale and F-Scale ratings match, then one is no more accurate than the other is, so **B** is wrong. An EF2 storm would cause more damage than fallen branches, so **C** is incorrect. **D** does not address the accuracy of EF-Scales, although radar readings are another factor used to determine EF-Scale ratings.

38. G
Natural Science: Inference   *Medium*

In paragraph 3, the author writes that the EF-Scale has enabled scientists to *broaden their damage-perspective lenses and evaluate a more substantial body of relevant data*, which supports **G** as the best answer. Scientists are *plagued by the difficulty of accurately measuring wind speed following a storm's fury*, so **H** is wrong. The *latitudinal and longitudinal paths of tornados* is only one factor in assessing a storm's EF-Scale, so **F** is too narrow of a choice. **J** is incorrect because the only tools discussed in the passage are the F-Scale and the EF-Scale.

39. B
Natural Science: Main Idea, Argument & Theme   *Medium*

The EF-Scale does not predict a tornado's path, and it does not allow remote measurements of wind speed, which means **A** and **D** are wrong. **C** is incorrect because the scale does not help scientists to measure tornado damage, but vice versa. Scientists assess the damage inflicted by a tornado to determine a storm's EF category. The best answer is **B** because the EF-Scale helps scientists to assess a tornado's intensity.

40. H
Natural Science: Specific Detail   *Easy*

H is correct because the author states in paragraph 6 that *the only tornado in history to measure EF5 occurred on May 4, 2007, in Greensburg, Kansas, producing estimated wind speeds greater than 205 miles per hour and destroying 95 percent of the town*. **F** is wrong because the EF-Scale was introduced in 2007, but the F-Scale was introduced in the 1970s. The author writes that *more than 1200 tornadoes* are reported in the United States every year, but no textual evidence suggests that 2007 had a *higher than average number of tornadoes*. **J** is incorrect because the EF-Scale only goes to EF5.

SCIENCE

1. D

Data Representation: Read the Chart   *Easy*

Figure 1 shows a rise in the global sea level over time. Figure 2 shows a decline in glacier length, beginning after 1850 and continuing steadily into the twenty-first century. This means that glacier length decreased at the same time that the sea level became higher, so **D** is the correct answer. **A** correctly describes a rise in sea level but incorrectly states that glacier length increased. **B** correctly describes a decrease in glacier length but incorrectly states that sea level became lower. Both parts of **C** are incorrect, because they state the *opposite* of the information presented in Figures 1 and 2.

2. J

Data Representation: Use the Chart   *Easy*

Figure 1 shows a steady increase in the global sea level over time. The line's trajectory will hit 1.8 cm by 2010. **J** is correct because it reflects this upward trend. **G** and **H** represent sea-level rises that occurred around 2000 and 2003, respectively, so both choices are incorrect. **F** is a misinterpretation of the data.

3. B

Data Representation: Read the Chart   *Medium*

This answer is found by subtracting the glacial area of the Southern Andes (30,000 km^2) from the glacial area of the Rocky Mountains (126,033 km^2). When we subtract 30,000 km^2 from 126,033 km^2, we get 96,033 km^2, so the correct answer is **B**. **A** is simply the glacial area of the Southern Andes, so that choice is incorrect. **C** is the difference between the area of the Rocky Mountains and the area of the Tropical Andes. **D** results from adding the area of the Rocky Mountains to the area of the Southern Andes, making that an incorrect choice as well.

4. G

Data Representation: Use the Chart   *Medium*

Kamchatka has been assigned a weight of 0.006. The Alps and Pyrenees have been assigned a weight of 0.004. Scandinavia must have an assigned weight that is in between the two, making **G** (0.005) the correct answer. **F** is too small, and **H** and **J** are too large.

5. D

Data Representation: Use the Chart   *Medium*

The line graph in Figure 2 shows that a dramatic change took place in 1850. Namely, the length of the glaciers went into a steady decline. The information presented in the first paragraph of the passage states that sea-level rise is a major sign of global warming and that melting glaciers contribute to this rise. Therefore, **D** is the correct answer. The melting of glaciers leads to a rise in sea level, not to a lowering, so **A** is incorrect. Neither **B** nor **C** is supported by the passage.

6. H

Research Summary: Read the Chart   *Easy*

The solution reached the equivalence point when 25 mL of the acid was added. Here, the graph shows a pH reading of 7 on the y-axis. At additions of less than 25 mL, the solution maintained a pH greater than 7, so **F** and **G** are incorrect. **J** is incorrect because with the addition of more than 25 mL of acid, the pH of the acid-base solution dropped below 7.

7. A

Research Summary: Use the Chart   *Easy*

Table 2 shows that all five strong acids have a pH of 0. Experiment 1 explains that these acids all had a concentration of 1 mol. Therefore, an unidentified 1-mol-strong acid solution would most likely have a pH of 0. **D** is incorrect, because according to Table 2, 14 is the pH of strong base solutions.

8. G

Research Summary: Use the Chart   *Medium*

G is correct. Experiment 3 involved a weak acid and a weak base. According to Table 1, CH_3COOH is a weak acid, and NH_3 is a weak base. **F** and **H** are incorrect, because both contain strong acids and bases. **J** is incorrect because HNO_3 is a strong acid.

9. D

Research Summary: Take the Next Step   *Medium*

This experiment would involve adding a strong acid to a weak base. According to Table 1, perchloric acid is a strong acid, and diethylamine is a weak base, so **D** is correct. **A** is incorrect because it contains a weak acid added to a strong base. **B** is incorrect because it contains a weak base added to a strong acid, and **C** is incorrect because it contains a strong acid added to a strong base.

10. F

Research Summary: Use the Chart   *Medium*

Figure 3 shows that as more acid is added to the base in the beaker, the pH drops from 14 to nearly 0. This drop occurs because the solution becomes more acidic. The addition of the strong base would serve to increase the pH of the acid-base combination in the beaker, because the solution would become more alkaline.

11. B

Research Summary: Use the Chart   *Difficult*

The graph in Figure 3 shows a steep drop in pH around the equivalence point. The drop in pH starts right before the equivalence point is reached. Between 24 and 26 mL of acid added, the pH drops from 11 to about 2. The drop in pH is very steep for this strong acid-strong base titration.

The graph in Figure 4, by contrast, shows a relatively smooth drop in pH. The pH starts at around 12 and ends at about 5. There is no steep drop in pH as is shown in Figure 3. Thus, for the weak acid-weak base combination, the drop in pH is less steep than for the strong acid-strong base combination. **B** is correct.

A is incorrect because in both Figure 3 and Figure 4, the pH drops below 7 after the equivalence point. **C** is incorrect because the weak acid-weak base combination, graphed in Figure 4, does not reflect a steep drop in pH. **D** cannot be concluded based on the results of Experiments 2 and 3. The results shown in Figures 3 and 4 appear to contradict the statement in **D**, because the slower change in pH occurs in Figure 4, where the initial pH was less than in Figure 3.

12. **H**

Data Representation: Read the Chart

In Figure 1, large negative ions are represented by the white bars in the top graph. In November 2005, the growth rate of these ions was nearly 15 nmh^{-1}. This means that the correct answer is **H**. The growth rate in July 2005 was high, but not as high as in November 2005, so **F** is incorrect. The growth rate in September 2005 was very low, so **G** is incorrect. The growth rate in July 2006 was also significantly lower than that in November 2005, so **J** is incorrect as well.

13. **A**

Data Representation: Read the Chart   *Easy*

Figure 2 shows that medium positive ions (represented by the white bars in the middle graph) had the smallest growth rate when the wind direction was between 0° and 30°. Medium positive ions had a larger growth rate between 120° and 150° than they did between 0° and 30°, so **B** is incorrect. **C** represents the smallest growth rate in medium *negative* ions, not medium positive ions, so it too is incorrect. **D** is incorrect because medium positive ions had a larger growth rate between 330° and 360° than they did between 0° and 30°.

14. **G**

Data Representation: Read the Chart   *Medium*

Looking at Figure 1, we see that for both positive ions and negative ions in February 2006, the growth rate of the large ions was significantly greater than the growth rate of the small or medium ions. The correct answer is **G**. The growth rate of the medium ions was actually smaller in February than in January, so **F** is incorrect. Likewise, **H** is incorrect, because the growth rate of the small negative ions was smaller in February than in January (and the growth rate of the small positive icons in February was about the same as in January). **J** is the *opposite* of the correct answer.

15. **D**

Data Representation: Use the Chart   *Medium*

The passage tells us that easterly winds blow at directions between 0° and 180°, and westerly winds blow at directions between 180° to 360°. Figure 2 shows that the growth rate of medium and large ions is, on average, greater in easterly winds than it is in westerly winds. **A** is incorrect because the growth rate of small negative ions is *smaller* than the growth rate of large negative ions in some instances. **B** is incorrect because the growth rate of large positive ions is *smaller* than the growth rate of large negative ions in some instances. Finally, **C** has it backward—the growth rate of large ions is greater in easterly winds than in westerly winds, not the other way around.

16. **H**

Data Representation: Use the Chart   *Difficult*

To answer this question, we need to use Figure 2. According to the bottom graph, a particle that experiences a growth rate of 15 nmh^{-1} when the wind is blowing at a direction between 120° and 150° is between 7 nm and 20 nm. The correct answer is **H**. **F** and **G** represent a misreading of the data. **J** is incorrect because the data are sufficient for answering the question.

17. B

Research Summary: Read the Chart   *Easy*

According to Figure 1, when tone mul1.5 was played, approximately 60% of the birds stayed more than 10 meters from the researchers, and approximately 30% did not approach at all. The correct answer is **B**. Most birds came closer than 10 meters when the control tone was played, so **A** is incorrect. Around 65% of the birds came closer than 10 meters when the ptone was played, so **C** is not correct either. **D** is incorrect because approximately half of the birds came closer than 10 meters when the noAM tone was played.

18. J

Research Summary: Read the Chart   *Easy*

According to Figure 2, 80% of the tested birds had a high response rate to the control song. The correct answer is **J**. The percentages in choices **F**, **G**, and **H** are all too low.

19. C

Research Summary: Read the Chart   *Medium*

Looking at Figure 1, we see that the bar for the noAM tone is divided almost perfectly in half. The correct answer is **C**. There was no scenario in which 100% of the birds approached closer than 10 meters, so **A** is incorrect. **B** and **D** represent a misreading of the data.

20. G

Research Summary: Use the Chart   *Medium*

In both experiments, the birds had the highest response to the control song. This means the correct answer is **G**. The birds had a low response to the mul1.5 song in the first experiment but not in the second, so **F** is incorrect. **H** is not supported by the data; the birds respond to the sounds, not to the researchers' presence. The birds have a higher response to the control tone than to the pure, synthetic tone, so **J** cannot be correct.

21. A

Research Summary: Use the Chart   *Difficult*

The birds had low responses to the songs with altered FM frequencies (mul1.5 and div2). In the second experiment, the birds did have high responses to the second half of a song, so **B** is incorrect. **C** and **D** represent a misreading of the data.

22. H

Research Summary: Use the Chart   *Difficult*

A white-browned warbler will approach closer than 10 feet when played the control tone, and it will call at less than 3 times the typical emission rate when played the div2. **F** has the first part correct, but the ptone causes the bird to call at more than 3 times the typical emission rate. **G** has the second half correct, but the first half incorrect. Both parts of **J** are incorrect.

23. D

Conflicting Viewpoints: Detail   *Easy*

In the second paragraph of the passage, Scientist 1 states that the results of the Maltoni Center study *confirm the findings of a previous study conducted by the same Italian research group.* **A** is incorrect, because thyroid cancer is not discussed in the passage. **B** is incorrect because Scientist 1 states that the study revealed an increase in cancer in rats that consumed aspartame. **C** is incorrect because it is not stated by Scientist 1.

24. H

Conflicting Viewpoints: Comparison   *Easy*

Scientist 1 concluded that the Maltoni Center study demonstrated that consumption of aspartame causes cancer in rats. This conclusion was based on the fact that rats who consumed aspartame demonstrated a higher incidence of certain cancers. Thus, Scientist 1 would be likely to conclude that aspartame causes bladder cancer, based on the increased incidence of bladder cancer found in the new study. Scientist 2, by contrast, views the aspartame consumption and increased cancer incidence only as correlated, not as causally linked. So, Scientist 2 would not be likely to conclude that a causal relationship exists in the bladder cancer study.

25. A

Conflicting Viewpoints: Detail   *Medium*

In paragraph 4 of the passage, Scientist 2 notes that both groups of rats studied demonstrated an increased incidence of cancer: those that consumed 100 milligrams of aspartame per kilogram of body weight per day and those that consumed 20 milligrams per kilogram of body weight. **B** is incorrect because paragraph 4 states that the incidence of cancer was also higher in rats that consumed 20 milligrams of aspartame per kilogram of body weight, but that the increased incidence was not statistically significant.

26. J

Conflicting Viewpoints: Inference   *Medium*

Scientist 2 states that the Maltoni Center study may not be applicable to humans because its findings were statistically significant only when rats consumed 100 milligrams of aspartame per kilogram of body weight per day. This amount, Scientist 2 notes, is more than what some individuals consume daily. Because the amounts ingested by the rats in the study are not necessarily typical for humans, Scientist 2 questions whether the findings can be applied to humans. Scientist 2 would be likely to argue that to be applicable, the conditions of animal tests should match those that humans might actually encounter.

   H is incorrect, because Scientist 2 raises no objections based on differences in physiology between rats and humans.

27. B

Conflicting Viewpoints: Comparison   *Medium*

Both Scientist 1 and Scientist 2 agree on the fact that the Maltoni Center study showed an increased incidence of cancer in rats that consumed aspartame. Scientist 1 states this in paragraph 2 of the passage, and Scientist 2 states this in paragraph 5.

The scientists differ in how to interpret the meaning of this correlation. **A** is incorrect, because Scientist 2 would likely disagree with this statement. **C** is incorrect, because Scientist 1 would likely disagree with this statement. **D** is incorrect, because neither scientist provides information to support this conclusion.

28. **F**

Conflicting Viewpoints: Comparison   *Medium*

Scientist 2 provides two arguments that contradict the arguments of Scientist 1. The first of these arguments is that the Maltoni Center studies do not necessarily apply to humans. The second argument of Scientist 2 is that correlation does not equate with causation. **F** expresses a main rationale of Scientist 2's second argument.

G and **H** are incorrect, because these arguments were not made by either scientist in the passage. **J** is incorrect, because Scientist 1 does not discuss the importance of proving a food harmful before it is considered unsafe.

29. **C**

Conflicting Viewpoints: Inference   *Medium*

Scientist 2 argues in general that the Maltoni Center study does not justify concern over the safety of aspartame. Scientist 2 would likely see these findings as weakening the conclusion that there is a significant correlation between aspartame consumption and increased incidence of cancer, because the incidence of malignant tumors is less significant for females than for males. **A** is the opposite of the correct answer. **B** and **D** are incorrect, because this finding does not relate to Scientist 2's argument regarding how to determine causation.

30. **F**

Research Summary: Read the Chart   *Easy*

The results for the bimodal synthetic lips and the bimodal synthetic face were nearly identical at –13 dB, so **F** is correct. The results are too far apart at –15 dB, –18 dB, and –19 dB to be considered "nearly identical," so **G**, **H**, and **J** are all incorrect.

31. **A**

Research Summary: Read the Chart   *Easy*

The bimodal natural face at –11 dB yielded a proportion of .09, which is the greatest proportion of correctly identified CVs in Experiment 1. The unimodal auditory presentation at –19 dB yielded the smallest proportion of correctly identified CVs, so **B** is incorrect. The bimodal synthetic face at –13 dB and the bimodal natural face at –18 dB did not yield as great a proportion of correctly identified CVs as the bimodal natural face at –11 dB, so **C** and **D** are both incorrect.

32. **H**

Research Summary: Use the Chart   *Medium*

All three of the experiments show that unimodal auditory presentations always result in the smallest proportion of correctly identified CVs. A bimodal synthetic face yields *fewer* correctly identified CVs than a bimodal natural face, so **F** is incorrect. Participants correctly identified more CVs when presented with bimodal faces than with bimodal lips, so **G** is incorrect. **J** has it backward—unimodal auditory presentations result in a *lower* proportion of correctly identified CVs than bimodal face presentations.

33. D

Research Summary: Use the Chart   *Medium*

The data in Experiment 3 support the hypothesis that bimodal natural lips yield only a slightly smaller proportion of correctly identified CVs than a bimodal natural face. The proportion is not the same, so **A** is incorrect. **B** is incorrect because the proportion of correctly identified CVs yielded by the bimodal natural lips cannot be described as "much larger." The proportion of correctly identified CVs yielded by the unimodal auditory presentation is much lower than that yielded by bimodal natural lips, so **C** is incorrect.

34. H

Research Summary: Use the Chart   *Medium*

The participant who identified a proportion of 0.2 CVs correctly at −16 dB during a unimodal auditory presentation could have taken part in either Experiment 1 or Experiment 3. Because the answer is either Experiment 1 or Experiment 3, **F**, **G**, and **J** are incorrect.

35. B

Research Summary: Take the Next Step   *Difficult*

Across all three experiments, the highest yields of correctly identified CVs occurred when participants were presented with the entire face of a human speaker. The presentations represented by choices **A**, **C**, and **D** do not yield high enough proportions of correctly identified CVs to be correct.

36. J

Data Representation: Read the Chart   *Easy*

Figure 1 shows that CO_2 emissions were close to 5 Tg in both January and December. **F** is incorrect, because June emissions differed from November emissions by about 5 Tg. **G** and **H** are also incorrect, because these pairs of months both show differences of 10 Tg or more in their emission levels.

37. B

Data Representation: Use the Chart   *Medium*

The ecologist's statement is not supported by Figure 2, because Figure 2 shows that Alaska had higher peak CO_2 emissions than did Oregon during the given time frame. Oregon recorded a peak of 23 Tg of CO_2 during one month of the 5-year period, whereas Alaska recorded a peak of close to 100 Tg during the period.

38. F

Data Representation: Use the Chart   *Medium*

Figure 1 shows two peak periods of CO_2 emissions. The first is in the spring, during March/April, and the second is in the summer and early fall, from July through October. The statement in **F** is consistent with these peak periods. If there are large numbers of fires in the spring and summer, this would explain why CO_2 emissions from fire are higher during spring and summer.

G is incorrect because Figure 1 shows low CO_2 emissions from December through February. **H** is incorrect because the average October CO_2 emissions are higher than those of June, so we would expect fewer fires in June than in October. **J** is incorrect, because this statement is not related to the data shown in Figure 1. Figure 1 displays CO_2 emissions by month, not information regarding the spread of fires geographically.

39. C

Data Representation: Use the Chart   *Medium*

For the month of April, Figure 3 shows the average CO_2 emissions in the following order from most to least: Central, Southeastern, Western, Midwestern, and Midatlantic. **B** and **D** are incorrect because during the month of April, emission levels in the Central region exceed those in Southeastern region.

40. H

Data Representation: Use the Chart   *Medium*

Figure 2 shows emissions greater than 20 Tg in Oregon in the month of July. **F, G,** and **J** can be eliminated, because none of these states had CO_2 emissions greater than 20 Tg during the months indicated.

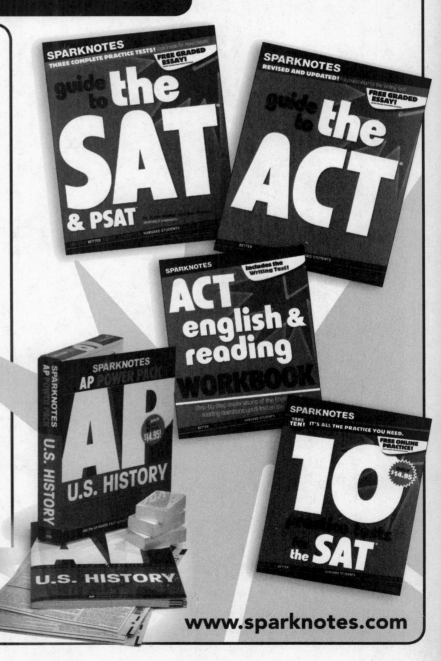